Corporate Risks and Leadership

Corporate Risks and Leadership

What Every Executive Should Know About Risks, Ethics, Compliance, and Human Resources

Eduardo Esteban Mariscotti

Routledge
Taylor & Francis Group

A PRODUCTIVITY PRESS BOOK

First published 2020
by Routledge
52 Vanderbilt Avenue, New York, NY 10017

and by Routledge
2 Park Square, Milton Park, Abingdon, Oxon, OX14 4RN

Routledge is an imprint of the Taylor & Francis Group, an informa business

Library of Congress Cataloging-in-Publication Data
A catalog record has been requested for this book

ISBN: 978-0-367-48037-0 (hbk)
ISBN: 978-0-367-49393-6 (pbk)
ISBN: 978-1-003-03823-8 (ebk)

Typeset in Minion Pro
by Deanta Global Publishing Services, Chennai, India

Contents

SECTION 3   Risks

Acknowledgments

Thanks to:

My wife, Lorena, for her patience, love, and support.

My children, Tomas, Bruno, Jacinta, and Clara because they inspire me every day.

My parents, Raul and Graciela. Thank you for being my guides, mentors, role models, and teachers. Thanks for always helping. The influence and impact on my life cannot be measured.

My brother Marcelo, family members, and friends with whom I have shared important moments.

Escuela Argentina Modelo and Professors Horacio De Leo and Carlos Maria Gelly y Obes, (1923–2014), models of virtue and honor.

The University Foundation of Rio de la Plata, which through its rigorous examinations and training seminars, helped me to expand my curiosity and knowledge of history, politics, economics, and international relations.

The Faculty of Law of the University of Buenos Aires, the British Council and the University of London in England, the School of Economics and International Business at the University of Belgrano, the Iacocca Leadership Program at Lehigh University in Pennsylvania, and Yale University in New Haven, because each of these institutions contributed in different ways to improving my education.

Jesuit Father Enrique Fabbri (1920–2015) who for more than 20 years led my wife and me in groups of engaged couples and married groups, and shared lessons on ethics and values.

Members of the radio program "Zona Republicana," and members of Grupo Participar, who over four years organized in the city of Buenos Aires 18 free public conferences with more than 30 business leaders, thinkers, intellectuals, economists, historians, and politicians to provide proposals to improve Argentina.

To my friend, the Chilean lawyer Gonzalo Smith, who in January 2014 suggested and insisted that once and for all, I work on my thesis to get my Master of Business Administration (MBA). The master's thesis, defended in July 2015 in front of a jury of professors at the University of Belgrano in Buenos Aires, was the basis and the starting point of this book.

All my former bosses, teachers, professional advisors, co-workers, and colleagues, from whom I have learned different aspects of leadership in organizations. In particular, I value my work experiences at Baker & McKenzie Argentina, Wilde Sapte Solicitors in London, Cablevision-FiberTel, Walmart Argentina, Walmart International, Walmart Latin America, Walmart US, and Cameron Smith & Associates.

Dr. Marcelo Dabos, Director of the Center for Studies in Business, Finance, Economics, and Marketing of the Graduate School of Business of the University of Belgrano, who approved my MBA thesis project at the beginning of 2014, and those people who took the time to read drafts of my book or thesis and sent me their suggestions or helped me in some way, especially: Raul Mariscotti, Griselda Lassaga, Julio Souto, Fernando Avelleyra, Tom of ProofreadingPal, Virginia Granillo Valdes de Quiroga, Robert Mahler, and Valeria Facetti.

I devote this book to those business and organizational leaders who consider ethical values and compliance a priority when making decisions every day.

Eduardo Esteban Mariscotti

About the Author

Eduardo Esteban Mariscotti is a lawyer, and he graduated from the University of Buenos Aires, Argentina. A native of Argentina, he earned a Master of Law (LLM) in International Business Law from the University of London in England with a scholarship from the British Council.

Eduardo also holds an MBA from the University of Belgrano in Buenos Aires, Argentina. He graduated from the Lee Iacocca Leadership Program for Future Leaders in Business and Industry at Lehigh University, Pennsylvania, and he took the Management Program for Lawyers at Yale School of Business, Connecticut.

Eduardo worked for Baker & McKenzie at the Buenos Aires Office and he took a six-month internship for international lawyers at Wilde Sapte Solicitors in London, England, in 1996.

He was Chief of the Legal Department of Cablevision, one of the biggest TV cable operators in Latin America from 1998 to 2003. From 2004 to 2011, he was General Counsel of Walmart Argentina (Director of Legal, Ethics, Compliance, and Labor Relations) and a member of the Walmart Argentina Executive Committee.

In 2011 he was transferred to Bentonville, Arkansas, to work at Walmart Home Office. At Walmart, from 2011 to 2017 he took on the roles of VP of International Compliance, VP and Latin America Regional Ethics Officer, and VP of Human Resources for the US market.

As VP of International Compliance, Eduardo designed and delivered a global compliance strategy for the organization, excluding the US market. He oversaw the development and delivery of compliance programs and headcounts in facilities around the world, and supervised the review and evaluation of compliance issues and concerns.

As VP of Ethics Latin America, Eduardo held responsibility for designing and executing an ethics program for over 400,000 associates spanning ten countries across the Latin American region. He supervised a 45-member team in creating, implementing, reviewing, and updating policies, tools, and procedures for an organizational ethics program.

Eduardo supervised Compliance Programs across Canada, Central America, South America, Africa, Europe, and Asia.

He managed large geographically dispersed teams with diverse skill sets and he invested time in training and mentoring people to ensure organizational growth and professional development.

His expertise in Legal and Corporate Risks is supplemented by his experience and qualifications in Business Law, Strategy, and Human Resources.

He works for Cameron Smith & Associates (CSA) in Arkansas, one of the best headhunting firms in the world. He helps companies to recruit top talent in the United States and around the world.

Eduardo was certified at the Society of Corporate Compliance and Ethics (SCCE) and at the Ethics and Compliance Officer Association (ECOA).

Eduardo wrote articles about legal, ethics, and compliance in legal publications and newspapers. He also wrote a paper for the International In-house Counsel Journal. Eduardo has given more than 100 lectures and presentations in legal management, risks, ethics, compliance, anti-corruption, diversity, and leadership.

Eduardo was a member of the Advisory Board of the Hispanic Initiative at Southern Methodist University in Dallas, Texas, and a member of the Board of Directors of the National Hispanic Corporate Counsel. At Walmart, he was Co-Founder and Treasurer of the Hispanic Officer Caucus.

Introduction

Since I received my law degree from the University of Buenos Aires in 1989, my work experience has been linked to the corporate world.

Between 1992 and 2003, I worked in the Buenos Aires office of the law firm Baker & McKenzie, I completed training for international lawyers at the law firm of Wilde Sapte in London, England, and I worked as a lawyer at Cablevision and Fibertel, Argentine TV cable and internet companies.

In 2004 I joined Walmart Argentina to be in charge of the Legal Department. In that role, I had the responsibility of leading the legal, ethics, and compliance matters and for some years also, labor relations. I had the opportunity to assemble a great team of law professionals that grew over the years to 16 people and we had the support of more than 30 law firms throughout the country. For just over seven and a half years I was also a member of the executive committee of the company and I learned a lot from my team, peers, and bosses – an interdisciplinary team of very talented professionals – about trade, leadership, strategy, finance, human resources, and the retail business in general. In those years Walmart Argentina grew from 11 to 65 stores, including those from the acquisition of a retail chain we completed.

In August 2011, my wife, my kids, and I moved to Bentonville, Arkansas, USA, to work as vice-president in the area of compliance for Walmart International.

From that role, I learned in greater depth the main compliance risks that Walmart's operations around the world were facing, and I had the chance to work with teams in South America, Central America, Mexico, Canada, England, Africa, and Asia in developing strategies to mitigate those risks.

My next work challenge in the United States began in late 2012 and until early 2015, when I took the role of vice-president of ethics for the region of Walmart Latin America, also in Bentonville, Arkansas, where our team took care of the strategy and coordination of ethics programs for more than 400,000 Walmart employees in nine countries.

I worked with Walmart leaders and their departments of ethics in Latin American markets where Walmart has operations to implement strategic plans and processes to further promote the ethical culture of the organization.

From February 2015 to February 2017, I took the position of vice-president of Human Resources in Walmart US and I completed a training program in the areas of human resources and operations. I had the opportunity to rotate through the different areas and visit stores and distribution centers. I completed training courses on leadership and human resources and I conducted training at a Supercenter. I represented the company at events and organizations; I shook hands with the president of the United States on two occasions, gave lectures at universities, participated in events on diversity, and collaborated in the development of the Hispanic talent inside and outside the company.

In the United States, I noticed that almost every week the *Wall Street Journal* reported problems of compliance and/or ethics in business that resulted in heavy financial penalties for organizations and criminal sanctions for some of its executives.

After I had worked for more than ten years on issues of ethics and compliance in a multinational company in Argentina and the United States, gained experience in risks in different international markets, learned from cases analyzed as well as from experts and consultants; obtained training by participating in the Master's in Business Law and Business Administration and in international seminars, continued reading specialist literature and earning certifications in ethics and compliance in the United States, as well as my work experience in leadership positions and human resources, I felt interest in sharing some ideas, experiences, knowledge, and learning.

I have asked myself, what do we do with the learnings and experiences that we acquire through the years in investigations, organizations, and training?

In this work, I have tried to organize and transmit in the best way I could, the information I have acquired in the area of corporate risks and leadership. And I have the intellectual need to share it.

My focus and commitment on this issue are based on the facts that (a) I worked several years in retail, which is a business with multiple risks, and (b) I had my main work experience in Argentina, an unpredictable country, one that is more vulnerable and unstable than any developed country.* This combination of working in the retail business and in Argentina helped deepen my interest in the multiple and changing risks facing organizations.

Retail is a business with profit margins usually less than 5%, and depending on the market where a business operates and the format used, it may even be less than 2%. Unlike the supermarket industry, businesses such as pharmaceutical companies, jewelry sales, and the oil industry typically have profit margins over 30%.

By having low-profit margins, interest in acting within the laws makes it an even higher priority because any event occurring due to lack of compliance (for example, theft, fraud, and/or fines for breaching the law) can put retail companies in an extremely vulnerable position.

Walmart is interesting as an ethics and compliance school not only because of the size of the organization but also because retail involves many customers, employees, suppliers, merchandise, regulations, and risks, and changes are constant.

The specialization in ethics and compliance is a fairly new topic outside the United States but grows each year in the corporate world because acting in an ethical, legal, and transparent manner – and controlling so that suppliers and subcontractors do the same – is a complex task that is of increasing concern to businesses.

At the beginning of 2018, Walmart operated nearly 12,000 stores in 28 countries and is one of the organizations with the most employees in the world, after the Department of Defense, which has about 3.3 million employees. The Chinese Army and Walmart are tied for second place with 2.3 million employees/members each.

Walmart has more employees than all the people of Trinidad and Tobago, Cyprus, and Luxembourg. Just one of its regions, Walmart Latin America, a few years ago had more than 400,000 employees, making that business

---

* Economist Paul Samuelson (1915–2009), winner of the Nobel Prize in Economics in 1970, proposed to classify countries into five categories: "They are the capitalist countries, the socialist orbit and the very heterogeneous Third World; but that is not enough, because in reality there are five systems: there are two more countries to consider separately: Japan and Argentina ... are so peculiar and so unpredictable that should be placed aside." Marcos Aguinis, *The Atrocious Charm of Being Argentine* (Editorial Planeta), 10. Some say that the Russian-American economist Simón Smith Kuznets (1901–1985), winner of the Nobel Prize in Economics in 1971, had already divided the countries into four categories: developed, underdeveloped, Japan, and Argentina.The GDP per capita of the Argentine Republic in 1895 was the highest in the world, above that of the United States (Maddison Project, www.ggdc.net/maddison/historical_statistics).

region comparable to or greater than General Electric, Citigroup, Home Depot, Target, or Ford Motor Company in the number of employees.

But there is also another unique aspect of Walmart. It is not only the world's largest private company in the number of employees but also in annual sales. Despite having been founded in 1962 – just over 50 years ago – it has been ranked number one for six consecutive years on the Fortune 500, *Fortune* magazine's annual ranking of the 500 largest US corporations by total revenue. If Walmart with its US$500 billion in annual sales were in a ranking of countries by gross domestic product, it would be in 25th place, beating Belgium, South Africa, Norway, Austria, Ireland, and Israel.*

The second-ranked company in *Fortune* magazine in 2018 is Exxon with US$244 billion in annual sales and is followed by Berkshire Hathaway with US$242 billion in annual sales.† That is, the aggregate of annual sales of the second- and third-largest companies in the world do not even equal Walmart's annual sales.

More than 37 million customers shop at Walmart stores daily. It's as if the entire population of Canada, Peru, and Poland shops at Walmart stores every day.

In addition to being the world leader in sales and employees, Walmart is a company that promotes diversity and inclusion. In a 2016 ranking of organizations that provide opportunities for diverse populations in the United States, Walmart was in the first place.‡

These examples serve to illustrate that working at Walmart is a unique experience, because of its size, diversity, and success. And this success is supported in the ethical culture of the company.

This does not mean the company does not have or has not had ethical and compliance problems. No company is perfect because it is almost impossible to control everything, and it gets harder as a company gets bigger. It is enough to point out by way of comparison that even in the most developed and safe countries, crimes are also committed.

Walmart invests heavily in controls to prevent risks and to create a work environment of respect for people, laws, values, and ethical principles. The company has invested heavily and improved its ethics and compliance

---

* "World Economic Outlook Database," International Monetary Fund, April 17, 2018.
† "Introduction to the New Fortune 500 List," Fortune.com/2018/05/21.
‡ "America's Top 50 Organizations for Multicultural Business," Diversity Business.com January 28, 2016. Thousands of companies participated in the selection process to name the company that provides greater opportunities in the United States.

program in recent years. In fact, the company has spent US$1.6 billion on FCPA and compliance related costs from 2012 to 2018, or around US$530,000 a day for six years.*

On June 8, 2016, the New York Stock Exchange announced the winners of the leading companies in governance, risk, and compliance, which are selected by an independent panel of experts. Walmart was the winner for having the best "Governance, Risk and Compliance Program" for large companies.†

In 2018, 6,600 Americans were asked to think of a company that they would consider being ethically responsible and naming the first one that came to mind. Walmart had the most mentions.‡

I mention these characteristics of Walmart so that you know the type of company in which I have worked for 13 years. In this book, I do not analyze the ethics and compliance program of Walmart or any particular company. What I analyze here is the cause and *raison d'être* of the ethics and compliance programs in organizations, as well as their main elements.

Ethical conflicts in organizations occur when leaders must make decisions that are often complex. The business world always has gray areas and employees must make decisions and then justify them. While business and ethics should go hand in hand, it has been argued that business ethics is an *oxymoron*, which in Greek means a contradiction in terms.§

The context of business has been changing for companies in recent years and following numerous corporate and accounting scandals, many countries have increased the number of national and international regulations designed to ensure transparency and compliance with the law.⁋ Because of the existence of these new regulations, the level of control, the severity of sanctions by governments, and the amount of the fines for non-compliance have increased dramatically.

---

* "Walmart Updates Ethics Report, CEO Says Company Will Never be Satisfied with Status Quo," Kim Souza, Talkbusiness.net/2018/04, April 26, 2018.

† Adam Sodowick, president of NYSE Governance Services, said: "NYSE Governance Services would like to congratulate the individuals and organizations that have truly exemplified the highest standards of compliance, ethics, and governance. Their dedication and noteworthy achievements truly set the bar for best practices and standards in corporate governance, which plays an integral role in a company's success and long-term value to its shareholders."

‡ "Walmart, Amazon, Target Named America's Most Ethical Companies," Tanya Gazdik, www.mediapost.com August 6, 2018. "The Ten Most Ethical Companies in America," morningconsult.com/form/the-10-most-ethical-companies-according-to-americans/.

§ Joseph W. Weiss, *Business Ethics*, 4th ed (Thomson, 2006), 14.

⁋ In the United States, some examples of these regulations are PCI DSS (Payment Card Industry Data Security Standard), SOX (Sarbanes Oxley Act), and FCPA (Foreign Corrupt Practices Act).

In parallel, with the technological revolution in communications, business management has become more transparent, and any negative event is uploaded to social networks and shared with an indeterminate number of people.

This change in the regulatory, sanctioning, and technological context has forced large companies to rethink risks, investments, and budgets to deal in this more complex environment.

In order to transition to this change, some companies have included ethics and compliance programs in their corporate agenda, along with marketing and sales plans, strategies, growth targets, investment plans, and/or talent acquisition.

While each industry has its particular risks, in this book, I describe the essential elements that any effective ethics and compliance program should contain.

This book is a source of information that connects yesterday with today. I share observations and lessons of the past in order to suggest corporate leaders implement effective ethics and compliance programs to protect their organizations and themselves.

This work may be also useful for business leaders, lawyers, and business and law students so that they are clear that behaviors have limits and the consequences of exceeding those limits are serious. In this book, I draw upon my experience and knowledge in the areas of compliance, ethics, human resources, and leadership. As the Italian genius, Leonardo da Vinci (1452–1519) said, "The acquisition of knowledge is always of use to the intellect, because it may thus drive out useless things and retain the good."*

This work has a holistic approach that I hope will help enrich the analysis of corporate risks from different dimensions and perspectives, from the Old Testament and Greek philosophers to the latest computer viruses. I use stories, illustrations, and examples.

The book covers theories of ethics but with an eye focused on practical application. Risks, ethics, and compliance are analyzed with an overall vision, connected to the reality of business life, without getting bogged down in abstract thinking or in technical and regulatory details.

Interest in business ethics has accelerated in recent years. Ethics and compliance are disciplines that have increasingly achieved greater recognition in organizations. Thus, due to the importance of risk

---

* "Leonardo da Vinci," www.goodreads.com/quotes.

management in the business world and the necessary involvement of the CEO and the board of directors, it seems appropriate that executives get access to a book about risks, ethics, compliance, and human resources directed not only to compliance experts but also to any organizational leader.

Some leaders make a false assessment of circumstances and underestimate risks. Hitler (1889–1945) benefited by having been underestimated for years when he still did not have enough power.* Once the risk was understood, it was too late.

The risks and problems of compliance and ethics in organizations are often underestimated. Just as integrity is fundamental for the development of nations, so it is for companies. Although ethics comes from philosophy, it has practical importance. It is an indispensable element in companies' decision-making process and is also a necessary measure of security and protection for the sustainable success of any organization.

The risk of costly investigations and fines for bribery and corruption in the supply chain can cause headaches, nightmares, and sleeplessness. The risks have multiplied, and the more you know about them and how to prevent them, the better control you will have over the organization.

This book is a wake-up call that allows business leaders to understand the benefits of implementing an effective ethics and compliance program that will help members of organizations to make the right decisions and act within the law. If they do, they can better prevent and react to the difficult obstacle course of risks, dangers, and threats that organizations face and that may jeopardize the sustainability, resilience, and survival of companies.

The book contains an introduction, four sections (Culture, Change, Risks, and Control covering 25 chapters), and the conclusion. The themes that are developed are values, culture, reputation, ethics, change, crisis, corporate risks, and best practices to control risks.

This book should be able to answer the following questions:

Why is an ethical corporate culture important?
Why is how we get the results important?
Why should you control the exercise of power in your organization?
What are the risks of the digitally hyper-connected world?

---

* Professor Vejas Liulevicius, *Utopia and Terror in the 20th Century*, University of Tennessee, The Great Courses, The Teaching Company, Part 2 (2003), 25.

Why must we be vigilant and react quickly when the risks are still small?

Why are vision, motivation, and commitment needed to overcome internal resistance and to implement changes in organizations?

Should we become more aware that we can be deceived?

How should we deal with uncertainty?

What kind of training, analysis, and questioning can improve decision-making?

What are the main compliance risks that organizations face?

What basic elements should an ethics and compliance program have to protect a company against risks?

Perhaps these questions could be summarized in two ways:

Why do business leaders need to be aware of corporate risks?

What should leaders do to maintain an organizational culture of integrity and compliance?

Compliance is the result of organizations complying with their obligations. As risks are plentiful and things can get worse quickly, a bad day can cause an immediate and significant loss in the market value of organizations. Organizational leaders must understand that companies have their flaws and imbalances, and if not corrected, they can cause irrecoverable damage to a company's reputation.

Business people are constantly dealing with moral challenges and questions about how to behave. It is necessary to create greater awareness of the importance of values, morals, and ethics. In some situations, acting ethically is not so obvious, and in this work, there are examples showing that the course of action to be followed in certain situations or dilemmas is not clear, and therefore ethical training is necessary.

It is not possible to completely eliminate uncertainties and many of them are outside of the management's control. Nevertheless, the recommendations suggested in this book attempt to reduce corporate risks, so that organizations are better prepared to survive to threaten, changing and dangerous environments, where doing the wrong thing has consequences.

Welcome to this trip through the world of risks, ethics, compliance, human resources, and history.

I hope this book can make a practical contribution to the effort to mitigate corporate risks.

If the message is understood, ethics and compliance will become part of the strategic priorities of your organization; and you will soon implement an integrity program that will better protect your company from the dangerous and unpredictable corporate risks that will lurk in the organization on the way to the future.

Section 1

Culture

1

Ethics and Values

1.1 ETHICS AND MORAL CONSCIENCE

For the Greek philosophers, wisdom was the search for knowledge. They reflected on the causes of things to explain the different phenomena of reality, such as the origin of the universe, the meaning of life, and the pursuit of truth.*

In the West, Thales of Miletus (625–547 BC) was the first philosopher. Thales is recognized as the first person in the Western world who attempted a rational and logical explanation to the different phenomena of the world, leaving aside mythical and supernatural explanations.† That is why it is said that Thales passed from the "myth" to the "logos," which is the use of "reason."‡

Eastern philosophy, meanwhile, emerged more or less at the same time. There are certain similarities between the two cultures as both pursue the desire of man to question the existence and the things around him.

In China, it is said that Confucius (551–479 BC) was the first philosopher. Confucius (Kung Fu Tzu) was a Chinese thinker who regretted the disorder, degeneration, decadence, and lack of moral standards of his time. Confucius said: "The rulers can only be great if they lead exemplary lives and are guided by moral principles. If the prince is virtuous the people will imitate his example. Being ethical is the ultimate goal."§

---

* The word *philosophy* comes from Greek and is composed of the words *filos* (love) and *sophia* (wisdom). Philosophy means "love of wisdom" and the invention of the term is attributed to the Greek mathematician and philosopher Pythagoras (569–475 BC) around the year 530 BC. Pythagoras was considered wise but replied that he was not wise, but rather someone who aspired to be wise.

† One night while watching the stars, Thales fell into a well and excused himself by saying that his eagerness to know the things of heaven made the things under his feet not be seen.

‡ After Thales there were many great philosophers in Greece, such as Pythagoras, Anaximander, Anaximenes, Heraclitus, Socrates, Plato, and Aristotle.

§ "Pact with the Devil," Interview with Peter Koestenbaum. Emeritus Professor of Philosophy at San Jose State University, California, *Management* (November–December, 1999): 131.

The *Tirukkural* or *Thirukkural* is a classic Tamil text* consisting of 1,330 couplets dealing with the virtues of an individual. It is considered one of the greatest works ever written in ancient times on ethics and morality.†

Philosophy is divided into different branches to respond to specific problems. *Ethics* is a branch of philosophy that reflects on and judges human behavior and values that apply to decision-makers. Ethics is the branch of philosophy that focuses on moral issues, in what is right and what is wrong.

The word *ethics* comes from the Greek *ethos* meaning *behavior*. For Aristotle (384–322 BC) ethos was the habit, character, mode of being, personality, or identity of the person derived from his way of behaving according to customs.‡

Ethics analyzes acts performed by a man and makes a judgment about them to determine whether an act or behavior has been ethically good or bad, right or wrong. Acting with ethics implies the requirement of complying with values.

Ethics helps us to reflect on the behavior of the human being and to determine if we have acted with integrity or not. Ethics focuses on behavior and asks what behavior is good or bad.§

The Spanish philosopher Adela Cortina says that "ethics task…is to show us how to deliberate well with the aim of making good choices."¶

Fernando Savater, Spanish philosopher and intellectual, in his book *Ethics for Amador*** defines ethics as "the art of discerning what is good and what is bad."

Organizational ethics expert and professor at the University of San Francisco, Marvin T. Brown, has said, "Although it may seem strange, the purpose of ethics is not that people are more ethical, but that they are able to make better decisions. Ethics is the process of deciding what to do."††

---

* The Tamils are an ethnic group native to the state of Tamil Nadu, in India, and the northeastern region of Sri Lanka. They speak mainly the Tamil language, and its history goes back two millennia ago. At present, its total number is 77 million people. es.wikipedia.org/wiki/Tamil_ (pueblo).

† The *Tirukkural* is divided into three volumes, it has 38 chapters. It was authored by the poet and philosopher Valluvar around the year 300 BC.

‡ "Ethos," Wikipedia.

§ British philosopher George Edward Moore (1873–1958) has written in his book *Principia Ethica* (1903) that the fundamental question of ethics is how to define "good." For Moore, it is impossible to define good and any definition of good is fallacious. es.wikipedia.org/wiki/George_Edward _Moore.

¶ Adela Cortina, *Business Ethics* (Editorial Trotta), 18.

** Ariel, 2014.

†† Adela Cortina, *Business Ethics* (Editorial Trotta), 86.

Individuals with their actions in the world of *being* may conflict with the world of *what should be*, the world of rules, norms, and consensus, i.e., the world of morality.

The word *moral* comes from Latin "mos" and its plural "moris" and means *custom*.* *Morality* is a set of customs and norms that are considered good in directing the behavior of people. Conduct is moral when aligned with customs and accepted standards.

While *morality* refers to the prescriptive and normative, to what *should be*; *ethics* refers to the descriptive, to *what it is*.

Ethics reflects wonders and judges whether an action or behavior is moral or immoral; that is if that action (*what it is*) is aligned to what *should be* according to rules, norms, values, or moral consensus.

Business Ethics is a branch of ethics that examines the ethical principles, standards, and set of values that govern the business behavior of an individual and also the ethical problems that arise in a business environment.

Ethics lawyer Michael Josephson has said that "ethics is a moral perspective that asks you to judge your conduct in terms of what is right or wrong, what's decent, what's good, what's honest."[†]

The French thinker Alexis de Tocqueville (1805–1859) traveled in 1831 to the United States for two years to study for the country's prison system. Tocqueville said: "Humankind feels permanent and general needs that have given rise to moral laws."[‡]

Some authors do not distinguish between morals and ethics and use the terms synonymously. Ayn Rand (1905–1982) was born in the Russian Empire and is the author of bestseller *Atlas Shrugged*.[§] In a work called "Ethics in our time" presented in 1961 at the University of Wisconsin, Rand said, "What is morality or ethics? It is a code of values that guide the actions and choices of men."

And what is the role of conscience? According to the mythological legend of the "Ring of Gyges" mentioned by the philosopher Plato (427–347 BC) in the *Republic*, people would be unjust if they could be invisible to the laws.[¶]

---

* It was the philosopher Marco Tulio Cicero (106–43 BC) who took the adjective ethicós, referring to custom, and coined the term *moralis*, from which derived moral, download.com/ethos/.

† Linda Trevino and Katherine Nelson, *Managing Business Ethics*, 5th ed (John Wiley & Sons, Inc. 2011), 346; Josephson, *Ethics in a Legalistic Society, Exchange* (Fall 1989), 3–7.

‡ Alexis de Tocqueville, *Democracy in America* (Folio), 206–07.

§ In the eighties, the Library of Congress conducted a survey asking what book had greater influence in the lives of the respondents. First in the ranking was the Bible; second was *Atlas Shrugged*.

¶ Gyges was a shepherd who found a gold ring and decided to keep it. When Gyges found that the ring had magical properties – when he gave the ring a few turns, it turned him invisible – he used the ring to kill the king and take over his kingdom.

Savater has said that "human beings do all the evil they let us do."*

Is it really so? Would you behave well yourself or would you engage in improper behavior if you couldn't get caught?

The ethical conscience in decision-making has been the object of analysis by different thinkers throughout history. You can read the thought of some of them in the footnote.†

Every day, every hour, we choose how to act. In ethical behavior, conscience is like an invisible hand that leads us to decide what to choose, it is a voice that speaks to us and tells us what we should do. It is an inner voice that everyone listens to and warns us of possible problems. It is like a compass that connects our behavior with our principles and values.

Many times, ethics goes through our conscience. The German priest and Doctor of Theology Anselm Grun said, "Trust in your conscience. It is the supreme rule by which you must make decisions. God himself has given them the conscience, the inner sense for what is right."‡

Sheldon "Shel" Silverstein (1930–1999) was an American poet and composer who wrote a poem called "The Voice," which says:

> There is a voice inside you
> That whisper all day long,
> I feel this is right for me,
> I know this is wrong.
> No teacher, preacher, father, friend
> Or wise man can decide
> What's right for you – just listen to
> The voice that speaks inside§

We differentiate what is good from what is wrong when we listen to our conscience.

Joseph Butler (1692–1752) was an English philosopher and bishop. Butler wrote that Thomas Hobbes (1588–1679) had an egoistic view of human nature. He argued Hobbes saw human beings as being violent,

---

* International Book Fair of Guadalajara in Mexico, November 29, 2011 http:// cultura.elpais.com.
† The Greek tragic poet Sophocles (496–406 BC) said: "There is no witness more terrible or prosecutor more powerful than the conscience."

    Roman politician and philosopher Marcus Tullius Cicero (106–43 BC) said that "my conscience has more weight for me than the opinion of everyone."

    The Liberator of Argentina, Chile, and Peru, Jose Francisco de San Martin (1778–1850) stated that "conscience is the best judge of a good man."

    Socrates (470–399 BC) said: "There is no better pillow than sleeping on a clean conscience."
‡ Anselm Grun, *¿Qué quiero? Coraje y Valor para Decidir* (Bonum, 2014), 151.
§ Sheldon Silverstein, *A Light in the Attic*.

self-seeking, and power-hungry. On such a view, there was no place for genuine altruism or benevolence or any conception of morality as traditionally conceived.

In the *Sermons*, Butler argues that human motivation is less selfish and more complex than Hobbes claimed. Moral conscience, Butler claims, is an inborn sense of right and wrong, inner light and monitor, and is received from God. Conscience tells one to promote both the general happiness and personal happiness. Butler argued that unethical and self-centered people who care nothing for the public good are usually not very happy.*

In Plato's *Apology of Socrates*, Socrates claimed to have a *daimonion* (literally, a "divine something") that frequently warned him – in the form of a "voice" – against mistakes but never told him what to do.†

Conscientious objection is the refusal to obey orders or laws or to perform acts or services invoking ethical or religious reasons. Conscientious objection is a subjective right to resist the mandates of authority when they contradict one's moral principles. It is a right that has to do with the intimate convictions of a person, whether moral or religious, that enables him or her to refrain from performing certain acts that have deep justification in international human rights treaties. Generally speaking, this right is related to freedom of conscience, thought, and religion. Objection, therefore, comes into play when there is a clash between a legal norm that obliges one to do and the ethical or moral norm that opposes that action.‡

In 1948, the issue of the right to "conscience" was dealt with by the United Nations General Assembly in Article 18 of the Universal Declaration of Human Rights. It reads:

> Everyone has the right to freedom of thought, conscience, and religion; this right includes freedom to change his religion or belief, and freedom, either alone or in community with others and in public or private, to manifest his religion or belief in teaching, practice, worship and observance.

In 1964 the boxer Muhammad Ali joined the Nation of Islam and in 1967, three years after being World Heavyweight Boxing Champion, he did not want to join the Armed Forces of the United States based on his religious beliefs and his moral rejection to the Vietnam War. He declared a *conscientious objection* which caused him to be arrested. He was accused

---

* en.wikipedia.org/wiki/Joseph_Butler.
† en.wikipedia.org/wiki/Daemon_(classical_mythology).
‡ es.wikipedia.org/wiki/Objeción_de_conciencia ("objection of conscience").

of treason and sentenced to spend five years in prison. He had to pay a fine of US$10,000, he was stripped of the boxing title, and his license to box was suspended. After being found guilty, Ali appealed his case to the Supreme Court of the United States where he finally won. His case was known as *Clay v. The United States*.[*]

In Uruguay, *conscientious objection* is applied to those doctors who, for whatever reason, reject the practice of abortion. The 2012 law, which legalized the voluntary interruption of pregnancy in Uruguay, indicates that gynecologists and health personnel who have conscientious objections to intervene in procedures may express it, being exempt from carrying out this practice.[†]

Philosophy considers conscience is a human faculty that allows one to decide actions and to be responsible for the consequences of them according to the conception of good and evil.[‡] The power of conscience allows us to recognize and judge what is wrong to avoid it and look for the good.

Titus Plautus (254–184 BC) was a Roman comedian who in the comedy *Asinaria* wrote the lines "Lupus est homo homini, non homo, quom qualis sit non novit," which has been translated as "A man is a wolf rather than a man to another man, when he hasn't yet found out what he's like."[§]

Thomas Hobbes (1588–1679) wrote in *Leviathan* (1659), "Homo Hominis Lupus," meaning that man is the wolf to another man. For Hobbes, every human being wants their own interest and leads him or her to permanent conflict with others.

Xun Zi who was born under the name of Xun Kuang (312–230 BC) was a Chinese philosopher who said that "Human nature is evil, and goodness is caused by intentional activity."[¶] That is to say, without a moral guide or education, people would perform immoral behaviors.

For St. Augustine (354–430) people are made in the image of God, but with an evil that lurks in us because of original sin. That's why St. Augustine said there is something in humans that is fundamentally evil.[**]

On the other side, many philosophers have argued that people are naturally good. Mencius (or Mengzi or Meng Ke (372–289 BC)) was a Chinese philosopher who asserted the innate goodness of the individual,

---

[*] es.wikipedia.org/wiki/Objeción_de_conciencia ("objection of conscience").
[†] es.wikipedia.org/wiki/Objeción_de_conciencia ("objection of conscience").
[‡] definicion.de/conciencia/ ("definition of conscience").
[§] en.wikipedia.org/wiki/Asinaria.
[¶] www.brainyquote.com/quotes/xun_kuang_333679.
[**] "Moral Decision Making" Professor Clancy Martin, *The Great Courses*, Guidebook, University of Missouri-Kansas City.

believing that it was society's influence – its lack of positive cultivating influence – that caused bad moral character.*

The Genevan philosopher Jean Jacques Rousseau (1712–1778) said that "People in their natural state are basically good. But this natural innocence, however, is corrupted by the evils of society."† The phrase alludes to the fact that man is a product of society and an evil society transforms people. Rousseau says this because each individual, when he or she is born, lacks a structure of moral thought and each person must capture the norms each society has. Therefore, according to Rousseau, people are not born with morality, they acquire them as they go deeper into society, and they acquire the social model's society imposes, leaving the state of "purity" that they had at birth.‡

Sigmund Freud (1856–1939) was an Austrian physician and neurologist, the creator of psychoanalysis. For Freud, morality is a reaction against the evil inherent in man and, therefore, a man had to develop ethical standards to make possible life in society. Freud said:

> Man is not a tender creature in need of love, who would only defend himself if attacked; but on the contrary, a being that has aggressiveness among his instincts. Therefore, the neighbor is … a temptation to satisfy his or her aggressiveness, to exploit the work of others without paying what it corresponds in return, to take advantage of sex without consent, to keep the property of others, to humiliate people, to cause suffering, to martyrize and to kill them: Homo Hominis Lupus.§

For Freud, culture seeks to dominate human aggression and the law is necessary to regulate human relations. Man will always live in a tension between the imposed culture and its natural reality:

> Culture dominates the dangerous aggressive inclination of the individual, weakening the individual; disarming him and making him watch over an intact lodged inside, like a military garrison in the conquered city.¶

---

* en.wikipedia.org/wiki/Mencius.
† www.azquotes.com/quote/1221297.
‡ "El Hombre Nace Bueno y la Sociedad lo Corrompe," Laura Vanin sociabilidadserhumano. blogspot.com.
§ "El Hombre en el Espejo: Un Acercamiento a la Ética de Sigmund Freud," Alejandro Ocampo, www.razonypalabra.org.mx; *El Malestar de la Cultura*, Sigmund Freud (Biblioteca Nueva, 1999), 102. ("The Man in the Mirror: An Approach to the Ethics of Sigmund Freud").
¶ Sigmund Freud, *El Malestar de la Cultura* (Biblioteca Nueva, 1999), 114–15 (*Discomfort of Culture*).

According to a Cherokee legend,* one morning an old Cherokee was teaching his grandson about life. "A fight is going on inside me," he said to the boy. "It is a terrible fight and it is between two wolves. One is evil, the other is good. The same fight is going on inside you, and inside every other person, too." The grandson thought about it for a minute and then asked his grandfather, "Which wolf will win?" The old Cherokee simply replied, "The one you feed."†

J. K. Rowling, the writer of *Harry Potter*, said, "Besides, the world isn't split into good people and Death Eaters. We've all got both light and dark inside us. What matters is the part we choose to act on. That's who we really are."‡

The American writer Mark Twain (1835–1910) said, "Every man is a moon and has a side which he turns toward nobody."§

Manichaeism was the name of a religion founded by the Persian Prince Manes (215–276). The Manicheans were dualists; they believed that in man there was an eternal struggle between two opposing principles: good and evil.¶

For San Augustine of Hippo (354–430), on the contrary, men have the capacity to do bad or good according to his will, in contrast to the Manichean dualism that affirmed that the interior of man was a battlefield where good and evil were intertwined in an eternal struggle and whose result depended on the action of man.

The Austrian psychiatrist Viktor Frankl (1905–1997) survived the Nazi concentration camps during World War II and in his book, *Man's Search for Meaning* wrote:

> From all this, we may learn that there are two races of men in this world, but only these two – the "race" of the decent man and the "race" of the indecent man. Both are found everywhere; they penetrate into all groups of society. … Man is that being who invented the gas chambers of Auschwitz; however, he is also that being who entered those chambers upright, with the Lord's Prayer or the Shema Yisrael on his lips.**

---

* The Cherokee are an indigenous group in North America.
† "Two Wolves," www.firstpeople.us; "Dos Lobos," shechangersoi.be; "Los Dos Lobos. Una Historia Cherokee," www.lcps.org.
‡ www.goodreads.com/quotes/840051-besides-the-world-isn-t-split-into-good-people-and-death; J. K. Rowling, *Harry Potter and the Prisoner of Azkaban.*
§ www.goodreads.com/quotes/237641-every-man-is-a-moon-and-has-a-side-which.
¶ "Maniqueísmo," www.significados.com y "Maniqueísmo," Wikipedia ("Manichaeism").
** www.brainyquotes.com.

The Argentine writer Ernesto Sabato (1911–2011) said that man constantly oscillates between good and evil. "Man ... is suspended between the search for good ... and the inclination for evil."*

Miep Gies (1909–2010), the Austrian who hid Anne Frank (1929–1945) and her family in Amsterdam during World War II, between 1942 and 1944, said:

> Helping people who are in danger is not a question of courage, but a choice between good and evil that every person should do in his life. Thanks to our help Anna lived two more years in which she wrote her diary which represents for millions of people a source of hope and inspiration.†

The Spanish philosopher Jose Ortega y Gasset (1883–1955) said, "With morality, we correct the errors of our instincts."‡

Johann Wolfgang von Goethe (1749–1832) was a German novelist, and his play *Faust* has become a classic of world literature that shows how good and evil coexist within our being and how people must choose which path to follow. The work refers to a German legend in which a man makes a pact with the devil and sells his soul for power, youth, pleasure, and knowledge.

Another book, *Arjuna's Dilemma* – written by Viasa – is based on the history of *Bhagavad Gita*, a Sanskrit text that is part of *Mahabharata* epic, a gigantic work that describes the history of India with life lessons passed down from generation to generation. Thousands of years ago in India, Arjuna, a young warrior prince, leads his army into a civil war against those who unjustly usurped his kingdom. Arjuna noted that among the enemies were relatives, teachers, and friends. He is paralyzed and feels compassion. He asks: "How could we be happy by killing our own kinsmen?" Arjuna gets into an ethical conflict between duty to do and want to do because what he wants to do is not what, apparently, he should do as his duty in his role as a warrior, his "dharma."§

---

* Ernesto Sabato, *La Resistencia* (Planet, 2000), Seix Barral. See also the conference given by the lawyer Esteban Russell at the "First Forum of Artificial Intelligence and Internet of Things in Intelligent and Sustainable Cities in Latin America." May 29, 2018. ("The Resistance").

† "Murió la mujer que escondió a Ana Frank y su Familia," www.lanacion.com.ar, January 13, 2010. ("The woman who hid Anne Frank and her Family died.")

‡ "60 Frases de Ortega y Gasset para entender su Filosofía," www.psicologiaymente.com.("60 Phrases of Ortega y Gasset to understand his Philosophy.")

§ *Dharma* is a term used in various religions such as Buddhism or Hinduism. It means law and if not satisfied with the dharma, the consequence will be bad karma (bad action).

The Uruguayan writer Eduardo Galeano, in a speech when he received the Stig Dagerman Award in Sweden in September 2010, said: "Hopefully we can be disobedient every time we receive orders that humiliate our conscience."*

The Bible relates that Judas Iscariot, one of the 12 apostles of Jesus of Nazareth, was the betrayer. According to the four canonical Gospels, Judas led the guards who arrested Jesus to the place where he was and told them who he was by kissing him. Because of his betrayal, Judas was rewarded with 30 pieces of silver.† But soon he felt guilty and repented. He wanted to return the money to the chief priests, but they did not accept it. Desperate, he committed suicide by hanging himself from a tree. Judas had the freedom to decide and decided to hand Jesus over for a few coins. His conscience led to suicide, and the name Judas became synonymous with treason.

Ethics helps us to answer two questions:

Can I?
Should I?

Not all that I want I can do, not all that I can do I should do.

There will be a peace of mind and conscience and ethical behavior in people when what we want is at the same time what we should do.

For example, imagine that your company is going to do business in a country where (a) you can hire children aged 12 years in factories for 12 hours a day, (b) the safety and hygiene conditions of factories are very bad but allowed by the law of the place, or (c) the company that wants to operate in that country will generate a great environmental contamination that is allowed by the local law, or (d) the factory requires the hiring of security companies that could be linked to the illegal drug business, although that security company is doing a legal business in that country. In all these examples you *could* do business in that country without violating local law, but *should* you?

It is not always enough and it is not a valid excuse to simply comply with the laws of the foreign countries where you act, and such compliance should not be a way to justify unethical behavior. Corporate leaders must be careful and perform an ethical analysis because they can comply with local laws and at the same time act unethically.

---

* clickalsur.wordpress.com October 31, 2014.
† *The Bible* Matthew 26:15.

Normally, legal systems reflect the ethics and values of society. Nevertheless, an ethical analysis is broader than a legal analysis because not everything that is approved by the law is necessarily ethical. For example, consider a company that obtains authorization from the regulatory body to market a product, but nevertheless the company learns that its product has a fault or defect that could generate some harm to the health of the consumer. Despite having "legal" authorization, it would be unethical to market the product.

It may be legal to set a high price and a high-profit margin on a basic product of the family food basket in a deprived area, although perhaps this is not ethical.

Some multinational companies conduct business in developing countries where the environment or working conditions are not regulated as they are in developed countries and where pollution or certain conditions of employment or forms of doing business may be legal.

That a public official designates his entire family in public positions may be legal, but not ethical. In many countries, racially discriminatory laws were legal, although never ethical.

Frederic Bastiat (1801–1850) was an important French economist who said: "When law and morality contradict each other, the citizen has the cruel alternative of either losing his moral sense or losing his respect for the law."[*]

Lynn Sharp Paine, professor at John McLean University, wrote in 1994 that in

> a 1991 case at Salomon Brothers…four top executives failed to take appropriate action when learning of unlawful activities.…Company lawyers found no law obligating the executives to disclose the improper ties. Nevertheless, the executives were forced to resign, for not having the moral authority to lead.[†]

The TV host and entrepreneur Oprah Winfrey[‡] gave a speech at Stanford University on June 15, 2008, where she stated:

> Every wrong decision I've ever made was a result of me not listening to the greater voice of myself. If it doesn't feel right, don't do it. That's the lesson.

---

[*] Frederic Bastiat, *The Law.*

[†] Lynn Sharp Paine, "Managing for organizational integrity," *Harvard Business Review,* 110 (March–April 1994).

[‡] She was one of the 15 most powerful women in the world according to *Forbes* magazine in 2014.

And that lesson alone will save you, my friends, a lot of grief. Even doubt means don't. This is what I've learned. There are many times when you don't know what to do. When you don't know what to do, get still, get very still, until you do know what to do.*

Lee Scott, a former CEO of Walmart Stores for nine years, said in 2005: "If someone asks you to do something that you know is wrong you must have the courage to say 'no'. We all have to do this, no matter our role or position within the company." Ronald Reagan had said, "We must have the courage to do what we know is morally right."†

It is said that a person or company is altruistic (from the French *altruisme*) when he/she or it seeks the good of others even at the expense of one's own. The term means to attend the other and was used by the French philosopher Auguste Comte (1798–1857) in the year 1851. The idea of altruism is that an individual should do the right thing because it is right or will benefit others, not because the individual will benefit from it.

Under the auspices of the Center for Ethical Business Cultures (formerly known as the Minnesota Center for Corporate Responsibility), a group of business leaders developed business principles to foster the fairness and integrity of business relationships. The Minnesota Principles Toward an Ethical Basis for Global Business were proposed in 1992 as a guide to international business activities.

The Preamble states that laws are necessary but insufficient guides for conduct, and the document affirms the legitimacy and centrality of moral values in economic decision-making "because, without them, stable business relationships and a sustainable world community are impossible." The general principles are as follows:

1. Business activities must be characterized by fairness. We understand fairness to include equitable treatment and equality of opportunity for all participants in the marketplace.
2. Business activities must be characterized by honesty. We understand honesty to include candor, truthfulness, and promise-keeping.
3. Business activities must be characterized by respect for human dignity. We understand this to mean that business activities should show a special concern for the less powerful and the disadvantaged.

---

* Stanford News, "Oprah talks to graduates about feelings, failures and finding happiness," June 15, 2008. https://news.standford.edu.
† Reagan, www.brainyquote.com.

4. Business activities must be characterized by respect for the environment. We understand this to mean that business activities should promote sustainable development and prevent environmental degradation and waste of resources.[*]

In language and form, the Minnesota Principles provided a substantial basis for the Caux Round Table, which is an international organization of business executives aiming to promote altruist ethical business practices and moral capitalism.[†] The mission of the organization is to promote ethical and sustainable business practices and facilitate trade based on the Japanese concept of *Kyosei*, which means working together for the common good. The introduction of the "Principles for Responsible Business" published in March 2009, says:

> Trust and confidence sustain free markets and ethical business practices provide the basis for such trust and confidence. But lapses in business integrity, whether among the few or the many, compromise such trust and hence the ability of a business to serve humanity's needs.
>
> Events like the 2009 global financial crisis have highlighted the necessity of sound ethical practices across the business world. Such failures of governance and ethics cannot be tolerated as they seriously tarnish the positive contributions of responsible business to higher standards of living and the empowerment of individuals around the world.
>
> The self-interested pursuit of profit, with no concern for other stakeholders, will ultimately lead to business failure and, at times, to counterproductive regulation. Consequently, business leaders must always assert ethical leadership so as to protect the foundations of sustainable prosperity.
>
> It is equally clear that if capitalism is to be respected, and so sustain itself for global prosperity, it must be both responsible and moral. A business, therefore, needs a moral compass in addition to its practical reliance on measures of profit and loss.[‡]

As Joanne B. Ciulla, professor of ethics at the University of Richmond, has said: "The really creative part of business ethics is discovering ways to do

---

[*] "The Minnesota Principles toward an ethical basis for Global Business," 1992. Mnethicsaward. org.

[†] It was founded in 1986 by Frederick Philips (former president of Philips Company) and Olivier Giscard d' Estain (INSEAD Business School).

[‡] "Principles for Business," Caux Round Table for Moral Capitalism, March 2009, updated in May 2010, www.cauxroundtable.org.

what is morally right and socially responsible without ruining your career and the company."*

Whether a company acts ethically is a significant factor in the average American's willingness to work for an employer, according to independent research released by the company LRN. More than one in three employed Americans have actually left a job because they disagreed with a company's business ethics.

The LRN ethics study provides evidence that links a company's ability to foster an ethical corporate culture with an increased ability to attract, retain, and ensure productivity among US employees.

A majority of workers – 94% – says it is "critical" or "important" that the company they work for is ethical. Eighty-two percent said they would prefer to be paid less but work for a company with ethical business practices than receive higher pay at a company with questionable ethics.

LRN CEO Dov Seidman says, "Our findings confirm that companies with a commitment to ethical conduct enjoy distinct advantages in the marketplace, including attracting and retaining talent."†

Mexican lecturer Miguel Angel Cornejo (1946–2015), a doctor in Molecular Biomedicine and a great promoter of the culture of excellence, says,

> Ethics have produced extraordinary results. Ethics in prices, quality, and services. The richest companies in the world are those that are the most ethical in the world. They do not deceive the consumers; they do not deceive the workers. Its central vector is ethics.

Why should organizations give importance to this issue?

Because when we make decisions, our way of thinking based on ethics, moral conscience, and values determines our behavior.

We act as we think.

1.2 VIRTUES AND VALUES

Adam and Eve were the first people who populated the earth according to Jewish and Christian beliefs. Pursuant to the book of Genesis, Adam was created on the sixth day and God decided he needed a companion.

---

* Andrew Stark, "What's the matter with business ethics," *Harvard Business Review* (May–June 1993).
† www.prsa.org August 3, 2006.

God put Adam and Eve in the Garden of Eden, Paradise, and to allow them to prove their loyalty and obedience gave them the mandate to eat from all the fruits of the trees of the garden, except one. The snake took advantage of this unique rule and tempted Eve to eat the forbidden fruit and then Eve shared it with Adam. This initial lack of obedience – Original Sin – carries them to the expulsion from Paradise, death, pain, embarrassment, and work. It was the first penalty for failure by doing wrong. Adam and Eve acted against the will of God and sinned.

According to the Old Testament of the Bible, another penalty for non-fulfillment occurred when Lot and his people were rescued by two angels from the destruction of Sodom. God asked them only not to turn their heads to look at the fire. But Lot's wife did not resist the temptation and turned her head and by disobeying the divine command, God made her a statue of salt.[*]

People sometimes succumb to ethical temptations and other times resist them. Eva and Edith, Lot's wife, were defeated for the temptation to do the forbidden. When Jesus was tempted in the desert, he refused with determination and conviction. After being baptized by John the Baptist, Jesus fasted for 40 days and nights in the Judaean Desert. During this time, Satan came to Jesus and tried to tempt him. The devil took Jesus to the top of a great mountain where all the kingdoms of the world could be seen. Satan said, "All these things I will give you if you fall down and do an act of worship to me." Jesus replies, "Get away, Satan!"[†]

Temptation is the impulse to sin. *The Bible*, which is full of teachings and proverbs, says in the New Testament, "For I know that good itself does not dwell in me, that is, in my sinful nature. For I have the desire to do what is good, but I cannot carry it out."[‡]

The Lord's Prayer, which is the most important Christian prayer taught by Jesus of Nazareth, ends by saying, "And lead us not into temptation but deliver us from evil. Amen."[§] In this way Catholics ask God to move them away from the paths that can lead them to sin.

Sin is the estrangement of man from God, the removal of what is right and straight.[¶] Evagrius of Pontus (345–399) was a Christian monk and ascetic who was born in the Roman province of Pontus. In 375 in Egypt,

---

[*] Genesis 19: 1–38.

[†] Matthew 4:10

[‡] Romans 7:18

[§] es.wikipedia.org/wiki/Padre_nuestro ("The Lord's Prayer").

[¶] For the Greeks and the Hebrews, sin was "failing in the goal, err on the target, not reach a goal."

to educate about Christian morality, he was the author of the first list of deadly sins, known as evil vices. Evagrius's list contained eight sins, but Pope Gregory the Great, or St. Gregory (540–604), reviewed the list of Evagrius of Pontus and reduced the sins to seven: arrogance, greed, envy, anger, lust, gluttony, and laziness.

These seven vices, or defects of man, have inspired the works of artists. For example, the supreme Italian poet Dante Alighieri (1265–1321) wrote *The Divine Comedy* between 1304 and 1321, a masterpiece of world literature that describes Dante's journey through Hell, Purgatory and Paradise, guided by the Roman poet Virgil (70–19 BC). Dante shows the characteristics of Hell, the place you are going to suffer in for having committed capital sins during life.

The Garden of Earthly Delights is a triptych of the Dutch painter Hieronymus Bosch (1450–1516). The left panel depicts a scene from Paradise of the Garden of Eden, the center panel is adorned by nude figures and different creatures, and the right panel illustrates Hell. The work of Bosch seems to be a warning against lust.*

In the homily given at the Mass celebrated at the Casa Santa Marta in April 2017, Pope Francis recalled that no one is clean, he said, "we are all sinners† and we must avoid falling into corruption, which leads to sin." His Holiness said, "Corruption occurs when sin enters our conscience and leaves no room for air."‡

Virtues are opposed to the seven sins. The word *virtue*, from the Latin *virtus*, refers to a positive quality. *Virtue* in the Greek language means *arête*: mastery or excellence. Ancient Greece gave great importance to the virtue of the excellence or fullness that a person can reach.

The first Greek philosopher who used the term *virtue* was Socrates (470–399 BC), and it meant what helps you to know what is good.

For Aristotle (384–322 BC) the idea of being good was not enough, but man should *do* good. At the beginning of *Nicomachean Ethics*, the Greek philosopher says that ethics is that part of philosophy that it is studied not so much to know it but to practice it. Aristotle argued that to achieve perfection and to live well it was necessary to cultivate virtues. The virtues are *good habits*. Genuine happiness requires the achievement of virtues.

---

* The painting has been housed in the Museo del Prado, in Madrid, since 1939.

† Jesus said, "He that is without sin among you, let him cast the first stone," John 8:2–11.

‡ "Papa Francisco: Todos Somos Pecadores y Podemos Caer en la Corrupcion." ("Pope Francis: We are all sinners and we can fall into corruption.") Miguel Perez Pichel, ACI Press, April 3, 2017, www.aciprensa.com.

Virtues (*aristeia*) are well-oriented *actions* and lead to perfection and excellence in human life. For Aristotle, those people who cultivate and practice virtues develop the excellence of character and happy life. On the other hand, those who fall into the vice of greed or avarice (*pleonexia*) do not achieve a good life.* For Aristotle, a person gets moral virtue when he or she has the habit of choosing excellence in any situation.

Eudaimonia is a Greek term that means happiness, well-being, or prosperity. Etymologically, it is composed of the words *eu* (good) and *daimōn* (spirit) and is the central concept in Aristotelian ethics, together with the word *aretē* (virtue or excellence). Aristotle considers that virtue and its practice are the most important component of eudaimonia, and also recognizes the importance of external goods such as health, wealth, and beauty.[†]

Aristotle develops his concept of virtue beyond that of Socrates. For Socrates virtue is a matter of knowing, a person who really knew what was right would do right. Socrates tended to identify virtue with knowledge, so if someone acted wickedly, that person must not have understood what goodness required. For Aristotle, instead, merely knowing what is right does not guarantee virtuous behavior and that people will do what is right. Virtue also requires a habit. Moral virtue is acquired through repeated actions and constant effort.[‡] For Aristotle, the knowledge of what is right is as important as good habits. Both are necessary to achieve happiness or *eudaimonia*.

The four cardinal virtues guide our conduct.[§] They are prudence, justice, fortitude, and temperance.

Prudence is the virtue that disposes us to choose correctly what we should do, say, and avoid. It helps us to discern right from wrong for each circumstance.

Justice is the virtue that leads us to give everyone his or her due and respect everyone's rights.

Temperance is the virtue that moderates our actions and dominates the will of the pleasures and instincts.

---

* en.wikipedia.org/wiki/Pleonexia.
† In contrast, the Stoics consider virtue as necessary and sufficient for eudaimonia and therefore deny the need for external goods. es.wikipedia.org/wiki/Eudaimonia. Stoicism is a philosophical school founded by the Greek Zeno of Citium (336–246 BC) in 301 BC. The goal of stoicism is to achieve happiness and wisdom dispensing with material goods.es.wikipedia.org/wiki/Staticism.
‡ Joseph W. Koterski, *The Ethics of Aristotle* (The Great Courses, Course Guidebook, 2001).
§ *Cardinal* in Latin means *fundamental*.

Fortitude is the virtue that gives us firmness in difficulties and constancy to do well. This virtue helps us to overcome obstacles and to face problems, and it gives us the courage to face risks.

Plato (427–347 BC), the Greek philosopher follower of Socrates and teacher of Aristotle, describes justice as the foundational virtue. According to Plato, only when justice is understood you can get the other three virtues.

Justice, the virtue that keeps the four together, is represented by the Italian painter and architect Raphael Sanzio (1483–1520) in a 1511 fresco called *Cardinal and Theological Virtues and the Law*, which is in the Vatican.*

Unlike values, the four virtues are universal, constant, and independent of individual and cultural considerations.

Axiology is the philosophical study of value. Values (from Latin *valere*, meaning *strength*) are principles and transmitted beliefs from generation to generation that helps a person to prefer and choose one thing over another or one behavior over another. Values are those qualities by which a person or thing is appreciated. *Value* is all that is "valued" as good, desirable, and necessary, and it reflects the interests and beliefs of each person or organization.†

Values are our guides to analyze and judge situations and facts, and they help us make good decisions where principles, convictions, and ethics prevail over particular interests.

For the Greek Sophist thought the truth was not universal and depended on the interpretation of each person. Good and evil, true and false, depended on the personal perspective with which the facts were valued. For the sophists "everything is relative," "the truth does not exist, only opinions exist" and "each individual perceives the world in its own

---

* In the painting, the virtues represented by the female characters are Prudence, Temperance, and Fortitude. Prudence is the female figure in the center. Temperance is on the right. Fortitude is on the left, holding tightly an oak, considered the epitome of robustness. Justice should be understood as represented by frescoes below the lunette.

† Scottish economist and philosopher Adam Smith (1723–1790) wrote that the word *value* had two meanings in relation to objects. On the one hand, it means the utility of a particular object, and on the other, the ability to exchange an object for other goods. Smith called the first definition "value in use" and the second "value in exchange." Thus, many things that have a higher value in use have a lower value in exchange. For example, Smith explained the diamond-water paradox: water has a great value in use but little value in being exchanged for something else (value in exchange). On the other hand, a diamond has a low utility but can be exchanged for many high-value goods. Adam Smith, *The Wealth of Nations* (Biblioteca de Economía. Folio, 1996), 73.

way and convenience."* For them, things were as they seem to everyone and knowledge is mediated by the personal, cultural, and historical characteristics of who judges the issues. There is no universally valid knowledge; everything is relative because knowledge is limited.

The German philosopher Frederich Nietzsche (1844–1900) made an exhaustive critique of the western culture. For Nietzsche, the values created by culture are false and morality is a force that has corrupted humanity. Nietzsche affirms the death of God and proposes *Nihilism*, which implies "living beyond good and evil."

All human beings have values; all believe that there is value in something. Each individual has his values and depends on cultural considerations. Values are more ambiguous and subjective than virtues since not everyone has the same values, but they can match. For example, justice is a virtue and can be a value to follow. Values are subject to culture, group, religion, habits, and traditions.

Americans celebrate Thanksgiving to commemorate the feast by Pilgrim settlers and their Native American guests in 1621 when the small band of English colonists gave thanks for surviving their first year in their new American home.†

---

* "The Sophists" Jesus Moises del Cid Robles, September 12, 2006, www.filosofia.mx.

† The Pilgrims were members of a radical faction of the English Separatist Church who broke from the Church of England because they considered it "too Catholic." The Pilgrim radicals were distinct from the "Puritans," who shared the belief that the Church of England was too Catholic but wanted to reform the church from within. Since failure to attend Church of England or Anglican services were against the law, the radicals, who called themselves "saints" rather than "Pilgrims," left England in 1608 and settled in Leiden in the Netherlands, where religious laws were less stringent. After a dozen years in the Netherlands, the leaders decided to emigrate to the New World where they believed economic opportunity was better and because they feared their children were becoming too secular and "too Dutch." They convinced English investors to finance a trip to establish a new English-speaking colony. It would become the second successful English colony in North America after Virginia, which was settled in 1607. After receiving permission from King James I, the Pilgrims set sail from Plymouth, England, in September 1620 aboard the *Mayflower*. "How much do you know about the Pilgrims and their legacy?" By Robert Raid, November 25, 2015, www.stripes.com/how-much-do-you-know-about-the-pilgrims-and-their-legacy-1.380430. The Pilgrims founded a colony at Plymouth, Massachusetts, but it is believed that they would not have survived without the help of the native Indians who lived there. When the United States obtained its independence from England in 1776, each state celebrated Thanksgiving on a different day. In 1863 President Abraham Lincoln fixed Thanksgiving Day for the entire country as the last Thursday of November. In 1941, President Franklin D. Roosevelt made Thanksgiving Day the fourth Thursday of November (not necessarily the last one). In the United States, Thanksgiving Day is one of the major holidays of the year. It is a day when families from all over the United States gather together and prepare traditional dishes, watch football on TV, and have a big meal with turkey stuffed in the oven as the main course.

The National Monument to the Forefathers, formerly known as the *Pilgrim Monument*, commemorates the *Mayflower* Pilgrims. Dedicated on August 1, 1889, it honors their ideals and values, later generally embraced by the United States. Located in Plymouth, Massachusetts, the 81-foot-tall monument was commissioned by the Pilgrim Society. On the main pedestal stands the heroic figure of "Faith" with her right hand pointing toward heaven and her left hand clutching the Bible. Upon the four buttresses also are seated figures emblematical of the principles upon which the Pilgrims founded their Commonwealth; counterclockwise from the east are Morality, Law, Education, and Liberty.[*]

Subjective values, such as beauty, depend on the eye of the beholder. Democracy is valued differently in the United States and China. A family photo or letter can be of enormous value to some person and that same photo or letter does not have any value for another person. Women can be valued differently in different parts of the world and that value changes according to times and places.

Susana Frisancho, a Ph.D. in developmental psychology from Fordham University, New York, argues that values are "spectacles" from which we can examine and understand reality. They guide our opinion and behavior and the way we see what is going on.[†]

Values such as honesty, loyalty, commitment, decency, respect, solidarity, and trust are essential to living in society and for the success of organizations. Values give us the perspective to make decisions at any time.

Tom Peters, writer, and American business consultant, comments in a study of outstanding companies,

> All great companies we studied have a clear idea of what they represent and take very seriously the process of forging values. We doubt that is possible to achieve excellence if they do not have clear values and if these values are not successful.[‡]

On December 12, 2003, the former secretary-general of the United Nations, Ghanaian economist Kofi Annan (1938–2018), made a speech at

---

[*] National Monument to the Forefathers en.wikipedia.org/wiki/ National_Monument_to_the_ Forefathers.

[†] "Education with values or Moral Education?" May–June 2002, www.oei.es.

[‡] Thomas Peters and Robert Waterman Jr., *In Search of Excellence* (Editorial Atlántida, 1994), 276.

the University of Tubingen, Germany, entitled "Do we still have universal values?" He said,

> The values do not exist to serve philosophers or theologians, but to help people to live their lives and organize their societies. Therefore, at the international level, we need mechanisms of cooperation strong enough to insist on universal values and be flexible enough to help people to do them in a way that can be effectively applied to their particular circumstances.[*]

People make different decisions based on their personal experiences. In companies, hundreds or thousands of conversations, decisions, and behaviors are carried out every day. Corporate values, which form the organization's culture, should serve as a guide, GPS, or advisor to behave and make the right decisions at all levels in the company to reduce the risk that the company, through its employees, might behave without complying with standards and ethics. People inspired by values would be more likely to act with integrity than people governed by rules.

Consultant Roger Herman, in his book *Keeping Good People*, says that "the successful companies of the future will be based on solid ethical principles. . . . Corporate values will be recognized as the blood that keeps people together."[†]

Corporate values give a sense of belonging to the people in the organization and help answer the following questions: Is the decision we are making fair? Are we being respectful of employees, customers, and suppliers? Are we being honest?

In an article, Attorney Milton Bordwin[‡] says,

> In the Quick Ethics Review of Texas Instruments, the law is the axis of the first question: Is it a legal operation? Overcoming the basic limits of legality, the analysis of Texas Instruments enters the field of values. Is it compatible with the values of the company? Will I feel bad if I do it? The questionnaire includes a warning: If you know it is wrong, do not do it!

Microsoft Corporation was founded by Bill Gates and Paul Allen in 1975 and its headquarters is located in Redmond, Washington, USA. Satya Nadella, CEO of Microsoft, wrote a letter to its employees, which says:

---

[*] www.un.org/press/en/2003.
[†] Roger Herman, *Keeping Good People* (Oakhill Press, 1999), 63.
[‡] Partner of Law Firm Rubin & Rudman, *Revista Gestion*, September–October 1998, 172.

> Our success depends on you. We set high ethical standards in Microsoft and expect every employee to live those standards. Complying with the laws and policies of the company are the first and most important job of every employee of Microsoft.*

Microsoft wrote on its website:

> What are the values? ... They are the beliefs that govern behavior. ... Before making a business decision, ask yourself: Is it consistent with our values and standards? Is it legal? Will I feel comfortable if others find out about the decision?†

Founded in 1892, the Coca Cola Company based in Atlanta, Georgia, USA, is the manufacturer of the most-consumed soft drink in the world. Its Code of Business Conduct says:

> If you ever have a doubt about behavior, ask yourself:
> Is it consistent with the Code?
> Is it ethical?
> Is it legal?
> Reflect well on me and the Company?
> Would I like to read about this in the newspaper?
> If the answer is no to any of these questions, do not do it.‡

3M (Minnesota Mining and Manufacturing) was founded in 1902 and is dedicated to research, development, and commercialization of innovative products. The company says:

> 3M employees ... must make good ethical decisions based on 3M's core values related to honesty, integrity, compliance with commitments, fairness, respect, concern for others and personal responsibility. When faced with the decision on the correct action to be taken, employees must be sure that they can answer "yes" to the following questions:
> Is this action consistent with 3M's corporate values not to compromise honesty and integrity? Will this action protect 3M's reputation as an ethical company? Can this action withstand public scrutiny if it were reported in the media?

---

* www.microsoft.com.
† www.microsoft.com.
‡ Code of Business Conduct, www.coca-colacompany.com, 4.

3M has a worldwide reputation as an ethical company that abides by the law, which does business with uncompromising integrity and honesty.*

People must recognize the ethical dimension of issues. The perception that something is unfair maybe indicating the existence of an ethical problem. Whenever you find yourself thinking about a *zero-sum game* situation, a situation in which there can only be one winner because what one wins another loses, it can be an indicator of an unfair decision.

Ethics is related to decision-making and an ethical business culture prioritizes what is right over what is convenient. Values are before money. Every time you confront an ethical issue, perform the ethical check-up such as the one used in Microsoft, Coca Cola, or 3M. Those questionnaires are a good guide for ethical decision-making.

Each person chooses to act rightly or wrongly when confronting value conflicts. Then he or she must justify his or her actions. Each person, with his or her own actions, can help to develop the virtues and moral values in the organization, to set an example and inspire other employees.

The Indian leader Mahatma Gandhi (1869–1948) said:

> Keep your thoughts positive because your thought become your words
> Keep your words positive because your words become your behavior
> Keep your behavior positive because your behavior becomes your habits
> Keep your habits positive because your habits become your values
> Keep your values positive because your values become your destiny†

Corporate leaders should "define what values should guide your organization. These will form the basis of the corporate culture you want to build."‡

The values on which the corporate culture is based, along with laws, policies, and internal procedures, define the framework in which businesses are done, the scope of the company's activity, and the border between correct and incorrect action.

We all make choices in life; the hard thing is sometimes to live with them. People need to think about the ethical and legal problems that restrict their actions.

---

* Code of Conduct Global Handbook, Be 3M, 12.
† Mahatma Gandhi, www.goodreads.com.
‡ "Three Simple Steps to Improve your Development Culture," Michael Volkov, Lauren Connell, January 10, 2018.

Ethics generally sets standards of conduct higher than those of the laws.

Values are not abstract concepts. Companies should decide what kind of values they want to defend and develop. Keeping values alive should be an organizational priority.

Values are critical guides to help us to judge situations and make decisions.

How important are the values in your organization?

1.3 JUSTICE

As I mentioned earlier, in ancient Greece there was a group of intellectuals called *Sophists* (a term meaning wise) who achieved great influence in Greek youth and were experts in rhetoric and dialectics. The sophists caused a turn in thought. They did not believe in absolute truth, for them everything was relative. They were interested in achieving prestige, social hierarchy, and earning money by teaching the art of oratory in their classes. They devoted themselves to teaching the art of persuasive discourse through argumentation techniques in favor of two sides of the same subject. For example, a disease is good and bad at the same time. It is bad for the patient, but it is good for the doctor.[*]

Three Sophist thinkers stood out above the rest, Protagoras (485–411 BC), Gorgias de Leontino (490–380 BC), and Isocrates (436–338 BC). Protagoras was the first of the professional sophists who received money in exchange for transferring his knowledge of rhetoric. Protagoras had Evatlo as his disciple in his academy. They agreed that in return Evatlo would pay Protagoras his fees when he won the first trial. As time passed and Evatlo did not get clients, Protagoras decided to sue his former student. If he won the trial the court would force Evatlo to pay him and if he lost, Evatlo would have won the first trial and for the agreement they had made, he would also have to pay him. Win or lose Protagoras would receive the fees.[†]

---

[*] Periodo Antropológico, Enrique Sepúlveda Torres, www.esepulveda.cl.tripod.com ("Anthropological Period").

[†] "The Judgment of Protagoras and Evatlo," Alejandro Gamero, www.la piedradesisifo.com, August 22, 2013. Eulato is sometimes known as Evatlo.

Against the sophists were Socrates (470–379 BC), Plato (428–347 BC), and Aristotle (384–322 BC)* who saw the rhetoric of the sophists as an instrument often used to manipulate the emotions of others and omit facts. They accused the sophists of manipulation.†

Plato (427–347 BC) in *The Republic* Book I, says

> "Do you think that a city or an army or a band of pirates or thieves or any association of this kind that propose a common goal through injustice, could carry it out if its components interact with each other with injustice?"‡

The personification of justice balancing the scales of truth and justice dates back to the goddess *Maat*, and later *Isis*, of ancient Egypt.§

In ancient Greece, *Dice* or *Dike* was the goddess who personified justice. In Greek mythology, *Dice* guarded the acts of men and approached the throne of Zeus with regrets whenever a judge violated justice. *Dice* protected the wise administration of justice.

Its equivalent in Roman mythology was *Iustitia* and ancient Rome adopted the image of that female goddess of justice.

It is said that Justice is blind, and it is usually depicted as a Lady of Justice who frequently adorns courts and tribunals wearing a *blindfold*, a *pair of scales* in her hand, and a *sword* in the other. Being blindfolded emphasizes that justice does not look at people but is the same for everyone. The blindfold represents faith, in which justice is, or should be

---

* *Rhetoric* is the name of a Greek treatise on the art of persuasion that was written in the fourth century BC by Aristotle and is attributed to enormous historical influence. "Rhetoric Aristotle," Wikipedia.

  The work deals with the art of speaking and persuading the others taking into account three modes: ethos, pathos, and logos.

  According to *Ethos*, the person proposing an argument must be trustworthy and respected as a professional who has knowledge about the subject under discussion. That is why he must achieve that the audience perceives him in a position of authority and integrity.

  Pathos takes into account the emotions of people. This mode of persuasion appeals to feelings of the audience such as happiness, sadness, hope, and pride.

  Logos is linked to the use of facts. This category includes data, information, statistics, important dates, and all kinds of reasoning. Many speakers rely on a statistic or a reliable source of information to justify their arguments. Logos relies on logical evidence resorting to the reason and intelligence of the audience.

  These three modes of persuasion summarize what a good speech should include: credibility, emotions, and reason. To generate credibility, a speaker must strike a balance between his logical and emotional arguments, www.centropolitico.org/modos-de-persuasion-credibilidad-ethos-emocion-pathos-y-razon-logos/.

† Today "sophism" is said to false arguments formulated with the purpose of inducing error. For example, "All young people drive badly."

‡ "Codes of Conduct," Guillermo Ceballos Serra. 3/2/2011. http: // ceballosserra.blogspot.com/.

§ es.wikipedia.org/wiki/Dama_de_la_Justicia ("Lady of Justice").

imposed objectively, without fear or favor, regardless of identity, money, power, or weakness. The balance implies that a case will be defined putting the arguments and evidence presented on each side of the balance. Finally, the sword means that justice shall punish the guilty with a hard hand.

At the suggestion of the American architect Cass Gilbert (1859–1934), the United States Supreme Court Building Commission selected American sculptor James Earle Fraser (1876–1953) to sculpt the two statues beside the steps of the monumental entrance to the Supreme Court Building situated in Washington D.C.

While developing his design, Fraser wrote to Gilbert, "I think … the figures must have a meaning, and not be perfunctory and purely decorative."*

The name of the two statues is *The Contemplation of Justice* and *Authority of Law*.

In *Contemplation of Justice*, Fraser described the female figure to the left of the main steps as "a realistic conception of what I consider a heroic type of person with a head and body expressive of the beauty and intelligence of justice." A book of laws supports her left arm and a figure of blindfolded Justice is in her right hand.

In *The Guardian or Executor of Law*, Fraser described the male figure to the right of the steps as "powerful, erect, and vigilant. He waits with concentrated attention, holding in his left hand the tablet of laws, backed by the sheathed sword, symbolic of enforcement through law." The Latin word for law, LEX, is inscribed on the tablet.†

The Roman jurist Domicio Ulpiano (170–228) said that people had "to live honestly, do no harm and give everyone his due. … Justice is the habit of giving everyone his due."

Roman politician and philosopher Marcus Tullius Cicero (106–46 BC) said, "Justice is a habit of the soul, observed in the common interest, which gives each his dignity. … Nothing is more beautiful than knowing the truth and nothing is more shameful than approving the lie and treating it for truth."‡

Marco Tullius Cicero (106–43 BC) and Aristotle (384–322 BC), both agreed that there were differences in laws in different jurisdictions, although in all of them there were universal precepts – such as the principle of equity – that it was adopted in every jurisdiction.

---

* www.supremecourt.gov/about/FraserStatuesInfoSheet.pdf.

† www.supremecourt.gov/about/FraserStatuesInfoSheet.pdf.

‡ The French painter and sculptor Georges Braque (1882–1963) said: "Truth exists. Only lies are invented."

As I pointed out when mentioning the cardinal virtues, Justice is a virtue that is guided by the truth and respect for the rights of individuals, giving each his or her due. Justice is one of the general principles of law and it is the origin of all legal systems, associated with the principles of fairness and impartiality.

The word *law* comes from the Latin word *directum* and means "what is well run, which does not deviate from the right path" or "what is according to the rule, to the law, to the norm," or "what does not deviate to one side or the other."*

Law is a normative and institutional order of human behavior inspired by the postulates of justice and legal certainty. Its character and content are based on social relationships in a certain place and time. The Austrian jurist and philosopher Hans Kelsen (1881–1973) said in his Pure Theory of Law that "the law is a normative order of human behavior; it is a system of rules that regulate behavior."†

The purpose of the law is to order behaviors and to regulate social relations and our behavior by establishing in the normative order what is allowed and what is prohibited.

The Digest, a legal work published in 533 by the Byzantine emperor Justinian (483–585), begins by saying that "The law is the art of good and fair."‡ And the *Institutes* of Justinian begins with a definition of Justice as "the set and constant purpose which gives to every man his due."§

King Solomon was the third and last king of the United Kingdom of Israel before the separation of Israeli territory into the kingdoms of Judah and Israel. Son of King David, who killed Goliath, Solomon managed to reign over a vast territory for nearly four decades. According to the Bible, Solomon was a young king when he took office and asked God for help. He asked for neither wealth nor long life, only wisdom: "Grant your servant a docile heart to judge your people, to discern between good and bad."¶

The book 1 Kings in the Bible** describes what King Solomon did to find the truth in a dispute between two women who claimed to be the mother

---

* es.wikipedia.org/wiki/Derecho.
† "Análisis de la Teoría Pura del Derecho de Hans Kelsen," Carla Santaella, www.monografias.com/trabajos87/analisis-teoria-pura-del-derecho-hans-kelsen/analisis-teoria-pura-del-derecho-hans-kelsen.shtml, July 2011. ("Analysis of the Pure Theory of Law by Hans Kelsen").
‡ es.wikipedia.org/wiki/Ius.
§ "The Institutes of Justinian," translated into English by J. B. Moyle (1913), www.gutenberg.org/files/5983/5983-h/5983-h.htm.
¶ The Bible, 1 Kings. 3.5–7.
** The Bible, 1 Kings. 3: 16–28.

of the same child. The two women lived together and had given birth to their children with a difference of three days. One night one of the babies died because the mother had leaned on her baby while she was sleeping. Realizing what had happened, the mother of the dead baby exchanged her baby with the other. Upon waking, the living baby's mother recognized that the dead baby was not hers and began to argue.

To solve the problem, King Solomon was asked to resolve the dispute. The king said, "Bring the sword and divide the body of the child in two. Give half to one and a half to the other."

The woman who was the living baby's real mother told the king: "My lord, give her the living child, do not kill."

The other woman told the king: "Neither I nor you, but divide."

The king said, "Hand over her the living child, not kill him. It's your mother." Solomon was able to see that the mother of the living child preferred to give him up rather than watch him die.

True justice is the art of giving fairness. The Chinese thinker Confucius (571–479 BC) said that "knowing what is right and not do it is the worst cowardice."

Socrates with his "Socratic method" of asking questions refuted the Greek sages many times and began to be imitated by young Athenians, thus transforming certain traditions of Greek society. His accusers put him on trial. According to Plato and Xenophon, the trial conducted in 399 BC was one of the most famous in Antiquity. Socrates was accused of having corrupted youth and denying the existence of gods. Plato led the protest against the arrest and death of Socrates attributing it to sophistic rhetoric. The jury was composed of 501 citizens. A majority of 280 found him guilty with 221 against. Socrates proposed to pay a fine as a sanction, but the accusers asked the jury for the death penalty. A total of 360 voted in favor and 141 against. Faced with injustice, Criton and many of his followers recommended he flee into exile, which would have been accepted by society, but Socrates refused because if he ran away he would be contravening one of the principles he held, never answer injustice with another injustice (disobedience to the laws).* Socrates advocated to always act with justice and respecting the laws stated: "it is better to suffer an injustice than to commit it."[†] That's why he drank the hemlock and died at 70.

---

* Francois L'Yvonnet, "Socrates, entre la Pena de Muerte y Suicidio Ejemplar," www.revistaaleph. com, June 26, 2009; es.wikipedia.org/wiki/juicio_de_Socrates. ("Socrates, between the Death Penalty and Exemplary Suicide" in Wikipedia, "Trial of Socrates").
† www.askphilosophers.org/question/1395.

The American writer Napoleon Hill said, "Socrates' decision to drink the cup of poison, rather than compromise his personal belief, was a decision of courage."*

The theologian and English judge, Thomas More (1478–1535), reflected on the injustice in the world and over 38 years wrote a book called *Utopia* in which he wanted to organize an ideal society on an island.

In 1535 More was put on trial by King Henry VIII (1491–1547). He was accused of high treason for not taking an oath to the Anglican Church, for opposing the king's divorce from Catherine of Aragon (1485–1536), and for not accepting Henry VIII as head of the new Church. More remained in prison in the Tower of London for 80 days and was beheaded on July 6, 1535. His head was boiled on a stick and displayed on London Bridge. More is considered an example of moral consistency; his integrity served the supreme ideal of justice as well as the defense of conscience against power.

On February 21, 1631, the Italian astronomer Galileo Galilei (1564–1642) publicized in Florence his *Dialogue*, where he mocks the geocentric theory that established that the earth was in the center and the Sun was spinning around it. His book, *Copernican*,† was considered scandalous. Galileo, aged 69, was required to appear before the court of the Roman Inquisition. On June 22, 1633, Galileo was forced to pronounce on his knees the abjuration of his doctrine before the commission of inquisitors, under the orders of Pope Urban VIII (1568–1644). Galileo was forced to say, "I Galileo Galilei abandoned the false opinion that the Sun is the center of the Universe and is motionless. I abjure, curse and detest such errors." When he stood up after this plea that was imposed on him, he said, "E Pur Si Muove" ("and yet he moves"), referring to the earth around the Sun. Galileo was sentenced to live under house arrest and the court ordered to burn all copies of his book.‡

The late 1600s saw the advent of a more modern adversarial system in England and American Colonies. The adversarial system resolves disputes;

---

* Napoleon Hill, *Think and Grow Rich*, Vermilion (Random House, 2004), 160–1.
† The Polish astronomer monk, Nicolas Copernicus (1473–1543) formulated in a work the Heliocentric theory (the earth moves around the Sun), which had been conceived in the first instance by the Greek astronomer and mathematician Aristarchus of Samos (310–230 BC). Copernicus published his work in 1543, the year of his death. "Nicolas Copernico," en.wikipedia.org.
‡ Es.wikipedia.org/wiki/galileo-galilei; also see "Galileo Galilei y el Juicio de Herejia que lo llevo a Prisión," Maricela Flores, www.de10.com.mx, February 15, 2018. Galilei died in 1642, the year in which the English physicist Isaac Newton (1642–1727) was born ("Galileo Galilei and the Heresy Trial that took him to Prison").

both sides argue their point of view by presenting conflicting views of fact and law to an impartial arbiter who decides which side wins what.*

The importance of Justice is undeniable and it is reflected in the thinking of Pope Francis, Jorge Luis Borges, Abraham Lincoln, and the Oath of Judges of the International Court of Justice.†

The administration of justice in decision-making should be a key objective in organizations. It involves making decisions that are fair when employees are hired, evaluated, promoted, and sanctioned. The American philosopher John Rawls (1921–2002) in *Theory of Justice* mentions the need for impartiality to achieve justice. Justice in organizations means fairness and impartiality in decisions, equal opportunities, and treating everyone equitably, without arbitrariness or privileges.‡

The American political philosopher at Harvard University Law School, Michael J. Sandel, said, "Justice is not only about the right way to distribute things. It is also about the right way to value things."§

Business leaders have the challenge of managing people who are different in their origin, way of thinking, culture, and personality. Part of the task of leaders is to make decisions related to group members and solve problems. And they must do so with justice.

All must be measured with the same yardstick of justice. Disciplinary sanctions in organizations must always be administered in a fair and

---

* Monroe H. Freedman, "Our Constitutionalized Adversary System," www.chapman.edu/law. In 1694 in England, the judges dressed in black to mourn the death of Queen Maria II (1662–1694) and that tradition has remained to date.
† Jorge Mario Bergoglio was the Archbishop of Buenos Aires before being appointed the 266th pope of the Catholic Church, and in his homily on May 25, 2006, he said: "Happy is he who practices justice. … Happy is he who hunger and thirst of justice that orders and pacifies, because he places limits on errors and faults, does not justify them; because he responds to abuse and corruption, does not conceal it; because he helps to solve and he does not wash his hands."
    Abraham Lincoln (1809–1865) in his address in Peoria, Illinois, in 1854, said: "Stand with anyone that is right; stand with him while he is right and part with him when he goes wrong."
    The International Court of Justice (ICJ) is the principal judicial organ of the United Nations, and its judges must make in the first public hearing the following oath: "I solemnly declare that I will perform my duties and exercise my powers as a judge, honestly and faithfully, with absolute impartiality and conscientiously."
    The Argentine writer Jorge Luis Borges (1899–1986) said "Once people are fair, we may not need Justice," The Last October Document, *Clarin*, October 20, 2018.
‡ In *Theory of Justice*, a group of people is imagined as meeting in an original position and their task is to decide which would be the principles of a society under which they will live, and "just society" is one of the principles chosen in such a context.
§ "Michael Sandel," Wikipedia. Sandel's course *Justice* was the university's first course to be made freely available online and on television. It has been viewed by tens of millions of people around the world, including in China, where Sandel was named the "most influential foreign figure of the year" (*China Newsweek*).

consistent manner. Similar situations should be treated alike. If there is no justice, employees' trust in the organization will erode.

Decisions made by business leaders should always be fair, impartial, and objective in each particular case and should adopt justice as a fundamental value for managing people.

1.4 COOPERATION AND TRUST

A credit agreement is a financial operation in which a person, the creditor, makes a loan for a certain amount of money to another person, the debtor, and in which the latter agrees to return the amount requested plus interests, in a term defined according to the conditions established for the loan.[*]

The word *credit* comes from the Latin *credititus* (from the verb credere: creer), which means "trusting thing." So "credit" in its origin means trusting or having confidence.[†] In economic and financial life there is credit when there is confidence in the ability to fulfill a contracted obligation.

At the beginning of the twentieth century, people had to pay cash for almost all products and services. In 1949, Frank X. McNamara, director of the Credit Corporation "Hamilton," went to have dinner with two friends at the Majors Cabin Grill restaurant in New York. When it was time to pay for dinner, McNamara discovered that he had forgotten his wallet and, in an embarrassing situation, his wife had to bring him the money.

A few months later McNamara founded Diners Club. The first Diners Club cards were delivered in 1950 to 200 people and accepted by 14 restaurants in New York. They were not plastic, but a type of paper with the conditions of acceptance on the back, including the credit limit. As trust in the means of payment grew, the concept of the card grew and, by the end of 1950, 20,000 people were using the Diners Club credit card.[‡]

---

[*] es.wikipedia.org/wiki/Crédito.
[†] es.wikipedia.org/wiki/Crédito.
[‡] Diners Club International, Wikipedia, "The first Credit Card, History," Felix Casanova, Hdnh.es "The credit card," www.expansion.com/2014/07/10/directives. In 1952 McNamara sold his shares in the company to his two partners for $200,000. The Diners Club credit card continued to grow and had no competition until 1958. In that year, both American Express and Banco Americard (later called VISA) appeared in the market.

Trust is the foundation of any relationship between individuals; it is the belief and confidence that a person will act in a certain way in a given situation. When someone trusts the other, one can predict the actions and behaviors of the other. This is how trade works, manufacturers, distributors, supermarkets, customers, credit card companies, banks; all form the links of the same trust chain that holds them together.

Who aspires to influence and convince other people to follow a determined course should build confidence making good decisions and aligning their statements and behavior with values.

When an important decision is made it is necessary to analyze in depth the situation in order to choose the best path according to the different alternatives and potential results. Because after making the decision it is necessary to face its consequences.*

Making good decisions and ethical choices in our work build trust in each other. A trusting environment allows sharing knowledge and information and it facilitates the growth and long-term development of enterprises and individuals.

The area of choice under uncertainty represents the heart of decision theory, which is closely related to the field of game theory.†

Game Theory is an area of applied mathematics that is used to study the interactions of individuals and decision-making processes. According to this theory, a game is a set of players, moves, optimal strategies, and rewards. Game theory studies behavior and rational interaction in situations of competition and cooperation and analyzes the best possible

---

* The "Theory of Decision," refers to the study of the behavior of decision-makers. The analysis of decisions in situations of uncertainty was analyzed and developed by the French mathematician Blaise Pascal (1623–1662) in his work *Pensées* (Thoughts) (1670).

† It was created by a mathematician, John von Neumann (1903–1957). Game theory did not really exist as a unique field until John von Neumann published *On the Theory of Games of Strategy* in 1928. Von Neumann addressed how to play the child's game of matching pennies. The game is played as follows: Two players each hold one penny behind their backs and decide which face of the coin they are going to reveal – heads or tails. They count to three, then show each other the pennies at the same time. If the pennies match – either both heads or both tails – then one of the players wins both coins. If the pennies don't match, then the other player wins both coins. You should expect to win only about 50% of the times. In the matching pennies game, in every interaction, one of the players wins and the other loses, and that's all that can happen. The matching pennies are a zero-sum game. In zero-sum games, the total benefit to all players in the game, for every combination of strategies, always adds to zero (more informally, a player benefits only at the equal expense of others). His paper was followed by the 1944 book *Theory of Games and Economic Behavior*, co-written with Oskar Morgenstern (1902–1977), which considered cooperative games of several players. en.wikipedia.org/wiki/Game_theory; en.wikipedia.org/wiki/Matching_pennies; Professor Connel Fullenkamp, *The Economics of Uncertainty*, The Great Courses (2015).

decision for a person when the costs and benefits for that person depend also on what others do.

Professor Barry Nalebuff of the Yale School of Management and Professor Adam Brandenburger of Harvard Business School have studied game theory and say:

> The game theory exists when there are many interdependent factors and we cannot make a decision regardless of many others.[*] The basic idea of game theory is the importance of focusing on others; that is, allocentrism. You have to take the place of the other players. We have to be allocentric... the ability is to bring together the two points of view: understanding both the egocentric and allocentric perspectives.[†]

Game theory involves two players in a situation where each does not know the move of the other, and they have the option to cooperate or defect from the game. If both cooperate to protect each other, they both receive a beneficial payoff.[‡]

Game theory prompts us to consider not just our own plans but the responses of others who have an interest in the outcome. Anticipating these responses should allow us to identify and select the strategy that maximizes our payoff.[§]

Try to imagine how the other players see the game and then make your decision. In addition to our own decisions, the decisions made by others are of fundamental relevance, as are how the players cooperate and the degree of trust that exists between players.

The *Ultimatum Game* is an experiment created in 1982 by the economists Werner Guth, Rolf Schmittberger, and Bern Schwarze of the University of Cologne in Germany to analyze people's sense of fairness when they make decisions. In this experiment, the first player receives a sum of money and proposes to another player how to divide the sum. The second player chooses to either accept or reject the proposal. If the second player accepts, the money is split according to the proposal. If the second player rejects, neither player receives any money. Let's illustrate the experiment with an example obtained from Linda Trevino and Katherine Nelson:

---

[*] Barry J. Nalebuff and Adam Brandenburger, *Coopetition* (Grupo Editorial Norma, 1996), 9.

[†] Barry J. Nalebuff and Adam Brandenburger, *Coopetition* (Grupo Editorial Norma, 1996), 88.

[‡] Stanley Ridgley, *Strategic Thinking Skills, Course Guidebook* (Drexel University, The Great Courses, The Teaching Company, 2012), 126.

[§] Stanley Ridgley, *Strategic Thinking Skills, Course Guidebook* (Drexel University, The Great Courses, The Teaching Company, 2012), 127.

Subject A receives 10 one-dollar bills and can give subject B any number of them. Subject B can choose to accept or reject A's offer. If B accepts they each get what was offered. If B rejects the offer, each gets nothing. It seems that A could offer B one dollar and keep the rest and B should accept the offer because getting one dollar is better than nothing.

But most A subjects offer B close to half the total, an average of 4 dollars. B subjects who are offered one or two dollars generally reject the offer. Therefore, people's sense of fairness seems to be driving both subjects' behaviors.*

This simple experiment serves to better understand the behavior of the human being. People do not act in a purely rational way since they reject monetary payments that improve their initial situation. People prefer to punish inequality and expect fair and balanced treatment.

The *Prisoner's Dilemma*, popularized in 1950 by the Canadian mathematician Albert William Tucker (1905–1995), is a problem of game theory (also known as decision theory) that shows the tension between individual and group advantages and also shows that if people do not trust each other and do not cooperate, they will act against their own interests.

The scenario of the Prisoner's Dilemma is that after a robbery, police detained two people. It is certain that at least one of the two suspects is the culprit. Each of the two persons is interrogated separately and is presented with the following:

If you plead guilty and the other person pleads not guilty, you will be ten years in prison and the other person will go free.

If you plead not guilty and the other person pleads guilty, you will go free and the other person will be ten years in prison.

If the two plead not guilty for trying to deceive the police, they will both be sent to prison for 15 years.

If the two plead guilty, the penalty will be five years for each one.

The prisoners must decide whether or not to confess. The separate and individual thought of each prisoner would lead everyone to make the decision that is best for each person. However, as we have seen, the best solution for both is that the two are declared guilty.

While each player seeks to optimize their own advantage, selfishness, competition, and lack of confidence hurt the players. Instead, cooperation, coordination, and complementarity among members of a team and the

---

* Linda Trevino y Katherine Nelson, chap 1, *Managing Business Ethics*, 5th ed (Wiley, 2011).

transparency of their actions build better results. If you want to go far, you need to go together.

Game theory makes it clear that cooperation is more important than individualism. If we act in silos, independent of each other, then we will not achieve maximum performance. We all depend on each other. To be successful and get the best results, we must collaborate cross-functionally and cross-geographically and we must communicate often and effectively.

The American author Peter Senge said, "Collaboration is vital to sustain what we call profound or really deep change, because without it, organizations are just overwhelmed by the forces of the status quo."*

For some animals, coordination and teamwork can be learned. Ants work well together and solve complex problems. They focus on the needs of the colony rather than on their own individual needs. Teamwork is dependent on trusting other folks to come through with their part.

Researchers at the University of Illinois at Urbana Champaign have been looking for ways to improve human coordination during disaster situations. These researchers attempt to draw inspiration from the collaboration patterns that honeybees and ants use in their decision-making process in order to develop coordination strategies in a chaotic situation.†

When geese migrating south to avoid the cold, they create a *V* structure because each bird produces an air stream that helps the goose behind it, and therefore it can increase their flight by more than 70%. If a goose falls out of formation, it feels the air resistance and immediately returns to the *V* structure to benefit from the goose that is in front. They work as a team and help each other with a great sense of community. That solidarity and sense of union make them more effective.

In organizations, the bonds of trust and an atmosphere of cooperation among employees create a better complementarity, performance, and results. Good teamwork produces a better result.

A popular legend tells that Mr. Fleming, a Scottish farmer, one day saved the son of a nobleman from drowning, and the latter, in gratitude, paid for Fleming's son's medical studies. Years later, the son of the nobleman, Winston Churchill, being prime minister of the United Kingdom, became seriously ill with pneumonia and was saved by the young Fleming, who administered the penicillin he had discovered.‡

---

* Peter Senge, Goodreads.com.
† "Honeybees Collaborate When Foraging, Selecting a New Hive Through Knowledge Sharing," Asknature.org/strategy/collaborative_for_Group_decisions, November 29, 2015.
‡ This story first appeared in 1950 in a US religious publication, *Devotion Programs for Youth*, in the chapter titled "The Power of Goodness."

Companies are not successful unless all members work together toward a common mission. All depend on each other.

The Dutch Maurits Hendriks, who was in charge of the men's hockey team of Spain,* one day visited with his team the Ferrari factory in Maranello,† where Formula One teams are trained and where he was able to observe the high degree of coordination and cooperation among the team members. He said:

> The training caught my attention. A team of twelve people has five seconds to change the wheels and fill the gas tank. In that short time, no one can make a wrong step because otherwise the team dynamic breaks. You have to understand exactly what your task is, but at the same time, know what the role of the others is.‡

In 2019, some Formula One teams change tires in less than two seconds.

Herbert Brooks Jr. (1937–2003) was the coach of the ice men hockey team at the University of Minnesota. Soon after Minnesota won its third college championship in 1979, Brooks was hired to coach the US Olympic team. He named several of his Minnesota players to the team as well as several from their rival, Boston University. Brooks trained a squad of college students' team with a strong emphasis on teamwork, a difficult thing to do because of the tough rivalry between the University of Minnesota and Boston University. Brooks told the players that they were to let go of old rivalries and start becoming a team where trust prevails among all. In 1980 his team won the gold medal-winning Olympic ice hockey at Lake Placid. The US Olympic ice hockey team's victory in semifinals over the favored Soviet professionals in 1980 was dubbed as the "Miracle on Ice."§

Robert Levering, co-founder of Great Place to Work, an institute that since 1992 has been dictated to the research and consulting to improving work environments, says "An excellent place to work is one in which you

---

* With that team, Hendriks won the titles of the Champions Trophy in 2004, the European Championship in 2005, and the bronze medal in the 2006 World Cup.

† Maranello is a town in Northern Italy. It is the home of the Scuderia Ferrari Formula One racing team.

‡ *La Nacion*, March 23, 2008, sports section, 14.

§ Upon the 25th anniversary of the Miracle on Ice, the Olympic ice arena in Lake Placid, New York, where the United States won the gold medal, was renamed Herb Brooks Arena. A statue of Brooks depicting his reaction to the victory in the "Miracle" game was erected at the entrance to the River Centre in Saint Paul, Minnesota, in 2003. Disney released a film about the 1980 Olympic team in 2004 called *Miracle*. Brooks served as a consultant during principal photography, which was completed shortly before his death. At the end of the movie, there is a dedication to Brooks. It states, "He never saw it. He lived it." Miracle, Wikipedia; Herb Brooks, Wikipedia.

trust people to whom you work, you are proud of what you do and enjoy the people you work with." Great Place to Work says, "Our data show that trust in the workplace is the best investment that the company can make. Confidence leads to better selection and recruitment of new employees, lower turnover, greater innovation and productivity, more loyal customers and higher profits."

Greek fabulist Aesop (620–564 BC) tells the fable of the scorpion and the frog.

A scorpion asked a frog to help him to cross a lagoon. The frog refused because it was a scorpion and the frog feared being attacked. But the scorpion promised not to hurt her and convinced her that it would make no sense to kill her because he would also drown. When the frog had swum halfway across, the scorpion stung the frog. The frog, surprised and pained, asked, "How could you do this? Both of us will die now" and the scorpion apologized, saying "I had no choice, it's my nature." Soon after, both disappeared underwater.

Was the scorpion someone to trust?

Companies should avoid having labor and commercial relations with people and companies who do not enjoy trust and a good reputation because the cost can be high. An investigation conducted in 2002 by the American Society of Association Executives (ASAE) revealed that transparency and trust are indivisibly linked because transparency is a means to generate a climate of trust.* When there is no transparency, confidence is lost, and the leadership and the company go into crisis.

Transparency of actions is vital for people to work collaboratively. Organizations must create a culture of trust wherein a collaborative network exists, people are respected, there are solidarity, cooperation, and team spirit; and every person gives the best of themselves for the benefit of all.

In Japan at the age of six, children walk to school in the company of older students. Thus, older students learn the importance of responsibility and cooperation. They all clean the school and its bathrooms. In this culture, it is very important to teach children to work as a team and to help each other. Generosity and respect for others are taught in Japan from childhood.

The American football coach Vince Lombardi (1913–1970) said, "Individual commitment to a group effort – that is what makes a teamwork, a company work, a society work, a civilization work."†

---

* Michael Ritter, *El Valor del Capital Reputacional* (Olivos, Ritter & Partners, 2013), 65.
† www.vincelombardi.com/quote.

The former player and coach of the National Basketball Association (NBA) Phil Jackson said, "Good teams end up being big teams when their members trust each other enough to give up the 'I' for 'us'."

Ginni Rometty, CEO of IBM, said, "Your value will not be what you know, it will be what you share."*

The Japanese chemist Kaoru Ishikawa (1915–1989) said that business quality is backed by ethical behavior: "I am an advocate of quality control based on the belief of virtue of people.... If a person does not trust his subordinates and imposes strict control ... the system does not work."

Starbucks, founded in 1971 in Seattle, is the world's largest coffee company. Starbucks understands that the way to be successful and get a great employee performance is by creating an environment of trust and loyalty among customers and employees. For Starbucks it is not enough to add talent; they must also build trust between them. For Starbucks, "the value of a trademark is 100% linked to the confidence that people have that the company will do what it said it was going to do."

The business of the French corporation Alstom is based on trust. In its code of ethics, the French Corporation says:

> Teamwork is the way we achieve our collective and individual objectives. Teamworking means collaboration at all levels of the organization and extends to our external partners.
>
> Alstom, with its activities, several management structures, units, production sites, and countries, is by definition a complex company. Trust is essential for the proper conduct of our business and the efficient management of our projects.
>
> Trust is closely associated with professionalism, integrity, compliance, and responsibility. Mutual trust between colleagues, management and external partners enables empowerment and the delegation of authority. In return, anyone exercising this delegation is accountable for the decisions taken, their actions and their consequences. When we work in a mindset of trust, we are open to our professional environment and ethical and transparent in our dealings.†

Trust is earned and built over time through what is said and done and through integrity, and it must be protected to maintain it.

Professor Jorge Etkin has written:

---

* quotefancy.com/quote/1548073/Ginni-Rometty.
† "Our Code of Ethics," Alstom, 2, www.alstom.com.

How can a company be run when the parties distrust each other? ... In that environment, delegating is like giving resources to your adversary.*

When there is no trust and credibility, shortcuts and illegality show up at all levels of the organization.

An analogy exists between the sustainable growth of a company and a country. To grow over time, countries require stable and predictable institutions that generate investor confidence.† Companies, meanwhile, to achieve sustainable growth require an institutional cultural base that generates confidence to attract investment and growth.

The German philosopher Max Weber (1864–1920) introduced culture in the analysis of social development:

A society evolves into development if the two protagonists of change – officials and businessmen – have a cultural attitude conducive to development.... If there is a professional and honest bureaucracy and a truly competitive business class, there are bases for development.‡

Robert A. Dahl (1915–2014), who was a professor of political science at Yale University and one of the most prominent American political scientists, said, "The United States was in its infancy an economically underdeveloped country in relation to England. Its priority, however, was to establish a Constitution and fulfill it. ... The resulting institutional security created a climate by which economic development would emerge."§

Francis Fukuyama, an American political scientist, explains that

one of the most important lessons we can learn from examining the economic activity is that the prosperity of a nation, as well as its ability to compete, is conditioned by a cultural characteristic: the level of confidence inherent in society.¶

For this author, "trust is like a lubricant that makes any group or organization to operate in a more efficient way."

---

* "Bases Conceptuales de la Gestion Socialmente Responsable" (Conceptual Bases of Socially Responsible Management), Jorge Etkin, *Saberes*, 1 (2009).
† The Austrian-Hungarian economist and philosopher Friedrich Hayek (1899–1992), Nobel Laureate in Economics in 1974, considered the development of institutions (justice, laws, the right to private property, contractual rights, etc.) as the necessary condition to achieve a "spontaneous order" that would enable economic growth.
‡ Mariano Grondona, *Corruption* (Editorial Planeta, 1993), 74.
§ Mariano Grondona, *Corruption* (Editorial Planeta, 1993), 75–6.
¶ Francis Fukuyama, *Trust: The Social Virtues and the Creation of Prosperity* (Free Press, 1995).

Some magazines, newspapers, and consultants measure business confidence. For example, *Forbes* magazine is specialized in the world of business and finance. Founded in 1917 by the Scottish journalist Bertie Charles Forbes (1880–1954), it annually publishes a list of the "100 Most Trustworthy Companies" among those publicly traded in the United States.

Another ranking called "The Most Trustworthy Companies in America" is produced by GMI Ratings and involves the review of accounting and corporate behavior of 5,000 companies listed on the New York Stock Exchange.

Other methods of calibration measure companies based on their reputation, integrity, and other non-financial criteria. For example, *Fortune* magazine creates a ranking of the most admired companies; the *Financial Times* creates another ranking on the most respected global companies; *Dow Jones* prepares an index on sustainability programs and environmental protection; Great Place to Work selects great places to work; Ethisphere rewards the most ethical companies.

Rankings ultimately measure a certain level of credibility, trust, and respect for the organizations listed in these rankings. The biannual Meaningful Brands Global Index made by Havas Media Group is also a great tool that analyzes 1,500 brands.*

Public relations firms – such as Edelman, founded in Chicago in 1952 and ranked number one globally by *The Holmes Report* – helps organizations promote confidence and protect their brands. For 18 years the *Edelman Trust Barometer* is a reference in the measurement of people's trust. In the Annual Global Survey conducted in 2018, Richard Edelman, president and CEO of Edelman wrote, "Nearly 7 in 10 respondents say that building trust is the number one job of the CEO's, ahead of high-quality products and services. … Nearly two-thirds say they want CEO's to take the lead on policy change."†

Countries are also measured by their degree of confidence. A country risk index attempts to measure the level of risk that a country has in foreign investments, which is related to the possibility that a sovereign state will be prevented or unable to meet its foreign obligations. The country risk is measured through the surtax paid for their bonds issued compared with

---

* www.meaningful-brands.com/en.
† "The Battle for Truth," Richard Edelman, Executive Summary Edelman Trustbarometer 2018 Annual Global Study, cms.edelman.com.

the rate paid by the US Treasury on its bonds. The lower the rate a country pays, the greater the level of confidence it will generate.

Many business people and thinkers emphasize the importance of trust in business. In the footnote, you can read their thoughts as examples.*

---

* Cavett Robert (1907–1997), founder of the National Speakers Association, said: "If my people understand me, I will achieve his attention. If my people trust me, I will achieve its action." John Maxwell, *Developing the Leader Within You* (Nelson, 1993), 39.

Warren Buffett, CEO of Berkshire Hathaway and one of the most influential people in the world, says that "confidence is like the air we breathe. When present, no note; but when it is absent, everybody notices."

Stephen M. R. Covey and Rebecca R. Merrill are the book authors of *The Speed of Trust*, in which they say: "Trust always affects two variables, speed, and cost. When confidence decreases, the speed decreases and cost increases. When confidence increases, the speed increases, and the cost decrease" (Free Press, 2006), 13.

Bill George, former CEO of Medtronic, says: "Trust is everything, because success depends on customer confidence in the products they buy, the employee confidence in their leaders, investor's confidence and the public trust in capitalism, if you do not have integrity, no one will trust you." Bill George, *The True North: Discover Your Authentic Leadership* (New York: John Wiley & Sons, Inc., 2007).

Jack Welch, the former CEO of General Electric, said of trust: "You know what it is when you feel it."

Robert Eckert, Mattel's former CEO for 11 years, stated: "When you get to work, your greatest responsibility should be to build trust. ... Trust is the key to creating the reputation of the company." Stephen M. R. Covey and Rebecca R. Merrill, *The Speed of Trust* (Free Press, 2006), 27 and 263.

The Irish Nail Fitzgerald, the former CEO of Unilever, said "you can have all the facts and figures ... but if you cannot attain trust, you are not going anywhere." Stephen M. R. Covey and Rebecca R. Merrill, *The Speed of Trust* (Free Press, 2006), 4.

French academic Laurence Cornu-Bernot says, "Trust is a hypothesis about the future behavior of the other. It is an attitude that concerns the future, to the extent that this future depends on the action of another."

American poet Susan Polis Schutz says, "We need to set the values of honesty and fairness when interacting with others. We need to establish a sound ethical foundation as a lifestyle. ... We need to create a world where we can trust each other again."

German philosopher Friedrich Nietzsche (1844–1900) said: "It does not bother me that you have lied to me, what bothers me is that now I cannot trust you."

Consultant and author James C. Hunter says, "Without basic levels of trust marriages and families are broken, businesses ruined and countries come down." James C. Hunter, *The Paradox* (Empresa Activa. Ediciones Urano, 2013), 70.

Jim Burke (1925–2012), former CEO of Johnson & Johnson, said, "You cannot succeed without confidence. ... Tell me any human relationship that works without trust, whether a marriage or friendship or social interaction. ... The same happens with business, especially businesses that relate to the public. ... Trust is the key to long term success." Stephen M. R. Covey and Rebecca R. Merrill, *The Speed of Trust* (Free Press, 2006) 6, 40.

For the German sociologist Niklas Luhmann (1927–1998), trust is a "mechanism of reduction of complexity that increases tolerance to uncertainty." Michael Ritter, *El Valor del Capital Reputacional* (Primera Edición. Olivos, Ritter & Partners, 2013), 73.

Chris Patten, the former British Parliamentary who was president of BBC Trust, has said, "The basis for the BBC's prestige in Great Britain is the confidence of the people in it if the BBC loses that, it's over." Michael Ritter, *El Valor del Capital Reputacional* (Edicion. Olivos, Ritter & Partners, 2013), 73.

The British consultant Stephen Bungay has said:

> There was a time which now seems long ago when the business was measured and predictable. The most important information was held in the center.... Today the environment is fast and uncertain. The most important information is held at the periphery and organizations are desperately seeking synergy through a mixture of cross-functional teams.*

In 2003 Sony was ten times bigger than Apple. Morten Hansen, a management professor at the Universities of Berkeley and INSEAD in France, points out in his book *Collaboration* that "Sony tried to respond to the iPod by developing Sony Connect, but the culture of internal competition frustrated their efforts." Apple, for its part, combined existing technologies in a new way and developed the iPod through the collaboration of different areas and departments of the company.

Emmanuel Lulin, SVP and Chief Ethics Officer of L'Oréal, has said that "Trust is the currency of ethics, so we must generate and maintain it."†

In organizations with a strong ethical culture, you can live and feel the prevailing values and a relationship of trust among its members that takes them to do the right thing. An effective team is not only a group of people working together but also a committed group where everyone trusts each other. In these organizations the employees are part of a group where everyone cooperates, they are supportive, they collaborate with each other, and they are committed to the company.

Would you follow someone you don't trust?

People want to work in organizations that they are proud of and in which they believe. A relationship of trust with customers, suppliers, and employees is an essential intangible asset for the sustainability and long-term success of a company.

Without honesty there is no trust, without trust there is no collaboration, and without collaboration, there is no business.

The consultant Dov Seidman says about trust: "Studies show that economic growth and prosperity in a society requires a minimum level of generalized trust. Without trust, investment ceases and economic activity grinds to a halt." *How: Why How We Do Anything Means Everything* (John Wiley & Sons, Inc., 2011).

Satya Nadella, CEO of Microsoft, wrote a letter to employees that says, "Trust is paramount in how we operate and conduct business with individuals, companies and governments. We build and maintain trust through our commitment to ethical conduct and acting with honesty and integrity."

* Stephen Bungay, "Mission Leadership," *Ashridge Journal* (Spring 2003).
† "Ethics Officers in all Large Companies?" Newsroom, Victoria University Wellington, October 8, 2018.

1.5 HONESTY AND INTEGRITY

What is the truth? The term *truth* is used to mean the coincidence between an affirmation and the facts.

Is the truth subjective or objective?
Is the truth relative or absolute?

We know that water wets and that fire burns, but sometimes the truth is not simple to decipher.

Honesty is a human quality that consists in behaving and expressing ourselves with sincerity, always respecting the truth and committing ourselves to it, even if it harms us. When integrity and honesty guide our decision process, then we will be more likely to make ethical decisions.

Always being honest will not be the simplest course of action, but it is the one that will give us integrity. To have integrity is related to *what we are* as human beings.

The American singer and composer Billy Joel composed the song "Honesty" in 1978. The song says that truth is harder to find than love. A verse says:

Honesty is such a lonely word.
Everyone is so untrue
Honesty is hardly ever heard
And mostly, what I need from you.

Honesty is a moral value linked to truth and transparency and is the opposite of lying and corruption. Honesty is an indispensable value for human relationships to develop in an environment of trust.

The Greek philosopher Epictetus (55–135 BC) said that life has two types of components: what depends and what does not depend on us.* Honesty, integrity, and self-control depend on us.

The Roman emperor Marcus Aurelius (121–180) wrote a literary work called *Meditations* where, remembering Epictetus, Marcus Aurelius said that there are acts that escape our control but there are others that man can control, such as maintaining an intelligent and fair behavior.†

---

* "El Estoicismo Existencial," www.filosofia.mx.
† "El Estoicismo Existencial," www.filosofia.mx.

People can control their integrity. To be reliable and credible, we must keep moral integrity, be honest, and tell the truth. If we lie and cheat, our punishment will be the loss of trust.

American journalist and writer Ivy Lee (1877–1934), personal adviser to John D. Rockefeller, said, "tell the truth because sooner or later the public will find out anyway."[*]

The Italian writer Carlo Lorenzini (1826–1890), known as Carlo Collodi, wrote *The Adventures of Pinocchio*, a children's story that deals with a wooden puppet that grew his nose every time he lied. That was his punishment.

The shepherd of Aesop's fable also suffered from a lack of confidence.[†] There is a popular saying that "at the mouth of the liar the truth becomes dubious." You can fool all the people some of the time, you can fool some people all of the time, but you cannot fool all the people all the time.

The person who repeats a lie can convince himself that it is the truth. If the lie is told and repeated to many people, the lie can become part of reality for these people. Because by telling the lie too many times people are convinced that it is true. Joseph Goebbels (1897–1945), the Nazi propaganda minister, said, "A lie told once remains a lie but a lie told a thousand times become the truth.… If you repeat a lie often enough, people will believe it."[‡]

There are people who tell lies and there are some people who say them because they have good reasons, like the pious lies to children, such as Santa Claus or Elf on the Shelf. Or the pious lie Nancy told her son Thomas Edison (1847–1931).[§] On the contrary, lies that are not pious are not said by an honest and sincere person. An honest person does not lie because it would go against his or her moral values. If we tell the truth, it is part of our past, but if we tell lies, they will be part of our future.

---

[*] Ivy Lee, www.azquotes.com.

[†] Aesop's fable of the young liar shepherd says that when he screams "Help, help" – because this time the wolf comes to eat the sheep – no one comes to help him because, with his previous lies, he had lost all credibility and confidence among the peasants.

[‡] Joseph Goebbels Quotes, www.azquotes.com/author/5626-Joseph_Goebbels.

[§] Legend has it that one day Thomas Edison came home from school and gave Nancy, his mother, a note from his teacher. Nancy's eyes filled with tears as she read the note and then read it to Thomas aloud: "Your son is a genius. This school is too small for him and doesn't have enough good teachers for training him. Please teach him yourself." Many years later Nancy died and Thomas while ordering the family's things found that letter from his teacher, opened it and read it: "Your son is *addled (mentally ill)*. *We won't let him come to school any more.*" Edison recalled that day, cried for hours and then he wrote in his diary: "Thomas Alva Edison was an addled child that, by a hero mother, became the genius of the century."

It is appropriate to remember this imaginary story that has a real message. One day four friends were walking where a party was being held in the village. Their names were Science, Fortune, Resignation, and Honesty.

Science suggested, "Friends, what happens if we lose each other? It would be good to agree on where each one will be if that happens."

Then Science said, "You can find me in the library."

Fortune said, "I will be in the millionaire's house."

Resignation said, "I'll be in the small, dirty, dirty house on the corner."

As Honesty remained silent, they asked: "And you? Where will we find you?"

Honesty answered: "If you lose me, you can hardly find me again."

The 2001 film *L'emploi du temps* (Time Out)* clearly shows how a lie destroys confidence. The film tells the story of Vincent, a middle-aged man who is fired after spending more than 11 years working for a prestigious consulting firm. Unable to admit that he has been fired, the unemployed executive pretends to go to the office every day. In fact, Vincent spends his time aimlessly on the roads of France and Switzerland, reading papers or sleeping in his car. As time progresses, Vincent invents increasingly elaborate lies to his wife and parents, plunging into a vicious spiral of deception, until he is discovered. When discovered, he also loses the credibility and trust of his family.

Thinkers and entrepreneurs have expressed the importance of honesty and integrity throughout history. In the footnote, you can read some selected opinions about the importance of honesty and integrity.†

---

* It was directed by Laurent Cantet.

† Thomas Jefferson (1743–1826), one of the Founding Fathers of the United States and its third president, said, "Honesty is the first chapter in the book of wisdom."

The English writer William Shakespeare (1564–1616) said that "no legacy is as rich as honesty."

Japanese businessman Konosuke Matsushita (1894–1989), founder of Matsushita Electric Industrial Company, Panasonic Corporation since 2008 and one of the most outstanding people in the history of the industry in Japan, says that "without personal integrity we can never be respected or respected by ourselves, however wise and capable we may be."

Seth Waugh, the former CEO of Deutsche Bank America, states, "Once I was told that when we need to take a complex and controversial decision we should always apply the following test: What would be the reaction of your mother if she read a story about you on the cover of the Wall Street Journal? She would be happy or sad? This test should be applied throughout the organization." Donald Trump, *The Way to the Top: The Best Business Advice I Ever Received* (Crown Business, 2004), 248.

Aristotle (384–322 BC) noted that "you cannot be and not be something at the same time and under the same aspect." Socrates (470–399 BC) said that "the key to greatness is to be actually we pretend to be." John Maxwell, *Developing the Leader Within You* (Nelson, 1993), 37.

A person acts with integrity when his or her behavior inside and outside the organization aligns with the values of doing the right thing, being honest and fair, telling the truth, and respecting others. We have integrity when we are consistent in all the situations we face, between what we say and do, both in public and in private. According to Angel Alloza, CEO of the Center for Reputation Leadership, "integrity consists in aligning what we say and what we do, our words and our actions."*

When Jack Welch, former CEO of General Electric, asked if he could be a good Catholic and at the same time a businessman, he answered, "I never had two agendas. There is only one way, the way of doing things right." *Jack. Straight from the Gut* (Warner Business Books, 2001), 381.

Experts Ken Blanchard and Marc Muchnick have pointed out that "integrity builds trust and respect," *The Leadership Pill* (Grijalbo, 2004), 53.

Thomas M. Joyce, former president and CEO of Knight Trading Group, says: "During my years at Merrill Lynch ... one of the main focuses was the ROI: Return on Integrity. Integrity is the basic foundation on which you build your career. We all make mistakes and occasional errors in the decisions we make in business, but we learn from them and we become better businessmen with accumulated experience ... . But the perceived lack of integrity is a death sentence in business." Donald Trump, *The Way to the Top: The Best Business Advice I Ever Received* (Crown Business, 2004), 134.

Donald Phillips said that "Lincoln reached success, admiration and a positive image by keeping unchanged its integrity and honesty," Donald T. Phillips, *Lincoln y el Liderazgo* (Deusto, 1993), 75.

"Zig" Ziglar (1926–2012) was a renowned American motivational speaker. Ziglar said that "with integrity you have nothing to fear, because you have nothing to hide."

American pastor and lecturer John Calvin Maxwell said that "when integrity is the referee, we are consistent." *Developing the Leader Within You* (Nelson, 1993), 36.

For the Roman philosopher Marcus Tullius Cicero (106–46 BC), sincerity was "the end to which every human being should aspire."

When Republican Gerald Ford (1913–2006) assumed the position of the 38th president of the United States in his inaugural speech after taking office on August 9, 1974, he said, "Honesty is, in the end, the best of policies."

Albert Einstein (1879–1955) said, "Try not to become a man of success but rather try to become a man of value," www.brainyquote.com/quotes/albert_einstein_131187.

Bruce N Pfau, a partner with Human Capital Strategy and Culture Transformation at KPMG, has pointed out, based on surveys conducted, that "employees feel that companies that run the business with honesty and integrity show much higher levels of commitment."

Francis Fay Vincent is a lawyer that was the CEO of Columbia Pictures and wrote in the *Wall Street Journal* a few years ago an article called "Ten Tips for New Executives," in which he said, "Tell the truth at work and in public. ... A lie almost always is soon uncovered and the damage to the reputation of the person who lies – and often to the organization he represents – is severe."

John Shad (1923–1987), former chairman of the US Securities and Exchange Commission between 1981 and 1987, said, "Ethics pays."

Pope Francis sent a message to the World Economic Forum in January 2014: "The international economic community can count on many men and women of great honesty and personal integrity, whose work is inspired and guided by noble ideals of justice, generosity, and care for the authentic development of the human family. I urge you to take advantage of these great human and moral resources and make them responsible for this challenge with determination and vision. ... I ask you that humanity uses wealth and not to be governed by it."

* "Un Esquema para Recuperar la Confianza," Angel Alloza, www.linkedin.com/pulse/un-sencillo-equema-para-la-recuperar-confianza-angel-alloza-phd, 22 de abril de 2018 ("A Scheme to Regain Confidence").

Integrity, from the Latin word *integrates* (*all*), implies one should always act honestly. Something is integral when it is complete and is not divided; it is one thing and not two parts. We have integrity when our beliefs and ethical actions line up.

If people are not ethical outside of work, they lose respect and trust. Ethics professor Denis Collins says ethical leaders are ethical at work and outside of work. Employees will judge the behavior of leaders outside of work in the same way that they judge their behavior at work. The way people behave outside of work reflects the kind of people they are.*

To act with integrity, we need to act honestly 100% of the time, both at work and in private life. Integrity cannot be turned on and off like a faucet; it must be constant. In the same way, it is not enough to correctly pilot 99% of the flights of an aircraft. If a leader acts with honesty 99% of the time and does not in the remaining 1% of the time, he or she will be judged by that 1%.

If I'm just honest in some actions, then I'm not a person with integrity. Integrity is what we are, honesty is what we do.

Ethical leaders never lie to their employees, their customers, or their suppliers. If they sometimes lie then they lack integrity. If they do not always treat people with respect, they are not acting with integrity. If they are not always fair with people, they are not acting with integrity.

We do not have integrity when we do the right thing only when somebody is watching us.

An "honor system" is a way of running a variety of endeavors based on trust, honor, and honesty. It is a system granting freedom from customary surveillance with the understanding that those who are so freed will be bound by their honor to observe regulations and will therefore not abuse the trust placed in them. A total honor system makes no checks on its users to verify their honesty, thereby easily allowing the system to be cheated.†

The first honor system in America was penned by Thomas Jefferson at the College of William and Mary. In some colleges, the honor system is used to administer tests unsupervised. Students are generally asked to sign an honor code statement that says they will not cheat or use unauthorized resources when taking the test. As an example, at Vanderbilt University students taking examinations are required to sign and include the

---

* "Business Ethics: How to Create and Ethical Organization," Denis Collins, Edgewood College, Udemy.com.

† en.wikipedia.org/wiki/Honor_system.

following pledge: "On my honor, as a student, I have neither given nor received aid on this examination."*

Some supermarket chains allow customers to scan their own groceries with handheld barcode readers while placing them in their own carts.†

Lack of moral integrity has not been seen only in entrepreneurs. Ethical scandals have also involved, for example, government officials, church people, and professional sports figures.

Bill Clinton was the 42nd president of the United States from 1993 to 2001. Under his leadership, the US economy grew. During his tenure, 22-year-old Monica Lewinsky was hired to work as an intern in the White House. Between 1995 and 1997, Lewinsky conducted a secret affair with Clinton, and the fact came to light because she told to a colleague, who recorded those conversations.

On January 26, 1998, Clinton denied the affair in a press conference on television, but later, on August 17, Clinton admitted he had an "improper physical relationship" with Lewinsky. The lies and infidelity with the intern (and the conflict of interest) affected the image of Bill Clinton, and some analysts said the Lewinsky affair and the morality vote may have had an impact on the defeat of Vice President Al Gore in the presidential election of the year 2000.

General David Petraeus was one of the most renowned American military leaders since World War II but resigned as director of the Central Intelligence Agency (CIA) on November 9, 2012, because of an extramarital affair with his biographer.

Dean C. Ludwig and Clinton O. Longnecker are co-authors of the article "The Bathsheba's Syndrome: The Ethical Failure of Successful Leaders" published in *The Journal of Business Ethics*.‡ In that biblical story, King David and Bathsheba, the wife of one of his soldiers, had a relationship, and he impregnated her.§ Ludwig and Longnecker argue that the psychological impact of power may unleash a dark side of leaders. Even leaders of high moral character

---

* en.wikipedia.org/wiki/Honor_system.

† en.wikipedia.org/wiki/Honor_system. In many places where an honor system is used, it has been found to be cost-effective. Many businesses and organizations using an honor system have determined that the cost of maintaining staff to enforce proper payment outweighs the losses caused by the percentage of the population who are willing to cheat the system.

‡ *The Journal of Business Ethics*, Vol. 12 Issue 4 (Kluwer Academic Publishing, April 1993) 265–73.

§ The Bible, II Samuel. Also see Mackubin Thomas Owens, "Why Did a Man We So Respected Succumb to Temptations?" November 13, 2012, www.nationalreview.com. Also see Donelson Forsyth "The Bathsheba Syndrome: When a Leader Fails." *Connections*, November 13, 2011.

may abandon their commitment to their values and succumb to the temptations of power.

Walmart's founder Sam Walton (1918–1992) said, "Personal and moral integrity is one of our basic fundamentals and it starts with each one of us. ... We have to have a basic foundation of integrity or sooner or later we will stumble."

Along the same lines, Lee Scott, CEO of Walmart between 2000 and 2009, said, "Integrity is more important than sales, profitability or increasing the stock price. Integrity is the main characteristic of any leader. You can overcome almost everything, but you cannot overcome the lack of integrity."

The engineer Mike Duke, who succeeded Scott as CEO during the years 2009–2013, said,

> If you work for Walmart, there is not a gray area between what is right and what is wrong. Or you do the right thing or not. We do not accept anything less than integrity. Our commitment to Ethics and Compliance is critical for our success; it is the way we earn trust and respect.

Walmart's former chairman of the board, Rob Walton, said in 2012 at the shareholders meeting: "Let me be clear: Acting with integrity is not a negotiable part of this business, it is our business."

The executive education authors James Kouzes and Barry Posner asked 75,000 people around the world what were the main qualities that a leader should have. The result of the survey was that *honesty* was considered the main feature and quality of any leader.[*] Honesty is even more important than the ability to inspire, intelligence, imagination, ambition, communication skills, quality of management, or courage. Those authors point out: "When we follow someone we believe is dishonest, we realize that we are compromising our own integrity."[†]

Five-time Formula One world champion Argentine Juan Manuel Fangio (1911–1995), who was born in Balcarce Province of Buenos Aires, was one of the best drivers of all time in the international motorsport. In an interview in 1989, Fangio said,

> When I was offered the post of president of Mercedes Benz Argentina, I said I could not do something I did not know. But Daimler-Benz insisted

---

[*] James Kouzes and Barry Posner, *The Leadership Challenge* (Jossey-Bass, 2003), 25.
[†] James Kouzes and Barry Posner, *The Leadership Challenge* (Jossey-Bass, 2003), 27.

and then I went to Germany and asked only one thing: employees with three qualities: strength, competence, and honesty. With these three conditions, you can do everything.*

Arturo Umberto Ilia (1900–1983) was a doctor and president of Argentina between 1963 and 1966. One of the main features of President Illia was his honesty and trustworthiness. Ilia said that to be useful "must be austere, selfless and modest." In 1966 his wife was seriously ill and Ilia did not want to use the money given by the state for his personal expenses because he believed that would rob the country, so he had to sell his car to meet the expenses.

The successful Mexican businessman Carlos Kasuga Osaka said,

> Why do you want to have in your company an accountant, a graduate, an engineer, a human resource with three masters if they are not honest? The longer you have them, the more damage they will cause you. … Values are the most important thing in humans.[†]

Warren Buffett, American investor, CEO, and major shareholder of Berkshire Hathaway, said, "We look for three things when we hire people. We look for intelligence, we look for initiative or energy, and we look for integrity. And if they don't have the latter, the first two will kill you."[‡]

Buffet ranks executives in four categories:

1. Those who achieve objectives and have values
2. Those who fail objectives but have values
3. Those who achieve goals but have no values
4. Those who fail objectives and do not have values.

Those who fall into categories 3 and 4 should be dismissed.

The Persian mathematician Muhammad Al-Khwarizmi lived between 780 and 850. On one occasion he was asked about the value of the human being, to which he replied:

> If he has ethics, his life is equal to 1.
> If he is also smart, add a 0 and its value is equal to 10

---

* "Entrevista a Fangio," Revista *La Nacion* (February 1989), German Sopena ("Fangio Interviewed")

† Conference at the Embassy of Japan in Mexico, 2009.

‡ "Warren Buffett looks for these traits in people when he hires them," *Market Insider*, January 4, 2017, www.markets. businessinsider.com.

If he is also rich, add another 0 and its value is equal to 100

If he is also a great person, add another zero to it and its value equals 1000

But if he loses the 1, which corresponds to ethics, you will lose all its value, because only the zeros will remain.*

If you are dishonest, sooner or later you will pay "by loss of reputation and perhaps even loss of liberty."† Honesty, sincerity, integrity, and justice are the roots and the basis on which trust and reputation are upheld. When employees feel that the company is honestly managed, the level of their commitment is greater. When customers observe that the company does not cheat them, sales are higher.

Marcus Aurelius (121–180) was one of the most prestigious emperors of the Roman Empire. Called "the Philosopher," he wrote a book called *Meditations*, where his thought is reflected. Marco Aurelio wrote, "If it is not right do not do it; if it is not true do not say it."‡

One can and should be successful and honest. Acting with integrity and in harmony with values, telling the truth and being fair and objective in decisions are essential for the development and sustainable growth of companies.

Controls are important, but people's ethics are even more so. Laura Kane, vice president of corporate communications of Aflac, said "We can forgive honest mistakes, but we can never forgive unethical behavior."§

When you think about what makes a company successful, culture is always an essential element. A corporate personality where honesty, credibility, and integrity prevail is needed to achieve long-term success.

No success justifies failing with ethics because any success that is not achieved ethically is no success at all.

Ethics is more important than gold.

Morality, values, ethics, and integrity are extremely important because they guide us to do the right thing.

Ethics is the essence and foundation of good leadership.

---

* Ignacio Mantilla, "Algebra y Ética," July 14, 2017, www.elespectador.com.
† Napoleon Hill, *Think and Grow Rich* (Vermilion, Random House, 2004), 142.
‡ www.goodreads.com/author/quotes/17212.Marcus_Aurelius.
§ "Ethics Communications Best Practices Report," *The Ethisphere Institute*, Page 3, report from "Best Practices in Ethics Communications Workshop," New York City, June 19, 2012.

2

Culture and Ethics

In 1798 Napoleon Bonaparte (1769–1821) undertook a trip from the Mediterranean to the East to block the routes of the British Empire. The French army went to Egypt and was composed not only of people in arms but also of professors and researchers recruited to gather information on Egyptian culture. In mid-1799 the campaign in Egypt continued its course, although without Napoleon since he had already begun his return to France. On July 15, 1799, the French arrived at a town near the port city of Rashid, known to the French as Rosetta. That day, under ground, a dark-colored rock with inscriptions in three different carved languages was found by a soldier of the French army. The first part was written in Egyptian hieroglyphs, the second fragment in demotic script, and a third inscription in ancient Greek. Until then ancient Greek and demotic were known, but not Egyptian hieroglyphics. The British commanded by Lord Horatio Nelson (1758–1805) cornered the French army in 1801, and the stone fell into British hands and was sent to London for display at the British Museum. For several years the hieroglyphics could not be deciphered, but thanks to the work of the Englishman Thomas Young (1773–1829) and the Frenchman Jean François Champollion (1790–1832), in 1822 the inscriptions were deciphered and they discovered it was a priestly decree in honor of Pharaoh Ptolemy V of the year 196 BC. The Rosetta stone solved the mystery of the Egyptian hieroglyphs and allowed us to understand its texts. By being able to decipher the hieroglyphic writing it was possible to know the history, the beliefs, the civilization, and the Egyptian culture.*

Culture consists of a set of habits, customs, and traditions based on beliefs and values that characterize an organization or a group of people.

---

* "History of the Rosetta Stone," www.allaboutarcheology.org; "Rosetta, the Stone that Deciphered Egypt," Ramon de Fontecha, July 20, 2014, www.elconfidencial.com.

It is like a pattern of behavior that is taken for granted. Actions, when repeated, become habits. Habits become customs and create cultures.

The United Nations Educational, Scientific and Cultural Organization (UNESCO) is based in Paris and is a specialized agency of the United Nations that was founded in 1945. Its declared purpose is to contribute to peace and security by promoting international collaboration through educational, scientific, and cultural reforms in order to increase universal respect for justice, the rule of law, and human rights along with fundamental freedom. UNESCO has defined *culture* as the "set of distinctive spiritual, material, intellectual, and emotional features of society or a social group, and that it encompasses, in addition to art and literature, lifestyles, ways of living together, value systems, traditions, and beliefs."*

Culture is a complex subject. It includes language, religion, values, customs, education, and institutions. Culture says who we are and is the way things are done in an organization, and it is reflected in stories, events, and behaviors that members of the organization carried out for years. Culture shows the way of being and is one of the most important things in any organization.

In the United States, there are more than 500 Native Americans or American Indian tribes recognized at the federal level. Each tribe has its own culture, language, beliefs, history, and music and food.

A great plurality of different cultures coexist in the world.

The Masai, for example, is a tribe of Kenya and Tanzania in Africa. They have the custom of spitting on their hands to greet the elderly and spitting on children to give them a good future.

In Brazil and Venezuela, the members of the Yanomami tribe often eat the ashes of the dead because they believe it will save the souls of these people.

In southern India, an Okali religious ritual consists of throwing babies from the terrace of a temple 15 meters high, as the family awaits below with a blanket to catch the infant. The belief is that this ritual will bring the infants a future with luck, health, and prosperity.

Sale of women is a common practice in some countries in Africa. In South Sudan, a 17-year-old girl was sold at an auction in exchange for 530 cows, 3 cars, and 10,000 dollars. The family offered it through Facebook as if it were the sale of a house.†

---

* UNESCO, Universal Declaration on Cultural Diversity, October 14, 2007; www.newworldenc yclopedia.org/entry/Culture; UNESCO, Wikipedia.
† "A Family Sold Its Daughter for 530 Cows, 3 Cars and 10 Thousand Dollars," www.lanacion.com. ar November 23, 2018.

Jon Huntsman is the founder of Huntsman Corporation, a company that in 2000 became the most important family company in the United States. Huntsman says in his book *Winners Never Cheat* that in Arunachal Pradesh, one of the 29 states of India, situated in the extreme northeast, live more than 100 tribes, each with its own culture, language, and religion. He says that for those "primitive" societies, honesty is an absolute value.[*]

The Maoris live in New Zealand and are known for the *haka* dance, which is a demonstration of tribal pride and unity. It consists of banging feet, sticking out the tongue, and clapping to accompany a song.[†]

Successful business people understand and respect cultural differences.

For Westerners, eating with cutlery is an essential etiquette, but for many Asians, eating with their fingers is a common tradition.

In some places in China, Vietnam, South Korea, or Switzerland, it is customary to eat dog meat, and in Hawaii, it is customary to eat cat meat. The Cambodians eat rats found in rice fields.

In Finland Donald Duck was once banned because he had no pants; in Ukraine, a spider web is a symbol of good luck and also a Christmas decoration, and in Singapore chewing or selling gum is prohibited.

In Egypt, for example, you express your appreciation for a plentiful meal by leaving some food on your plate, indicating that your host has generously provided more food than you can consume.

American business people sometimes feel uncomfortable when negotiating with people from the Middle East, who tend to stand closer to others than is generally acceptable in the United States.[‡]

In Thailand, Asia, for example, the location of buildings is often determined by astrologers. Thais also believe that all the wood in a building should come from the same forest. In Malaysia, production runs in a plant can be halted when a goat is sacrificed and its blood sprinkled on the factory floor to drive away evil spirits.[§]

In Buddhist, Hindu, and Muslim cultures, many events are simply considered "acts of God," and so plant workers may be less motivated to

---

[*] Jon M. Huntsman, *Winners Never Cheat* (Pearson Education, 2001).
[†] The rugby team of New Zealand, the All Blacks, uses the *haka* as a rite minutes before their matches.
[‡] K. Blanchard, C. Schewe, B. Nelson and A. Hiam, *Exploring the World of Business* (Worth Publishers, 1996), 86.
[§] K. Blanchard, C. Schewe, B. Nelson and A. Hiam, *Exploring the World of Business* (Worth Publishers, 1996), 86–7.

take accident prevention measures on the factory floor since accidents are fated and cannot be avoided.*

In Portugal, it is not uncommon for a businessperson to come to a meeting later than the appointment time, but in Sweden, appointments are kept to the minute.†

Globalization and migration are changing and evolving cultures.

For example, Hispanics in the United States have been influencing American culture. Think of the names of some cities and states of the United States: Colorado, Nevada, San Diego, Florida, San Antonio, Santa Barbara, San Jose, etc. The Hispanic population has been growing. In 1980, it was 6% of the US population, 9% in 1990, 12% in the year 2000, and 18% in 2017. This process of change has also increased the teaching of the Spanish language in schools, TV programs in Spanish, Hispanic stores and popularity of soccer. Hispanics in the United States already number more than 55 million, more than the total population of Spain.

One of the most accepted definitions of *organizational culture* is from MIT psychologist professor at the Sloan School of Management, Edgar Schein:

> Organizational culture is the pattern of basic assumptions that a particular group invented, discovered or developed in the process of learning to solve its problems of external adaptation and internal integration and that worked well enough to be considered valid and, therefore, to be taught to new group members as the correct way to perceive, think and feel in relation to these problems.‡

According to the analyst and Canadian psychologist Elliot Jacques (1917–2003), organizational culture is composed of the traditional way of thinking and doing things that, to a greater or lesser extent, all members of the organization share and new members must learn, accept, and respect it.

Satya Nadella, CEO of Microsoft, wrote that "each one of us shapes our culture through our words and actions."§

---

* K. Blanchard, C. Schewe, B. Nelson and A. Hiam, *Exploring the World of Business* (Worth Publishers, 1996), 87.
† K. Blanchard, C. Schewe, B. Nelson and A. Hiam, *Exploring the World of Business* (Worth Publishers, 1996), 86.
‡ Edgar H. Schein, "Coming to a New Awareness of Organizational Culture," *MIT Sloan Management Review*, January 15, 1984, sloanreview.mit.edu/article/coming-to-a-new-awareness-of-organizational-culture/.
§ www.microsoft.com.

Airbnb CEO Brian Chesky has said that "culture is the sharing way of doing things. The beliefs that never change…. Culture is about repetition. It is repeating over and over the things that really matter at the company."[*]

The Ethics Resource Center has said, "ethical culture is the unwritten code that tells employees how to think and act how things are actually done around here."[†]

To the extent that there is correspondence and alignment between the values of employees and the organizational culture, the worker's commitment to the organization will be greater.

The American consultant Francis Fukuyama defined *social capital* as the set of shared values among members of a group that permits cooperation among them.

In 1976, the American anthropologist Edward T. Hall developed the analogy of the "cultural iceberg." Below the surface of the iceberg are the invisible elements of culture: values, beliefs, thoughts, and principles; and on the tip of the iceberg above the water are visible behaviors of culture, easy to identify, which are projected to the outside and are perceived by those who interact with the organization (for example, languages, arts, literature, religion, music, dress, dance, or sports).[‡]

To build a strong organizational culture, a company needs to include consistency between the invisible and the visible, and between ideas, values, words, actions, and behaviors of employees.

Senior executive Torben Rick has written that "organizational culture is like the wind, it is invisible, yet its effects can be seen and felt."[§]

The pioneering consultant on diversity in business, R. Roosevelt Thomas Jr. (1945–2013), said, "corporate culture is a kind of tree, its roots are assumptions…its branches, leaves, and seeds are behavior. You can't change the leaves without changing the roots."[¶]

John Kotter and James Heskett, professors at Harvard Business School, meanwhile, have identified two levels in culture. In the visible level appear behavioral patterns of employees, and in the invisible level shared values show up.[**] Kotter and Heskett conducted a study of how organizational

---

[*] Guest speaker at Stanford University, November 19, 2015.
[†] "Ethics Resource Center National Business Ethics Survey of Social Networks" (2013), 39.
[‡] "Iceberg Model of Culture," www.globaltradeandlogistics.org and also "Edward Hall's Cultural Iceberg Model," www.spps.org.
[§] www.torbenrick.eu/blog/culture/organizational-culture-is-like-the-wind/.
[¶] R. Roosevelt Thomas Jr., "From Affirmative Action to Affirming Diversity," *Harvard Business Review*, March–April 1990, 8.
[**] J. F. Stoner, R. E. Freeman and D.R. Gilbert Jr., *Administration*, 6th ed (Pearson, 1996), 203.

culture influences their economic performance and analyzed Hewlett-Packard, Xerox, ICI, Nissan, and other major corporations. They concluded that shared values in companies positively influence their economic success.[*]

The practice of sports forces players to comply with the rules of the game and accept the culture of fair play. For example, the "Laws of the Game" of rugby says:

> It is through discipline, control and mutual respect that flourish the spirit of the game. ... These are the qualities that forge the fellowship and sense of fair play, essential for long-term success and survival of the game. They can be considered traditions and virtues of old stock but have stood the test of time and at all levels in which the game is played, they remain as important to Rugby's future as they have been throughout its long and distinguished past.[†]

The "Fundacion Espartanos" is an NGO created by the Argentine lawyer Eduardo "Coco" Oderigo in 2009 and through the practice of rugby seeks to reduce the rate of criminal recidivism of prisoners at the time of regaining their freedom. It has been proven that the rate of recidivism in the crime of those prisoners participating in the Espartanos program is reduced from 65% to 5%. Rugby teaches prisoners the values of respect for others, trust, companionship, effort, teamwork, and compliance with rules. Rugby changes them.[‡]

Milton Friedman (1912–2006)[§] said, "The company only has one social responsibility: to use their energy and resources to activities that increase their profits, provided they respect the rules of the game ... and engage in an open and free competition without deception or fraud."[¶]

Good corporate culture helps employees make the right decisions and prioritize the values of honesty, truth, justice, legality, and respect over results and execution.

---

[*] John Kotter y James Heskett, *Corporate Culture and Performance*, (NY Press, 1992).

[†] Rugby Union, "Laws of the Game," www.laws.worldrugby.org.

[‡] www.fundacionespartanos.org. Currently, the program operates in 50 prison units in Argentina, and more than 2,000 players participate in it. The program is expanding to Portugal, Italia, Uruguay, Chile, Perú, and Spain.

[§] American economist, professor at the University of Chicago, and winner of the Nobel Prize in Economics in 1976.

[¶] J. F. Stoner, R. E. Freeman and D. R. Gilbert Jr., *Administration*, 6th ed (Pearson, 1996) and also see Milton Friedman, "The Social Responsibility of Business Is to Increase Profits," *The New York Times Magazine*, September 13, 1970.

It is preferable to lose than to win unfairly. In 2003 the Danish soccer team played against Iran. When the first half was going to end, an Iranian player mistook a whistle from the crowd as being the referee's half time signal and picked the ball up with his hands in the penalty area. The referee gave Denmark a penalty kick, but following consultation with national team coach Morten Olsen, the player Morten Wieghorst missed the penalty on purpose as a token of fair play. Denmark ended up losing that match 1 to 0. Morten Wieghorst was named 2003 Player of the Year in Denmark and received a 2003 Olympic Committee fair play award for missing a penalty kick on purpose.* The Denmark soccer team did not want to win at any cost.

The Hippocratic Oath is taken by those who graduate in medicine and promise to be ethical in their practice. According to Galen of Pergamum (129–201), who practiced medicine in Rome, Hippocrates (460–370 BC), one of the most outstanding figures in the history of Greek medicine, wrote this oath, whose content has been updated throughout the centuries. Among other things it says:

> Into whatever homes I go, I will enter them for the benefit of the sick, avoiding any voluntary act of impropriety or corruption. ... Whatever I see or hear in the lives of my patients, whether in connection with my professional practice or not, which ought not to be spoken of outside, I will keep secret, as considering all such things to be private.†

In May 2009, a group of MBA students at Harvard Business School created a voluntary commitment to promote responsible business ethics. The MBA Oath was made with the purpose that the business be conducted in a responsible and ethical manner and that MBAs think about what it means to be a manager, a leader, and a professional. Among other things, the oath says:

> I will refrain from corruption, unfair competition or business harmful to society. ... I will protect the human rights and dignity of all people affected by my Enterprise and I will oppose discrimination and exploitation. ... I will protect the right of future generations to ... enjoy a healthy planet.‡

---

* en.wikipedia.org/wiki/Morten_Wieghorst.
† "Greek Medicine," www.nlm.nih.gov.
‡ www.mbaoath.org.

The MBA Oath was not the first to be implemented in a business school. The Thunderbird School of Global Management's honor oath has been in effect since June 2006 and says:

> As a Thunderbird and a global citizen, I promise: I will strive to act with honesty and integrity, I will respect the rights and dignity of all people, I will strive to create sustainable prosperity worldwide, I will oppose all forms of corruption and exploitation, and I will take responsibility for my actions. As I hold true to these principles, it is my hope that I may enjoy an honorable reputation and peace of conscience. This pledge I make freely and upon my honor.[*]

The values of the organization limit the actions of its members. As consultant Fred Kofman says, "Respect for the essential values imposes restrictions on our behavior."[†]

When people drive a car, it is easy for them to make the decision to stop if the traffic light is red and not to stop if it is green. But the decision is not so clear and the driver can be uncertain – and decide wrongly – when it is yellow. In business, not everything is green and red, or black and white. There are also yellow and gray, and a successful ethical culture helps determine whether the gray is black and white, or if the yellow is green or red. The reason we are educated in values and principles is because they will guide us and help us make the right decisions and have the courage and values to face difficult situations.

As authors Kouzes and Posner point out, values serve as guides for action:

> Values inform our decisions as to what to do and what not to do; when to say yes, or no, and really understand *why* we mean it. If you believe, for instance, that diversity enriches innovation and service, then you should know what to do if people with differing views keep getting cut off when they offer up a fresh idea. If you value collaboration over individualistic achievement, then you'll know what to do when your best salesperson skips team meetings and refuses to share information with colleagues. If you value independence and initiative over conformity and obedience, you'll be more likely to challenge something your manager says if you think it's wrong.[‡]

---

[*] Thunderbird Oath of Honor, https://thunderbird.asu.edu.
[†] Fredy Kofman, *La Empresa Consciente*, (Punto de Lectura, 2001), 135 ("The Conscious Enterprise").
[‡] J. M. Kouzes and B. Z. Posner, *Leadership the Challenge*, 3rd ed (Jossey-Bass, 2002), 48.

The American writer Dale Carnegie (1888–1956) in his book *How to Win Friends and Influence People* (Out of Pocket, 2006), tells the following story:

> Theodore Roosevelt said that when as President he had a serious problem, he usually reclined in his chair and looked at a big picture of Lincoln on the desk in the White House and wondered, what would Lincoln do if he were in my place?. How could he solve the problem?

When the governing board of the University of Virginia is faced with a difficult decision, they are guided by the university's founder Thomas Jefferson, and they ask "What would Mr. Jefferson do?"*

My father used to say that if you find yourself in a difficult situation and you do not know what decision to make, ask yourself what Jesus of Nazareth would have done in a similar situation.

So, if you face an ethical dilemma, you can decide what is right or wrong in the same way that an ethically ideal person would. What would the Pope, the Dalai Lama, or Mother Teresa of Calcutta do in a similar situation?

The film *Courageous* raises ethical issues.† In one scene, the boss calls an employee to his office and tells him that if he makes certain accounting movements (improper and unethical), he will be promoted. The boss asks him to think about it and to answer the next day. The employee needs desperately to increase his income because the salary he receives is not enough to support his family. When he returns home, the employee, distressed, shares the situation with his wife. He does not want to accept the imposed condition, but he believes that if he does not accept it, not only will he not be promoted, but he will be fired. His wife, anguished, tells him that they desperately need the money, but she supports him on his decision not to accept the proposal.

The next day, the employee meets his boss and he tells him that he really wants the promotion but cannot accept the request because it is not the right thing to do. His boss looks at his employee seriously, and after a few seconds of silence tells the employee that he will be promoted because the employee had passed the ethical test. The boss wanted to be sure to have someone with integrity for the position.

---

* Linda Trevino and Katherine Nelson, *Managing Business Ethics*, 5th ed (John Wiley and Sons Inc, 2011), 156.
† Directed by Pastor Alex Kendrick and premiered in 2011.

When ethics is embodied in employees, they are more likely to make the right decisions consistent with principles and values, even in high-pressure situations.

The film *The Insider* of 1999* deals with a case in which the tobacco company Brown & Williamson, a subsidiary of British American Tobacco, was condemned by the American justice system for adding ammonia, a substance that increases addiction to tobacco.[†] Lowell Bergman, producer of *60 Minutes*, a news program on the CBS network, asks Jeffrey Wigand, Ph.D. in biochemistry and former vice president of research and development of the tobacco company Brown & Williamson, to report on the harmful consequences of nicotine and ammonia added to the cigars to make them more addictive. Wigand must choose between speaking and doing what conscience dictates, or not speaking and not risking his severance and medical coverage paid by the company through a confidentiality contract signed with the tobacco company. However, to relieve his conscience, on February 4, 1996, Wigand appeared on the program *60 Minutes* and stated that Brown & Williamson[‡] had intentionally manipulated its tobacco blend with chemicals such as ammonia to increase addictive effects on cigarette smoke.[§]

In the American television series *Lost*,[¶] surgeon Jack Shephard observes a patient die while she is operated on by his father, also a surgeon. After the operation, Jack's father justifies himself by telling Jack the patient died because she was in a very poor condition. Jack replies that the patient died because his father inadvertently damaged an artery, and that happened because his father was drinking before the operation and his hand shook under the influence of alcohol. The father tells Jack that, due to her poor condition, she was going to die anyway. He also adds that if Jack shared what he said, his medical license would be withdrawn for the rest of his life.

Jack has an ethical and conscience problem. Should he declare the truth about the cause of the patient's death in the operating room, or, on the contrary, do what his father asked to protect him?

---

[*] The film was directed by Michael Mann.

[†] The chemical compound was banned in cigarettes in 1997 and is listed in the United States by the FDA among substances whose addition for use in food by humans is prohibited.

[‡] In 2004 Brown & Williamson merged with R.J. Reynolds creating Reynolds American, Inc.

[§] en.wikipedia.org/wiki/Jeffrey_Wigand; es.wikipedia.org/wiki/Brown_%26_Williamson.en.wiki pedia.org/wiki/The_Insider_(film).

[¶] *Lost*, 2004, Bad Robot Productions, Touchstone Productions ABC Studios.

In the TV series *House of Cards*, Douglas "Doug" Stamper, chief of staff of the president of the United States, asks an employee to make a phone call requesting something that is illegal.

The employee answers: "I'm not doing this. It is not just the law. It is ethics."

Doug replies: "Then change your ethics, or you can resign and your deputy can make this call."*

If someone is forced to do something illegal or that does not conform to his or her values, there will be a conflict or a problem, and the way that dilemma is solved can have serious consequences for the organization and for the individual. The decisions that are made can affect the quality of life of society, so they must always be reasoned, duly evaluating their potential impacts. As decisions have consequences, it is advisable to always stay true to the ethical compass.

The ethical culture of an organization expands and is reinforced when leaders set a tone of integrity and earn the trust of employees. Organizational culture influences the behavior of employees. If the company has a strong ethical culture, then employees are more likely to make decisions aligned with the values of fairness, honesty, and respect, and the company will have a better chance of surviving in the future.

Executives, professionals, consultants, and institutions have referred to the importance of organizational ethical culture. Examples of their comments are provided in the footnote.†

---

* *House of Cards*, Chapter 45, Season 4, Episode 6.

† John Gardner, professor of psychology, said: "In any community, some people are more or less hopelessly bad and others more consistently good, but the behavior of many people will be deeply influenced by the moral climate of the moment." (John Gardner, *Leadership* (Editorial Grupo Latino Americano, 1989), 236.

Donald Keough, former president of the Coca Cola Company, said: "Men and women can flourish for periods of time, but eventually their lack of moral and humility destroys them. You cannot build a strong and long-term business on a rotten foundation." *The Ten Commandments for Business Failure*, (Penguin, 2011), 77.

Alejandro Melamed, a specialist in human resources, said: "While the impact of ethics, in different fields, was studied for many years, the conclusion is that long-term leadership, ethically and morally right, generates more successful organizations in general, and more successful enterprises in particular." *Empresas más Humanas*, (Grupo Editorial Planeta Booket, 2010), 55.

Austrian writer and consultant Peter Drucker (1909–2005) emphasized the importance of culture in business and said that "culture eats strategy for breakfast."

Philip Selznick, professor of sociology and law at the University of California, Berkley, said that "well understood survival is a matter of maintaining the values and distinctive identity." In *Search of Excellence*, ed. Thomas Peters and Robert Waterman Jr. (Atlantis, 1994), 277.

"The Institute for Global Ethics, based in Maine, United States, notes that "an organization formed without ethics is like a cabin built without nails: no matter how solid it may seem, it slowly crumbles."

At L'Oréal, the world's largest cosmetics company, ethical behavior is as important as its economic performance or the quality of its products. The ambition of the company is to be an exemplary organization that integrates ethics at the heart of its business practices. The French company says:

> Our ethical principles shape our culture, support our reputation and must be known and recognized by all employees of L'Oreal.
> Integrity, because acting with integrity is vital to build and maintain trust and good relations.
> Respect, because what we do has an impact on the lives of many people.
> Value, because ethical questions are rarely easy, but must be addressed.
> Transparency, because we must be always truthful, honest and able to justify our actions and decisions.*

After acquisition of one company by another or a merger, cultural differences could become an obstacle to the integration of those companies. Jack Welch was CEO of General Electric between 1981 and 2001, and during that period the company turnover increased fivefold from US$26,000 million to US$130,000 million.† Welch said: "I made acquisitions that did not work. Sometimes I bought companies with bad cultures and failed because when I bought, I did not think about the culture. I thought about the numbers, but not about the culture."

Doug McMillon, CEO of Walmart, noted in 2015 at Stanford Graduate School of Business that "one of the downside aspects of an acquisition is the cultural alignment issue. We cannot buy a business that does not believe what we believe, because that can create a lot of problems."

Herb Kelleher (1931–2019), co-founder and former CEO of Southwest Airlines, illustrated his vision of the difference between strategy and culture. Kelleher said, "Napoleon and his generals in Paris decided to invade Russia as part of its imperialist strategy, but they needed a million French soldiers to march into Russia. Culture is what made the troops march."

Futurist and English doctor Patrick Dixon, said: "Our society has come to see that a strategy to create shareholder value without a clear mission based on solid ethical values is complete nonsense. In fact, it is one of the fastest ways of destroying a global business."

Consultant Nikos Mourkogiannis has pointed out that "companies that declare a moral purpose but do not practice it suffer crisis and paralysis; their staff receive inconsistent and even contradictory directives." *Revista Gestion*, March–April 2006, 36.

* www.loreal.com.

† Welch was elected the executive of the twentieth century by *Fortune* magazine in 1999.

The purpose of a corporation cannot be to maximize shareholder returns only. The goal of a corporation should be to maximize shareholder return by doing the right thing.

Economist Milton Friedman wrote that a corporate executive's responsibility "will be to make as much money as possible while conforming to their basic rules of the society, both those embodied in law and those embodied in ethical custom."*

The establishment of a strong ethical culture is a continuous process that should involve all levels of leadership of the organization. In this way, the great majority of company leaders can achieve honest, fair, and objective behavior within the framework of the law and internal policies.

Culture impacts the way problems are solved, on how the company works and makes decisions, and begins with the transmission by leaders of the basic values and principles that cannot be compromised.

Employees can speak different languages and have different customs, but the ethical culture and respect for and collaboration with the other will be the binding factor that will make the company, even if it is very large, seem small.

An employee must challenge a boss's order to do something wrong. The culture must be above positions because the ultimate goal of ethical culture is to protect the organization against misconduct.

No employee of the company is above the organization's standards. The lawyer John Adams (1735–1826) was one of the Founding Fathers of the United States, its first vice president, and its second president. Adams wrote that the United States is "a government of laws, not of men." No person or group is above the law. The "rule of law" implies that all citizens, whether or not they are leaders, must comply with the laws. Similarly, in an organization, the president and the CEO must comply with the ethics code and internal policies. No one is above them.

Sam Walton said, "At Walmart, a man or a woman can affect the future. I am concerned; we must maintain the culture and the things we believe. Our future depends on our associates."

To perform well, teams require good leaders. Leaders inspire confidence when they create a culture where each member of the team can feel comfortable expressing their point of view.

---

* Milton Friedman, "The Social Responsibility of Business Is to Increase Its Profits," *The New York Times Magazine*, September 13, 1970.

Corporate culture plays an important role in attracting and retaining employees, in the relationship with suppliers, and in customer loyalty. It is essential for the long-term success of the business.

A successful company has principles, values, and beliefs that remain in time and carries forward a business strategy that changes, modifies, and adapts to the changes of the environment. Like a compass that marks the north, the values do not change, and the company must protect them. We must never change our commitment to the highest standards of professional conduct. Even when we strive to improve performance in a highly competitive world, we must always act according to our values.

The traditions involve patterns of coexistence to keep certain values intact over time, which are part of the identity of organizations. For example, it is part of the tradition of the Catholic Church to require members to obey the Ten Commandments and the failure to do so is considered a sin; in companies, their principles and values are also inflexible. Then, as it is called "sin" for the breach of religious precepts and "crime" for the breach of legal norms, it is called an "unethical act" for the breach of the principles and moral values established by organizations.

Consultant and American writer Jim Collins of Stanford University, says: "Successful companies that remain in time preserve their core values and purpose, while its strategy and operating practices must constantly adapt to the changing world."[*]

Business strategies change to adapt to the market, but the commitment of a company and its leaders to its values should not change. Professor Jorge Etkin has pointed out that "values have to do with the credibility and reliability of the organization in an uncertain and changing environment."[†]

Executives, authors, and consultants have agreed on this topic, and examples are provided in the footnote.[‡]

---

[*] Jim Collins, *Good to Great* (Harper Business, 2001), 195.

[†] Jorge Etkin, "Bases Conceptuales de la Gestion Socialmente Responsable" (Conceptual Bases of Socially Responsible Management), *Saberes*, 1 (2009).

[‡] 1 – Tim Cook, the current CEO of Apple, said in an interview, "The greatest contribution of Steve (Jobs) is the Company and its culture. ... Everything can change except for the values." Interview with the CEO of Apple. *La Nación*. April 13, 2015.

2 – The CEO of DuPont, Ed Breen, has said that "while our Company evolved and changed over the last 214 years, our commitment to our core values has been constant." Introductory Letter, DuPont's Ethics Code.

3 – John H. Tyson, who was CEO of Tyson Foods, said that "our company endures because our culture endures."

4 – John Young, former CEO of Hewlett-Packard, said: "Our basic principles have remained intact since they were created by the founders. We have distinguished between core values and practices. Core values do not change, but practices can change." Jim Collins and Jerry Porras, *Built to Last*, (Collins Business Essentials, 2002), 46.

Thomas J. Watson (h) (1914–1993), CEO of IBM for almost 20 years, was an American businessman who, among other honors, received the Presidential Medal of Freedom in 1964. In his book *A Business and Its Belief*, he wrote about his experience at IBM. Watson said:

> We could speculate at length about the cause of the decline and fall of a company. Technology, changing fashions and tastes are factors that contribute.... Its importance is indisputable. But I doubt they are decisive factors.

> How can you keep this common cause among the many changes that occur from one generation to another? Consider any good organization, one that has lasted many years. I think we will find that its longevity is due not to their organization or their administrative skills, but to the power of what we call beliefs and the importance they have for their employees.

---

5 – Jim Collins and Jerry I. Porras said successful corporations "distinguish between their values and core purpose (which never changes) of its operating practices and business strategies (which must constantly change to meet the changing world)." *Built to Last*, (Collins Business Essentials, 2002), 220. The authors resemble these two complementary forces with two concepts of Taoism, *yin*, and *yang*, two forces that interact and achieve balance and where the *taijitu* is its form of representation.

> This is therefore my thesis: I firmly believe that to survive and achieve success, an organization needs a series of strong beliefs on which to base all their policies and actions. Secondly, I think the most important factor in the success of a company is the faithful adherence to these beliefs. And finally, I think that if an organization aims to meet the challenge of a changing world, you must be willing to change everything except those beliefs throughout your life.*

Watson's successor, Lou Gerstner Jr., CEO of IBM between 1993 and 2002, also noted: "I saw in my time at IBM that culture is not only an aspect of the game, it is the game."[†]

Companies must invest in a culture of integrity that impacts the conduct of its employees. According to a report of CEB, in companies with a strong culture of integrity, employee misconduct is reported 51% more times than in companies with a perceived lower ethical culture.[‡]

Building a culture of integrity fortifies organizations against risks. The British futurologist Patrick Dixon said, "Strong ethics keep corporations healthy. Poor ethics make companies sick. Values are the immune system of every organization."[§]

Cultivating ethics is essential in organizations so that their members can better analyze the consequences and the impact of their decisions and behaviors.

Leaders must also lead to the diffusion of the organization's culture. Alexander the Great (356–323 BC) was the first leader to realize the importance of expanding culture, in this case the Greek culture, by building a universal empire in the fourth century BC. Like Alexander, multinational organizations must work so that the culture of integrity is disseminated, shared, and made consistent among different lines of business, markets, regions, and/or countries where it operates.

The more effort organizations put into the diffusion of ethics, the more likely it is that their employees will perceive it. One of the problems faced by global organizations is that corporate culture is usually stronger and better understood by the employees who work in the home office and its surroundings. When business units are located far from the parent company, the understanding of corporate culture normally decreases.

---

* Thomas Peters and Robert Waterman Jr, *In Search of Excellence*, (Editorial Atlántida, 1994), 276.
† Louis Gerstner Jr., *Who Says Elephants Can't Dance?* (Harper Business, 2002).
‡ www.cebglobal.com CEB (formerly Corporate Executive Board) is a subsidiary of Gartner, an American research and advisory firm that provides information technology.
§ Patrick Dixon, "32 Mind-Blowing Patrick Dixon Quotes," https// brandongaille.com.

Benoit Mandelbrot (1924–2010) was a Polish-born mathematician known for his work on the fractal geometry of nature.* A *fractal* is a geometric object whose basic, fragmented, or irregular structure is repeated at different scales. A property of fractals is self-similarity; thus, the same subject appears in an infinite number of scales. Some natural structures are fractal-like, such as coastlines, mountains, or trees. Each of the branches of a tree is a smaller version of the main trunk of the tree.†

Companies should aim to achieve a *fractal expansion* of organizational culture so all of its business areas replicate the culture from the home office, and the company gets a consistent, comprehensive, and uniform culture in all its business units.

Deloitte's 2016 annual report on global trends in human capital says: "The new CEOs and HR leaders of organizations are focused on creating a shared culture, a work environment that engages its people."‡

Napoleon Hill (1883–1970) said, "When a seed is planted in fertile soil, it germinates, grows and multiplies itself over and over again, until that one small seed becomes countless millions of seeds of the same brand."§

Donald Soderquist (1934–2016), former chief operating officer of Walmart Stores between 1988 and 1998, said, "To build a great company we must create a culture where everyone shares the same values, goals, and expectations of success. . . . Culture has an impact on the bottom line. Culture is what differentiates Walmart."¶

Fons Trompenaars and Charles Hampden-Turner in their book *Building Cross-Cultural Competence* discussed a study of cultural attitudes that revealed differences between citizens of different countries.** The study sought to understand better and more clearly how the culture of each country reacts regarding loyalty and regulations.

The following situation was proposed:

---

* The French mathematician Gaston Maurice Julia (1893–1978) was the first to study fractals. Fractal derives from the Latin *fractus*, meaning broken or fractured.
† The leaves of the trees are formed by smaller leaves similar to it, and this structure can be seen in the bushes of different plant species. Another example would be the clods created by drought in a lagoon; they are made up of other smaller ones like them. Another example is broken ice, because it is divided into similar smaller fractures. The same applies to the shell of a turtle.
‡ "Global Human Capital Trends 2016," Deloitte University Press, 1.
§ Napoleon Hill, *Think and Grow Rich* (Vermilion, Random House, 2004), 50.
¶ www.Soderquist.org.
** Charles Hampden-Turner and Fons Trompenaars, *Building Cross-Cultural Competence* (Yale University Press, 2000), 15, 16. The case is also mentioned in the Dov Seidman book *How* (John Wiley & Sons, 2007), 29, 30.

A friend of yours is driving a car and you are with him.

Your friend runs over a pedestrian.

You know he was driving at least 35 miles per hour in an area of the city where the speed limit is 20 miles per hour and you are the only witness.

The lawyer of your friend tells you that if you declare under oath that your friend was driving only 20 miles per hour, your friend would be saved from serious consequences.

What is the right thing to do? Be loyal to your friend or tell the truth?

In countries with a strong Protestant tradition and stable democracies like the United States, Switzerland, Norway, Finland, Sweden, and Australia, 80% thought it was right to tell the truth in court. In South Korea, Russia, or Bulgaria, by contrast, 80% thought that helping your friend was the right thing to do. The Japanese, meanwhile, said that the right thing to do was to ask your friend to have the courage to tell the truth.

When the leaders of multinational companies ask their employees to "do the right thing," the phrase can be interpreted, depending on the culture of each country, like loyalty to a friend or to law enforcement.

When followers of Aristotle (384–322 BC) told him that Plato (427–347 BC) thought differently about a topic, Aristotle did not prioritize the loyalty to his friend over what he considered the truth and answered, "Plato is a friend, but truth is a better friend."*

Even though Aristotle thought that friendship was among the highest and most moral of goods that life has to offer, he thought that friendship is something that takes place between two people, but the truth is something greater than any number of people. The truth is something that everyone depends on and has intrinsic value. Aristotle stated, "It is our sacred duty to honor truth more highly [than friends]."†

Loyalty to someone should not mislead us into doing what is wrong, because as individuals we must have greater loyalty and commitment to the values of truth and justice.

Behavior that may be correct in one culture may not be correct in another, and what is good or bad may vary from one culture to another because the values, principles, and beliefs are different and relative to each

---

* en.wikipedia.org/wiki/Amicus_Plato,_sed_magis_amica_veritas. In Latin, the phrase is known as: "Amicus Plato, sed magis amica veritas." Aristotle was a student of Plato and tutor of Alexander the Great.

† Professor Clancy Martin, *Moral Decision Making* (The Great Courses, Guidebook, University of Missouri, Kansas City, 2014).

culture. That's where the idea of "ethical or cultural relativism" comes from, which implies that values are relative and what is right or wrong can vary with culture.

Communicating a message so that it is interpreted similarly and penetrates evenly throughout the organization is one of the complexities multinational companies must overcome. The way in which employees perceive and interpret the culture of the company can vary, and the possibility this happens is greater when there is a high turnover of employees, the employees are in different regions and countries, they speak other languages, or when the training and communication of the principles and culture of the organization are neither frequent nor effective.

For some people, *doing the right thing* would be to fulfill the business plan, to achieve the sales plan, or to get the expected gains. For other people, *doing the right thing* means to act according to law and the company's principles.

Neville Isdell, the former CEO of Coca Cola, said that "for any global company, there is nothing more important than understanding the culture of the country where it is operating." Isdell says regarding his experience in the Philippines, that in the Philippine culture, "yes" means "I'm listening," it does not mean "I agree with you."[*]

The understanding of the local language is important. A US airlines pitched its waiting areas as "Rendezvous Lounges," but in the version used in Brazil these became "Rooms for lovemaking."[†] Ford experienced slow sales when it introduced the "Ford Comet" in Mexico under the name "Caliente."[‡]

It is necessary to know the body language and cultural differences before traveling to other countries. For example, in the West, if we move the head from top to bottom, we communicate an affirmation, and if we move it from side to side, we communicate a negation. In some places in India, the meaning of these gestures is the reverse. The same happens in Bulgaria, people move their heads up and down to say "no" and from one side to the other to say "yes."

---

[*] Neville Isdell, *Inside Coca Cola* (New York, St. Martin's Press, 2011), 70.
[†] K. Blanchard, C. Schewe, R. Nelson and A. Hiam, *Exploring the World of Business* (Worth Publishers, 1996), 86.
[‡] Alan M. Rugman and Richard M. Hodgetts, *International Business, A Strategic Management Approach* (McGraw Hill, Inc., 1995), 125.

The OK sign with the raised thumb (thumbs-up), which means "in agreement," does not have the same meaning in Turkey as in the West.* In Turkey, that gesture means that a person is homosexual. In Turkey, also, it is offensive to point to objects or people with the index finger, as well as showing the sole of the foot or the sole of the shoes.

The joining of the index finger and thumb to form an O means "okay" in the United States, money in Japan, and "I will kill you" in Tunisia.†

In some countries of Europe, the gesture of a finger turning on the temple meaning madness can be punished by law. In some Arab countries, touching the mustache may be a sexual insinuation.

In Asia, it is not appropriate for a couple to show their affection in public places. In Japan, if you receive a professional card, you have to take a few seconds and read it to show deference.

Latin Americans generally greet with a hug or a kiss. Americans generally greet each other with a handshake. Arabs maintain greater eye contact than in the West. In Russia it is normal to give three kisses and even kisses on the mouth between men, as did, for example, the secretary-general of the Communist Party of the Soviet Union Leonid Brezhnev (1906–1982) and Erich Honecker (1912–1994), the president of the State Council of the German Democratic Republic, in 1979.

Understanding not only the legislation but the different cultures of the places where we conduct business is essential if we want to be successful. We must see from the perspective of the other, have more empathy, and communicate the corporate culture more effectively.

Sweden has a 99% literacy rate, and so a company can safely advertise its product in various magazines and newspapers. But in Yemen, in Asia, the literacy rate is about 54%. Here, an approach based on visual media such as picture posters would be more appropriate. Even then, cultural problems can occur.

This happened when a company, hoping to market baby food in Central Africa, designed a picture of a cute baby from a local tribe on the jar. But local consumers had little experience with the culture of packaging and came to believe that the picture on the package represented its contents. They concluded that the baby food jars contained processed baby.‡

---

* In 1839 in the *Boston Morning Post* his editor wrote "Ok – all correct." Then, during the War of the Secession (1861–1865) when the troops returned to the barracks without soldiers killed, on a blackboard they wrote OK ("0 Killed").

† John D. Daniels and Lee H. Radebaugh, *International Business, Environments and Operations*, 7th ed (Addison Wesley Publishing Company, 1995), 65.

‡ K. Blanchard, C. Schewe, R. Nelson and A. Hiam, *Exploring the World of Business* (Worth Publishers, 1996), 85–6.

A global business must be adapted to different products and strategies for different foreign markets.

Different cultures require a global communication strategy that can be adapted to the different nations, and therefore, selling the same product, the same way, everywhere, to gain economies of scale in production and marketing is not necessarily always the best decision. The assumption that consumers around the world may have the same wants and needs might be wrong. See the following example:

> Australian media mogul Rupert Murdoch, who launched the Fox TV network in America, initially beamed his Star TV satellite network into Asia with a one-size-fits-all approach of offering English-language programming. But losses resulted. So, the strategy was altered, by customizing music programming to local tastes.
>
> Syrupy love ballads were broadcast to Taiwan.... Chinese viewers were provided with more gymnastics, soccer, and track, while in India, where the British influence remains strong, Star broadcasted more cricket matches. Movies were made in Mandarin for Hong Kong and in Hindi for India.*

In Japan, for example, Procter & Gamble used an advertisement for Camay soap in which a man meeting a woman for the first time compared her skin to that of a fine porcelain doll. Although the ad had worked well in South America and Europe, it insulted the Japanese.†

Understanding the cultures of the countries where the business is conducted is, therefore, essential to be able to clearly and effectively communicate also the values of the company to reduce unethical behaviors.

Why do people perform unethical acts? Sometimes the reason is that certain people try to profit personally from a given situation. Other times the reason is lack of training in ethical issues, and the individual, when making a decision, does not recognize the ethical dilemma and makes a mistake.

Ethics training allows individuals to develop their ability to conduct ethical reasoning and understand the impact of their decisions. It allows them to anticipate and prevent problematic situations.

Another reason people act unethically is the existence of an organizational culture that allows or encourages unethical behavior. For example, if it is known that certain employees steal merchandise from the

---

* K. Blanchard, C. Schewe, R. Nelson and A. Hiam, *Exploring the World of Business* (Worth Publishers, 1996), 92–3.
† Donald A. Ball and Wendell H. McCulloch Jr., *International Business, the Challenge of Global Competition*, 6th ed (IRWIN, 1996), 271.

company's distribution center and nobody cares or does anything, it could encourage other employees to do the same in the future, because if bad behavior is not disciplined, other people will replicate it.

On the other hand, a strong organizational ethical culture often influences behaviors and discourages or diminishes actions outside the ethics of individuals. Employees are influenced by how others behave, and so a strong ethical culture in the workplace is important to promote ethical behavior among members of the company.

The Ethics Resource Center (ERC) mentions that

> the vast majority of people act based on the circumstances in their environment and the standards set by their leaders and peers, even if it means compromising their personal moral ideas. Good people do bad things if they are put in an environment that does not value values if pressured to believe that they don't have any choice but to get the job done, whatever it takes.*

The ERC showed in the 2007 National Business Ethics Survey that a strong ethical culture in organizations reduces misconduct by more than 50% and that percentage is even higher and reaches 65% when the company has in addition to an ethical culture an effective program of ethics and compliance that supports it.

Success in executing a business strategy has never been more dependent upon an ethical culture and effective risk management. Gary Hill, principal, Ethics & Compliance Practice, at Solutions House, says, "If there is any one lesson I have learned in more than 30 years in the field of ethics and compliance it is that it's all about culture."

Culture is powerful and determines how individuals will behave. Therefore, without an ethical and compliance culture, organizations will always be at risk. Ethical character and social responsibility are features of organizational culture. As Professor Jorge Etkin says, they are "a trait of its identity."†

As Deloitte points out, "Without a culture of integrity, organizations are likely to view their ethics and compliance programs as a set of check-the-box activities, or even worse, as a roadblock to achieving their business objectives."‡

---

* *The Importance of Ethical Culture; Increasing Trust and Driving Down Risks* (The Ethics Resource Center, 2010). Mentioned by Latour Lafferty in the paper "Ethics and Culture."

† Jorge Etkin, "Bases Conceptuales de la Gestion Socialmente Responsable," (Conceptual Bases of Socially Responsible Management), *Saberes*, 1 (2009).

‡ "Building World-Class Ethics and Compliance Programs: Making a Good Program Great," www.deloitte.com.

Marianne M. Jennings JD, professor of business ethics at Arizona State University, says, "A poor ethical culture breeds ethical breaches. Ethical breaches then often lead to legal violations. Too often accompanying both is financial collapse."*

It is necessary to ensure a culture that prevents ambition from being above ethics and that prevents relaxation in ethical standards.

It is necessary to have a standard to follow, but the will to follow it is also necessary.

Michael Rake, former chairman of the board of KPMG International and current chairman of the BT Group, says,

> The focus is not on internal controls but on the culture of the organization. . . . When a person is under pressure and has to meet a certain goal, no matter what happens, their behavior will depend on the style imposed by the head of the company and the culture of the organization.†

Warren Buffet has regularly sent a letter to his managers reminding them that culture will determine how an organization behaves. In one of those letters, Buffet writes, "There is plenty of money to be made in the center of the court. If an action is questionable or close to the line, just assume it is outside the line and forget it."

The following *cultural loop* shows that corporate values, beliefs, and principles disseminated within the organization are the basis for decisions and behaviors:

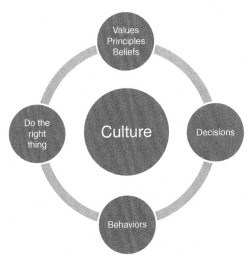

---

* See Latour Lafferty, "Ethics and Culture."
† "Reglas claras y transparentes," May/June 2004, www.gestion.com.ar. Interview with Michael Rake, 124 ("Clear and Transparent Rules").

If the company has a mature ethical culture disseminated within the organization, it will generate a new loop of trust, a good reputation, and effective leadership that will lead to high performance over time.

When the company does the right thing by acting ethically, it becomes a reliable place for employees, customers, suppliers, and shareholders.

Standards and internal policies must be implemented in the different business units and geographies with the same degree of compulsion so the different industries and regions in which the company operates can be united by a common culture.

Behavior is the consequence of culture. The leaders of organizations must ensure that people are treated well, be decent, speak the truth, compete within the rules of the game, be honest and fair, and create a climate that encourages exemplary behavior, which forms the basis for discouraging harmful behavior. Roger W. Ferguson Jr., president and CEO of TIAA-CREF, said:

> In the end, what matters most are not rules, but how people actually behave. And what is it that determines how employees behave? Behavior is driven by a company's values and culture. That's why values and culture are the ultimate keystones of governance. They are what lead people to do the right thing, even when nobody is looking. ... Companies can have the most extensive processes and procedures, but if they have the wrong people in

positions of leadership or if those people do not behave with transparency and integrity, they won't necessarily have a culture that promotes doing the right thing.*

Ethical leadership is essential to achieve success in organizations. The way a leader behaves and his moral authority has an impact and influences the business culture. When leaders act ethically, the organization is more likely to achieve a culture based on trust and respect for people and laws. This leads to a corporate culture that rejects immorality and corruption.

Life has rules, play fair.

Our values lead our behavior. If an ethical culture expands and grows, the company will have a competitive advantage that will guide employees to make good decisions and reduce the possibility of misconduct.

Culture is the soul of any organization and, therefore, an ethical culture is the most important thing for any company.

---

* Roger W. Ferguson Jr., *Business Ethics and the Financial Service Sector: The Way Forward* (The Raytheon Lectureship in Business Ethics at Bentley University, April 2, 2013).

3

Reputation and Ethics

Reputation is the information or opinion one has of someone or something, regardless of whether the information is true.

The reputation of a company is the image it has built of itself over time, through its values, its history, its members, its actions, its quality, its service, customer and employee's satisfaction, and good practices.[*] In order to sell their products or services, companies must generate confidence in their potential customers. A positive image is built through a constant behavior during a period of time that is aligned with moral values.

Companies are worth as much for their tangible assets as for intangibles, and a good reputation is one of those intangible attributes that cannot be bought.

The Technological Institute of Monterrey, in Mexico, has pointed out that the reputational value of a company represents its main source of economic value.[†]

We are in the "era of ethics, not aesthetics."[‡] Organizations create their reputational information through their history of compliance behavior.

The book of Proverbs in the Old Testament of the Bible says, "A good name is more desirable than great riches; to be esteemed is better than silver or gold."[§]

In *Othello*, a play by the greatest English writer William Shakespeare (1564–1616), Iago states:

Who steals my purse steals trash; 'tis something, nothing;
Twas mine, 'tis his, and has been slave to thousands;

---

[*] "Reputación y Valores," Sembrarvalores.org, October 18, 2016 ("Reputation and Values").
[†] "El Valor de la Reputación," Ankromgroup.com, October 13, 2016 ("The Value of Reputation").
[‡] "El Valor de la Reputación," Ankromgroup.com, October 13, 2016 ("The Value of Reputation").
[§] The Bible, 22:1.

But he that filches from me my good name
Robs me of that which not enriches him,
And makes me poor indeed.*

A Greek poet, Hesiod, who lived around 700 BC said that "a bad reputation is lifting a light load, heavy to carry and difficult to download."†

US President Abraham Lincoln (1809–1865) stated: "Character is like a tree and reputation like a shadow. The shadow is what we think of it, the tree is the real thing."‡

Reputation, like a forest, takes many years to grow but can burn and disappear in minutes. A Japanese proverb says that "a reputation of a thousand years may depend on the behavior of one hour" and Benjamin Franklin (1706–1790) said: "It takes many good deeds to build a good reputation and only one bad one to lose it.§ ... Glass and reputation are easily cracked and never well mended."¶

A good reputation is a recognition that it is made from the behavior of the company with its customers, employees, suppliers, and the community. A good name is the most valuable thing one can have. Socrates (470 BC–399 AC) said, "Regard your name as the richest jewel you can possibly be possessed of ... but if you once extinguish it, you will find it an arduous task to rekindle it again."**

Therefore, the phrase of Ellevest CEO Sallie Krawcheck is very accurate: "If it comes down to your ethics vs. a job, choose ethics. You can always find another job."††

The Economist Intelligence Unit created a report published by Deloitte in 2005 that stated,

> If the opinions of customers, employees, analysts, regulators, and other key stakeholders shift against a company, the negative impact wrought by a bad reputation can send shock waves through nearly every aspect of the organization – from recruiting the best talent to stock value and consumer opinion – up to and including its ability to survive.‡‡

---

* *Othello*, Act 3, Scene 3.

† www.akifrases.com.

‡ www.reputationxl.com and www.goodreads.com.

§ www.brainquote.com.

¶ www.goodreads.com.

** www.goodreads.com.

†† www.quotetab.com/quotes/by-sallie-krawcheck#klJxahGztvheTzGY.97.

‡‡ "The Strategic Importance of Reputational Risk," Economist Intelligent Unit white paper, Risk Intelligence Series, Issue 22. Deloitte, 2005.

Former professional golfer "Maestro" Roberto De Vicenzo (1923–2017) was born in 1923 in the province of Buenos Aires, Argentina. De Vicenzo won 230 golf tournaments, including four tournaments on the PGA Tour and the British Open. On April 14, 1968, after the last round of the Masters in Augusta, Georgia, De Vicenzo did not review his golf card as completed by his playmate Tommy Aaron, who wrote by mistake four strokes on the 17th hole instead of the three that De Vicenzo had made. He finished with 65 shots, but his card accounted for 66. De Vicenzo signed the card and presented it without noticing the error of the stroke added by Aaron.

According to the rules of golf, if a card has more golf shots than those actually incurred, the score declared by the golfer is accepted (if the card has fewer golf shots than those actually incurred, the player would be disqualified).

De Vicenzo, who in the field had tied for first place, finished second because of the extra shot in his card and; therefore, Bob Goalby won the Augusta Open without a playoff. When De Vicenzo learned about Aaron's mistake he did not blame him and merely expressed a phrase that became famous: "how stupid I am."*

Roberto De Vicenzo said later, "I made the mistake when analyzing the card before signing it. Nobody else is responsible." In 2014, when he was celebrating his 91st birthday he commented: "I have traveled a lot and I learned that the first duty was to respect the regulations. If one is able to do this in life, not only in golf, you will not have problems."†

Like De Vicenzo, business leaders must always respect and accept the laws and procedures – the rules of the game – to maintain a reputation for integrity, the basis for sustainable growth.

Julius Caesar (100–44 BC) took extraordinary care to eliminate negative perceptions toward him. Publius Clodius Pulcro (93–52 BC) was a general of the Republic of Rome who fell in love with Pompeia Sila (140–85 BC), the second wife of Julius Caesar, after the death of his first wife, Cornelia (97–69 BC). On one occasion at a women's party, Clodius Pulcro tried to get close to Pompeia disguised as a woman but was discovered and escaped. Believing that his wife was deceiving him, Julius Caesar separated from Pompeia because of rumors of her behavior. Greek historian

---

* Bob Goalby, winner of the tournament, once said: "Roberto, because of you I never won the Masters. You were the true champion." De Vicenzo has been part of the World Golf Hall of Fame since 1989 and always enjoyed an unblemished reputation.
† April 23, 2014, www.berazategui.gov.ar.

Plutarch (46–120) wrote that Caesar said, "Caesar's wife ought not even to be under suspicion."*

Perception gives us meaning, a reality to what we perceive with our senses, like a picture in our mind of something or someone.

The Scottish philosopher David Hume (1711–1776) argued that we judge things to be good or bad not because of certain moral external reality, but because of the event in question affects us.

The American psychologist Chris Argyris (1923–2013), professor emeritus at Harvard Business School, called *the ladder of inference* a thought process by which people draw conclusions and act from certain selected data based on their beliefs and prejudices. According to Argyris, the way we think is like a ladder. On the step is what is observable. We climb a step and select data on which we focus the observation. Then we climb another step and add to that observation of our beliefs. On the fourth step, assumptions are made based on our beliefs and data. In the following steps, people draw their conclusions and finally carry out an action. The *inferential ladder* shows us the process of how we mentally ascend from observations and our perceptions to decisions and actions.

The following conundrum was asked to a group of people: A father and son travel in a car and have a serious accident. The father dies and the son is taken to a hospital to perform an emergency operation. They call a medical expert, but when the person arrives and sees the patient, the doctor says "I cannot operate on him, he is my son."

The majority of the responses to the riddle were, "It cannot be" or "It is impossible, the father of the kid is dead."

The right answer is that the doctor is the child's mother. Most people (men and women) associated "medical eminence" with "a man." But the medical eminence was in fact a woman.†

How accurately does our mental representation of reality reflect actual reality?

There was once a man who had a cabin in the mountains. Every Saturday morning, the man drove his red Porsche to his cottage through

---

* www.evostudies.org.

† The Attorney Milton Bordwin, who also has written on this matter, says that even for the leader of the Roman Republic Julius Caesar (100–44 BC), caring perception and reputation were very important: "Julius Caesar did not believe in the attributed infidelity of his wife. Anyway, he divorced, admitting that Caesar's wife must be above suspicion." Milton Baldwin, "Above Suspicion," *Gestion,* September–October 1998.

† Video of BBC Mundo-Inma Gil and Carol Olona. Sources: Tinu Cornish, Borah Belle, and Mahzarin Banasi.

a dangerous path of tight corners. One Saturday morning the man was heading to his cabin, and suddenly, on the other side of the curve, a car approached, almost out of control and zigzagging. The man slowed the Porsche, and from the out of control car approaching him, a woman stuck her head out the window and shouted, "Pig!"

"What?" he replied and almost instantly added, "You're a pig too!" Meanwhile, she sped up her car and continued on her way. The man with the Porsche, angry, pressed the accelerator, sped around the curve, and … he crashed into a pig.*

The man driving the Porsche thought the woman had insulted him, but, in fact, she had actually attempted to alert him about the dangers of a pig on the road. He did not hear what she wanted to say. His own thoughts and his prejudices blocked his mind. The perception of the reality of the two was completely different.

Not everything is always what it seems. According to the Chinese, three mirrors form the image of a person: the first shows how one looks to oneself, the second shows how others see you, and the third reflects the truth.†

Perception is a complex mechanism conditioned by the psychology, experiences, and beliefs of individuals. The mental image is subjective, and it is our perception which becomes our reality. Two people can look at the same thing and see something totally different. The same reality may be different depending on who looks at it, how it is looked at, and where one looks at it.

Some people may believe graduation from college is necessary to succeed in business. However, this perception does not necessarily match reality. Neither John D. Rockefeller nor Henry Ford, nor Steve Jobs, nor Bill Gates, nor Paul Allen, nor Mark Zuckerberg, nor Michael Dell, nor Walt Disney, nor Ted Turner, nor Richard Brandson, to name but a few, are or were university graduates.

Our vision of reality is conditioned by how we interpret what happens around us and "our" reality is formed in our mind. Albert Einstein (1879–1955) said "reality is merely an illusion, albeit a very persistent one."‡

There is no one way of seeing things; each of us interprets reality differently. It depends on the different mental models of people.

The idea of mental models was originated by Kenneth Craik (1914–1945) in his book published in 1943 entitled *The Nature of Explanation*.

---

* Joel Arthur Barker, *Paradigms* (McGraw-Hill, 1999), 227–28.
† Robin Sharma, *The Monk Who Sold His Ferrari* (Sudamericana, 2010), 102.
‡ www.goodreads.com.

A mental model is a mechanism of thought by which a person creates his representation of reality. It is the perspective of each individual who sees or thinks about a thing based on their personal circumstances, experiences, customs, and culture.

The mental model is created from our imagination and influences our decisions. Thus, if a person thinks that money is the most important thing, he will act to obtain it regardless of the damage it may cause, because according to his mental model only with money that person is happy.*

The socialist regime and the capitalist regime can be good or bad, depending on the perception and mental models of each one. The number 6 might be a numeral 9, depending on how you see it. As in art or with the Rorschach test,† each person interprets images subjectively, influenced by one's prejudices and by what he or she wants or can see. Some images can mean different things depending on who looks at them.

The vertical-horizontal illusion is the tendency for observers to overestimate the length of a vertical line relative to a horizontal line of the same length.

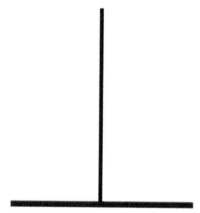

Different *perceptions* of reality and the different ways people see, feel, and/or think things can explain why people behave differently or have distinct comments on identical circumstances. The Heriot-Watt University, in Edinburgh, Scotland, presented a paper that suggests that reality is not objective and it depends on who is looking at it.‡ Everyone sees something

---

* Es.wikipedia.org/wiki Modelo_Mental ("Mental Model").
† Technique and method of psychological diagnosis created by Swiss psychiatrist and psychoanalyst Hermann Rorschach (1884–1922). It was first published in 1921 and is primarily used to assess personality. It consists of a series of sheets that have ink stains characterized by their ambiguity.
‡ "Un Estudio Cientifico Demostro Que la Realidad no Existe" ("A Scientific Study Demonstrated that Reality Does Not Exist"), March 7, 2019, www.clarin.

different and makes different choices. The world is not what it is but what we think it is.

On the morning of January 12, 2007, at the subway station L' Enfant Plaza in Washington D.C., one person took a violin and performed a small recital of six classical melodies over 45 minutes. Although hundreds of people walked by him, very few stopped to listen to him, and by the end of his presentation, he had collected US$32. That violinist was the American Joshua Bell, one of the best in the world. Two days earlier he had performed at Boston's Symphony Hall at an average ticket price of US$100 per seat. This experiment was organized by the *Washington Post* to analyze the perception of people when a given situation occurs in an unexpected context. Our perceptions can make us miss great opportunities.

In an old parable, six blind wise men encountered an elephant and started to touch the body to understand what it was. Each touched a different part and then compared their observations.

One of them crashed against the elephant's hardback and said, "It's like a wall." The second, feeling the tusk, shouted, "This is so round and smooth that the elephant is like a spear." The third touched the twisted trunk and shouted, "The elephant is like a snake." The fourth extended his hand to the knee and said, "It is clear that the elephant is like a tree." The fifth, who touched the elephant's ear, said, "Even the blindest of men would realize that the elephant is like a fan." The sixth, which touched the tail, said, "The elephant is very much like a rope."

And so the wise men discussed, and each had a particular perspective on reality. Like the blind wise men, man is unable to know the whole of reality; people may perceive the same situation differently and transform it into their reality.

Austrian psychologist Paul Watzlawick (1921–2007) said, "The belief that one's own view of reality is the only reality is the most dangerous of all delusions."*

"I only know that I know nothing" is a famous phrase attributed to the Greek philosopher Socrates (470–399 BC) that reflects how conscious he was of his own ignorance.†

According to the French philosopher Rene Descartes (1596–1650), we must adopt a skeptical position:

---

* www.goodreads.com.
† en.wikipedia.org/wiki/I_know_that_I_know_nothing.

Not only don't I know anything, but I am positioned in such a way that what I think I know is probably laden with error, misapprehension, and confusion.... Accept nothing as true except what presents itself with clarity and vividness that is irresistible.*

Ray Kroc (1902–1984) joined McDonald's in 1954 and managed to transform it over the years into the most successful fast-food company in the world. In 1960 the company sold US$76 million worth of food annually, but its profits were only US$159,000 annually. It was the financier Harry Sonneborn (1916–1992) who changed Kroc's perception of his business. McDonald's does not make a profit from the sale of hamburgers and fries; the real "business" is real estate: renting the land where McDonald's stores will be built. Kroc changed his perspective and began to see his own business differently.†

Reputation is a consequence of the good or bad perception of a person or a brand. Reputation is said to be the perception of integrity. Reputation is how others see you. Therefore, the perceptions that others have about the organization are of great importance.

That is why corporate leaders must understand the importance of the phrase, "I do not care what it is, I care what it looks like."

The Greek philosopher Socrates (470–399 BC) said, "The way to gain a good reputation is to endeavor to be what you desire to appear."‡

The Italian politician and historian Nicolas Machiavelli (1469–1527) said, "Everyone sees what you appear to be, few experience what you really are."§

Roman emperor Marcus Aurelius (121–180) said, "Everything we hear is an opinion, not a fact. Everything we see is a perspective, not the truth."¶ The judgment, opinion, or concept that we form about something has a lot of power over us. The Greek Stobaeus of the Roman province of Macedonia at the beginning of the fifth century said, "Unfortunately, opinion has more strength than truth."

People see reality from different perspectives. The way clients view an organization does not always coincide with how the organization sees itself. A company's reputation stems from the perception of reality that

* Daniel N. Robinson and The Great Courses, "Descartes and the authority of reason," *The Great Ideas of Philosophy*, 2nd ed (Oxford University, The Great Courses), Lecture 26, 407.
† "The Founder," film directed by John Lee Hancock (2016).
‡ www.brainyquote.com/quotes/socrates_385050.
§ www.goodreads.com/quotes/158433-everyone-sees-what-you-appear-to-be-few-experience-what.
¶ www.goodreads.com/author/quotes/17212.Marcus_Aurelius.

is built on the mental maps of customers and is the result of behavior developed by the organization over time.

Vincent Covello, president of the Center for Risk Communication, says, "For companies, the perception of their customers is their reality. And what is perceived as real for their customers is real in its consequences for the company."[*]

A few years ago, *Apertura* magazine asked the lawyer Hector Mairal, partner of the law firm Marval O'Farrell and Mairal, his opinion on his election as the best lawyer in Argentina by the vote of his colleagues. He replied, "This is like golf, you play and another one completes the scorecard." One acts, and the image projected becomes a reality in the minds of others.

Ethics helps to maintain a good reputation, to add value to the brand and to give long-term sustainability to the organization. Reputation is of paramount importance, and therefore most corporate leaders are sensitive to any event that may damage it.[†]

The protection of a company brand is a priority because each brand has an emotional connection with customers and a certain history that expresses belonging to a particular product, company, or service. David Aakkeer, the author of *Building Strong Brands*, states that "the strongest brands require the support and shared the care of the entire organization."[‡]

The possibility an event may affect the trust of the company is called "reputational risk."[§] As a consequence, there is a risk of financial loss due to the company's adverse perception due to unacceptable business practices, lack of transparency, errors in dealing with customers, in choosing its partners, or in decision-making. The consequences of a bad reputation can be very negative.

Roger & Me is a documentary film released in 1989, directed by Michael Moore. It portrays the economic and social impacts produced when General Motors, led by its CEO Roger Smith (1925–2007), decides to close its car plants in the city of Flint, Michigan. As a result of this decision,

---

[*] Michael Ritter, El *Valor del Capital Reputacional* (Olivos, Ritter & Partners, 2013), 49 ("The Value of Reputational Capital").

[†] Robert G. Eccles, Scott C. Newquist and Roland Schultz, "Reputation and Its Risks," *Harvard Business Review*, 104 (February 2007).

[‡] Pablo Gracia Beccar and Julio Souto, Thesis Magister Institutional Communication. "Relación entre la Imagen Pública y el Mercado de Consumo" (UCES. 2001): 10 ("Relationship between the Public Image and the Consumer Market").

[§] Michael Ritter, El *Valor del Capital Reputacional* (Olivos, Ritter & Partners, 2013), 223 ("The Value of Reputational Capital").

30,000 employees are out of work and the city of Flint is economically devastated. Smith decided to close 11 factories in the United States and open 11 in Mexico with disastrous social, economic, financial, and reputational consequences. CNBC called Smith "one of the worst American CEOs of all time."[*] In 2013 he was listed on *Fortune*'s list of "10 worst auto chiefs"[†]and in 1995 consumer advocate Ralph Nader said Roger's Smith tenure "was one of the darkest in General Motors' history for customers, workers and for residents of GM's factory towns."[‡]

Moore's documentary can be used effectively to teach how certain decisions and actions can have extremely negative external and internal consequences.

Kevin O'Leary, chairman at O' Shares and Shark on Investments, mentioned in a video the importance of protecting company's brands.

> A few years ago, if you experience something you didn't like about a product, you picked up the phone and called customer service and you complained. That's not what happens today. When a customer is unhappy with your company they go online, to every website, every rating agency and they go crazy on you. The damage is almost irreparable. You have spent years building a brand…you have to spend energy and money to fix it.…30% of the time when a customer is flailing at you online, it's not a customer, it's your competitor. They are trying to take you down and steal your market share, and it's nasty cruel. Companies have to spend a lot of money even if they are small, making sure that their brand is protected. Your brand is your life. If everybody assails your brand, your business dies, it's that simple.[§]

In 2009 Tiger Woods was for the eighth consecutive year the highest-paid athlete in the world. Until that time, large companies used Tiger's image, among them were Nike, Accenture, Gatorade, Gillette, American Express, and Tag Heuer. In November 2009, the number one image of golf began to collapse following a car accident outside his Isleworth, Florida mansion that uncovered Tiger's infidelities. "According to Wikinvest.com quoting a study from the University of California, companies that sponsored Woods

---

[*] www.imdb.com and https: vikivisually.com.
[†] Alex Taylor III, "History's 10 worst auto chiefs," April 3, 2013, Fortune.com.
[‡] Michael Maynard, "Roger B. Smith, ex-chief of GM dies," December 1, 2007. www.nytimes.com.
[§] "30 years ago, if you pissed off a customer," Kevin O'Leary video, ABC's Shark Tank.

lost between US\$5 billion and US\$12 billion worth of market value after the sportsman's scandal."*

Andrea Bonime-Blanc, the CEO of GEC Risk Advisory, says, "Smart organizations are prepared for when a reputational risk occurs. These organizations understand why there was a risk and how things can be improved in the future."†

According to Michael Ritter, a former Siemens executive, "According to 959 executives from 11 countries … consulted in 2006 by KRC Research, seven out of ten top managers think it is much more difficult to recover a bad reputation than to win and maintain it."‡ Ritter has written that according to an investigation by Burston-Marsteller in 2004 called *The Road to Reputation Recovery*, executives of 150 global companies were surveyed and it was concluded that even if the company takes the appropriate measures, on average, it would take more than five years to regain lost prestige.§

A solid reputation helps companies attract the best talent, be an attractive investment, and be seen as a responsible and positive member of the community.

Since 2007, the Reputation Institute publishes the Annual RepTrak, which are rankings of companies with the best reputation in the world *and in the United States*. In the 2018 world ranking, Rolex from Switzerland was first and, in the United States, the highest ranking went to Campbell Soup Co.¶ The RepTrak examines more than 7,000 companies. The Institute was created in 1997 by Charles Fombrun and its ranking is an authoritative source for measuring the reputation of companies around the world.** The Reputation Institute states that "reputation is more than an abstract concept; it is a corporate asset that is a magnet to attract customers, employees, and investors."†† In a global survey conducted in 2012 by this institute, it was concluded that "83 percent of respondents said that the

---

* Michael Ritter, *El Valor del Capital Reputacional* (Olivos, Ritter & Partners, 2013), 293 ("The Value of Reputational Capital").

† Andrea Bonime-Blanc, *The Reputational Risk Handbook* (Doshort, 2014), 109.

‡ Michael Ritter, *El Valor del Capital Reputacional* (Olivos, Ritter & Partners, 2013), 296 ("The Value of Reputational Capital").

§ Michael Ritter, *El Valor del Capital Reputacional* (Olivos, Ritter & Partners, 2013), 310 ("The Value of Reputational Capital").

¶ www.reputationinstitute.com/us-reptrak.

** www.reputationinstitute.com/about.

†† Joseph Weiss, *Business Ethics*, 4th ed (Thomson, 2006), 171. The words of the executive director of the Reputation Institute.

decision to work or invest in the company is conditioned by the perception they have of it."[*]

But the Reputation Institute is not the only recognized entity that measures the reputation of companies. Since 1999 the Harris Poll has been publishing the "Reputation Quotient" that quantifies the reputation of the 100 most visible companies. The Reputation Quotient classifies the reputation of companies taking into account six dimensions: (i) The quality and innovation of their products and services; (ii) the trust and respect that awakens; (iii) its work environment; (iv) the projection of growth; (v) the vision and leadership; and (vi) the social responsibility with the community and the environment.[†]

Being in the top places in these rankings is of interest to many business leaders because they know it is recognition to a good job done in the previous year. For example, Amazon founder and CEO Jeff Bezos, in his letter to the shareholders of 2018, noted, "The Harris Poll released its annual Reputation Quotient, which surveys over 25,000 consumers in a broad range of topics from workplace environment, to social responsibility, to products and services, and for the third year in a row, Amazon ranked #1."[‡]

The academic Daniel Diermeier in his book *Reputational Rules* says,

> Once the company faces a reputational crisis, people pay attention not only to what is happening but also to what was done before to prevent it. This perspective should be incorporated into the decisions made today because through the decisions we make today we are creating facts that are the basis of our history tomorrow.[§]

The prestige of an institution is linked to its reputation and the good opinion and trust that are built. In order to maintain a good image and trust, the company must act fairly and impartially with its employees and suppliers. It must offer quality products and services, and be honest and not try to fool customers with misleading ads. A good reputation should be protected.[¶]

---

[*] Michael Ritter, *El Valor del Capital Reputacional* (Olivos, Ritter & Partners, 2013), 49.

[†] theharrispoll.com/reputation-quotient/.

[‡] www.sec.gov/Archives/edgar/data/1018724/.

[§] Daniel Diermeier, *Reputational Rules* (Mc Graw Hill. 2011), 185.

[¶] "Special Report: Mastering Risk: The Challenge of Protecting Reputation," *Financial Times*, September 30, 2005, says: "Because it's easy for executives to think and plan financial risk but difficult to understand the intangible risks, which can destroy the shareholder value."

Maintaining a good reputation, in the long run, is essential for businesses. Jeffrey Immelt, former CEO of General Electric, in a letter accompanying the company's 2002 annual report, said: "We spend millions each year to improve our training, ensuring compliance with standards and reinforcing the values … to preserve our culture and to protect one of our most valuable assets: our reputation."

The long-term success of organizations is strictly linked to their reputation. It is the responsibility of each member of the organization to protect it by acting with integrity. In that way, the image of the company is positively reflected.

On February 21, 1991, Paul Mozer, executive of the investment bank Salomon Brothers, made illegal offers of bonds to the US treasury and the executive director of Salomon had to resign. Warren Buffet, who was a shareholder of the bank, was appointed as a new executive director. Soon, he gathered the bank executives and told them:

"Lose money for the firm, and I will be understanding, lose a shred of reputation for the firm, and I will be ruthless."* "Each one of you is expected to inform me immediately of any illegal infringement or moral breach of any employee."†

If a good reputation is lost, trust, talent, credit, and customers are also lost with it. Important personalities in the business world talk about reputational risk and endorse the importance of keeping a good reputation, as highlighted in the footnote examples.‡

---

* "La Debacle de Salomon Brothers," Artibus Consulting, www.ArtibusConsulting.com ("The Debacle of Salomon Brothers"). "This is the moment America met Warren Buffett," Myles Udland, www.financie.yahoo.com April 30, 2019.

† "Las Medidas Que no Tomo Kenneth Lay de Enron," knowledgeawharton.com.es, March 7, 2003 ("The measures that Kenneth Lay did not take from Enron").

‡ 1 – Keith Darcy, senior adviser to Deloitte & Touch and former executive director of the Ethics and Compliance Officer Association (ECOA), has written that "reputational risk is as high today as the financial, operational or strategic." "Managing Global Ethics and Compliance as an Asset, Not an Expense," *Risk and Compliance Journal*, Deloitte, May 19, 2014, *The Wall Street Journal*.

2 – The CEO of the Centre for Reputation Leadership, Angel Alloza, says that "mismanaged reputation can wipe out a company." "Reputational Risk Management Is a Strategic Imperative," November 3, 2016. This professor at the University of Malaga refers to a work of the British company AON wherein this global risk firm states that "damage to reputation and corporate brand is considered the main risk facing organizations today." "AON Risk Solutions," April 2005, AON Global Risk Management Survey.

3 – Sam Walton (1918–1992) said, "Don't compromise your reputation, it is a precious commodity. Don't compromise your integrity. Have a good name."

4 – American writer and psychologist Robert Greene has pointed out, "Reputation is a treasure to be carefully collected and hoarded. … You must protect it strictly, anticipating all attacks on it," Robert Greene, *The 48 Laws of Power* (Penguin Books, 2000), 92.

5 – The investor Warren Buffett has said that "we can lose money, but not our reputation."

Companies face a fast-moving environment where complex issues can quickly damage even the strongest reputations. Those unpredictable events might undermine the credibility of organizations and impact negatively their bottom line. Companies are not always prepared to face these crises when they occur.

The biggest threat to a company's reputation is that it does not have adequate control systems that prevent it from understanding what is happening inside and outside the organization. If a company has reputational problems, it will lose the confidence of customers, employees, suppliers, and partners.

The new economy based on constant innovation requires better management controls on intangible assets such as ethical conduct. Potential clients are better informed today and want to do business with ethical organizations, where the goods and services offered are ethically produced. To act ethically and to maintain the confidence of consumers and their own employees, organizations must reinforce the dissemination of the values and moral principles.

An organization with a good reputation is a consequence of the actions of ethical leaders who see reality from the perspective of values and who implement controls and protocols that hinder inappropriate behaviors and allow timely reactions.

Because when scandals erupt, there is no turning back, and the repair costs, economic and reputational, can be high.

A good reputation, such as credit or trust, takes years to build and can be lost in an instant.

4

Theories on Ethics

Philosophers have had diverse perspectives on ethics. As mentioned earlier in this book, in ancient Greece the sophists were interested in perfecting the technique of discourse, argumentation, and rhetoric and were criticized by classical philosophers because for the sophists the truth was always relative. The ultimate goal of the sophists was to win the lawsuit without considering whether they manipulated the facts or whether the arguments used were true or not.

Epicurus (341–270 BC) was an ancient Greek philosopher. For Epicurus, the purpose of philosophy was to attain a happy and tranquil life, characterized by *ataraxia* (peace and freedom from fear) and *aponia* (the absence of pain). Epicurus was a hedonist,[*] he taught that what is pleasurable is morally good and what is painful is morally evil.[†]

Also, when Plato explains the ideal project of the State, he justifies that the leaders can lie if they have a good reason and they do it to generate something good for the community. Plato, therefore, justifies that the rulers distort the information to people and legitimize the lie if it aims to achieve the good of the State. Plato, in *The Republic*, argues the leader of a society can tell noble lies to citizens when what is sought is their welfare. "If it is lawful for anyone to lie, it will only be those who govern the city, authorized to do so with respect to their enemies and fellow citizens."[‡]

Niccolo Machiavelli (1469–1527) was a philosopher and writer born in Florence, Italy. In 1513 he wrote his famous treatise on political doctrine entitled *The Prince*, published in 1531, after his death, in Rome. Although scholars say that Machiavelli never said it, he is credited with the phrase

---

[*] The Greek word *Hedon* means pleasure.

[†] en.wikipedia.org/wiki/Epicurus.

[‡] Miguel Catalan, "Genealogía de la Noble Mentira" (2004), journals.openedition.org/amnis/399 ("Genealogy of the Noble Lie").

"the end justifies the means." The phrase sums up his idea that when the ultimate goal is important, any means are valid to reach it. His ideas refer to those who act in their own interest regardless of whether the consequences of their actions affect third parties.

Machiavelli believed that the decision of whether or not to lie did not rest on moral principles and he argued that there was nothing morally wrong about telling a lie if it was a viable option and the most practical way to achieve one's goals.*

German philosopher Friedrich Nietzsche thought that many good things can be achieved only through deception. Statements do not have an inherent moral quality and are good or bad according to the circumstances.†

The French political scientist and historian Alexis de Tocqueville (1805–1859) in *Democracy in America* said, "I see others who … want to find what is useful without worrying about if it is right."‡

The Irish philosopher Francis Hutcheson (1694–1746), the Scottish philosopher David Hume (1711–1776), the English philosophers John Gay (1699–1745), William Paley (1743–1805), Jeremy Bentham (1748–1832), and John Stuart Mill (1806–1873), the American philosophers William James (1842–1910) and Richard Brandt (1910–1997), among others, considered that the most important aspect of human behavior was the outcome. That way of thought was known as *utilitarianism* or the *ethic of responsibility*.

Utilitarianism is a philosophical doctrine that places utility and the final result as the principle of morality, putting the result before the norms. Utilitarianism determines whether an action is moral by estimating the positive or negative consequences of it.

For utilitarianism nothing should be regarded as intrinsically right or wrong, but we should rather evaluate the usefulness of things from the perspective of maximizing happiness and pleasure and minimizing pain. The utilitarian theory of ethics restricts its considerations to weighing costs and benefits and focuses only on the final effect (the benefits of each decision must outweigh its costs), without focusing on the intrinsic values of actions, human rights, or the dignity of people. From the utilitarian

---

* Professor Clancy Martin, *Moral Decision Making*, The Great Courses, Guidebook (University of Missouri-Kansas City, 2014).

† Professor Clancy Martin, *Moral Decision Making*, The Great Courses, Guidebook (University of Missouri-Kansas City, 2014).

‡ Alexis de Tocqueville, *La Democracia en America (Democracy in America)*, 12th ed (Fondo de Cultura Economica, 2011), 38.

perspective, an ethical act is that which produces the greatest good for the greatest number. Utilitarianism might be considered a developed form of hedonism promoted by Epicurus (341–270 BC) who advocated a life where pleasure was the goal of life and it would be maximized.

David Hume (1711–1776) said, "Beauty is no quality in things themselves: It exists merely in the mind which contemplates them, and each mind perceives a different beauty."* Hume's theory of moral sentiments is the basis of Bentham's utilitarian ethics. Jeremy Bentham (1748–1832) formulated the utilitarian doctrine, embodied in his work *Introduction to the Principles of Morality and Legislation* (1789) where he advocated that human acts, rules, or institutions, should "be judged according to the utility they have … according to pleasure or suffering, they produce in people."†

From that simplification, Bentham proposed to formalize the analysis of political, social, and economic issues, based on measuring the usefulness of each action or decision. This would be the foundation of a new ethic, based on the enjoyment of life and not on sacrifice or suffering. For Bentham, that was the measure to know if an act was good or bad.

"Nature has placed mankind under the governance of two sovereign masters, pain and pleasure. It is for them alone to point out what we ought to do, as well as to determine what we shall do." Ethics becomes, for Bentham, a matter of calculation of consequences or consequentialism.‡

Bentham argued an individual should evaluate the likely consequences of his or her action and try to act in such a way as to maximize pleasure and minimize pain. In Bentham's formulation, an act is ethical if and only if it produces the greatest pleasure for the greatest number of people. Bentham's intellectual influence continued through his godson, John Stuart Mill.

Mill, one of the most influential philosophical writers in the English language, said that the ultimate test of a course of action is whether the action is useful. Mill said that to differentiate from animals that seek pleasure, the word *pleasure* should be replaced by happiness. In Mill's

---

* David Hume Quotes, www.goodreads.com.
† He was recognized as a child prodigy by his father when he found him at his desk reading several volumes of the History of England. At the age of three, he read treatises, played the violin at five, and studied Latin and French. By his express wish, his skeleton, fully clothed and with a wax head (the real one was mummified), is kept in a glass case at the University College of London en.wikipedia.org/wiki/Jeremy_Bentham.
‡ en.wikipedia.org/wiki/Jeremy_Bentham. Consequentialism is a theory of ethics that holds that the moral value of an action is determined by the consequences of that action.

formulation, utilitarianism advocates for the greatest happiness for the greatest number of people. However, the happiness of many may justify the unhappiness of a few.

For the utilitarian theory, lies were ethical if they were useful and this is justified when lies allow better results than telling the truth. For Mill, lies are justified when the good consequences outweigh the bad ones and what is pursued is a greater benefit. For example, it is ok to lie if is used to save a life. For Mill, stealing would be justified if it is to feed the hungry.

David Hume and John Stuart Mill considered that God gave people the freedom of choice to seek their happiness and well-being. Freedom of choice should prevail in any circumstance, and even should be acceptable and useful in suicide, to end a life of pain and torment.

For the German philosopher Max Weber (1864–1920) the ethics of responsibility is that the statesman agrees, even by means rejected by ethics, to achieve a *supra-individual* goal, which is the good of the community. Max Weber clarified that, however, the ethic of responsibility should have limits. So, for example, Weber quoted Niccolo Machiavelli and the sacrifice of the salvation of the soul for the benefit of the greatness of the city; but Weber also quoted Martin Luther when he confronted the Catholic Church before the Diet of Worms: "Here I stop, it is not right to act against conscience, I cannot do otherwise."*

The utilitarian ethics or ethic of responsibility that, as we saw, emphasizes that the action is correct if it produces good results and happiness for the majority (*good-based theory*), is opposed to the ethical theory that understands an action is correct if its motives and intentions are correct, without interesting consequences or results of the action (*right-based theory*). This ethics theory is the *ethics of conviction*, represented by the influential Prussian philosopher Immanuel Kant (1724–1804).

As Professor Osvaldo Agatiello says, "While the ethics of conviction is absolute and does not take into account the possible consequences of political action, the ethics of responsibility allows the individual to sacrifice their principles if this can avoid greater evils."†

For Kant people have the ability to reason and differentiate in each situation if something is good or bad, and therefore the distinction between good and evil is innate to men. In most cases, people will act

---

* Assembly of the Princes of the Holy Roman Empire held in Worms (Germany) in 1521, where the German professor Martin Luther was invited to retract, but he defended his position of Protestantism.
† Osvaldo Agatiello, "The Ethics of Responsibility," January 2016.

in accordance with the good, according to certain norms and values that they have internalized as members of society.

Kant's theory is an example of a deontological moral theory. This theory holds that morality is determined by moral principles above and beyond the consideration of consequences. Deontological moral theories are opposed to utilitarian theories; that is, that something is right because it happens to achieve a good or desirable outcome. According to the deontological theory, the rightness or wrongness of actions does not depend on their consequences but on whether they fulfill a duty or moral obligation. The value of the goodwill is independent of its consequences.

Kant attributes ethical value to the facts by their very essence. Thus, the facts are good or bad according to the intention of the person who performs them, regardless of the consequences.

For Kant, duty is more important than the result. This deontological ethics (in Greek *deon* means *duty* or *necessary*), or principle of universalism, argues that the right should always be done regardless of the consequences.

Deontologists do not want people to damage the process that leads to an outcome. For this theory, for example, you should never lie under any circumstances.

Kant considers moral law, not as a means to seek pleasure or avoid pain, but as a way of doing the right thing. This theory emphasizes the importance of respect for human rights and that people need to make responsible choices.

For Kant, man is rational and free to choose how he should act and Kant's theory is based on the principles on which his actions are based. If their intentions are aligned with universal moral principles, the action is moral.

The basis of Kantian ethics is "Act only in accordance with that maxim through which you can at the same time will that it become a universal law."* Kant advised we should act in such a way that the maxim of our actions would be instituted as a universal law of nature. Act in a way that the principle on which the action is based would guide all actions everywhere and at all times.

Kant understood that there was a supreme principle of morality, and he referred to it as "Categorical Imperative" (an absolute and unconditional obligation). An act is morally justifiable if that act can be universalized

---

* en.wikipedia.org/wiki/Categorical_imperative. See also, "Kantian Ethics" www.csus.edu and www.e-torredebabel.com/. historia de la filosofia.

and applied to all human beings in all places at all times. Any maxim or principle by which an individual intends to act must be subject to the test of universalization.

Kant argued certain moral precepts are unconditionally and objectively a necessary right, without considering desires, motives, purpose, results, or the *utility* those actions may produce. For Kant, moral maxims are universal and they guide our actions. Moral precepts are not dependent on the contingent facts of the world and they are applicable to all imaginable situations. The moral maxims have their own authority and are based on the universal principles of justice, honesty, and respect. For an act to be moral it must be based on those universal principles or maxims.

Kant believed that certain types of actions like murder, theft, or lying were absolutely prohibited always, even in cases where those actions would be justified.

For Kant, if my action does not respect human beings, then I must not perform the action. Men need to do the right things all the time; men are *moral* beings.

Kant argued that suicide is a moral wrong. If a person destroys himself in order to escape from painful circumstances, he or she uses his or her person merely as a means. For Kant, an individual is never a means to an end, but always an end unto himself.*

For Kant, each person is a moral authority, so everyone should be treated with respect.†

Saint Augustine (354–430), born in Tagaste, present-day Algeria, had a similar vision. In the City of God, Saint Augustine attacks the Roman tradition, including myths such as that of Lucretia Lucretia, a lady who, after being raped by the son of the last king of Rome, committed suicide by stabbing herself with a dagger. For the Romans, Lucretia was the worthiest model of moral integrity. Not for Saint Augustine, who considers that her death added crime to another crime, because "whoever kills himself, kills a man and, therefore, contravenes the divine law."‡

The Algerian philosopher Albert Camus (1913–1960) wrote in 1942 an essay entitled "The Myth of Sisyphus," where he discusses the question of

---

* "Means to an End," Wikipedia.
† Kant was a methodical man. He got up, ate, and went to bed every day at the same time. And just as punctual was his afternoon walk, at five in the afternoon, not a minute more or a minute less. So much so that it was said that their walks served the neighbors to put their clocks on time. www.educa.madrid.org.
‡ es.wikipedia.org/wiki/Agustín_de_Hipona.

suicide and the value of life. Sisyphus in Greek mythology made the gods angry for his cunning nature and as punishment he was condemned to lose his sight and to perpetually push a large mountain stone up to the top. Once at the top, the stone rolled down to the valley and there Sisyphus had to pick it up again and push it back to the top indefinitely.

Sisyphus is aware of the futility of his life. The Myth of Sisyphus is a metaphor that describes an overwhelmed man and whether life should be lived or if the absurdity of life needs suicide. For Camus, suicide must always be rejected; the absurd requires constant confrontation and rebellion. Camus sees Sisyphus as someone who, despite the anguish, absurdities, and punishments, wants to live and continues to push.*

In 1933, nine million Jews lived in the countries of Europe that would be occupied by Germany during World War II. In 1945, six million, or two out of every three European Jews, had been killed.

The film *Schindler's List* tells the story of Oskar Schindler (1908–1974), an entrepreneur who managed to save the lives of more than 1,200 Polish Jews during the Holocaust.† When the Nazi army invaded Poland, Schindler reached an agreement with the director of a labor camp to use Jewish labor from Krakow. Over the months, Mr. Schindler understands the reality experienced by Jews in the concentration camp and begins to use his fortune to bribe the Nazis and "buy Jews" to save them from the death camps. Schindler tries to solve his problem of conscience by hiring Jews in his utensils factory to save them from death.

Bribing is illegal, but what made it valid for Schindler to avoid the murders?

The actions of Schindler would be justified under the ethics of responsibility of Anglo-Saxon thinkers as they agreed to use non-ethical methods to achieve a higher goal. By contrast, the "ethics of conviction" would refuse these actions because, according to Kant, what should prevail is always ethical conduct in all situations, not the outcome.

During World War II, typhus was a disease so feared by the Germans that they declared "quarantine" on the area where a suspicious outbreak occurred, and they immediately suspended the deportation and the recruitment of infected persons to the Polish Jewish labor and extermination camps.

---

* es.wikipedia.org/wiki/El_mito_de_Sísifo ("The myth of Sisyphus").
† Directed by Steven Spielberg in 1993, it won seven Oscars, including the Academy Award for Best Picture.

In 1940 the Polish physician Eugeniusz Lazowski (1913–2006) practiced medicine in the village of Rozwadow, Poland, and was responsible for reporting outbreaks. In 1941 Lazowski found the first case of typhus in the area. He took a blood sample and sent it to a laboratory controlled by the Germans. With the help of his colleague, Dr. Stanisław Matulewicz, he found that if a patient were injected blood with typhus, although he or she would test positive, the patient would not develop symptoms of the disease. Then it occurred to Lazowski to start injecting samples of blood with typhus to patients with influenza so that the blood test would be positive and thus they would avoid Nazi recruitment.

The first time Lazowski and Matulewicz used the typhus injection, they sent the blood sample to the Nazi lab, and two days later they received a telegram saying "Danger, Typhus! Isolate the patient. It is impossible to step on German soil." From this result, the doctors designed a plan to pseudo-infect a large number of Poles with influenza and typhus-like symptoms, telling the patient that the injection was to increase their resistance. Soon Lazowski took the blood sample and sent it to the laboratory. In this way, many patients achieved a false positive influenza result without anyone knowing. At one point the Germans sent medical inspectors to the area to verify the high number of cases of illness and the few deaths, but they did not discover the deception.

At the end of the war, Lazowski settled in Chicago, in 1958, as a professor of medicine at the University of Illinois, and Matulewicz went to Zaire. In 1977 Lazowski would tell this story in a microbiology journal.[*]

The actions of Drs. Lazowski and Matulewicz that prevented the extermination of Polish Jews would also be justified by the ethics of responsibility, because, like Schindler, they used ethical methods to achieve a higher objective.[†]

By learning about these theories of ethics and morality, we can be better prepared to analyze and recognize and understand moral problems and ethical challenges. The following graphic is divided into two main theories

---

[*] Gregorio Doval, *Fraudes, Engaños y Tinos de la Historia* (Nowtilus Saber, 2011), 30–2. ("Frauds, Deceptions, and Tinos of History.")

[†] Another example to prevent the extermination of Jews was the making of the movie *La Porta del Cielo* ("The Gates of Heaven"), an Italian film directed by Vittorio de Sica. Filming began in 1943, during the German occupation of Rome. Vittorio de Sica contracted 300 extras; all Jews persecuted by the Nazi regime. To avoid the deportation and death of the Jews, Sicca prolonged the filming while waiting for the arrival of the allies to Rome, which occurred on June 5, 1944. en.wikipedia.org/wiki/ the_Gates_Of_Heaven.

about ethics, with key representatives outlined for each (based on what they have written, said, or done).

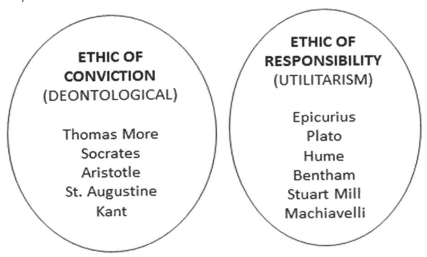

Before making a decision, it is convenient to take into account these theories about ethics and ask yourself some questions:

Does the action to be taken respect universal values?
What would be the consequences of the action if it were executed?
Who benefits and who is harmed by the decision?
What decision would an ideal, ethically perfect person make?
What does the voice of your conscience say?

5

Ethical Debates

The Spanish philosopher Fernando Savater in one of his books tells a story of Swiss philosopher Jean Jacques Rousseau (1712–1778) that is about an ethical decision, a matter of conscience, which reads:

> Rousseau invites us to imagine that there is a Mandarin over ninety years old, cruel and wicked to intolerable extremes in China.
>
> Suddenly you get a button and if you press it, the Mandarin will die and, also, you will win the lottery. The next day you will be rich and the Mandarin will be dead. No one can accuse you of anything. You don't have any relation to either China or the Mandarin.
>
> You do not know him; you've never seen him and only you know that there is a link between a lottery prize and the death of an old despot somewhere in remote China. Rousseau's question is: What will you do? Would you press that button?*

The Austrian neurologist Sigmund Freud (1856–1939) also referred to the term "kill the Mandarin," attributed to Rousseau.† Freud said, "What would you do if you could, without being noticed, invisibly, kill a Mandarin in China with just thinking about it and this would bring you great advantages?"

Imagine that in order to eliminate poverty and suffering in much of the world, all you have to do is push a button. When you prepare to press the button, you are informed that if you do, even if the majority of the population of the world ceases to be poor, a girl will suffer terrible tortures for the rest of her life. If you were a supporter of the ethic of utilitarian

---

* Fernando Savater, *Ethics of Urgency* (Ariel, 2012), 28.
† The term could also be from the French writer Francois-Rene, Vicomte de Chateaubriand (1768–1848).

responsibility, you would push the button because it would be best for the majority. On the other hand, if you were to defend the ethics of Kant's convictions, you would never press the button because its consequences would be immoral.

To analyze these two schools of thought, the American philosopher Robert Nozick of Harvard University (1938–2002) discusses an ethical dilemma:

> During a war, I capture an enemy. I know that he knows where a nuclear bomb that will explode in my city is located, but I can only get that information if I torture him. What should I do?

Following Kant's ethics of conviction, the enemy should not be tortured, although failure to do so would cause the death of thousands of people. But according to the ethic of responsibility of Anglo-Saxon philosophers, you should ask and analyze what is more important, saving the lives of thousands of people or not torturing an enemy of war.* For the utilitarians who preach the ethics of responsibility, the terrorist must be tortured because by torturing him, information can be obtained to save thousands of lives.

The English philosopher Jeremy Bentham (1748–1832) has been regarded as the "father" of the "ticking time bomb" argument. Bentham wrote in his 1804 essay "Means of Extraction for Extraordinary Occasions":

> For the purpose of rescuing from torture a hundred innocents, should any scruple be made of applying ... torture, to extract the information from the mouth of one criminal?†

Those in favor of torture justify its use if they have a terrorist in custody who possesses critical knowledge, such as the location of a time bomb or a weapon of mass destruction that will soon explode and cause great loss of many lives.

Opponents to the argument rely on legal, philosophical/moral, and empirical grounds to reaffirm the absolute prohibition of torture because there is uncertainty about its effectiveness.

---

* This ethical dilemma and analysis are posed by Professor and Doctor of Law Mariano Grondona in his book *Corruption* (Planeta, 1993), 82, 83. A similar ethical dilemma can be seen in en.wikipedia.org/wiki/Ticking_time_bomb_scenario.

† en.wikipedia.org/wiki/Ticking_time_bomb_scenario.

Richard Posner, judge of the United States Court of Appeals for the Seventh Circuit, wrote in *The New Republic,* "If torture is the only means of obtaining the information necessary to prevent the detonation of a nuclear bomb in Times Square, torture should be used – and will be used – to obtain the information."[*]

Some human rights organizations, professional and academic experts, and military leaders have absolutely rejected the idea that torture is ever legal or acceptable. They reject the proposition that certain acts of torture are justifiable.

The United Nations Convention against Torture and Other Cruel, Inhuman or Degrading Treatment or Punishment,1984, explicitly states in Article 2.2 that:

> No exceptional circumstances whatsoever, whether a state of war or a threat of war, internal political instability or any other public emergency, may be invoked as a justification of torture.[†]

Psychologist and philosopher Lawrence Kohlberg (1927–1987), professor at the University of Chicago, Yale, and Harvard,[‡] used moral dilemmas to analyze the reasoning of his students.[§] Kohlberg supported the idea of promoting an open debate about issues that generate conflict to stimulate the development of ethical reasoning. To that end, Kohlberg used the Heinz dilemma:

A woman has a special type of cancer and will die soon but there is a medicine that doctors think can save her; it is a remedy a pharmacist in the same city just discovered.

The pharmacist is charging ten times what it cost him to produce it: It costs US$1000 to produce it and he is charging US$10,000 for the drug.

The husband of the sick lady, Mr. Heinz, appeals to everyone who knows to borrow money, but can only collect US$2,500. Then he tells the pharmacist that his wife is dying and asks him to sell the drug cheaper or let him pay later.

The pharmacist says: "No, I discovered it and I have to make money with it."

---

[*] en.wikipedia.org/wiki/Ticking_time_bomb_scenario.

[†] www.ohchr.org/en/professionalinterest/pages/cat.aspx.

[‡] Kohlberg founded the Center for Development and Moral Education at Harvard and was noted for his theory of the stages of moral development.

[§] For his research, he used some of the contributions of the Swiss psychologist Jean Piaget (1896–1980) to the study of morality in Psychology.

Heinz is desperate and thinks about stealing the drug for his wife.

What should Heinz and the pharmacist do?

By 2005, Merck, one of the largest pharmaceutical companies in the world, was the manufacturer of Mustargen and Cosmegen, two drugs that were used by approximately 5,000 cancer patients and generated annual sales of about US$1 million. In August of that year, Merck sold off the two cancer drugs to Ovation, a smaller pharmaceutical firm. Merck agreed to continue manufacturing those drugs if requested by Ovation. After the deal was completed, Ovation raised the prices of both products more than 100%.*

A few years ago the patent office of the government of India confirmed the issuance of compulsory licenses that allow the generic manufacture of a drug against kidney and liver cancer, rejecting the arguments of Bayer that is the owner of the product patent. The government of India made the decision to allow generic production of the patented drug after Bayer stipulated a price for the product of about US$5,500 per month, which was unattainable for Indian patients. With the compulsory license granted by the patent office, the price was reduced by more than 95%, so the cost of the treatment was reduced to US$175 per month. Bayer receives a royalty of 6% of sales from the Indian manufacturer and the generic can only be sold in India. Bayer executive Marjin Dekkers has pointed out, "It's essentially a robbery."†

India is not the first country that decides to break patents on medicines. Brazil in 2007 and Thailand in 2006 decreed compulsory licenses for drugs with the argument that they needed to manufacture them at low prices to combat the AIDS epidemic.‡

Is it ethical to violate the right to property and to produce generic medicines for patents when their prices turn out to be too high for thousands of sick people in certain countries?

Some conflicts and moral dilemmas generate a strong debate in society. As values are subjective and based on a personal point of view, for certain sectors of society certain actions can be morally and legally correct and for another sector those same actions are not.

---

* Max H. Bazerman and Ann E. Tenbrunsel, "Ethical Breakdowns," April 2011, www. Hbr.org.
† "India Garantiza el Acceso de Medicamentos Frente a una Patente de Bayer," March 4, 2013, www. msf.com; Diario *El Mundo*, January 24, 2014, www.elmundo.es. ("India Guarantees Access to Medicines against a Bayer Patent").
‡ "La Farmacia de los Pobres Desafía al Gigante Bayer," Ana Gabriela Rojas, March 12, 2012, www. elpais.com ("The Pharmacy of the Poor Challenges the Giant Bayer").

Let's analyze slavery. An international treaty of 1926 declared slavery – that is, one person owns the slave – illegal. However, even today slavery still exists and it is estimated that there could be some 27 million slave people in the world. For example, one of the countries that maintain slavery is Mauritania, in Africa. Around 4% of the population of Mauritania – 150,000 people – are slaves. It is also estimated that there are between 90,000 and 300,000 slaves in Sudan, in Africa. In 1989, a woman or child of the Dinka tribe in Southern Sudan "cost" US$90. Months later the "price" of individuals fell to US$15 due to excess supply. Once enslaved, these people are forced to change religion and must learn another language. Since 1995, Christian Solidarity International Organization* buys slaves to free them by paying US$50 each.

Lincoln said, "If slavery is not unjust, then nothing is unjust."[†]

According to the Greek historian Herodotus (484–425 BC), what is right and what is wrong is always relative and related to the circumstances existing in a place and a particular moment in history.

For Kant slavery could never be justified because it is something morally wrong, everywhere and under any circumstances.

A majority of people would declare slavery to be morally wrong today; however, the institution of slavery was allowed in the past. In ancient Greece the philosophers owned slaves, and in America Thomas Jefferson and George Washington also owned slaves.

Although slavery may be allowed by some countries today, is slavery ethical? Was slavery ethical in the past?

Pornography and prostitution are also issues of debate.[‡] For some people, both pornography and prostitution are morally unacceptable but not for others.

In the United States, each state legislates the legality or not of pornography, but child pornography is never allowed. In China, pornography is banned and illegal.[§] Pornography provokes a strong rejection in certain cultures and is considered immoral because it denigrates the person.

---

* Christian Solidarity International (CSI) was founded in 1977 in Switzerland as a Christian human rights organization that advocates for and helps victims of religious persecution, enslavement, victimized children, and victims of natural disasters. www.csi-usa.org.

[†] en.wikiquote.org/wiki/Abraham Lincoln; Joshua Cohen, *The Arc of Moral Universe* (Harvard University Press, 2010),3.

[‡] Pornography is the filming or photography of sexual relations. Prostitution is the occupation of people who have sex in exchange for money.

[§] "Pornography," Wikipedia.

In most countries, prostitution is illegal, as is pimping which consists of obtaining economic benefits from prostitution at the expense of another person. However, some countries such as the Netherlands or Germany regard prostitution as a legitimate and regulated activity. In 1949, the United Nations General Assembly adopted the Convention for the Suppression of the Traffic in Persons and of the Exploitation of the Prostitution of Others, stating that prostitution and the accompanying evil of the traffic in persons for the purpose of prostitution are incompatible with the dignity and worth of the human person and endanger the welfare of the individual, the family, and the community.*

Take another example of ethical debate, the case of marriage between people of the same sex.

Is it morally good or bad? Should it be approved by law?

The debate over the legality of same-sex marriage is one of the most agitated in the Western world. There are those who believe that marriage is an essentially heterosexual institution that reflects the union between a man and a woman. They argue that the word *marriage* comes from the Latin "matrem" (mother) and "monium" (quality of) and therefore two people of the same sex could never constitute a marriage. Alfonso X of Castile, called the Wise (1252–1284) in *The Seven Parties*, left in writing the etymological definition of marriage,

> Matris and Munium are two words from the Latin of what I call marriage, which means a mother's job. And the reason why marriage is called marriage and not patrimony is this: because the mother suffers more work with the children than the father, because as the father begets them, the mother suffers great embargo with them while bringing them in the belly, and suffers very great pains when it has to give birth and after they are born, it takes great work in raising them herself, and in addition to this, because the children, while they are small, need the help of the mother than the father. And because all these above-mentioned reasons fall to the mother to do and not to the father, for that reason it is called marriage and not patrimony.†

On the other hand, those in favor of the legality of homosexual marriage argue that prohibiting the use of the word *marriage* to the union between

---

* As of June 4, 2017, the agreement has been ratified by 82 countries. "Prostitution," Wikipedia.
† "Marriage," Etymologies of Chile.net/marriage. The dictionary of the Royal Spanish Academy defines marriage as "The union of man and woman agreed by certain rites or legal formalities, to establish and maintain a community of life and interests." www.dle.rae.es.

two people of the same sex would be discriminatory. Twenty-five countries currently allow marriage between same-sex couples.* Therefore, a marriage between persons of the same sex will be considered something morally correct or incorrect depending on the values and the perception with which each individual evaluates the situation.

Another controversial issue is the voluntary interruption of pregnancy or abortion – the ending of fetal life through elective abortions.

Etymologically, abortion comes from the Latin *abortus*, formed by the prefix ab (deprivation) and ortus (birth), that is, "deprivation of birth."

Is abortion morally good or bad? Is abortion a homicidal act? Should it be approved by law?

In ancient Greece, the Hippocratic Oath for doctors said that women would never have an abortion.† In the first century BC the Roman general Lucius Cornelius Sulla Felix (138–78 BC) prohibited the abortive practices and condemned them with severe penalties.‡

Roe v. Wade case is the name of the judicial case of 1973, by which the United States Supreme Court decriminalized abortion in that country by a divided decision of 7 against 2.§

In 1970, in the United States, a lawsuit was filed in Texas where two newly graduated lawyers from the Law School of the University of Texas, representing Norma L. McCorvey (1947–2017) (known by her pseudonym "Jane Roe"), claimed for their right to abortion induced by rape. At that time, in Texas, only rape was accepted as an exception to allow a legal abortion.

Henry Wade, the district attorney of the County of Dallas, Texas, represented the State of Texas and opposed abortion.

The District Court of the County of Dallas, Texas, ruled in favor of Jane Roe without establishing changes or restrictions in the legislation on induced abortion

In 1970, a lawsuit was filed in Texas where lawyers represented Mrs. Norma L. McCorvey ("Jane Roe") claiming the right to abortion induced by rape. The District Court ruled in favor of Jane Roe, but without establishing changes in the legislation on induced abortion. "Jane Roe"

---

* Among them, Germany, Argentina, Australia, Canada, Colombia, Spain, the United States, the United Kingdom, South Africa, the Netherlands, Sweden, and Uruguay.
† Almu del Campo, "La Medicina, el Aborto e Hipócrates," September 24, 2014, www.arguments.es/cultura de la vida. ("Medicine, Abortion and Hippocrates").
‡ "El Aborto en Roma," universalis.mforos.com ("Abortion in Rome").
§ es.wikipedia.org/wiki/Caso_Roe_contra_Wade ("Roe vs. Wade").

gave birth to her daughter – whom she gave for adoption – while the case was being adjudicated.

The case was repeatedly appealed to the Supreme Court of Justice of the United States, which finally, in its resolution of January 22, 1973, established that women have the right to free choice – understood as "right to privacy or privacy" – to carry or not carry a pregnancy to term.

The resolution of the case *Roe v. Wade** is considered historic because it annulled the laws that penalized abortion in the different states and prevented legislation against it since it could be considered as a violation of the constitutional right to privacy, protected by the Fourteenth Amendment of the Constitution of the United States. The judges ruled that women are free to make reproductive decisions without state interference. The decision forced the modification of all federal and state laws that proscribed or restricted abortion and that were contrary to the new decision.[†]

Hugh Hefner, the founder of *Playboy*, acknowledged his funding for the trial. He said, "Playboy was probably more involved in Roe vs. Wade than any other company."[‡]

In 1995, the plaintiff in the case, Norma McCorvey,[§] changed her position on abortion and said her statement was not true and was exploited by her lawyers, who sought to change the legislation that prohibited abortion in the State of Texas.

She quit her job at an abortion clinic and appeared in 2005 before the Supreme Court to review the 1973 ruling, arguing that she had not been raped and that abortion caused great harm to women and destroys life. Her request was denied.[¶]

Sarah Weddington, one of the attorneys who litigated the *Roe v. Wade* case in the Supreme Court,[**] explained in a speech at the Institute of Educational Ethics, in Oklahoma, why she used the false charges of rape,

---

* The name of the district attorney of the County of Dallas was Henry Wade who represented the State of Texas and opposed abortion.

[†] "Roe vs. Wade," Wikipedia. The precedent, "Griswold v. Connecticut" of 1965 established that a Connecticut law criminalizing the use of contraceptives violated the right to marital privacy.

[‡] es.wikipedia.org/wiki/Norma_McCorvey.

[§] Her father abandoned her when she was a girl and her mother was an alcoholic. Within ten years of age, she committed a crime and was institutionalized. Upon returning home, she was raped by her mother's cousin. At 16 she married her boyfriend and after having a daughter she got divorced. Two years later she had a second daughter whom she gave up for adoption. In 1969, she became pregnant for the third time and it was what caused the *Roe v. Wade* case. Her third daughter was also given up for adoption. McCorvey died from a heart attack in 2017.

[¶] Matias Bauso, "The Story of Jane Roe, the Woman Who Legalized Abortion in the United States and Became a Pro-Life Icon," August 8, 2018, www.infobae.com.

[**] The other lawyer was Linda Coffee.

up to the Supreme Court: "My conduct may not have been entirely ethical. For what I thought were good reasons."*

The *Doe v. Bolton* case is a judgment of the United States Supreme Court that nullified the abortion law of the state of Georgia. The Court's decision was made public on January 22, 1973, the same day as the decision on the famous *Roe v. Wade* case.

The plaintiff, a pregnant woman who adopted the pseudonym "Mary Doe" to protect her identity, sued Georgia's Attorney General, Arthur K. Bolton, as responsible for enforcing the law.

The anonymous plaintiff was later identified as Sandra Cano, a 22-year-old woman, mother of three children, and nine weeks pregnant at the time of the lawsuit.

The ruling was passed with the same 7-2 majority (with the opposing votes of Justices Byron White and William Rehnquist) that repealed the Texas abortion law in the *Roe v. Wade* case.

Sandra Cano explained that she is pro-life and that her lawyer, Margie Pitts Hames, tricked her into filing the lawsuit. In 2003, Sandra Cano filed a petition to reopen the case. The District Court denied the petition, and Cano appealed. When the Court of Appeal also rejected the motion, Cano requested that the case be reviewed by the Supreme Court, which refused to take into consideration Sandra Cano's attempt to revoke the decision.†

Jointly, Roe and Doe declared abortion as a constitutional right of the United States, which resulted in the repeal of most anti-abortion laws passed in other states.

Regardless of the legality of abortion, the problem generates a great ethical dilemma. Since the Supreme Court decision in 1973, there have been more than 40 million legal abortions performed in the United States. The practice has divided the nation with a moral debate associated with the rights that fetuses have.

For those who consider the embryo as a human being, abortion is a crime. For those who consider that the embryo is not a person, the woman has the choice to decide what to do with her body.‡ They argue that since the woman carries the embryo, she can get rid of it.

Is it correct to say that a minute before birth there is no human being, but a minute later there is?

---

* es.wikipedia.org/wiki/Norma_McCorvey.

† es.wikipedia.org/wiki/Caso_Doe_contra_Bolton.

‡ Luis Rojas Marcos, "The Human Dilemma of Abortion," *El Pais*, May 26, 1991, www.elpais. com.See also "Scientific Arguments against Abortion," www.outono.net July 19, 2016.

Bernard Nathanson (1926–2011) was an American obstetrician and gynecologist who came to practice or supervise 75,000 abortions in different clinics, private homes, and hospital centers in the United States. In one of those abortions, he took the life of his own son or daughter – a child conceived with a girlfriend.*

He was the director of the Center for Reproductive and Sexual Health, the largest center for abortion practices in the world. Nathanson founded an organization to reject the laws against abortion and had influence in society and in the aforementioned resolution *Roe v. Wade* that recognized the right to induced abortion.

However, with the development of technology in the mid-1970s, Nathanson had the opportunity to observe an abortion in real time and this led him to reconsider all his abortionist actions.

In 1984 he directed and narrated the movie *The Silent Scream* and then developed a second documentary called *The Eclipse of Reason*. In 1996, he published a book called *The Hand of God*, which explains the transition from being an abortion activist to a champion of the campaign against abortion. Nathanson has pointed out that abortion is:

> The most atrocious holocaust in the history of the United States…the killing of the fetus while fighting for its life, of unborn children who are human beings and who have as much right as an adult to legal protection from conception…interrupt pregnancy only it can be seen as the elimination of a member of our species.†

In his presentations against abortion, Nathanson shows how a baby in the maternal uterus tries to avoid being reached by the instruments of the abortionist doctor.

Abby Johnson was one of the directors of the Planned Parenthood clinic in Bryan, Texas, and worked there for eight years. In September 2009, she was asked to assist in an ultrasound-guided abortion at 13 weeks gestation, which she finds to be disturbing.

According to Johnson, they had to meet a certain number of abortions (abortion quota) per month because 50% of Planned Parenthood's income, she pointed out, comes from abortions. She said,

---

* Robert George, "Bernard Nathanson: A Life Transformed by Truth," February 27, 2015. www.thepublicdisclosure.com.
† Hector D'Amico, "The Story of Bernard Nathanson, the Doctor of the 75,000 Abortions That Became a Pro-Life Leader." *La Nacion*, May 5, 2014. Wikipedia, "Nathanson." William Grimes, "B.N. Nathanson, 84, Dies; Changed Sides on Abortion," February 21, 2001, www.nytimes.com.

> At the affiliate, I worked at, we sold the whole body for US$200 per fetus.... [W]e had the capacity to perform about 75 abortions every day, 6 days a week.... [W]hen you're working inside an industry like that, you become very dark, and you stop seeing just the heinous acts that you're participating in.*

After that personal experience in September 2009 that touched her conscience, she resigned her job and became a pro-life activist.† The movie *Unplanned* is based on the book of the same name written by Johnson.‡

Nicolás Jouvre de la Barreda, Ph.D. in Biological Sciences from the Complutense University of Madrid and professor of Genetics at the University of Alcalá, said, "When a fetus is crushed to cause an abortion, what is crushed is the life of a human being."§

Luis F. Leujone, professor of genetics at *La Sorbonne*, has written that

> Accept the fact that with fertilization begins the life of a new human being is no longer subject to discussion. The human condition of a new being from its conception until the end of its days is not a metaphysical affirmation, it is simple experimental evidence.¶

In some countries such as Canada, the United States, Uruguay, India, and most of the countries of Europe, abortion is legalized at the request of women during a certain gestation period. On the contrary, in most countries in Latin America, Africa, the Middle East, Oceania, and Asia, abortion is illegal and penalized. The most populous countries in the world, China and India, encourage adoption instead of abortion.**

Abortion generates hundreds of millions of dollars a year. The number of induced abortions around the world annually is about 46 million.††

---

* Richard Enos, "Former Clinic Manager Reveals Planned Parenthood's Business Model: Abortion Quotas & Selling Fetuses," March 27, 2019, www.collective-evolution.com.
† Planned Parenthood operates over 600 clinics in the United States and is present in 12 countries. It is the largest single provider of abortions in the United States. In the 2014–2015 annual report, the organization stated that it performed 324,000 abortions. en.wikipedia.org/wiki/Planned_Parenthood.
‡ *Unplanned*, directed by Chuck Konzelman y Cary Solomon (2019). The book was published by Tyndale House Publishers (2011).
§ February 18, 2010, www.religionenlibertad.com/noticias/7191/cuando-se-tritura-un-feto-para-provocar-un-aborto-lo-que.html ("when a fetus is crushed to cause an abortion").
¶ "¿El Aborto, es aborto?" Alberto Benegas Lynch (h). www.libertadyprogresonline.org/2016/09/14/el-aborto-es-aborto/ 10 de julio de 2019. (¿"Is Abortion, abortion?").
** In China, for example, 570,000 newborns were abandoned in 2012. "Bernard Nathanson," Wikipedia.
†† "Other legislations,"www.web.archive.org/ abortions and see "Legislation on the practice of abortion in the world," www.es.wikipedia.org.

In May of 2019, a law passed in the state of Alabama defies the ruling of the Roe case. The law prohibits the interruption of pregnancy and criminalizes with up to 99 years in prison the doctor who practices it.[*] Kay Ivey, Governor of Alabama, in enacting the law, said:

> Today, I signed into law the Alabama Human Life Protection Act. To the bill's many supporters, this legislation stands as a powerful testament to Alabamians' deeply held belief that every life is precious & that every life is a sacred gift from God.[†]

Mother Teresa of Calcutta (1910–1997) pointed out that "The greatest threat that peace suffers today is abortion because abortion is to make war on the child, the innocent who dies at the hands of his own mother."[‡]

What should prevail, the right to privacy and freedom of choice of women or the respect for human life and the right to be born? Is the mother the owner of her son's body? Is it correct to impose the death penalty on a human being who is harmless and innocent and who has not killed anyone?[§]

Ronald Reagan (1911–2004) said, "I have noticed that everyone who is for abortion has already been born."[¶]

Euthanasia comes from the Greek "eu" (good) "Thanatos" (death). It means "Good Death." Euthanasia is an act or omission that aims to intentionally cause the death of a person suffering from an incurable disease to prevent further suffering.

Is euthanasia morally good or bad? Should it be approved by the laws?

Eluana Englaro (1970–2009) was an Italian woman who was in a vegetative state due to a traffic accident from January 18, 1992, to the date of her death in 2009. Given the irreversible situation of the daughter, her father supported the possibility of suspending the food supply and letting her die. On November 13, 2008, the Supreme Court of Italy granted

---

[*] "Ultima Ofensiva en EEUU Contra el Aborto: Alabama se acerca a la Prohibicion Total," elpais.com/sociedad.

[†] Caroline Kelly, "Alabama governor signs nation's most restrictive anti-abortion bill into law," May 15, 2019, www.cnn.com/2019/05/15/politics/alabama-governor-signs-bill/index.html @ GovernorKayIvey.

[‡] "Madre Teresa: el aborto amenaza la paz," es.catholic.net/op/articulos/63186/cat/286/madre-teresa-el-aborto-amenaza-la-paz-.html#modal ("Mother Teresa: abortion threatens peace").

[§] Jorge Arturo Quarracino, "Despenalización del aborto. Con una carta demuelen los argumentos de Lanata." Marzo 10, 2018 ("Decriminalization of abortion. With a letter demolish the arguments of Lanata").

[¶] Ronald Reagan Quotes, www.goodreads.com.

Eluana's father the right to disconnect her from the machines that allowed her to remain alive. The decision was met with immediate opposition from the Italian government and the Catholic Church. Cardinal Ennio Antonelli, president of the Pontifical Council for the Family, pointed out that,

> Eluana is in a vegetative state, but it is not a vegetable. It is a person who is sleeping. The person, even in such a state, maintains all his dignity. The person is valuable in itself, not because of what it consumes or produces, or because of the pleasure or satisfaction, it may give others.[*]

Eluana passed away on February 9, 2009.

Another well-known case was one of Dax Cowart. In 1973 when he was 25 years old he was severely burned. Mr. Cowart's burn injuries included both hands, eyes, and ears, and two-thirds of his skin area. Cowart said, "I was burned so severely and in so much pain that I did not want to live." Mr. Coward was in the hospital for 14 months and he begged his doctors to end treatment and allow him to die. Although blind, hearing impaired, and without functioning hands, Mr. Cowart studied and earned a law degree from Texas Tech University in 1986 and got married. Mr. Cowart's life and his reflections on what has happened to him continue to challenge medicine's understanding of itself as a moral practice.[†]

Wang Shubao, from China, miraculously woke up after 12 years in coma caused by a car accident in 2006. During the 12 years his mother, Wei Mingying, never left him.[‡]

The World Medical Association considers euthanasia an act contrary to ethics. In a "Declaration on Euthanasia" made at the 38th World Medical Assembly in Madrid, Spain, in October 1987, the Assembly noted that "Euthanasia, that is, the deliberate act of putting an end to a patient's life, even at his own will or at the request of his relatives, is contrary to ethics."[§]

Euthanasia is illegal in most countries of the world. The Netherlands was the first country in the world to legalize euthanasia in 2001. In that

---

[*] "Vatican cardinal pleads for life of Italian Terri Schiavo," *Catholic News Agency*, February 2009, www.catholicnewsagency.com/news/ Vatican.

[†] en.wikipedia.org/wiki/Dax_Cowart. A documentary of his plight titled *Please Let Me Die* was filmed in 1974, with a follow-up documentary titled *Dax's Case* filmed in 1984.

[‡] "Un Hombre Despertó después de 12 años de estar en coma bajo el cuidado de su madre," 20 de noviembre de 2018, www.lanacion.com.ar. (A man woke up after 12 years of being in a coma under the care of his mother," November 20, 2018, www.lanacion.com.ar).

[§] "Euthanasia," Wikipedia.

country, euthanasia can be granted from 12 years of age, provided that the person has expressed the desire to stop living and that a doctor considers that the suffering is unbearable. In 2017 more than 6,500 people chose euthanasia to end their lives in the Netherlands.*

Today it is allowed in other European countries such as Belgium, Luxembourg, and Switzerland. In Colombia and Canada, it is also legal. In 1994, Oregon was the first state in the United States to allow assisted suicide for incurable patients.†

Is euthanasia morally good or bad? Should the right of family members prevail to decide to kill a sick person so the sick patient does not suffer or should the right to life for the sick person prevail?

The death penalty or capital punishment consists of causing the death of a convicted person as punishment for the commission of a crime. A death penalty is a form of revenge designed to reestablish equality. The exact retribution to a person that has been victimized, like the *lex talionis*: "Eye for an eye, tooth for a tooth."‡ The death penalty seeks to balance justice because if the murderer is not killed, the murderer's life would be valued more than the life of the murdered person.

Is the death penalty passed by law morally good or bad?

Those in favor of the death penalty believe it is a form of fair punishment for the crime committed and a way of warning people about the consequences of certain serious criminal acts. According to its supporters, the death penalty reduces crime and prevents the repetition of the improper act by the same individual.

Isaac Ehrlich is an American economist that has done research in the economics of crime and the death penalty. He studied execution and murder rates between 1933 and 1969 and concluded that "an additional execution per year ... may have resulted in 7 or 8 fewer murders." Ehrlich's study was criticized because crime went up between 1960 and 1969 in states that had the death penalty in place and in states that did not.§

* "Holanda: Le Conceden la Eutanasia a una Adolescente Victima de Violencia Sexual," 4 de junio de 2019, www.lanacion.com.ar ("The Netherlands: Euthanasia Awarded to a Teen Victim of Sexual Violence"), June 4, 2019.

† "Only five countries of the world and some states of the United States allow euthanasia," May 16, 2016, www.information.com/world. Other states that also allow it are Washington, Montana, and Vermont.

‡ Professor Clancy Martin, *Moral Decision Making*, The Great Courses, Guidebook (University of Missouri-Kansas City, 2014), Lesson 19.

§ Professor Patrick Grim, *Questions of Value*, the State University of New York at Stony Brook, The Great Courses, Course Guidebook, Lecture 18, 70.

Those who are against the death penalty argue human life should not be eliminated under any circumstances. They argue the death penalty does not reduce homicides nor is it a just penalty since it deprives certain people of something irreplaceable: life. They proclaim the state has no right to take life because it would put the state in the place of the criminal to carry out revenge. They also add that the irreversibility of the death penalty implies the impossibility of compensating convicts of judicial errors and, therefore, the possibility of executing innocent people.

In his *Reflections on the Guillotine*, written in 1957, the French philosopher Albert Camus (1913–1960) takes a position for the abolition of the death penalty. The essay opens with a description of Camus's father's reaction to witnessing the execution of a convicted murderer. At first Camus's father fully supported the decision, but after witnessing the event he was left in a state of shock for several days. Throughout the essay, Camus expresses his own shock and disgust at the brutality of the guillotine.

Camus's main point in his argument against capital punishment is its ineffectiveness. Camus points out that in countries where the death penalty has already been abandoned, crime has not risen. Camus also argued the threat of death is insufficient to prevent people from committing crimes and it is reduced to an act of revenge that only breeds further violence.

He likened this act of state revenge to the concept of an eye for an eye and stated justice should be based on law and principles and not instinct and emotions.

Camus suggested the maximum penalty should be being set at labor for life due to the possibility of judicial error. A life of work, in the opinion of Camus, is more severe than death but at least it carries the possibility of being reversed. He argued that "Capital punishment is the most premeditated of murders, to which no criminal's deed, however, calculated, can be compared."[*]

The death penalty has been abolished in most European and Latin American countries. But in 31 states of the United States, in Guatemala, and in most of the Caribbean states, it is in force. In Asia and Africa, it is allowed in several countries. In total, 58 countries in the world use it. In China, human trafficking and serious cases of political corruption are punishable by the death penalty. In 2007 in North Korea, the director of a company was publicly executed in a sports stadium before 150,000 people

---

[*] en.wikipedia.org/wiki/Reflections_on_the_Guillotine.

as punishment for having made phone calls abroad.* The most commonly used methods for executing death sentences include lethal injection, electrocution, gas chamber, hanging, decapitation, and shooting.

Another controversial issue is that of artificial insemination. Artificial insemination in humans is the technique of assisted reproduction that consists of a procedure by which semen is delivered to the ovum using non-natural techniques.†

On July 25, 1978, Louise Brown was born in the English town of Oldham, the first test-tube baby in history. Her conception had been produced in a laboratory nine months earlier by the technique of in vitro fertilization. The specialists extracted an ovule from their mother and attached it to sperm on a laboratory plate and then it was implanted in the maternal uterus to start the gestation process.‡

The birth of Louise opened a new stage in the treatment of sterility. Currently, assisted reproduction techniques include sterility treatments in which ovules and sperm are manipulated. In 1984 in California, a child was born conceived by a donated ovum, and in Australia, a woman gave birth to a baby from a frozen embryo. In 1994 a 62-year-old Italian woman had a child for a donated ovum that was fertilized with her husband's sperm.

Those who criticize artificial insemination point out the dignity of the human person is denaturalized since procreation becomes a technical act without interpersonal relationships. Those who support artificial insemination argue that science solves the problem of the sterility of many couples.

> Is artificial fertilization morally good or bad? Should it be approved by the laws?
> Is everything technically possible, ethically good?
> Should we do whatever we can do?§

Mary Shelley's novel, *Frankenstein* (1818), was inspired by the work of the Italian physician Luigi Galvani (1737–1798), who had experimented with electricity in frogs. Shelley's book was the first that raised a relevant issue: Should science have moral boundaries?

---

* Wikipedia, "Capital Punishment."
† Spanish Royal Academy Dictionary, www.dle.rae.es.
‡ "Louise Brown," Wikipedia.
§ Riano Galan and Nunez Cubero Bol Pediatr, "Assisted reproduction techniques. Ethical dilem-
  mas," 2004, 185–92, www.sccalp.org.

In November 2018 the Chinese scientist He Jiankui claimed that he had managed to modify the DNA of human embryos and two twin girls (Luly and Nana) had been born. He told *The Associated Press* that he modified the embryos of seven couples with HIV – the virus that causes AIDS – and they underwent in vitro fertilization using a technique called CRISPR, to block the gene that allows HIV to enter the cells. The experiment was strongly criticized by the international scientific community and by the Southern University of Science and Technology, the institution where He Jiankui works.

By modifying human embryos, these changes can be transmitted to the descendants of these people and open the possibility of altering the human species. The modification of genes can introduce undesirable effects in people and their descendants. He Jiankui said: "Genetic surgery should be used for healing. Improve the IQ or select the color of the hair or the eyes ... should be prohibited. I understand that my work will be controversial, but I think families need this technology."

Matthew Porteus, a stem cell researcher at Stanford University, pointed out that this announcement about the birth of genetically modified children highlights the weaknesses of the current regulatory system and he said, "This is not the way I would like science to advance." Southern University reported that they will investigate what happened, noting that Jiankui would have "seriously violated academic ethics and codes of conduct."*

Is it OK to modify human embryos to try to prevent AIDS?
Can science and technology be used to manipulate human nature?

Cloning is the process by which identical copies of an organism, cell, or molecule are obtained. With the cloning of Dolly the sheep in 1996 through nuclear somatic cell transfer (SCNT), the idea of human cloning also became a passionate ethical debate.

Would possible human cloning be morally good or bad?
Should human cloning be approved by law?

The Symbionese Liberation Army (SLA) was a left-wing urban guerrilla that emerged in California in 1973 and its symbol was a seven-headed

---

* "Debate Ético: En China dicen haber creado bebas modificadas genéticamente," Macarena Vidal Liy, November 26, 2018, www.lanacion.com.ar ("Ethical Debate: In China, they say they have created genetically modified babies").

cobra. Its most notorious actions were the murder of the director of the Oakland Schools, the robbery of the Bank of Hibernia, and the kidnapping of Patty Hearst. Hearst was kidnapped on February 4, 1974. Two months later she was photographed with a rifle during the bank robbery and in September 1975 she was arrested, and the SLA dismantled. At the trial, Hearst stated that she had been locked in a closet and subjected to sexual abuse. However, she helped the terrorist group and she pleaded that her actions were the results of *Stockholm Syndrome*, a psychological reaction in which the victim of a kidnap develops a strong affective bond with his captors.* Despite her plead, Hearst was sentenced to 35 years in prison and many years later pardoned by President Bill Clinton.†

Was Patty responsible for her criminal actions or they "brainwashed" her during captivity? Did Patty have altered mental conditions when she robbed the bank?

We can continue with more debatable issues. For example, is it ethical to lend money at a disproportionate interest rate? From which amount the interest rate of a loan becomes usurious or immoral? Is it ethical that a company that produces shoes in Asia pays wages that are legal in the country of production, but are below the individual's basic needs? Is it ethical to fire a third of the company's employees to boost profits for its owners? Is it ethical to conduct experiments with animals? Is it ethical to lock them in zoos and aquariums? Can a clothing marketing campaign be ethically considered if it indirectly promotes anorexia in girls? Can it be considered an anti-ethical act when it is carried out under coercion or when it is carried out by a person with serious mental problems? ‡

As you can see with these examples, intellectual property, slavery, pornography, prostitution, homosexual marriage, abortion, euthanasia, artificial fertilization, death penalty, human cloning, Stockholm Syndrome's situations, money loans, and animal's rights are some of the issues that generate an ethical debate in society and where to take a

---

* On August 23, 1973, Jan Erik Olsson attempted to assault the Credit Bank of Stockholm, in Sweden. After being cornered, he took four bank employees as hostages. They were tied with ropes for five days until the police released them. See "Stockholm Syndrome," Wikipedia. The psychiatrist Nils Bejerot, adviser of the Swedish police during the assault, crashed the term *Stockholm Syndrome* to refer to the reaction of the hostages in captivity. According to data from the Federal Bureau of Investigation (FBI), about 27% of the victims of kidnappings have this type of reaction.

† "Patty Hearst," Wikipedia.

‡ For Aristotle (384–322 AC) we are responsible for actions that we have done voluntarily (the action is not done under compulsion or coercion).

stand on whether each of them is morally good or bad will depend on the perception, the point of view, and the scale of values of each person. There is no unanimity about what is good or bad, fair or unfair, moral or immoral.

Henry Hazlitt (1894–1933) was an American journalist who wrote about business and economics. Hazlitt's major work in philosophy is *The Foundations of Morality*. Hazlitt said, "Liberty is the essential basis, the sine qua non of morality. Morality can only exist in a free society; it can exist to the extent freedom exists."* Only the free man can be moral when he is free to choose between good and evil.

The morality or immorality of an act will depend on the values of each one. For example, the Russian novelist Leon Tolstoy (1828–1910) was a promoter of nonviolence that had great impact on Gandhi, or Martin Luther King Jr. Tolstoy was a precursor of naturism and vegetarianism. Tolstoy said, "A man can live and be healthy without killing animals for food; therefore, if he eats meat, he participates in taking animal life merely for the sake of his appetite. And to act so is immoral."†

Some ethical questions are not easy to solve and test our ability to make the right decisions. For example, suppose you are aware of an illegal or unethical action of one of your co-workers, and the company's code of ethics forces you to report it to your boss. Or imagine your company developed an edible product that can be very successful, although an internal report indicates the possibility the product contains carcinogenic components. If the sale of the product is suspended, it is most likely the company will go bankrupt; but if it goes on sale, that product can end up causing lethal consequences for those who consume it.

What decision should you take?

An ethical dilemma many times comes upon us unexpectedly. Bob McCoy was an executive of Morgan Stanley who spent three months hiking in the Himalayas through Nepal in 1983. During the Nepal hike, something occurred that had a powerful impact. When he and a friend approached a difficult pass to attain the highest point of the climb, one of the teams in front of them came back from the pass with an Indian holy man wearing little clothing, a sadhu, who was almost frozen and barely alive, suffering from hypothermia. He had been lying on the ice.

---

* Gary Galles, "Henry Hazlitt on liberty: 21 choice quotes," Foundation for Economic Education, November 28, 2018, www.fee.org.

† es.wikipedia.org/wiki/León_Tolstói.

The New Zealander that brought the body slung across his shoulders wanted to get across the pass before the bright sun melted the snow and he said, "I have done what I can. . . . You care for him. We are going on."

McCoy took a carotid pulse and found that the sadhu was still alive. McCoy and his group wrapped the sadhu in warm clothing and gave him food and drink. McCoy told his friend, Stephen, he was concerned about withstanding the heights to come and wanted to get over the pass. Some members of the group followed McCoy and they arrived safely to the summit. Stephen and other members of the group stayed with the sadhu and tried to help him move down toward a village. They carried the sadhu down to a rock and pointed him toward a hut another 500 feet below. They left him there. Stephen and the rest of the team arrived at the summit an hour after McCoy did. When Stephen met McCoy, Stephen said, "How do you feel about contributing to the death of a fellow man?" McCoy replied, "Is the sadhu dead?" "No," replied Stephen, "but he surely will be." *

McCoy and Stephen never learned whether the sadhu lived or died.

A group of people went through an unexpected moral dilemma and they made wrong decisions under pressure and stress without thinking all the consequences. They made the decision to go up to the summit instead of carrying the man back down off the mountain to safety.

The sadhu story raises a lot of questions, but the story should always remind us that if there is a tension between values and goals, values should always prevail.

In 2009 a group of Italian climbers was trapped by a snowstorm 400 meters from the summit of Aconcagua, a mountain located in the province of Mendoza in the west of Argentina with an altitude of 6,960 meters, the highest summit in the Americas. A rescue group managed to rescue them, except the group's guide, a 31-year-old Argentine, who was injured. A video taken by one of the people in the group shows how, due to the difficulties that had to be overcome, the guide was abandoned even though alive.

The video sparked a controversy about the action of the mountaineers. The father of the deceased guide condemned the rescuers and climbers, saying, "They abandoned him like a dog." In the video, one of the rescuers

---

* Bowen H. McCoy, "The parable of the sadhu," *Harvard Business Review*, September–October 1983. AT&T and the American Red Cross used this story in their ethics training. See also Clancy Martin, "Moral decision making," The Great Courses, Guidebook (University of Missouri-Kansas City, 2014), 50–51.

says, "We are freezing, we are 400 meters to the summit and he does not move. He is dying." Rescuers considered the guide had no chance of surviving, and because rescuing him involved too great a risk for the rest of the participants, they decided to abandon him at almost 7,000 meters in the middle of a strong storm, where it was difficult to breathe.

Ethical analysis can be complex, and one can be wrong. Experienced rescuers felt incapable of saving the guide's life because of the extreme weather conditions. The question that we must ask is if the decision made by the rescuers was the correct one or if something else could have been done.*

Although our circumstances limit us, they cannot force us, as free human beings we are, to follow one line of action over another. For this reason, as the French philosopher Jean-Paul Sartre (1905–1980) argued that we chose in the midst of anguish; we know we must choose and the election will have consequences.[†]

Does your company have a plan for dealing with contingencies?

Kirk O. Hanson, professor of social ethics at Santa Clara University, gave an example of how you can be prepared to deal with ethical conflicts:

> If you are placed in a difficult ethical situation at work, one approach is for you to go first and ask, Did I understand you correctly? Do you want me to falsify this record? ... Isn't that going to get us in trouble? You act dumb and ask more questions. At some point, the manager you are dealing with might either realize they are in some really tough territory and could get in trouble for asking you to do that.[‡]

The American aerospace businessman Norman Augustine, former chairman de Lockheed Martin, says, "I would never suggest that ethics is simple. Not only does one have to know the right things to do, but one must also have the moral fortitude to do it."[§]

---

* "Investigan la muerte de un montanista abandonado a 7.000 metros de altura," February 18, 2009, www.eleconomista.es; "Montañero muere abandonado a 7000 metros de altura," El mundo TV, February 10, 2009, www.El Mundo.com, "La muerte del alpinista abandonado en la montaña," YouTube ("They investigate the death of an abandoned montanista at 7,000 meters of height"; "Mountaineer dies abandoned at 7000 meters high"; "The death of the abandoned mountaineer in the mountain").

† es.wikipedia.org/wiki/Mala_fe_(Sartre).

‡ Kirk Hanson's speech, "The six ethical dilemmas every professional face," speech delivered at the Center for Business Ethics at Bentley University, February 3, 2014.

§ Art Weiss and Marjorie Doyle, "Organizational ethics: who needs it?" SCCE Compliance & Ethics Institute. September 26, 2016, slide 25.

The following account took place in the Caribbean Sea in an anti-submarine warfare frigate of the North Atlantic Alliance, during the Cold War. The person who wrote and told me this story was at that time in the ship and witnessed the following ethical dilemma:

On a Sunday afternoon of a routine patrol in the Caribbean, the frigate received an assignment from Senior Command to locate and follow a potential underwater Soviet submarine very likely to be heading towards the island of Cuba.

The frigate deployed sonobuoys and sonars and after a moderate interval, the surveillance systems recognized the presence of an underwater object navigating on a course towards Cuba and the tracking mission was on.

But an unexpected development came to disturb the mission. Surface's radars identified a small boat dead on the water ahead of the frigate.

As the frigate approached the small boat it became apparent that the boat and seafarers on board were unsafe and in peril.

The Commanding Officer ordered the launching of a small patrol and boarding craft to make an assessment. It was determined that there were 44 passengers on the boat and the boat was not seaworthy and slowly sinking. The mast for the sail was a tree branch. The sail had several bed sheets that were stitched together. The passengers were potential Haitian refugees that had intended to navigate to Florida.

Transferring forty-four personnel from a boat still floating presents a more complicated regulatory and administrative challenge than lifting few shipwrecks from the water. Larger numbers also bring the inherent risk of a sizable number of unknown people becoming unruly after having being brought onboard. And also, there is the issue of the interruption of the military mission of tracking the submarine. Lastly, there was the political issue of refugees from Haiti in the Caribbean Sea during the Cold War.

The Commanding Officer needed the authorization from the Chain of Command to move the passengers from the boat to the frigate.

For the next two or three hours, there ensued a very vocal argument among the senior officers on the bridge of the ship on what the correct course of action should be. There were three or four who advocated for leaving the boat and the 44 passengers where they were and for the continuation of the military mission.

Another three or four officers argued that leaving the 44 humans in their derelict craft was a guaranteed death sentence by drowning.

After much arguing, we received authorization to pick up the potential shipwrecks and to continue the submarine tracking mission. So we did. We fed them, cleaned them up and made it so they would be warm. The mission was pursued to completion. We were able to discharge the forty-four human beings at an allied installation in the next 24 hours or so.

This event happened so many years ago. I have not forgotten it. Neither have most of the shipmates that were present that afternoon. We meet as Veterans with some frequency and we think this was one of the best opportunities in our lives to do something meaningful and valuable to other human beings.

I'm still glad that God gave me the opportunity to be on that ship, present on that bridge that afternoon. I cannot imagine what every single day of the following decades of my life would have been like for me if I had not been on the side of the fighting to pick up the 44 Haitian refugees.

Decisions many times are not easy, ethical analysis can be complex, and anyone can be wrong, even more, when decisions are made under stress and tense situations.

To reduce the margins of error, it is convenient to reflect and analyze the different alternatives before acting.

Training in ethics, through practical cases and simulations, helps people to incorporate ethics in the decision-making process to thereby better protect the organization.

6

"How" to Achieve Results

In ancient Rome, it was common for urine collected in public latrines to be used for industrial purposes. The urine was used by the tanners of skins, as well as by the laundresses, who used it to clean and bleach wool togas because of their ammonia content.

In order to afford the wars and the construction of the Roman Colosseum, the Roman emperor Vespasian (9–79) decided to impose a tax on the buyers of the urine that was poured into the latrines of Rome and was collected in the Maximum Sewer. From then on, the artisans who needed the urine in their businesses had to pay the new urine tax.

Vespasian's son, Titus, complained about the disgusting nature of the tax and reproached his father. Then, Vespasian held up a gold coin and asked Titus whether he felt offended by its smell. When Titus said "No," Vespasian replied, "Yet it comes from urine." He also said, "Pecunia non olet" (money does not smell).

The phrase "money does not smell," means that money is money, wherever it comes from, regardless of its origin.*

Is it important *how* we achieve our goals?

Robin Hood was a thief who lived hiding in Sherwood Forest near the city of Nottingham, in England, in the Middle Ages. With his bow and arrow, he robbed the rich to help the poor.†

---

* *Pecunia non olet* ("money does not smell"). https://es.wikipedia.org/wiki/Pecunia_non_olet. The name of Vespasiano is still associated today with public urinals in France (vespasienne), Italy (Vespasiano), and Romania (vespasiene). "El Dinero No Tiene Olor" ("Money Has No Smell"), https://latincaste.jimdo.com/el-dinero-no-tiene-olor/.

† According to legend, he had to take refuge in the woods to defend the prisoner King Richard I of England, known as Richard the Lionheart (1157–1199) of his brother John Lackland (1166–1216). There is no good evidence that Robin Hood existed, although there are documents that describe that during the year 1266, the Sheriff of Nottingham chased outlaws who stole in the forests of Sherwood and had taken the name of Robin Hood.

On the other hand, Colombian drug trafficker Pablo Escobar Gaviria (1949–1993) became one of the richest people on earth with a fortune of over US$25 billion. During his youth, when he was poor, he told his friends, "If when I am 25 years old, I do not have a million pesos in my pocket...I will shoot myself."[*]

For Robin Hood and Pablo Escobar, the important thing was the ultimate goal, regardless of the means to achieve it.

The Congo Free State was an African colonial domain, a property of King Leopold II of Belgium (1865–1909), administered privately by that king between 1885 and 1908.[†]

During the period in which it was administered by Leopoldo II, the territory was subjected to indiscriminate exploitation of natural resources (especially ivory and rubber), in which native labor was used exclusively, in conditions of slavery and exploitation. The usual procedure was to take hostages, mostly women and children, who could be rescued only by delivering certain quantities of rubber. Leopold II allowed all kinds of atrocities and justified any action to get ivory and rubber, including torture, mutilation, and murder, terrorizing the population to meet his target.

Although it is impossible to make accurate calculations, historians have mentioned figures close to ten million dead. It was a slaughter, annihilation, genocide, a mass murder.[‡]

In 1890 the American historian George W. Williams (1849–1891) made the first complaint about the calamities he saw in the Congo. Years later, the scandal broke in Europe with the publication in the press of the stories and data collected by writers, diplomats, and the work of the British journalist Edmund Dene Morel (1873–1924), who convinced the European and US governments to begin to investigate and oppose the extermination that was taking place. Diplomatic maneuvers and the pressure of public opinion got the Belgian king to relinquish his personal rule over the Congo, which went on to become a colony of Belgium under the name of Belgian Congo in 1908.

For Leopoldo II, any method to get ivory and rubber was valid. For him, any end justified the means. Goals should be obtained without harming values. The *what* does not justify any *how*. The results must never be above

---

[*] *Pablo Escobar: The Drug Lord*, Netflix series.

[†] In 1908, the territory was ceded to Belgium.

[‡] "Leopold II of Belgium," Wikipedia; "Leopoldo II y su Genocidio en El Congo," https://revista-dehistoria.es/leopoldo II – y-su-genocidio; "La Brutal Vida de Leopoldo II," www.elconfidencial.com ("Leopold II and His Genocide in the Congo"; "The Brutal Life of Leopoldo II").

the procedures to achieve them and they must be obtained respecting the rules of the game. A short-term mentality can lead to winning now but losing later.

China has the largest overseas fishing fleet, with 2,460 vessels. Satellite night photos show the lights of large fleets at the edge of the economic exclusion zones of several countries in Latin America. The waters of Chile's Easter Island are coveted by Asian fishers looking for tuna and swordfish, and in Peru and Argentina, giant squid or cod are the species coveted by Asian vessels.

In 2013, Mexican authorities seized US$2.25 million in illegal totoaba bladders, and in 2015, Ecuadorian authorities reported on the confiscation of nearly 100,000 illegal shark fins.[*] According to statistics from the Food and Agriculture Organization (FAO) of the United Nations, about 50% of global catches are illegal.

Former CEO of GE, Jack Welch, has written: "Mission announces the direction in which we move and progress, and values describe the behavior that takes us there."[†] Welch said: "There is no secret in the what; the secret is in the how."[‡]

Frank Knight (1885–1972) was an American economist founder of the Chicago School. Nobel Prize winners Milton Friedman (1912–2006), George Stigler (1911–1991), and James Buchanan (1919–2013) were all students of Knight at that University. Knight, the author of the book *Risk, Uncertainty and Profit*, says, "With uncertainty doing things... the primary problem is deciding what to do and how to do it."[§]

John Zenger and Joseph Folkman, renowned professionals in the field of performance and leadership, said: "In organizations with integrity... great emphasis is placed on honesty and ethical behavior. Success is measured not only in terms of achieving results but also considering how to get them."[¶]

The consultant Jim Collins explains:

> Public corporations face incessant pressure from the capital markets to grow as fast as possible, and we cannot deny this fact. But even so, we've found in all our research that those who resisted the pressures to succumb

---

[*] Daniel García Marco, "The Huge Illegal Operation of Chinese Fishing Vessels in Latin American Waters," *BBC Mundo*, March 21, 2016, www.bbc.com.

[†] Jack Welch, *Winning*, (BSA, 2005), 26.

[‡] Dov Seidman, *How* (John Wiley & Sons, Inc., 2011), 51.

[§] Ronald Harry Coase, *The Nature of the Firm* ("Economica" Journal of LSE (London School of Economics), 1937).

[¶] John Zenger and Joseph Folkman, *The Extraordinary Leader* (Alfaomega, 2010), 151.

to unsustainable short-term growth delivered better long-term results by Wall Street's own definition of success, namely cumulative returns to investors.*

In 1972 during Richard Milhous Nixon's (1913–1994) term as the 37th US president, there was a political scandal that culminated in his resignation. On June 17, 1972, a security guard discovered five spies in the Watergate Hotel in Washington, D.C., where Democratic Party leaders were meeting. *Washington Post* reporters then discovered that the Nixon administration had ordered spying on political opponents and recorded their conversations. When it seemed inevitable the Congress would prosecute him on charges of obstruction of justice, Nixon decided to resign in August 1974, being replaced by his vice president, Gerald Ford. Nixon was the first president to resign in US history.

Michael Ritter, a German consultant, former Siemens executive, and an expert on reputational issues, commented on the pressures suffered by John Daniel Ehrlichman (1925–1999), an aide to President Nixon, who was sentenced to prison for conspiracy, obstruction of justice, and perjury for the Watergate crisis. Ehrlichman said in a report,

> The pressures can reach the point where you seriously consider suicide. I considered it. It is a very lonely, very depressing situation to be under the spotlight of the media like the *Wall Street Journal*, those who constantly write editorials about you.[†]

In a study conducted by experts James J. Hoffman, Grantham Couch, and Bruce T. Lamont, sponsored by Florida State University, these experts said:

> Every day, members of any organization, consciously or unconsciously, make ethical decisions. With each decision, although they do not perceive it, they are shaping their own future, the future of their peers and the organization to which they belong. The way in which ethical problems are solved will affect the company's customers, the shareholders who invested in it and the society as a whole.[‡]

---

* Jim Collins, *How the Mighty Fall* (Collins Business Essentials, 2009), 54.
† Michael Ritter, *El Valor del Capital Reputacional* (Olivos, Ritter & Partners, 2013), 270. Interview of Martin Fitzwater in *Naked Washington: Power, Press, and Presidency*, ABC, 1996 ("The Value of Reputational Capital").
‡ Revista Gestion (Gestion Magazine), "The glass with which you look," May 1999.

Companies with a strong ethical culture do not support cheating because cheating means to deceive and take advantage of a breach of the rules. Every leader must ensure the pressure of competition and the objectives set never justify deceit or lack of integrity. Sometimes in organizations, members cross the line of ethical behavior because they are too focused on the bottom line.

Achieving results is very important, but it is important how you get to them. People should never compromise their values, even if it affects the bottom line.

George W. Merck, the founder of the American pharmaceutical company Merck & Co, said in 1950, "We try to never forget that medicine is for the people. It is not for profits. The profits will follow."[*]

Kenneth Blanchard and Norman Vincent Peale have written: "Managing only for profit is like playing tennis with your eye on the scoreboard and not on the ball."[†]

Assistant Attorney General for the Criminal Division Leslie Caldwell said, "There are companies that put its profit margins ahead of its business ethics."[‡]

Kirk O. Hanson is the executive director of the Markkula Center for Applied Ethics and professor of social ethics at Santa Clara University. He said in a lecture at Bentley University in 2014:

> How far are the CEO's really willing to go to give up profit to be ethical? Are they willing to give up business in Asia if they can't do it without bribing? Are they willing to not release a product because they are not sure what its effect will be?
>
> You can make a lot of money either by acting ethically or unethically, so why not be ethical? That suggests that it's possible to have a business that operates ethically and still makes money.[§]

The American economist and marketing specialist Philip Kotler has said that "It's more important to do what is strategically correct than what is immediately profitable."[¶]

---

[*] www.merck.com/about/our-people/gw-merck-doc.pdf.
[†] Kenneth Blanchard and Norman Vincent Peale, *The Power of Ethical Management* (William Morrow and Company Inc., 1988), 106.
[‡] At the 22nd Annual Ethics and Compliance Conference held in Atlanta on October 1, 2014.
[§] Kirk Hanson's, "The six ethical dilemmas every professional face," speech given at the Center for Business Ethics at Bentley University, February 3, 2014.
[¶] Philip Kotler, *Marketing Direction*, Millennium ed (Pearson, 2001), 63.

German engineer and inventor Werner von Siemens (1816–1892) said, "I will not sell the future in exchange for short-term profit."*

The Lord's Prayer (also called Our Father, Pater Noster) is a venerated Christian prayer, which, according to the New Testament, Jesus taught as the way to pray. At the end it says, "Lead us not into temptation." Through that phrase, Catholics ask God to move them away from the paths that lead to sin.

The temptation is the desire to perform an immediately pleasant action but probably harmful in the long term. Temptations are inevitable and we all have to face them. Jesus was tempted in the desert but He did not give in; Judas was tempted to betray his master and he did. Temptations will always exist and the issue is to know the correct way to act in the face of these temptations.

To build trust, credibility, and transparency, company leaders must pay attention to *how* the objectives are achieved. When members of a company are committed to the organization's ethical standards, they will not only think of financial results for the next quarter or year-end, but they will also think about how to achieve those results. They will be interested not only in the goals but also in the processes to achieve those goals.

How do we play the game?

Antonio Machado (1875–1939), a leading Spanish poet, said, "Doing things well is more important than doing them."†

Corporate culture and ethical principles must be well communicated within the organization so that decisions and even internal policies can be challenged when they do not match corporate values and principles. Look at this situation that happened to a US Bank customer in Portland, Oregon, during Christmas Eve, in 2019:

A customer's check was being held by US Bank until it could be verified. The customer was almost out of gas so he drove to a gas station and waited there, praying for his funds to be released so he could fill his tank and drive home. The customer was desperate; he needed US$20 to join his family for Christmas Eve.

The customer called the bank's customer care number for help, and a call center representative put him on hold and went to talk to a supervisor about the situation. The supervisor said, "It's Christmas Eve, let's get this guy home." The supervisor gave the call representative permission to meet the customer at the gas station and give him US$20 in cash.

---

* es.wikiquote.org/wiki/Werner_von_Siemens.
† www.sabidurias.com and www.akifrases.com.

The customer was surprised by the kind gesture. That gesture, however, would cost the employees their jobs.

A few days after that, a regional manager fired the supervisor and the call center representative for violating a US Bank internal policy that prohibits employees from leaving work to meet with unknown customers.

The US Bank received widespread criticism over the decision taken with its employees. It has apologized and offered both employees their jobs back. A US Bank statement said:

> Our recent employment decision in Oregon did not reflect who we are as a company. U.S. Bank fell short of our and other's expectations and we sincerely apologize.
>
> Our CEO has personally spoken with both employees and asked them to rejoin the company. ... We are beginning a re-evaluation immediately of our policies and how they are applied to be certain they are flexible and put the customer first, while remaining consistent with our obligation to safeguard customer assets and ensure the safety of our employees.*

Internal policies and their interpretation should never go against corporate values, principles, and ethics.

On Sunday, April 9, 2017, United Airlines flight 3411 from Chicago to Louisville, Kentucky, had been oversold. Following the procedure, the airline requested that four passengers voluntarily agree to leave their seats in exchange for a voucher of US$800 and a hotel night, offering a new flight the next day. United got only three passengers to accept the offer and made the decision to choose the fourth passenger randomly. They chose a 69-year-old Chinese physician who was forcibly expelled. As a result, the passenger suffered a concussion, a broken nose, and two lost teeth, and he ended up bloodied. After being interviewed, he mentioned that he did not want to fly again and that being dragged off the plane was "more horrifying than the Vietnam War...being dragged down the aisle was more horrifying and harrowing than what I experienced when leaving Vietnam."†

Smartphone images were taken by other passengers on the plane and uploaded to the internet to show how security personnel expelled the

---

* "A Bank Employee gave $20 to a Customer in Need. She and her Supervisor were Fired," Minyvonne Burke, www.nbcnews.com/news , February 8, 2020.
† "United Airlines passenger says being dragged off the plane was more horrifying than Vietnam War," www.independent.com.uk, April 14, 2017. Also, "United Airlines Passenger, Worse Than Fall of Saigon" www.bbc.com, April 13, 2017.

passenger by dragging him semiconscious down the aisle like a suitcase. United Airlines did not seem to understand the risk of making certain decisions in the era of transparency. Many people have a smartphone and these behaviors can be filmed and uploaded to the internet; social networks and the internet can show a horror movie in seconds. Videos of the event uploaded to YouTube received more than three million views in the first five days.

United's actions pose the following questions:

What is the culture of that company?
Do they have the right to disrespect the decision of people and decide for them?
Does the end justify the means?

Values and ethical principles should be the basis of business policies and decisions. As Professor Jorge Etkin says, "In an organization without principles or values, the right thing is whatever it turns out to be."*

Companies that put customers first, prioritize respect for the individual and customer service, and promote that culture internally are less likely to suffer mistakes in the decisions of their employees. A well-publicized strong ethical culture and respect for the individual in the organization would hardly have permitted what happened on April 9, 2017, on United Airlines flight 3411.

The cost of making bad decisions can be expensive. The UA share price fell 4% in the early days after the event, close to US$1 billion in market capitalization. The perception of people and the press, in general, was what happened to that particular passenger could happen to any other United Airlines customer.

Will United learn from its mistake? Will they work to strengthen a more humane culture? The CEO must play a key role in driving these changes. If United does not make big changes in its processes and culture, it will face the risk of returning, as in 2011, to the "Most Hated Companies in America" ranking.

The values disseminated and shared within the organization are the guide, funnel, or filter for decision-making. Pressures to keep equity prices high, meet business and sales plans, accelerate growth, and outperform

---

* Jorge Etkin, "Bases Conceptuales de la Gestion Socialmente Responsable" (Conceptual Bases of Socially Responsible Management), *Saberes*, 1 (2009), 9.

competition can increase the risk of creating a workplace where decisions that are inconsistent with ethics are made.

The work environment influences the decisions that individuals make in relation to ethics.

As Andrew Stark, professor at the University of Toronto-Scarborough, points out, "Ethics and interests can conflict."* If organizations do not emphasize the importance of fair play, it is feasible that a member of the company will try to fulfill plans or objectives without addressing the right ways to achieve them. Excessive pressure and focus on results can derail any company.

In an article published by *Gestion* magazine in 1996,† Jackie Wills referred to the ethical standards of the Esso Company. It reads: "The standards of ethics and business performance of Esso ... have a section on business ethics that says: We will not tolerate any employee who obtains good results disobeying the laws or executing immoral agreements."

The Ghanaian Kweku Adoboli was a bank operator that made the UBS Bank in London lose US$1.9 billion in 2011, and in 2012 he was sentenced to prison for recording fictitious transactions. In an interview with the BBC, Adoboli declared that the "system" led him to act that way, mainly by strong pressure for profit. He said: "Operators are driven to make huge profits and are rewarded for it. Clearly, in the financial sector, there is a conflict between the goals they set and the possibilities of achieving them."‡

The ethics program is doomed to failure if the company executives do not support the ethical standards of the organization for the employees.

In a speech made in 2004, Stephen Cutler, Director Division of Enforcement US Securities and Exchange Commission, said, "We have often seen instances of managers demanding results and what employees heard was results at any cost, including results without complying with the rules."§

The attention of leaders should not only be focused on the final product or end result, but also on the processes and behaviors on the way to reaching the goal. The attention and emphasis should not be placed solely

---

* Andrew Stark, "What's the matter with business ethics?" *Harvard Business Review* (May–June 1993), 6.
† Jackie Wills, "How a good behavior is achieved?" *Gestion Magazine* (July–August 1996), 143.
‡ "Making Money No Matter How," www.lanacion.com.ar, August 13, 2016.
§ Stephen M. Cutler, "Tone at the top: getting it right," speech given at SEC Staff: Second Annual General Counsel Roundtable, Washington, D.C., December 3, 2004.

on company sales and profits. Leaders must be clear in communicating to their work teams *how* things should be done in the organization, focusing on *how* to achieve the results. It is essential to avoid statements like, "Do whatever it takes" or "Get it done, and I don't care how you do it."

More important than having is being. Business is not just about money. Doing good is good business. Remember Google's philosophy: "You can make money without doing evil."[*]

The important thing is the way results are achieved. Therefore, it is the responsibility of business leaders to clearly communicate to employees, partners, and suppliers that the earnings, objectives, and plans must be met in a manner consistent with corporate values and legislation in force.

Results must always be obtained in a legitimate and fair manner.

Success without integrity is not a success.

---

[*] "Ten Things We Know to Be True," www.google.com.

Section 2

Change

7

The Challenge of Adapting to Constant Change

Once a king said to the wise men of the court that he wanted to order a diamond ring, and he wanted to keep inside the ring a message that could help in times of despair. It had to be a short message so that he could leave it under the stone. His wise men were great scholars and they thought and looked in their books, but they could not find anything.

The king had an old servant who had also been a servant of his father. The king felt respect for the elder and asked him about the ring and message. This old man said he knew a message that had been given once. The man wrote it in a small roll, folded it, and passed it to the king saying, "Do not read it. Keep it hidden in the ring. Open it for the first time only when all else has failed, when you cannot find a way out of a situation."

That moment came quickly. The territory was invaded, and the king lost his throne. He fled on his horse to save his life. He came to a place in the forest and remembered the ring. He opened the paper and found the little message, which said, "This too shall pass." The king folded the paper, put it back in the ring, and soon gathered his armies and reconquered the kingdom.

The day he entered the city, there was a great celebration with music and dancing, and the old man, who was at his side, asked the king to read the message of the ring again. The king asked why he should do that now if he was victorious and not in a desperate situation. The old man said:

> This message is not only for desperate situations, but it is also for pleasant situations. It is not only for when you are defeated, but is it also for when you've succeeded. It is not just for when you're the last, but also for when you are the first.

The king opened the ring and read the message "This too shall pass."

Amid the crowd celebrating, the king felt the same peace and silence of the forest. Pride had disappeared, and he understood the message: "Everything changes and passes."*

Nicolas Fouquet (1615–1680) was the powerful superintendent of finance of King Louis XIV (1638–1715). On August 17, 1661, Fouquet gave the king a party at his house. This was a sumptuous celebration with 1,000 guests. The banquet was supervised by Francois Vatel (inventor of the Chantilly cream) and among the guests were Moliere, La Fontaine, and Madame de Sevigne.

Louis XIV was so angry to see so many splendors that a few days later Fouquet was accused of embezzlement and arrested.†

Voltaire wrote, "When the evening began, Fouquet was at the top of the World. By the time it had ended, he was at the bottom."‡

Nothing is forever.

Like the stock price of listed companies, your Twitter followers, or the price of Bitcoin, everything is moving and changing. When a bird is alive, it eats the ants, but when it dies, the ants will eat the bird.

The Greek philosopher Heraclitus of Ephesus (535–484 BC) stated:

> Everything flows. Everything is in motion and nothing lasts forever. Therefore, we cannot descend to the same river twice, because when I descend to the river for the second time, neither I nor the river is the same.... There is nothing permanent except change. Everything is always changing.§

We live in a world where everything is constantly moving, although we do not always perceive it. The pace of change we are experiencing is exponential and has also affected business management. Change means moving from one state to another, leaving certain structures, procedures, and behaviors to acquire new ones. Organizations must change to adapt to new contexts and meet new needs. As the Irish writer George Bernard Shaw (1856–1950) said, "Progress is impossible without change."¶

---

* Jaime López Gutiérrez and Marta Inés Bernal Trujillo, *The Fault of Cow* (Colombia, Intermediate Editors, 2006), 216–19.
† Nicolas Fouquet, www.wikipedia.com.
‡ Robert Greene, *The 48 Laws of Power* (Penguin Books, 2000), 3.
§ Euripides (480—406 BC), one of the great Greek tragic poets of antiquity, also said that "everything changes in this world, inconsistent is human life and subject to many mistakes."
¶ www.brainyquote.com.

Carl Sagan (1934–1996) was an astronomer born in New York, author of the documentary and the book *Cosmos*. Sagan said, "The Earth is the most beautiful place we know. But that beauty has been sculpted by change: The smooth change, almost imperceptible, and the sudden and violent change. In Cosmos, there is no place that is safe from change."

Just as we do not perceive that the earth moves, sometimes we do not notice the changes that are taking place in the world and in the environment of our company.* The universe is always changing, we are always changing, but we want to remain the same. What seems stable and quiet is not, and there is a flow of events that we cannot control, such as the rotation of the earth or the passage of time.

Look at these examples:

1. In 1987 there were five billion people on Earth, but 200 years before, the world's population was one billion people.
2. In 1900 only 5% of the inhabitants of Earth lived in cities; in the year 2016, more than 50% do.
3. Today the most representative or typical person in the world is from China, is male, and is 28 years old. But in 2030, that statistic will change and the most typical person will be a representative from India.†

The imponderables of chance can be estimated through probability calculations, analyzing data, and statistical models. But these calculations are never accurate, such as when estimating the production and trade of raw materials, cereals, or fuels or foreseeing potential economic, labor, and environmental movements. The future is unpredictable, uncertain, and unexpected.

The German physicist Werner Karl Heisenberg (1901–1976) won the Nobel Prize for Physics in 1932. Heisenberg formulated the *uncertainty principle*, which states that it is impossible to simultaneously measure accurately the position and velocity of a particle. The more you know about the speed of a particle, the less you know about its position.

---

* The place where we live, Earth, seems to be not moving, but it is not still. It rotates, turns, and changes. Not only does the earth orbit the sun, but it also rotates on its axis, from right to left, from west to east, and a full turn lasts 23 hours, 56 minutes, and 4 seconds. We rotate at the same speed as the earth, but we do not perceive that speed because the earth rotates at a constant speed. Earth rotates at a linear velocity, measured from Ecuador of 1,666 kilometers per hour, or about 0.5 kilometers per second. As it approaches the poles, the speed of the earth decreases.

† *The World's Most Typical Person*, National Geographic video. YouTube.

Living with uncertainty and change, organizations cannot make an accurate diagnosis or control or dominate what will happen. The facts do not have to be a linear continuation of the past. Because one cannot determine with certainty what will continue, what will change and will be new, leaders must work to adapt and be prepared for the uncertainty.

In economics and finance, the concept of *imperfect information* or *market failure* is used when one does not have complete knowledge of prices, products, and quantities. Companies are not fully aware of the risks to which they are exposed, and the information they have is imperfect.

The British mathematician Alfred Marshall (1842–1924) in his book *Principles of Economics* analyzed the functioning of markets and price formation. His method allowed him to study the effect of a given function if the other variables and factors remained *ceteris paribus*,* because otherwise, it would be difficult to disentangle the effect of each individual variable. Leaving aside all fixed variables except one allowed him to simplify reality to understand the complex phenomenon of constant change.

In 1957 the Standard's and Poor's index was created, one of the most important stock indexes in the United States. The index reflects the changes in the average value of the shares of the 500 largest companies listed on the US Stock Exchange, weighted according to the market capitalization of each.†

Of the 500 largest companies that were part of that index in 1957, only 75 were in the ranking in 2000.‡ That is to say, only 15% of the 500 companies remained in the ranking 43 years later.

It is necessary to reinvent and innovate frequently. Of the 500 companies that were part of the Fortune 500's list in 1955, only 50% remained 30 years later.

Those who win today will not necessarily win tomorrow. The business world moves with an exponential speed no one can foresee. Nothing is permanent.

In the 1940s, four out of five cars were built in America. In 1960, only half were made in America. And by 1990, less than one-fourth of the world's cars came from America.§

---

* *Ceteris paribus* means that the other factors held unmodified, constant.
† That is, the share price of each of those companies multiplied by the number of shares issued, which provides the total value of the shares of each company.
‡ Nassim Nicholas Taleb, *The Black Swan* (Random House, 2010), 308.
§ K. Blanchard, C. Schewe, B. Nelson and A. Hiam, *Exploring the World of Business* (Worth Publishers, 1996), 15.

In 2001, the five largest companies by market capitalization were General Electric, Exxon, Citi, Microsoft, and Walmart. Only one of them was technological. In 2017, the five largest companies by market capitalization are all technological: Apple, Google, Microsoft, Amazon, and Facebook.[*]

The Dow Jones Industrial Average (DJIA) is one of the stock indices created by Charles Henry Dow (1851–1902), publisher of *The Wall Street Journal* and co-founder of Dow Jones & Company.

The DJIA measures the performance of the 30 largest US-based public companies. The human resources expert, David Van Rooy, says, "Companies at the DJIA have changed forty-eight times since the index was founded in 1896. More than half of the organizations were replaced in the last twenty years."[†]

Richard N. Foster, a former executive of Mc Kinsey and Co. and author of the book *Creative Destruction*, states that by 2027, 75% of Fortune 500 companies will be companies that do not exist today.

Illegal organizations must also innovate to survive. This is the case, for example, of drug traffickers, who must innovate permanently as they distribute the drug so as not to be discovered. For example, drugs were found in rotten tomatoes covered with lithium fat to mislead drug dogs.[‡]

In 2017, the Colombian Navy found the first electric submarine used to transport cocaine in the basin of the San Juan and Baudo rivers, in the area bordering Panama. It was an 11-meter green boat that could sail 3 meters below the surface and transport up to 3 tons of coca.[§] In November 2019 another narco-submarine with 3,000 kilos of cocaine was intercepted in Spain waters.[¶]

Liquid cocaine has been found in jeans and cardboard boxes where jeans were kept. The authorities reviewed the clothes but threw the boxes, which were then picked up by the narcos to recover the drug. Cocaine is also hidden in creams and gels.[**]

---

[*] Paul Ausick, "Market Cap of 5 Largest US Companies Up 36% in Most Recent Year," October 29, 2017, finance.yahoo.com.

[†] David Van Rooy, Trajectory (Amacom [American Management Association], 2014), 129–30.

[‡] September 11, 2019, www.clarin.com.

[§] "El Submarino, el Parásito, el Pitufeo y otros Métodos que Invento Pablo Escobar para Traficar Droga y siguen Vigentes," de mayo de 12, 2019, www.infobae.com ("The Submarine, the Parasite, the Pitufeo and other Methods that Pablo Escobar invented to traffic drugs and are still in force," May 12, 2019).

[¶] "El Narcosubmarino LLevaba mas de Veinte Dias de Navegacion desde Colombia hasta Pontevedra," RTVE.ES 25 de noviembre de 2019. ("The Narco submarine had more than Twenty Days of Navigation from Colombia to Pontevedra,") RTVE, November 25, 2019.

[**] "El Submarino, el Parásito, el Pitufeo y otros Métodos que Invento Pablo Escobar para Traficar Droga y siguen Vigentes," de mayo de 12, 2019, www.infobae.com ("The Submarine, the Parasite,

The anti-narcotics police at the El Dorado International Airport in Bogotá, Colombia, confiscated a painting of the Virgin Mary and a Bible where pink cocaine was hidden (2CB).*

Organizations need to learn, take risks, and innovate to grow and change in the future.

A future that is uncertain and uncontrollable.

Neither magic nor horoscopes or astrology can provide certainty about what will happen because human beings cannot control or predict the future. We are neither Nostradamus (1503–1566)[†] nor Jules Verne (1828–1905),[‡] the magician Rasputin (1869–1916), the magician Houdini (1874–1926), Prometheus,[§] Sir Edmund Halley,[¶] Cassandra,[**] the blind Bulgarian clairvoyant Baba Vanga (1911–1996), or an old diviner of the tribe.

Throughout history, mathematicians, astrologers, prophets, physicists, cardinals, and theologians have predicted dates on which the end of the

---

the Pitufeo and other Methods that Pablo Escobar invented to traffic drugs and are still in force," May 12, 2019).

* "El Submarino, el Parásito, el Pitufeo y otros Métodos que Invento Pablo Escobar para Traficar Droga y siguen Vigentes," de mayo de 12, 2019, www.infobae.com ("The Submarine, the Parasite, the Pitufeo and other Methods that Pablo Escobar invented to traffic drugs and are still in force"), May 12, 2019; "En Biblia, Narcos Pretendian enviar 2 kilos de 2CB a EEUU," 19 de Abril de 2019 ("In the Bible, Narcos wanted to send 2 kilos of 2CB to the US," April 19, 2019), www.eltiempo.com/justicia/conflicto-y-narcotrafico/en-una-biblia-camuflaron-dos-kilos-de-cocaina-rosada-351364.

† This French physician and astrologer, whose real name was Michel de Notre dame, was one of the most famous authors of prophecies, especially after publishing in 1555 his book *Les Prophecies*, which led to the queen of France Catherine de Medici (1519–1589) summoning him to court to draw up the horoscope of their children. The son of Nostradamus was known as Nostradamus the Young, and in 1574, he predicted to the knight D'Espinay Saint Luc that the village of Pouzin in Vivarais would be destroyed by a fire. The young Nostradamus was discovered when he wanted to cause a fire to fulfill his prediction, and D'Espinay Saint Luc killed him. This story of the son of Nostradamus is mentioned on page 244 of Gregorio Doval's book *Frauds, Cheats and Tinos of History* (Nowtilius Saber, 2001).

‡ French novelist Jules Verne discovered future worlds in his novels. For example, he predicted that large cities would be illuminated by electric lights and prophesied in his novel *From the Earth to the Moon* in 1865 the arrival of man on the moon as well as the creation of the submarine and the helicopter. In 1863, he wrote a futuristic novel called *Paris in the Twentieth Century* about a young student of literature who lives in a glass skyscraper in a city where there are high-speed trains, gas cars, calculators, and a global communications network. This novel was discovered in 1989 and published in 1994.

§ Demigod of Greek mythology.

¶ In 1705 Sir Edmund Halley (1656–1742) correctly predicted that the famous comet of 1682 would return 76 years later, in December of 1758. Halley had used the Law of Universal Gravitation of Isaac Newton (1642–1727) to foresee the behavior of the comet spinning around the sun.

** In Greek mythology, Cassandra was the daughter of the king of Troy and to whom Apollo granted the gift of prophecy. en.wikipedia.org/wiki/Cassandra.

world would come, and no one has been right.* Many world personalities have opined about the impossibility of foreseeing the future. Some of them are mentioned in this footnote.†

The prediction and precise prognosis of certain events that will happen in the future are not possible as there is no astrologer, oracle, seer, prophet, or Wall Street analyst‡ who has a special power to anticipate future events and who can accurately predict the future.

In 1972, an international group of academics calling themselves "The Club of Rome" published a report, funded by the Volkswagen Foundation, called *The Limits to Growth*. Since its publication, some 30 million copies of the book in 30 languages have been purchased. After reviewing their computer simulations, the research team came to the conclusion that given business, as usual, the limits to growth on earth would become evident by 2072. The report has been criticized by academics, economists, and businessmen. Critics claimed that history proved the projections to be incorrect, which was based on the belief that the book predicted economic collapse by the end of the twentieth century.§

---

* In the book *Frauds, Cheats and Tinos of History* (Nowtilus Saber, 2011), 223–28, Gregorio Doval mentions the names of more than 30 people who predicted dates for the end of the world. See also Massimo Polidoro, *Enigmas and Mysteries of History, Review*, April 2014, 229–34.

† 1 – Professor Paul Samuelson (1915–2009) was the first individual winner of a Nobel Prize in Economics in 1970. Samuelson said that it was not possible to predict the future. Humorously, he said: "Economists have correctly predicted nine of the last five recessions."

2 – Niels Henrik Bohr (1885–1962), a physicist born in Denmark who made contributions to understanding the atomic structure and quantum mechanics and in 1922 won the Nobel Prize in Physics, joked by pointing out that "forecasting is very difficult, especially if it is about the future."

3 – Lawrence "Yogi" Berra (1925–2015), a famous American baseball player who played 19 seasons in Major League Baseball (MLB), humorously said, "It is difficult to make predictions, especially about the future."

4 – Winston Churchill (1874–1965) said, "The politician must be able to predict what is going to happen tomorrow, next month and next year and explain later why it was that what he predicted did not happen."

5 – Alvin Toffler (1928–2016), considered the "world's most famous futurologist" by the *Financial Times*, author of *The Third Wave* and *Future Shock*, said "anyone who says that can predict the future is probably a member of the club of charlatans, because human events are full of surprises and casualty, conflicts, setbacks, and disorders."

6 – Peter Drucker (1909–2005) said, "all we know is that the future will be different."

7 – Charles Handy, Irish thinker, said, "you cannot see the future as a continuation of the past because the future will be different. … We have to get rid of the way we handled the past to be able to handle the future."

8 – The Uruguayan Fernando Parrado, a survivor of the tragedy of the Andes of October 13, 1972, has said: "It is not known what will happen tomorrow," *La Nacion*, October 30, 2008, ExpoManagement.

‡ Wall Street firms employ analysts whose job is to predict the future. They produce estimates for both revenue and EPS for major companies.

§ "The Limits to Growth," Wikipedia.

There are no statistics, algorithms, theorems of probabilities, laws of large numbers, or mathematical models that can project trends about the future without mistakes. Although you cannot predict or know the future with precision, corporate leaders however have to prepare and try to anticipate what will come.

Leaders should try to understand the environment, trends, and innovations. They should try to detect changes that may be either a business opportunity or a competitive nightmare. But also, a leader must be always prepared to anticipate and manage the ethics and compliance risks to which any organization is exposed.

You should always be ready to anticipate and reduce uncertainty.

It is called "futurology," the science that studies the future and plans actions to influence it. It analyzes the causes of changes to try to improve possible future scenarios and determine their probability.[*]

Some professionals, centers, and organizations exist that investigate or have investigated the dangers and risks of the future. For example, the Centre for the Study of Existential Risk is a research center at the University of Cambridge, England, that was created for the study of disasters and risks that threaten the human species.[†] Also, the World Future Society (WFS), founded in 1966, is the largest organization in the field of the future and has members in more than 80 countries. Based in Maryland, the WFS investigates how technological and economic developments are shaping the future and through the magazine *The Futurist* tries to explain the changes.

The World Economic Forum in its annual report, called *Global Risk Report*, each year describes the overall risks in the world; i.e., events that could cause a negative impact on different countries or industries in the next ten years. The World Economic Forum asks 800 experts each year what those risks are and their degree of likelihood and impact. For example, conflicts between states, the water crisis, data theft, climate change, unemployment, epidemics,[‡] the price of oil, weapons of mass destruction, and the food crisis, among others, are mentioned.

The Chinese philosopher Confucius (551–479 BC) believed that the key to long-lasting integrity was to constantly think since the world is continually changing at a rapid pace.[§]

---

[*] The Polish writer Stanislaw Lem (1921–2006) took care of the problems of the future and cybernetics and in the 1960s wrote *Summa Technologiae*, a philosophical essay trying to "examine the thorns of the roses yet to flourish."

[†] The founders of the center were Huw Price (professor at the University of Cambridge), Sir Martin Rees (astronomer), and Jaan Tallinn (co-founder of Skype).

[‡] The Spanish flu of 1918 took 20 million lives.

[§] en.wikipedia.org/wiki/Ren_(Confucianism).

British scientist Sir Arthur Clarke (1917–2008), author of science fiction works as *2001: A Space Odyssey*, said, "The only way to discover the limits of the possible is to go beyond them into the impossible."*

In a few years, the world will be very different. Can we adapt to the pace of current change?

Thomas Friedman[†] says all the knowledge centers on the planet are connecting to a global network,[‡] wherein the strongest and the fastest will survive. Friedman tells that a Chinese manager of a fuel pump factory in Beijing posted the following African fable translated into Mandarin, on his factory floor:

Every morning in Africa, a gazelle wakes up.
It knows it must run faster than the fastest lion or it will be killed.
Every morning a lion wakes up.
It knows it must outrun the slowest gazelle or it will starve to death.
It doesn't matter whether you're a lion or gazelle.
When the sun comes up, you'd better be running.[§]

Like a ping-pong ball or as a tennis player running after every ball, companies have to move constantly to be able to stay in the game.

When an organization perceives change threatening certainty, there is some resistance in the system because change threatens stability and balance. But even if the company is very large, if it does not adapt, it runs the risk of extinction. The dinosaurs were large, dominated the earth, and became extinct. The dodo bird did not adapt to change and also disappeared.[¶] Civilizations of the past, such as the Roman Empire, ceased to exist.

An armadillo crossing a night route is paralyzed by the lights of the trucks, does not adapt to the changing environment, does not move, and dies by being run over.

---

* www.brainyquote.com.
[†] Friedman is a journalist for *The New York Times* and a Pulitzer Prize winner. The Pulitzer Prizes are awarded for achievements in journalism, literature, and musical composition in the United States. They were established in 1917 under the provisions of the will of the Hungarian-born American publisher Joseph Pulitzer, and Columbia University in New York City is in charge of their administration.
[‡] Thomas Friedman, *The World Is Flat: A Brief History of the Globalized World in the 21st Century* (Penguin Allen Lane, 2005).
[§] Thomas Friedman, *The World Is Flat* (Picador Edition, 2007), 137.
[¶] The dodo is an extinct species of flightless bird of Mauritius in the Indian Ocean. The extinction of the dodo in the late seventeenth century has become the archetype of extinct species by humans.

The British naturalist Charles Robert Darwin (1809–1882) wrote the book *The Origin of Species in Terms of Natural Selection* in 1859. Darwin said that "It is not the strongest species that survives, nor the most intelligent that survives. It is the one that is the most adaptable to change."*

Although changes may be uncomfortable, in a hostile, unpredictable, and complex environment, of unprecedented changes, it is necessary to adapt and change to survive. Roberto Goizueta (1932–1997) was the chairman of the board and CEO of the Coca Cola Company from 1980 to 1997, and under his leadership, the company became the number one corporation in the United States. Goizueta said: "What has always been will not necessarily always be forever."†

In 2000, Yahoo was much bigger than Google. That year, Yahoo had a market value of US$125 billion and Google of around US$1 billion. But in 2016 Google had a market value of US$500 billion and Yahoo was sold to Verizon for lightly more than US$4 billion, or less than 4% of Yahoo's market value in 2000.

Since 2000, American newspapers have lost 40% of their daily circulation. With the internet, journalism is suffering from a strong reconversion, like most companies.

The Greek historian Herodotus (484–425 BC) said that "circumstances rule men, men do not rule circumstances."‡

Companies must be able to change quickly based on external circumstances because the change from the outside of the company has been coming at an ever-increasing speed. Business leaders must be vigilant and detect changes in the environment to adapt, accommodate, change with, and move with them. Leaders must be protagonists and not victims of change. They must continue to innovate. Although things have worked so far, this is not an excuse not to keep changing and leave the security of the known. Living is moving. The slower we move, the greater the risk of disappearing.

The lawyer, Austrian writer, and consultant Peter Drucker (1909–2005) has said that "To survive and succeed, every organization will have to turn itself into a change agent. The most effective way to manage change is to create it."§

---

* www.wealthygorilla.com.

† www.brainyquote.com

‡ www.brainyquote.com/quotes/herodotus_131102.

§ www.fastcompany.com.

Sam Walton (1920–1992) pointed out "You can't just keep doing what works one time. Everything around you is changing. To succeed, stay out in front of change."*

At Walmart's Annual Shareholders Meeting, Doug McMillon, CEO of Walmart, said in 2014:

> We will lead with urgency to get ahead of change. ... We can think about it in three parts: *now, new* and *always*. We need to get better at what we're already doing *now*. We also need to invent the *new*, to bring together the digital world of eCommerce with the physical world of our stores. And we will *always* stay true to Walmart's purpose and values.

To generate change, we must think critically about the status quo and challenge existing paradigms in an organization, because the circumstances and context are constantly changing.

At one time, to perform an experiment, five monkeys were left in a room. In the middle of the room, the experimenters placed a ladder and, on top of the ladder, a bunch of bananas. Each time one of the monkeys went up the stairs to look for bananas, the experimenters sprinkled the rest of the monkeys with a jet of cold water. After a while, the monkeys assimilated the connection between climbing the ladder and cold running water, and when one of them started up the stairs in search of bananas, the rest of the monkeys prevented him violently. It got to the point that no monkey wanted to climb the ladder to get the bunch of bananas.

The experimenters removed one of the original five monkeys, introduced a new one into the room and stopped spraying cold water. The new monkey tried to climb quickly up the stairs in search of bananas, but as the others noted its intentions, they pounced on him and beat him down without the jet of ice water making its appearance. After the new monkey repeated this experience several times, it understood that it was better to give up climbing the ladder.

Then the experimenters replaced, one by one, the initial monkeys that had felt the jet of cold water. Under the blows received by the old monkeys, the new monkeys who entered the room refused to climb the ladder to find the bananas.

There came a time when all the old monkeys from the initial experiment had been replaced, and none of the remaining had ever received a stream

* www.azquotes.com.

of ice water. The experimenters found that none of the new monkeys dared to climb the ladder to grab bananas because they would receive blows from the other monkeys for no reason since none of them had been sprinkled with running cold water. They did not go up to get the bananas just because the situation had always been like this.

The experiment, true or not,* mentioned by professors Gary Hamel and K. Prahalad in their book *Competing for the Future*, graphically poses why things are done in a certain way, without modifying or challenging the status quo.

A leader must ask why a certain control or process is in place or why there is no other or none. Sometimes certain policies and processes exist only because they once were effective. It is imperative to challenge and distrust existing procedures. The American inventor Thomas Alva Edison (1847–1931) challenged the status quo. When an employee asked him to explain the process to perform a task, Edison replied: "Hell, there are no rules here. We are trying to accomplish something!"[†]

Lyall Watson (1939–2008) was a South African botanist, biologist, and zoologist. In 1979 he published *Lifetide: The Biology of the Unconscious*, a book in which he recounts an experiment with a colony of monkeys on an island near Japan. Watson wanted to change the feeding of the monkeys, so they fed them potatoes. But as the monkeys noted that potatoes were dirty with earth and sand, the animals rejected them. After a while, a young monkey washed a potato in the river and ate it. Over time, the young monkey taught other young monkeys how to wash the potatoes. First, just a group did so, but then many other monkeys imitated them and washed the potatoes.

The day the 100th monkey washed and ate the potato, a strange phenomenon was observed; all other monkeys began to wash the food massively. The critical mass was 100 monkeys; from there, the information spread at high speed, and the change was massive.[‡] The *100th monkey effect* was the name of the hypothetical phenomenon by which a new behavior or idea spreads quickly, by unexplained means, once the idea and behavior reach a group of 100 people.

Successful companies challenge the comfort zone of the familiar, comfortable, and stable, and they embrace innovation and change. Noting

---

* "That Five Monkeys Experiment Never Happened," www.throwcase.com.
† www.brainyquote.com.
‡ The Indian doctor Deepak Chopra popularized this legend.

the changing environment, one will be better prepared to adapt and be proactive to change behaviors, systems, and processes.* All processes can be improved, constantly challenged, and rethought to be effective in solving problems.

For the January 2000 Super Bowl, 14 dot-com companies paid an average of US$2.2 million per television spot. In the Super Bowl the following year, and with the crisis of the internet bubble, only three dot-com companies paid for ads.

The former US president Dwight Eisenhower (1890–1969) said: "The world moves and ideas that were once good are not always good."† The world, the environment, and life are not linear. The future is different from the past that we know. The past is that past and the future has curves we cannot predict or forecast just because we know the past.

Organizations face uncertainty and to mitigate risks, companies obtain data and information to evaluate options to a given situation. The data came from the past and there is no guarantee that the future will behave in the same way. Success and performance in the past do not guarantee success and performance in the future, because the future is not written, and no one can predict with certainty what will happen. However, using data and information from the past is better than not using it. Any situation can change rapidly from positive to negative due to the presence of unlikely events. After the US President Donald Trump sent an unexpected tweet where he said "I'm a Tariff Man" (I am a man of tariffs) in the middle of a trade war with China, stocks on Wall Street immediately retreated more than 3%.‡

In life, it is necessary to manage uncertainty. The former president of the People's Republic of China Mao Tse Tung (1893–1976) said that "There are no straight roads in the world; we must be prepared to follow a winding road"§ and Archibald Joseph Cronin (1896–1981), a Scottish novelist and physician, said that "life is not a straight and easy corridor we travel free and unhampered, but a maze of passages."¶

---

* The "Global Innovation Index" (GII), prepared by INSEAD, Cornell University, and the World Intellectual Property Organization, compares the environment for innovation and change in different countries. Switzerland, England, Sweden, the United States, the Netherlands, Finland, and Singapore led the ranking of the GII of 2015.
† www.eisenhower.archives.gov.
‡ "Stock Markets Plunge after Trump's Tariff Man Tweet," NYPost.com, December 4, 2018. The Dow Jones dropped 3.1% and Nasdaq fell 3.8%.
§ "10 Frases Célebres de Mao," www.muyinteresante.es ("10 Famous Phrases of Mao").
¶ www.goodreads.com.

Statistics deals with analyzing and interpreting data and drawing conclusions from observations, but one cannot totally rely on them to predict the future. In the eighteenth century, the Marshal Duque de Lorges suffered from gallstones and found out there was a Dominican friar named Jacques Beaulieu who treated this pathology by performing an operation. The marshal did not trust the healer, so he decided to find 20 patients with the same disease and submitted them to the operation. All of them healed within a few weeks. This made the Duke of Lorges gain confidence and had the friar operate on him. However, the duke died the day after the operation.[*]

The American writer Mark Twain (1835–1910) said that "there are three kinds of lies: lies, damned lies, and statistics."[†]

Ram Charan, a consultant born in India, a Harvard professor, and advisor of global corporations, in a talk organized some years ago by the World Business Forum in Buenos Aires, said, "Uncertainty is here to stay. There is no perfect forecast. Think about how to work on offense."

In the ambiguous and complex world in which we live, a leader must be prepared to face storms, because what has been projected can change quickly and if reasonable preventive measures are not taken in time, the company will fall into quicksand.

Patrick Dixon, a British futurologist, author of the book *Futurewise*, said,

> The risk of a business being hit by a low probability, high impact event is far higher than most boards realize because the number of potential wild cards is so great … take hold of the future or the future will take hold of you.[‡]

Singularity University is an institution that is located in Silicon Valley, founded in 2008 by the North American inventor Raymond Kurzweil. It educates leaders in technology to develop solutions to the problems of humanity. Singularity University raises the question: "Are you ready for the coming changes?"

That question is what any businessman must pursue permanently. Sometimes leaders do not interpret the changes that are taking place and that may be happening behind their backs.

---

[*] Manuel J. Prieto, *Curistoria: Curiosidades y Anécdotas de la Historia* (Evohe Ddaska, 2008), 18 ("Curiosities and Anecdotes of History").

[†] en.wikipedia.org/wiki/Lies,_damned_lies,_and_statistics.

[‡] Patrick Dixon, "32 Mind-blowing Patrick Dixon Quotes," December 23, 2016, brandongaille.com.

Plato (427–347 BC) was for ten years a disciple of Socrates (470–399 BC).[*] In the book *The Republic*, Plato explains the *Allegory of the Cave*. A group of men have been imprisoned in a cave since birth, with chains that hold their necks and legs so that men can only look to the wall that is in the back of the cave, unable to turn their heads.

Plato says that behind the chained prisoners there is a fire that illuminates the cave and a corridor where people walk with different objects. The chained men can see only the shadows of people and objects reflected on the wall of the cave, and they believe these shadows of objects are the only truth. But when one of the prisoners is released, he sees that the reality is very different outside the cave, different from what the rest of the prisoners see.[†]

As if they were in the cavern, or in an ivory tower, or in a palace or on top of the mountain, leaders working in the headquarters of companies may have a particular and inaccurate perspective and point of view on what is happening in the organization. Sometimes from the cavern of the corporate office, executives believe they know what is happening in and around the organization, but many times the reality is they do not know the changes that occur at full speed inside and outside it. Sometimes the perception they have is that everything is under control and that the information received is reliable. But it can be an illusion. Reality may be different, and what they think is happening is different from what is actually happening.

Many times in organizations the higher you climb the corporate ladder, the more distant you are of the reality of what happens in the various business units. You receive partial, distorted, and limited information, which is taken as the only truth.

Referring to the importance of information and transparency, former United States Court of Justice Judge Louis Brandeis (1856–1941) said, "Sunlight is said to be the best of disinfectants."[‡]

As noted by the writer and pedagogue Jaime Barylko (1936–2002), "We are surrounded by appearances. . . . You want to know the truth, what is hidden behind appearances. In Greek it is said Aletheia, the des-covered, that is, the truth."[§]

---

[*] His name was "Aristocles" but called him Plato because of his broad shoulders. Plato was an athlete who at some time was sold as a slave. He founded a philosophical school called Academy, in the gardens of the Greek hero Akademos in Athens.

[†] Allegory of the Cave, Wikipedia; "Plato's Cave Allegory by Markus Maurer."

[‡] "Justice Louis Brandeis," www.brandeis.edu.

[§] Jaime Barylko, *The Philosophy* (Planet Booket, 1997), 10.

Andy Grove (1936–2016), former CEO of Intel, said, "Most CEOs are in the center of a fortified palace and news from the outside has to percolate through layers of people from the periphery where the action is."*

Knowing how to listen is a key aspect for the best functioning of any organization. Become a good listener can be a great challenge. A good leader listens to his collaborators and asks the right questions. Whoever feels heard increases their self-esteem and their commitment to the leader. Also, the act of listening allows knowing concerns and significantly reduces potential conflicts. By listening we allow other people to express their views, we show our attention and help to create a positive bond between the parties. The best leaders also listen to their customers because they know they can get new ideas from them to innovate and improve. We have two ears and one mouth because we are supposed to listen twice as much as we talk.

Walmart founder Samuel Moore Walton (1920–1992) understood that well. He told his managers in the home office, "Listen to those who work in our stores. They know what's going on."

The Hindu consultant Ram Charan said that "If leaders are not connected with reality, they fail."

Chilean psychiatrist Claudio Naranjo has pointed out, "Ignorance is not seeing what happens. It's blindness."†

Richard Buetow (1931–2002), former director of quality at Motorola, said, "I do not sit on top of a mountain and get these visions of what we ought to do. I have to find out from other people. I have to do a lot of listening."

When Louis Gerstner took over as top executive at IBM, he started listening to customers. He talked to thousands of customers and he told his top 24 managers to, as he put it, "bear hug" five customers and report on their findings. Each manager told his employees to bear hug more customers, and so on until everyone was talking to customers.‡

Duke Energy's president and CEO, James E. Rogers, instituted a series of what he called "listening sessions" when he was the CEO and chairman of Cinergy (which later merged with Duke). Meeting with groups of 90–100 managers in three-hour sessions, he invited participants to raise any pressing issues. Through these discussions, he gleaned information that

---

* thewaiterspad.com.

† Congreso del Futuro 2017. Santiago de Chile ("Congress of the Future 2017").

‡ K. Blanchard, C. Schewe, B. Nelson and A. Hiam, *Exploring the World of Business* (Worth Publishers, 1996), 22.

might otherwise have escaped his attention. At one session, for example, he heard from a group of supervisors about a problem related to uneven compensation. Having heard about the conflict directly from those affected by the problem, he could instruct his HR department to find a solution right away.[*]

The consultant David Cottrell in his book *Monday Morning Leadership* refers to the situation that is generated in the *management land*, where things are not always what they seem.[†] In management land, people easily lose perspective, and it is difficult to discover the truth of what happens on the periphery. A leader must escape the management land and be in touch with the truth.

When companies do not have adequate control systems, managers located in the headquarters are probably the last to know about the problems, and they will know only a portion of what actually happens.

The Institute of Business Ethics has noticed that

> There is often a disconnection between the perception senior leadership has of the issues and those of their employees. Those at the top tend to overestimate the level of communications around ethical issues within their organizations and as a result, are somewhat biased about how well the issues are addressed on the ground. Closing the gap in perceptions between leaders and their workforce is crucial in effectively implementing ethics into all parts of an organization.[‡]

Risks, as well as customer needs, change. Organizations must implement adequate warning and alarm systems that allow them to access real-time information. These control systems are essential to shed light on the dark and allow leaders to make quick reactions to negative events. Companies cannot ignore uncertainty and assume their companies operate in stable and predictable environments.

Leaders must be prepared to prevent and deal with the unexpected and improbable because those can affect their business strategy. Leaders should do as the prisoner released from the cavern, get out of the dark and see the light of reality, leave management land and escape from appearances. They must observe around them, listen and understand the environment, so

---

[*] Boris Groysberg and Michael Slind, "Leadership Is a Conversation," *Harvard Business Review,* June 2012, hbr.org/2012/06/leadership-is-a-conversation.

[†] David Cottrell, *Monday Morning Leadership* (CornerStone Leadership Institute, 2002), 37.

[‡] "The 4 Key Business Ethics Themes You Need to be Aware of in 2018," Simon Webley IBE Research Director, Institute of Business Ethics, March 2, 2018.

they are not surprised by the innovation of their competitors and/or by the lack of compliance with legal orders or the lack of ethics of its employees, partners, or suppliers.

Small changes in the business environment can generate modifications in the services, products, business strategy, or risk management. With the coming of new technologies and globalization, companies and industries can suddenly become obsolete.

American economist and engineer Michael Porter, a professor at Harvard University, points out that without a well-crafted plan, one cannot survive in the business world.* The lack of understanding of abrupt changes in the competitive environment can lead to failure in the execution of a business strategy.

Companies that do not change, do not adapt, or have a rigid response to the changing environment can disappear or lose drastic market share, so the anticipation of crises is a great competitive advantage. Changes are occurring at a faster pace and companies need to stay a step ahead of trends to be competitive.

In *Capitalism, Socialism, and Democracy*, the Austrian economist Joseph Schumpeter (1883–1950) popularized the term *creative destruction* to describe "the process of industrial mutation that incessantly revolutionizes the economic structure from within, incessantly destroying the old one, incessantly creating a new one."†

Technology becomes obsolete if companies do not adapt fast to the new business environment. Companies that once revolutionized and dominated new industries saw their profits fall and their domain vanished when their competitors launched improved products.

The disruptive transformation process accompanies innovation.

As Professor Connel Fullenkamp said, "The typewriter business was destroyed by the introduction of personal computers and film business was destroyed by the introduction of digital photography."‡ The explosion of the internet in the 1990s increased the range of media choices available and many magazines and newspapers disappeared around the world.

---

* Porter analyzes the five market forces that can threaten an industry: (i) the threat of new competitors entering the market, (ii) rivalry between competitors, (iii) threat of substitute products, (iv) the power of supplier negotiation, and (v) the bargaining power of consumers.
† en.wikipedia.org/wiki/Creative_destruction.
‡ Professor Connel Fullenkamp, *The Economics of Uncertainty*, Lecture 22, The Great Courses (2015), 155.

The cassette tape replaced the 8-track, only to be replaced in turn by the compact disk, which was undercut by downloads to MP3 players, which is now being usurped by web-based streaming services.*

Companies like Kodak, Pan Am, Concorde, People Express, Blackberry, Polaroid, Tower Records, Toys R US, Daewoo, Yahoo, Motorola, Nokia, Atari, AOL, MySpace.com, Palm, Sears, and Blockbuster were leading companies for years, but they didn't innovate on time.

Some of those companies collapsed and went bankrupt, and others are on the verge of extinction. The history of these slow-moving companies is a warning light that shows us nothing is forever.

Leaders need to be open to seeking input and stay in touch with fresh opinions and perspectives. As Brigette Hyacinth says, "Titans as Blackberry, Kodak and Nokia have paid the price for leaders who refused to listen. Their leaders operated in a bubble."†

When someone is arrogant, indifferent to others, and self-centered, that person can be considered narcissistic. In Greek mythology, Narcissus was a young man who fell so much in love with himself that he drowned while trying to kiss his image reflected in the clear water of a lake.

Companies with a narcissistic culture do not look at what happens around them because they believe that nothing they can learn from their competitors.

When Narcissus was born, his mother, Liripe, took him to the blind prophet Tiresias and asked him for a prophecy, "Will he have a long life?" He responded with, "He'll have a long life as long as he never knows himself."‡

Perhaps, as some people think, what the prophet meant was that Narcissus would have a long life if he did not love himself so much. Companies will have a long life if they stop looking at themselves, they learn about what is happening around them and execute the best ideas, even if they are not their own.

Many companies find it hard to innovate; they stay in their micro-world and ignore the changes around them. They prefer tradition to innovation.

Managers of large and midsized companies need to adopt the entrepreneurial spirit of smaller companies to gain the flexibility and

---

* en.wikipedia.org/wiki/Creative_destruction. Warner Music reveals streaming income has overtaken downloads, *The Guardian*, May 12, 2015.
† Brigette Hyacinth, "Never punish loyal employees for being honest," July 18, 2018.
‡ "The Second Story of Echo and Narcissus," October 29, 2012, https://thelastpsychiatrist.com/2012/10/the_story_of_narcissus.html.

creativity to pursue new opportunities or avoid new problems. Innovation involves changes in products, in the quality of the work process, and in the empowering of employees.*

If you miss a critical bend on the road, you may never catch up. While Nescafe was focusing on changing their coffee cans, Starbucks became America's number one coffee brand.

Hungarian Andy Grove (1936–2016), co-founder of Intel, said that "In the future, there will be two kinds of companies, the fast and the dead."† "Business success contains the seed of its own destruction. The more successful you are, the more people want a chunk of your business and then another chunk and then another until there is nothing."‡

David Glass (1935–2020), a former CEO of Walmart Stores, gave *Fortune* magazine in 2004 the following example:

> Kmart was better than any of us. But it did so well that one of its executives said in the latter part of the 70s that the only way they were vulnerable was if they changed from what they were doing. So, they just decreed that no one could change anything. They sat for about five years running stores but did not change a thing. All of us copied everything they were doing and improved upon it. Kmart woke up five years down the road, looked around and saw there were retailers better than they were. They just never caught up.§

US investor David S. Rose has said that "Any company designed for success in the 20th century is doomed to failure in the 21st."¶

The German Michael Ritter, an expert communication consultant, says,

> Perhaps the greatest external threat to corporate reputation lies in the organization itself and in its inability to analyze the changing environment, to understand how it can affect it and how it will evolve in the near future, fundamental aspects that allow the anticipation of critical issues emerging from these changes.**

* K. Blanchard, C. Schewe, B. Nelson and A. Hiam, *Exploring the World of Business* (Worth Publishers, 1996), 28.
† "Business Expertise," www.e-bigfish.com.
‡ Andrew Grove quotes, www.goodreads.com.
§ "The Most Underrated CEO Ever," *Fortune*, April 5, 2004, 24.
¶ "David S, Rose," www.goodreads.com/quotes.
** "El Valor del Capital Reputacional" (Olivos, Ritter & Partners, 2013), 237 ("The Value of Capital Reputation").

William C. Ashley, professor at Northwestern University, and James L. Morrison, professor of educational leadership at the University of North Carolina, wrote *Anticipatory Management: 10 Power Tools for Achieving Excellence into the 21st Century*, in 1995, in which they say:

> Even big organizations with considerable internal resources have failed to anticipate dramatic outside shifts and have faced the unanticipated checkmate. For example, GM failed to heed signals in the late 1960s of a potential energy crisis, as well as the increasing attractiveness of small, fuel-efficient Japanese cars. Ignoring these signals cost GM almost 30% of its U.S. market share.
>
> Sears in the 1970s continued to "fiddle" with self-branded merchandise, monolithic department stores, and catalog delivery systems, while customers asked for name-brand merchandise and for more quality in products and services.[*]

The history of quartz wristwatches is yet another example of how we should address signals and react to threats in the environment. As explained by the consultant Joel Baker:

> In 1968 the Swiss had more than 65% of unit sales in the world market for watches and 80% of profits. They were the world leaders in the manufacture of watches. By 1980, its market share had dropped from 65% to 10%.
>
> What happened? The mechanical mechanism was about to give way to the electronic mechanism.
>
> It was the Swiss who invented the electronic quartz movement at their research institute in Neuchatel, Switzerland, but when they introduced the revolutionary idea to Swiss watchmakers in 1967, it was rejected.
>
> After all, it did not have springs, it did not need shafts, it did not require gears, it worked with batteries, and it was electronic.
>
> The researchers exhibited their invention at the World Congress of Watchmaking, Seiko saw it and the rest is history.[†]
>
> For Japan, which had less than 1% of the world clock market in 1968, it was a unique opportunity.[‡]

---

[*] www.horizon.unc.edu.

[†] At Christmas in 1969, the Seiko Quartz-Astron 35SQ was presented, the first quartz wristwatch on the market, which lost only five seconds each month. Made of gold, its price was US$1,250, the price of a car. Its launch slogan was "Someday, all clocks will be like this." In 1920, Warren Marrison and J. W. Horton built the first quartz watch at Bell Telephone Laboratories. Seiko used his Quartz Crystal QC-591 model to time the Tokyo Olympics in 1964. But in 1967, the first two prototypes of quartz wristwatches, Beta 1, appeared.

[‡] Joel Arthur Barker, *Paradigms* (McGraw Hill, 1999), 20.

Everything that the Swiss were good at – the manufacture of gears, axles, and springs – was now irrelevant.

In less than ten years, the Swiss future in making watches, which seemed so safe, so profitable, so dominant, was destroyed. Between 1979 and 1981, fifty thousand of the sixty-two thousand Swiss watch manufacturers lost their jobs.[*]

Taoism is a philosophy of life system that has influenced the Far East for 5,000 years based on the teachings of the Chinese philosopher Lao Tse. Lao Tse said, "If you realize that all things change, there is nothing that you will try to hold on to."[†]

Nokia, a Finland's telecom company, was for 14 years the leader in the global telephone market. However, its belated evolution and lack of insight into new trends led it to lose 63% of market share by the end of 2007. Nokia was forced to lay off 20,000 employees and was on the verge of bankruptcy in 2012 because it did not know how to get on the fast and thriving train of smartphones and tablets in due course.

In 2013 at the press conference where it was announced that Microsoft was acquiring the Nokia phone division, Stephen Elop, Nokia's CEO, finished his message by saying, "We did not do anything wrong, but somehow, we lost."[‡]

In his bestseller *Who Moved My Cheese?* Spencer Johnson said, "Smell the cheese often so you know when it is getting old."[§]

Jeff Bezos, Amazon's CEO, has said that "The dangerous thing is not to evolve."[¶]

Jack Welch, ex-CEO of General Electric, said:

If the rate of change on the outside exceeds the rate of change on the inside, then the end is near. Today the rate of change is eclipsing most organizations and they can't keep up.[**]

Doug McMillon, CEO of Walmart, pointed out:

This is a period of significant change at Walmart. I think the pace and magnitude of our changes are critical to the company's future as we adapt to

---

[*] Joel Arthur Baker, *Paradigms* (McGraw Hill, 1999), 18–19.
[†] "Lao Tzu," www.brainyquote.com.
[‡] www.leadership-choices.com.
[§] www.goodreads.com/work/quotes/3332594-who-moved-my-cheese.
[¶] "5 Frases de Jack Welch," www.crearmiempresa.es ("5 Jack Welch quotes").
[**] "Jack Welch Got It Right … Even for Customers," www.ceotoceo.com.

an environment that is changing more quickly all the time. We are changing how we work and what we do without changing our purpose and our
values.*

Are business leaders prepared to react to changes in the environment?

Change is difficult, but the world evolves quickly, and to survive you have
to adapt. Companies that live by staring at their navel will lose. Because
nothing is permanent, organizations must be prepared to react, adapt, and
change all the time; otherwise, they may end badly.

Kodak invented digital technology for photo cameras in 1975, but Kodak
did not know or could not or did not want to carry out the change so as
not to affect the photographic film business. Ninety percent of its income
came from the sale of photo rolls.

Adaptability is necessary to manage change.

Sometimes companies sell very successful products, but suddenly a new
trend appears and the company must decide whether or not to invest in it.
If this new trend is finally consolidated and the company has not invested
on time, it may be too late to change.

One of the great resistances to change is precisely that sometimes we can
refuse to see the world as it is. The Italian political philosopher Nicholas
Machiavelli (1469–1527) said, "Men will not look at things as they really
are, but as they wish them to be and are ruined."[†]

William Deming (1900–1993) was an American engineer and university
professor, diffuser of the concept of total quality, and his name is linked
to the development of Japan after World War II. Deming taught Japanese
managers how to use statistics to assess and improve quality.

PDCA (plan, do, check, adjust) is a four-step management method used
for the control and continuous improvement of processes and products.
PDCA is also known as Deming Cycle, although Deming always referred
to it as the *Shewhart Cycle*.[‡] For Deming, continuous improvement should
be a permanent goal in organizations.[§]

---

* "What I've learned since becoming CEO," Walmart CEO, Letter to Shareholders, 2019 Annual
  Report.
† Niccolo Machiavelli Quotes, www.goodreads.com/quotes.
‡ American engineer Walter A. Shewhart (1891–1967).
§ The Deming Prize is the longest-running and one of the highest awards on TQM (Total Quality
  Management) in the world. It recognizes both individuals for their contributions to the field of
  TQM and businesses that have successfully implemented TQM. It was established in 1951 to honor
  W. Edwards Deming. His teachings helped Japan build its foundation by which the level of Japan's
  product quality has been recognized as one of the highest in the world. en.wikipedia.org/wiki/
  Deming_Prize.

The consultant Rafael Aguayo, a student of the Deming method, has written: "Sometimes a radical change can only be accepted when disaster strikes. People simply are not willing to throw away their old ideas and adopt radically different ones when everything seems to be acceptable, or not too bad."*

The context changes and the company must change and what worked in the past may not work anymore in the future. As noted earlier, the manufacturers of Swiss mechanical watches did not attend or understand the threat, did not react or adapt to change.

In 1522 in Bicocca, west of Milan, the Spanish soldiers clashed against their French and Swiss enemies. As part of the French army, there were 15,000 Swiss mercenaries. On the Spanish side were 4,000 arquebusiers. The Swiss advanced against the imperial soldiers while the arquebusiers fired without ceasing. The Swiss withdrew with 3,000 casualties while the Spaniards suffered none. This battle began to show the efficiency of the arquebus† compared to the arms of the time and changed war in Europe.‡

During World War II, a Mongol cavalry corps faced a German infantry division on November 17, 1941, in Mussino, southwest of Klim, in Russia. The Mongol cavalry raised their sabers and launched 2,500 meters from the Germans at a gallop. On the snow-covered fields of Mussino, a terrible spectacle began. Riders flew through the air. Horses are killed by grenades and machine guns. Two thousand horses and riders of the two regiments of the 44th Mongolian Cavalry Division lay dead on the snow. In that battle, 2,000 Mongolian soldiers and no German soldiers died. The Mongols realized that fighting on horseback was no longer effective.

A leader should not fall into a *cognitive catch*, a phenomenon of blindness due to lack of attention, whereby the observer is too focused on a task and not on the environment that surrounds it.

Neurologist and psychiatrist Austro-Hungarian Rudolf Balint (1874–1929) said,

> It is a well-known phenomenon that we do not notice anything happening in our surroundings while being absorbed in the inspection of something; focusing our attention on a certain object may happen to such an extent

---

* Rafael Aguayo, *The Deming Method* (Vergara, 1993), 174.
† The arquebus was a form of long gun that appeared in Europe during the fifteenth century. An infantryman armed with an arquebus is called an arquebusier.
‡ From that battle comes the expression "this is a bicocca" to express something that is easy or cheap. Manuel J. Prieto, *Curistoria: Curiosities and Anecdotes of History* (Evohe Ddaska, 2008), 84.

that we cannot perceive other objects placed in the peripheral parts of our visual field.*

Change blindness is a perceptual phenomenon that occurs when a change is introduced, and the observer does not notice or detect it.

Ulrich Neisser (1928–2012) was a German psychologist, considered the father of cognitive psychology, i.e., the mental processes linked to knowledge. In 1975 Neisser asked five students from Cornell University to watch a video in which two groups of three basketball players passed the ball. One group of players had white shirts and the other black. The students watching the video had to count how many times the target players passed the ball. The five students who watched the video focused so much on the direction of the ball that only one of them noticed a gorilla-clad individual walking through among the basketball players as they made the passes. Neisser's experiment[†] served to demonstrate that people intently focused on an area or subject do not see changes because they have "blindness for lack of attention."[‡]

Daniel James Simons is a professor in the Department of Psychology at the University of Illinois and is known for his studies on change blindness and how people can be unaware of information right in front of their eyes. His studies have revealed how people can fail to notice unusual events when their attention is too focused on other tasks and the new events are unexpected. For example, in one situation, an experimenter was asking directions to a pedestrian on a college campus, and after ten seconds, they were temporarily interrupted by two people carrying a door between the experimenter and the pedestrian. While the experimenter was blocked by the door, another experimenter took his place and continued the conversation with the pedestrian after the door had passed. Only 7 of the 15 pedestrians who were interviewed noticed the change of experimenters. The other eight pedestrians did not notice that they were now with another person and continued the conversation as if nothing had happened.[§¶]

---

[*] Daniel Simons and Christopher Chabris, "Gorillas in Our Midst: Sustained Inattentional Blindness for Dynamic Events," *Perception*, 28 (1999): 1059–74.

[†] A similar study to that of Neisser were conducted by professors Daniel Simons and Christopher Chabris.

[‡] This phrase was coined by Arien Mack and Irvin Rock in 1998.

[§] Daniel J. Simons and Daniel T. Levin. "Failure to detect changes to people during a real-world interaction," *Psychonomic Society Inc.* (1998): 644–46.

[¶] You can see a video of this experiment on YouTube. *The Door Study*, Simons and Levin, 1998.

Executives can be too focused on the details of sales, spending, and growth and be blind to the risks or gorillas that cross in front of them, as demonstrated in the Neisser experiment.*

Donald Rumsfeld, a former US Secretary of Defense, said on February 12, 2002, at a press conference, regarding the lack of evidence that the Iraqi government had provided weapons of mass destruction to terrorist groups,

> We know there are known knowns, there are things we know, we know.... There are known unknowns, that is to say, we know there are some things we don't know. But there are also unknown unknowns, the ones we don't know we don't know.†

Unknown unknowns are those risks that are unexpected and are not anticipated because they should not occur.

The pace of change in which we live is accelerated and exponential and to be able to survive it is necessary to innovate and change. Transformational leaders leave the comfort zone and modify the status quo to anticipate the future. It is necessary to do it, not only to be competitive, but also to be able to survive.

Every leader should ask himself:

Is there any better way of doing things?
Is it necessary to change the processes?
Can we do things differently?
Changes can be risks or opportunities.
Companies need to have adequate alert systems to be able to access information on time and thus be prepared to react successfully and prevent crises. They need to implement programs that allow them, like submarines, to see below the surface.

---

* David Van Rooy in his book *Trajectory* (Amacom, 2014, 36) wrote about this experiment that is mentioned by Max Bazerman and Dolly Chugh in an article published in *Harvard Business Review*.
† "There are known knowns," Wikipedia. Donald Rumsfeld Unknown Unknowns, YouTube.

8

The Challenges of Legal and Technological Changes

8.1 LEGAL CHANGES

Humanity throughout history has felt the need to organize, regulate, and limit the conduct of society through a set of rules called the law, which is constantly evolving.

Zaleucus was a Greek lawgiver, said to have devised the first written Greek law code, the Locrian Code. According to legends, he punished adultery with the forfeiture of sight. When his own son was condemned of this, he refused to exonerate him; instead, as the punishment of the law was to blind two eyes, he ordered to blind one of his son's eyes and one of his own, for having raised a son who committed adultery.*

In the year 1754 BC, King Hammurabi of Babylon (1810–1750 BC) created the Code of Hammurabi, the first code of laws in history that ended private revenge and for the first time, a central government established penalties. It also created the *presumption of innocence*, since the accused had the opportunity to provide evidence.

This code was carved from a block of basalt of about 2.4 meters high by 1.9 meters wide; it had 3,600 lines and contained 282 laws. The king ordered copies of the code to be left in the streets of the city so all the people knew the law and its punishments.

One of these laws established the "law of talion,"† a penalty for which the aggressor suffers damage equal to that caused, and the first attempt to establish proportionality between the damage done and the punishment received. The best-known phrase of the law of talion is the biblical passage, "Eye for an eye; a tooth for a tooth."

---

* en.wikipedia.org/wiki/zaleucus.
† Lex Talionis.

Law 195 of the Hammurabi Code provided that if a child beat his father, the child's hands would be cut off. Law 196 stated that "If a man destroys the eye of another man, they shall destroy his eye." Law 197 of the code stated that if a bone of a person is broken, the bone of the aggressor would be broken too.

Another of its laws condemned to death the person who sold beer in bad conditions.*

In the fourteenth century BC, Moses received on Mount Sinai in Egypt the Ten Commandments, a Decalogue of ethical principles written on two stone tablets that have played an important role in Judaism and Christianity† because they establish the moral limits to human behavior to make life easier in society. An act is correct if it is consistent with the wishes of God reflected in the Decalogue.

The Romans, meanwhile, also established a legal system, a set of rules governing the Roman people since the founding of Rome (753 BC), which lasted until the sixth century, when the Emperor Justinian made a monumental compilation of all Roman law.

The French civil code known as the Napoleonic Code was adopted in 1804. It had 2,281 articles and was one of the world's best-known codes.‡ Its main feature was the same law should be applied to all inhabitants of the same nation. The Code of Napoleon was a pioneer in the universal legislation for the clarity of its text and the strength of its content, and it was a model of successive civil codes in more than 20 countries.

Napoleon Bonaparte (1769–1821) said: "My true glory is not to have won forty battles.... What will not vanish, which will live forever, is my Civil Code. Only my Code, in its simplicity, has done more to France than all laws before me."§

The conscience of each person to do the right thing is not enough to achieve an orderly society. Regulations and laws are also necessary. For example, the conscience of each one would not be enough for citizens to comply on time with the payment of their taxes. That is why laws are created to establish sanctions in case of noncompliance.

Laws serve the function of regulating human behavior and promoting order. The English philosopher Thomas Hobbes said, "We need rules in

---

* The Code of Hammurabi was discovered by French archaeologists in 1902 in Susa, Persia. It is displayed at the Louvre Museum in Paris.
† Narrated in Chapters 19, 20, and 24 of the Book of Exodus in the Old Testament of the Bible.
‡ A code is an ordered set of rules.
§ Matthew Weber, "Napoleon Bonaparte Dies in Exile (1821)," historycollection.co/.

society because without them life would be lonely, poor, dirty, brutal and short."*

The regulations are not only a limit but also a guide to act correctly. In this way, failure to comply with regulations carries a penalty. The social order and the freedom of individuals and organizations depend on the rules that set certain limits on individual freedom for the benefit of society as a whole.

Legal regulations and internal company policies, as well as the values and principles on which organizations are based, provide the framework, the border, and the limit in the business field. If that line is crossed, the company – and the employees who cross the line – must face the consequences.

When companies behave in a way that society considers unethical, governments intervene, enact laws, and create regulatory bodies with the intention that these actions do not happen again.

Legal systems usually fall into one of three categories: common law, civil law, and theocratic law.

Common law is based on tradition, precedent, and custom, and the courts fulfill an important role in interpreting the law. Legal interpretations are based on past court decisions. The United States and Canada have common law systems.

The civil law system, operating in over 70 countries, is based on a very detailed set of laws that are organized into a code that reduces the interpretation.

The two legal systems differ primarily in that common law is based on past judicial decisions applied to the facts, whereas civil law is based on how the law is applied to those facts.

An example of an area in which the two systems differ in practice is contracts. In a common law country, contracts tend to be very detailed, with all contingencies spelled out. In a civil law country, contracts tend to be shorter and less specific because many of the issues that a common law contract would cover already are included in the civil law.†

In theocratic systems, religious laws govern the legal system. Muslim law, which is followed in 27 countries, is based on the teachings of the Koran which governs all parts of life.

---

* Geoffrey Brennan and James M. Buchanan, *La Razon de las Normas* (Folio, Biblioteca de Economia, Union Editorial, 1987), 42. *The Reason of Rules* (Cambridge University Press, 1985).

† John D. Daniels and Lee H. Radebaugh, *International Business, Environments and Operations*, 7th ed (Addison Wesley Publishing Company, 1995), 84.

The government provides a system of laws to protect its interests, safeguard private property, and enforce contracts. The government passes laws and imposes regulations on businesses, defining the ways they can set prices, hire and fire employees, advertise to customers, and discharge waste products. Country laws govern the establishment of firms; taxation; environmental, health, and safety standards; minimum wages; and trademarks.

Professors Blanchard, Schewe, and Nelson, say:

> Laws addressing the conduct of business relate to nearly every business activity, from the hiring and paying of employees, to their safety on the job, to the safety of products advertised and sold to consumers, to the use of the natural resources needed to create products and services, to the disposal of unwanted by-products.
>
> These laws attempt to capture our society's notions about the fair treatment of individuals, the right of employees not to be injured by their work, the right of consumers to receive safe and pure products, and the responsibility of all of us to conserve and protect the natural world.*

In recent decades, governments have increased regulations, the amounts of fines for noncompliance, and the level of control on business. After each company scandal, governments reacted with a series of fines, legal actions, and new regulations to prevent a similar incident from happening again.

No firm can function effectively without understanding the legal system of the country in which it is doing business. The complexity of being in compliance is given in not only that the legal framework is constantly changing but also the rules are often ambiguous and difficult to understand.

For instance, as a legal director and compliance officer at Walmart Argentina, part of my job consisted of supervising the company's compliance with the different regulations at the national, provincial, and municipal levels. Regulatory risks in retail trade are quite varied. Some of the aspects to be controlled are the following:

How is it regulated in each jurisdiction where we have stores selling meat? Should the meat on sale in stores be chopped and cut in front of the customer at a counter or not regulated? How is the sale of eggs regulated

---

* K. Blanchard, C. Schewe and R. Nelson, *Exploring the World of Business* (W. H. Freeman & Co., 1996), 105.

in each jurisdiction? Should they be sold refrigerated and displayed in refrigerators? Are there special regulations for the commercialization of sunglasses? What is the legal procedure for presentation to the regulatory bodies of cosmetic products, cleaning products, and enamels? In which jurisdictions are health checkpoints for pest controls and agricultural diseases required? Are there any prohibitions on the entry of meat with a bone in Patagonia? Are there restrictions on the sale of alcoholic beverages? Hours, days, ages? How should prices be published, what information should be included on the shelves and in graphic advertising, TV, and radio? Are there any municipal fees for the distribution of the flyers? What regulations exist for the opening of a pharmacy? What labeling regulations should be followed for toys, electronics, food, cosmetics, cleaning products, and textiles? What maximum percentage of lead can a fishing rod contain? What percentage of phthalate is allowed in toys and childcare products containing phthalate as plasticizer? What are the environmental regulations in the handling of hazardous and pathogenic waste, a dump of water, and gaseous emissions? What is the compliance program for private label suppliers? What is the regulation for the sale of mopeds? Are there restrictions for the commercialization of fruits due to the "fruit fly"?

A tangle of rules and regulations marks the field in which a company must play. The ambiguity and contradiction of laws is a risk in itself. Although governments should work to reduce risks, some regulations increase it with laws that generate more problems than those that are trying to solve.

The Roman principle *pacta sunt servanda* is a Latin phrase of ancient Rome, and it means "the pact obligates"; that is any agreement must be fulfilled by the parties. The Roman rule wanted to provide predictability and confidence in commercial relations. It is one of the fundamental principles of civil law in contractual matters because if obligations and commitments are not respected, then bad faith, distrust, abuse of law, and lack of certainty would be generated.

The English philosopher Thomas Hobbes (1588–1679) said that when a pact has been made, breaking it is unfair and the definition of injustice is nothing other than breaking the covenant.*

---

* Geoffrey Brennan and James M. Buchanan, *La Razon de las Normas* (Folio, Biblioteca de Economia, Union Editorial, 1987), 141, *The Reason of Rules* (Cambridge University Press, 1985).

Legal certainty is a warranty given by the states that people, goods, and rights will be protected and that if such protection does not occur, those rights will be repaired. That is, it is a certainty that companies and individuals have a right that their legal status will not be changed except by established procedures previously published. Uncertainty decreases productivity, increases the cost of credit, requires more controls, makes communication among employees more difficult, demotivates them, raises tensions, and creates conflicts.

Lack of trust leads to destructive meetings, errors, poor communication, lack of commitment, and fear, and it creates structural conditions that lead people to behave improperly.

Some principles derived from legal certainty and certainty of the law include the non-retroactivity of the law (the laws do not apply or affects an act done prior to the passing of the law),* the definition of offenses and penalties, constitutional guarantees, *res judicata*,† prescription rights, and clarity and no contradiction of rules.

These problems of legal uncertainty, complexity, ambiguity, and inconsistency of regulations are multiplied when we refer to multinational companies, also subject to the change of laws of the countries in which they operate. Legal risks have become important because of increasingly complex business regulations worldwide.

An example of the unpredictability of legislative changes and the need to adapt quickly is what happened to Walmart in India. In August 2018, Walmart announced the acquisition of 77% of the shares of the Indian e-commerce company Flipkart for the astronomical sum of US$16 billion. Six months later, on February 1, 2019, the Indian government changed the rules for the e-commerce business. For example, the sale of exclusive products in certain portals was prohibited and it was forbidden to offer products sold by companies with which the owners of the e-commerce platform have a shareholding. Due to these legal changes, Flipkart is obliged to modify its business model. Walmart President Doug McMillan said: "In terms of the regulatory environment, we are disappointed with

---

* The opposite of this principle of law is an *ex post facto* law, which is a law that retroactively changes the legal consequences of actions that were committed before the enactment of the law. In criminal law, it may criminalize actions that were legal when committed. *Ex post facto* laws are expressly forbidden by the United States Constitution.

† Res judicata or res iudicata, also known as claim preclusion, is the Latin term for a matter already judged. In the case of res judicata, the matter cannot be raised again, either in the same court or in a different court. A court will use res judicata to deny consideration of a matter. "Res Judicata," Wikipedia.

the recent change in law. ... But the team has worked to ensure we are in compliance with the new rules."*

The customs of the countries in which multinational companies operate must also be taken into account when applying their codes of conduct. Behaviors accepted in certain countries may not be aligned to the culture, values, and principles of organizations. For example, accepting a simple coffee from a supplier at a business meeting is a common custom in certain Latin American countries. However, that simple act could be considered for an American company as a "gift from a supplier to its employees," which could be considered an unacceptable act by some codes of conduct. However, if the coffee is not accepted, it could be considered an act of lack of courtesy with the supplier.

The Basel Committee of Banking Supervision (2005) defines *compliance risk* as:

> the risk of legal or regulatory sanctions, material financial loss or loss of reputation a bank may suffer as a result of its failure to comply with the laws, regulations, rules, related-self regulatory organization standards and codes of conduct applicable to its banking activities.[†]

The complexity increases when a company is listed on the stock exchange or provides a public service with additional specific regulations to be filled. For example, if the company is publicly traded in the United States, it must comply with the Sarbanes-Oxley Act of 2002.[‡]

The Sarbanes-Oxley Act increased penalties for companies in case of financial manipulation and gave greater independence and responsibility to boards. Under this law, the key executives of a company must sign the financial and accounting statements, verifying their veracity and making themselves accountable in case of a lack of accuracy. The CEO and CFO certify in each quarterly or annual report filed with the Securities and

---

* "New E-Commerce Rules: Walmart Disappointed, But Hopes to Work with Govt. on Pro-growth Policies," *Money Control News*, May 7, 2019.

† Basel Committee on Banking Supervision, *Compliance and the Compliance Function in Banks*," April 2005 (Bank for International Settlements), Introduction, point 3. www.bis.org/publ/bcbs113.pdf.

‡ The Sarbanes-Oxley Act is a US law also known as the Reform Act of the Public Company Accounting and Investor Protection. It was created in order to monitor the companies listed on the stock exchange and to prevent the value of the shares be altered questionably. Its purpose is to prevent fraud and bankruptcy, protecting the investor. This law is named after two congressmen and was a legislative reaction to establish new controls and penalties for fraud and financial scandals in large companies.

Exchange Commission they have read and analyzed the report based on their knowledge, it does not contain false information and has not omitted important information.

Many other regulations also apply to businesses in the United States. Some of the most important are the Gramm Leach Bliley Act, the Payment Card Industry Act, the Fair Credit Reporting Act, the Fair and Accurate Credit Transactions Act, the Health Insurance Portability and Accountability Act (HIPPA), and the Genetic Information Non-Discrimination Act.

Since 1976, the Office of the Inspector General of the US Department of Health and Human Services (OIGHS)[*] has guided efforts to combat fraud and abuse in health services and public and private health plans in the United States. This body has developed guidance documents of compliance to strengthen internal controls and ensure compliance with regulations.

The board of directors of a company must also perform surveillance of compliance and ethics programs and assess whether the CEO and executives of the company maintain and promote a culture of integrity. The Federal Sentencing Guidelines require that the board "is knowledgeable about the content and operation of the compliance and ethics program."[†]

The Committee of Sponsoring Organizations of the Treadway Commission, an NGO known as COSO, that seeks to prevent fraud in its 2009 report said:

> The role of the Board of directors in enterprise-wide oversight has become increasingly challenging as expectations for board engagement are at all times highs...but the complexity of business transactions, technology advances, globalization, speed of product cycles and the overall pace of change have increased the volume and complexities of risks facing organizations over the last decade.[‡]

---

[*] Office of Inspector General of the US Department of Health and Human Services. The website is http:// OIG.HHS.GOV.

[†] www.ussc.gov. Guidelines Manual, November 1, 2011. The Federal Sentencing Guidelines are rules that set out a uniform sentencing policy for individuals and organizations convicted of felonies and serious misdemeanors in the United States federal court system. The Guidelines are the product of the United States Sentencing Commission, which was created by the Sentencing Reform Act of 1984. The Guidelines' primary goal was to alleviate sentencing disparities.

[‡] "Effective Enterprise Risk Management Oversight: The Role of the Board of Directors," report of the Committee of Sponsoring Organizations of the Treadway Commission, 2009. Mentioned by Donna Boehme in her paper "Board Engagement: Training and Reporting: Strategies for the Chief Ethics and Compliance Officer."

In the United States, the shareholders of Caremark International Inc. launched a lawsuit alleging that the company's board of directors breached their duty of care by failing to put in place adequate internal control systems. According to the lawsuit, that lack of supervision allowed crimes to be committed which imposed fines on the company. The Delaware Chancery Court ruled in this case in 1996 that the company should have an effective program of compliance, and board members could be responsible if there were a situation or event that hurt the company and that could have been avoided with "reasonable supervision." Therefore, the board of directors of the company could be liable for breach if it were shown that there was a lack of supervision in the area of compliance. Directors would default on their duty of supervision if they (i) knew or should have known that they were violating the law in the organization or (ii) did not perform actions in good faith to prevent or remedy the situation and (iii) those errors contributed to the losses.

Caremark is an important case in the United States corporate law and discusses a director's duty of care in the oversight context. It raised the question, "what is the board's responsibility with respect to the organization and monitoring of the enterprise to assure the corporation functions within the law to achieve its purposes?" Caremark is widely known and cited for this vision of the duty of oversight and is one of the reasons why corporations strengthened their ethics and compliance programs.*

Topics of compliance in recent years have entered the agendas of executive committees and boards of directors of companies, not only because new regulations and court rulings have established new limits on business but also because in case of default on those new regulatory frameworks and judgments, the amounts of the fines could seriously affect a company's financial results and business reputation.

The impact on the bottom line is mainly due to two factors that have deepened in recent years: (i) the millions of dollars in fines payable that have been imposed by regulators and (ii) the transparency generated by new technologies and social networks, which make any errors or negative events regarding a company and/or its employees known immediately by millions of people.

---

* "Caremark International Inc. Derivative Litigation," Delaware Court of Chancery, September 25, 1996, Wikipedia.

Many companies did not notice these changes were occurring in the environment, and they paid the consequences with CEO layoffs, reputational problems, steep drops in share prices, millions in fines, class action suits, and business closures. Big companies such as Intel, Abbott, Enron, AIG, Siemens, Johnson & Johnson, Pfizer, The Time Warner, Glaxo Smith, and BP have in recent years been fined more than a billion dollars each by various regulatory agencies.

After years of litigation, those who had suffered illnesses and health problems associated with silicone implants began class actions that led to agreements for an amount around US$3 billion to be paid by the implants' manufacturers Dow Corning, the Baxter Healthcare Corporation, and Bristol-Myers Squibb.

Tobacco companies also reached a settlement in 1998, derived from a class action, in the amount of US$206 billion to be paid over 25 years. The master settlement agreement includes the major tobacco companies: Brown & Williamson Tobacco Corporation, Lorillard Tobacco Company, Philip Morris Incorporated, R. J. Reynolds Tobacco Company, Commonwealth Tobacco, and Liggett & Myers.

The world has changed and the severity of sanctions is a threat that organizations should avoid.

Due to the increasing complexity of laws and regulations from different governmental entities and countries, companies must ensure they act in compliance with the new regulatory requirements related to their business.

To begin to understand the new threats, risks, and dangers, organizations began implementing ethics and compliance programs that enable them to prevent and protect themselves from situations that could make them more vulnerable in the future.

8.2 TECHNOLOGICAL CHANGES

In the early nineteenth century, data errors had serious consequences; for example, a faulty navigation table could cause shipwrecks.

In 1822 the British mathematician Charles Babbage (1791–1871) produced a machine that could collect and print mathematical tables almost without human intervention. Babbage believed that a machine could do faster and more accurate mathematical calculations than a person, and years later he created a prototype machine (analytical engine) that had memory and the main parts of a computer.

In the late nineteenth century, American engineer Herman Hollerith (1860–1929) used electricity to create a machine to compute census data from 1890 and then founded a company that would later be called IBM.

Alexander Graham Bell (1847–1922) revolutionized the history of communications by patenting the first telephone. Since he had been a child, Bell expressed interest in the problems of communication because his father was engaged in speech therapy and his mother was deaf. Bell worked tirelessly in order to transmit sound at a distance, and with the help of Thomas Watson and the financial support of the parents of two of his deaf students (one would become his future wife), he designed a device capable of transmitting voice and sound electronically.*

It 1876 Bell was working in his laboratory when, in response to an error when handling an electrical device, he exclaimed: "Mr. Watson, come here, I need you." Watson was working with a sound receiver elsewhere and clearly heard the voice, and that day there was a revolutionary change in the evolution of communications.

From 1876 to today, technological change has accelerated, which has left many leaders and companies disoriented and paralyzed in recent years.

As time passes, the lapse in which technological changes occur is increasingly smaller and impacts on companies, which must continually adapt to survive.

As the theory of evolution – so-called *interrupted gradualism* – says, evolutionary change is gradual, but at certain times its slowness is interrupted by rapid acceleration. Technological development is unpredictable and it has a direct impact on processes, trade, and economy.

The transatlantic flight from New York to Paris by Charles Lindbergh (1902–1974) in 1927, for example, marked a before and an after in the history of air navigation and the first commercial airlines began to

---

* On June 11, 2002, the US Congress adopted Resolution 269, which recognized that the inventor of the telephone was the Italian Antonio Meucci and not Alexander Graham Bell. Meucci submitted a patent caveat for his telephonic device to the US Patent Office in 1871, but there was no mention of electromagnetic transmission of vocal sound in his caveat. In 1876, Alexander Graham Bell was granted a patent for the electromagnetic transmission of vocal sound by electric current. Meucci studied the principles of electromagnetic voice transmission for many years and was able to realize his dream of transmitting his voice through wires in 1856. He installed a telephone-like device within his house in order to communicate with his wife, who was ill at the time. Meucci intended to develop his prototype but did not have the financial means to keep his company afloat in order to finance his invention. His candle factory went bankrupt, and Meucci was forced to unsuccessfully seek funds from rich Italian families. However, military expeditions led by Garibaldi in Italy had made the political situation in that country too unstable for anybody to invest. Meucci published his invention in the New York Italian-language newspaper *L'Eco d'Italia*.

develop. In 1935 Pan Am inaugurated the passenger service across the Atlantic Ocean.*

The American philosopher and historian Thomas Kuhn (1922–1996) published a book in 1962 called *The Structure of Scientific Revolutions*† and its publication was a landmark event in the history of scientific knowledge. Kuhn challenged the then prevailing view of progress in science. Scientific progress was viewed as "development-by-accumulation" of accepted facts and theories. Kuhn argued for an episodic model in which periods of continuity in normal science were interrupted by periods of revolutionary science. These revolutionary discoveries totally replaced previous theories and created new *paradigms* that changed the rules of the game. After some time, at some point, a new solution gains enough adherents in the world of science, so a new scientific revolution generates a new paradigm.

Andy Grove (1936–2016), former CEO of Intel, in his book *Only the Paranoid Survive*‡ said that a "Strategic Inflection Point" occurs when in the life of a business its fundamentals are about to change. New technology appears that changes the paradigm, so a major change, a turning point, occurs and one has to adapt to the change, to the new. The strategic inflection point can mean an opportunity to rise to new heights or it may just as likely signal the beginning of the end.§

In 1958 the engineers Jack Kilby (1923–2005)¶ and Robert Noyce (1927–1990) developed the idea of the integrated circuit, which meant the existence of several transistors within the same microchip. In April 1965 the magazine *Electronics*, in a document prepared by the co-founder of Intel Gordon Moore,** anticipated in subsequent years an increase in the

---

* On May 20, 1927, at 8 a.m. the plane *The Spirit of St. Louis* took off at the Roosevelt airfield in New York. Piloting the plane was the American aviator Charles Lindbergh (1902–1974) who had proposed to fly from New York to Paris when he learned that a hotelier in New York had offered US$25,000 to the first person to make that nonstop flight. Lindbergh had to stay awake in a tiny cabin where there was no place to stretch his legs, but he could overcome the cold of the night and he could stay awake. On May 21 at 5:22 p.m. the plane landed in Paris where there was a crowd. In the first four days, US newspapers wrote more than 250,000 notes on the event. When he returned to New York, a parade was held where more than 1,800 tons of chopped paper were thrown. Lindbergh received more than 3.5 million letters in his house.

† Thomas S. Kuhn, *The Structure of Scientific Revolutions* (The University of Chicago Press, 1962), Wikipedia.

‡ Andrew Grove, *Only the Paranoid Survive* (Random House, 1996), 32.

§ Andrew S. Grove, Quotes, www.goodreads.com.

¶ In 2000 he won the Nobel Prize in Physics.

** Gordon Moore is a member of the National Academy of Engineering of the United States and the Royal Society of Engineering, UK, and he has been awarded the National Medal of Technology and the Presidential Medal of Freedom in the United States for his contributions to the world of electronics and leadership in the development of reports based on MOS transistors.

complexity of integrated circuits and a reduction in their costs. Ten years later, in 1975, Moore noted that the number of transistors on a chip would double every 24 months, and their cost, despite the increased complexity, would continue to decline exponentially, making integrated circuits increasingly cheap to produce.* These findings became known as Moore's Law, that is, a computer that costs US$3,000 today is worth half that the next year and will be obsolete in two years.

Although the Russian-American writer Isaac Asimov (1920–1992) forecasted the development of the internet and personal computers, he could not anticipate the speed and pace of growth. The internet's origins date back to 1969 when the first connection of computers known as ARPANET (Advanced Research Projects Agency Network) between UCLA and Stanford University in California was established.

The science fiction writer Arthur C. Clarke (1917–2008) in an interview conducted by ABC in 1974 predicted that by the year 2001 people would have personal computers from which they could access all the information needed.[†]

Michael Leonidas Dertouzos (1936–2001) was a Greek computer scientist who in 1976 predicted that in the mid-1990s there would be a personal computer in one out of four homes; although his most surprising prognosis came in 1980 when he predicted the internet.[‡]

On March 12, 1989, the English engineer Tim Berners-Lee, working at CERN, in Switzerland, wrote a proposal on the architecture of the web with the aim of finding a system that would help the communication and dissemination of information among researchers.[§]

What are the threats and dangers of this change related to new technologies?

The aforementioned Asimov (1920–1992) showed concern when he said, "The saddest aspect of life right now is that science gathers knowledge faster than society gathers wisdom."[¶]

---

* Transistors are switches that control the flow of electrical signals. By reducing the size of transistors, microprocessor speed is improved, and production cost and energy consumption are reduced. The transistors used today are between 60 and 90 nanometers (a billionth of a meter). In some years, they will measure 6 nanometers, equivalent to a size 20, a thousand times smaller than a human hair, and their cost will be reduced.

† "Arthur C. Clarke predicts the internet," ABC Interview 1974, YouTube.

‡ es.wikipedia.org/wiki/Michael_Dertouzos.

§ Berners-Lee is currently a professor of computation at the University of Oxford and at MIT.

¶ Issac Asimov Quotes www.brainyquotes.com; todayinsci.com.

Klaus Schwab, the engineer and German economist, executive director of the World Economic Forum, wrote the book *The Fourth Industrial Revolution* in which he analyzes the transformational changes that will generate in the world new technologies, robotics, artificial intelligence, and the digitalization of production.*

The Institute for the Future of Humanity, University of Oxford, England, is also working on these issues. Led by the Swedish philosopher Nick Bostrom, it investigates the greatest threats to human survival as a species. In the document entitled "Existential Risk as a Global Priority," Bostrom states that we are entering a technological era that can challenge the future of humanity and could exceed our ability to manage its consequences. For example, biotechnology and nanotechnology could generate chain reactions and affect the whole world. Bostrom said in a BBC article:

> With new technologies, there are advantages but also risks. It's a matter of scale: we live in an interconnected world: news and rumors are spread at the speed of light. Therefore, the consequences of an error … are more unconscionable than in the past. We are at the level of children in terms of moral responsibility, but at the level of adults in technological capacity.†

Artificial intelligence (AI) is exhibited by machines that automate processes with high productivity and efficiency. But, unlike human beings, intelligent systems do not take into account empathy or emotional elements.

Artificial intelligence is the intelligence exhibited by machines. Unlike human beings, intelligent systems do not take into account emotional elements and do not forget the goal they must achieve.

Deep Blue was a supercomputer developed by the US manufacturer IBM to play chess and that used an artificial intelligence algorithm. "Deep Blue versus Garry Kasparov," is the name for the famous chess matches between the IBM Deep Blue supercomputer and the Chess World Champion, Garry Kasparov. The first match was played in February 1996 in Philadelphia, Pennsylvania, and Kasparov won it. In 1997, a second match was played and on that occasion, the Deep Blue supercomputer, which had been improved since the previous match, won against Kasparov.‡

---

* In the report called "Global Innovation Barometer" published by General Electric for five years and with the opinion of some 4,000 experts and executives, 70% of respondents had positive expectations for the fourth industrial revolution.

† "How Mankind Will Be Extinguished," *BBC World*, April 28, 2013, www.bbc.com.

‡ "Deep Blue versus Garry Kasparov," Wikipedia; see also theconversation.com/twenty-years-on -from-deep-blue-vs-kasparov-how-a-chess-match-started-the-big-data-revolution-76882.

In February 2011, Watson, another supercomputer created by IBM, managed to win a three day competition by playing in the television program *Jeopardy*, in which he defeated the two top champions in the program's history. Unlike Deep Blue, Watson had to be programmed with a vast amount of information, and with an artificial intelligence engine capable of deciding on its own the most appropriate response to each of the program's proposals.[*]

DeepMind Technologies is a British artificial intelligence company, which developed the Alpha Go software and was acquired by Google in 2014. Two years later, Alpha Go was the computer that beat the South Korean professional Go player Lee Se-dol, world champion of the game. The triumph of DeepMind set a milestone because it was the first time a computer beat a human being in that game.[†]

Transhumanism (H+) is an international cultural and intellectual movement that aims to transform the human condition through the development and manufacture of technology that improves human capabilities, both physically and psychologically or intellectually. This movement believes human beings can become capable of transforming themselves into beings with extensive capabilities, deserving of the "post-human" label.[‡]

The most famous novel by the British writer Aldous Huxley (1894–1963), *Brave New World*, published in 1932, anticipates the development of reproductive technology through drugs that radically change society. The story begins with a group of students visiting the London conditioning center, where a scientist shows them the technique of artificial reproduction. The perfect organization of society has been determined from birth and the government manipulates reproduction. Children from very young are conditioned by orders in their dream to accept their place in society, so there is harmony. War and poverty were eradicated and all are permanently happy.

---

[*] "Watson," en.wikipedia.org; also see blog.ted.com/how-did-supercomputer-watson-beat-jeopardy-champion-ken-jennings-experts-discuss/.

[†] Lalo Zanoni, "Inteligencia Artificial: Los Numeros y Los Casos mas Increibles de la Tecnologia que Cambiara Todo" ("Artificial Intelligence: The Most Incredible Numbers and Cases of Technology That Will Change Everything"), June 1, 2019, www.infobae.com; see also Louis Coppey, " What Does AlphaGo vs Lee Sedol Tell Us About the Interaction between Humans and Intelligent Systems?" March 15, 2018, https://medium.com/point-nine-news/what-does-alphago-vs-8dadec65aaf; see also, en.wikipedia.org/wiki/Lee_Sedol.

[‡] The contemporary meaning of the term *transhumanism* was forged by one of the first professors of futurology, Fereidoun M. Esfandiary (1930–2000), known as FM-2030, who thought of "the new concepts of the human" around 1960.

However, the paradox is that all these things have been achieved after eliminating many others: the family, cultural diversity, art, the advance of science, literature, religion, philosophy, and love.*

Gattaca is an American science fiction drama film from 1997 that resembles the novel *Brave New World* in relation to genetic manipulation.

The argument is that people decide to have children with the help of genetic engineering so their children have better physiognomy, health, and opportunities to get great jobs and earn more money, as they have to compete against other people also improved at birth with the advances of genetic engineering.

The film tells the story of a child born naturally and must fight to compete against the other children who received genetic help from before birth, even against his own brother who is the favorite of his parents.

The child grows and can only get cleaning jobs in companies, but one day working on cleaning a private astronaut training academy, he enrolls in the academy, with an elaborate scheme of fraud and deception, to be able to dodge system controls, which seek to discard any person who is not perfect and does not have good genes in society.†

The debate on artificial intelligence and robotics is becoming increasingly relevant. Yuval Harari, a tenured professor in the Department of History at the Hebrew University of Jerusalem,‡ wrote:

> Most jobs that exist today might disappear within decades. As artificial intelligence outperforms humans in more and more tasks, it will replace humans in more and more jobs.
>
> The crucial problem is creating new jobs that humans perform better than algorithms. Consequently, by 2050 a new class of people might emerge – the useless class. People who are not just unemployed, but unemployable.§

Technology has increased the pace of everything. The big future changes that lie ahead and their impact on society raise concerns, fears, and uncertainties.

---

* es.wikipedia.org/wiki/Un_mundo_feliz.

† es.wikipedia.org/wiki/Gattaca.

‡ His book, *Sapiens: A Brief History of Humankind* was published in English in 2014 and it has since been translated into some 45 additional languages.

§ Yuval Noah Harari, "The meaning of life in a world without work," May 8, 2017, www.theguardian.com/technology.

In May of 2018, Uber suspended the operations of its autonomous vehicles in Arizona, USA, after a woman died after being hit by one of its vehicles on March 18, 2018, in Tempe, Arizona.[*] After that incident, Nvidia also suspended the tests with their autonomous cars on public roads.[†]

A few days after the accident in Arizona, another incident occurred, this time by an engineer who was driving a Tesla Model X with the automatic system activated. This accident generated new doubts about the safety of autonomous driving systems. After knowing this new event, Toyota also suspended operations with autonomous vehicles in San Francisco, California, and Ann Arbor, Michigan.[‡]

When analyzing artificial intelligence from an ethical perspective, it is convenient to differentiate the "robotics" from the "ethics of the machines." The ethical analysis of robotics must include the moral behavior of human beings when they design, build, and use artificial intelligence. For its part, the ethics of machines refers not to the behavior of human beings, but to the autonomous behavior of machines created with artificial intelligence.[§]

Some experts have questioned the use of robots and weapons with artificial intelligence for military combat. Scientists like Elson Musk, Stephen Hawking, Max Tegmax, and Stuart Russell have warned about the dangers in the use of artificial intelligence weapons as they could trigger a catastrophe. In an open letter signed by hundreds of experts, they point out that "a military arms race with Artificial Intelligence will not benefit humanity."[¶]

On February 16, 2017, the European Parliament approved a Resolution on Robotics in which it establishes an Ethical Code of Conduct where, among other principles, it establishes the need to protect human beings from the damage caused by robots.[**]

---

[*] "Uber suspende operaciones de Vehículos Autónomos en Arizona," May 25, 2018, www.20minutos. com; "Arizona Suspende Operaciones de Vehículos Autónomos de Uber," March 27, 2018, www. elfinanciero.com.mx ("Uber suspends operations of Autonomous Vehicles in Arizona"; "Arizona Suspends Uber Autonomous Vehicle Operations").

[†] "Porque suspende Nvidia las pruebas de autos sin conductor en vías públicas," March 23, 2018, es.digitaltrends.com ("Why Nvidia suspends tests of cars without a driver on public roads").

[‡] "Segundo Accidente Mortal de un Coche Autónomo en Menos de una Semana," March 31, 2018, www.huffingtonpost.es ("Second Deadly Accident of an Autonomous Car in Less than a Week").

[§] "Inteligencia Artificial," Wikipedia ("Artificial Inteligence").

[¶] "Científicos Alertan sobre el Avance de Armas de Inteligencia Artificial," July 28, 2015, www. eluniverso.com ("Scientists Alert on the Advance of Artificial Intelligence Weapons").

[**] "Resolución del Parlamento Europeo con recomendaciones destinadas a la Comisión sobre normas de Derecho Civil sobre Robótica," February 16, 2017, www.europarl.europa.eu ("Resolution of the European Parliament with recommendations to the Commission on rules of Civil Law on Robotics").

Just as in 1975 a group of geneticists met in Asilomar, California, to develop an ethical framework for biotechnology, four decades later the Future of Life Institute brought together experts in Artificial Intelligence in the same city to develop a series of ethical principles. One of the conclusions of the debate in Asilomar was that Artificial Intelligence should be used for the common good of humanity and the more serious the potential risk, the stricter must be the systems of control and risk management.*

Harvard University and the Massachusetts Institute of Technology (MIT) jointly offer a course on the ethics and regulation of artificial intelligence. The University of Texas at Austin has a subject entitled "Ethical Foundations of Computer Science"; Stanford University published in September 2016 a report called "Artificial Intelligence and Life in 2030," and it has developed a computer science ethics course; Cornell and New York universities also have ethics courses applied to technological changes. What is transmitted in these courses is the awareness of the effects and ramifications that technological innovation may produce in society.[†]

The French writer Antoine de Saint Exupery (1900–1944) said, "The machine does not isolate man from the great problems of nature but plunges him more deeply into them."[‡]

Professor of mechanical engineering at the University of Texas at Austin, John Goodenough, creator of lithium-ion batteries used in cell phones, says,

> Technology is morally neutral – you can use it for good and for evil. … You can use it to explode bombs under somebody's vehicle. You can use it to steal a bank account. As scientists, we do the best we can to provide something for society. But if society cannot make the moral decisions that are necessary, they only use it to destroy themselves.[§]

The German chemist Fritz Haber (1868–1934) was awarded the Nobel Prize for Chemistry in 1918 for having developed ammonia synthesis that

---

* "Ética e Inteligencia Artificial en la Robótica: Un Debate Abierto," www.thinkingheads.com ("Ethics and Artificial Intelligence in Robotics: An Open Debate").

† Natasha Singer, "Porque hay que Enseñar Ética como Materia de Computación, Según Silicon Valley," *La Nación*, February 26, 2018 ("Why Ethics must be taught as a Computer Subject According to Silicon Valley").

‡ www.brainyquote.com.

§ Lindsay Ellis, "Welch Foundation lauds Goodenough for battery research that changed the world," October 22, 2017, www.houstonchronicle.com.

allowed the manufacture of fertilizers. But these chemical processes were also used for the manufacture of chemical and toxic weapons. In World War I, Haber was directly responsible for the use by Germany of poisonous gases despite being prohibited by the Hague Convention of 1907. In 1915, when his wife, doctorate in chemistry, learned Haber was supervising the use of dichloride gas for the war, she committed suicide in the garden of her house.* Haber said, "During peacetime, a scientist belongs to the world, but during wartime he belongs to his country."†

What is the responsibility of scientists concerning the development of chemical and biological weapons?

The Argentine toxicology specialist Edith Valles, following the Hague Ethical Guidelines for the Prohibition of Chemical Weapons, has stated,

> A scientist must behave ethically regardless of whether it is in time of peace or war. It should always act for the benefit of humankind and the environment by applying the highest ethical principles, being responsible for the non-use of the chemical sciences for illicit purposes.‡

On August 2, 1939, the Hungarian physicist Leo Szilard (1898–1964) and Albert Einstein sent a letter to the President of the United States, Franklin D. Roosevelt, warning of the danger that Germany might develop atomic bombs and suggesting to Roosevelt the United States should start their own nuclear program. This is how the Manhattan Project was born with US\$6,000 of initial capital.

The American Robert Oppenheimer (1918–1988) led the "Manhattan Project" aimed at developing the first atomic bomb, which began in 1941. Oppenheimer supervised 5,000 engineers and technicians, including some of the most recognized scientists at that time, including the Italian-American Enrico Fermi (1901–1954), the Hungarian-American John Von Neumann (1903–1907), and the American Richard Feynman (1918–1988). The team of scientists retreated to the town of Los Alamos and on June 16, 1945, they tested the bomb in Alamogordo, New Mexico. After the explosion of atomic bombs in Hiroshima and Nagasaki, Japan, also in 1945 – by which more than 100,000 people died in a matter of seconds – Oppenheimer pointed out with a deep sense of guilt, he said "Physicists

---

* Fritz Haber, Wikipedia.
† Peter Herrick, "The Responsibility of the Scientist," EMBO Reports, www.ncbi.nlm.nih.gov/pmc/articles.
‡ Lucas Gianre, Uniciencia, www.uniciencia.unc.edu.ar/2016/Septiembre. See also www.opcw.org.

have known sin" and recalled the Hindu scripture Bhagavad Gita: "I became death, the destroyer of worlds."* Oppenheimer had to coexist with this ethical problem and over the years became an opponent of nuclear weapons.[†]

Argentine journalist Tomas Eloy Martinez (1934–2010) wrote:

> Those doubts, which were his illness and his martyrdom, draw an endless Greek tragedy, in which a man realizes that has created a force similar to God's, and he spends his life fleeing from it, terrified.[‡]

Mahatma Gandhi (1869–1948) said business without morality and science without humanity destroy the human being.[§]

Physicist Ana Maria Cetto Kramis has urged, "Do not let the conscience fall asleep....We should not be idle to stop the use of science and technology for armaments."[¶]

The German Albert Einstein (1879–1955), Nobel Prize for Physics in 1921, reflected on the danger of nuclear weapons and said:

> At present, physicists who participated in the construction of the most tremendous and dangerous weapon of all time, are overwhelmed by a similar feeling of responsibility, not to mention guilt.
>
> I made a grave error in my life when I signed the letter to President Roosevelt recommending atomic bombs; but there was some justification, the danger of the Germans doing it.... If the enemies of mankind did it before, given the Nazi mentality, they would have consummated the destruction and slavery of the rest of the world.
>
> Atomic energy for the moment is a threat. Whatever is good, as it should be. It may intimidate the human race to put order in their international affairs, which without the pressure of fear, would not occur.
>
> Atomic war is likely to...bring destruction on a scale that has never been possible before, which can hardly be conceived and to which little

---

* Estephanie Gutierrez, "Manhattan Project," February 17, 2017, www.de10.com.mx; Hector Rago, "The Eternal Guilt That Persecuted the Father of the Atomic Bomb," June 10, 2016, "Manhattan Project," Wikipedia. Other scientists who used their knowledge to create destructive weapons were, for example, the American Hungarian Edward Teller (1908–2003) considered the "Father of the H-bomb" and the Russian Andrei Sakharov (1921–1989) known as the "Father of the Soviet atomic bomb."

† Matias Bauso, "La Culpa que Persiguió al Padre de la Bomba Atómica hasta el último instante de su vida," February 17, 2019, www.infobae.com ("The Blame That persecuted the Father of the Atomic Bomb until the last moment of his life").

‡ Matias Bauso, "La Culpa que Persiguió al Padre de la Bomba Atómica hasta el último instante de su vida," February 17, 2019, www.infobae.com ("The Blame That persecuted the Father of the Atomic Bomb until the last moment of his life").

§ "The mirror of Gandhi," Joose Scharenberg, January 29, 2014, sloyu.com/blog/english/2014/01/29/mirror-gandhi/.

¶ "Scientists Have an Ethical Responsibility to the Development of Chemical Weapons," www.decs.unam.mx, September 27, 2013.

civilization will survive. Perhaps two-thirds of the population of the earth will be annihilated.*

The lawyer Esteban Russell, in a conference on artificial intelligence held in Buenos Aires in May 2018, remembered the Argentine writer Ernesto Sabato (1911–2011) who said, "The technical growth of man, if it is not accompanied by an equivalent ethical growth, is a danger to the subsistence of mankind."†

Technological innovation permanently redefines the limit of what is possible, and therefore it is not easy to predict and control the future.

In a recent interview, the CEO of Daimler Benz (Mercedes Benz) said that his company's competitors are Tesla, Google, Apple, and Amazon. Soon it will not be necessary to buy a car, a car will be contacted by phone and the car will take you to your destination. Cities will need fewer parking lots and will be less noisy. The transport industry foresees the incorporation of robots in land, rail, and air transport.

Soon, domestic chores will be performed by robots and smart homes. Agriculture is being automated and in medicine, robots are performing surgeries.‡

Shoe companies will start making shoes with 3D printers. In China, a six-story 3D building has already been built.

In the state of Wisconsin, USA, judges have an assistant called Compac that was developed by Northpointe Inc., which consists of an algorithm that analyzes data and estimates the possibilities a defendant will re-offend in the future.§

In Cleveland, Ohio, judges are guided by artificial intelligence algorithms. These algorithms can examine judicial data to predict how defendants will behave. The algorithm aims to reduce decisions influenced by race, gender, or even clothing of the accused.¶

---

* Estephanie Gutiérrez, "Manhattan Project," February 17, 2017, www.de10.com.mx; Héctor Rago, "The Eternal Guilt That Persecuted the Father of the Atomic Bomb," June 10, 2016; "Manhattan Project," Wikipedia. Other scientists who used their knowledge to create destructive weapons were, for example, the American Hungarian Edward Teller (1908–2003), considered the "Father of the H-bomb," and the Russian Andrei Sakharov (1921–1989), known as the "Father of the Soviet atomic bomb."

† "Primer Foro de Inteligencia Artificial e Internet de las Cosas en Ciudades Inteligentes y Sustentables en Latinoamérica." May 29, 2018 ("First Forum of Artificial Intelligence and Internet of Things in Intelligent and Sustainable Cities in Latin America").

‡ "Humanoides y Robots. Inteligencia Artificial, Robótica y Mujeres: Una Nueva Revolución," October 8, 2018, www.clarin.com ("Humanoids and Robots. Artificial Intelligence, Robotics, and Women: A New Revolution").

§ Mitch Smith, "In Wisconsin, a Blacklash Against Using Data to Foretell Defentant's Futures," June 22, 2016, www.nytimes.com.

¶ "Gobernar con Inteligencia Artificial," February 14, de 2018, www.thenewnow.es ("Rule with Artificial Intelligence").

In a police station in Washington D.C., a case was reopened, thanks to a Machine Learning application called Rekognition, developed by Amazon Web Services (AWS). In 48 hours, the machines reviewed more than 300,000 photos to find the suspect of a crime, which was finally found and convicted.[*]

In China, in a short time in some police stations instead of police, there will be an Artificial Intelligence system that will be in charge of keeping the station running 24 hours. It will not be necessary to show any identification; by means of facial recognition applications, the system scans the face of citizens.[†]

Some robots are being used for the care of children in daycare centers and elderly people in nursing homes. In China, an automaton called *Chaoneng Xiaobai* interacts with television presenters and analyzes data in the news program that is broadcasted in the Guangxi region.[‡]

In November of 2018, a television announcer created by a computer presents the news in the Chinese agency Xinhua. The virtual presenter can work 24 hours on the website and social networks. The humanoid created with artificial intelligence has a monotone voice, is dressed in a suit and tie, wears glasses, and moves his mouth and head.[§] His English language version started his first program saying: "Hello Everyone. I'm an English IA Anchor. . . . I will work tirelessly to keep you informed."[¶]

The English mathematician Alan Mathison Turing (1912–1954) said that in a short time we will not know if we are communicating with a machine or with a human being.

A humanoid robot named Sophia is scheduled to speak at the 20th Annual Regional Audit Conference, hosted by the UAE Internal Auditors Association in Dubai from April 12–14, 2020.[**]

---

[*] Lalo Zanoni, "Inteligencia Artificial: Los Numeros y los Casos mas Increibles de la Tecnologia que Cambiara Todo" ("Artificial Intelligence: The Most Incredible Numbers and Cases of Technology That Will Change Everything"), June 1, 2019, www.infobae.com.

[†] Lalo Zanoni, "Inteligencia Artificial: Los Numeros y los Casos mas Increibles de la Tecnologia que Cambiara Todo" ("Artificial Intelligence: The Most Incredible Numbers and Cases of Technology That Will Change Everything"), June 1, 2019, www.infobae.com.

[‡] "Un Robot con Inteligencia Artificial Conducirá un Noticiero de la TV China," www.clarin.com/tecnologia ("A Robot with Artificial Intelligence Will Lead a China TV News").

[§] "China revela un Periodista Virtual que Presenta las Noticias Gracias a la Inteligencia Artificial," November 9, 2018, www.clarin.com ("China reveals Virtual Journalist Presenting News Thanks to Artificial Intelligence").

[¶] "China's AI news anchor vows to 'work tirelessly to keep you informed'," November 9, 2018, www.msn.com; see also www.youtube.com/watch?v=eB29ZVDOFfU&t=21s.

[**] "Robot to Talk AI at Audit Conference," Matt Kelly, March 7, 2020 www.radicalcompliance.com/2020/03/07/robot-talk-ai-audit-conference/; ww.uaeiaa.org/conference-detail.htm?20

The Venezuelan MIT engineer Jose Luis Cordeiro has indicated that by 2029, we will have a mixed civilization of humans and machines and Mars will be colonized, and by the year 2045 humans could "achieve immortality," that is, all diseases will be cured.*

Google CEO, Sundar Pichai, said, "artificial intelligence is one of the most important things humanity is working on. It is more profound than electricity or fire."†

New technologies advance faster than our capacity to assimilate them and it is a great challenge to be able to adapt at the speed that circumstances require. In 2017, in the admission test to enter the best university in Japan, a robot scored better than 80% of the students.‡ We must live with the anxiety that generates the impossibility of eliminating the surprise of what's to come.

The mobility of employment, capital, products, and technology has made businesses more and more global.

Messenger pigeons§ and the control of the globalization of news mainly through television and CNN are part of the past. The power has been scattered. Technological advances have passed control of the information from the television chains to individuals.

On April 30, 1973, the American engineer Martin Cooper, systems manager of Motorola, made the first call from a cell phone in history. Cooper called Joel Engel, from Bell, against whom he competed in creating the first mobile phone. Motorola's cell phone, which weighed 1 kilogram, went on sale in September 1983 at a cost of US$3,995 and in the first year, 3,000 units were sold.¶

The degree of connectivity, led by Generation M,** is unprecedented. The transfer of multimedia information (audio and video) grows over the network with increasing force.

Blackberry phones and video conferencing began the revolution in communications 20 years ago. With the power and mass of the internet and uncontrollable social networking, millions of people are informed

---

* Jose A. Gomez, "In 2045 the Man Will Be Immortal," July 22, 2014, www.elmundo.es/ciencia.

† Catherine Clifford, "Google CEO: A.I. Is More Important Than Fire or Electricity," February 1, 2018, www.cnbc.com/2018/02/01/google-ceo-sundar-pichai-ai-is-more-important-than-fire-electri city.html; see also www.entrepreneur.com/article/308041.

‡ #MiEmpleoMiFuturo, "Un Documental Sobre Robots," Youtube ("Documentary about Robots").

§ In World War I (1914–1918), 500,000 pigeons were used to send messages.

¶ "Así fue la Primera Llamada por Celular, a 45 años de un Hecho Histórico," April 3, 2018, www. clarin/tecnologia ("This was the First Call by Cellular, 45 years of a Historic Fact").

** Millennium, multicultural, and mobile.

immediately of any event, which has generated an exponential increase in our ability to relate. Information is just a click away.

With the web, access to knowledge has been decentralized, and the distances between people, countries, and cultures were shortened. Videos, photos, and any kind of information and images can be uploaded to the internet and forwarded by social networks to millions of people in a matter of seconds. With the internet, information is distributed, multiplies, and flies without barriers. Social networks *horizontalized* the information that previously came from radios, newspapers, and television.

It is not surprising that changes take place, but what surprises are (i) the speed of the changes, which makes it difficult to adapt, and (ii) the type of changes, which went from being predictable and incremental to transformational. These data prove it:

1. In 2005 the figure of one billion users connected to the internet was reached. In 2010 it reached two billion users, in 2014 it was three billion people, and in 2019 it reached five billion users. In 2019 more than 51% of the world's population (four billion people) was connected to the internet.[*]
2. At the end of 2017 people sent 195 billion emails per day.
3. In 2017 there were more than 30 million people online on Skype at any time of day and over 3 billion Google searches are performed per day.[†]
4. The words written daily on Twitter fill a book of over 10 million pages; 560 million tweets were sent per day in 2017.
5. It is estimated that by 2020, there will be about six billion people with smartphones; i.e., with the internet in their pockets. New technologies allow the streaming of videos and images from any place, and any individual becomes a journalist with only a smartphone. More than four billion phones have a camera and can record videos and upload them to the internet.

---

[*] www.internetlivestats.com, www.internetworldstats.com; "Dia de Internet: Se Envian 41 millones de Mensajes en WhatsApp por Minuto y otros Datos Curiosos de la Red de Redes," 17 de Mayo de 2019, www.clarin.com/tecnologia; "Esto es todo lo que Ocurre en un Minuto en Internet," 17 de mayo de 2019, www.infobae.com/america/tecno. ("Internet Day: 41 million Messages are sent on WhatsApp per Minute and other Curious Data of the Network of Networks," May 17, 2019, www.clarin.com/tecnologia; "This is all that happens in a minute on the Internet," May 17, 2019, www.infobae.com/america/tecno.)

[†] Dave Ulrich, Jon Younger, Wayne Brockbank and Mike Ulrich, "Next generation HR," Chapter 1 in *HR from the Outside In*.

6. The fifth generation of mobile technologies – 5G – will allow speeds ten times higher than current 4G technology.

7. Due to the development of cell phone cameras, more than 10% of all images in the history of photography were taken in the last 15 months.

8. If Facebook were in a ranking of countries by population, it would be the most populous in the world, with two billion users in 2018. At the end of 2017, there were 10,000 times more photos on Facebook than in the US Library of Congress. Every minute Facebook users send roughly 31.25 million messages and watch 2.77 million videos.[*]

9. In 2017 WhatsApp had more than one billion users, Messenger 800 million, and Instagram had more than 500 million users. Every day more than five million photos are uploaded to Instagram.

10. Every minute, 188 million emails and 750,000 tweets are sent, 1 million photos are uploaded to Snapchat; 1 million people look at Facebook; 4.5 million videos are watched on YouTube; 360 thousand people use Instagram; and 41 million messages are sent on WhatsApp.[†]

11. By the end of 2017 more than 24 hours of video were uploaded to YouTube per minute, about 500 million people played 100 million hours of video per day, and the same year YouTube exceeded 1 billion users. Some YouTubers, such as Swedish Felix Kjelbeng (nicknamed "Pew Die Pie"), have more than 40 million subscribers.

We live in an era of hyper-connectivity. In this digital and communications revolution, every day as much data are created as in the first 2,000 years of humanity. D Wave Systems of Canada is the first company to market quantum computers. Microsoft, Google, and IBM are investing millions of dollars in new technology that will enable them to make ten trillion[‡] transactions per second vs. one billion of operations per second with

---

[*] "21 Big Data Statistics & Predictions on the Future of Big Data," January 25, 2018, www.newgenapps.com.

[†] "Dia de Internet: Se Envian 41 millones de Mensajes en WhatsApp por Minuto y otros Datos Curiosos de la Red de Redes," 17 de Mayo de 2019, www.clarin.com/tecnologia; "Esto es todo lo que Ocurre en un Minuto en Internet," 17 de mayo de 2019, www.infobae.com/america/tecno. ("Internet Day: 41 million Messages are sent on WhatsApp per Minute and other Curious Data of the Network of Networks," May 17, 2019, www.clarin.com/tecnologia; "This is all that happens in a minute on the Internet," May 17, 2019, www.infobae.com/america/tecno.)

[‡] 1,000,000,000,000.

the current technology. In this transparent and hyper-connected world, everything moves with increasing speed.

Amazon was a few years ago only a vast river in Brazil and Alibaba was just a character in the book of Middle Eastern and South Asian tales called *One Thousand and One Nights*. Amazon and Alibaba are the two big giants of the e-commerce industry. Wikipedia, Google, Twitter, Yahoo, Skype, WhatsApp, Facebook, YouTube, LinkedIn, Instagram, Snapchat, Periscope, Slack, apps, blogs, tablets, drones, smart and satellite phones have changed communications forever.

Technological advancements keep the world informed no matter where the news originates. The spread of information on the internet expands like an epidemic – impossible to control, information moves uncontrollably at full speed, and the transparency achieved by technology has left individuals and organizations exposed as never before.

China and Silicon Valley are leading this technological change race.

Uber, the largest taxi company, does not own any vehicles. Alibaba, as mentioned, one of the world's largest retailers, does not own inventory. Facebook, the leading media company, does not own any content. Netflix, one of the major film companies, does not own most of its platform.

Technology threatens our privacy. Our actions can be tracked and analyzed by credit card and debit card records. The world became a kind of *Big Brother** show where privacy does not exist as if the companies were surrounded by cameras and microphones 24 hours a day. In this transparent context, all are known or will be known, and everything remains in view. The media and the people are always watching, and any small misstep can grow dangerously.

The era of transparency has the advantage of formidable access to information available on the web, but at the same time, there is no secret that lingers for a long time; privacy is threatened by billions of online interconnected observers, and companies are exposed.

The book *The Naked Society*, written by the American journalist Vance Packard (1914–1996) and published in 1964, was the first book to discuss how the new technology, such as hidden microphones and concealed cameras, was being used to invade people's liberties. Packard wrote that privacy was "evaporating."[†]

---

* *Big Brother* is a television program in which, for about three months, a group of people live together in a house, totally isolated, and with cameras watching them 24 hours a day.

† Charlotte Andriesse, "Privacy: Do We Really Care?" February 28, 2018, www.goodreputations.nl/privacy.

In the same vein, Myron Brenton said in *The Privacy Invaders* that "we arc at the threshold of what we can call the fishbowl era."* We live in a time where almost everything is transparent, amplified, and visible. We are heading toward a world without secrets, where nothing can be hidden under the carpet and there is no margin for error.

In the article "The Age of Transparency," Gonzalez Biondo says:

> In 2004 it was known that the Kryptonite padlocks for bikes could be opened with a simple pen. In a few hours, internet videos proliferated showing how to do it. Traditional media lifted the story a few days later, but by then millions of people had seen the online version of one of the blogs in which it appeared. Kryptonite took more than a week to respond that it would replace the locks. Estimated cost? Ten million dollars, almost half of projected earnings for the year.†
>
> When everything is in sight, integrity, honesty, trust, social responsibilities … are conditions of survival as necessary as efficiency, productivity, and profitability.‡

Any company, institution, or person is free to see their image wrapped up in a serious crisis in a few hours due to the speed of movement of the news on the internet.

Companies play with all information in sight, which flows uncontrollably and where everything is recorded and registered. Technological change in communications makes not only opportunities but also risks grow exponentially in terms of their potential impact.

An error that appears on social networks can produce either a headache or put in risk a career or a brand with years of trajectory.§

At present, companies are more vulnerable, not only because of the difficulty of adapting to technological changes but also because of the possibility of being trapped in this new transparent, digital, and uncontrollable context, where everything is known.

---

* "Fuera de control," *Revista Gestion*, September–October 2008, 83 ("Out of Control").
† Graciela Gonzalez Biondo, "La Era de la Transparencia," *Revista Gestion*, September–October 2008, 50, www.gestion.com.ar ("The Era of Transparency").
‡ "Fuera de control," *Revista Gestion*, September–October 2008, 83 ("Out of Control").
§ Fernan Saguier, "El Valor del Periodismo se Mantiene Intacto," *La Nación*, August 3, 2018 ("The Value of Journalism Remains Intact").

9

The Challenge of Internal Change: Vision, Motivation, and Execution

On September 20, 2015, Pope Francis met with 5,000 Cuban youths and told them, quoting a Latin American writer, that people had two types of eyes: one of flesh and one of glass. With the one of flesh, we look at what happens around us, and with the one of glass, we see what we dream.

An effective leader is the one who looks at the horizon and imagines the opportunities, threats, risks, and challenges that can cross his or her path, and takes those measures that reduce uncertainty.

A leader plans how to reach the desired goal because, as the Canadian author Robin Sharma says, "Who fails in planning, plans his failure."* Unlike King Midas,† an effective leader must have a proper strategy to achieve his or her goal.

The French emperor Napoleon Bonaparte (1769–1821) pointed out that the art of war was a science in which nothing worked out unless it was calculated and meditated on previously. Before organizational change is initiated, the potential consequences of the change must be carefully considered. Organizational leaders must resolve this tension between driving change or maintaining the status quo. A process of organizational change and changes in strategies, processes, technology, and people can give good results or changes that lead to disaster.

A business leader must be traditionalist and progressive at the same time. They must act with balance so that the traditions and changes can coexist in the organization. But the leader should not be swayed by the

---

* Robin Sharma, *The Monk Who Sold His Ferrari* (Sudamericana, 2010), 177.
† King Midas wanted to have all the gold in the world and one day asked God to turn everything he touched into gold. God gave the power to him, and so he turned stones, garments, the door of his house, and even the dog who went out to greet him to gold. And when he wanted to eat food, it became gold.

temptation to change things if that change was not analyzed properly because the consequences can be disastrous.

Coca-Cola made the worst change in its history when it launched the New Coke in 1985 and received some 1,500 customer calls daily for a month complaining about the product change.

In 2002 PepsiCo launched Pepsi Blue, a berry-flavored soft drink that was promoted by the singer Britney Spears. However, since the drink was made with Blue 1, a controversial and prohibited coloring agent banned in several countries, the sale was discontinued in the United States and Canada in 2004.

In 1998 Richard Branson, founder of the British multinational Virgin Group, introduced the soda Virgin Cola in Times Square in New York City, driving a tank that he crashed into a wall of coca-colas. Coca-Cola reacted quickly, increasing spending in marketing and negotiating with its distributors. In 2001, Virgin Cola left the American market and Virgin sold the product license in 2007.[*]

The merger of AOL with Time Warner in 2000 during the internet boom, the merger of Daimler AG with Chrysler in 1998, Ford's investment in the Edsel model, Quaker Oats' purchase of Snapple tea drinks, or the restructuring Roger Smith oversaw at GM are examples of changes that were bad for those organizations.

On the contrary, the changes can also be very positive. Steven Ortiz, a 15-year-old high school student from Glendora, California, used Craigslist's online service to exchange an old cell phone he had received as a gift. First, he exchanges it for another phone, then he swapped that second phone for an iPod Touch, then the iPod for a bicycle, then the bicycle for a MacBook, the MacBook for a golf cart, the golf cart for a Ford Bronco, and finally he exchanged the Ford Bronco for a Porsche Boxster.

A total of 14 exchanges took him from an old cell phone to a Porsche in two years.[†]

The American philosopher and composer Michael Friedman has said, "Concentrate on finding your goal, then concentrate on reaching it."[‡]

---

[*] "Virgin Cola, El Intento de Destronar a Coca Cola y Pepsi que Nunca llego a España," elrenostalgico.wordpress.com; "Mi Mayor Fracaso fue querer Derrotar a Coca Cola con Virgin Cola," August 5, 2013, www.iprofesional.com ("Virgin Cola, the Attempt to Dethrone Coca-Cola and Pepsi that Never Arrived in Spain"; "My biggest failure was wanting to Defeat Coca-Cola with Virgin Cola").

[†] Ben Wojdyla, "How a 17-year-old Craigslist Swapped an Old Phone for a Porsche," July 20, 2010; jalopnik.com/5591644/how-a-17-year-old-craigslist-swapped-an-old-phone-for-a-porsche?

[‡] Michael Friedman, www.quotes.net/authors.

Changes are advancing rapidly around us, many times without us realizing it. If the organization continues doing what it knows and only pursues short-term goals without noticing the changes in its environment, it can take the company to the precipice.

Organizations must constantly seek alternatives to be able to successfully commit themselves to an increasingly demanding market. Customers, technology, and competitors tirelessly change. Therefore, companies must carry out transformations that allow them to gain an advantageous position in a market that is constantly evolving.

But it's not just about changing; you have to change in the right direction. It is necessary to manage change through good planning and strategy. Change is not easy, but it is necessary and generates growth opportunities. We need to adapt to new trends. Change and growth are linked together.

Optimism and enthusiasm are generators of change. Former UK Prime Minister Winston Leonard Spencer Churchill (1874–1965) stated, "A pessimist sees the difficulty in every opportunity; an optimist sees the opportunity in every difficulty." He also said, "Success consists of going from failure to failure without loss of enthusiasm."[*]

The English poet William Ernest Henley (1843–1903) suffered from tuberculosis that resulted in the amputation of his left leg below the knee. After his leg was amputated, Henley was told that his other leg required a similar procedure. He decided to go to another doctor who managed to save his leg. While recovering in the hospital, he was moved to write the verses that became the short poem "Invictus."[†] The end of the poem says,

> I am the master of my fate:
> I am the captain of my soul.

The poem has inspired great leaders. Mandela, for example, often read this poem while in prison to stay strong. Mandela was also inspired by the German Jewish girl Anne Frank (1929–1945). Mandela said,

> During the many years my comrades and I spent in prison, we derived inspiration from the courage and tenacity of those who challenge injustice even under the most difficult circumstances. As my colleague, Govan Mbeki indicated at the Port Elizabeth exhibition, some of us read

---

[*] Winston Churchill, Quotes, www.brainyquote.com.
[†] en.wikipedia.org/wiki/William_Ernest_Henley.

Anne Frank's Diary on Robben Island and derived much encouragement from it.*

Great leaders are great dreamers and a strong impulse, desire, and determination lead them to realize their dreams.

Thomas Alva Edison (1847–1931) has been described as America's greatest inventor. He made 1,000 unsuccessful attempts at inventing the light bulb. When a reporter asked, "How did it feel to fail 1,000 times?" Edison replied, "I didn't fail 1,000 times. The light bulb was an invention with 1,000 steps."†

Most people know Henry Ford because of the Ford Motor Company. But in 1899, at the age of 36 years, Ford formed his first company, the Detroit Automobile Company that went bankrupt. He didn't give up.

Walt Disney was fired in 1919 from his job at the Kansas City Star paper because he "lacked imagination and had no good ideas."‡

The American writer Napoleon Hill (1883–1970) said that "Our only limitations are those we set up in our own minds."§

At 11 months of age, the Australian Michael Crossland was diagnosed with cancer in the central nervous system. Doctors said to his mom that he had only a 4% chance of survival. As a last resort, her mother accepted that Michael be part of a cancer test drug together with the other 24 kids. Within 30 days, 20 out of the 25 children had passed away. Within 90 days, 24 out of the 25 kids were dead.

Michael was the only survivor. The doctor said to his mother that he will never go to school, he will never play sports, and if he reaches his teenage years it would be a miracle. After many years of illness and treatment, at age 12, Michael suffered his first heart attack and at 19 his second heart attack. This second heart attack ended his successful baseball career in America. Despite all of this, Michael Crossland later built a life of exceptional achievements in the world of banking and finance and is an example of determination, vision, and desire to achieve the impossible, no matter the size of the obstacles that lay ahead.¶

Truly, the size of the inconveniences and obstacles does not matter if there is enough energy and determination.

---

* Address by President Nelson Mandela at the opening of the Anne Frank Exhibition at Museum Africa, Johannesburg. www.mandela.gov.za/mandela_speeches/1994/940815_annefrank.htm.

† "Thomas Edison's." www.uky.edu. It is said that Thomas Edison was afraid of darkness.

‡ "12 famous people who failed before succeeding," www.wanderlustworker.com.

§ Napoleon Hill, *Think and Grow Rich* (Vermilion, Random House, 2004), 33.

¶ Michael crossland.com.

According to the biblical narrative, David (1040–966 BC), a small shepherd, faced Goliath in what it seemed unequal combat. Israel was at war with the Philistines and a warrior over 2 meters tall named Goliath of Gath challenged the Israelite army for 40 days by proposing that they choose their best man to face him. In the words of Goliath, if he was defeated and killed by the Israelite, the Philistines would be slaves of Israel, but if he stayed and killed the chosen one by Israel, the Israelites would be slaves of the Philistines.

David appeared before King Saul who authorized him to accept the challenge of Goliath. David, refusing the use of armors, went to the battlefield with his sling and five stones. David defeated Goliath using a sling and a stone and his victory shows how to overcome the problems and difficulties that seem impossible.[*]

Determination and convictions also had Alexander the Great (356–323 BC). His father had prepared him to reign, giving him military training and entrusting to the Greek philosopher Aristotle (384–322 BC) his intellectual training.

In the year 335 BC, when arriving at the coasts of Phoenicia, Alexander had to face one of his biggest battles.

Upon disembarking, he realized that enemy soldiers exceeded his army three times and that his men were unmotivated and frightened. Alexander ordered that all his ships be burned. While the vessels were consumed in flames and sinking in the sea, he gathered his men and said:

> Watch how the boats burn. That is the only reason why we must win because if we do not win, we will not be able to return to our homes and none of us will be able to reunite with our families again. … We must emerge victorious in this battle since there is only one way back and it is by sea. When we return, we will do it in the only way possible, on the ships of our enemies.[†]

The army of Alexander won in that battle and returned to his land aboard the conquered ships.[‡]

---

[*] "David," Wikipedia. "Goliath," Wikipedia, The Bible (I Samuel 17, 49–50).

[†] Jorge S. Casillas, "El Origen Histórico de la Expresión Quemar las Naves," www.abc.es, 30 de septiembre de 2014 ("The Historical Origin of Expression Burn the Ships," September 30, 2014).

[‡] years later the leader of the Roman Republic Julius Caesar (100–44 BC) used the same resource. After crossing the English Channel, he disembarked with his legions in Britain. He made his soldiers stop when they reached Dover and ordered them to watch as the fire consumed the ships in which they had arrived. Burned the only means to retreat, they could only advance and conquer. The Spanish Hernán Cortés (1485–1547), when he made the conquest of Mexico (1521), sank most of his ships to discourage any attempt to return.

Vision inspires, motivates, and moves forward. As the American business consultant Warren Bennis (1925–2014) put it, "Leadership is the capacity to translate vision into reality."* The Italian sculptor and painter Miguel Angel Buonarroti (1475–1564), known as Michelangelo, is considered one of the greatest artists in history. Among his works are the sculptures *El David* and *the Pieta* and frescoes of the vault of the Sistine Chapel. Michelangelo had a clear vision of what he wanted to do. He said:

> In every block of marble I see a statue as plain as though it stood before me, shaped and perfect in attitude and action. I have only to hew away the rough walls that imprison the lovely apparition to reveal it to the other eyes as mine see it.†

Arjuna was one of the heroes of the Hindu epic poem *Mahabharata*. He was a masterful archer of great integrity. On one occasion, a teacher decided to test his students by hanging a wooden bird from the branch of a tree. One by one, he asked the students to point their bow at the eye of the bird and describe everything they saw. The students described the garden, the tree, the flowers, and the branch of the tree from which the bird hung, as well as the bird itself. When Arjuna's turn came, he told his mentor that all he saw was the eye of his prey.

All his concentration was on the target.

Publius Ovidius Naso (43–17 BC) was a Roman poet. His work *The Metamorphosis* tells the story of Pygmalion, king of Cyprus and sculptor, who long sought a woman to marry provided she was perfect. Frustrated in his quest, he finally decided not to get married and devoted his time to creating sculptures to compensate for the absence of a wife. One of these sculptures he made was so perfect that Pygmalion fell in love with the statue. Pygmalion begged Aphrodite, the Greek goddess of love, to allow him to marry her. Because of that love, one day the marble breathed, opened its eyes, smiled, and came to life in the form of Galatea.

The Pygmalion effect is studied in psychology, and it means that if someone believes something with firmness and conviction, they can make it happen. The psychologists Robert Rosenthal, Lenore Jacobson, and David McClelland conducted studies in schools and concluded those students, who were stimulated more, achieved better results and grades. A person who feels appreciated will always do more than is expected.

---

* "Top 10 Warren Bennis Quotes of All-time," paulsohn.org.
† Michelangelo Gallery, www.michelangelo-gallery.com.

On the other hand, if instead of encouraging those students are criticized, their results will be lower.*

Successful leaders achieve *The Pygmalion Effect* in their work and in the work of their teams, an unconscious force by which they achieve the best of themselves, believe in their abilities, advance in the objective, and manage to exceed expectations.

Enhamed Mohamed Yahdih is a Spanish Paralympic athlete who at the age of eight years suffered a retinal detachment that caused him blindness. At nine he started swimming.† After having obtained four gold medals in the Beijing 2008 Paralympic Games, Enhamed is considered the best Paralympic swimmer in history. In the 100-meter butterfly race in Beijing, he had to face a Chinese swimmer who was encouraged by 17,000 people. When asked how he had faced that challenge, he said:

> As I did not see or understand the seventeen thousand Chinese spectators, I proposed to imagine that they were Spaniards and that they had come to see and support me.
>
> I visualize everything up to the last detail. I visualized the 100 meters butterfly swimming race sixteen thousand times. When you visualize something that you love it so much, your brain tries to get your actions to be equal to what you are imagining. Not everything is a matter of view; it is a matter of vision.‡

Motivation and vision are important to achieve results.

A group of frogs traveled through the forest when suddenly two of them fell into a deep well.

The other frogs gathered around the hole and when they saw how deep it was, they told the fallen frogs they were going to die and that their efforts would be useless.

However, the two frogs tried to leave the hole with all their strength until one of them paid attention to what the frogs told her, she gave up and died.

The other frog continued to jump with as much effort as she could. The frogs shouted at her that it was useless, but the frog jumped more and more with force until she managed to get out of the hole.

---

* es.wikipedia.org/wiki/Efecto_Pigmalión y "¿Que es el Efecto Pigmalión?" Norberto Abdala, Revista Viva, Clarín, www.clarin.com November 12, 2017 ("What Is the Pygmalion Effect?").

† "Enhamed Enhamed," es.wikipedia.org.

‡ "Como Convertirnos en las Personas Que Queremos Ser" ("How to Become the People We Want to Be"), Enhamed Enhamed, Conference organized by BBVA and EL PAIS, April 2018, YouTube.

When she came out of the hole, the others asked her in amazement if she did not listen to what they were saying. The frog explained that she was not listening well and that she believed that the others were encouraging her to try harder and harder to get out of the hole.*

The American writer William Ward (1921–1994) has pointed out: "The experienced mountain climber is not intimidated by a mountain – he is inspired by it."† The mountains were created to be conquered, adversities to be overcome, and problems and crises to be solved.

All this is achieved with clear vision and determination.

One of the main causes of the failure of many dreams and projects is the lack of sufficient determination. In the presence of obstacles and difficulties, the objective is left aside.

At the time of the gold rush in the United States,‡ a man named Darby went West to look for gold and get rich. After several weeks of searching, he discovered a gold mine in Colorado. As he needed appropriate machines to remove it, he covered the mine and returned to his city to raise money from family and friends.

When he returned to the place with the machines, he could not find the gold again. During several weeks he performed perforations without achieving any positive results. Finally, he decided to quit. He sold the machinery to a junk man for a few hundred dollars and took the train back home.

The junk man called in a mining engineer to explore the area where the drilling had been done. The calculations made by the engineer showed the gold existed and it was "only three feet from where Darby had stopped drilling."§ The gold was found there and Darby lost a fortune because he abandoned the search less than a meter away from where the gold was located.

Thomas Edison (1847–1931) said, "Many of life's failures are people who did not realize how close they were to success when they gave up.... Our greatest weakness lies in giving up. The most certain way to succeed is always to try just one more time."¶

---

* Jaime Lopera Gutiérrez and Marta Inés Bernal Trujillo, *La culpa es de la vaca* (Intermedio Editores. Colombia, 2006), 54–55 ("It Is Cow's Fault").

† William Arthur Ward, www.brainyquote.com.

‡ Period of mass migration of workers to the west in search of gold between 1848 and 1960.

§ Napoleon Hill, *Think and Grow Rich* (Vermilion, Random House, 2004), 5–6.

¶ www.brainyquote.com/quotes/thomas_a_edison_109004; www.brainyquote.com/authors/thomas_a_edison.

Leaders with a clear vision and determination can achieve great impact. There are stories that inspire people to achieve goals that seem impossible. These are some of them:

For many years the Italian navigator Christopher Columbus (1433–1506) asked the monarchies of France, England, and Portugal to help him finance a new route to Western Asia. Columbus did not let himself be overcome by adversity and he finally persuaded the Spanish kings Fernando de Aragon (1452–1516) and Isabel de Castilla (1451–1504) to finance the trip.[*]

Padma Shri Jadav "Molai" Payeng is a forestry worker from Jorhat, India. Over the course of 39 years, he planted and tended trees on a sandbar of the river Brahmaputra. Today that desert is a forest, called Molai forest after him. The forest is located near Kokilamukh of Jorhat, Assam, India, and encompasses an area of about 1,360 acres/550 hectares. Molai forest now houses Bengal tigers, Indian rhinoceros, deer, rabbits, monkeys, and several varieties of birds.[†] Payeng had a vision almost 40 years ago, plant a jungle in a desert. He says, "I never thought that my small initiative would make such a difference one day."[‡] Thanks to his vision and execution, Payeng turned a desert into a forest. In 2015 Payeng was honored with Padma Shri, one of the highest civilian awards to citizens of India in recognition of their contribution to the country.[§]

The Irish explorer Ernest Shackleton (1874–1922) made a trip to cross the Antarctic across the South Pole in 1915. He published a notice in the press in 1913 to recruit his crew saying: "Men Wanted. for hazardous journey, small wages, bitter cold, long months of complete darkness, constant danger, safe return doubtful, honor and recognition in case of success. Ernest Shackleton."[¶] He received 5,000 applications.

The motto of the expedition was "fortitudine vincimus" (we will overcome by resistance). His ship, the *Endurance*, sailed from England in August 1914. The expedition that was going to be 120 days ended up becoming a nightmare of almost 2 years in extreme conditions. On January 19, 1915,

---

[*] Columbus discovered America on October 12, 1492, when he disembarked on the island of San Salvador or Guanahami in the Bahamas. Columbus knew that the earth was not flat. The Greek philosopher Pythagoras (569–475 BC) had claimed 2,000 years before that the earth was round and those observations had been endorsed by Aristotle (384–322BC). Columbus made four trips to America.

[†] "Jadav Payegn," en.wikipedia.org/wiki/Jadav_Payeng.

[‡] Partho Bruman, "An Assamese Who Created a Woodland in a River Island Is the Forest Man of India," April 27, 2015, www.theweekendleader.com/Heroism/2155/forest-maker.html.

[§] "Jadav Payegn," en.wikipedia.org/wiki/Jadav_Payeng.

[¶] en.wikiquote.org/wiki/Talk: Ernest_Shackleton; en.wikipedia.org/wiki/Ernest_Shackleton.

the ship was immobilized by ice in the Weddell Sea and on November 21, 1915, the ship sinks and leaves the men on the ice. Shackleton's leadership proved so effective that even in extreme circumstances lasting two years, all 28 men who left England managed to return.*

The Austrian psychiatrist Viktor Frankl (1905–1997) was sent in 1942 to a Nazi concentration camp and managed to survive even when he worked 12 hours a day, even under snow with temperatures below zero.†

Frankl frequently used a phrase of the German philosopher Friedrich Nietzsche (1844–1900): "He who has a why to live can bear almost any how."‡

On September 12, 1962, at Rice Stadium in Houston, Texas, US President John F. Kennedy launched a major challenge to 35,000 people. He said:

> We choose to go to the Moon in this decade and do the other things, not because they are easy, but because they are hard; because that goal will serve to organize and measure the best of our energies and skills, because that challenge is one that we are willing to accept, one we are unwilling to postpone, and one we intend to win, and the others, too.§

Effective leadership consists of having a vision, sharing it, and getting the rest of the people to align in that direction.

When John F. Kennedy visited NASA space center for the first time, in 1962, while touring the facilities, he introduced himself to an employee and said, "Hi, I'm Jack Kennedy. What are you doing?"

"Well, Mr. President," the janitor responded, "I am helping to put a man on the moon!"¶

---

* After camping on the ice for months, Shackleton went with his people in lifeboats to Elephant Island in South Shetland, 550 kilometers from where the *Endurance* had sunk, where the group could step mainland after 497 days. Elephant Island was an inhospitable place, so Shackleton left most of the people there and with five men he undertook a 1,300-kilometer trip in a boat named *James Caird* to the whaling stations of South Georgia Island, in distressing conditions of survival. For more than two weeks they navigated the ocean waters at the mercy of marine storms that threatened to overturn the boat. On May 9 they managed to set foot in the south of the island and Shackleton and two of his men began a 51-kilometer hike through mountainous terrain. After walking for 36 hours they reach the Stromness whaling station to ask for help. Shackleton sent help to pick up the three men who were on the south coast and with the help of a Chilean ship and a British whaler; they arrive at Elephant Island on August 30, 1916, and rescued the other 28 men.
† In 1946 his book *Man's Search for Meaning* was published in German. The Library of Congress in Washington declared it one of the ten most influential books in the United States.
‡ www.brainyquote.com/quotes/friedrich_nietzsche.
§ en.wikipedia.org/wiki/We_choose_to_go_to_the_Moon.
¶ "JFK and the Janitor: The Importance of Understanding the WHY That Is Behind What We Do," November 26, 2014, www.beqom.com; John Nemo, "What a NASA Janitor Can Teach Us About

That without a doubt is to share a vision. All employees must feel that they are part of the organization's major objectives. The vision is what mobilizes and allows achieving the goals.

The Pursuit of Happyness is a 2006 American biographical drama film based on the true story of Chris Gardner's journey from homelessness to a successful stockbroker. The movie has a message of "Never give up." In one of the scenes of the movie, he said to his son:

> Don't ever let someone tell you that you can't do anything.
> You got a dream, you gotta protect it.
> You want something, go get it. Period.*

The Uruguayan Fernando "Nando" Parrado and Ricardo Canessa had a clear objective when they went out to seek help walking through the Andes Mountains 60 days after flight 571 of the Uruguayan Air Force, Fairchild Hiller FH 227, crashed on October 13,1972 to 6,000 meters high in the mountains. After walking 60 kilometers for ten days, enduring the snow, the cold, the height, and the hunger, they are observed by a muleteer with a river in between. The muleteer attaches sheets of paper and a pencil to a stone and throws it to Parrado. Parrado writes a message where he says:

> I come from an airplane that fell in the mountains. I am Uruguayan. We have been walking for 10 days; I have a friend hurt higher up the road. There are 14 injured persons on the airplane. We have to get out of here fast and we do not know how. We do not have food. We are weak. When can we go and look for them? Please, we cannot even walk, where are we?

The Chilean muleteer threw him some bread and went to seek help and to inform there were 16 survivors of the accident of the Andes.

As Ricardo Canessa said,

> For society it was impossible that we had hit the mountain and we were still alive, it was impossible that we could endure that cold, it was impossible to

---

Living a Bigger Life," December 23, 2014, www.bizjournals.com.

* Gardner's book of memoirs, *The Pursuit of Happyness*, was published in May 2006. The 2006 motion picture *The Pursuit of Happyness*, directed by Gabriele Muccino and starring Will Smith, is based on the book. The unusual spelling of the film's title comes from a mural that Gardner sees on the wall outside the nursery his son attends. He complains to the owner of the daycare center that "happyness" is incorrectly written and should be changed. Gardner now travels all over the world 200 days a year as a motivational speaker. Gardner has spoken in over 50 countries. www.en.wikipedia.org/wiki/The_Pursuit_of_Happyness.

cross that wall of snow, rocks, and ice...they come to ask me how we did to survive and they go with a simple answer: we never stop thinking about escaping.*

A vision shows us goals that seem impossible. There are stories that inspire and mobilize people to persevere, be optimistic, execute, and achieve their goals.

How did Anne Frank (1929–1945) maintain her optimism about the Nazi occupation? In the *Dairy of a Young Lady*,† she wrote:

> At such moments I don't think about all the misery, but about the beauty that still remains.... It's a wonder I haven't abandoned all my ideals, they seem so absurd and impractical. Yet I cling to them because I still believe, in spite of everything, that people are truly good at heart.‡

How did Jose de San Martin (1778–1850) and his army cross more than 3,500 meters over 500 kilometers of the Andes Mountains under an intense cold and then defeat the Spanish army in the Battle of Chacabuco?§

How did 33 miners trap 69 days deeper than 700 meters to survive?¶

---

* Pablo Vierci, *La Sociedad de la Nieve*, Editorial Sudamericana, 2008, 30, 36. The father of Roberto Canessa, the cardiologist Juan Carlos Canessa (1928–2009), on December 22, 1972, got in a taxi in Buenos Aires, Argentina, and told the driver that he was the father of one of the boys who fell on the mountain. The driver, then, looking at him in the rearview mirror, asks: "Have you heard? ... Two appeared.... It is on all the stations." As the driver turned on the radio, the first thing Canessa heard was, "Roberto Canessa and Fernando Parrado are the two survivors who arrived at Los Maitenes." Completely uncontrolled, Canessa threw himself into the front seat to hug and kiss the driver, who had to put the brakes on the car, and they began to cry. See Pablo Vierci The Snow Society, Editorial Sudamericana (2008), 141/2.

† Annelies Marie Frank Hollander, known as Anne Frank (1929–1945), was a German Jewish girl known for her Diary, where she recorded the two years she had to hide with her family from the Nazis in Amsterdam during the World War II. When Ana was discovered by the secret police of Nazi Germany, the Gestapo, she was sent with her family to the concentration camps, where she died of typhus in March 1945. Miep Gies (1900–2010), the Austrian who hid Anne Frank and her family in a hiding place in the back of his company in Amsterdam between July 1942 and August 1944, was the one who kept Ana's Diary until her father returned. But after Ana's death in the Bergen-Belsen concentration camp, when her father Otto Frank returned to Amsterdam, Miep Gies handed Otto the diary. In 1947 Ana's work was published by her father, the only survivor of the family, and the book was translated into more than 55 languages.

‡ www.goodreads.com.

§ The crossing of the Andes is considered one of the greatest feats of military history.

¶ On August 15, 2010, the collapse of the San Jose mine, 30 kilometers from Copiapo in northern Chile, left 33 miners trapped 720 meters deep. The Chilean government started the search work without knowing if the miners were alive and it was speculated that they would have food for three days. On August 22, after several failed attempts at drilling, a probe achieves the objective and the same day a note is received from the miners who said, "We are fine in the shelter the 33."

How did the Mexican architect Bosco Gutierrez Cortina survive after being kidnapped, threatened with death, and held in a box of 3 square meters for 257 days?*

How did Mother Teresa (1910–1997) devote himself to charity in Calcutta, India, for more than 45 years and manage to rescue 60,000 poor and sick people from the streets?† Mother Teresa said: "We ourselves feel that what we are doing is just a drop in the ocean. But the ocean would be less because of that missing drop."‡

How did the Italian violinist Niccolo Paganini (1782–1840) continue playing his violin when he had already broken three strings? Paganini symbolizes those who continue ahead in the face of difficulties. When everything seems impossible you can awaken the "Paganini" that exists inside us to overcome obstacles.

How did Tony Melendez learn to play the guitar with his toes and then be able to perform a concert before Pope John Paul II and 6,000 people?§

How did athlete Heather Dorniden do after stumbling and to be in the last place missing 200 meters (in an athletics race of 600 meters) and finish winning the race?¶

---

* Bosco Gutierrez Cortina was kidnapped in August 1990 after leaving a church in Mexico City. Cortina said, "The day and night were confusing because they turned on and off the light when they wanted. I offered my suffering to God every day and, when I thought, I realized that Christ had suffered much more than me and that he had given his life for me when he was crucified. Thanks to prayer I had the strength and I could pray for the captors. From that moment, I felt the need to try to survive this situation."

† Mother Teresa of Calcutta (1910–1997) was born in the Republic of Macedonia (Yugoslavia) under the name of Agnes Gonxha Bojaxhiu and at the age of 18 opted to change her name to Teresa, in reference to the patron saint of the missionaries, Therese of Lisieux (1873–1897), the Discalced Carmelite Saint Therese. In 1929, Mother Teresa traveled to Calcutta to understand the needs of the poorest and sickest. In 1950 she founded the "Missionaries of Charity," and her dedication was total until her death. Mother Teresa was awarded the Nobel Peace Prize in 1979. She challenged with her actions the conscience of humanity. The news produced a national joy.

‡ www.brainyquote.com/quotes/mother_teresa_121243.

§ Tony Melendez, Nicaraguan guitarist, composer, and singer, became famous for his ability to play the guitar with his feet. Tony has no arms because he was affected by Thalidomide. The medicine was prescribed to her mother during pregnancy to calm her nausea. His performance for Pope John Paul II was famous at the Amphitheater University of Los Angeles on September 15, 1987. After Tony finished playing *Never Be the Same*, the Pope surprisingly jumped off the stage, approached him, kissed and congratulated him. The words of the Pope were: "Tony, you are truly a very courageous young man. You are giving hope to all of us. My wish for you is that you continue to give hope to the people." Tony Melendez sings for Pope John Paul II - 1987. www.youtube.com/watch?v=hEkDS3V3Nh4.

¶ Heather Dorniden, an athlete from the University of Minnesota (2008). Watch "Atleta cae se levanta y gana la carrera" (Athlete falls up and wins the race), www.youtube.com/watch?v=G01RIcVIF7o Watch "Inspiring Heather Dorniden Takes a Fall but Still Wins the Race," www.youtube.com/watch?v=xjejTQdK5OI.

How did Zamperini (1917–2014) survive, during World War II, 47 days on a raft in the middle of the Pacific Ocean after dropping the plane in which he was traveling to the water and then endure forced labor and mistreatment in the concentration camps in Japan?*

How did the soldier Rowan deliver the letter from the president of the United States to the head of the Cuban rebels called Garcia who was hiding in the jungle of Cuba in 1899? Rowan toured the island from coast to coast and three months later returned from Cuba with Garcia's response. The "Letter to Garcia" highlights the importance of commitment and willingness to meet the objectives.†

Abraham Lincoln (1809–1865) had a vision of what he wanted for North America: a united country without slaves. To achieve this, he had to endure the Civil War between the North and the South of the country. In the month of July 1863 the Union army, under the leadership of Major General George Meade, defeated the Confederate army of General Robert Lee at the Battle of Gettysburg and some 50,000 soldiers died in the bloodiest Civil War. The people of Gettysburg built a huge cemetery in memory of those killed in that war and organized a ceremony to which they invited President Lincoln to say a few words. A total of 15,000 people gathered and at the end of the speech, Lincoln pointed out:

> These dead shall not have died in vain – that this nation, under God, shall have a new birth of freedom – and that government of the people, by the people, for the people, shall not perish from the earth.‡

The influence and source of inspiration of Lincoln's speech in Gettysburg have been so great that even the formula "government of the people, by the people, and for the people" has been used to define democracy and was adopted by the constitution of the French Revolution. Lincoln with his vision and leadership achieved the union of the United States.

---

* Louis Silvie Zamperini (1917–2014) was an American athlete who participated in the 1936 Berlin Olympic Games in the 5,000 meters race. In the final he broke the lap record with 56 seconds, being at 19 years old the youngest American Olympic athlete of the specialty until that time. Hitler was impressed with the record and asked to meet him and shake his hand. His story of self-improvement was narrated by Laura Hillenbrand in the book *Unbroken: A World War II Story of Survival, Resilience, and Redemption*, which has sold more than 13 million copies. The book was taken to the cinema in 2014 under the name of *Unbroken* (2014).

† The story is told in El periodicomedierraneo.com and in "La Vida es un Supermercado" Luis Puchol (Coleccion Vital, 2005), 12.

‡ "Gettysburg Address," Wikipedia.

What motivates leaders to face a problem and not give in to difficulties?
What mobilizes them to think big and then build their dream?
How trust and perseverance are achieved in order to influence others?
How do we get inspiration and motivation to move forward despite the
negative reactions of bosses or peers?
How do you overcome frustration and persist with an idea?

Change has always been resisted. Anyone who must convince the CEO
or a board of directors of the desirability of implementing or improving a
risk control program will probably have to overcome conflicting opinions,
adversity, and questioning. Is it a mission impossible? No, but maybe you
need to swim against the tide.

Creating a compliance and ethics structure can be a difficult task,
especially in organizations with results-oriented cultures. It is not easy
to achieve approval for investments in employees, systems, processes,
suppliers, communication tools, and training. It is reasonable that internal
resistance will be generated; and then a motivated and inspired leader
with determination, passion, and influence will be required to champion
the project.

In seminars and conferences on ethics and compliance in the United
States and Latin America, frustrated compliance officers are heard because
their CEOs reject their proposals for risk control programs since they do
not consider it a priority or find it expensive. In the face of this situation, it
is imperative to persevere and not be discouraged. To achieve objectives, it
is necessary to overcome obstacles, motivated by the vision that is desired
to achieve.

Motivated people are like an electric shock, they energize. The German
philosopher Georg Friedrich Hegel (1770–1831) said that "Nothing great
in the world has ever been accomplished without passion."*

The French writer Antoine de Saint Exupery (1900–1944) said: "If you
want to build a ship, don't drum up people to collect wood and don't
assign them tasks and work, but rather teach them to long for the endless
immensity of the sea."†

French novelist Jules Verne (1828–1905) said, "There are no impossible
obstacles; there are just stronger and weaker wills, that's all."‡

---

* Georg Hegel, Quotes, www.brainyquote.com.
† www.brainyquote.com.
‡ www.goodreads.com.

An old Chinese proverb says that "A journey of a thousand miles begins with a single step."*

The will is like water that passes over obstacles and always reaches its destination.

The Latin phrase *aut viam inveniam aut faciam* means "I will either find a way or make one."

Leadership is not about looking over your shoulder and living in the past. Leadership is about looking over the horizon and envisioning the future.

Vision guides leaders but also lets them know where they are now and what steps they must take to cross the gap to realize that vision.

The founder and CEO of Amazon, Jeff Bezos, says the success of his company in part is due to having a mindset focused on the future. Bezos says,

> I've built my work so I do not have to be attracted to the present. I can stay for two or three years in the future.... Due to our emphasis on the long term, we can make decisions differently to some companies.†

Also, the CEO of Walmart, Doug McMillon, points out:

> We are playing a long game. Our priority is to position our company for long-term success. History has shown us that companies that focused too much on the short term were doomed to fail.
>
> Managing our business on a daily basis is important, but our most important strategic decisions are made in light of what we want our company to become for the next generation.‡
>
> If I go back and look at how I've spent my time, it changed quite a bit from five years ago, and I'm much more focused on the future.§

Transformational leaders can change and carry out the revolution in their companies. They always keep an eye on their goals and they will need to overcome difficulties, obstacles, and problems.

---

* en.wikipedia.org/wiki/A_journey_of_a_thousand_miles_begins_with_a_single_step.
† www.cnbc.com/2018/04/26/why-amazon-ceo-jeff-bezos-doesnt-focus-on-the-present.
‡ "What I've Learned Since Becoming CEO," Walmart CEO, Letter to Shareholders, 2019 Annual Report.
§ *Fortune* Interview: "Walmart CEO Doug McMillon on Automation, Training 2.2 Millon Workers, and the Tragedy in El Paso." Brian O' Keefe on August 19, 2019. www.fortune.com.

At the end of the movie *The Terminator*,* Sarah stops at a gas station, and a boy takes a picture with a Polaroid camera. The boy says that a storm is coming, and Sarah responds "I know."

Like Sarah, the compliance officer knows the storm that the company may suffer if preventive measures against risks are not implemented.

What should be the attitude toward risks?

Success in business lies in vision and values. Change requires courage and leaders with dreams and passion are those who generate it.

The vision of an organization with a good culture and reputation thought for the long term and for the next generation requires taking the initiative and leading strategic changes that protect the company and its members.

---

* *The Terminator* is an American science fiction film and action thriller from 1984 and directed by James Cameron.

10

Be a Proactive Leader

The Maslow pyramid or hierarchy of human needs is a theory proposed by the American psychologist Abraham Maslow (1908–1970) in his 1943 work *A Theory of Human Motivation*, wherein the author formulates a hierarchy of human needs and argues that as basic needs are met (bottom of the pyramid), people begin to address higher and less basic needs.

Maslow describes the scale of needs in five levels. Each level of a need motivates our behavior until that particular need is satisfied. Once that point is reached, the next level of need will motivate our behavior until we fulfill it and then try to meet the next level.

The first need is *physiological* (breathing, feeding, sleeping). The second need is *security* and *protection* (physical security, protection of assets and property, stability, reduction of threats). The third need is *social relationships* (friendship, family, and couple). The fourth need is *esteem* (respect, appreciation, trust, recognition, reputation). The fifth need is *self-realization* (problem solving, creativity).

If this theory is transposed to the hierarchy of needs of organizations, the company will also achieve its own realization when it meets the previous needs.

In order to meet the second basic need for survival (security and property protection, stability, and reduction of threats), companies must have an effective risk protection program.

Noah was the only righteous man of his generation at a time when the earth was plunged into violence. Around the year 2300 BC and by God's instructions, Noah built an ark of cypress wood and, thanks to it, was one of the eight survivors of the great universal flood created to destroy the

descendants of Adam and Eve, as told in the Bible in the Book of Genesis.*
Noah was prepared, and he anticipated the flood and the storm.

Effective leaders hope to navigate difficult times. They will not always
have quiet seas to bring their ship to good port, and therefore they must
take the necessary precautions to overcome the storms of life.

One of the 12 apostles chosen by Jesus of Nazareth, Matthew, says in the
Gospel of St. Matthew:

> Before the flood, and until the day Noah entered the ark, people ate, drank
> and married. But when they least expected it, the flood came and took
> them all away.
>
> Understand that if the owner of a house knew at what time of night the
> robber would arrive, he would remain awake and would not allow anyone
> to enter his house to steal. So also, be prepared.†

Ulysses, the legendary Greek hero of the epic poem *The Odyssey*, had to
overcome multiple risks to which he was exposed. Thanks to his cunning,
he managed to avoid the continuous problems that he had to face and
managed to escape the Sirens, whose song made the listener go crazy.
Their sound was irresistible and attracted the sailors to the rocks where
they ended up sinking the ships. Ulysses prepared himself by anticipating
the risks and ordered his men to cover their ears with wax except him. He
ordered his men to tie him to the mast because he would not be able to
resist the singing of the sirens.

Like Ulysses or Noah, the organization must be able to plan and
anticipate risky events, establishing the necessary controls to be able to
face them successfully. Instead of suffering in the storm, you should dance
in the rain.

Thomas Hobbes (1588–1679) was an important English philosopher
and thinker of the seventeenth century who reflected on the need to be
cautious. Hobbes said that "Although the wicked were less in number
than the righteous since we cannot distinguish them, it is necessary to be
suspicious, to be cautious, to anticipate always and defend even the most
honest and just."‡

---

* The Bible, Genesis 6: 6–7 God said to Noah, "But I will sign my covenant with you, and you will
  enter into the ark with your wife, your children and the wives of your children. You will put in the
  ark a pair of every living thing or of all the animals so that they can survive with you. You will take
  male and female."
† The Bible, Matthew, 24:37–44.
‡ Brennan-Buchanan, *The Reasons of Rules* (Biblioteca de Economía, Editorial Folio, Cambridge
  University Press), 98.

Roberto Goizueta (1932–1997), who as CEO of Coca-Cola between 1980 and 1997 led the company to become the number one corporation in the United States, said: "If you take risks, you may fail; but if you don't take risks, you will surely fail. The greatest risk of all is to do nothing."*
Aligned with this thought, Facebook founder Mark Zuckerberg has pointed out that "The greatest risk is not taking any risk. ... In a world that is changing really quickly, the only strategy that is guaranteed to fail is not taking risks."†

Brazilian novelist Paulo Coelho is one of the most-read writers in the world and has sold over 200 million books translated into 81 languages.‡ Coelho says that "The world is in hands of those who have the courage to take the risk of living their dreams."§

John Augustus Shedd (1859–1928) was an American author and professor who said, "A ship in port is safe, but that's not what ships are built for."¶

Companies must make decisions and take risks in environments of uncertainty. As Professor Fullenkamp points out,

> We cannot get rid of all the risk and uncertainty in our lives. Every company has to take some kind of risk in order to create wealth and prosperity. ... [T]he growth and development of economies rest to a great extent on innovation, which is a fundamentally risky activity.**

Aversion to total risk would imply doing nothing, so success depends on taking risks.

Doug McMillon, CEO of Walmart Inc., said:

> There is no growth without change, and there is no meaningful change without risk. So, get comfortable with an intelligent level of risk. Otherwise, the law of diminishing returns sets in as always doing the same thing the same way takes over.††

---

* www.azquotes.com; www.goodreads.com.
† www.brainyquote.com.
‡ Paulo Coelho, Wikipedia.
§ sabidurias.com/cita/es/192299/paulo-coelho.
¶ en.wikiquote.org/wiki/John_Augustus_Shedd.
** Professor Connel Fullenkamp, *The Economics of Uncertainty* (Duke University, The Great Courses, The Teaching Company, 2015), 5 and 24.
†† "What I've learned since becoming CEO," Walmart CEO, Letter to Shareholders, 2019 Annual Report.

Companies must have a mitigation system and controls to protect themselves from unexpected events and find a balance between taking and controlling risks.

Zero risks do not exist, so business risks must be properly controlled and managed.

Former chairman of the board of KPMG International, Michael Rake, says: "Good corporate governance means achieving the right balance by taking risks without exposing the company to disproportionate risks."[*]

Being the president of the United States has its risks. From George Washington to the current president, among these 45 men,[†] 4 of them (9%) have been assassinated during their tenure: "Abraham Lincoln (1865), James A. Garfield (1881), William McKinley (1901) and John F. Kennedy (1963) .... If we add that nine Presidents have survived attacks during their mandates, and those who were killed, there are 30% of the Presidents."[‡]

When the president of the United States travels around the world, he assumes risks, but at the same time, the US government anticipates and takes control measures to protect him. For example, the president uses bulletproof suits made with a lightweight and flexible fiber that allows him to walk smoothly. The water he usually consumes abroad is taken from Washington, and at the dinners, he is attended by his own waiters (Secret Service agents).

The vehicle that carries the president is known as "the Beast" or "Cadillac One." The windows of this car are shielded with five layers of glass and polycarbonate. The car has protection against attacks using radiation, chemical, and biological weapons. The car weighs seven tons and is considered the safest in the world. Its structure is capable of resisting the impact of bombs and shots and has a system to activate bombs, automatic weapons, and gas. The limousine floor is prepared to resist mines, grenades, and explosive artifacts. The car also has oxygen tanks and a blood supply compatible with that of the president in case a transfusion is needed. Its tires are reinforced with Kevlar and the chauffeur, trained by the Secret Service, is in a driving cabin that is reinforced with a door with the thickness of a jet. The Beast was manufactured by General Motors and has a cost of US$1.5 million per unit.[§]

---

[*] "Reglas Claras y Transparentes," interview with Michael Rake, May–June 2004, 124, www.gestion.com.ar ("Clear and Transparent Rules").

[†] Donald Trump is the 45th president of the United States.

[‡] Manuel Prieto, *Curistoria 2* (Manuel J. Prieto, 2017), 96.

[§] "Como es La Bestia," www.infobae.com 25 de noviembre de 2018 ("How is the Beast").

The Strategic Petroleum Reserve (SPR) is an emergency fuel storage of petroleum maintained underground in the states of Louisiana and Texas by the United States Department of Energy (DOE). It is the largest emergency supply in the world, with the capacity to hold up to 727 million barrels.

The United States started the petroleum reserve in 1975 under Fords' presidency, after oil supplies were interrupted during the 1973–1974 oil embargo, to mitigate future supply disruptions.*

If due to a crisis the United States could not import oil, the country could keep running for more than 30 days.†

The US government tries to anticipate, prepare, and prevent risks or be ready to react to unexpected events.

The market is dominated by factors that are beyond the company's control, but organizations must be prepared and take the necessary protective measures to deal with risks.

In war, the environment is unpredictable; everything changes quickly. When soldiers go to the front, they take risks, but at the same time, they protect themselves. The VUCA acronym is used in military vocabulary to reflect volatility, uncertainty, complexity, and ambiguity in certain situations.

Companies must be prepared to anticipate the attacks, risks, and even ambiguous threats that may occur in the future.

Considered the best French general during the time of Louis XIV, Maurice of Saxony (1696–1750) said that "War must be fought without leaving anything to chance."‡

The military strategist and philosopher of ancient China Sun Tzu (544–496 BC) noted in his book *The Art of War* that one should always be alert and observe the movements of the enemy.

Pierre Yves Hittelet, CEO of the coaching organization R-Each, wrote an article about leadership lessons based on the military experiences of Jocko Willink and Leif Babin, members of the US Navy military elite that led American and allied soldiers during the battle of Ramadi in Iraq. Hittelet says:

---

* In October 1973, Syria and Egypt were at war with Israel (Yom Kippur War). Because Israel received US support, Arab countries suspended the export of crude oil to the West, which caused oil prices to go from the US$3 to the US$12 per barrel.
† The United States uses 20 million barrels per day. Every day, the United States produces 12 million barrels and imports 10 million barrels.
‡ John Laffin, *Grandes Batallas de la Historia* (El Ateneo, 2004), 197 ("Great Battles of History").

The more precautions are taken to anticipate problems and mishaps, the higher the chances of success. It is thus the leader's responsibility to plan for a maximum number of scenarios and alternative plans so as to adapt to a situation that can change at any moment.

For a Navy Seal, there is nothing worse than indecision.... [I]t is not possible to remain paralyzed and not take any decisions.... There is a real danger in letting a situation degenerate due to a lack of firmness and decisiveness. Jocko and Leif, both well versed in decision making and maximum risk, recommend making a decision rather than "wait and see." ... [T]he more one waits, the more the situation degenerates and more everybody suffers from it.*

Every year about one million people die from malaria, Zika, dengue, or West Nile virus. The risk of acquiring any of these during a trip is variable, depending on the destination, the time of year, and the measures of anti-mosquito protection taken (repellents and preventive drugs). In the same way that many travelers take steps to avoid acquiring malaria, organizations must be prevented to protect themselves against the risks to which they are subjected.

When competitors participate in adventure-risk races Eco-Challenge style whereby groups of people run 300 miles (500 kilometers) through inhospitable areas, trekking, diving, living in the jungle, and sleeping 20 hours in nine days, the teams are sufficiently prepared and motivated to reach their goals. Companies must also know how to manage the risks and overcome the obstacles and thorns that are encountered along the way as if it were a hurdle race or rafting in fast and turbulent rivers.

The Greek historians Timothy of Tauromenius (356–260 BC), Diodorus Siculus (first century BC), and the Roman philosopher Marco Tulio Cicero (106–43 BC) relate the legend of Damocles, a courtier in the service of King Dionysius I (430–367 BC), a tyrannical king at Syracuse, Sicily. Damocles envied the king and propagated the idea that the sovereign was very fortunate by the luxuries and comfort with which he lived and by having so much power and wealth.

One day the king was informed of what Damocles said and then offered him to exchange the roles for a few hours so that he could enjoy the pleasures he envied. That same night, a banquet was held, and Damocles was served like a king. When the banquet was well advanced,

---

* Pierre Yves Hittelet, "12 Leadership Lessons to Learn from the NAVY SEALs," INC.COM, May 25, 2017, 10.

Damocles noticed that a sharp sword hung tied by horsehair directly over his head.

Damocles immediately lost his appetite for the delicacies when he saw the threatening sword, and he asked the king to leave his post.

The sword of Damocles exemplifies the constant threat, the imminent danger that can lead unexpectedly to a tragic end.

Companies that do not have adequate risk protection systems are balancing on a rope, moving through a minefield, a block of brittle ice, or with a sword dangling over their heads.

According to the poem "Aquileida," written by the poet Estacio (45–96) in the first century, when Achilles was born his mother Tethys tried to immortalize it by immersing him in the Styx. An Oracle had revealed that the son of Thetis would be much stronger than his father. The legend says that the Styx lagoon made invulnerable any part of the body that was immersed in it. Thus, Thetis bathed her son Achilles in the lagoon and he achieved invulnerability, except for the right heel by which his mother grabbed him by submerging him and thus became his only vulnerable point.*

Achilles became famous for beating any rival that crossed him, but the carelessness of his mother would make him pay with his life, thus fulfilling the Oracle that also predicted that the life of Achilles would be celebrated but ephemeral.

In the Trojan War, during the final battle fought between Greeks and Trojans, after defeating and killing Prince Hector, Achilles was mortally wounded by a poisoned arrow thrown by Paris, Hector's younger brother, who went to strike on his right heel.

The expression "Achilles heel" refers to a vulnerable point.[†]

Do companies have their Achilles heel?

A leader must avoid having Achilles' heels and be prepared and on alert to face the risks, deceptions, and betrayals of the Judas Iscariots and Dick Dastardly's of this world.[‡] Like the Toba volcano,[§] everything can change

---

* es.wikipedia.org/wiki/Tetis_(nereida); ¿De dónde viene la expresión "talón de Aquiles"? ("Where does the expression "Achilles heel" come from?") December 7, 2012, blogs.infobae.com/grecia-aplicada/2012/12/07/cual-es-tu-talon-de-aquiles/index.html; es.wikipedia.org/wiki/Estigia_(río).

† es.wikipedia.org/wiki/Aquiles y es.wikipedia.org/wiki/Talón_de_Aquiles.

‡ Dick Dastardly (Pierre Nodoyuna) is the villainous fictional character of the cartoon The Wacky Races that competed with a Super Ferrari and in the races made traps to try to win them.

§ The volcanic eruption of Toba on the island of Sumatra 73,000 years ago deforested almost all of central India. The volcano Toba threw ash into the atmosphere within a radius of 800 cubickilometers. It created a crater 100 kilometers long by 35 meters wide, which is now the largest volcanic

overnight or in a matter of seconds, and to avoid being unprotected from such change, successful companies execute their strategies with adequate protection and thus manage risk in an increasingly volatile, chaotic, and unpredictable world.

Life is full of surprises and setbacks, and therefore it is necessary to act proactively and implement changes that help to prevent rather than react to problems. While it is not possible to know with certainty when and how the risk and its danger will come, it is necessary to prepare to deal with a variety of possible contingencies and risks. The more prepared and prevented you are, the fewer surprises you will have to face.

The Argentine engineer Roberto Servente (1920–2014) was 39 years old when in 1959 he decided to take the first flight of the Austral Company that connected the cities of Buenos Aires and Mar del Plata, in Argentina. It was a recycled Curtis plane from World War II where, with the crew included, 59 people were traveling. The plane took off at ten o'clock in the middle of a big storm. Halfway, the flight attendant informed the passengers that the plane should return to Buenos Aires due to technical problems. The plane began to lose altitude, the right-wing broke, and the plane fell into the sea. The crash into the water was so hard that 54 passengers died on impact. Engineer Servente put himself in a fetal position and saved his neck. The darkness was total. Servente had broken the fibula, several ribs, the clavicle, and he was bleeding from his head, but he managed to get rid of the jacket and pants and began to swim. He swam for more than four hours until he reached a cliff. His reaction to the unexpected, his attitude and optimism, saved his life and he was the only survivor of the accident.*

Carlitos Páez, one of the 16 survivors of the plane crash of 1972 in the Andes Mountains, said:

> Infinity of times I have asked myself which is the most recurrent characteristic of the limit test that I had to live in the mountains. And I always

---

lake in the world. Ashes from this cataclysm have been found in India, the Indian Ocean, the Bay of Bengal, and the South China Sea. Sulfur volcanic aerosols hampered solar radiation for six years. This and other effects almost instantly started an ice age that, according to evidence found in Greenland ice cores, lasted approximately 1,800 years.

* In 1995, a Lear plane carrying Ricardo Romanelli and six other people to the city of Paraná, in Argentina, fell into the Rio de la Plata on another night of cold, wet, and rain. Romanelli spent two hours in the water, in the dark, and in the rain came swimming to the coast with acute hypothermia. He was the only survivor. Romanelli said that the strongest teaching of the accident was "the determination of the human being to get out of a crisis situation when he realizes that help, from outside, will not come." "Live to Tell It," May 3, 2010, www.apertura.com.

come to the same conclusion: the unforeseen. Nothing that happened was in anyone's plans.*

The Perfect Storm is a 2000 film[†] based on an actual event in October 1991. Some fishermen of swordfish from Gloucester, Massachusetts, sailed calmly offshore on the boat *Andrea Gail* while a gigantic storm was forming with waves over 25 meters high without the crew knowing, and unfortunately, the end was tragic.

The expression *perfect storm* has also applied to business, to negative circumstances that can create maximum tension. Like tornadoes, tsunamis, or earthquakes, we do not know when the magnitude of the crisis that will happen can occur, but by then the organization should be prepared to be protected.[‡]

It is necessary to visualize problems, imagine the situations, and anticipate them in order to face the unexpected and unwanted risks. You should assume you can get in the eye of the perfect storm and the worst might happen.

In an unpredictable, changing, and volatile world, like the financial markets, no one knows exactly what can happen and leaders must make decisions to try to control the future with the best information they know and have available from the past and of the present. If leaders do not make decisions, it increases the risk that the organization will be impacted by events that lead to a crisis. The inaction of leaders can raise the risk of a company's losses.

Innovation expert Daniel Burrus has said:

> No matter who you are or what you do, you can anticipate. Therefore, do not wait for your future to unfold randomly, only to end up in a place you do not want to be.... Look at what you can do rather than what you cannot.[§]

---

* Pablo Vierci, *La Sociedad de la Nieve* (Editorial Sudamericana, 2008), 209 ("The Snow Society").
† The film was directed by Wolfgang Petersen.
‡ In the past 15 years, an earthquake in Iran killed over 40,000 people; another in the Kashmir region between India and Pakistan killed 80,000 people; one in Gujarat, in India, killed almost 20,000 people; one in Sichuan, China, killed about 70,000 people; and one in Haiti killed more than 300,000 people. A tsunami killed more than 230,000 people on the Indian Ocean coast, and another in Japan a few years later killed about 18,000 people. Hurricane Katrina killed 2,000 people in New Orleans. A cyclone in Burma killed about 200,000 people; a heatwave in Europe left about 40,000 dead and in Russia killed about 50,000 people.
§ Daniel Burrus, "The New Principles of Leadership," March 27, 2014.

While we can't always control what happens in the environment, we can control how to react to it. The best way to plan and anticipate is to put in place a protection system that identifies potential problems, to attack them when they are small threats before they grow and become unmanageable crises.

In 1938, British prime minister Neville Chamberlain (1869–1940) did not understand the magnitude of the threat presented by giving in to Hitler's demands to annex part of Czechoslovakia to Germany to prevent invasion and war. But Hitler, by securing the transfer of territories and people, managed to secure three million potential soldiers, got the Skoda armament factories, obtained vast territories without firing a bullet, and surrounded Poland. With this concession, Chamberlain did not achieve anything. He only increased the risk and danger. He did not stop Hitler or achieve peace. Winston Churchill (1874–1965) summed it up by saying in the Parliament: "You were given the choice between war and dishonor. You chose dishonor and you will have war."[*]

The writer, lecturer, and professor, Steven Covey (1932–2012) in his book *The 7 Habits of Highly Effective People* regarded proactivity as the first of the habits of effective people.[†] Proactive leaders are ahead of events, they are convinced of what they need to change and they execute. Planning allows you to anticipate and think of strategies to prevent and respond to improbability, anticipate scenarios, and create mitigation plans.

Strategic planning uses different methods, such as (i) scenarios to describe the future, (ii) the Delphi technique for consensus-building, and (iii) computer simulations of reality. These tools serve to analyze the threats of the environment, create contingency plans, and respond to crisis situations.

Attorney Andrew Gilman, president of CommCore Consulting Group, said, "In most companies executives... believe that nothing bad can happen to them. They seem to overlook the fact that planning and preparation make a big difference in overcoming an unexpected event that can lead to serious problems."[‡] It is the responsibility of leaders to build in the organization the necessary design so that if negative events happen, the impact is mitigated.

---

[*] "Winston Churchill," www, goodreads.com.

[†] www.stephencovey.com.

[‡] Andrew Gilman, "De la amenaza a la oportunidad," Revista Gestión May–June 2004, 78 ("From Threat to Opportunity").

In 1996, New York City mayor Rudolph Giuliani created the Office of Emergency Management (OEM) to respond to potential major incidents such as terrorist attacks. This initiative was a great help when the attack on the Twin Towers on September 11, 2001, happened. OEM Director at that time, Jerome Hauer, pointed out, "We looked at every conceivable threat that anyone on the staff could think of, be it natural or intentional."

American lecturer John Maxwell said that "A test of a leader is the ability to recognize a problem before it becomes an Emergency. . . . Under excellent leadership, a problem seldom reaches gigantic proportions because it is recognized and fixed in its early stages."*

The American economist Milton Friedman (1912–2006) of the University of Chicago and Nobel Laureate in Economics in 1976 popularized the phrase "There's no such thing as a free lunch,"† which means that any benefit has an associated cost. No one picks the roses without feeling their thorns.

Making decisions requires trading off one goal against another. In 1976, Gary Becker (1930–2014), an economist at the University of Chicago, said that human beings analyze incentives and disincentives to make decisions.‡ People make decisions based on their benefits and costs.

The fate of the organization is not written. Leaders decide with their effort and attitude. We are the boss of our attitude and attitude influences performance. Attitude is more important than the aptitude, in such a way that the attitude itself will determine the aptitude.

An anonymous reflection called "The Stone and the Man," in one section, says: "The distracted stumbled with her, the entrepreneur built with her, Michelangelo made the most beautiful of the sculptures; in all cases, the difference was not in the stone but in the man."§

The Chilean psychologist and lecturer Pilar Sordo tells the story of Jaime, a blind man who Pilar Sordo asked to write down in a notebook all the good things that happened to Jaime every day. When after a few days Sordo saw the notebook, she was surprised. Among the good things Jaime had written were:

---

* Vault, theleadershiphub.com, "Test of a Leader: Recognized a Problem Before It Becomes an Emergency."
† www.brainyquote.com.
‡ "En el Tema de Corrupción la Culpa no es 50% y 50%," Juan Carlos De Pablo, August 26, 2018, www.lanacion.com.ar ("On the Corruption Topic, Guilt is not 50% and 50%").
§ "La Piedra-Reflexión," www.lavidalucida.com ("The Stone – Reflection").

The temperature of the shower in the morning; The wonder of drying with a dry towel; The power to get into a bed with clean sheets; The exquisite satisfaction of getting into a bed with freshly washed pajamas; The texture of tomato sauce at lunch; The laughter of a child in the distance; The kindness of a cashier in the supermarket; The sparks of a coca-cola hitting my nose; The sun hitting my face when I walk; The smell of toast in the morning.

As the story of Jaime teaches us, happiness is a personal decision and has to do with the attitude we have every day.

The Dutch lecturer Victor Kuppers has pointed out "Knowledge adds up, experience adds up, but attitude multiplies."[*] Kuppers says his favorite phrase is from Mother Teresa of Calcutta: "Let no one ever come to you without leaving better and happier. Be the living expression of God's kindness: kindness in your face, kindness in your eyes, and kindness in your smile."[†]

The following story is also related to a positive attitude.

A writer lived near the sea and every day went out walking early on the beach. One morning he saw in the distance a young man who was enthusiastically grasping some of the sand and throwing it into the sea. He approached him and asked: "What are you doing?"

The young man said to him,

Today many starfish appeared lying on the beach, the sun will be very strong and the tide begins to descend, if I do not pick them up and send them to the sea, they will dry and die. That's why I'm returning them to the sea.

The writer said to him, "You are still very young. Don't you realize that there are thousands of starfish lying on the beach right now? Do you think it will be worth your effort to be throwing them one by one to the sea?"

The young man did not say anything. He bent to catch a starfish, and with the same enthusiasm, he threw it very far into the sea. He came back and said, "Sir, for that starfish that returned to the water, it was worth it. It will not die and will have a new opportunity."

The writer did not know what to answer and left.

The next morning the writer went to walk to the beach like every day and found the young man again throwing starfish into the sea. The writer

[*] "Actitud," Victor Kupper, Ted x andorralavella, www.youtube.com.
[†] www.kuppers.com/1/quien_soy_1090570.html and Mother Teresa www.goodreads.com.

picked up a starfish, threw it far into the sea, and helped the young man throw the starfish one by one into the sea for the rest of the morning.*

Like the writer and young man in the story, the company leader must choose between being an observer and leave things as they are, doing nothing, or acting and protecting their starfish.

Some organizations are reluctant to implement controls and prevention programs against fraud and other risks because they consider them an unnecessary expense. The most heard excuse is: "We are a big and successful company; we do not need and we do not have resources for a compliance program."

Many companies are not well prepared to deal with crises because their executives believe that nothing bad can happen to them. Their leaders think that they should not make corrections or improvements in their companies because things are going well. Actually, they do not see the dangers due to their ignorance, or because they prefer not to see them.

The implementation of a compliance program can be expensive, the imprudence of not having it can self-generate costly problems. Former US Deputy Attorney General Paul McNulty said, "If you think compliance is expensive, try non-compliance."†

The correct implementation of an integrity program constitutes a suitable means to prevent the commission of crimes, exercise supervision and control, and strengthen the culture of integrity within the company. A well-executed integrity program plays a decisive role against corruption.

Consultant Andrew Gilman has pointed out: "Some companies prefer to ignore the specter of a crisis; others are preparing and transforming adverse circumstances into opportunities."‡

It is necessary to act and anticipate hazards before problems begin.§ Even if everything goes well, we should not forget the words of the business

---

* "The Star Thrower Story by Joel Barker," www.starthrower.com.
† Preeti Wadhawan, "Keys to Building a Robust Compliance Culture," April 9, 2018, www.corporatecompliance.org.
‡ Andrew Gilman, "De la amenaza a la oportunidad," *Revista Gestión*, May–June 2004, 78 ("From Threat to Opportunity").
§ The German physicist Albert Einstein (1879–1955) said, "The world is a dangerous place to live; not because of the people who are evil, but because of the people who don't do anything about it." Albert Einstein, Quotes, www.brainyquote.com.Leonardo da Vinci (1452–1519), the scientist, painter, sculptor, and inventor born in Florence, author of *The Mona Lisa* and *The Last Supper*, two of the most famous paintings of all time, said that there are three classes of people: "Those who see, those who see when they are shown, those who do not see." Leonardo Da Vinci, Quotes, www.brainyquote.com.

consultant Tom Peters who said, "If you sense calm, it's only because you are in the eye of the hurricane."*

In the book *Good Luck* consultants Alex Rovira Celma and Fernando Trias de Bes point out, "Since creating good luck is creating circumstances ... good luck depends on you."†

Creating circumstances helps improve the organization's risk control system. You must take action and create them. The choices we make will make the difference between success and failure. In the footnote are examples of some interesting phrases about it.‡

Recognizing the problem is essential for responding to the company's threats.

Someone said, "If you want to be happy, put your effort into controlling the sail and not the wind."§

Jack Welch said, "Control your own destiny or someone else will."¶

There was once a forest where lived three piglets that were brothers. To protect themselves from the eventual visit of a wolf, they decided to build their houses.

One of them built his house of straw and finished it quickly. He did so because he thought the wolf's visit was impossible.

The second pig built the house of sticks, and although it took a little more time and effort, he finished the house quickly because he considered unnecessary to spend more time on it. The fact that a wolf might appear was highly improbable.

The third pig designed the house of bricks. It took much more time and investment to build it. The third pig believed the appearance of a wolf was a probable risk, and if the wolf appeared and the pig was not prepared, he would die.

---

* Tom Peters, *The Tom Peters Seminars* (Vintage Books, Random House Inc., New York, 1994), 271.

† Alex Rovira Celma and Fernando Trias de Bes, *La Buena Suerte*, 17th ed (Empresa Activa, 2004), 98 ("The Good Luck").

‡ 1 – Canadian writer Robin Sharma has said, "Never be a prisoner of your past. Become the architect of your future." Robin Sharma, Quotes, www.goodreads.com.2 – "Life is about taking options and the destiny of each of us depends on the choices we make." Robin Sharma, *El Monje que Vendió su Ferrari* (Sudamericana, 2010), 33.3 – Walt Elias Disney (1901–1966), founder of The Walt Disney Company, said that "The way to start is to quit talking and begin doing." www.brainyquote.com.4 – The Dalai Lama is the spiritual leader of Tibetan Lamaism or Buddhism. Dalai Lama has said that "There are only two days in the year that nothing can be done. One is called yesterday and the other is called tomorrow." quotes.justdharma.com.5 – American consultant and writer Jim Collins says, "We cannot predict the future. But we can create it." Jim Collins and Morten Hansen, *Great by Choice* (Harper Business, 2011), 1.

§ Robert Moscatelli, *The Quote Manual* (Authorhouse, 2012), 167.

¶ Jack Welch, Quotes, www.brainyquote.com.

One day the improbable appeared – the wolf!

To eat the piglets, the wolf destroyed the first two houses blowing just a few breaths. They managed to escape and reach the house of the one who had built his house of brick. The wolf pursued them, but when it blew and blew, it could not destroy the house of brick. When it wanted to enter by the chimney, the fire surprised him.*

If we make an analogy of this classic fable of the three little pigs with compliance, of the three houses, only the last one warned against risk and had an effective plan.

The other two houses disappeared because they did not take the threats seriously – the impossible event or improbable event – the arrival of a wolf. Are organizations prepared to react when the wolf appears?

Matthew the Evangelist was one of the 12 apostles chosen by Jesus of Nazareth and the author of the Gospel of St. Matthew, written in Aramaic. St. Matthew comments on the following parable of Jesus:†

> A prudent man built his house on the rock. And the rain came and rivers came and blowing winds and beat against that house and did not fall because it was founded on rock.
>
> And everyone who hears these words and does not do it will be compared to the foolish man who built his house on the sand; and the rain came down, and the rivers came and the winds blew, and they beat upon that house, and he fell and his ruin was great.

Companies should not be a house of cards. They must build on a firm and secure basis to reduce the multiple risks to which they are exposed and that can ruin them.

Organizations operate in a complex, transparent, regulated environment with obstacles, and business leaders must have the tools to mitigate the risks they face and take the necessary actions to protect the company from constant change.

The Greek philosopher Epictetus (55–135) said, "We cannot choose our external circumstances, but we can always choose how to respond to them."‡

---

* *The Three Little Pigs* was included in *The Nursery Rhymes of England* (London and New York, c.1886), by James Halliwell-Phillipps, Wikipedia. The Wolf blows down the Straw house in a 1904 adaptation of the story. Illustration by the British artist Leonard Leslie Brooke (1862–1940).

† The Bible, Matthew 7:24–27.

‡ www.goodreads.com.

The Greek aphorism Know *Thyself** is attributed to Socrates (470–399 BC) and means that we must know our weaknesses in order to learn to master them. Organizational leaders must ask themselves whether their companies have the systems and processes necessary to reduce weaknesses and risks. There is always a need for improvements in control systems in any organization. This is how companies create their own storms and then they do not understand why it rains.

A life without control is probably short life. The British philosopher and thinker Bertrand Russell (1872–1970) said, "A life without adventure is likely to be unsatisfying, but a life in which adventure is allowed to take whatever form it will is sure to be short."[†] Growth and risks are closely linked, and companies must take risks but also reasonable precautions to prevent and control "bad luck."

José Hernández writes in 1872 the narrative poem *El Gaucho Martín Fierro* and then, in 1879, *La Vuelta de Martín Fierro*, both considered in their entirety the masterpiece of Argentine gaucho literature. Martin Fierro said in one of his verses:

> I warn you to be on your guard in life:
> You can never tell what corner
> Your enemy's lurking in.[‡]

The Irish philosopher and politician Edmund Burke (1729–1797) said, "The only thing necessary for the triumph of evil is for good men to do nothing."[§]

Warren Buffett, the most successful investor of our time, believes that risks must be taken, "if they are calculated risks."[¶]

Benjamin Franklin (1706–1790), an American scientist and one of the Founding Fathers of the United States,[**] said, "By failing to prepare, we prepare to fail."[††] He also said, "Instead of cursing the darkness, light a candle."[‡‡]

---

[*] It was inscribed in the forecourt of the Temple of Apollo at Delphi according to the Greek writer Pausanias.

[†] Bertrand Russell en.wikiquote.org.

[‡] sparrowthorn.com/MartinFierro_PART_TWO.pdf.

[§] www.brainyquote.com.

[¶] Mukul Pandya and Robbie Shell, *Lasting Leadership* (Knowledge Wharton, 2005), 215.

[**] In spite of having received formal education only until ten years old, in the year 1772, he was chosen to be a member of the Academy of Sciences of Paris.

[††] The writer Alan Lakein said, "Failing to plan is planning to fail," www.brainyquote.com.

[‡‡] www.goodreads.com, www.brainyquote.com.

Organizational leaders must act with intelligence to master the potential risks they may face. When Alexander the Great (356–323 BC) was 13 years old, he was able to tame a black horse called Bucephalus that no one could dominate. He could do it because he understood the animal feared its own shadow, and in order to mount it, he did so in front of the sun.

When termites build their anthills, they try to protect themselves. The writer Fernando Savater says: "Since the termite body is soft because it lacks the chitinous shell that protects other insects, the anthill serves as a collective shell against certain enemy ants, better armed than they."*

Earth's atmosphere protects life on the planet. It consists of several gases that are called air, and its main elements are nitrogen (78%) and oxygen (21%). The atmosphere is important to the warming of the earth. If there were no atmosphere, the temperature of the planet would be 22 °C below zero. The atmosphere not only acts as a protective shield against meteorites but also protects life on earth by absorbing part of the ultraviolet solar radiation through the ozone layer scattered in the atmosphere.

The lightning rod, invented by Benjamin Franklin (1706–1790) in 1752, is an instrument whose purpose is to drive lightning to the earth so that it does not cause damage to structures. Companies must design their own lightning rod, their atmospheres, their anthills, their systems of protection against risks, whose effectiveness must be continuously monitored because threats move and change. Organizations should invest in structures, systems, processes, and training to mitigate risks that may interfere with their business plans. Companies must invest in compliance.

Economic theory teaches people have unlimited wants but resources are limited. While companies should prioritize where to place their resources, it must also be noted that resources are limited to repair the damages generated by a misconceived and negligent administration. It is necessary to allocate resources to protect the bases for the organization's growth and development.

In humans, antibodies are molecules or proteins that have the function of detecting foreign particles, bacteria, viruses, parasites, pathogens, or antigens that invade the body and then repel the infection. A good immune system is made up of organs, tissues, proteins, and cells – white blood cells or leukocytes – that are like soldiers fighting bacteria who attack, surround, and destroy infectious germs and microorganisms that invade the body's systems and cause disease.

---

* Fernando Savater, *Ethics for Amador* (Ariel, 2008), 20, 21.

Like the human body, the company must generate an immune system that serves as a defense against infections, bacteria, or viruses that intend to contaminate it. Like the antibodies to fight Ebola or cancer in the human body, companies must also develop their vaccines, antibodies, and white blood cells to combat the risk of contracting the viruses and parasites that can affect them.

As Michael Ritter says, "Risk management is to a crisis, as preventive medicine is to sickness."[*] No doctor can assure his or her patient will not get sick the next winter, but if one takes care of him or herself and gets vaccinated against the flu, he or she will have less chance of getting sick.

An ethics and compliance program is like an antibody that protects companies.

When you buy a computer, one of the first things you do is install an antivirus, which acts as an immune system for different types of risks.

In July 2002 the consulting firm McKinsey & Company conducted a survey called "Global Investor Opinion" which stated, "most investors would pay more for companies that exhibit high standards of governance."[†]

After generating a change and implementing a solid compliance program, Siemens gained confidence in the market and improved its market share and profits. In 2007, lawyer Peter Solmssen faced the challenge of rebuilding the compliance role at Siemens. He pointed out that "investigators discovered one or two cases where the person paying the bribes was a compliance employee."[‡]

The Siemens Program proved to be an antibody against corruption and competitive advantage. The company showed a correlation between a good "corporate governance and corporate performance program."[§] Companies with good corporate governance have higher profitability.

The US Constitution is the oldest federal Constitution currently in force in the world. It was adopted on September 17, 1787, by the Constitutional Convention of Philadelphia, Pennsylvania, and then ratified by the people at conventions in each state. One of the objectives of the delegates was to create legislation that would last over time. The Preamble says, "We, the people of the United States, in order to form a more perfect union, establish justice, insure domestic tranquility, provide for the

---

[*] Michael Ritter, *El Valor del Capital Reputacional* (Olivos, Ritter & Partners, 2013), 211 ("The Value of Reputational Capital").

[†] Michael Emen, "Corporate governance: The view from NASDAQ." "An overwhelming majority of investors are prepared to pay a premium for companies exhibiting high governance standards."

[‡] A. Clege, "El Gerente de Etica," *Financial Times*. Published in *El Cronista* on June 13, 2011.

[§] Ethiopis Tafara and Robert J. Peterson, "The True Value of Corporate Governance."

common defense...." In the United States, the Department of Defense was founded in 1947 and is the institution in charge of protecting the security of the country. Business leaders must create the tools to provide security to their organizations against the various internal and external risks they face.

James Collins and Jerry Porras point out in their book *Built to Last*, "Great executive directors are less concerned with strategies, business models, products, or immediate financial results than with creating large institutions that serve for a long time."* That is what a visionary leader must do: create the design and institutions that remain in the company.

As James Kouzes and Barry Z. Posner say, "The most significant contribution leaders make is not simply to today's bottom line; it is to the long-term development of people and institutions so they can adapt, change, prosper, and grow."†

MIT Professor Peter Senge says in his book *The Fifth Discipline*,

> Imagine that your organization is a ship and that you are the leader. What role do you play? I have asked this question to many groups of managers. The most common response is, of course, the "Captain." However, there is a role whose importance overshadows that of others: The designer of the ship. Nobody has a bigger influence.‡

Companies must design their own ship and implement an effective program of protection against internal and external risks that must adapt to their industry and be updated permanently so as not to be obsolete when new risks arise. The key is to find the design each organization needs to mitigate the different risks.

Each organization operates in certain geographical regions, under different regulations, and in different industries, and it faces different threats from which it should be protected. Insurance and hedging contracts§ are instruments that can reduce the impact and economic consequences in case of certain risks. But organizations, in addition to insuring against certain hazards, must build their *protective shield*, a

---

* Jeffrey E. Garten, *The CEO Mentality* (Editorial Norma, 2001), 166.
† J. M. Kouzes and B. Z. Posner, *The Leadership Challenge*, 3rd ed (Jossey-Bass, 2002), Preface.
‡ Peter Senge, *The Fifth Discipline* (Granica, 1990), 420.
§ Hedging against a risk means using instruments in the market to offset the risk of any adverse price movements. Hedging is a transfer of risk without buying insurance policies. For example, someone accepts to absorb potential losses from price drops in exchange for potential gains from price increases, and the other party ensures a uniform price during the term of the contract.

system of protection and prevention against the risks of lack of ethics and compliance. A protection system that reduces the *risk of occurrence* and, in case of occurrence, mitigates its effects, prevents the damage from spreading and eliminates the reason that causes it.

When Alexander the Great (356–323 BC) went to the Persian Empire in 333 BC, he conquered Phrygia (current Anatolia in Turkey) and faced the challenge of untying a knot that had been made by Gordias, King of Gordius. Alexander, instead of trying to untie it, solved the problem by cutting the knot with the sword. Cutting the Giordano knot implies execution and resolution to solve the cause of a problem.

Problem prevention and resolution is a skill of the effective leader, and success will be driven by excellent planning and execution of the strategy.

As Rudolph Giuliani, the mayor of New York during September 11, 2001, terrorist attack, said, "As a leader, there is something that can be done to prevent future disasters."*

American actor Bradley Whitford delivered a speech in May 2004 to graduates of the University of Wisconsin-Madison in which he said, "You have a choice. You can either be a passive victim of circumstance or you can be the active hero of your own life."†

Nicholas Machiavelli (1469–1527), the Italian historian and politician, said in his work *The Prince*:

> What all-wise princes must do: they not only have to worry about present problems but also about future ones. If you set them, you can easily remedy them. But if you wait to have them over, the medicine does not arrive in time, because the disease has become incurable.‡
>
> A wise prince should not be idle in times of peace, but with a wit to get a capital from which he can lay hands on adversity so that, should his fortunes change, he may find him ready to resist it.§ Princes become great when they overcome the difficulties and obstacles that oppose them.⁋

In 1513 Machiavelli pointed out, "If we knew the problems as soon as they appear it would be easier to remedy. But, when lack of knowledge allows

---

* Rudolph Giuliani, *Leadership* (Miramax Books, 2002), 93.
† "Spring Commencement: Transcript of Address by Bradley Whitford," May 15, 2004, University of Wisconsin-Madison news.wisc.edu.
‡ Niccolo Machiavelli, *The Prince* (Ediciones Nuevo Siglo, 1994), 22.
§ Niccolo Machiavelli, *The Prince* (Ediciones Nuevo Siglo, 1994), 89.
⁋ Niccolo Machiavelli, *The Prince* (Ediciones Nuevo Siglo, 1994), 119.

them to grow until anyone can recognize them; then, there is no more time to find the remedy."*

Australian consultant Matthew Kelly[†] says that we were born to be the best version of ourselves. Corporate leaders must also ask themselves what they need to do to make the best version of their companies.

To survive in this chaotic, changing, and risky world, you must be permanently alert and guarded.

To ensure the security of the country, the US government created a scale called Defense Readiness Condition (DEFCON) that has five levels of alertness and availability of the Armed Forces according to the seriousness of the situation. DEFCON 5 stands for peacetime, and DEFCON 1 means impending conflict with a maximum alertness level. For example, after the September 11, 2001, terrorist attacks, the level was raised to the DEFCON 3, and during the Cuban missile crisis, DEFCON 2 was declared.

American psychologist and writer Robert Greene has pointed out, "Always be alert to potential attacks and thwart them before they happen."[‡]

Janus, in Roman mythology, was a god guardian of all gates and represented with two faces facing the sides. Organizational leaders, like Janus, should be able to look in both directions at once, to handle danger from whatever it comes. "No days unalert. Nothing should catch you by surprise because you are constantly imaging problems before they arise."[§]

Hungarian-American businessman Andy Grove (1936–2016), former CEO of Intel, said, "Success breeds complacency. Complacency breeds failure. Only the paranoid survive."[¶] An entrepreneurial leader must be paranoid, obsessive, and maniac about the risks that surround the company and protect from them as best he or she can so the company can survive. An effective leader designs the organization to face with greater probability of success the risks and dangers to which it is exposed.

Walmart CEO said. "We could go away at any minute."** Doug McMillon keeps a photo on his phone that lists the top ten retailers in the United States over the past few decades. The picture helps to remind him how so many companies come and go. Walmart has been in the number one

---

* Michael Ritter, *El Valor del Capital Reputacional* (Olivos, Ritter & Partners, 2013), 229 ("The Value of Capital Reputation").
† Kelly is the founder of Floyd Consulting and the Dynamic Catholic Institute. Kelly wrote the book *Rediscover Catholicism*, which has sold millions of copies throughout the world.
‡ Robert Greene, *The 48 Laws of Power* (Penguin, 2000), 37.
§ Robert Greene, *The 48 Laws of Power* (Penguin Books, 2000), 20.
¶ Andy Grove, Quotes, www.brainyquote.com.
** Lauren Thomas, "We could go away at any minute," November 19, 2019, cnbc.com.

spot since the 1990s when it overtook Sears. McMillon said that Walmart has a "healthy paranoia" to stay ahead of rivals. He said, "You see the rise and fall of Sears and others. ... [I]t's just a reminder that this can happen to us too."*

Business needs to innovate and adapt constantly. Complacency is the kiss of death in business. That's why the founder of Amazon, Jeff Bezos, wrote in a 1999 shareholder letter, "I constantly remind our employees to be afraid, to wake up every morning terrified."†

Indra Nooyi, former CEO of Pepsi, in a 2016 Bloomberg Interview, said:

> I'm always afraid that if I fail, I may have to go back to something that I don't want to. ... [T]hat fear always motivates me and so I drive myself to be better and better at my job every day.‡

The American writer and psychologist Spencer Johnson said: "I now know the need to adapt more quickly because if you do not adapt in time, it is very possible that you can no longer do it."§

The American cartoonist James Thurber (1894–1961) said, "Let us not look back in anger, nor forward in fear, but around in awareness."¶

An effective leader is proactive and anticipates crises that can affect compliance with business strategies and plans. For a proactive leader, solutions are before problems.

Effective leaders make the necessary changes to protect the company, to anticipate the future, to surf the waves, and to overcome the chaos. They will be ready to extinguish the fire.

Effective leaders analyze trends and make strategic decisions based on his or her predictions about what will come next. They have implemented systems and processes that allow them to see the deer or gorilla that crosses in front of him or her on the road or the missile that is targeting them.

Effective leaders pay attention to the small signs and risks on the horizon to react in time and avoid chaos. They are on alert, anticipate, and change.

---

* Lauren Thomas, "Here's the one photo Walmart's CEO keeps on his phone to stoke Healthy Paranoia in the race against Amazon," December 7, 2018, www.cnbc.com.
† Ruth Umoh, "Why Jeff Bezos wants Amazon employees to wake up every morning terrified," August 28, 2018, cnbc.com.
‡ Ruth Umoh, "Why Jeff Bezos Wants Amazon Employees to Wake Up Every Morning Terrified," August 28, 2018, cnbc.com.
§ *Who Moved My Cheese?* 47th ed (Active Company, 2000), 79.
¶ www.brainyquote.com/authors/james_thurber.

11

Small Can Be Dangerous

11.1 CAUSALITY AND SYSTEMIC EFFECT

An old proverb says, "If you want to know the past, look at the present that is the result. If you want to know the future, look at the present that causes it."

Causality is a relationship between two successive events; the first (cause) gives birth to the second (effect). A precedes B.

According to this principle, things do not occur in isolation but are linked to each other in a process of interaction whereby some things are the consequence of others. If we want to change the effect, we must change the cause that generates it.

The Greek philosopher Socrates (470–399 BC) 2,000 years ago said the "law of causality" shows that every effect or event has a prior cause. The universe appears to be governed by this law as there is a *causal relationship*, or *causal connection*, a *boomerang effect* or *action-reaction* between facts and results, between stimuli and responses.*

The Stoics were the representatives of a philosophical tendency that emerged in ancient Greece around the third century BC. For the Stoics, the Universe is governed by rational laws, according to the law of causality where everything happens for a cause. In the causal chain of events, everything happens in a certain way. The choice of Stoic life consists in saying "yes" to the Universe. The only choice we have is how we receive each of the events. What happens in the world does not depend on the individual; it is governed by universal reason. For the Stoics, it only remains to accept how things happen. Thus, we can choose to live against nature and against reason and be unhappy. Or we can live a happy life and accept

---

* In Buddhism and Hinduism, *karma* (meaning *"action"*) creates an energy that then returns to someone; that is, if you do something good or bad, then good or bad returns to you.

destiny. The way we react to what happens to us is our "moral intention." Therefore, the maxims of Stoic morality are intended to strengthen the individual: to endure pain, hunger, and sorrow.[*]

Pierre Simon Laplace (1749–1827) was a French physicist and mathematician, a representative of *scientific determinism*. This school of thought believes that despite its complexity and unpredictability, the world evolves according to predetermined rules and that all events are subject to the universal laws of causality by which some are derived from others: All events are determined by a cause-consequence chain. Laplace said: "We may regard the present state of the universe as the effect of its past and the cause of its future."[†] For causal determinism, given certain past events and natural law, current events could not have been otherwise.

When the cause-effect processes are analyzed, we must avoid falling into simplifications and hasty and erroneous conclusions.

The Latin phrase *Post Hoc Ergo Propter Hoc* is a fallacy that means "After this, therefore, because of this." The fallacy assumes that, if A happens before B, then A is the cause of B. However, if something happens before a certain event, it may not be sufficient evidence to justify the causality.

Another fallacy of legal Latin is the phrase *Non-Causa Pro Causa* which means "not the cause for the cause." This fallacy occurs when it is reasoned that A is the cause of B. However, there may be a combination of causes or variables that trigger an effect. As a consequence of this fallacy, wrong conclusions can be drawn through insufficient or manipulated data to attempt to arrive at a result.

To avoid falling into fallacies in the cause-effect relationship, different methods are used. Let's see some.

Japanese Professor Kaoru Ishikawa (1915–1989) was an industrial chemist expert in the implementation of appropriate quality systems in business processes and he is considered the father of the scientific analysis of the causes of problems in industrial processes. The cause-effect diagram called *Ishikawa Diagram* (or *fishbone* for its resemblance to a fish skeleton) was developed by Ishikawa in 1943 and is used to identify possible causes of a problem. Because we need to address the root cause of difficulties rather than their symptoms, the *fishbone method* allows us to eliminate the symptoms and discover the root cause of a problem.[‡]

---

[*] "Los estoicos: características principales, www.historiasminimalistas.com.("The Stoics: Main characteristics").

[†] "Laplace's Demon," The Information Philosopher, www.informationphilosopher.com.

[‡] "Ishikawa Diagram," Wikipedia.

Another method to determine the cause of problems is the *five-way method*, developed by Sakichi Toyoda (1867–1930) at Toyota, which is a technique that serves to explore the cause and effect relationships underlying a problem. The goal is to determine the cause of a defect or problem by repeating the why question, and each answer is the basis of the next question.*

In negotiations, for example, it is important to be able to distinguish between *positions* (what people want, a fixed idea) and *interests* (*why* people want what they want). *Interests* explain *why* someone takes a certain position and the underlying motivation of *positions*.† Interest-based negotiation is a strategy that focuses on developing mutually beneficial agreements based on the interests of the disputants.‡

Also, to tackle a systemic problem, it is necessary to understand its deep roots. If we ask *why?* several times, it will force us to keep going until we reach the cause of the problem.

Just as the ancient philosophers wondered about the causes and the why of things, business leaders must also ask and understand the causes and the why of problems.

Dante Orlandella and James T. Reason of the University of Manchester hypothesized *the Swiss cheese model* of accident causation used in risk management in aviation, engineering, and healthcare. This hypothesis holds that an organization's defenses against the risks of accidents are constructed by a number of barriers, represented as slices of cheese, and the holes in the slices represent the weaknesses of the defense system. Accidents occur when the holes in the cheese slices momentarily align, allowing a "trajectory of accident opportunity," and that is when the risk materializes as an accident. This model suggests that most accidents are caused by the sum of the following: (i) *influence of the organization* (e.g., reduced training costs), (ii) *lack of oversight* (e.g., a driver without experience driving on a rainy night), (iii) *preconditions* (e.g., a driver is tired or tires should be replaced); and (iv) *specific acts* (e.g., a driver has not pressed the brake pedal).§

FMEA (Failure Mode and Effect Analysis) is a methodology developed in the late 1950s to analyze failures in military processes. FMEA seeks to (i) identify ways in which a process can fail, (ii) estimate the risks of

---

* "5 Whys," Wikipedia.
† "Interests vs Positions," www.watershedassociates.com.
‡ Web.mit.edu/negotiation.
§ "Swiss Cheese Model," Wikipedia.

the causes of such failures, (iii) create a control plan to prevent failures, and (iv) prioritize and register actions to be undertaken. Although initially developed for the military, FMEA has since been used in different industries and at NASA.

Sigma (σ) is a Greek letter meaning a statistical unit of measurement and represents the standard deviation of a process. *Six Sigma* is a quality process improvement methodology developed by the engineer William Smith Jr. (1929–1993) at Motorola Inc., and whose objective is to reduce or eliminate defects or failures in the delivery of a product or service to the customer through practices that emphasize the understanding, measurement, and improvement of processes.*

An effective leader analyzes, identifies, and works on the *root causes* of problems and carries out corrective and preventive measures so a similar issue does not happen again. The background of the crisis must be analyzed, and the problems must be attacked during their incubation period.

Sometimes a problem is generated by a cause that is not directly linked to it.

A story goes that a mouse looked through a hole in the wall of a farmhouse and noted that the farmer and his wife had bought a mousetrap. Terrified, the mouse ran to the farm to warn the rest of the animals that there was a mousetrap in the house.

The hen lifted her head and said it was a mouse problem, and she was not harmed at all.

The lamb replied, "I'm so sorry; I will remember you in my prayers."

The mouse then turned to the cow, which replied that she was not in danger.

The mouse turned to his mouse hole depressed.

That night, the farmer's wife heard a noise and rushed out of her bedroom and caught something.

---

* At a Six sigma level there are 3.4 defects per million opportunities. The goal of Six Sigma is to reach a maximum of 3.4 defects per million events or opportunities (DPMO).

  You can classify the efficiency of a process based on its sigma level:
  - 1 sigma = 690,000 MPD = 68.27% efficiency
  - 2 sigma = 308,000 DPMO = 95.45% efficiency
  - 3 sigma = 66,800 DPMO = 99.73% efficiency
  - 4 sigma = 6,210 DPMO = 99.994% efficiency
  - 5 sigma = 230 DPMO = 99.99994% efficiency
  - 6 sigma = 3.4 DPMO = 99.9999966% efficiency

In the dark, the woman did not realize she had caught a snake, and it bit her. The farmer then laid his wife down and wanted to make a soup, so he killed the chicken. Then as her health worsened, her neighbors visited her, and to feed them, the farmer killed the lamb. The woman died, and many people went to her burial, so the farmer sacrificed the cow to feed their friends.

As in the mousetrap story, in organizations, the different business units are interconnected. Actions or events within a sector of the organization may impact other parts of the entity. In a company, an employee depends on the rest, and as consultant Tim Irwin says, "The behavior of employees impacts on other employees."[*]

The human body is a system with interconnected organs, muscles, bones, and nerves and the problem of one organ may affect all of them. The world is also a set of complex, interrelated, dynamic, and discontinuous organs where what happens is not always expected and logical. The global economy is also interconnected. As the famous phrase says, "If the US sneezes, the world catches a cold." Financial crises have shown the extent to which international economies are interconnected, globalized, and integrated into world markets.

Barry Nalebuff, professor at the Yale School of Management, and Adam Brandenburger, professor at Harvard Business School, have said: "We all interact with everyone, directly or indirectly, in search of their various purposes. Everything is, finally, after all, connected to everything else."[†]

John Donne, an English poet who lived 400 years ago, wrote: "No man is an island entire of itself; every man is a piece of the continent, a part of the main."[‡]

Organizations are complex systems composed of many elements that interact with each other in a chaotic environment where balance and stability do not exist.

All the members of the company depend on each other in doing the right thing, and if someone makes the wrong decision, it can affect the rest of the organization.

Peter Senge, a graduate engineer at Stanford University and MIT professor, has written that the organization is a system, an organism

---

[*] Tim Irwin, *Derailed* (Nelson Free, 2009), 187.
[†] Barry Nalebuff and Adam Brandenburger, *Coo-petencia* (Grupo Norma 2005), 339.
[‡] John Donne, "No Man Is an Island," web.cs.dal.ca.

with subsystems and components that interrelate. Therefore, solutions to business problems must be complete; otherwise, the solution will not have the desired effect or be effective.

Professor Senge tells the story of the carpet seller. A rug merchant saw his most beautiful carpet had a lump in the center. He stood over the bulge to flatten it and succeeded. But the lump reappeared elsewhere. He jumped on the bulge again and it disappeared momentarily, only to reappear elsewhere. The merchant jumped, again and again, spoiling the carpet with his frustration. Finally, he lifted a corner of the carpet, and out came an angry snake.*

Senge says:

> Unfortunately, the most common leaders ... have little ability to encourage systemic understanding. ... They manage almost exclusively on the level of facts.
>
> Under his leadership, the organization goes from one crisis to another. ... They are dominated by reactivity to the facts. His experience involves jumping from one crisis to another ... with no control over destiny.†

Understand how the systems work helps to understand how organizations work.

As Steve Jobs (1955–2011) said in 2005 at Stanford University, the dots are connected. They are linked within a system and depend on each other, and the changes in one of them are the cause of changes in others. The solutions to problems should be sought with a systemic view.

To change the effect; it is necessary to act on the cause that generates it. As the company is a system, any legal or ethical breach committed by an employee or supplier in any corner of the planet can affect and damage the reputation, finances, and future of the company.

11.2 THE SMALL CAN BE DANGEROUS

The *Boiling frog* is a fable describing a frog being slowly boiled alive. The premise is that if a frog is put suddenly into boiling water, it will jump out,

---

* Peter Senge, *The Fifth Discipline* (Granica, 1990), 77.
† Peter Senge, *The Fifth Discipline* (Granica, 1990), 437.

but if the frog is put in tepid water which is then brought to boil slowly; it will not perceive the danger and will be cooked to death.

The story is used as a metaphor for the inability or unwillingness of people to react to or be aware of threats that arise gradually.* Just as the frog reacts to major changes but does not with slow and small changes, sometimes business leaders react only to obvious changes in the environment but not if they are slow and gradual.

When the Japanese began to import cars in the North American market, nobody in Detroit paid enough attention because it was something small. Today, Asian cars capture 45% of the North American market.

A wise king of ancient warned, "*Nobody* trips *over mountains*. It is the small pebble that causes you to *stumble*."[†]

Author Thomas Cleary, Ph.D. in Asian languages and civilizations from Harvard University, says,

> The fact that no attention is paid to small problems usually is the reason that so many have remorse. Worrying about the problems when they have occurred is like when a sick person is seeking treatment once their situation has become critical.[‡]

The impact of small things cannot be underestimated. Who has not experienced the nuisance of a stone in a shoe, a contact lens misplaced, or the presence of a mosquito in the room when one tries to fall asleep? It is necessary to act and react while problems are small or even just potential problems because the insignificant can become giant.[§]

In 1982, GE's former CEO Ian Wilson, said,

> Without an appropriate response from business, today's society's expectations become part of tomorrow's political agenda, legislative issues the next day, and in judicial sanctions the day after. As the [alert] signals become more intense, the organization's choices are reduced and responsibilities are increased. Therefore, the sooner you can identify emerging issues, the more options you will have.[¶]

---

* "Boiling Frog," Wikipedia.
† Thomas Cleary, *The Tao of Politics* (Imgesa, 1992), 48–49. www.sparkpeople.com.
‡ Thomas Cleary, *The Tao of Politics* (Imgesa, 1992), 48–49.
§ A leader must know how to differentiate what is small and potentially harmful and risky, from what is not, because big things also start small. Recall that Walt Disney (1901–1966) said, "I just hope that we do not lose sight of one thing; it all started with a mouse."
¶ Michael Ritter, *El Valor del Capital Reputacional* (Olivos, Ritter & Partners, 2013), 229.

A small change can have a huge impact.

Hugh Hefner (1926–2017) founded *Playboy* magazine in Chicago in 1953, after *Esquire* executives denied him a US$5 increase in his salary. He transformed *Playboy* into a media giant and a big competitor of *Esquire*.

In 2006 the Italian airline Alitalia reported that the price of the business class ticket from Toronto, Canada to Cyprus was US$39, instead of US$3,900. Before the error was corrected, 2,000 customers took advantage of the offer. The cost of Alitalia was US$7.7 million.

Rudolph Giuliani, mayor of New York in the period 1994–2001, said that we must attack the problems when they are small to prevent small issues from becoming into major disasters.[*]

British prime minister Winston Churchill (1874–1965) said that "Although most of the predicted catastrophes never happen that which looms becomes a problem to be solved."[†]

Robert Goodin and Frank Jackson in their essay "Freedom from Fear" cite the "one percent doctrine" of former US vice president Dick Cheney. This doctrine says that even if there is a low likelihood that something will happen, we must do our best to prevent it from happening. Cheney says: "If there is a one percent chance that terrorists have a weapon of mass destruction and there has been a small probability of such occurrence for some time, the US must act as if it were true."[‡]

According to legends of ancient Greece, when Pandora married Epimetheus, she received as a gift a box with instructions not to be opened. However, Pandora opened the box and released from inside the world's ills. To open *Pandora's Box* means that a small action can lead to serious consequences, and that which seems small grows more and more.

There are different names to mean how a problem can grow excessively and become an uncontrollable threat.

Thus, the term *domino effect* is used to reflect an action that produces consequences in a chain. The effects of a primary accident are increased, giving rise to several secondary accidents more serious than the primary.

A *cascade effect* occurs when one of the parts of a system fails and causes the problem to be amplified. Other parts also fail and generate an unstoppable chain of events.

---

[*] Rudolph Giuliani, *Leadership* (Miramax Books, 2002), 50.

[†] Michael Ritter, *El valor del Capital Reputacional* (Olivos, Ritter & Partners, 2013), 211.

[‡] Amartya Sen, "The Idea of Justice," fourth part, *Harvard Business Review* (2007): 401.

The *risk multiplier effect* occurs when the consequences of a particular risk in a business unit quickly spread to other units.*

A small rolling snowball at first has difficulty adding snow, but as it grows, it improves its ability to take on more snow and gains in speed and size. A *snowball effect* then occurs when something small gains momentum and, if not stopped in time, grows exponentially.

The bankruptcy of a bank can generate panic that leads to a domino effect that exposes the interbank system to systemic risk.

Pandora's Box, the cascade effect, the domino effect, the risk multiplier effect, and the snowball effect show how a small action can be expanded and eventually affect the entire system, which is interconnected.

Aristotle (384–322 BC) said that "The least initial deviation from the truth is multiplied later thousand-fold."†

Sometimes flashing lights are seen that anticipate the existence of small crises or problems. When this happens, you must act quickly because if the problem is ignored, it is very likely it will grow.

Immunology is a branch of biology that deals with the immune system. This system consists of a set of structures, tissues, and cells inside an organ that allows it to recognize anomalies and alien elements and to give an immediate response, thus maintaining an internal balance against dangers and aggressions. In organizations, it is important to develop an *immunological memory* in corporate leaders that helps protect the company from corporate risks. In that way, leaders will become aware that anomalies or complications must be prevented or fought from the beginning.

Melanoma is a type of skin cancer that occurs when cells begin to grow out of control and beyond the normal. To avoid melanoma, first, it must be prevented with the use of sunscreens. But if melanoma does occur, it must be attacked when it is still small and remove it with surgery. If the melanoma grows and there is metastasis, the possibility of cure decreases.

Public or sovereign debt is an obligation of a state against other countries or individuals for loans it has received. If those debts are not paid when they are small, they can lead to serious problems for countries and their populations. For example, Argentina's foreign debt was US$7 billion in

---

* In economics, it is known as the *multiplier effect* to all increases produced in the national income of a country due to increased consumption, investment, or government spending.
† creatingminds.org/quotes.

1976 and grew over the years. In 2001 the country went into default on its foreign debt when the debt amounted to US$144 billion.

Former US president Bill Clinton said in his memoirs, "The globalized world in which we live is inherently unstable, which means that at the same time it is full of opportunities and destructive forces."*

Chaos theory deals with complex, dynamic, and sensitive systems to variations in initial conditions, preventing prediction in the long term. A problem can grow and grow to create chaos.

In chaotic systems, a minimal change in the initial conditions makes the system evolve differently from what was expected. This theory shows the world does not follow the model of the watch, a universe of order, predictability, and harmony. There are, on the contrary, uncertain circumstances, jumbled, unstable, nonlinear, and unpredictable, that can create chaos in the system.

A British folk poem† may help explain this theory:

> For want of a nail, the shoe was lost
> For want of a shoe, the horse was lost
> For want of a horse, the rider was lost
> For want of a rider, the message was lost
> For want of a message the battle was lost
> For want of a battle the kingdom was lost.

The poem is about how a nail caused the loss of a kingdom, illustrating how something seemingly insignificant, can mean a lot.

Natural phenomena such as the movement of clouds or the movement of leaves in the wind are so disorderly and chaotic that they seem to defy any attempt to find laws that govern nature.

The chaos theory challenges the *scientific determinism* of Laplace (1749–1827) because it shows that systems with similar initial conditions can lead to different, unpredictable, and complex behaviors in the long term.

A slight difference in the initial conditions can change the final result. In 1903 the French mathematician Jules Henri Poincare (1854–1912) claimed that certain minor inaccuracies in initial conditions can lead to

---

* Bill Clinton, *Mi Vida* (Random House, 2009); Michael Ritter, *El valor del Capital Reputacional* (Olivos, Ritter & Partners, 2013), 21 ("The Value of Reputational Capital").

† A paragraph extracted from *Jacula Prudentum* (1651), a compilation of proverbs made by George Herbert (1593–1633), a poet, orator, and priest of Welsh origin.

large differences to the outcome. A small disturbance in the initial state could lead to a radically different state. On one occasion, Poincare's work was published, and the editor detected small inaccuracies. The work was republished with the inaccuracies corrected, which led to new discoveries by Poincare and the beginning of chaos theory.

Sixty years later, the American mathematician and meteorologist Edward Lorenz (1917–2008), a scientist at MIT, worked on a model that would allow him to predict the behavior of climate variations. In 1963 Lorenz worked on a model in order to predict the climate in the atmosphere and, using computers, tried to see the behavior of those equations. At that time computers were slow, so "Lorenz went to drink a tea while the computer did some calculations and when he came back he met a figure that is now known as the Lorenz attractor."[*]

Lorenz thought he had made a mistake when he ran the program and tried again and again until he reached the conclusion the simulations were very different from very similar initial conditions. The only change in some decimals produced very different results. In 1972 he presented a paper called "Predictability," which asked whether the flutter of a butterfly in Brazil could set off a tornado in Texas.

The *butterfly effect* seeks to demonstrate that a variation in one of the initial conditions of a given system can cause the system to develop completely differently, to the point that the final terms are radically modified.

Just as a small seed can grow a tree, a small action can generate chaos of enormous magnitude. A small event can grow out of control if the cause of the problem is not resolved quickly, which can lead to unpredictable consequences.

As artificial intelligence is made up of algorithms and formulas that process data so that if there is an error or failure in the programming of the data, the conclusion will be erroneous. For example, in 2016 Google was criticized when its image recognition system confused photos of gorillas with people and the issue was spread by twitter. The user wrote "My Friend Is Not a Gorilla," and attached the photo. Google had to apologize and promised to solve the error in the algorithm. It was not the only problem for Google. Journalist Carole Cadwallard told *The Guardian* newspaper that when she entered in Google the question "Did the Holocaust Happen?" the search engine showed an article from a neo-Nazi

---

[*] "Chaos Theory and Pattern," December 29, 2015, www.serorganizacional.com.ar.

site with the title "The 10 Reasons Why the Holocaust Didn't Happen." Google had to modify the algorithm.*

The Mars Climate Orbiter (MCO) was a NASA probe launched from Cape Canaveral on December 11, 1998, which was due to arrive on Mars on September 23, 1999. The purpose of the trip was to study the atmosphere and climate of Mars. But there was a small mistake on the part of the probe control team on Earth that caused an accident that cost the United States more than US$125 million.

On November 10, 1999, a NASA review board released a report detailing the suspected issues encountered with the loss of the spacecraft. The board found that the problem was in the software controlling the orbiter's thrusters. The software calculated the force the thrusters needed to exert in *pounds* of force. A separate piece of software took in the data assuming it was in the metric unit: *newtons*. NASA engineer Richard Cook, who was the project manager for Mars exploration projects at the time said, "Everyone was amazed we didn't catch it." Propulsion engineers, like those at Lockheed Martin who built the craft, typically express force in pounds, but it was standard practice to convert the newtons for space missions. One pound of force is about 4.45 newtons. Engineers at NASA's Jet Propulsion Lab assumed the conversion had been made and didn't check.†

Mahatma Gandhi (1869–1948) was a lawyer born in New Delhi. Once, in South Africa, on his way to Pretoria by train, Gandhi was sent off the train at Pietermaritzburg station because he refused to move from first to the third class, intended for people of color. On another occasion, traveling in a stagecoach, he was beaten by the driver because he refused to give up his seat to a white passenger. He also suffered other indignities when he was denied accommodation at various hotels because of his race.

These experiences brought Gandhi into direct contact with the problems faced by people of color in South Africa, a country where he lived over 20 years, working as the legal representative of Indian traders. Having suffered from racism, prejudice, and injustice in South Africa, he began to question the social situation in India.

---

* "Racist, Machist, and Extremist Algorithms: Do We Need to Teach Ethics to Robots?" Desiree Javmovich, July 5, 2018, www.infobae.com. Microsoft also had problems. The company had to silence Taym a bot for twitter. After taking action he went from being nice to attack users of the platform. "I Just Hate Everyone." A bot (apheresis of a robot) is a computer program that automatically performs repetitive tasks through the internet. es.wikipedia.org/wiki/Bot; "Why Microsoft's 'Tay' AI bot went wrong," www.techrepublic.com/article/why-microsofts-tay-ai-bot-went-wrong/.

† Lisa Grossman, "Nov 10, 1999; Metric Math Mistake Muffed Mars Meteorology Mission," October 11, 2010, www.wired.com.

The Gandhian nonviolent movement had a strong influence on securing the independence of India from the British Empire in 1947 and was also the inspiration of other leaders, such as with the Civil Rights Movement led by Martin Luther King Jr. and in the struggle against apartheid in South Africa led by Nelson Mandela.

It all started with a small incident on a train in Pretoria.

Rosa Parks (1913–2005) was an important figure of the movement for civil rights in the United States. In 1955 in Montgomery, Alabama, Parks refuses to obey a public bus driver who had ordered her to move to the back of the bus to give up her seat to a white person. Rosa Parks went to prison for refusing to give the seat and was accused of disturbing the peace. In response to the jailing of Rosa Parks, a relatively unknown Baptist minister, Martin Luther King Jr., led a protest to public buses in Montgomery, where he summoned the African-American population not to take buses. A year later, in 1956, the Supreme Court of the United States declared segregation in transportation unconstitutional.

It all started with an incident on a bus. Rosa Parks's history became the spark that ignited the protests against racial discrimination in the United States in 1955 and 1956. A seemingly small act can be the beginning of great change and revolution.

The flapping of a butterfly can cause a tornado. One should not underestimate the impact of what may seem small and should pay attention to the changes that occur. The challenge of the unknown, the uncertain, the improbable, and unstable, should be addressed long before circumstances become out of hand. If processes are implemented to act quickly and proactively, the change will not be a surprise.

Spencer Johnson, author of the book *Who Moved My Cheese?*, describes the importance of detecting the change and act quickly. He says:

> "We must remain vigilant to detect when small changes begin and thus be better prepared for the big change that can occur."[*]
> "Always stay vigilant and observe small changes, it will help you adapt to the great changes to come."[†]
> "If you do not change you may disappear.[‡] Anticipate change. Get ready."

---

[*] *Who Moved My Cheese?* 47th ed (Empresa Activa, 2000), 79.
[†] *Who Moved My Cheese?* 47th ed (Empresa Activa, 2000), 76.
[‡] *Who Moved My Cheese?* 47th ed (Empresa Activa, 2000), 51.

Organizations are complex systems composed of elements that interact with each other in a chaotic environment. Nothing happens in isolation, the facts are linked together, some are the cause or consequence of others.

Every day a small action, an error, or a seemingly small problem can evolve and grow over time, generating an unpredictable change that could lead to serious damage or a catastrophe for the future of the company.

Tommy Lascelles, who was the Buckingham Palace majordomo, said to Queen Elizabeth II, "it's in the small things that the rot starts."*

Every small fault, every little infraction, and the early signal should be a warning and an indicator of potentially more serious and systemic problems.

Companies must implement efficient controls that allow them to anticipate, warn, and react quickly to the existence of threats or dangers, so as to prevent them from growing dangerously and unexpectedly.

What should be the degree of protection of your organization?

How is the profitability of your business protected?

What is the prevention strategy to reduce the likelihood of a potentially serious and disruptive event from happening?

If the event happens, what processes are implemented to limit or reduce its impact?

How big can the problem grow?

---

* *The Crown*, Netflix.

12

Learning from Crises to Change

Until 1697 it was believed that swans should be white because all the records reported swans with white feathers.

However, a Dutch expedition led by explorer Willem de Vlamingh in 1697 discovered black swans in Australia.

The Lebanese researcher and mathematician Nassim Nicholas Taleb developed a theory of the *Black Swan* concept to refer to any surprise and highly improbable event, one that is unexpected, is difficult to predict, that we tend to ignore, and has high impact and magnitude.*

The black swan theory is a metaphor that describes events that come as a surprise and has a major effect.

There are unpredictable acts that can alter the equilibrium. For example, "Acts of God" = natural events such as floods, earthquakes, hurricanes; and Force Majeure = "Acts of Man" such as war, terrorist actions, labor disputes, interruption of electricity, or communication systems.†

The Y2K computer problem in 2000, climate change, chemical and biological attacks, the Ebola, Coronavirus (COVID-19), or SARS viruses, the threat of terrorism and hydrogen bombs, and other unexpected situations of maximum risk and minimum control could create a crisis at any time.

If organizations are not prepared, they will be more vulnerable to dangerous and unexpected situations, to a black swan event, or to a Tuesday the 13th event.‡ They will be more exposed to crises.

---

* Nassim Nicholas Taleb, *The Black Swan* (Random House, 2010).
† "Acts of God vs. Force Majeure," forum.wordreference.com and www.lawctopus.com/academike/understanding-differences-act-god-force.
‡ For the ancients, something bad could happen on the 13th, an event that would create damage. For the inhabitants of the Babylonian empire (1792–539 BC) – Iraq and northwest Syria today – the number 13 is represented with a raven, a symbol of bad luck. Around 700 BC, a poet of ancient Greece, Hesiod, recommended farmers not plant on the 13th of the month. At the Last Supper, Jesus of Nazareth was with his apostles, and they were 13 in number, and one of them

Says former Siemens executive Michael Ritter: "Managers and executives...are paid to solve the small crises that are presented to them on a day-to-day basis. However, their skills are really put to the test the day they face a truly serious crisis."[*]

A surprise is a gap between what we expect will happen and what does happen.[†] A surprise may generate a crisis, and the surprising crises in business life are more common than usually thought.

Oxford Metrica is a US AON group company that has been working for two decades to advise companies based on the analysis of negative effects on reputation and market value. In 2011, Oxford Metrica calculated companies have in a five-year period an 80% probability of suffering considerable damage to its reputation, including a loss of more than 20% of its market value, due to at least one negative event occurring suddenly and inadvertently.[‡]

A crisis is an abrupt and important change in the development of an event. Crises can damage the reputation of a company and, like fire, can grow wildly at an astonishing rate. A crisis can produce a dangerous change, and how to address those challenges will define the quality of a leader's management.

It is useful to remember some known crises to analyze what can be learned from them.

12.1 THE CUBAN MISSILE CRISIS

The world began to experience a major crisis on Tuesday, October 16, 1962, when US President John F. Kennedy was informed of aerial photographs of Soviet military bases in Cuba taken by a U-2 spy plane. The Soviets were preparing nuclear missiles with enough scope to attack large cities in the

---

betrayed him. The Code of Hammurabi does not mention this number. Some airlines skip the number 13 on seats, and in some hotels and buildings, the 13th floor is eliminated.

[*] Michael Ritter, *El valor del Capital Reputacional* (Olivos, Ritter & Partners, 2013), 258 ("The Value of Capital Reputation").

[†] Stanley K. Ridgley, *Strategic Thinking Skills* (The Great Courses, Course Guidebook, The Teaching Company, 2012), 111.

[‡] Michael Ritter, *El valor del Capital Reputacional* (Olivos, Ritter & Partners, 2013), 267; *Oxford Metrica Reputation Review*, 2011. The calculation is based on the "Global 1000" list (which lists the thousand most important companies in the world) and the data of the Ernst & Young consulting firm study "Risk that Matter" ("The Value of Capital Reputation").

United States. After the failure of the invasion of Cuban exiles in Bahia de Cochinos (1961), the Soviet government decided that year to establish a military force on Cuban soil, which included missiles, nuclear warheads, bombers, fighter jets, other military units, and almost 50,000 soldiers.

An agreement with the USSR was reached when Kennedy publicly promised he would not invade Cuba if the USSR removed the missiles and offered a secret pact to withdraw US missiles from Turkey, avoiding a third world war.

The crisis showed that one of its causes was the need to maintain more fluid and direct communication between the USSR and the United States. In 1963 a "red telephone" was created, a direct line of communication between the White House and the Kremlin, to expedite the conversations between both powers to try to prevent conflicts during periods of crisis.

"Never before had there been such a high probability that so many lives would end suddenly. Had war come, it could have meant the death of 100 million Americans, more than 100 million Russians, as well as millions of Europeans,"*wrote Professor Graham Allison of Harvard University in *Essence of Decision*, a book about the 13 days of the crisis.

The Cuban Missile Crisis was portrayed in the film *Thirteen Days* in the year 2000.

12.2 APOLLO 13

The Apollo 13 spacecraft was launched on April 11, 1970, at 1:30 p.m. from the Kennedy Space Center in Florida, USA, and was the seventh manned mission of the Apollo program and the third with the goal of landing on the moon.

On its way to the moon, 200,000 miles (321,868 km) from Earth, the crew turned on the fans of the hydrogen and oxygen tanks, and 93 seconds later, the astronauts heard an explosion accompanied by fluctuations in electrical energy. Oxygen tank number 2, one of the two tanks located in the service module, had exploded. The cables that went to the fans inside tank 2 were short-circuited by a damaged Teflon insulation, and the tank dome broke. The damage to the service module caused the landing to be abandoned.

---

* Graham T. Allison, "Essence of Decision," *The Science of Public Policy*, Tadao Miyakawa (Routledge 2000), Chapter 5, 85.

For four days, the three crewmen lived one of the most incredible survival dramas in history. Despite the critical situation for limited energy, heat loss in the cabin, and lack of potable water, the crew managed to return safely to Earth on April 17 of 1970.

Why did such an accident happen?

Tank 2 suffered an accidental fall during its handling by an operator the year before the launch. Although the fall was only five centimeters, it was enough to damage one of the internal components in the filling system, and deterioration occurred in the insulation in the cables connected to the system that removed oxygen.

Jim Lovell, commander of Apollo 13, said

> Human error is a virus that can be immersed in the best defined of the plans.... We must accept some risk and be aware that the unforeseen will always be there.... We must keep in mind that at some point in the future we will hear these words again: Houston, we have a problem.*

To suffer abrupt changes is part of the business activity, and in this case, a five-centimeter error turned into a tragedy.

12.3 THE IBM CASE

IBM is an American multinational technology company founded in 1911 that manufactures and markets hardware and software for computers and offers computer consulting. In 1975 IBM launched the IBM 5,100 portable computer, a device weighing 25 kilograms for the corporate market. In 1977 the first personal computers through companies such as Apple, Atari, or older companies such as Commodore, who envisioned a niche market, began to appear. In 1980, due to the market growth of personal computers, IBM decides to enter the market.

While until then IBM had designed and built 100% of their computers with proprietary technology, to meet their project of entering and positioning themselves in the personal computer market on schedule, IBM contracted suppliers for the different components of their future IBM PC personal computer. For this purpose, it hired Intel to provide the processor

---

* "Apollo 13, the Most Successful Failure of the Space Race," May 25, 2015, www.El Mundo.es.

and a small company called Microsoft to supply the operating system. Microsoft bought the operating system from a programmer named Tim Paterson of Seattle for US$50,000, made some adaptations, and called it MS-DOS (Microsoft Disk Operating System).

Thus, was born the first IBM personal computer, and it was a success. The expected income was US$240,000 in a period of five years. However, that figure was reached in a month and made IBM the sector leader.* While the quality of the computer was similar to those existing in the market, the difference was the IBM brand, which was known and reliable.

But IBM made a mistake that cost them dearly, and its leadership in the sector lasted only two years. In the rush to market and due to a lack of foresight, IBM had accepted Microsoft's proposal only to assign a license to use the operating system. That is, IBM did not buy the Microsoft MS-DOS product or contract for its exclusive use, an error that went unnoticed and would come back to haunt IBM.

By 1984 Microsoft had already granted MS-DOS licenses to more than 200 manufacturers of computers that began to hit the market, many similar to IBM PC computers, all at competitive prices and with the MS-DOS operating system. IBM realized Microsoft's success was its own nightmare as more and more competitors entered the market. In 1993 IBM announced losses of about eight million dollars, at that time a record company loss in US history.

The story of the personal computer provides a lesson: Pay attention to small details. As an old saying goes, the devil is in the details and a small mistake can create a big risk that dangerously affects a company's future.

12.4 THE DELL CASE

In June 2005 the American journalist Jeff Jarvis bought a Dell brand laptop and purchased an extended warranty service contract. His computer soon began to fail, and Dell's customer service did not respond well to his claim. After fruitless efforts, he decided to publish on June 21 on his blog *buzzmachine.com* a comment that read, "Dell lies, Dell sucks," to share his experience as a customer. Shortly after, blog followers commented on similar experiences. First, there were ten, and then there were hundreds

---

* Elisabet Rodriguez, "The Origin of IBM," www.maestrostheweb.com.

who complained of similar problems with Dell. Jarvis returned his computer, bought another brand of laptop, and posted an open letter to the founder and chairman of Dell Inc., Michael Dell.

The situation began to rebound in the media and to impact the stock price of Dell. Because of the bad press, in two months the share price of Dell dropped from US$40 to US$20. Sometime later, Dell interacted with customers on Jarvis's blog and also created its own blog.

Jarvis's blog and letter turned into a major fiasco for Dell. A single consumer may take a multinational company close to hell if the company does not react and change fast.

12.5 UNITED BREAKS GUITARS

Fifteen years ago, when any unsatisfied consumer commented to his or her friends and relatives about a problem, those who learned about his or her experience were a relatively small group. Today, everything has changed. Due to the development of the internet, a complaint can reach millions of people in a short time.

In 2008, the Canadian musician Dave Carroll was in the Chicago airport with his band for a connecting flight through United Airlines to Omaha, Nebraska. United Airlines personnel damaged his Taylor guitar, and he submitted a claim to the company. The answer to Carroll's complaint was that because it had been made after 24 hours, by company policy, United Airlines could not do anything. For nine months the musician claimed he was due compensation from United Airlines for having broken his guitar without any success.

On July 6, 2008, Dave Carroll uploaded to YouTube a protest song called "United Breaks Guitars," where he took out his frustration. On only the first day, his video had been seen by 150,000 people, and the song positioned itself at number one on iTunes downloads the week of its release.

Carroll's public claim brought down the share value of United Airlines down 7% in the first four days of the crisis, which represented a loss of the company's market value of more than US$100 million. United Airlines then offered compensation of US$3,000, which Carroll rejected. His goal, he said, was to change the company's customer care policies.

The situation generated strong negative publicity for United Airlines and positive publicity for Carroll, who began lecturing about his case and published a book entitled *United Breaks Guitars*, like his song, along with a web platform where consumers could leave their complaints.

In August 2015 the video had 15 million visits.

The flapping of a butterfly transformed into a tornado.

United Airlines announced that it would use Carroll's video for customer care training.*

Social networking is a powerful communication tool. Dissatisfied customers can transform something small into something large and dangerous.

The sooner the leaders deal with the problems, crises, and claims, the lower the damage they will generate in their companies.

12.6 RMS *TITANIC*

In 1898 the American writer Morgan Robertson published a book called *The Wreck of the Titan*. It tells the story of a huge transoceanic ship built with the idea that it could never sink. That transatlantic luxury liner made its maiden voyage from Britain to New York in April with 2,000 people on board. In the novel, the huge ship hits an iceberg of gigantic proportions, and almost all passengers and crew die for lack of lifeboats. The ship's captain was named Smith.

Fourteen years later, that novel was going to be almost a copy of reality.

The RMS *Titanic*, the largest ocean liner ever built, with unparalleled luxury, set sail on April 10, 1912, from Southampton, England, to New York with 2,223 people on board. As it was considered unsinkable and indestructible, it had only lifeboats to accommodate 1,178 people, about half of the people traveling.

The captain of the *Titanic*, E. J. Smith, said in 1907, "In all my years at sea...I never saw any shipwreck, I never wrecked, nor have I ever encountered a situation that threatened to end with some kind of disaster."†

But the past does not necessarily repeat or determine the future.

Four days after starting its first voyage, the *Titanic* crew began to receive messages from other ships warning of several icebergs.

---

* July 24, 2009, www.bbc.com.
† Nassim Nicholas Taleb, *The Black Swan: The Impact of the Highly Improbable* (El Cisne Negro, Paidos), 90.

On April 14, 1912, while the ship sailed at full speed, Captain Edward J. Smith retired to his room to rest at 9:20 pm. At 11:40 pm, the indestructible ocean liner hit an iceberg. The ship broke in half and 2 hours and 45 minutes after the collision, the ship sank.

The 1,514 people lost their lives in this tragedy, not only by the collision with the iceberg but also from the absence of sufficient boats and/ or lifejackets.* The warnings received by the crew were not taken into account, and the disaster occurred.

The survivors of the biggest shipwreck in history were found by the transatlantic RMS *Carpathia* at 3:30 a.m..†

After the disaster, there was a reaction from the regulatory authorities, significant improvements in maritime safety were implemented and the International Convention for the Safety of Life at Sea was agreed to.

The wreck of the *Titanic* shocked the world by the high number of deaths and mistakes. No organization is too big to fail or to have disaster strike, and everyone should take their precautions.

Unlike what happened to the *Titanic*, organizations must address the signals and implement controls and response plans to improbable situations in order to prevent and react to an unlikely but possible crisis.

12.7 PEARL HARBOR

The surprise attack of December 7, 1941, by the Imperial Japanese Navy against the naval base of the United States at Pearl Harbor, Hawaii, was carried out before 8:00 a.m. with 353 aircraft. For two hours, the Japanese bombs managed to damage or sink eight American battleships that were in the port, as well as cruisers and destroyers. The 6 major naval bases on Oahu, one of the islands of Hawaii, were ruined, 188 aircraft were destroyed, 5 warships sank, and more than 2,400 people lost their lives.

---

* Seven percent of the dead were women. The *Titanic* was the first ship to send an SOS, which means "Save Our Souls."

† On July 17, 1918, *Carpathia* was part of a convoy headed for Boston when it was attacked by a German submarine 120 miles west of Fastnet, an island in Ireland. Three torpedoes sent *Carpathia* to the bottom of the sea. Its remains were discovered in 2000 in 540 feet of water some 220 miles off the east coast of Ireland.

What is striking is that Americans had at least five opportunities to prevent the tragedy several hours before the attack.

Messages from Tokyo were intercepted in Washington, periscopes were seen near the entrance of Pearl Harbor, the conning tower of a foreign submarine was also seen, spots were discovered on the radar screen, and messages that were sent arrived later to their destinations.

In the period 1939–1941, Ricardo Rivera Schreiber (1892–1969) was the Peruvian ambassador to Japan. At that time, the embassy had the services of a Japanese translator who was a cousin of an employee of the Ministry of the Japanese Navy. In January 1941 the translator told the chief of staff of the Peruvian embassy the following: "Powerful Japan. Japan goes to war and will destroy the American fleet in the middle of the Pacific." The chief of staff relayed the information to Ambassador Rivera Schreiber.*

A few days later, a friend of the ambassador, a Japanese professor at Tokyo University, mentioned to Rivera that his country was "on the brink of a disaster that would bring ruin forever" and added, "Admiral Isoroku Yamamoto (1884-1943) had drawn up a plan to attack the American fleet in Pearl Harbor and had a drill in one of the southern islands of Japan."[†]

The two versions match. Then Rivera Schreiber informed the US ambassador to Japan Joseph Clark Grew (1880–1965), who sent a telegram to the American secretary of state Cordell Hull (1871–1955) where he said: "An official of the embassy was informed by my Peruvian colleague that Japanese military forces were planning a massive surprise attack on Pearl Harbor ... the plan looked fantastic (unreal)."[‡]

The telegram was not given importance and was taken as a mere rumor.

On January 24, 1941, almost 11 months before the Japanese attack on Pearl Harbor, Frank Knox, who was then secretary of the US Navy, wrote: "In the event of a war with Japan, it is quite possible that hostilities begin with a surprise attack on the fleet or the Pearl Harbor naval base, with inherent possibilities of becoming a major disaster."[§]

In the book *Secret Stories of the Last War* by *Reader's Digest*, it was written:

---

* Pierina Pichi, "Ricardo Rivera Schreiber, the Peruvian who warned the US of Ties to Pearl Harbor," *BBC World*, December 7, 2015.
† Pierina Pichi, "Ricardo Rivera Schreiber, the Peruvian Who Warned the US of Ties to Pearl Harbor," *BBC World*, December 7, 2015.
‡ The telegram can be read among the diplomatic documents of *Foreign Affairs of the US*, digitized by the University of Wisconsin. Pierina Pichi, "Ricardo Rivera Schreiber, the Peruvian Who Warned the US of Ties to Pearl Harbor," *BBC World*, December 7, 2015.
§ Manuel J. Prieto, *Curistoria: Curiosities and Anecdotes of History* (Evohe Ddaska), 68.

Even now the issue is discussed. However, apart from what the high command did or did not do in Washington and Pearl Harbor, the truth is that possibilities existed to avoid disaster. Missed opportunities. The best way to avoid disaster is actually very simple: we must learn to recognize the warning signs when presented to our view.*

12.8 MALVINAS

The Malvinas War was an armed conflict between Argentina and the United Kingdom, which took place in the Malvinas/Falkland Islands, South Georgia, and the South Sandwich Islands between April 2 and June 14, 1982. The origin of the war was the attempt by Argentina to recover the sovereignty of the islands, which the United Nations considered disputed territories.

Did the then president of Argentina get information or signals sufficient to understand that a war with Britain would be a wrong decision and that, instead, should continue the advanced diplomatic negotiations?

On April 2, 1982, the facto president of Argentina, Leopoldo Fortunato Galtieri (1926–2003), received a call from the president of the United States, Ronald Wilson Reagan (1911–1989) at 10:10 pm. During the investigation of the book *Malvinas: The Secret Plot*, the authors had access to a "minute" of that dialogue.† President Reagan in that telephone conversation transmitted to President Galtieri the following:

> Mr. President, I have reliable news that Argentina will take a measure of strength in the Falkland (Malvinas) Islands. I am, as you will understand, very concerned about the impact that an action of this type could have.
>
> I want to express to you, Mr. President, the concern of the United States and the need for an alternative to the use of force.
>
> My government is ready to offer its good offices to resume talks and reach a solution. If your government deems it appropriate, I can send Vice President Bush to Buenos Aires for talks and begin to find a negotiated solution to the situation.
>
> Moreover, in the context of the United Nations, we can also find a suitable formula. Ambassador Kirkpatrick is ready to assist the parties in this

---

* P. Weiss, "Secret Stories of the Last War," *Reader's Digest*, 1963, 134.
† Cardoso-Kirschbaum and Van der Kooy, *Malvinas: La Trama Secreta* (Sudamericana-Planeta, 1983), 96 ("Malvinas: Secret Plot").

process. You know well Ambassador Kirkpatrick, Mr. President, and know how she could work in this direction.

I think it is my duty to warn you that Britain is prepared to respond militarily to an Argentine landing.

The conflict will be tragic and will have serious hemispherical consequences. I do wish to point out clearly, then, that the relationship between your country and mine will suffer severely.

Britain, Mr. President, is a very close friend of the United States and the new relationship that keeps Washington with Argentina today will be irremediably damaged.*

The US ambassador in Buenos Aires, Harry Shlaudeman, made a last attempt to avoid the war and met with President Galtieri on the early morning of April 30, 1982, after midnight, at the headquarters of the army. In that meeting, that lasted nearly two hours, the ambassador warned: "If this continues, tomorrow we will announce several measures against Argentina." A few hours later Galtieri answered him: "The Navy is hungry to get into action."[†]

That same Friday, April 30, President Reagan announced open US support for Britain. The bombing of Puerto Argentino began on the first of May, and on May 2 two torpedoes sank the cruiser *General Belgrano*. The ending was predictable and sad. The balance of the war in human lives was 900 people killed: 649 Argentine soldiers, 255 British, and 3 civilian islanders.[‡]

Did the Argentine military government understand the risks and consequences of starting a war against England?

12.9 SEPTEMBER 11, 2001

The twin towers of the World Trade Center in New York were built in 1976 by the American architect Minoru Yamasaki (1912–1986). On September

---

* Cardoso-Kirschbaum and Van Der Kooy, *Malvinas: Secret Plot* (A South American Planet, 1983), 97–100.
[†] Hugo Alconada Mon, "Como fue la Noche en la que Pudo Haberse Evitado la Guerra," *La Nacion*, April 30, 2007 ("How was the Night in which War Could Have Been Averted").
[‡] In the UK, the victory in the confrontation helped the government of Margaret Thatcher (1925–2013) to be reelected in the elections of 1983. In Argentina, the defeat in the conflict precipitated the resignation of Galtieri and the end of the military board that governed the country.

11, 2001, the emblematic twin towers were brought down by two jetliners, hijacked by terrorists that hit them.

On July 22, 2003, a commission of the US Congress released a 900-page text related to the attacks that killed 3,019 people and injured nearly 6,000. The paper reported that the three major agencies of US intelligence – the CIA, the FBI, and the NSA – had clues about Al Qaeda operations, but they never shared the information due to the lack of communication and coordination among them. The report claims that due to the mistakes of these national security services, the opportunity to thwart the September 11 plot was lost. The document reads:

> The United States never considered the possibility of a terrorist attack on a large scale in its own territory. Although the intelligence services had relevant information on the attacks before September 11, they could not concentrate on them. Neither had they proved to have enough initiative to deal with new transnational threats.
>
> An FBI contact rented an apartment in San Diego to two of the hijackers, without having the slightest suspicion of their activities. The CIA and the NSA, each on its side and without informing the FBI, had watched these two members of the terrorist network.*

Members of the terrorist group who were monitored had obtained entry visas into the United States and had opened bank accounts there, attained driver's licenses, and conducted aviation courses in Arizona and Minneapolis, Minnesota. For lack of coordination and cooperation among the agencies, the controls did not work, and the threats were not properly attended to. If the protection system had worked, the attacks perhaps could have been avoided.

12.10 CHALLENGER

The space shuttle *Challenger* accident occurred on Tuesday, January 28, 1986. The disaster happened over the Atlantic Ocean off the coast of central Florida and is considered the most serious accident in the history

---

* Isabel Piquer, "Todo el Control que Funciono Mal," *Pagina 12*, July 25, 2003, www.Pagina12.com. ar ("All the Control that Work Wrong").

of space exploration. The shuttle disintegrated seconds after launch, killing all seven crew members.*

Could the accident have been prevented?

Discovery's flight a year earlier, in 1985, had taken off with temperatures of 11 °C, almost out of the limit recommended by the supplier, the Morton Thiokol Company, which manufactured the solid-fuel motors. Low temperatures caused *Discovery*'s joint to become rigid, and they did not expand fast enough to seal the O-rings, releasing gases that partially damaged them. If the seals had been worn one millimeter more, there would have been a disaster. Company technicians had warned that launching a rocket below certain temperatures presented a serious danger.†

Did the NASA officials hear the warning?

On January 27, 1986, the day before the launch of the *Challenger*, temperatures at the Kennedy Space Center fell below 0 °C, and the entire launchpad remained covered in ice. Upon hearing this, the engineer of the contractor Morton Thiokol, Roger Boisjoly, requested a teleconference with NASA officials to prevent the launching of the next day. In this communication, Boisjoly tried to convince NASA to postpone the launch.

Seeing that it was possible the launch could be delayed by Boisjoly's questions, NASA, due to political commitments and scheduling problems, pressed the supplier Morton Thiokol to move forward with the launch.

Boisjoly, angry, showed images of *Discovery* so the managers would be aware of what was going to happen. At that moment, a manager of contractor Thiokol made a statement to Boisjoly to end the discussion: "Take off your engineering hat and put on your management hat."‡

That night when he got home, Boisjoly's wife asked him if anything was wrong because of his mood, and his response was, "No, nothing, just that tomorrow will be a launch and the astronauts will die."§

The next day, after the launch, there was a spectacular explosion. The compartment in which the crew was traveling shot out intact in a fireball and continued to climb five kilometers before falling.

---

* The shuttle had two solid rocket fuels. These rockets were made up of several sections that were then coupled. To prevent fuel gas from escaping through the joints, each joint contained two toric joints that, when expanded by heat, sealed the space.

† "El Accidente del Challenger," https://memoriahisterica.wordpress.com ("The Challenger's Accident").

‡ www.nasaspaceflight.com/2007/01/remembering-the-mistakes-of-challenger.

§ "El Accidente del Challenger," https://memoriahisterica.wordpress.com ("The Challenger's Accident").

Six months after the disaster, the Rogers Commission prepared a 225-page report of the investigation into what happened. It was determined that the cause of the accident was the failure of one of the O-rings in the booster rocket, which made hot pressurized gases enter into contact with the external tank. The O-rings were not prepared for the low temperatures on the day of launch. The commission also concluded that warnings had not been heeded. The warning signs were not taken into account, and the disaster could have been avoided.

Roger Boisjoly (1938–2012), the mechanical engineer who had given the warning on the effect of low temperatures on the O-rings, after leaving his employer Morton Thiokol, started lecturing on ethics. The accident is used as an eyewitness case to discuss safety engineering.*

12.11 COLUMBIA

On January 16, 2003, the shuttle *Columbia* was launched from the Kennedy Space Center with seven crew members. Within 82 seconds of taking off, it suffered the impact of pieces of foam insulation made of polyurethane that had detached from the outer tank and hit the left-wing. According to NASA, the fragment had a weight of 1 kilogram and hit at more than 800 kilometers per hour. The blow pierced a pair of panels and caused a hole of 25 centimeters in diameter.

After 16 days of a scientific mission and during re-entry to the earth's atmosphere, the hole in *Columbia* allowed the entrance of extremely hot gas that melted the internal aluminum structure of the left-wing and led to the destruction of the shuttle, which disintegrated in the air.

The detachment of pieces of insulation had occurred during previous flights with minor damage, and, therefore, NASA did not consider it as risk, and control of missions did not give it more importance. The final research report criticized NASA for not listening to the suspicions of its technicians. For example, a space agency engineer warned the shuttle was in danger two days before the accident. Security specialist Robert

---

* Bob Ebeling was the other engineer at NASA's contractor Morton Thiokol that had tried to stop the launch. He said in 2016, "If they listened to me and waited for a weather change, it might have been a completely different outcome." Ebeling retired soon after *Challenger*'s accident and he suffered depression. "30 Years after Explosion Challenge Engineer Still Blames Himself." Howard Berkes, www.npr.org January 28, 2016.

Daugherty sent emails alerting NASA to the possible damage caused by the impact of objects on the left-wing of the spacecraft during takeoff.

The article "NASA Was Able to Avoid the Columbia Accident" says

If they had evaluated well the risk that the impact of the piece of foam caused, listening to the suspicions of some engineers that were reflected in electronic messages they would have asked the observation of damage with military satellites and they could have sent the shuttle Atlantis to rescue the crew.*

12.12 EXXON VALDEZ

The *Exxon Valdez* was an oil tanker, owned by ExxonMobil, that on March 24, 1989, at 12:04 a.m. ran aground in Prince William Bay in the Gulf of Alaska, and after hitting the Blight Reef coral reef, spilled 40 million gallons of crude oil (257,000 barrels) over 2,000 kilometers of coastline. Alaska had experienced the worse ecological tragedy in its history. Damage to wildlife in the area threatened the food chain that the fishing industry was supported by and threatened ten million birds and waterfowl, hundreds of otters, sea lions, and whales.

The research report of the National Transportation Safety Board (NTSB) revealed that the cause of the accident was the captain had left in command two crew members who had not rested the mandatory six hours. The ship was on autopilot, and lookouts warned about the incorrect position of the vessel twice. It has been noted the captain was drunk when the tragedy happened,† and when he wanted to right the ship, it was too late.

The Court of Appeals of San Francisco considered the irresponsible behavior of Exxon, by putting a chronic alcoholic in command of his supertanker with millions of barrels of crude oil to sail the pure and rich fishing waters of the bay Prince William deserved severe penalties.‡ The Supreme Court of the United States in 2008 ordered the company to pay about US$500 million in damages.§

---

* "La NASA pudo Evitar el Accidente del Columbia," *El País*, August 27, 2003 ("NASA was able to avoid the Columbia Accident").
† "Exxon Valdez, the Tragedy Is Not Over Yet," March 24, 2014, www.veoverde.com.
‡ IN RE: the EXXON VALDEZ, http://caselaw.findlaw.com/us-9th-circuit.
§ Adam Liptak, "Damages Cut against Exxon in Valdes Case," June 26, 2008, www.nytimes.com.

The disaster also generated a legislative reaction, the Oil Pollution Act of 1990, which states that owners and operators of tankers must submit for approval response plans to the risks of oil.

12.13 GERMANWINGS

Germanwings is a low-cost German airline, a subsidiary of Lufthansa, and was founded in 1997. On March 24, 2015, Flight 9525, operating a German Airbus A320-211 aircraft, departed at 10:01 a.m. from Barcelona El Prat airport en route to Dusseldorf International Airport with 144 passengers, 2 pilots, and 4 crew members. The plane crashed in the French Alps of Provence.

Could the airline have taken the necessary steps to avoid the accident?

Andreas Lubitz, one of the pilots of that plane, had visited 41 doctors in the 5 years prior to crashing the plane into the mountain. Only 30 days before the tragedy, he had had an appointment with 7 doctors, and according to the final report of investigation, 2 weeks before the accident, a doctor recommended Lubitz be transferred to a psychiatric hospital.

Lufthansa knew the pilot's history of depression.[*] Marseilles prosecutor Brice Robin said at a press conference, "Lubitz deliberately crashed the plane and killed 149 people."[†]

12.14 LAMIA

On November 28, 2016, a plane from Lamia, which had left Santa Cruz, Bolivia, in the direction of Medellin, Colombia, crashed at Cerro Gordo, 17 kilometers from the airport of Rionegro, near Medellin. The Brazilian soccer team of Chapecoense was traveling on Lamia Flight 2933, and 71 people lost their lives in the accident. The cause for the accident was the failure to follow the air safety protocol: making a flight without the

---

[*] "Lufthansa Knew about Killer Pilot's Depression," March 27, 2015, www.thetimes.co.uk; "Lufthansa Knew of Co-pilot's Previous 'Severe Depression' in 2009," www.washingtonpost.com by Anthony Faiola and Michael Birnbaum March 31, 2015; www.lavozdelderecho.com 03/29/2015.

[†] www.lanacion.com.ar, June 11, 2015.

obligatory fuel reserve. The irresponsibility of the pilot and the lack of controls resulted in a perfectly avoidable tragedy.

At the Santa Cruz airport, the inspector considered the flight plan unsafe; however, the plane took off. Landing in Bogota to refuel would have ensured flight safety but would have also triggered a $25,000 fine for flying under the permitted fuel level. The fact that the pilot was also a shareholder of the company might have made him value the expense more than the danger. According to the Colombian newspaper *El Tiempo*, "The entrepreneurial mentality had more weight than the instinct of the pilot."*

As a result of the accident, the airport authorities of Bolivia suspended the operating license of Lamia, removed the authorities of the General Direction of Civil Aviation, and began an investigation. It was later learned the pilot had an arrest warrant in Bolivia.

The Cuban Missile Crisis, Apollo 13, IBM, DELL, United Airlines, Titanic, Pearl Harbor, Malvinas War, September 11, Challenger, Columbia, Exxon Valdez, Germanwings, and Lamia are some examples that show us the importance of paying maximum attention to details and changes in the environment to avoid serious crises.

George Santayana (1863–1952), Spanish philosopher, poet, and novelist, in his work *The Life of Reason*, pointed out, "Those who cannot learn from history are doomed to repeat it."[†]

Leaders must attack the causes of problems and learn from the lessons of history and past mistakes. The good side of crises is that they usually have a solution, an expiration date, and a lesson for the future. This is endorsed by the sayings of different personalities throughout history. Some examples are detailed in the footnote.[‡]

---

* www.eltiempo.com, December 4, 2016.
† en.wikiquote.org/wiki/George_Santayana.
‡ 1. Saint Pio de Pietreicina (1887–1968) said, "Blessed the crises that made you grow."
  2. Microsoft founder Bill Gates said, "It's okay to celebrate success but it's more important to pay attention to the lessons of failure."
  3. Augustine Og Mandino (1923–1996), a psychologist and writer born in Italy, said that "every obstacle is a comrade in arms that forces you to be better." *The World's Greatest Salesman* (Editorial Diana, 1982), 34.
  4. Authors Charles Poissant and Christian Godefroy point out, "It is not shameful to make a mistake. It is to make the same mistake twice. If you have thoroughly analyzed the reasons for failure, you will understand better what will lead you to success." *My First Million* (Editorial Atlantida, 1986), 153.
  5. The Egyptian philosopher, physician, and theologian Maimonides (1138–1204) said that "if there is a wrong situation there, try not to fall into the same error."
  6. Canadian lawyer and writer Robin Sharma notes that "all adversity teaches us a lesson," *The Monk Who Sold His Ferrari* (Editorial Sudamericana, 2010), 31.

For Tracy Carter Dougherty, former director of ethics at Lockheed Martin Corporation, it is good for managers to wonder what they would do if they had to face a major crisis "because it will inevitably happen.... Something happens like that in a matter of time."[*]

The tragedy of Titanic, Pearl Harbor, the Malvinas Islands War, September 11, the Challenger and Columbia crashes, Exxon Valdez, Germanwings and Lamia's accidents could have been avoided.

Chesley B. Sullenberger III, the pilot who safely landed a plane on the Hudson river in 2019, said in an interview, "It is not surprising that before a crisis, there are indications of real deep problems that have their roots in leadership."[†]

Surprises, crises, and failures can often be evaded.

Edward De Bono, the Maltese psychologist at Oxford University, says:

> Things can go wrong. The facts may not be as expected. Unfortunately, unpredictable interferences can occur.[‡] ... One can analyze the past, but one has to design the future. The more information we get, the better it will be for our decisions and actions. If the information is clear and complete, there will be a natural flow towards decision or action.[§]

Learn and analyze the mistakes of the past, to design the future. Henry Ford (1863–1947), the founder of the Ford Motor Company, is considered the father of mass production chains. He was born into a family of Irish immigrants who lived on a farm and failed several times before founding Ford Motor Company. In 1893, he designed the first vehicle powered by

---

7. The American writer Napoleon Hill (1883–1970), who was an adviser to President Franklin Roosevelt and author of one of the best-selling books in history, *Think and Grow Rich*, stated that "Most great people have achieved their greatest success just one step beyond their greatest failure."

8. Lido Anthony "Lee" Iacocca (1924–2019), born in the United States, is one of the most representative people in the automotive industry. Iacocca was the creator of the hit Ford Mustang and Chrysler Minivans. Iacocca says in his book, "Mistakenness is part of daily life and it is impossible not to make mistakes from time to time. We can only hope that they do not have unreasonable consequences and that one does not repeat the same mistake twice." Iacocca. *Autobiography of a Winner* (Grijalbo Bantam, 1984), 57.

[*] Dayton Fandray, "El Compromiso con los Valores," *Revista Gestión*, March–April 2001, 122 ("The Commitment to Values").

[†] David Gelles, "I Honestly Don't Trust Many People at Boeing: A Broken Culture Exposed," January 13, 2020, nytimes.com.

[‡] Edward De Bono, *Ideas for Thinking Professionals* (Paidos, 1994), 129.

[§] Edward De Bono, *Ideas for Thinking Professionals* (Paidos, 1994), 35.

gasoline, but his company disappeared because of the low quality of cars and their high prices.

In 1908 Ford developed the first Ford Model T that required 12 hours of work. In 1913 he patented the assembly line for mass production and achieved remarkable efficiencies. By 1917 half of the cars in the United States were Model T's. In 1920, Ford produced one Model T per minute and by 1925, each Model T left the assembly line every five seconds.* Ford sold more than 15 million cars. Ford said that "*failure* is simply the opportunity to begin again, this time more intelligently."[†]

The Mayan civilization was one of the most important in history, had great knowledge of astronomy[‡] and mathematics, possessed a hieroglyphic writing system, and built impressive buildings. The Maya sages knew that in the teachings of the past was the knowledge to live the future better.

Yuval Harari, an Israeli historian, and professor in the Department of History at the Hebrew University of Jerusalem, wrote,

> We study history not to know the future but to widen our horizons, to understand that our present situation is neither natural nor inevitable. ... The best reason to learn history is not in order to predict the future, but to ... imagine alternative destinies.[§]

The best organizations are those that learn from experience and change.

We must learn from the failures of the past and the causes that generate crises so that mistakes are not repeated. The past is for learning, the future is for doing.

The Greek philosopher Heraclitus of Ephesus (535–475 BC) said: "If you do not expect the unexpected, you will not recognize it when it arrives."[¶]

"And now, the end is near, and so I face the final curtain. ... Regrets I have had a few," sang Frank Sinatra (1915–1998) in the song "My Way."

If you act preventively there will probably be no regrets. There is no need to complain or run after events, we must anticipate the "unlikely" threats on the horizon to protect the company.[**]

---

* J. Stoner, R. Freeman and D. Gilbert Jr., *Management*, (Prentice-Hall, Pearson, Addison, Wesley, Longman, 1966; Prentice-Hall Hispanoamericana SA, 31).
† www.brainyquote.com/quotes/henry_ford_121339.
‡ Without the help of technology, the Mayans specified the duration of the solar year as 365 days.
§ "Yuval Noah Harari Quotes," www.goodreads.com.
¶ www.azquotes.com/quote/658201.
** Michael Ritter, *El Valor del Capital Reputacional* (Olivos, Ritter & Partners, 2013), 233 ("The Value of Reputational Capital").

It is necessary to be proactive, design, and execute a plan that prevents, controls, and prepares the company to neutralize the adverse conditions to avoid having to regret it tomorrow.

The American philosopher Wayne Dyer (1940–2015) said that "you cannot always control what goes on outside. But you can always control what goes on inside."[*]

Intelligence was given to people to question things.

Why did the crisis happen?

Has the context changed?

Is the company prepared to react quickly to negative threats and events?

Do we learn from mistakes and failures?

What happened to a competitor or supplier can happen in the company?

Are organizations prepared to react to the coming of the wolf, the gorilla, the black swan, the perfect storm, or the "bad luck"?

You must choose to be a victim or protagonist of the change.

The problem is not so much the risks, but the attitude toward them. The immense downside costs to a company from the lack of an effective program against risks must be the incentive to move it forward.

Corrective and preventive actions must be taken to coexist with the circumstances and uncertainty. We do not know what may happen tomorrow, or what kind of crisis we have to face.

The environment is volatile and it is necessary to read the signals and threats well to face risks successfully.

If the company is not duly prepared to react to negative threats it may quickly fall like in a roller coaster.

---

[*] www.brainyquote.com/quotes/wayne_dyer.

Section 3

Risks

13

Corporate Risks: Unit 1

A risk is a state of uncertainty that can affect an organization's ability to achieve its objectives. Risks are a chance of loss and are part of a company's life.

All organizations must face the uncertainty of risks and must be able to identify them in order to neutralize them and prevent them from negatively impacting the company.

Risks increase the cost of doing business. Therefore, investing in security and risk control is cheaper than paying the consequences. The ability of organizations to anticipate threats and to respond and adapt to risks depends on the control program implemented.

An effective leader goes through the OODA cycle, reflects on the knowledge gained, is proactive in identifying threats and obstacles to his or her plan, and makes decisions to anticipate the changes that may prevent compliance with the company's strategy.*

Because business and its risks constantly change, controls must be continuously reevaluated. A leader must review existing risks in order to improve prevention and carry out all necessary measures to minimize and control the hazard.

Lanny A. Breuer, Criminal Division Attorney of the Department of Justice, has said:

> An effective compliance and ethics program is one that prevents fraud and corruption in the first place but when such compliance program has not

---

* Colonel John Richard Boyd (1927–1997) was a combat pilot of the United States Air Force and adviser to the Pentagon, and his theories have influenced business. The OODA (observe, orient, decide, and act) loop is a process that Boyd developed from his observations on aerial combat in the Korean War. The OODA decision cycle consists of observing data, analyzing them to form an idea or thinking, choosing a course of action, and finally making decisions. This model has been implemented for the combat pilots and the firing of intercontinental missiles. The underlying idea is the advantage to the one who executes quickly.

done so, there are defined policies in place to quickly detect, fix and report the [FCPA] violations. Additionally, an effective compliance program should not be static but dynamic to meet changing business circumstances, such as when a company might move to do business in a high-risk country. Effective compliance programs should also be ever-evolving through continued assessments, as the compliance world grows and matures.*

As Professor Lynn Paine of Harvard Business School explains, business risks are multiple and include counterfeit records, hazardous products, abusive behavior, unsafe workplace conditions, conflicts of interest, theft, environmental issues, etc.†

The particular risks of organizations are influenced by the type of industry in question. For example, a supermarket chain may consider stealing from employees and/or poorly stored and inedible food as their main risks. An oil and gas company may consider environmental risks and worker health and safety issues as among its most important dangers. For a cable television or telephone company, perhaps the price arrangement and agreement of operating areas with competitors are among its main potential conflicts. A bank may consider insider trading (gaining privileged information to gain advantages from the purchase or sale of securities) or money laundering (making funds or assets obtained through illicit activities appear as the result of legitimate ones) as their priority risks. The list of potential threats that could have a negative impact on a business is vast and increasingly worries top management.

In 2010, *The Economist* presented a report called "The Age of Compliance," which states that "more than ever, boards and senior management want to understand the overall risk exposure."‡

Some leaders underestimate the level of risk and compliance and ethical issues in their organizations. But it is utopian to assume the company is immune to bad behavior. Corruption, fraud, theft, tax evasion, or illegal work are part of this dilemma.

Some of those leaders who are not convinced they should invest in an ethics and compliance program suffer from *cognitive dissonance*, a concept

---

* Mentioned by Latour Lafferty, a partner in Holland and Knight Law Firm, in his paper, "Culture and Ethics." Also "An Effective FCPA Compliance Program – Thoughts of Lanny Breuer," June 2, 2010, http://fcpacompliancereport.com/2010/06.
† You can see the interview with Professor Lynn Paine in "Where Morals and Profits Meet: The Corporate Value Shift," interview by Carla Tishler, Harvard Business School, November 18, 2002, www.hbs.edu/faculty/Pages/profile.aspx.
‡ "The Age of Compliance" (The Economist Intelligence Unit, 2010), 13.

that in psychology refers to the tension a person has when he or she has two ideas at the same time that are contradictory to each other. For example, one idea that tells him or her not to invest the money in the program and one idea that tells him or her it is necessary to do so.

In a 2011 report by the Economist Intelligence Unit, which resulted from a worldwide survey of 385 senior corporate executives, concluded that "few companies have the big picture needed for effective risk and compliance management."*

It is necessary to identify and understand the risks in order to know how to anticipate and deal with them. In order to be able to adjust controls and supervision, leaders need to know what risks to prevent and manage.

Business leaders must not only see the objective but also the obstacles, black holes, and risks that prevent them from achieving their strategy. Being alert to risks will allow companies to react quickly and survive.

While sometimes a piece may be missing to assemble the puzzle, the first step in analyzing the risks is to identify them and classify them by type of risk.

This work does not intend to focalize on certain risks that, although they are important for companies that face them on a daily basis, are not considered compliance, ethics, or human resources risks. For example these include: (i) credit risk (someone owes money and cannot pay back); (ii) market risk (the possibility of suffering losses due to changes in the price of assets); (iii) foreign exchange risk (to buy an asset priced in the currency of another country); (iv) the risk of interest rates (an increase in the interest rate that must be paid); and (v) liquidity risk (running out of cash to be used to pay debts).

Below you can find different corporate risks of compliance, ethics, and human resources, which, if not controlled, can turn into nightmares.

13.1 LACK OF LICENSES, PERMITS, AND CERTIFICATIONS

To work legally, businesses need a certain type of authorization, license, or operating permit at the municipal, state, and/or federal level.

---

* "Few Companies Admit to Risk and Compliance Failures in the Last Three Years," June 16, 2011 (The Economist Intelligence Unit).

Legislation normally requires, for example, the license granted by the Fire Department on certain fire safety measures*; those required to install signage (size, location, lighting, etc.); the necessary permits for the sale and preparation of food and the sale of animals; specific licenses for certain businesses (media, medicines, transportation, tobacco, alcohol, firearms); environmental authorizations for industrial waste and for logging and tree plantations; permits for alarm installations, for construction and repair of buildings, and for the use of soil, excavations, and drainage, etc.

Thus, it is usual to close businesses of all kinds (buildings, restaurants, service stations, casinos, nightclubs, hotels, clubs, commercial establishments, etc.) for operating irregularly or for lacking enabling licenses.

Elizabeth Holmes is a young American entrepreneur, who had thought to study medicine but the fear of needles and blood made her change her mind. She founded and was the executive director of Theranos, a health technology services, and clinical laboratory company. Theranos offered the extraction of blood through a device called Edison, without the use of needles. The company used nanotainers, containers that collected microliters of blood.[†]

The company offered a quick, painless, and cheaper method than a conventional blood draw, with a slight prick in the index finger, without using syringes.

In 2013 the company signed the largest commercial deal in its history with Walgreens, the second-largest US pharmacy chain with over 8,000 establishments. The intention was that Walgreens customers could take blood tests in their stores. *Fortune* valued Theranos at more than US$9 billion, and *Forbes* wrote that Holmes, with 50% of the stock, was "the world's youngest self-made billionaire."[‡] Theranos had already performed 6 million blood tests.

In February 2015, an editorial in the *Journal of the American Medical Association* (JAMA) written by John Ioannidis (a professor at Stanford

---

[*] For example, buildings must conform to the building code to obtain planning permission, usually from a local council. The main purpose of building codes is to protect public health, safety, and general welfare as they relate to the construction and occupancy of buildings and structures. "Building Code," Wikipedia.

[†] Sergio Ferrer, "El Escándalo de la Joven Que engañó a todos con Theranos, su startup de Medicina," April 7, 2016, www.elconfidencial.com/tecnologia ("The scandal of the young woman who cheated everyone with Theranos, her medical startup").

[‡] www.forbes.com/profile/elizabeth-holmes/

University School of Medicine) criticized Theranos for not having published an article in biomedical journals.*

The Wall Street Journal in an article published in October 2015 questioned and discovered the company sold dozens of tests, and none had been approved by the Food and Drug Administration (FDA).†

An investigation by CMS (Centers for Medicare & Medicaid Services) found that Theranos did not store the blood at the correct temperature and had poorly qualified personnel without required licenses to review the results of the blood tests. Besides, the company's laboratory did not meet the expected hygiene standards.

The FDA immediately temporarily suspended Theranos' activity because it jeopardized the patient's health.

NBC News interviewer Maria Shriver told her: "You are dealing with people's lives. You are dealing with test results that doctors use to prescribe medicine based on that."‡

In June 2016, after months of doubts about the technology used by the company, investigations of several federal agencies and accusations of medical risk and even fraud, *Forbes* reviewed the estimate of the net worth of Holmes's fortune of US$4500 million and reduced that amount to zero.§

Given the lack of confidence in Therano's business, on July 7, 2016, the government revoked the certification and permits of its laboratories, and Elizabeth Holmes, the so-called Steve Jobs of Biotechnology, was disqualified from running laboratories for two years. Holmes agreed to a settlement with federal regulators that bans her from being an officer or director of any public company for ten years and requires her to pay a US$500,000 penalty.¶

If companies do not have permits or have expired permits and licenses required by current legislation to operate, organizations are exposed to economic sanctions, merchandise hijacking, establishment closure, and

---

* Javier Jiménez, "El Fraude de los diez mil millones de Dólares. Elizabeth Holmes, Theranos y el Futuro de la Biotecnología," July 14, 2016, www.xataka.com ("The Fraud of the ten thousand million Dollars. Elizabeth Holmes, Theranos and the Future of Biotechnology").

† John Carreyrou, "Hot Startup Theranos Has Struggled with Its Blood-Test Technology," October 16, 2015, www.wsj.com.

‡ April 18, 2016, www.today.com/video/theranos-ceo-elizabeth-holmes-i-m-devastated-about -blood-test-issues-668286019825.

§ Sergio Ferrer, "El Escándalo de la Joven que engañó a todos con Theranos, su startup de medicina," April 7, 2016, www.elconfidencial.com/tecnologia ("The scandal of the young woman who cheated everyone with Theranos, her medical startup").

¶ "SEC Changes Theranos CEO Elizabeth Homes with Fraud," *The Wall Street Journal* (March 14, 2018).

even imprisonment for those directly responsible. The type of penalty for noncompliance will depend on each jurisdiction.

Organizations must always take into account the requirements of permits and licenses at the national, provincial or state and municipal levels to avoid noncompliance. They must also ensure the permits obtained do not expire and are renewed on time.

13.2 WORK AND ACADEMIC BACKGROUND

Control and security in the processes of hiring human resources are very important.

Marilee Jones, the dean of admissions at the MIT,* resigned in April 2007 after it was discovered that in her curriculum vitae, she had declared certain academic credentials that she did not possess. She said, "I misrepresented my academic degrees when I first applied to MIT 28 years ago and I did not have the courage to correct my resume."† One of her functions was to monitor the veracity of the applications submitted by students who wanted to enter the university. Ms. Jones had been making speeches around the US to promote her book where she wrote "Holding integrity is sometimes very hard to do because the temptation may be to cheat or cut corners." Phillip Clay, MIT's chancellor, said, "In the future, we will take a big lesson from this experience."‡

RadioShack, based in Texas, is a chain of electronics goods. A former CEO of that company included in his curriculum vitae that he had studied psychology and theology. In February 2006, with eight months in office, he was forced to resign for differences between reality and his resume. The Chairman of the board of Radio Shack said that "one of the most important things we have as a corporation is integrity and trust. We have to get it back."§

Yahoo was founded in 1994 by two graduate students from Stanford University. In 2012, the CEO resigned due to problems with his curriculum

---

* The Massachusetts Institute of Technology (MIT) is a private research university in Cambridge, Massachusetts. The MIT was founded in 1861, in response to the increasing industrialization of the United States.

† Tamar Lewin, "Dean at MIT Resigns, Ending a 28-Year Lie," April 27, 2007, www.nytimes.com.

‡ Tamar Lewin, "Dean at M.I.T. resigns, ending a 28-year lie," April 27, 2007 www.nytimes.com.

§ Floyd D. Norris, "RadioShack Chief Resigns after Lying," *New York Times*, February 21, 2006. "One of the most important things we have as a corporation is integrity and trust. We have to restore that back to the company."

vitae. Papers submitted to regulatory agencies and the company indicated that he had a computer engineering diploma from a Boston university, but he could not prove it.*

A former CFO of Veritas Software Corporation (*veritas* means *truth*) had not obtained an MBA from Stanford that appeared in his resume and had to leave the company.†

A senior Monster.com executive included on the website an executive MBA from Harvard that did not match those offered by that college.‡

Appearances can be deceiving. Conducting due diligence, verifying referrals, as well as work, criminal, and academic records of employees helps avoid costly hiring and recruitment errors and protects the reputation, trust, and interests of the company.

Denis Collins, professor of business ethics at Edgewood College, recommends asking the candidate's references the following question: "Would you hire him?"§

During the interview process with potential future executives, candidates should be asked how to solve certain hypothetical ethical dilemmas.

When the company carries out internal promotions, it should consider how the candidates performed, and this analysis must include ethical behavior.

The organization should try to reduce the risk of hiring and/or promoting those who can damage the culture, reputation, and finances of the organization.

13.3 DECEPTIVE ADVERTISING AND DANGEROUS ADVERTISING

Ethics is critical in marketing and advertising practices. Misleading marketing – like all unethical actions – can only work in the short term,

---

* Cony Sturm, "El CEO de Yahoo mintió en su currículum, no es ingeniero en computación," *Empresas*, May 4, 2012 ("The CEO of Yahoo lied in his résumé, he is not a computer engineer").
† "Veritas CFO Out on False Resume," *CNN Money*, October 3, 2002.
‡ Reuters, January 16. Online job search company Monster.com, which has some 20 million resumes in its database, needs to do some fact-checking of its own resumes, *BusinessWeek* reported. The website of Monster.com's parent company, TMP Worldwide Inc., lists the chairman as having an "executive MBA/OPM" from Harvard Business School, but the school does not have such a degree, *BusinessWeek* said in its January 27 issue.
§ Denis Collins, "Business Ethics: How to Create an Ethical Organization," Udemy.com.

because in the long term the reputation, loyalty, and trust of the client will always be compromised.

Some examples of unethical practices may include the exaggeration of features and benefits of products or services. Gillette, for example, had problems with the marketing practices used to promote the M3 Power Razor (M3P). The company had to pay US$7.5 million to reach a conciliatory agreement in a class action for alleged deceptive commercial announcements related to the promotion of that product in the years 2004 and 2005.

The Swiss Nestle SA marketed its breastfeeding formula in developing countries, and then some issues emerged. The formula needed sanitary water, but many mothers were not aware of that, so they mixed the formula with polluted water. As a consequence, babies had health problems. In the 1970s, a boycott was targeted on Nestle's baby formula, and in 1974 a book titled *The Baby Killer Scandal* was published by War on Want in the United Kingdom* as part of the propaganda against Nestle. According to that book, the cause of infant illness and death was the baby formula milk, although the argument could not be proven later in court.

It is necessary for companies to conduct marketing campaigns and promotions that are honest because honesty is the only way to build trust and long-term relationships with customers. Therefore, marketing management must ensure that the advertising is not false or wrong because nobody should be fooled by the products or services offered, or by the prices, payment options, and/or inaccurate statements.

Also, companies must be careful not to carry out advertising campaigns that may lead to irresponsible actions.

Abercrombie & Fitch, with its headquarters in Ohio, is a casual clothing brand for young people and has over a thousand stores in the world. Classist and sexist marketing and comments of its executives caused the company to be attacked by the press. In 2006, in an interview, the company's CEO provoked criticism, when he said:

> That's why we hire good-looking people in our stores. Because good-look-ing people attract other good-looking people, and we want to market to cool, good-looking people. In every school there are the cool and popular kids, and then there are the not-so-cool kids. Candidly, we go after the cool kids. ... Are we exclusionary? Absolutely.†

---

* waronwant.org/resources/baby-killer.
† en.wikipedia.org/wiki/Abercrombie_%26_Fitch.

Domino's is an American pizza restaurant chain founded in 1960 and the largest pizza seller worldwide.

Domino's Pizza had guaranteed that customers would receive their pizzas within 30 minutes of placing an order. If not, their money would be refunded. In 1992, the company settled a lawsuit brought by the family of an Indiana woman who had been killed by a Domino's delivery driver, paying the family US$2.8 million. In another 1993 lawsuit, brought by a woman who was injured when a Domino's delivery driver ran a red light and collided with her vehicle, the woman was awarded nearly US$80 million but accepted a payout of US$15 million. The 30-minute pizza guarantee was dropped that same year because of the "public perception of reckless driving and irresponsibility."*

13.4 INSIDER TRADING

Another risk faced by the organizations is that employees conduct *insider trading* of securities listed on the stock exchange. The "insider" gets reserved or privileged information and uses it (directly or indirectly through third parties) to obtain a personal benefit by trading shares or securities listed on the stock exchange. Inequality is then generated because those who know the information is not public are in an advantageous position with respect to the general public, violating the transparency and equality between investors. To avoid this problem, regulators use sophisticated computer systems and examine telephone records to discover insider trading.

The Australian philosopher Peter Singer reflects on how the excessive ambition of people can lead them to commit unethical acts. Says Singer:

> Consider the life of Ivan Boesky, the multimillionaire Wall Street dealer who in 1986 pleaded guilty to insider trading. Why did Boesky get involved in criminal activities when he already had more money than he could ever spend? Six years after the insider-trading scandal broke, Boesky's estranged wife Seema spoke about her husband's motives in an interview with Barbara Walters for the American ABC Network's 20/20 program. Walters asked whether Boesky was a man who craved luxury. Seema Boesky thought not, pointing out that he worked around the clock, seven days a week, and never took a day off to enjoy his money. She then recalled

---

* en.wikipedia.org/wiki/Domino%27s_Pizza.

that when in 1982 Forbes magazine first listed Boesky among the wealthiest people in the US, he was upset. She assumed he disliked the publicity and made some remark to that effect. Boesky replied: "That's not what's upsetting me. We're no-one. We're nowhere. We're at the bottom of the list and I promise you I won't shame you like that again. We will not remain at the bottom of that list."*

Joseph Nacchio, a former CEO of Qwest Communications, was convicted of insider trading related to his time as CEO of Qwest Communications International and spent more than four years in prison. Prosecutors said he sold US$52 million worth of Qwest stock in early 2001 without publicly disclosing that the company wasn't going to achieve its lofty revenue goals that year. Shareholders lost millions when the stock tanked.†

Martha Helen Kostyra is another example. Kostyra, better known as Martha Stewart, is an American businesswoman, television presenter with a fortune estimated at more than US$5 billion. The Securities and Exchange Commission accused Martha Stewart of insider trading when she sold shares of the biotech company ImClone Systems on December 27, 2001, after receiving material non-public information from the president of the company who was a friend of her daughter. The day following her sale, the stock value of that company fell 16%.

In March 2004 Stewart was found guilty of felony charges of conspiracy, obstruction of an agency proceeding, and making false statements to federal investigators, and was sentenced in July 2004 to serve a five-month term in a federal correctional facility.‡

Anyone with knowledge of confidential, material information can violate insider trading laws if they disclose material non-public information to third parties who may then trade stock based on that information or if they themselves trade stock based on that information.

To know if the information is "material," ask yourself if such confidential information makes you think of buying or selling the stock of any company.

If the answer is affirmative, it is very likely to be material information.

* Peter Singer, "The Drowning Child and the Expanding Circle," *New Internationalist*, April 1997, www.utilitarian.net/singer/by/199704--.htm. Boesky was one of the wealthiest brokers in New York. However, in 1986, federal inspectors discovered that an employee of the Drexel Burnham Lambert, Inc. company had been transferring inside information to Boesky. en.wikipedia.org/wiki/Ivan_Boesky.

† Mark Harden, "Joe Nacchio Speaks Out on Prison, Broken Justice System," April 29, 2015, www.bizjournals.com/denver/news/2015/04/29/joe-nacchio-speaks-out-on-prison-broken-justice.html.

‡ en.wikipedia.org/wiki/Martha_Stewart.

13.5 ANTITRUST – ANTIMONOPOLY

Antitrust law attempts to encourage free-market competition to achieve low prices. The general approach of this set of laws is preventing companies from obtaining monopoly powers.

Pricing and market-sharing arrangements between competitors that restrict competition and seek to abuse a dominant position are behaviors that are prohibited by most laws.

The law wants to protect trade from anti-competitive activities that harm consumers and are detrimental to the general economic interest.

What alternatives exist in substitute goods?

The American economic historian John Chamberlain has said: When "the customer can substitute a metallic product for a plastic one…the decisive test of a correct anti-trust decision is to determine whether or not there are really viable alternatives."*

Competition laws are responsible for regulating trade by prohibiting agreements between competitors, abuse of dominant market position, and certain mergers of companies.

The aim of antitrust rules is to promote fair competition among existing companies in a market and to promote goods and services at the lowest possible price.†

For example, antitrust rules may be violated when a company pressures suppliers to increase prices to competitors, when exclusivity contracts are executed with suppliers when the company's market share is already very high, or if the company executes agreements with competitors on prices, zones, and employee hiring.

Setting prices below cost must be made in accordance with current legislation.

In the United States, for example, 27 states do not have laws that prohibit selling below cost. In 20 states, it is allowed to sell below cost only if it is to match a competitor (but not to sell below the competitor); and in three states, it is prohibited to sell below cost even to match a competitor.

Any agreement to set high prices by collaborating with other competitors is illegal in many countries.

---

* John Chamberlain, *Las Raíces del Capitalismo* (Folio, Biblioteca de Economía, 1996), 162. *The Roots of Capitalism* (Unión Editorial).

† One measure of the degree of economic concentration of a market is the Herfindahl and Hirschman Index. If the index is very high, it expresses an uncompetitive and concentrated market.

Another illegal practice that interferes with free-market competition is bid-rigging collusion between one bidder and the buyer in order to gain a contract. This is an illegal practice in which competing parties collude to choose the winner of a bidding process while others submit uncompetitive bids. Bid-rigging stifles free-market competition, as the rigged price will be higher than what might have resulted from a competitive bidding process. As such, bid-rigging is detrimental to consumers and taxpayers who bear the cost of higher prices and procurement costs. Bid-rigging is illegal in a majority of countries as a form of market manipulation.

The term *trust* refers to the merger of different companies to form a single company in order to control an economic sector and exercise a monopoly.

In the United States, government regulation of business competition began with the passage in 1887 of the *Interstate Commerce Act*, in order to regulate the powerful railroad companies that threatened to gain monopoly power.

The first federal antitrust law was the *Sherman Act*, passed by the US Congress in the year 1890. This law declared illegal any contract that would limit interstate commerce, such as agreements between competitors to set prices, arrange tenders, or distribute customers.

In 1914, the US Congress passed two new antitrust laws: the *Federal Trade Commission Act* (a government commission with the power to investigate and take legal action against companies suspected of unfair trade conducts) and the *Clayton Act*, which prohibited practices that would lead to price increases, diminish business options, or slow down innovation.

Two business practices were declared illegal. The first one was "tying contracts," which force buyers to purchase unwanted products in order to purchase the products they do desire. The second one was an "interlocking directorate," a situation in which the same people sit on the boards of directors of two competing firms*; therefore, it might have anti-competitive effects like the coordination of business decisions or the exchange of sensitive information.

In 1976, the US Congress passed the *Antitrust Improvements Act* (*Hart-Scott Rodino Act*), which required any company wishing to merge with another should notify the Federal Trade Commission (FTC) prior to the

---

* K. Blanchard, C. Schewe, R. Nelson and A. Hiam, *Exploring the World of Business* (Worth Publishers, 1996), 107.

merger in order for it to analyze the effects of the merger on the market to avoid creating unfair competition. The FTC disallows some proposed mergers every year, either preventing them completely or requiring the companies to sell off a part of their business in order to avoid becoming too large and powerful in their market.

One of the most famous cases in antitrust history was *US v. Standard Oil of New Jersey*. Supposedly Standard Oil had monopolized the oil industry and increased the price of oil to consumers. In 1911, the Supreme Court of the United States confirmed the structure and performance of Standard Oil conformed to the term *monopoly* and demanded its dismemberment. Thus, the holding company was divided into 34 independent companies. Two of these new companies were the Jersey Standard, which eventually became Exxon and the Vacuum Oil and Standard Oil of New York (Socony), which years later would become Mobil.

The *US v. American Tobacco* case is similar in many respects to that of Standard Oil. The company was originally founded in 1902 when Imperial Tobacco of the United Kingdom and American Tobacco of the United States agreed to merge as the British American Tobacco Company Ltd. But also in 1911, the company was declared a monopoly and the group was forced to split and liquidate their shares.

In South Korea, in 2002–2003, Hyundai Motor Company used its dominant position so that 26 subcontractors had to lower their prices. South Korea's antitrust regulator fined Hyundai US$1.85 million and also required Kia Motors to pay US$5 million to its subcontractors.

In Chile, in January 2012, Chile's Free Competition Court (TDLC) determined that the three main drug chains had set prices in the drug distribution market. The regulator punished them with US$19 million in fines for coordinating the dates they were going to increase the price of medicine in each of these companies.

In recent years, some multinational companies had to face multimillion-dollar sanctions for antitrust issues. For example, Microsoft in 2006 had to pay a fine of almost 900 million euros to European regulatory authorities, and in 2009, that amount was exceeded by a penalty imposed on Intel of over 1 billion euros.

In June 2017, Google received a record US$2.7 billion fine from the European Commission for abuse of its dominant position in the online search market.

Companies must pay due attention to antitrust laws, in the different countries in which they operate, to avoid significant fines.

13.6 CONFLICTS OF INTEREST AND NEPOTISM

A conflict of interest situation occurs in a company when certain personal activity of an employee is in conflict with the interest of the organization that employs him or her. Conflicts of interest should be avoided because they can affect trust, objectivity, and impartiality in decision-making.

This happens, for example, when an employee accepts gifts from a supplier or potential supplier, which could influence the objectivity of the employee's decisions when selecting suppliers. There may also be a conflict of interest when an employee has financial interests in a competitor or supplier company or when he or she is working for both a company and its competitor.

Another example of a conflict of interest would be a sentimental relationship of an employee with his or her boss because it could generate the perception that the employee receives favoritism. Favoritism affects the objective decision-making process and damages the morale of working groups and their productivity. In November 2019 McDonald's CEO was fired for "consensual relationship" with an employee.[*]

David Gelber, JD, founder of the consulting firm Skout Group, says,

> Most employees want to feel committed to their work environment. However, if they feel that in their workplace, they do not feel connected and there is no commitment to it, people stop thinking about the general interest and start looking at themselves, regardless of the rest.[†]

The Chicago-based Boeing Company is the world's largest commercial and military aircraft manufacturer and is one of NASA's leading service providers. In 2005 a former CEO of the company was fired for having maintained extramarital relations with an employee.[‡]

In 2007, the World Bank suffered a crisis due to a conflict of interest from its president, who resigned after receiving strong pressure due to the rapid rise in the ranks of his girlfriend who worked for the Bank. His girlfriend's salary increased from nearly US\$133,000 to US\$180,000

---

[*] Hannah Knowles, "Mc Donald's CEO Fired for Consensual Relationship with Employee," November 4, 2019, www.washingtonpost.com; Amelia Lucas, "McDonald's Stock Falls after CEO Is Fired for Misconduct with Employee," CNCB.com, November 4, 2019.

[†] David Gelber Jr., "Overview of Compliance and Ethics Practice," 1.4., *Society of Corporate Compliance and Ethics Manual*, 2nd ed.

[‡] "Boeing's CEO Forced to Resign over His Affair with Employee," March 8, 2005, Wsj.com.

and with the first annual review, her salary was US$193,590 tax-free. A World Bank commission of inquiry released a report concluding that the employee's salary "exceeded the range" stipulated by the institution's rules. The president of the bank resigned in a five-page communiqué saying he hoped the crisis would identify "some of the areas of government and human resources where reforms are needed."[*]

Ethical companies value transparency and objectivity in selecting employees, suppliers, and partners and ensure there is a fair and objective selection process at all levels of the organization.

Nepotism is the preference that some public officials have for employing family members; regardless of the merit, they have to occupy the position. It is believed the concept derives from the ancient Greek "nepos" (nephew) or from the Roman emperor Julius Nepos (430–480).

The choice of relatives in family businesses can be a wise decision because they know the values and family culture (positive nepotism). But in general, the concept of nepotism is negative. This occurs when preference is given to family and friends to occupy positions or jobs in the government, organizations, and companies without considering whether they meet the appropriate requirements, preparation, experience, and skills.[†]

Leaders of countries and organizations must avoid nepotism because family members may impair objectivity when making business decisions.[‡]

Business decisions must be based on what is in the best interest of the company and not for personal gain or benefit. By discouraging and avoiding conflicts of interest, corporate leaders send a clear message about their loyalty to integrity and their determination to do what's right.

---

[*] May 28, 2007, www.elmundo.es/mundo dinero, ("World money").

[†] Throughout history there have been many cases of nepotism. For example, in the tyranny of the Greek Peisistratus (607–527 BC), in order to protect his authority, he handed over the highest political charges to members of his family and friends. The Greek philosopher Plato (427–347 BC) appointed his nephew as director of the Academy instead of his best disciple Aristotle (334–322 BC). In Roman times, General Pompey (106–48 BC) gave important responsibilities to his son-in-law Quintus Caecilius Metellus Scipio Nasica (100–46 BC) and was therefore denounced by the military Mark Antony (83–30 BC) before the Senate. Pope Callixtus III (1378–1458) converted two of his nephews into cardinals. Also, Pope Paul III (1468–1549) promoted his two grandchildren of 14 and 16 years old as cardinals. Napoleón Bonaparte (1769–1821) named his brother Joseph Bonaparte (1768–1844), known as Pepe Botella (Joe Bottle), for his love for alcohol, king of Spain.

[‡] For example, in January 2018, Argentine President Mauricio Macri signed a decree preventing his ministers from having close relatives in the government and those who had been appointed needed to resign. This type of initiative seeks to avoid the perception of the existence of favoritism and a lack of transparency. Macri said, "We will lose valuable people but we have to set the example."

13.7 RETALIATION TO WHISTLEBLOWER

The First Amendment to the US Constitution guarantees freedom of expression by prohibiting Congress from restricting the rights of individuals to speak freely.*

All employees of organizations should be able to report in good faith and without fear of retaliation any misconduct, including violations of laws and internal policies.

There is an ethical problem when an employee makes a complaint or questions a co-worker's actions or a provider and because of this he or she suffers retaliation; that is, a reprisal or persecution for having made that complaint.

One of the ethical problems or moral conflicts employees may face is a co-worker or supplier is performing an illegal act that harms the company and there is a risk that an employee who makes a complaint or who questions other employees or suppliers suffers *retaliation*; that is, persecution for having made a complaint.

The company must communicate to all employees that no reprisals will be tolerated against those who, in good faith, file complaints about the possible existence of improper conduct.

Employees must perceive that the organization has all the conditions, culture, and support to ensure their complaints and inquiries will be analyzed seriously without retaliation.

Otherwise, employees will not make complaints because they distrust the system, fear retaliation, or the loss of their job.

Retaliation against the complainant may consist of different actions; for example, a decrease in benefits, assignment, removal, or reduction of certain tasks, a negative performance evaluation, poor treatment, threats, physical or property damage or dismissal.

Employees who misuse the reporting system and file allegations they know are false, to harm the accused, must be punished.

For Aristotle (384–322 BC), courage is a disposition to confront danger without being paralyzed by fear.† If employees are afraid to share their concerns or prefer not to communicate them because they assume they are not taken seriously, this would be a clear indicator the company does

---

* During colonial times, English speech regulations were rather restrictive. The English criminal common law made criticizing the government a crime.
† Joseph W. Koterski, *The Ethics of Aristotle* (The Great Courses, Course Guidebook).

not have an adequate ethical culture. Silence can be a symptom of fear. If that happens, unethical behavior is not reported because there is no trust in the functioning of the reporting system and/or in the leadership of the organization.

13.8 CONTROL OF SUPPLIERS AND COMMERCIAL PARTNERS

Companies must ensure an appropriate audit or due diligence during the pre- and post-acquisition of companies. Likewise, the dangers related to the supply of goods and/or services must be considered since they can negatively affect the reputation of the company. Even companies with excellent internal controls can be exposed to unnecessary risks when integrity requirements are not followed along the entire supply chain.

One of the most difficult problems facing any company is to ensure the purchase of products from suppliers is done in the right way, so that the price of these products and/or services is not the only predominant element in the selection of suppliers. There are other important considerations, like quality and integrity, and in some circumstances, organizations need to avoid the cheapest option to ensure that level of supplier commitment.

Selecting suppliers adequately and transparently, controlling them, and ensuring compliance with environmental, labor, safety, and hygiene laws will prevent headaches. For example, controlling working conditions at product factories, controlling illegal logging to obtain wood (or if the timber is being obtained from a sensitive region – as in Russia where Siberian tiger habitat is endangered); the loss of cypress forest along the coasts; child labor, workers exposed to unsafe levels of cadmium, excessive hours of work, inadequate safety, violations of human rights, etc., are all compliance issues requiring attention.

General Electric has an "Integrity Guide for Suppliers, Contract Personnel and Consultants" that outlines the commitment assumed by a GE provider in complying with applicable law.

Chiquita Brands is a company that produces and distributes bananas, and its headquarters is located in North Carolina. The company paid nearly US$1.7 million between 1997 and 2004 to the United Self-Defense Forces of Colombia, known as AUC a paramilitary terrorist group, for the protection of its employees in the banana plantations in Colombia. The

AUC has been responsible for some of the worst massacres in Colombia's civil conflict and for a sizable percentage of the country's cocaine exports. The US government designated the right-wing militia a terrorist organization in September 2001. In addition to paying the AUC, Chiquita made payments to the National Liberation Army, or ELN, and the leftist Revolutionary Armed Forces of Colombia, or FARC. As a consequence of that, in 2007 Chiquita Brands was fined with US$25 million. The company finally sold its Colombian banana operations in June 2004.*

In the United States, the Dodd-Frank Act of July 2010 and in EU other regulatory initiatives require companies to audit their supply chains and report whether they sell or manufacture products containing *conflict minerals*, that is, certain minerals extracted from Central Africa. This is because the money from the sale of those minerals would be used to finance armed groups that undermine human rights. The regulations require companies to conduct due diligence to determine the origin of conflict minerals such as gold, tin, tungsten, and tantalum, used for the manufacture of electronics and jewelry.

In California, the California Transparency in Supply Chains Act went into effect in 2012 and requires companies with worldwide annual revenues of US$100 million or more to report on their specific actions to eradicate slavery and human trafficking in their supply chains. The law requires a company to disclose on its website its initiatives to eradicate slavery and human trafficking from its direct supply chain for the goods offered for sale.

In the UK, *The Modern Slavery Act* 2015 is an Act of the Parliament that applies to public and private companies, regardless of which sector they operate in and whether or not they were incorporated in the UK. These companies are required to comply with the provisions of the Act if they have a global net turnover of over 36 million pounds and the company carries on business or any part of their business in the UK. Companies who meet these criteria have an obligation to publish a "Slavery and Human Trafficking Statement" every year, six months after the end of the company's financial year. In such statement the company should outline the steps taken to ensure that slavery and human trafficking are not taking place within its supply chain or any part of their business.†

---

* "Chiquita Admits to Paying Colombia Terrorists," March 15, 2007, www.nbcnews.com; Matt Apuzzo, *Chiquita to Pay $25M Fine in Terror Case* (The Associated Press), March 15, 2007, www.washingtonpost.com.

† Natasha Reurts, "The Modern Slavery Act 2015: Overview and Future Developments," *Bright Line Law*, June 22, 2017. Also www.lexology.com.

Suppliers must be subject to audits. The ISO 9001:2015 is the international standard that regulates quality management systems. This standard recommends that companies keep documented information about the performance of their suppliers.

Companies need to take the necessary control measures; if a supplier fails to comply with current regulations, it can lead the contracting company to a serious crisis of trust and reputation, which could even affect its own subsistence.

13.9 ANTI-MONEY LAUNDERING, DRUG TRAFFICKING, AND TERRORISM

Money laundering is the attempt to conceal or disguise the nature, location, source, ownership, or control of funds derived from illegal activities such as fraud, corruption, terrorism, or narcotics trafficking. Money laundering can occur through transactions involving various methods and financial instruments, including money orders and money transfers or purchase or sale of merchandise.

Ambrosiano Bank was an Italian bank founded in 1896 by Italian banker and lawyer Giuseppe Tovini (1814–1897) and was named Ambrosiano in honor of St. Ambrose (340–397), bishop of Milan. Tovini's purpose was to create a Catholic bank that serves as a counterweight to the lay banks in Italy, and his goals were to offer "moral organizations, pious jobs, and religious bodies installed for charitable aid."* The bank was known as the "bank of priests."

In 1978, the Bank of Italy prepared a report on the Ambrosiano Bank on irregularities that led to criminal investigations. In 1982, it was discovered that the bank could not explain the provenance of US$1,287 billion. The bank traditionally used by the clergy for charity became a large money launderer, with large loans given to ghost companies. Other loans were used to finance companies based in Panama, others in European tax havens. There were companies that borrowed hundreds of millions of dollars from Banco Ambrosiano.

Soon the Milan magistrate investigating the case was killed. The president of the Bank Roberto Calvi fled the country with a false passport,

---

* en.wikipedia.org/wiki/Banco_Ambrosiano.

and the personal secretary of Calvi left a note of complaint to Calvi before losing his life by falling from his window. Calvi, meanwhile, was found hanging from the Blackfriars Bridge in London.

The bank was declared insolvent in 1982.

Organizations should prevent the risk of illegal transactions with third parties who launder funds from illicit activities, and they must have anti-laundering programs in place with policies, procedures, training, audits, and the obligation to report any suspicious transactions to the government. Failure to comply with anti-money laundering laws and regulations exposes a corporation to potential liabilities.

In 1986, Ronald Reagan, the 40th president of the United States, signed *Executive Order Number* 12.549.* According to this directive, debarment and suspensions are sanctions that the central government can apply against organizations and individuals who have committed fraud or a criminal offense in violation of federal law.

International financial institutions also fight against these risks. In the information note of April 2014, the World Bank Office of Suspension and Debarment reported that since 1999 the World Bank has sanctioned more than 600 companies and individuals and these penalties lead to the disqualification by other multilateral development banks.

In the United States, there is the *Clinton list* (*Specially Designated Narcotics Traffickers or SDNT list*) of 1995 that consists of a list of companies and related persons to have relations with money coming from the drug trafficking in the world. The list was created by former President Bill Clinton as part of a series of rules to take action against drugs and money laundering. The natural or juridical persons appearing on this list cannot make financial transactions nor have commercial business with the United States, and the American companies that have a relation with them commit a crime.

Following the terrorist attacks of September 11, 2001, *Executive Order Number 13.224* led to the creation of a list of persons, companies, and groups that may be connected with terrorism. This order prohibits anyone in the United States from conducting business with any personnel, entity, or group on the list, which is made by the Treasury Department's Office of Foreign Assets Control (OFAC). The OFAC list is constantly updated

---

* In the United States, an executive order is a directive issued by the president of the United States that manages operations of the federal government and has the force of law.

with thousands of names, and American multinational companies should periodically review it.

In May 2013 at the Barajas Airport in Madrid, the Ukrainian Arthur Budovsky, founder of online payment company Liberty Reserve, was arrested. Budovsky was the author of one of the largest money-laundering cases in history, totaling about US$6 billion. To access Liberty Reserve's electronic payment system, the user could open an account with only a date of birth and an email address. The cost was a commission of 1% per transfer. Also, if you paid US$0.75, you could hide the account number of the user to make the operation untraceable. By the time of Liberty Reserve's closure, more than 55 million transactions had been carried out.

The lack of controls caused the system to be used by criminals who laundered profits in different currencies obtained from illicit businesses such as piracy, drug trafficking, or child pornography. "The company was designed to help criminals carry out illegal transactions and money laundering from illicit activities," according to documents released by the Manhattan district attorney.*

In 2014 BNP Paribas pleaded guilty to illegally processing transactions from 2004 to 2012 through the US financial system from countries that were under US economic sanctions such as Sudan, Iran, and Cuba.

Assistant Attorney General George Caldwell said,

> BNP Paribas deliberately disregarded US law, of which it was well aware, and placed its financial network at the services of rogue nations, all to improve its bottom line. Remarkably, BNP continued to engage in this criminal conduct even after being told by its own lawyers that what it was doing was illegal.†

Department of Justice punished BNP with a historic US$8.9 billion fine, reflecting the amount that it illegally moved through the US financial system.

The Financial Action Task Force on Money Laundering (FATF) is an intergovernmental institution known by its French name, *Groupe d'action financière sur le blanchiment de capitaux* (GAFI). It was created in 1989 by the G-8, and its purpose is to develop policies to help combat money laundering and terrorist financing. The primary mission of the FATF is to focus on preventing the use of the banking system and other

* *BBC World*, May 29, 2013, www.bbc.com.
† "Risky Business: Top 10 Corporate Crackdowns," *Censible*, July 20, 2017, www.learn.censible.co.

financial institutions for money laundering arising from drug trafficking. It has developed a series of recommendations with concrete measures, including the adaptation of national legal systems and regulations, to help detect, prevent, and punish the misuse of the financial system for money laundering.

13.10 UNPAID WORK, ILLEGAL WORK, AND POOR WORKING CONDITIONS

The International Labor Organization (ILO), founded in 1919, is a specialized agency of the United Nations that deals with labor and industrial relations issues. Chilean lawyer Juan Somavia, who was the director-general of this body, stated that the ILO's main goal is to promote opportunities for decent and productive jobs "in conditions of freedom, equity, security, and human dignity."[*]

The labor exploitation consists of receiving a payment lower than that corresponding to the work done by law[†] and includes small abuses to slave labor.

There is a risk of illegal work if the employee works consecutive days without complying with the daily legal rest (which normally is 12 hours) and the mandatory weekly rest; or no breaks are granted during the workday; or collective bargaining agreements are not complied with; or the employee performs more tasks than for those hired for; or carries out unpaid work or receives noncompetitive remuneration; or when he or she suffers a constant delay in payments or does not have work permits and/or the required work visas.

There are more than 185 million children in the world who are victims of child labor, who carry out activities detrimental to their physical,

---

[*] "The ILO at a Glance," www.ilo.org; "Report of the Director General: Decent Work," August 17, 2015, www.ilo.org/public.

[†] I am not referring to the concept of surplus value of Karl Marx. Marx (1818–1883), a philosopher, intellectual, and militant German Communist, is considered one of the most influential people in history. His best-known writings are the *Manifesto of the Communist Party* and *The Capital*. Marx developed his theory of the economy of capitalism based on the idea of labor exploitation. It called *surplus value* the value that the worker generates for his labor and that is greater than the money that he receives for his effort. That is to say, the value of unpaid labor is left to the hands of a capitalist who, according to Marx, through surplus value accumulates money and exploits the worker.

moral, and mental health. Hard-working conditions create problems in these children such as premature aging, malnutrition, depression, and drug addiction.

Employers of child labor exercise absolute control over them and minors are often victims of physical and mental violence. Some children will probably be condemned to become illiterate adults without having the possibility to grow in their social and professional life.

In Cambodia, women workers in textile factories faint after sewing for 14 hours in a sector that occupies 600,000 women in that country. Some 5,000 fainting incidents have occurred in textile factories in Cambodia between 2012 and 2014.

> It was very hot and humid at the factory. The fan did not work that day and the temperature in the sewing area was unbearable. I saw other workers faint near me. I felt dizzy, with a headache. I could not breathe. The next thing I remember is waking up in the hospital, where I was being supplied with fluids and oxygen.

This 23-year-old employee fainted with 60 of her colleagues at a factory in November 2012.*

In 2011, *Wired* technology magazine released an article titled "One Million Workers. 90 Million iPhones. 17 Suicides."

The British BBC conducted an investigation and highlighted the working conditions of workers assembling devices for Apple in China and tin miners in Indonesia. The report informed that workers were being exploited with shifts of more than 12 hours and with children picking up the tin.† Apple has been working to improve the working conditions of its suppliers after complaints in Foxconn about long working hours and overcrowding conditions at the plants.‡ To reduce risk, Apple conducted audits of its direct suppliers and the companies that supply material to those suppliers.

In the1990s, many of Nike's contractors were in Indonesia. The factories employed mostly girls and young women, who received an entry-level salary of US$1.80 a day for sewing the shoes. It cost Nike about US$17.50 to produce the shoes, which usually sold for between US$45 and US$80.

---

* "Work until Fainting in Factories in Cambodia," June 21, 2015, www.elmundo.es.
† Richard Bilton, "Apple Failing to Protect Chinese Factory Workers," *BBC News Business*, December 18, 2014.
‡ December 19, 2014, www.lanacion.com.ar.

A *New York Times* article asked, "If Nike, which profits from these shoes, does not take responsibility for the people who make the shoes, who does?"[*]

In 1995 Nike started production of balls in Pakistan. The following year a *Life* magazine article denounced Nike for employing children to sew soccer balls in that country. The report stressed that the children received about 60 cents (0.45 euros, depending on the exchange rate) per day to produce two balls. Nike's response to the scandal was to sign an exclusive agreement with a single supplier that pledged to ban the work of people under the age of 18. Ten years later, the US Company broke off relations with a Pakistani supplier with repeated cases of subcontracting in workshops that did not meet the conditions demanded.[†]

In 2001, a BBC documentary uncovered occurrences of child labor and poor working conditions in a Cambodian factory used by Nike. The documentary focused on six girls, who all worked seven days a week, often 16 hours a day.[‡]

In January 2020, the Chipotle restaurant chain was fined for child labor, employing adolescents under 18 for more than 48 hours per week in different locations in the state of Massachusetts. The fines were for almost US$2 million.[§]

Canadian author Naomi Klein is the author of the book *No Logo*, published in 2000, in which she criticizes the behavior of corporations.

At the beginning of the book is a phrase of Indonesian architect and writer Yusuf Bilyarta Mangunwijaya (1929–1999) that said on July 16, 1998, "You might not see things yet on the surface, but underground it's already on fire."[¶]

Naomi Klein says, "Job creation as part of the corporate mission, particularly the creation of full time, decently paid, stable jobs, appears to have taken a back seat in many major corporations, regardless of company profits."[**]

---

[*] K. Blanchard, C. Schewe, R. Nelson and A. Hiam, *Exploring the World of Business* (Worth Publishers, 1996), 116. "Just Undo It: Nike's Exploited Workers," *New York Times*, February 13, 1994, F11.

[†] "Ética y Moda: el caso Nike," May 3, 2013, www.modaes.es ("Ethics and Fashion: The Nike Case").

[‡] en.wikipedia.org/wiki/Nike,_Inc.

[§] Noah Manskar, "Chipotle Fined $1.3 Million for Thousands of Child Labor Violations," nypost. com, January 28, 2020; Jordan Valinsky, "Chipotle Cited with 13,253 Child Labor Law Violations in Massachusetts," CNN Business, cnn.com, January 28, 2020.

[¶] Naomi Klein, *No Logo* (Picador USA, 2000).

[**] www.goodreads.com.

Founded in 1997, Social Accountability International (SAI) is a global nongovernmental organization advancing human rights at work.* SAI created a SA 8000 Standard that establishes minimum conditions to achieve a healthy work environment and contains, among others, rules on the duration of working hours and child and forced labor. Certification is voluntary and can be obtained by multinational companies to improve their image, their productivity, and the recruitment of workers.[†]

Another important document is the so-called Global Compact. This instrument was announced by the secretary-general of the United Nations in 1999 in Davos and aims to create global corporate citizenship that can reconcile the interests of companies and the values of society.

It is a free-standing document, and the adhering companies are committed to implementing its principles which, inter alia, relate to the protection of human rights, the elimination of forced labor, and the abolition of child labor.[‡]

Organizations should monitor and prevent the risk of violating labor laws and basic human rights related to employees (child labor or illegal workplace practices) of the company itself and of its suppliers.

---

* sa-intl.org.
[†] www.sa-intl.org.
[‡] www.unglobalcompact.org.

14

Corporate Risks: Unit 2

14.1 SECURITY AND SAFETY IN THE WORKPLACE

Companies must provide a workplace that does not pose unreasonable risks to the security, safety, and health of their employees, so they must meet certain standards established by legislation.

If employees do not feel secure in their work, the company cannot expect from them a high level of creativity or concentration and commitment to their tasks.

The prevention of occupational risks should identify and control the risks associated with the production process and promote the necessary measures to avoid them.

In industries such as manufacturing, construction, or extraction of natural resources, the lack of safety in the workplace is one of the main risks, and companies should be able to monitor compliance with current legislation. Companies are responsible for providing a safe environment for their employees.

Safety must be more than a slogan; it must be a commitment of the leaders to maintain a safe and adequate work environment where the safety procedures are permanently complied with. A negligent action or ignorance of the occasional risks to which the company is exposed may be the cause of an unexpected but foreseeable loss.

From the nineteenth century, the rapid industrialization of the American economy, coupled with the introduction of heavy machinery, increased the number of injuries on the job.

Herbert William Heinrich (1886–1962) was a pioneer of industrial safety in the United States. Heinrich's Law or Pyramid says that in a workplace, for every accident that causes a major injury or death of a person, there are 29 incidents that cause minor injuries and 300 accidents have no risk of injury at all. After Heinrich reviewed thousands of accident reports, his work showed that 95% of the events were caused by unsafe acts, and he argued employers had to optimize the prevention of accidents, even those that cause minor injuries, because he said there was proportionality between these and the serious ones. For each serious accident, there are previous warnings from minor accidents.

Frank E. Bird (1921–2007) was an American scientist who authored different theories on industrial safety and occupational risk prevention. He is known mainly by his Pyramid of Bird, who, after analyzing more than 1,750,000 damages or incidents, concluded that for each fatal accident that generated permanent disability, there were 10 serious accidents, 30 minor accidents, and 600 incidents that did not cause injury or damage. This means in the face of many minor incidents, there will be some serious accidents.

Bird's conclusion is if the base of the pyramid is reduced, it is possible to reduce the most serious accidents; and to do so, all employees must collaborate in the preventive action and correct unsafe acts in order to reduce the chances of accidents. For example, they must ensure emergency doors are not blocked, that stairs are safe, and that products do not spill.

In 1968, a coal mine explosion killed 78 workers in Farmington, West Virginia. This tragedy helped to reveal the extent of preventable danger some workers faced; at the same time, it focused public attention on the ravages of black lung disease among mine workers. In 1969 the federal government entered the arena of workplace safety with the *Coal Mine Health and Safety Act*.[*]

In March 2005, the explosion at a British Petroleum (BP) plant in Texas ended with the death of 15 people and injured another 180. An independent inquiry determined BP did not have an efficient security process.[†] The Chemical Safety Board (CSB) concluded that safety concerns

---

[*] K. Blanchard, C. Schewe, B. Nelson and A. Hiam, *Exploring the World of Business* (Worth Publishers, 1996), 115.

[†] An explanation of the cultural problems presented in BP can be found in the report to the BP board, "The Report of the BP US Refineries Independent Safety Review Panel," and in the March 2007 report of the US Chemical Safety and Hazard Investigation Board, "Investigation Report: BP Refinery Explosion and Fire."

in BP equipment were known to managers prior to the Texas refinery accident.*

On October 26, 2007, BP reached a global settlement with US authorities to pay fines totaling US$380 million for violations of existing legislation related to the unfortunate explosion of its refinery and losses in its pipelines. A number of print media sources highlighted the scandal in which BP was involved over several months.†

On April 16, 2014, an accident occurred on the Sewol ship near South Korea; the ferry carried 475 people, a load three times the maximum weight allowed. By such imprudence, more than 250 people died. The captain of the ferry was sentenced to 36 years in prison.

Three Mile Island incident was an accident at the nuclear power plant of the same name on March 28, 1979, in the state of Pennsylvania and remains the most serious nuclear accident in the United States. It all started around 4:00 a.m. on March 28, 1979, when there was a failure in the secondary circuit of the Three Mile Island nuclear power plant, and there is some consensus in affirming the accident was aggravated by the incorrect decisions made by the operators. A cascade of errors transformed the problem into a disaster that might have been avoided.

Cleaning the reactor took 14 years, up to 1993, at a total cost of US$975 million to eliminate 100 tons of radioactive fuel.

As a result of the accident, the training of nuclear reactor operators was changed, a new safety protocol was established, and new standards were set for nuclear power plants to be safer.

The plant accident occurred a few days after the release of the movie *The China Syndrome*, which is about a similar fictional incident.‡ In the film, the protagonists try to raise public awareness of the insecurity of the plant. During a scene, a nuclear security expert says an accident could force the evacuation of the population in an area "the size of Pennsylvania."

The term *asbestos* refers to a group of fibrous natural minerals of great commercial utility due to their extraordinary resistance to stress and chemical attack. For these reasons, asbestos is used in the insulation of buildings, as an additive in plastics and in the automotive industry.

---

* "CBS investigation of BP Texas City refinery disaster continues as organizational issues are probed," October 30, 2006.
† "BP Hopes $380 m Settlement Will Draw a Line under Scandals," *Financial Times*, October 26, 2007. Also, Sheila McNulty, "Blowdown: How Faults at BP Led to One of America's Worst Industrial Disasters," *Financial Times*, December 19, 2006; and Ed Crooks, "How Storm Clouds Gathered over Sun King," *Financial Times*, January 12, 2007.
‡ *The China Syndrome* is a 1979 American disaster thriller film directed by James Bridges.

In 1899, in London, Dr. Montague Murray noted the negative health effects of asbestos. In the early 1900s, researchers began to notice a large number of early deaths and lung problems in cities with mines where asbestos was extracted.

Johns Manville is an American corporation founded in 1858 that manufactures insulation, roofing materials, and engineered products. For much of the twentieth century, Johns Manville Corporation was the global leader in the manufacture of asbestos-containing products, including asbestos pipe insulation, asbestos shingles, asbestos roofing materials, and asbestos cement pipe.

In 1929, Johns Manville's employees began claiming disabilities due to lung diseases, and during the 1960s, 1970s, and 1980s, the company faced thousands of individual and class action lawsuits based on asbestos-related injuries such as asbestosis, lung cancer, and malignant mesothelioma. In the late 1970s, court documents proved that the asbestos industry officials knew of asbestos dangers since the 1930s and had concealed them from the public. Manville voluntarily filed for Chapter 11 bankruptcy protection in 1982.

Approximately 100,000 people in the United States have died or suffered from terminal illnesses as a result of exposure to asbestos in the construction of ships.

The World Health Organization estimates that around 125 million people worldwide have been exposed to asbestos in their jobs for more than 60 years, despite the known link of this mineral with cancer and other lung diseases.

In Bangladesh, one of the poorest countries in the world where 160 million people live with an average monthly wage of 50 euros per month,* hundreds of workers have died since 2005 due to fires and landslides in textile factories. In that country, there was a major controversy about the working conditions and safety of the textile industry because many factories do not have fire equipment or emergency exits.

On April 24, 2013, a building collapsed in the Dhaka district of Savar, Bangladesh. The eighth floor structure collapsed; 1,134 people were killed; and another 2,500 were injured. The Rana Plaza building had four clothing factories, a bank, and several shops. Cracks in the walls were detected on April 23, 2013, but the supervisors ignored them and asked the workers to go back to work the next day.

---

* Approximately US$56.

"Clean Clothes Campaigns"* launched a global action to improve building safety and fire prevention in Bangladesh, and to this campaign 192 multinational companies adhered. The agreement obliges the signatory companies to pay US$500,000 every year for five years, and 1,600 factories that supply global brands must be inspected.

With the rise of industrialization and mass production, at the end of the nineteenth century, the economy of the United States attracted millions of immigrants and since 1930 laws were passed to protect workers.

A job is much more than the exchange of work for money and a safe workplace; it is a basic human right. The doctrine of contractual freedom prevailing at that time was challenged and in 1935 the Wagner Law (National Labor Relations Law) was enacted. This statute guarantees the basic rights of private-sector employees to organize in unions, participate in collective bargaining to obtain better terms and conditions at work, and take collective action, including strike.

In the United States, the Occupational Safety and Health Administration, known as OSHA in the Department of Labor, was created in 1970. OSHA attempts to balance the need for employees to work in a safe environment and, on the other hand, employers' desire for the government to interfere as little as possible in their activity.

OSHA's mission is "to assure safe and healthy working conditions for working men and women by setting and enforcing standards and by promoting training, outreach, education, and assistance."† Under OSHA, employers have a responsibility to provide a safe workplace, and companies must comply with OSHA safety and health standards. OSHA protects workers from toxic chemicals and other hazards to safety at work.

North American federal and state statutes regulate workplace hazards to avoid or minimize employee injury and disease. These laws refer to problems caused by machinery, hazardous materials, the smoke of the cigarette, and noise. All these laws place the burden on employers to maintain a safe and healthy workplace.‡

Since its inception, OSHA has made significant progress. Injuries, illnesses, and deaths in the workplace have decreased significantly.

---

* The Clean Clothes Campaign is an organization that covers a broad spectrum of perspectives and interests, such as women's rights and consumer advocacy.

† en.wikipedia.org/wiki/Occupational_Safety_and_Health_Administration.

‡ "Employment Law," legal-dictionary-the freedictionary.com/wage+and+Hour+regulations.

In 1970, in the United States, the number of worker deaths was 38 people per day, while in 2015 it was reduced to 13 workers per day.*

In the United States, employers must comply with the standards established by OSHA or assume the risk of civil and criminal penalties.

Another risk against security is the attack by intruders with guns.

In 2019 there's been an average of more than one mass shooting per day in the United States according to the Gun Violence Archive, a nonprofit that counts incidents in which at least four people other than the shooter were injured or killed.†

Active-shooter incidents have been growing in the last years according to the National Center for Health Statistics.‡

An Active-Shooter Response Training may help to save lives. Training classes provide preparation and a plan for organizations on how to move proactively and handle the threat of aggressive intruders or an active-shooting event. Organizations also have cameras and sensor-based security systems that help to prevent threats.

Look for things you can do to improve the safety and security of your customers and employees.

Their health, safety, and security are more important than the next earnings report.

14.2 INTELLECTUAL PROPERTY

During the eighteenth century, many credited the German mathematician and philosopher Gottfried Leibniz (1646–1716) with inventing the study of calculus. Leibniz was the first to publish papers on the topic in 1684

---

* www.osha.gov/oshstats/commonstats.html. In the European Union, the Agency for Safety and Health at Work (EU-OSHA) was established in 1994, and it also has the function of making workplaces safer.

† Abby Versoulis, "I Wish We Could Stop Teaching This," What It's Like to Attend an Active-Shooter Training after the El Paso and Dayton Attacks," August 19, 2019, www.time.com.The Gun Violence Archive includes information on gun violence nationally, defensive use, officer-involved shootings in addition to mass shootings going back to 2014. Gunviolencearchive.org.The Mother Jones Database of Mass Shootings covers mass shootings in the United States from 1982 to present. www.motherjones.com.The FBI releases annual reports on active-shooter incidents, with state-by-state details, details on shooter behavior, and conclusions on trends. www.fbi.gov/file-reposito ry/active-shooter-incidents-2000-2018.pdf/view.

‡ Active shooters incidents represent around 2% of all gun deaths annually in the United States, compared to suicides (60%) and homicides (30%). www.cdc.gov/nchs/fastats/injury.htm.

and 1686. But when the Englishman Isaac Newton (1643–1727) published his book *Opticks* in 1704, a debate arose. Newton claimed he wrote about it in 1665–1666 and accused Leibniz of plagiarizing one of his early drafts.* Leibniz went to the Royal Society, the oldest scientific society in the United Kingdom, founded in 1660, to resolve the dispute, but without noticing the president of that institution was Isaac Newton. The Royal Society accused Leibniz of plagiarism. However, over time, the authorship of the calculus has been attributed to both thinkers.

Intellectual property is related to the creations of the mind: inventions, literary, and artistic works, as well as symbols, names, and images. Intellectual property rights allow the creator, or the owner of a patent, trademark, or copyright, to be protected and enjoy the benefits derived from his work or invention.

Trademarks are words, symbols, and designs that identify a product or business. If registered with the US Patent and Trademark Office, trademarks can be legally owned and protected in the United States. For example, the Nike name and curving line symbol are trademarks.[†]

Copyrights are rights to written work, software, films, music, paintings, photographs, sculptures, and architectural design. To protect their rights in the United States, authors or legal owners of such work must register it with the US Copyright Office.

Patents are exclusive rights to make, use, and sell new inventions for several years. Inventors or their employers must prove to the US Patent and Trademark Office that their inventions are genuine. If they do so, they receive protection from competitors. For example, Xerox patented the plain-paper copier and dominated the photocopier market until its patents expired in the early 1980s.[‡]

These three types of intellectual property encourage innovation by helping people and businesses profit from their original ideas and inventions.[§]

---

* "Ten Famous Intellectual Property Disputes," www.smithsonianmag.com.

[†] K. Blanchard, C. Schewe, B. Nelson and A. Hiam, *Exploring the World of Business* (Worth Publishers, 1996), 116.

[‡] K. Blanchard, C. Schewe, B. Nelson and A. Hiam, *Exploring the World of Business* (Worth Publishers, 1996), 116.

[§] These rights are enshrined in Article 27 of the Universal Declaration of Human Rights, which contemplates the right to benefit from the protection of the moral and material interests resulting from the authorship of scientific, literary, or artistic productions. Likewise, the importance of intellectual property was recognized for the first time in the Paris Convention for the Protection of Industrial Property (1883), and in the Berne Convention for the Protection of Literary and Artistic Works (1886).

The way countries protect intellectual property varies enormously and can be a source of conflict. In some countries, intellectual property is protected by using it. In other countries, ideas and names are protected only if they are registered in the country. In other countries in Asia, intellectual property can be used by anyone and no protection exists.*

Intellectual property is protected by laws as an incentive for people who invest time and money in developing new products. The progress of humanity depends on its capacity to create and invent new technological and cultural works. When countries legally protect intellectual creations, economic development and the quality of life of people improve.

Piracy is the unauthorized use or reproduction of copyrighted or patent material.

Chinese firms in the 1990s forged sunglasses similar to the Ray-Ban that Bausch & Lomb made, and called them "Ran Bans." Other forgers produced toothpaste with the "Cologate" brand to confuse it with Colgate toothpaste.†

"Happy Birthday to You" is a song written by the American sisters Mildred and Patty Hill in 1893. The original title was "Good Morning to All." According to the *Guinness Book of World Records*, "Happy Birthday to You" is the most popular song in the English language and has been translated into multiple languages.

Not everyone knows, however, that the copyright of the song was recorded in 1935 and acquired in 1988 by Warner Music for US$25 million. From then on, whoever wanted to use the song for a film, theatrical production, television show, or for musical greeting cards had to pay Warner a royalty for the rights of use.

For example, in 1995 the American Society of Composers, Authors, and Publishers (ASCAP) wanted to charge the Girl Scouts for singing the song in their camps. Warner's rights were extinguished in 2015 in the United States when former judge George H. King ruled that Warner had no rights to the song, and it became public domain. Warner then stopped receiving about US$2 million a year for the copyright to the song.

The World Intellectual Property Organization (WIPO) is a specialized agency of the United Nations, created in 1967, dedicated to promoting the use and protection of works of the human intellect. Headquartered

---

* K. Blanchard, C. Schewe, B. Nelson and A. Hiam, *Exploring the World of Business* (Worth Publishers, 1996), 84.

† K. Blanchard, C. Schewe, B. Nelson and A. Hiam, *Exploring the World of Business* (Worth Publishers, 1996), 84.

in Geneva, Switzerland, it is in charge of the administration of 26 international treaties dealing with various aspects of the regulation of intellectual property.

WIPO considers *trade secrets* as all confidential business information that gives a company a competitive advantage.

As the World Intellectual Property Organization says, "the intellectual property system helps establish a balance between the interests of innovators and the public interest, creating an environment in which creativity and invention can flourish for the benefit of all."*

Confidential information includes non-public commercial information that, if improperly disclosed, could be useful to competitors or harmful to the company, its suppliers, customers, or another third party or material to a reasonable investor's decision to buy or sell company's securities or securities of a business partner. For example, earnings, forecasts, business plans and strategies, significant restructurings, potential acquisitions, formulas, pricing, sales, research and product development, and undisclosed marketing activity would all qualify as confidential information.

There are millions of patents, trademarks, and industrial models registered in the world. New product designs, customer lists, or production processes are other examples of secret information.

For over a hundred years, the secret formula of Coca-Cola has remained one of the best-kept commercial secrets in the world. The story begins when pharmacist John Pemberton (1831–1888), hoping to cure his headaches and nausea, invented the Pemberton Coca wine, a drink that included cola nut and cola wine that was conceived as a medicinal beverage. In 1886, when Atlanta passed the alcohol ban, Pemberton reformulated the drink to remove alcohol, called it Coca-Cola, and it was sold in Georgia pharmacies.

Asa Griggs Candler (1851–1929), one of the first presidents of the Coca Cola Company, bought the formula for US$2,300 in 1887.[†] Since the 1920s, the document with the formula was locked at a bank in Atlanta,

---

* "Que es la Propiedad Intelectual," Organización Mundial de la Propiedad Intelectual, www.wipo.i nt/edocs/pubdocs/es/intproperty/450/wipo_pub_450.pdf ("What is Intellectual Property, "World Intellectual Property Organization").

† In 1916 and after 24 years at the helm of Coca-Cola, Griggs decided to leave the management of the company and to run for mayor of Atlanta. A year later he gave most of his shares to his children, but they had them for only a few years: in 1919 they sold them for US$25 million to Woodruff Syndicate, a consortium of banks. Robert Woodruff (1889–1985) was the president of the Coca Cola Company from 1923 to 1954.

but in 2006 Coca-Cola took the formula to a vault specifically built for that purpose in the company's museum, the World of Coca-Cola, in the same city of Atlanta. The vault has a palm scanner, a numeric code padlock, and a huge steel door. Inside is another safe with more security methods. And inside of that, a metal box contains what its owners call "the best-kept secret in the world": the "7X super-flavorful flavor" that gives Coca-Cola its flavor.*

Trade secrets are an important competitive advantage, and when Coca-Cola protects its secret formula, it also strengthens its brand.

US federal prosecutors have charged Chinese tech giant Huawei, one of the world's largest manufacturers of telecom equipment and smartphones, with racketeering and conspiracy to steal trade secrets. The charges accuse Huawei of stealing intellectual property such as source code and robot technology from six US tech companies.†

The indictment says Huawei helped the North Korean government build and maintain a wireless telecommunications network. It also said Huawei set up a bonus program that rewarded employees for stealing confidential information from competitors, based on the value of the information obtained.‡

The Chinese company has faced allegations that its wireless networking equipment could contain backdoors enabling surveillance by the Chinese government. Huawei has also faced allegations that it has engaged in corporate espionage to steal competitors' intellectual property, and in 2019 was restricted from performing commerce with US companies, over allegations that it willfully exported technology of US origin to Iran in violation of US sanctions.§

---

* Coca-Cola has noted that only two executives know the formula at any given time, although it has never released names or positions. According to an advertising campaign, they cannot travel on the same plane at the same time.

† Jeanne Whalen, "U.S. charges China's Huawei with Racketeering and Conspiracy to Steal U.S. Trade Secrets in new Indictment," www.washingtonpost.com/technology/2020/02/13/us-charges -chinas-huawei-with-conspiracy-steal-us-trade-secrets-new-indictment/, February 13, 2020.

‡ Jeanne Whalen, "U.S. charges China's Huawei with Racketeering and Conspiracy to Steal U.S. Trade Secrets in new Indictment," www.washingtonpost.com/technology/2020/02/13/us-charges -chinas-huawei-with-conspiracy-steal-us-trade-secrets-new-indictment/, February 13, 2020.

§ In 2003, Cisco's General Counsel traveled to Shenzhen to confront Huawei's founder with evidence of Huawei's theft of Cisco IP. The evidence included typos from Cisco's technical manuals that also appeared in Huawei's. After being presented with the evidence, it was replied "coincidence." In February 2003, Cisco Systems sued Huawei Technologies for allegedly infringing on its patents and illegally copying source code used in its routers and switches. According to a statement by Cisco, by July 2004 Huawei had removed the contested code, manuals, and command-line interfaces and the case was subsequently settled out of court. en.wikipedia.org/wiki/Criticism of_Huawei.

In addition to protecting their business secrets, companies must take precautions so their employees do not appropriate the invention or trade secrets for their competitors or third parties. If a trade secret is acquired via industrial espionage, its acquirer will be subject to legal liability for having acquired it improperly. A few years ago, a former Coca-Cola executive assistant was sentenced to eight years in prison for attempting to sell trade secrets to Pepsi for US$1.5 million. Employees play an essential role in protecting the intellectual property of companies.

The Spanish engineer Jose Ignacio Lopez left General Motors (GM) and was hired by Volkswagen. After a while, GM filed a lawsuit in the United States and Germany for trade secret infringement. Lopez was accused of industrial espionage and for having seized secret plans.[*] After three years of negotiations and litigation, the companies reached an agreement under which Volkswagen would pay GM US$100 million.[†]

In May 2018, Apple won Samsung's patent trial on the invention of smartphone technology. After seven years of starting the trial, the sentence forced Samsung to pay US$539 million to Apple. Tim Cook, CEO of Apple said the lawsuit was about values, and that the company, "chose legal action very reluctantly and only after repeatedly asking Samsung to stop copying our work."[‡]

14.3 SMUGGLING AND TAX EVASION

Countries need to control the import and export of goods because when they enter the country legally, the state can collect taxes and duties and, therefore, have enough resources to sustain the state apparatus. However, this does not happen if the merchandise enters the country and avoids customs control and without paying the corresponding tariffs. It is called smuggling the illegal transportation of objects across an international border in violation of applicable laws or regulations. The verb *smuggle* comes from Dutch *smokkelen* ("to transport goods illegally").[§] In popular perception, smuggling is synonymous with illegal trade.

[*] José Comas, "Volkswagen espera hoy la dimisión de Superlópez," November 29, 1996, www.elpais. com ("Today, Volkswagen waits for the resignation of Superlopez").

[†] Robyn Meredith, "VW Agrees to Pay $100 Million in Espionage Suit," January 10, 1997, www. nytimes.com.

[‡] Joel Rosenblatt and Mark Gurman, "Apple's $539 Million in Damages Is a Big Win over Samsung," *Bloomberg*, May 24, 2018.

[§] "Smuggling," Etymology, en.wikipedia.org.

Customs laws are in place to control the importing of goods and import taxes, known as "duties." The purpose of customs laws is to protect the economy, residents, jobs, and the environment (such as stopping foreign pests or diseases) by controlling the flow of goods into and out of the country.[*]

Companies that conduct international business must comply with the regulations governing exports and imports. The laws that control exports, for example, prohibit the transfer from the country of certain strategic products, defense products, or certain technologies.

Alphonse Gabriel Capone (1899–1947), known as Al Capone or Al "Scarface" Capone, nicknamed due to the scar on his face caused by a knife, was born in Naples, Italy, and was the most dangerous gangster who lived in Chicago. In 1919, criminals in Chicago were engaged in alcohol smuggling, and representatives of police and justice were associated with criminals. With the death of mobster Johnny Torrio, Al Capone became the head of the Chicago Mafia at the age of 26, a millionaire, with hundreds of gunmen at his service and 18 bodyguards who guarded him day and night. He had an enormous infrastructure that cost him US$800,000 a month.

Al Capone was once asked if he was involved in alcohol smuggling and replied, "All I ever did was sell beer and whiskey to our best people. All I ever did was supply a demand that was pretty popular. ... Some of the leading judges use the stuff."[†]

In 1929 President Herbert Hoover (1874–1964) and Treasury Secretary Andrew Mellon (1855–1937) decided to do whatever it would take to put Al Capone behind bars. They devised a plan based on the 1927 Supreme Court decision in *United States v. Sullivan* ruled that any criminal activity that generated an income was subject to income taxes.

Capone was pursued by Treasury agent Eliot Ness (1903–1957) and his men known as the Untouchables.[‡]

---

[*] criminal.findlaw.com/criminal-charges/smuggling-and-customs-violations.html.

[†] ww.myalcaponemuseum.com.

[‡] Capone's attempt to bribe the agents of Ness was exploited by Ness as publicity, obtaining for his team the nickname of "The Untouchables" by the media. There were several assassination attempts on Ness and one of his close friends, Cam Allison, was killed. es.wikipedia.org/wiki/Eliot_Ness.With the corruption among the police officers, Ness examined the records of all the treasury employees to form a reliable team, initially, 50, later reduced to 15 and finally only 9 men.Frank J. Wilson led the tax investigation. Wilson and his team examined over two million documents and evidence acquired a number of raids on Capone's establishments over a six-year period. Their strategy was to show that Capone spent a large amount of money, which served as a sign to the jury that the money must come from some undisclosed location. en.wikipedia.org/

One agent managed to infiltrate among the men of Al Capone and gathered evidence of illegal income and tax fraud. As Al Capone had never paid taxes, he was brought to trial in 1931. Capone was indicted on 23 counts of tax evasion from 1924 to 1929. The trial was widely covered by the press. Attempts were made to bribe the jury. After 9 hours of deliberation, Al Capone was acquitted of the crime of murder but sentenced to 11 years in prison for tax evasion and tax fraud.*

Organizations can evade taxes in different ways, for example, a sub-declaration of profits, depositing undeclared sums in tax havens, using front men and trusts, or lying with respect to the country of residence. It is said that there is a *tax haven* when a state or territory is characterized by a tax regime favorable to citizens or companies that are not resident but domiciled there for legal purposes. A feature of a tax haven is the existence of banking secrecy and data protection laws so strict that the records of shareholders and directors of companies do not appear in public records.

Placing money in a tax haven does not necessarily imply an illegal act when the taxing agency of the country that is harmed is notified; however, it is common to use offshore companies to hide assets, money from illicit activities, or money from the Treasury.

Tax havens have been accused of serving tax evaders who hide their identities in offshore phantom corporations, trusts, foundations, and bearer shares.

According to the International Monetary Fund, in tax havens, there are deposited sums higher than the GDP of the United States or even 25% of the world's private wealth.

Oxfam International is an NGO founded 70 years ago in Oxford, England. It works to reduce inequity and poverty in the world. In a 2014 statement, Oxfam points out that the 20 largest European banks only

---

wiki/Frank_J._Wilson.*The Untouchables* is the name of a 1987 American gangster film directed by Brian De Palma, based on the book *The Untouchables*, an autobiographical memoir about Eliot Ness co-written by Oscar Fraley, published in 1957.

* Al Capone served two years in prison in Atlanta and eight years on Alcatraz Island in San Francisco, California. When he was transferred to the feared Alcatraz, it was impossible for him to gain privileges or contact the outside. That powerful criminal who years before controlled Chicago became just prisoner number 85 and was forced to follow penitentiary discipline. By then he had been diagnosed with syphilis that he refused to treat for fear of injections. The worsening of his health relegated him to the infirmary of the prison, where he spent the last years of his sentence lying on a cot, lonely and elusive. When he left in 1939, his wife moved him to his luxurious Miami mansion. He could barely walk, he was not joking, and saliva flowed from his mouth. His mental deterioration was irreversible, and he died on January 25, 1947, at his house.

report a quarter of their profits in tax havens such as Hong Kong, Bermuda, Cayman Islands, or Luxembourg to avoid or reduce tax payments.

In the Bahamas, there are over 120,000 companies registered and over 80,000 in the Cayman Islands. The Ugland House located at 121 South Church Street, George Town, Cayman Islands, has only five floors and is the home of more than 18,800 companies.*

The main reasons why companies create an offshore company are to give more privacy to their owners and directors, to lower the tax burden, and to accelerate the formation of the company, because these jurisdictions do not require many legal requirements. Normally, in 24 hours, the company is constituted and the only payment made is an annual maintenance fee.

In tax havens, taxes are symbolic; there is fiscal secrecy and domiciled companies have no physical presence. An offshore company cannot conduct business in the territory where it is incorporated since it would become an onshore company, i.e., the tax haven would tax it like any other company registered in that country.

Of course, not all tax evasion cases come from tax havens. For example, former Chilean president Augusto Pinochet (1915–2006) was investigated by the US Senate and found to have 125 secret bank accounts at Riggs Bank in Washington D.C., where he had deposited more than US$20 million. In January 2005, the bank agreed to pay more than US$15 million for not reporting suspicious activities and accounts maintained by the former president.[†]

In May 2014, a US court imposed on the Swiss bank Credit Suisse a record fine of US$2.88 billion for helping 22,000 American customers evade taxes and for the lack of cooperation with the authorities in the investigation. This fine is considered the highest sanction imposed on a financial institution for a tax fraud case and was due in part to the bank's hidden assets and destroyed documentation. Credit Suisse issued a statement in which it accepted responsibility for the facts and committed to preventing this situation from happening again in the future. US attorney general Eric Holder said during a press conference that Credit Suisse

> developed complex safety nets for its clients and employees and tax evaders took advantage of this to commit their crimes. They did not meet our requirements for declassification of documents; they destroyed important

---

* en.wikipedia.org/wiki/Ugland_House.
† en.wikipedia.org/wiki/Riggs_Bank.

bank records and allowed transactions to repatriate many funds from evaders.*

Organizations must ensure that they have adequate tax advice to be in compliance and to avoid falling into illegality.

14.4 COMPUTER VIRUSES, CYBERCRIME, AND DIGITAL INFORMATION

The protection of confidential information is an asset that companies must take care of. Leakage of information may be due to negligence, ignorance, or infidelity of employees when sharing secret data with the press or the competition.

It is a great challenge for companies to process and monitor large volumes of information in the cloud, mobile, and virtual environments.

Data Privacy Day or Data Protection Day is an international event that occurs every year on January 28, and its purpose is to raise awareness and promote privacy and data protection best practices. January 28 because on January 28, 1981, was signed in Europe *The Convention for the Protection of Individuals concerning Automatic Processing of Personal Data* (Convention 108).†

Other conventions have been also regulating the privacy of information. For example, *The Convention on Cybercrime* (2004), also known as the Budapest Convention on Cybercrime, is an international treaty seeking to address the internet and computer crime by increasing cooperation among nations.

Privacy including data protection is also protected by the *European Convention on Human Rights* since 1950. Article 8 provides a right to respect for one's "private and family life, his home and his correspondence."‡

In 2018, the *Personal Data Protection Regulation* (GDPR) became effective in the European Union, and I will refer to it later.

---

* "The Biggest Fine in History to a Bank for Helping to Evade Taxes," May 20, 2014, www.bbc.com; "Risky Business: Top 10 Corporate Crackdowns," *Censible*, July 20, 2017, www.learn.censible.co. Another bank, the Deutsche Bank and 10,000 of its clients were sentenced in 2003 by the Frankfurt Court, in Germany, to pay more than 200 million euros for non-payment of taxes.
† en.wikipedia.org/wiki/Data_Privacy_Day.
‡ www.echr.coe.int/Documents/Convention_ENG.pdf.

Allianz Global Corporate & Specialty (AGSC) is a leading global corporate insurance carrier that publishes the annual Allianz Risk Barometer. The 2019 survey shows that cyber risk is a core concern for business leaders.*

Companies must take the necessary preventive actions against cybercrime and hackers and permanently adapt their security systems.

Facebook was involved in one of the biggest leaks of data in history and it all started with an innocent personality test.

In March 2018 *The New York Times* and *The Guardian* newspapers published revelations from a former employee of English-based marketing consultancy Cambridge Analytica.

According to their statements, the consulting firm collected personal and private information from 50 million Facebook users without permission through an application called "This Is Your Digital Life" – an online personality test and that supposedly had statistical and academic ends.

To complete the test the user was required to log in to Facebook and then the user's personal information was sent to Cambridge Analytica without the proper user's permission.

After this situation spread, Facebook shares fell more than 7% on Wall Street. Facebook suspended the Cambridge Analytica account and had to respond to accusations and possible class actions and fines for failures in computer security and in protecting the privacy of information.

Mark Zuckerberg, the founder of Facebook, said in a statement, "We have a responsibility to protect your data and, if we cannot, then we do not deserve to serve you."†

A new attack exposed 50 million of Facebook's users in September 2018. The attackers were able to take over the accounts and use them exactly as if they were the account holders, like posting or viewing information shared by any of that account's friends. Facebook fixed the issue and informed the FBI, regulators, and the Irish Data Protection Commission about the breach, a step required by the general data protection regulation (GDPR).

Mark Zuckerberg, CEO of Facebook, said: "The reality here is we face constant attacks from people who want to take over accounts or steal

---

* Agsc.allianz.com.

† Rafael Mathus Ruiz, "Mark Zuckerberg Is Responsible for the Facebook Scandal," *La Nacion*, March 21, 2018; "7 Keys to Understanding Facebook Scandal and Cambridge Analytica," March 20, 2018; "How to Use Cambridge Analytica: A Personality Test to Collect Private Information from Millions of Users," *BBC World*, March 21, 2018, www.lanacion.com.ar; "5 Keys to Understanding the Cambridge Analytica Scandal that Caused Facebook to Lose $37 Billion in a Day," *BBC World*, March 21, 2018, www.bbc.com/world.

information … we need to do more to prevent this from happening in the first place."* In a CNN interview Zuckerberg said, "This is going to be a never-ending battle."†

Facebook has doubled the number of people working on security.

Should Facebook have taken more preventive measures to protect the privacy of its user's data?

The Federal Communications Commission (FCC) is set to propose millions of dollars in fines against four major cellphone carriers (AT&T, Sprint, T-Mobile, and Verizon) for selling customers' real-time location data. In May 2019, all four carriers were hit with a class-action lawsuit for selling data.

The *New York Times* revealed in May 2018 that the carriers were selling this information to companies that used it to track people without their knowledge or consent. The trade in location data has emerged as a sensitive privacy issue because it affects millions of people and can reveal personal relationships and visits to doctors.‡

WikiLeaks is an international organization founded in 2006 by Julian Assange and has more than 12 million documents and it publishes on its website anonymous reports that usually reveal possible unethical behavior of governments or companies. In April 2010, for example, WikiLeaks released a 38-minute video recorded in 2007 with images about certain abuses committed by US troops when an Apache helicopter shot 12 civilians in Iraq.§ More than four million people watched the video in the first 72 hours when it was uploaded to YouTube.

WikiLeaks has said:

> We are convinced that a government based on transparency aims at reducing corruption and stable democracy. We are convinced that it is not only the citizens of a country who maintain the honesty of their government, but that is also the task of the citizens of other countries, who observe and control those governments.

---

* "Facebook Hack Exposed 50 Million Users' info and Accounts on Other Sites," *Heather Kelly*, September 28, 2018, www.cnn.com.

† "Mark Zuckerberg: Security on Facebook is Never-Ending Battle," Dylan Byers – Laurie Segall, April 4, 2018, www.money.cnn.com.

‡ Sara Morrison, "Verizon, T-Mobile, Sprint, and AT&T could be facing big fines for selling your location data," https://www.vox.com/recode/2020/2/27/21156609/verizon-t-mobile-sprint-att-f ined-location-data, February 27, 2020; Jennifer Valentino-DeVries, "F.C.C. to Fine Cellphone Carriers for Selling Customers' Locations," https://www.nytimes.com/2020/02/27/technology/ fcc-location-data.html?smtyp=cur&smid=tw-nytimes, February 27, 2020.

§ April 5, 2010, www.bbc.com.

Public examination forces institutions to behave ethically. Otherwise, they would be more irresponsible and reserved. Which manager would risk performing secret or corrupt transactions knowing that these can be discovered?

WikiLeaks can become the most powerful intelligence service on earth.

WikiLeaks will inform citizens about the established power over truth in the world.

WikiLeaks will be the outlet for any member of a government, for any bureaucrat or employee of a corporation who is informed of embarrassing issues that the institutions want to conceal and which the public needs to hear about.

What the conscience cannot contain and that is unfairly disguised as an institutional secret, WikiLeaks transmits it to the whole world.*

One of the largest document leaks in the history of journalism is called the Panama Papers. Conducted in April 2016, it exposed 11 million confidential documents of the Panamanian law firm Mossack Fonseca.

The documents were sent by an unidentified source to the German newspaper *Suddeutsche Zeitung* which shared them with the International Consortium of Investigative Journalists. The filtered records were reviewed by 350 journalists around the world and contain information on 214,488 offshore entities. The documents revealed multiple possible cases of asset concealment and profit and tax evasion by various officials, personalities, and world leaders.

One of the founders of the Mossack Fonseca Law Firm, created in 1977 and from where the documents were extracted, has denied any wrongdoing. He said his firm has no responsibility for what its clients do with their offshore shell companies once they've bought them. He compared the firm to a "car factory," and said that blaming Mossack Fonseca for what people do with their companies would be like blaming a car maker "if the car was used in a robbery."†

On November 5, 2017, a new leak called Paradise Papers was made public; millions of confidential electronic documents were sent to the German newspaper *Suddeutsche Zeitung*, who once again shared them with the International Consortium of Investigative Journalists. These documents came from the Appleby Offshore Law Firm. The records include emails, contracts, balance sheets, and information about investment funds.

---

* www.wikileaks.org.

† "The VICE News Guide to the Panama Papers," *Tess Owen*, www.news.vice.com/article/panama-papers, April 5, 2016.

On the website offshoreleaks.icij.org, anyone can now access information that was hidden by more than a half-million offshore companies. The archives bring to light secret details about the financial lives of companies, millionaires, and celebrities.

As explained above, resorting to offshore companies or opening a bank account in a tax haven is not in itself an illicit activity. But if the beneficiary of the operation does not declare his, her, or its assets to the tax authorities, they may be committing crimes of evasion or money laundering.

The movie *WarGames* of 1983 shows how a young hacker enters the computer systems of the US government.* This science fiction film was one of the first to point out the dangers of hacking to which organizations would be subjected years later.

Some of the main risks arising from the digital environment are the following:

Skimming is the theft of information from the magnetic stripes of credit cards in order to clone the card for fraudulent use. The personal data stolen from the magnetic strips on the card of the person who was the victim of the fraud are copied on a chip of another credit card.

Hacking allows the attacker remote access to the infected computer through a *trojan*, a malicious software (malware) that penetrates the computer and self-install to copy data and commit fraud.† The goal of the Trojan is to control the machine and send the information to the hacker's address without the victim being warned. About 80% of computer attacks are carried out using this method that activates a program or file that seems to have a useful or desirable function to encourage the user to install the program or open the file. In the background, however, it silently performs unauthorized actions (its *payloads*), without the user's knowledge or consent, to destroy the hard disk or to delete files.‡

In November 2016, malicious software violated the security of smartphones with the Android system and acquired data stored in more than one million Google accounts. The infection occurred when the user

---

* *WarGames* is a 1983 American Cold War science fiction directed by John Badham. The film follows David Lightman (Broderick), a young hacker who unwittingly accesses WOPR (War Operation Plan Response), a United States military supercomputer originally programmed to predict possible outcomes of nuclear war. Lightman gets WOPR to run a nuclear war simulation, believing it to be a computer game. The computer, now tied into the nuclear weapons control system and unable to tell the difference between simulation and reality, attempts to start World War III. en.wikipedia.org/wiki/WarGames.

† The term *Trojan* comes from the Trojan War, something that is hidden.

‡ www.f-secure.com/v-descs/trojan.shtml.

installed an application infected by Googilan malware on an Android device.

In Mexico, the so-called Dark Tequila Anejo was a malware used to steal financial information and in Brazil, malware known as BRata had access to Android phones.*

Phishing is a form of abuse characterized by a fraudulent attempt to acquire confidential information. The term *phishing* comes from the English word *fishing* and refers to the user's attempt to "bite the hook." The phisher poses as a trustworthy company or person and tries to capture credit card information, Social Security numbers, and passwords. Users register their data on fake websites of banking entities created by hackers and steal the confidential information of the user. With the confidential information obtained, they spend the money and credit of their victims. Between 2004 and 2005, more than one million computer users in the United States were affected by phishing.

Sometimes hackers violate the Domain Name System (DNS) server software and redirect the domain name to another web page, identical in appearance to the one that the user wants to use but created to obtain private data as credit card numbers or user passwords.

In 2006, a computer worm took over some pages from the Myspace website and redirected the links in a way that stole the information that users entered. Worms are replicated in the computer system, creating a large-scale effect. The first computer worm in history occurred in 1988 when the Morris worm infected a large number of servers.†

On March 26, 1999, a virus called "Melissa" was inside a file called "List. doc" that contained a password to access different web pages. Melissa caused more than US$80 million in damages, and its author was sentenced to prison.

On May 4, 2000, the "I Love You" virus was created in the Philippines, and ten days later it had infected 50 million computers. When the file was opened, the virus was auto-mailed to the email addresses that the user had in his or her calendar.‡

---

* Vanesa Listek, "Ciberdelitos: Se Registran 49 Amenazas por Minuto en la Argentina," 1 de diciembre de 2019, lanacion.com ("Cybercrimes: 49 Threats Per Minute are Recorded in Argentina", December 1, 2019).

† Its creator was a student named Robert Tappan Morris, who was sentenced to three years in prison and obtained probation, 400 hours of community service, and a fine of US$10,050.

‡ Other dangerous computer viruses were, for example, the Code Red and Nimda of 2001, Sol Slammer of 2003, and Conficker of 2008.

On October 21, 2016, a massive attack of hackers against the DNS servers of the provider Dyn, which hosts domains of web platforms, affected the navigation of half of the world's internet users.

A Botnet is a network of computers infected by malicious code and controlled by the attacker. Each infected system (zombie) executes the orders received. Botnets are often used to send spam and perform distributed denial of service (DDoS) attacks, which puts a website out of the user's reach. The most frequent DDoS attacks occur when many computers request information of a site at the same time, the server does not supply, and it collapses. When users enter the name of the site they want to access, the server does not respond. Twitter, Starbucks, Amazon, *The New York Times*, or CNN and millions of people were infected by this code.

Among the most dangerous software used for phishing is the *Exploit Kit*, which allows an attacker to take advantage of a system crash and steal information or install malicious code. The Exploit Kit can be acquired in the illegal market of hackers by a pair of Bitcoins.* Crypto-currency is intangible and is not supported by any government or dependent on a central issuer. The users of this digital currency through their exchanges (supply and demand) provide the value, and an algorithm measures Bitcoin movements and transactions in real time.† Due to its decentralization nature and anonymity, Bitcoin has become the preferred means of payment to carry out illegal transactions.‡

Smishing is similar to phishing but is done via a text message, like SMS. If the recipient accepts the message, the smisher begins to extract information.

Computer viruses are computer programs that infect system files with the intention to alter the normal operation of a computer without the user's permission and destroy the data stored on that computer. The first computer virus attacked an IBM 360 Series machine and was called

---

* Digital exchange coin created by Satoshi Nakamoto, in 2009. Nakamoto could be the pseudonym of a person or a group of people.
† Bitcoin is backed by Blockchain technology. Blockchain is a distributed database between interconnected computers that form a network and where all the nodes register the same data. It is called Blockchain because it consists of a chain of transaction blocks where all the information is stored. If someone wanted to modify some data, they would have to hack all the computers, which would be impossible. The information is encrypted to ensure your safety.
‡ The first transaction registered with Bitcoins was made in 2010 when a resident of California published in a forum that he would send Bitcoins to whoever sent two pizzas to his house. A person from London sent the pizzas and received 10,000 bitcoins that today amount to several million dollars. Bitcoin has a limit of 21 million coins, which should be reached in 2030.

Creeper. He would send out a message saying "I'm a creeper.... Catch me if you can."

Ransomware is a malicious software that encrypts and hijacks files and information from phones and computers and prevents the user from having access to them. The software is installed by clicking on malicious links. This software gives a cybercriminal the ability to lock a computer from a remote location and encrypt files by removing the control of the information and stored data from the owner. Then to recover the hijacked information, the owner has to pay. If the ransomware is detected in time, it can be deleted without giving it time to encrypt. *Jackware, Petya, Wannacry, EternalBlue, BlueKeep, Nyetya, Ryuk,* and *Keylogger* are types of ransomware malicious codes.

These viruses exploit the vulnerability of operating systems on networked computers and spread the damage quickly around the world.

In 2019, 205,280 organizations submitted files that had been hacked in a ransomware attack – a 41 percent increase from the year before, according to information provided by Emsisoft, a security firm that helps companies hit by ransomware. The average payment demanded to release files was US$84,115 by the end of 2019.*

The FBI warned ransomware attacks are becoming more and more sophisticated. For example, (i) ransomware forced a cargo transfer facility to shut for more than 30 hours after attackers took control of the industrial systems critical to process operations, (ii) several banks have been unable to make foreign currency conversions after a supplier was targeted by ransomware known as *Sodinokibi,* or *REvil,* (iii) a ransomware known as *Snake* or *Ekans* is focused on freezing the software responsible for industrial processes at oil and petroleum companies.†

On May 12, 2017, Telefonica de Espana's headquarters in Madrid and several British hospitals were affected by ransomware, and in January 2017, a Los Angeles hospital had to pay US$17,000 to free the computer files that had been encrypted.

Petya attacked companies in Ukraine and Russia and infected the Boryspil International Airport in Kiev. The Merck laboratory was also a victim of global hacking, as was the British multinational advertising company WPP and the port of Rotterdam.

---

* Nathaniel Popper, "Ransomware Attacks Grow, Crippling Cities and Businesses," https://www.nytimes.com/2020/02/09/technology/ransomware-attacks.html, February 9, 2020.

† Nathaniel Popper, "Ransomware Attacks Grow, Crippling Cities and Businesses," https://www.nytimes.com/2020/02/09/technology/ransomware-attacks.html, February 9, 2020.

The text of the Petya virus says:

> If you read this text, then your files are no longer accessible because they have been encrypted. Maybe you're busy looking for a way to recover your files but do not waste your time. No one can recover them without a decryption service.
>   We guarantee that you can recover all your files safely and easily, all you need to do is send the payment and buy the decryption key.

This virus could be associated with the Trojan Loki Bot that steals personal information (users and passwords) of the encrypted machines.

Financial services companies in the United States lost an average of US$23.6 million due to cybersecurity breaches in 2013.* In 2014, global credit and debit card fraud losses exceeded US$16 billion, of which more than 48% occurred in the United States.†

Leon Panetta, former US secretary of defense, addressed the US Congress on June 14, 2012, and said:

> We are literally the target of thousands of cyber-attacks every day. I'm very concerned with the potential in cyber to be able to cripple our power grid, to be able to cripple our government systems, to be able to cripple our financial system, which would practically paralyze this country. And as far as I'm concerned, that represents the potential for another Pearl Harbor.‡

Ted Koppel is an English-American journalist who in 2015 wrote a book called *Lights Out*. In his book, Koppel raises the possibility of a cyberterrorist attack that causes chaos for millions of people with dramatic consequences such as darkness, loss of refrigeration and food, and problems in communications, bank transfers, and running water. In other words, Koppel raises the risk of a cyber-attack that leaves a country or an entire region without electricity.

A few months after the book was published, on December 23, 2015, the first cyber-attack of this type occurred on an electric power plant in Ukraine, which cut the electricity supply in half the households in the Ivano-Frankivsk region. More than 200,000 people were left without electricity as a result of hackers using a code known as the *Black Energy Trojan*.

---

* www.revisasumma.com.
† www.nilsonreport.com.
‡ David Childers, "Cyber Compliance: What Every CEO, CRO, and CLO Need to Know."

One of the first cyber-attacks occurred at the Natanz nuclear plant in Iran in 2010. The Stuxnet virus was introduced to the plant when one of the plant's nuclear engineers connected a USB infected with that virus. The computer worm broke centrifuges used to enrich uranium. Siemens has made a Stuxnet detection and disposal tool available to the public.*

The Nuclear Threat Initiative is an organization founded by American businessman Ted Turner and former US senator Sam Nunn, whose aim is to strengthen global security by reducing nuclear, biological, and chemical weapons. In January 2016, this organization published a study that stated nuclear plants in many countries are at risk of being hacked by not having adequate protection against cyber-attacks.

The Center for Strategic Studies in Washington D.C. maintains a registry of cyber-attacks with losses of more than US$1 million and in 2018 they accounted for more than 100.†

Seventy state and local governments across the United States, including the city of New Orleans, suffered ransomware attacks in 2019.

Local governments are more frequently opting to pay the ransomware rather than rebuild their systems. After seeing Atlanta spend US$2.6 million to restore its systems rather than pay the US$52,000 ransom, many officials have decided that it's cheaper to pay the hackers.‡

Two Florida cities paid a combined US$1.06 million to hackers over ransomware attacks. In New Bedford, Massachusetts, hackers demanded a US$5.3 million ransom and rejected the city's offer of US$400,000 to restore its systems.§

"Because of the ransomware attacks recently, we've now made decisions to back up more frequently," said Kenn Kern, the New York County district attorney office's chief information officer. The office used to back up all its files once a day at 3 a.m., but now does it twice a day and is considering doing it more frequently.⁵

---

* Jose Porretti, "Ejercitos de Hackers y Ataques Ciberneticos: el Mundo ante un Nuevo Estilo de Guerra sin Reglas ni Limites," 21 de Septiembre de 2019, www.infobae.com ("Army of Hackers and Cyber Attacks: the World in a New Style of War without Rules or Limits", September 21, 2019).

† Jose Porretti, "Ejercitos de Hackers y Ataques Ciberneticos: el Mundo ante un Nuevo Estilo de Guerra sin Reglas ni Limites," 21 de Septiembre de 2019, www.infobae.com ("Army of Hackers and Cyber Attacks: the World in a New Style of War without Rules or Limits"), September 21, 2019.

‡ Alfred Ng, "Ransomware froze more cities in 2019. Next year is a toss-up," www.cnet.com/news/ra nsomware-devastated-cities-in-2019-officials-hope-to-stop-a-repeat-in-2020/ December 5, 2019.

§ Alfred Ng, "Ransomware froze more cities in 2019. Next year is a toss-up," www.cnet.com/news/ra nsomware-devastated-cities-in-2019-officials-hope-to-stop-a-repeat-in-2020/, December 5, 2019.

⁵ Alfred Ng, "Ransomware froze more cities in 2019. Next year is a toss-up," www.cnet.com/news/ra nsomware-devastated-cities-in-2019-officials-hope-to-stop-a-repeat-in-2020/, December 5, 2019.

Today many countries have a cybersecurity team in their national defense systems.

Large companies handle millions of customer transactions every hour. The ethical concerns raised by Big Data relate to capturing data, data storage, data analysis, search, sharing, transfer, visualization, querying, updating, privacy, and data source.*

Target Corporation, founded in 1962 in Minneapolis, Minnesota, is one of the largest retailers in the United States. The company suffered a cyber-attack during the 2013 Christmas season that affected 70 million customers and was one of the largest in US business history. Names, phone numbers, and email addresses were stolen. Target proposed paying up to US$10,000 in damages to each of the customers who were affected by the theft and who could prove that they were harmed by the theft of their data.† The retail company announced it hired a CIO to guide the transformation of the company's information technology and provided details on improvements on security as a result of the event that occurred in 2013 due to failures in data protection.‡ Target in the same statement said that it was actively seeking an information security director and a compliance director.

Yahoo, the internet company founded by two students at Stanford University in 1994, suffered two cyber-attacks in 2013 and 2014 affecting three billion users. Among the extracted data were names, phone numbers, and birthdays.§

In 2016 Uber was hacked, and data of more than 50 million of its customers were stolen.

In 2017 the consumer reporting agency of Atlanta, Georgia, Equifax announced that the information of 145 million people was compromised by a cyber-attack. As a consequence, sensitive information such as names, Social Security numbers, date of birth, and addresses had been stolen. Equifax took six weeks to announce the hack and a few days after three company executives sold their shares. The CEO of the company had to resign and one of the executives of the organization said: "We should have been quicker, more frequent and more transparent in our customer

---

* "Big Data," Wikipedia.
† "Victims of Cyber Attack on Target Could Receive Up to $10,000," *CNN Money*, March 19, 2015.
‡ April 29, 2014, pressroom.target.com/news.
§ Information provided by Yahoo on October 3, 2017.

communications immediately following the incident."* Equifax reached a US$700 million settlement with US regulators over that breach.

Marriott also suffered one of the biggest corporate data breaches in history in November 2018. Marriott's guest reservation database system was hacked, exposing the personal information of approximately 500 million guests. The New York Attorney General said it has opened an investigation into the data breach and class action lawsuits might materialize against the company.†

In July 2019 Capital One announced that a hacker had accessed about 100 million credit card applications, and investigators say thousands of Social Security and bank account numbers were also taken.

"Although some of the information in those applications (such as Social Security numbers) has been tokenized or encrypted, other information including applicants' names, addresses, dates of birth and information regarding their credit history has not been tokenized," the FBI complaint said. The bank told the bureau that the data includes "likely tens of millions of applications and approximately 77,000 bank account numbers."‡ Some specialists say that the incident could have been avoided or reduced if certain security measures had been taken.§

Hamza Bendelladj is a famous Algerian hacker who used the nickname BX1 or *the Smiler Hacker*. Bendelladj used a computer virus called the *SpyEye* to be able to commit large-scale thefts. This virus infected computers, stole passwords, and emptied accounts. Thanks to SpyEye, Bendelladj managed to extract millions of dollars in money from bank accounts, to close about 8,000 French sites, and to hack websites of the foreign ministries of European countries in order to grant visas to young people in Algeria. Bendelladj also took control of the Israeli government's websites and transmitted classified information to the Palestinian resistance. Part of the looting was intended to financially support nongovernmental organizations in Africa, and he even donated millions of dollars to Palestinian NGOs. Bendelladj for some is a terrorist

---

* Danielle Wiener-Bronner, "How Major Companies Handle and Botch Public Relations Crisis," April 23, 2018, www.money.cnn.com; Danielle Wienner-Bronner, "Equifax Turned Its Hack into a Public Relations Catastrophe," September 13, 2017, www.money.cnn.com.

† Jordan Valinsky, "Marriott Reveals Data Breach of 500 million Starwood Guests," *CNN Business*, November 30, 2018, www.cnn.com.

‡ Devlin Barrett, "Capital One Says Data Breach Affected 100 Million Credit Card Applications," July 29 at 7:36 p.m., www.washingtonpost.com.

§ Desiree Jaimovich, "Cómo Sucedió el Hackeo al Banco Capital One, uno de los más Grandes de los Ultimos Tiempos," July 30, 2019, www.infobae.com ("How Hacking Happened to the Capital One Bank, one of the Largest of Last times").

and for others is considered an internet Robin Hood, for the financial and migratory aid provided to Algerians.

After being sought by the FBI, Interpol, and Mossad, Bendelladj was arrested by Thai police at a Bangkok airport in January 2013 and extradited to the United States and prosecuted for cybercrimes, embezzlement of banks, removal of classified information of the Israeli government, and issuing visas of the French government for Algerians.

Bendelladj has been in prison in the United States since May 2013, serving a sentence of 15 years and an additional 3 years of probation. In their report, the US Department of Justice estimated the "SpyEye" virus had stolen approximately US$1 billion.*

Not everyone understands the importance of computer security and the vulnerability of systems. There is no real awareness of the danger of not securing information.

Ariel Torres, a technology journalist, has written that as a result of computer attacks in recent years:

> The health benefit company Anthem lost 80 million records; The British National Health Service (NHS) lost 26 million medical records; Netflix lost 19 episodes of "Orange is the new Black," Disney lost a full-length film that was about to be released; Ashley Madison lost 33 million user accounts, to E-bay lost data of 145 million members; from JP Morgan was extracted financial information of 76 million individuals and 7 million companies; Home Depot lost 56 million credit card numbers of its customers; Friend Finder lost 412 million emails and their corresponding passwords. In 2014 Yahoo lost data on 500 million accounts of its users.†

Rami Efrati, a former member of the Israeli Defense Forces and CEO of Firmitas, a cybersecurity company, has said that "a person was able to hack the system from an iPhone and turn off a turbine."‡

According to a report by Panda Security, a leading Spanish computer security company, in one quarter, 18 million new instances of malware emerged, or 200,000 new threats daily.§

---

* en.wikipedia.org/wiki/Hamza_Bendelladj.
† Ariel Torres, "Wanna Cry: The Lessons that We Still Do Not Learn," *Diario La Nación*, May 20, 2017.
‡ Muriel Balbi, "Ciberdelito: 10 consejos de un experto Israelí para protegerse de los ataques de hackers," January 17, 2017, www.infobae.com ("Cybercrime: 10 tips from an Israeli expert to protect against hacker attacks").
§ July 29, 2016, www.zonamovilidad.es.

Cybercrime continues to grow, evolve, and improve, and organizations must take appropriate measures to slow down its progress and avoid blocking or theft of stored information. "Anonymous" and "Lazarus" are examples of international cybercrime organizations.

Ransomware attacks have proved hard to identify; however, the US Department of Justice has indicted hackers in Iran, North Korea, and Russia.*

After the problems suffered by cities and large companies such as Facebook, Target, Uber, Yahoo, or Equifax in relation to the preservation of personal data, there is great concern about the protection and good use of customer data. This concern led governments to react by implementing new and more regulations that prohibit the disclosure or misuse of information and data about people.

In May 2018, the *Personal Data Protection Regulation* (GDPR) became effective in the European Union. This directive seeks to harmonize the data privacy laws in the countries that belong to the European Union and it establishes obligations that companies must comply with to protect the personal data they store or process from residents of the European Union. The regulation applies to users residing in the European Union, regardless of where the company that provides the service is located. For example, if a North American company sells services to an individual residing in the European Union, the North American company must comply with the GDPR regulations.† This regulation requires the express consent of individuals so that organizations can use their personal data. The users may also request companies to delete their personal data (the user's right to be forgotten). The regulation also establishes that companies must have prepared a data breach incident response plan in case of an event of a violation of personal data and also companies have to designate a Data Protection Officer (DPO).

If a security breach occurs, the regulation requires companies to notify corresponding authorities within 72 hours of the breach event. Failure to comply with the regulations could generate millions in penalties for companies that can amount to 20 million euros or 4% of the company's turnover, whichever is greater. Complying with this new regulation is not cheap. The International Association of Privacy Professionals has

---

* Nathaniel Popper, "Ransomware Attacks Grow, Crippling Cities and Businesses," https://www.nytimes.com/2020/02/09/technology/ransomware-attacks.html, February 9, 2020.

† Andrew Rossow, "The Birth of GDPR: What Is It and What You Need to Know," May 25, 2018, www.forbes.com.

estimated that the Fortune 500 companies have spent close to US$7 billion to prepare for this new regulation.

Aanand Kishnan, CEO of Tala Security, said, "GDPR went into full effect in May 2018, and in 2019 the EU has fined Google 50 million Euros, British Airways 180 million Euros, and Marriott 100 million Euros." GDPR puts the onus on companies to secure data or face penalties.*

The state of California took the lead in data regulation. The California Consumer Privacy Act (CCPA) entered into force on January 1, 2020 and according to it, certain companies must disclose what information they collect, for what business purpose they do, and with which third party they share that data.†

Kaspersky, a global cybersecurity company with more than 270,000 corporate clients, believes that the cyber threat is likely to target investment apps, online financial data processing systems, and cryptocurrencies. According to Kaspersky, the healthcare industry should focus on protecting medical records, corporate security teams should pay more attention to cloud infrastructure, and telecommunications should be prepared to assess risks that will come with wider adoption of 5G.

There are concerns regarding the 5G technology. 5G stands for fifth generation. 5G promises to deliver a much faster service than its predecessor 4G. 5G is 200 times faster than 4G. That means, for example, you can download an entire movie in about one second.‡

The German economist Daniel Gros said,

> Today's information technology systems are highly complex: current smartphone chips have more than eight billion transistors, and operating systems have more than 50 million lines of code. Moreover, many of these systems contain components supplied by hardware and software vendors from around the world. In practice, this creates multiple possible entry points for malicious attacks and data leaks, using "backdoors" that can be exploited to gain control of a device. And if backdoors cannot be detected and monitored, then entire 5G networks are potentially vulnerable, too.§

---

* Nate Swanner, "5 Cybersecurity Trends that Will Dominate 2020, According to Experts," January 8, 2020, thenextweb.com.
† The United States does not have any centralized, formal legislation at the federal level regarding personal data protection, but does regulate the privacy and protection of data through the US Privacy Act, the Safe Harbor Act, and the Health Insurance Portability and Accountability Act.
‡ Marcia Wendorf, "The Danger of 5G: 5th Generation Cellular Technology Might Be a Threat to Public Health," June 14, 2019, interestingengineering.com.
§ Daniel Gros, "We Must Tackle the Risks of 5G before National Security Is Compromised," August 29, 2019, europeanceo.com.

As a Kaspersky expert says, "There is nothing inevitable in potential upcoming threats, it is just important to be properly prepared for them."*

It is necessary to act proactively to protect personal data and companies must take precautions; for example, by (i) creating backups and copies on external disks and the cloud; (ii) updating antivirus and operating systems; (iii) not entering sites that the browser considers risky; (iv) creating strong passwords combining numbers, letters, and symbols; (v) not clicking on links that offer prizes or with unknown senders; (vi) creating authentication systems with codes or received by text message on the phone; (vii) ignoring alert windows that claim that the computer is in danger and that to save it you must click or call a certain phone; (viii) installing the security update MS17-010;† (ix) training employees to understand the risk to double-click on suspicious digital files; (x) using artificial intelligence systems, algorithms, and machine learning to prevent attacks on operating systems; (xi) taking precautions so that no information is sent to false email addresses or that no money is deposited in false bank accounts, almost identical to the real ones‡; and (xii) encrypting data when they are in transit to the cloud.

A company must protect the information of customers, partners, employees, and the company itself, preventing unauthorized access.

It only takes one wrong click to implant malware. Businesses need to prioritize data security because of hacker attacks and viruses. However, there is a tendency to value privacy too late when it has already been lost.

---

* usa.kaspersky.com.

† This update resolves vulnerabilities in Microsoft Windows. The most serious of these vulnerabilities could allow remote code execution if an attacker sends specially crafted messages to a Microsoft Server Message Block 1.0 server. support.microsoft.com/es.

‡ The so-called CEO Fraud is to send an email to an employee in the Finance area posing as the CEO of the company. The email requests that funds be transferred from the company to a bank account controlled by the scammers. The email refers to the confidentiality of the subject because it is a merger, an acquisition, or other confidential transaction. See "Como es la Estafa Digital por la cual Empresas Argentinas Perdieron Millones de Pesos," Sebastian Davidovsky, www.lanacion.com.ar, December 19, 2018 ("How is the Digital Scam by which Argentine Companies Lost Millions of Pesos").

15

Corporate Risks: Unit 3

15.1 SAFETY OF PRODUCTS AND SERVICES

Companies must provide safe products and services to their customers and employees, and for companies that produce or market products, the lack of product safety is a risk.

When businesses agree to sell consumers a specific quality of goods or services for a specified price, consumers expect to receive the promised product, and they expect that the product will not have any unexpected or hidden harmful effects. Businesses selling products to consumers are legally constrained by implied warranty, the expectation that their products are fit for normal use even if no written guarantee is provided.[*]

The whole process of manufacturing, loading, and transporting to distribution centers and to the stores, carries risks. Defective products, those without legal authorizations, and those not complying with legal labeling and precise instruction on their use can affect the reputation of the company.

Shortening a drug's trial period to market it quickly can endanger the health of the population and cause serious harm. The same happens if you give an incorrect medication or if errors are made with dosing. In 2017 more than 47,000 Americans died as a result of an opioid overdose.[†] Pharmaceuticals must have the knowledge to support people to use opioids safely and effectively.

---

[*] K. Blanchard, C. Schewe, B. Nelson and A. Hiam, *Exploring the World of Business* (Worth Publishers, 1996), 108.

[†] "National Institute of Drug Abuse," www.drugabuse.gov/drugs-abuse/opioids January 2019.

Medical errors are the third leading cause of death in the United States after cardiovascular disease and cancer. According to information from the *British Medical Journal*, in the United States, there are 250,000 annual deaths due to medical mistakes.[*]

Potassium bromate is a salt composed of bromate and potassium ions and was patented as a bread improver in 1914. In 1982 Japanese scientist Yuki Kurokawa showed potassium bromate caused cancer in rats and could be carcinogenic to people, so it is prohibited for use in the food codes of many countries.

Distributors in the toy industry have experienced problems with the safety of products imported from China. For example, the use of lead paint is prohibited for certain products in Western countries[†] and toys with plasticizers such as phthalate can be toxic to children.

Many companies have dealt with the problems generated by unsafe products. Here are some examples:

Mattel: In 2007, Mattel Inc. announced some of its toys manufactured by third parties contained lead in the paint. This resulted in their massive recall. The toy recall had estimated damage of US$110 million due to the lost sale during the holidays, and the market value of Mattel dropped.

Firestone: The company was founded in the late nineteenth century and it is headquartered in Ohio. Firestone was one of the leading tire suppliers in the United States for more than 70 years. In 1988 the company was acquired by Bridgestone. Firestone manufactured tires for Formula 1 vehicles from 1950 to 1974, when the tires were recalled due to several fatal accidents. A new series of crashes caused by Bridgestone/Firestone tires in 2000 led Bridgestone to remove 6.5 million tires used to equip Ford Explorer vans after 148 deaths in the United States were apparently caused by a defect in their tires.[‡]

"The problem," said George Whalin, president of Retail Consultants, "is tied to Firestone's attitude toward consumers. Once the managers had received the communication from the US authorities, they had to

---

[*] "Los médicos, tercera causa de muerte en los Estados Unidos," May 4, 2016, www.elmundo.es ("Doctors, third cause of death in the United States").

[†] Eric Lipton and Louise Story, "Toy Makers Seek Standards for US Safety," *New York Times*, September 7, 2007; Eric Lipton and Gardiner Harris, "In Turnaround Industries Seek US Regulations," *New York Times*, September 16, 2007.

[‡] www.nytimes.com, January 12, 2001.

immediately block the production of Firestone's tires; however, they continue producing the tires three more months."*

Regarding the recall of the defective tires, the CEO of Bridgestone Yoichiro Kaizaki said: "I decided on this move to strengthen our management in a rapidly changing global environment and win back the trust of our customers and shareholders."†

His successor, Shigeo Watanabe, said: "The biggest agenda will be to regain the brand image and trust."‡

Ford Pinto: The Ford Pinto was a compact car launched in 1971 in the United States to compete against small imported Japanese cars. Manufacturing would be done in record time (25 months), about 18 months faster than a standard car. It was a great success, and in the first year, Ford sold more than 400,000 units.

But the car had several critical defects; the fuel tank was behind the rear axle, and in a collision, the car exploded easily; the doors were also blocked, and the occupants were trapped in the flames.

The company was aware of these safety problems in the tests prior to its commercialization and was warned by its engineers, but the company's managers evaluated the potential costs and financial benefits of manufacturing the car and concluded that fixing the failures was more expensive than paying potential compensation for accidents that might happen.

In this way, as explained by Professor Patrick Grim, in pre-production, a different location of the fuel tank was considered, but the idea was rejected because it took up too much space. The problem could also have been solved at the cost of US$11 per car with a fire-prevention device in the gas tank. Ford's decision not to fix the problem was based on a cost-benefit analysis that calculates potential benefits and potential costs for each available option. The potential cost of the US$11 fix was expected to come to US$137 million. The potential benefit was calculated at US$49.5 million because Ford predicted 2,100 vehicles burned without the extinguisher, 180 serious burn injuries, and 180 burn deaths.§

---

* "Bridgestone Decided to Remove the Tires from the Ford Explorer," August 11, 2000, www.lanacion.com.ar.

† "Bridgestone President Kaizaki to Resign," abcnews.go.com/Business..

‡ Hiki Tanikawa, "Chief of Bridgestone Says He Will Resign," January 12, 2001, www.nytimes.com.

§ Burn injuries were estimated at US$67,000 and the value of human life was estimated at US$200,000 (which was the value of human life used in the 1972 report from the National Highway Traffic Safety Administration). *Questions of Value*, Professor Patrick Grim, The State University of New York at Stony Brook, *The Great Courses*, Course Guidebook, Lecture 8, 28–9.

Ford did not take enough ethical consideration for human lives that could be at risk into account and decided to go ahead with the production of cars. As a result of this decision, 12 people died, and many were injured. Ford began to face trials and to have reputational problems.

In 1978 the US Department of Transportation announced that the Pinto fuel system had a safety defect and Ford removed 1.5 million vehicles. Ford's reputation was damaged, and the company had to spend hundreds of millions of dollars to pay for the trials.* Around 117 lawsuits were filed against Ford related to the accidents generated by the defect in the fuel tank of the Ford Pinto.†

Linda Trevino and Katherine Nelson wrote,

> Organizational decision-makers must rely on quantitative analysis in making business decisions. But their reliance on numbers, to the exclusion of ethical considerations, is problematic and contributes to an unethical culture. Attempts to reduce complex decision making to quantitative terms aren't uncommon, especially in a highly competitive business environment.‡

Toyota: The Toyota Motor Corporation was founded in 1937 by Kiichiro Toyota, and in 1957 his cousin Eiji Toyoda became the head of the company and expanded worldwide. In 2008 the Japanese automaker was ranked No.1 on a list of the 600 largest companies in the world for having the best reputation.§

In 2010, Toyota had to call 2.3 million vehicles in the United States due to the spontaneous acceleration in some models manufactured between 2007 and 2010. The flaw in the safety of the acceleration pedals of the Toyota and Lexus vehicles could have been the cause of about a dozen deaths.

As a result of the scandal generated by these security issues, Toyota had to pay the US Department of Justice US$1.2 billion after reaching an agreement.⁵ The lack of safety generated an impact on Toyota's reputation as a safe, high-quality brand.

---

* Max H. Bazerman and Ann E. Tenbrunsel, "Ethical Breakdowns," April 2011, www.HBR.org.
† en.wikipedia.org/wiki/Ford_Pinto.
‡ Linda Trevino and Katherine Nelson, *Managing Business Ethics*, 5th ed (John Wiley & Sons, Inc., 2011), 179, 104.
§ Matthew Kirdahy, "The World's Most Reputable Companies," June 4, 2008, www.forbes.com.
⁵ *Fox News*, September 30, 2014.

General Motors: General Motors had to recall about 800,000 of its small cars due to faulty ignition switches, which could shut off the engine during driving and prevent the airbags from inflating. The company continued to recall more of its cars over the next several months, resulting in nearly 30 million cars worldwide recalled and paid compensation for 124 deaths.* The fault had been known to GM for at least a decade prior to the recall being declared. GM learned of the defect in the development phase prior to the production of the vehicle. GM agreed to forfeit US$900 million to the United States. GM gave US$600 million in compensation to surviving victims of accidents caused by faulty ignition switches.

GM's spokesperson noted, "General Motors is fully committed to learning from the past and adopting the highest standards of quality and performance, now and in the future."†

Grunenthal: Thalidomide is a drug used mainly for the treatment of some types of cancer and was released in 1957 in West Germany under the name of Contergan, marketed by the pharmaceutical company Grunenthal. The product was supposed to soothe nausea, insomnia, and gastritis and was being prescribed to expecting mothers.

Shortly after the drug was sold in Germany, thousands of babies were born with malformations, and only 40% of those children managed to survive. The Thalidomide catastrophe was the worst tragedy in the history of the German pharmaceutical industry, which produced some 10,000 malformations,‡ and generated the creation of new regulations to control the use and sale of drugs.

Johnson & Johnson: Johnson & Johnson is a multinational company based in New Jersey, founded in 1866. Its name comes from the surnames of the founders of the company and is a manufacturer of pharmaceuticals, personal care products, perfumes, and baby products.

Johnson & Johnson produced Tylenol, the best-selling analgesic in the United States. Tylenol was a leading product that accounted for almost 20% of the company's profits and accounted for almost 40% of the

---

* en.wikipedia.org/wiki/General_Motors_ignition_switch_recalls.

† Gregory Wallace, "GM oculto falla de Saturn Ion," March 3, 2014, www.espansion.mx/negocios ("GM hidden failure of Saturn Ion").

‡ See the Book of Adrian Slywotzky, *Value Migration* (Paidos, 1997), 162. See also the article "Grunenthal Asks Forgiveness of the Victims of Thalidomide," September 4, 2012, www. Compromisorse.com.

market share. In 1982, someone replaced Tylenol capsules with cyanide capsules and seven people who took Tylenol died in Chicago. The leading product, the product customers trusted, was transformed into a poison, a contaminated medicine that killed its buyers.

Hundreds of articles related to the tragedy of Tylenol were published in US newspapers and there were hours of television coverage of this news. In the first week of the crisis, the majority of the US population heard and learned about the deaths caused by the consumption of contaminated Tylenol.*

The company handled the situation well by putting the customers first. Johnson & Johnson ordered the withdrawal of all the capsules on sale, created a communication campaign, installed a 1-800 telephone line, organized press conferences, and created new security packaging. Tylenol became the first product in the industry to use resistant packaging.

In 2010, Johnson & Johnson paid millions of dollars in commissions to doctors to recommend Risperdal to certain patients to increase their sales.† The company apparently promoted the use of Risperdal to certain patients when it had not yet received final approval from the FDA (the US Food and Drug Administration)‡ and had to pay more than US$2.2 billion in fines.

In August 2017, a jury in Los Angeles, California, convicted Johnson & Johnson and ordered it to pay US$417 million because their baby powder caused ovarian cancer in a 63-year-old woman. Johnson and Johnson would face more than 4,500 complaints related to baby powder, and although the company has appealed the ruling, reputational damage has already occurred.§ In 2018 the company was found liable for having traces of asbestos in their talcum powder products. A Missouri judge ordered the healthcare giant to pay US$4.14 billion in punitive damages for not having warned its customers that talc could cause ovarian cancer. Johnson & Johnson was also ordered to pay the women compensatory damages of US$550 million. Twenty-two women testified in Court. The women said decades of use of baby powder and other cosmetic talc products caused their diseases. They alleged the company knew its

---

* The issue continued to appear in the media. See "Tylenol Killings Remain Unsolved and Unforgotten after 30 Years," *US News*, October 11, 2013.
† www.medicaldaily.com, July 20, 2010.
‡ US Food and Drug Administration.
§ "L.A. Jury Hits Johnson & Johnson with $417 Million Verdict over Cancer Link to its Talc," *Los Angeles Times*, August 22, 2017.

talc was contaminated with asbestos since the 1970s but failed to warn consumers about the risks.*

Pfizer: The US pharmaceutical company Pfizer Inc. was founded by German immigrants in 1849 in Brooklyn, New York, and since 1942 produces penicillin worldwide.

In 1996, Pfizer used its new antibiotic Trovan against meningitis in 200 sick children who were in a hospital in Kano, Nigeria. Eleven of these children died, and others suffered malformations. Pfizer had no written authorization from the parents of the children, from regulatory bodies, or from Nigerian authorities. Pfizer's test would not have met the protocols of the 1964 Declaration of Helsinki, promulgated by the World Medical Assembly.

The Declaration contains a set of ethical principles that guide the medical community. For example, some of these principles state that

> medical research is subject to ethical standards that promote and ensure respect for all human subjects and protect their health and rights. ... While the primary purpose of medical research is to generate new knowledge, this goal can never take precedence over the rights and interests of individual research subjects.†

In 2009 Pfizer pledged to pay US$75 million to families as compensation.‡

Years ago, Pfizer launched the drug for use and treatment without the approval by the FDA. In 2012 the pharmaceutical giant agreed to pay US$2.3 billion to reach an out-of-court settlement. Pfizer's chief attorney said, "We regret certain actions of the past, but we are proud of what we did to strengthen our internal controls."§

Merck: In 2004, Merck, one of the world's largest pharmaceutical companies, recalled Vioxx. The reason was that the consumption of this drug could lead to cardiovascular problems and heart attacks. In 2007,

---

* Jonathan D. Rockoff and Sara Randazzo, "J&J Hit with $4.7 Billion Jury Verdict in Baby Powder Suit," *The Wall Street Journal*, July 12, 2018. "J&J Shares Drop after Jury Orders Company to Pay nearly US$4.7 Billion in Missouri Asbestos Cancer Case," www.cnbc.com.
† World Medical Association, "WMA Declaration of Helsinki-ethical Principles for Medical Research Involving Human Subjects," www.wma.net.
‡ "Pfizer to Pay $75 Million to Settle Nigerian Trovan Drug – Testing Suit," July 31, 2009, www.washingtonpost.com; "Pfizer to Pay $75 M in Trovan Settlement – Source," *Reuters*, www.reuters.com.
§ "A Fine Record for Pfizer," *BBC World*, September 2, 2009, www.bbc.co.uk.

Merck created a compensation fund of US$4.85 billion to address 27,000 lawsuits filed against its anti-inflammatory drug.

Intel Corporation: Founded in 1968, Intel is the largest manufacturer of microprocessors for personal computers. In October 1994, mathematics professor Thomas Nicely of Lynchburg College of Virginia wrote a memo to Intel reporting that their Pentium chips were producing inaccurate results.[*]

Intel initially denied the existence of the problem, remarked the insignificance of the defects, and refused to replace the defective microprocessors. The microprocessor error was known as Pentium FDIV Error, and Intel Pentium users demanded replacement. The solution to the problem ended up costing Intel US$475 million. Then it was learned that the company had identified the error six months before Professor Nicely warned the company.[†]

Dell: Dell is a North American multinational company that manufactures and sells personal computers. The company grew over the years to become one of the largest PC vendors in the world.

In 2006, a video of a Dell laptop spontaneously combusting was reported at a conference in Osaka, Japan. When the video came to the media, Dell responded by saying the problem was an isolated incident. A month later, another Dell laptop exploded in Illinois, and a few days later, something similar happened in Singapore. A few weeks later, Dell announced the recall of defective products and 4 million Sony batteries.[‡]

Samsung: Samsung is a giant conglomerate of companies founded in 1938 in South Korea. The group's sales are estimated at 17% of South Korea's GDP. Samsung Electronics, founded in 1969, is the largest business unit within the Samsung group and employs about 500,000 people.

The company launched 2.5 million Galaxy Note 7 smartphones in the middle of 2016, but two weeks after the launch of the product, it had to suspend the phone's manufacture and proceeded to recall the phones. Due to a manufacturing defect in the placement of rechargeable lithium-ion batteries, the positive and negative terminals – anode and cathode – came

---

[*] The memo of October 30, 1994, that Nicely sent to Intel can be viewed at www.trnicely.net. The memo says, "Bug in the Pentium FPU," and addresses Intel as "To whom it might concern."

[†] Alicia Borghi, "The Biggest Scandals in the Technology Industry," April 2011.

[‡] Alicia Borghi, "The Biggest Scandals in the Technology Industry," April 2011.

into contact, and the apparatus overheated, exploded, and ignited. A Galaxy Note 7 exploded in a hotel in Australia; another triggered a car fire in Florida, and a child in New York hurt his hands.

In Louisville, Kentucky, the smartphone of a Southwest Airlines passenger going to Baltimore, Maryland, began to heat and burned part of the carpet of the airplane, which generated smoke and forced the cancellation of the flight and evacuation of the passengers. The scandal caused several airlines to ban these phones in their aircraft because of the risk of fire.

In two days, the South Korean company lost more than US$15 billion of stock market capitalization, and the price of its shares dropped 11% in two days. The images of charred phones flooded social networks, aggravated the situation, and affected the image of Samsung as a quality brand.

Monsanto: The Monsanto group was found guilty of negligence by a California jury and sentenced to pay US$81 million for the damage caused to an individual suffering from cancer who attributes his illness to his exposure to the Round-Up for years. Round-Up is an herbicide based on glyphosate. The lawsuit alleged Monsanto knew or should have known about the risks of the product and did not provide adequate warnings. The plaintiff's attorneys noted the jury sent a message to Monsanto that "it needs to change the way it does business."*

McDonald's: McDonald's opened its first fast-food restaurant in 1940 in San Bernardino, California, and currently serves about 60 million customers per day in some 33,000 establishments in more than 100 countries around the world.[†]

On February 27, 1992, Stella Liebeck, a 79-year-old woman from New Mexico, USA, ordered a cup of 49-cent coffee at a McDonald's drive-up with her grandson in the car.

She placed the cup of coffee between her legs, and when she removed the lid to add sugar and cream, she spilled the contents of the container over her knees. Her cotton trousers absorbed the boiling liquid and held

---

* A former California gardener was compensated with $78 million when the state court jury found that Round-Up caused his cancer. Monsanto faces hundreds of similar lawsuits in the United States. "Monsanto Sentenced Paying USD81 Million for Negligence," March 27, 2019, www.info-bae.com; "Sentence to Monsanto for Not Warning that Herbicide May Produce Cancer," March 28, 2019, www.elpais.com.

[†] Its global presence led the magazine *The Economist* to produce the Big Mac index that compares the cost of living of countries through the price of a hamburger.

it against her skin, burning her thighs, buttocks, and groin. Liebeck was taken to the hospital, where she was found to have third-degree burns on 6% of her skin and had to stay in the hospital for eight days, during which time she lost 20 pounds. Her treatment continued for two more years.

Liebeck wanted McDonald's to pay for hospitalization and treatment costs and asked for US$20,000 as compensation, but McDonald's only offered US$800. A trial took place in 1994. Liebeck had filed a lawsuit accusing McDonald's of "gross negligence" for selling coffee that was "unreasonably dangerous" and "poorly crafted." Liebeck's lawyers presented to the jury their arguments that 180 °F (82 °C) coffee could produce third-degree burns in about 12 to 15 seconds.

The judge awarded damages at US$640,000 and called McDonald's conduct "careless, monstrous and deliberate."[*] The parties finally agreed on a confidential amount before an appeal was decided.

In June 2011, HBO premiered *Hot Coffee*, a documentary that thoroughly analyzed the Liebeck case.[†]

Cars, medicines, computers, and telephones are not the only products that can create risks. Companies that produce or market food and drinks should ensure the products are not contaminated.

Dasani is a brand of bottled water marketed by the Coca Cola Company, which was launched in 1999. In March 2004, two months after its launch in Great Britain, some 500,000 bottles of Dasani water had to be withdrawn in the United Kingdom after finding high levels of bromate, a chemical that could increase the risk of cancer.

Food poisoning is said to occur when food or water with bacteria, parasites, viruses, or toxins is ingested. Foods in poor condition, poorly cooked, or poorly washed can represent a source of bacteria and viruses and produce illness in those who consume them.

Each year 600 million people suffer from some type of food poisoning, that is, 1 in 10 people living in the world. Of that group, 400,000 die and 25% of those deaths are children under 5 years old, according to data provided by the World Health Organization.[‡]

---

[*] Jonathan Rosenfeld, "Liebeck v. McDonald's: The Hot Coffee Controversy," May 11, 2015, www.rosenfeldinjurylawyers.com/news/liebeck-v-mcdonalds-the-hot-coffee-controversy; "Liebeck v. McDonald's Restaurants," en.wikipedia.org/wiki/Liebeck_v._McDonald%27s_Restaurants.

[†] Directed by Susan Saladoff.

[‡] December 3, 2015, www.who.int/en/news-room/detail/03-12-2015-who-s-first-ever-global-estimates-of-foodborne-diseases-find-children-under-5-account-for-almost-one-third-of-deaths.

The three most frequent pathogens that cause the highest number of deaths annually are (i) *Salmonella* with more than 50,000 deaths, (ii) *Escherichia coli* (*E. coli*) with more than 37,000 deaths, and (iii) *Norovirus* with more than 35,000 deaths. The regions most affected are Africa and Southeast Asia, with two-thirds of the deaths from food poisoning.

Salmonellosis, caused by the bacterium *Salmonella*, is the main cause of foodborne disease.* People get salmonellosis due to the consumption of contaminated animal foods (eggs, meat, poultry, and milk) and the consumption of vegetables if contaminated with manure.

The prevention of diseases caused by these pathogens requires control measures at all stages of the food chain, from agricultural production to processing, manufacturing, and preparation of food in both commercial establishments and households.

The consumer is not only interested in purchasing food, in addition, consumers are also interested in knowing *how* that food was obtained or prepared. The causes of food contamination are many, among which is the use of chemical agents to protect crops (some of them very toxic pesticides), a broken cold chain,† cross-contamination, or the presence of pests and rodents in places where food is produced, stored, or marketed.‡

Here are some examples of food companies that suffered this type of problem:

McDonald's: In July 2014, the company sold meat not fit for consumption in China, where it operates about 2,000 restaurants. The scandal erupted after it became known that a Chinese supplier was supplying McDonald's with meat in poor condition and systematically forged the expiration date. McDonald's global sales were reduced by 3.7% that year due to the beef scandal, which negatively impacted its branches in China and Japan.

The Spinach from San Benito: In September 2006, there was an outbreak of foodborne, an illness caused by *E. coli* bacteria found in uncooked spinach in 26 US states. By October 6, 2006, 199 people had been infected

---

* Both salmonellosis and *Salmonella* are a *Latinization* of the name of Daniel Elmer Salmon (1850–1914), an American veterinarian.
† A cold chain or cool chain is a temperature-controlled supply chain. An unbroken cold chain is an uninterrupted series of refrigerated production, storage, and distribution activities, along with associated equipment and logistics, which maintain a desired low-temperature range. en.wikipedia.org/wiki/Cold_chain.
‡ The 2008 documentary *Food Inc.*, directed by the American film director Robert Kenner, presents a critical vision on the American food industry.

including 3 people who died and 31 who suffered a type of kidney failure called hemolytic uremic syndrome after eating spinach contaminated with *E. coli* 0157: H7, a potentially deadly bacterium that causes bloody diarrhea and dehydration. The outbreak was traced to spinach grown on a 50-acre farm in San Benito County, California, which potentially originated from irrigation water contaminated with cattle feces or from grazing deer.*

Peanut Corporation of America: Peanut Corporation of America (PCA) was a peanut-processing business with headquarters in Virginia, USA. Between 2006 and 2009, as a result of a *Salmonella* contamination event, 9 people died and at least 714 people fell ill, all from food poisoning after eating products containing contaminated peanuts of PCA. This contamination triggered one of the most extensive food recalls in US history, involving 46 states, more than 360 companies, and more than 3,900 different products manufactured using PCA ingredients. On February 13, 2009, Peanut Corporation of America ceased all manufacturing and business operations and filed for bankruptcy liquidation. The CEO was sentenced to 28 years in prison for his role in the nationwide outbreak.[†]

Chipotle: In 2015, the Chipotle Mexican Grill chain of restaurants suffered different outbreaks of *E. coli*, salmonella, and norovirus in some of its restaurants in the United States, and 47 people became ill. The company decided to close 43 restaurants to conduct an investigation and pledged to strengthen its food safety processes.

Jack in the Box: Jack in the Box is a fast-food restaurant franchise founded in 1951 in San Diego, California, with about 2,000 restaurants in the United States. The company experienced a serious crisis in 1993 after 4 children died and about 600 people became ill due to an epidemic of *E. coli* caused by contaminated meat. Victims experienced fever, vomiting, and bloody diarrhea. Jack in the Box had to close dozens of restaurants, and the company introduced new regulations for its franchises on food preparation and a control process to ensure food safety.

Domino's Pizza: Domino's was founded in 1960 and is the second-largest pizza chain in the United States after Pizza Hut. It has 10,000 establishments with franchises in more than 60 countries.

---

* "2006 North American *E. coli*: 0157: H7 Outbreak in Spinach," en.wikipedia.org/wiki.
† "Peanut Corporation of America," en.wikipedia.org/wiki/ Peanut_Corporation_of_America.

In April 2009, two Domino's Pizza employees in North Carolina performed inappropriate activities with the dough, and the video was uploaded to social networks. By the time the video was deleted from YouTube, over a million people had viewed it and had reported the subject to the mass media such as NBC and *The New York Times*.

In February of 2015, another incident occurred in a Domino's restaurant in Peru: "We had already eaten a half pizza when I realized that among the tomato sauce, pepperoni and cheese there was a dead cockroach," the Peruvian customer told the *BBC World*.[*] The customer reported the incident to the store manager and then posted a photo of the cockroach on the pizza on his Twitter and Facebook accounts. His complaint went viral on social networks, resulting in the temporary closure of all Domino's franchises in Peru. The company then undertook to perform an audit of all its processes and facilities by an independent institution. The company suffered the snowball effect, where a cockroach on a pizza in a local in Lima caused the closure of all Domino's stores in Peru.

Another type of risk is food fraud. For example, in Spain in 1981, people consumed colza oil that had been intended for industrial rather than food use. It was sold as "olive oil" by street vendors at street markets and was used in salads dressings and for cooking. The outbreak killed over 600 people.[†]

In 2013, in Europe, foods advertised as containing beef were found to contain undeclared or improperly declared horse meat. The issue came to light on January 15, 2013, when it was reported that horse DNA had been discovered in frozen beef burgers sold in Irish and British supermarkets. While the presence of undeclared meat was not a health issue, the scandal revealed a major breakdown in the traceability of the food supply chain, and the risk that harmful ingredients could have been included as well.[‡]

Other cases of food fraud include milk, honey, coffee, tea, fish, or orange juice. Likewise, inorganic foods may be labeled and sold as organic. That is also a fraud.[§] For example, a businessman from Daventry (UK) was sentenced to 27 months in prison for selling organic foods that were not. The businessman purchased non-organic products from different

---

[*] BBC World, April 4, 2015, www.bbc.co.uk.

[†] en.wikipedia.org/wiki/Toxic_oil_syndrome.

[‡] en.wikipedia.org/wiki/2013_horse_meat_scandal.

[§] The US Farnacopean Convention has developed a food fraud prevention guide to mitigating its effects.

supermarkets and then marketed the products throughout the United Kingdom as if they were organic.*

The Food and Drug Administration (FDA), formed in 1906, is the US federal agency responsible for protecting and promoting public health through the control and supervision of food safety, tobacco products, dietary supplements, prescription and over-the-counter pharmaceutical drugs, vaccines, biopharmaceuticals, blood transfusions, medical devices, electromagnetic radiation emitting devices, cosmetics, animal foods, and veterinary products.[†] The FDA enforces the *Federal Food, Drug, and Cosmetic Act* (FD&C), a set of laws passed by Congress in 1938.

In the United States, the 1972 *Consumer Product Safety Act* (CPSA) established the United States Consumer Product Safety Commission (CPSC) with the power to develop safety standards and pursue recalls for products that present unreasonable or substantial risks of injury or death to consumers. CPSC can ban products and has jurisdiction over more than 15,000 different consumer products. The CPSA excludes from jurisdiction those products that expressly lie in another federal agency's jurisdiction, for example, food, drugs, cosmetics, medical devices, tobacco products, firearms and ammunition, motor vehicles, pesticides, aircraft, and boats.[‡]

In 2008, the *Consumer Product Safety Improvement Act* became effective. Among other provisions, this law protects whistleblowers who take certain actions to raise concerns about consumer product safety. The law requires manufacturers and importers of all children's products to have batches of their products tested by an independent certified laboratory.[§]

In order to improve the consumer protection of food products, the *Global Food Safety Initiative* (GFSI) was launched in 2000. GFSI is a private nonprofit organization that establishes food safety standards that have become a standard for the food industry and help to reduce costs and improve consumer confidence. Certifications awarded by the GFSI exceed the Food and Drug Administration and US Department of Agriculture (USDA) standards, and many multinational companies require their food suppliers to obtain GFSI certification in their factories and facilities.

---

* www.ecoticias.com/agricultura-ecologica/17629/Dos-anos-de-prision-por-fraude-con-alimentos-organicos-uk.

[†] en.wikipedia.org/wiki/Food_and_Drug_Administration.

[‡] These products may fall under the purview of agencies such as the US Food and Drug Administration, the US Bureau of Alcohol, Tobacco, Firearms, and Explosives, the US Department of Agriculture, the US Department of Transportation, the US Environment Protection Agency, and the US Federal Aviation Administration. "Consumer Products Safety Act," en.wikipedia.org/wiki/Consumer_Product_Safety_Act.

[§] "Consumer Products Safety Act," en.wikipedia.org/wiki/Consumer_Product_Safety_Act.

It is important that in the event of a crisis, the company reacts quickly and puts the focus on maintaining or recovering the trust of customers.

If the company does not succeed, it will not be able to survive.

15.2 ENVIRONMENTAL POLLUTION

Environmental pollution consists of the presence of chemical, physical, or biological substances in the environment, which is harmful to health, to the welfare of the population, as well as to animal and plant life.

In 1854, the most violent outbreak of cholera occurred in England, and as a result, 700 people died in less than a week in an area of 0.5 kilometer in diameter. John Snow (1813–1858), an English physician, identified the source of cholera and found that cases of this disease were grouped in areas where the water consumed was contaminated with feces. Snow mapped the water wells in the Soho district, locating one on Broad Street, and when he managed to close the water pump on that street, cholera cases dropped significantly. Snow showed that cholera was caused by drinking water contaminated with fecal matter.

Water is necessary for the development of different forms of life and poor water management in obtaining or preserving this vital element produces its contamination.

The film *Civil Action* (1998) is about a real case of water pollution that occurred in Woburn, Massachusetts, in the 1980s. Companies near a river in Woburn released polluting products, trichloroethylene, that caused cases of leukemia and health problems for the local population.[*] The polluting companies went bankrupt when they could not afford the compensation awarded to victims and the total cleaning of the contaminated area.

Another film based on a true story, *Erin Brockovich* (1999), refers also to a real case of water pollution produced in Hinkley, California, by the Pacific Gas and Electric Company that produced 600 seriously sick people.[†] A chemical, chromium, was in drinking water and that substance came from the factory. The judicial case was reconciled for the sum of US$333 million in 1996.[‡]

---

[*] en.wikipedia.org/wiki/A-civil-Action (2000) Film directed by Steven Zaillian and based on the book of Jonathan Harr.

[†] en.wikipedia.org/wiki/Erin-Brockovich-(film) Film directed by Steven Soderbergh.

[‡] Erin Brockovich lectures on environmental issues.

In both cases, large companies contaminated the water and injured the people who consumed it.

The Australian moral philosopher Peter Singer concerned with the damage occurring to the environment wrote the following thought in 1997:

> The atmosphere and the oceans seemed, until recently, to be elements of nature totally unaffected by the puny activities of human beings. Now we know that our use of chlorofluorocarbons has damaged the ozone shield; our emission of carbon dioxide is changing the climate of the entire planet in unpredictable ways and raising the level of the sea; and fishing fleets are scouring the oceans, depleting fish populations that once seemed limitless to a point from which they may never recover. In these ways, the actions of consumers in Los Angeles can cause skin cancer among Australians, inundate the lands of peasants in Bangladesh, and force Thai villagers who could once earn a living by fishing to work in the factories of Bangkok. In these circumstances the need for a global ethic is inescapable.[*]

An ethical life has better goals. We want to live on a planet where air, water, and food are safe and pollution is not a risk to its inhabitants. Organizations are part of this planet and should avoid damaging the environment.

Management of hazardous waste like corrosive liquids, pesticides, insecticides, aerosols, spray paint, insect spray, fuel, flammable solids, chemicals, oil, and fluorescents tubes should follow policies on waste management.

As the population grows, so does the demand for natural resources, which creates an environmental impact that threatens the ecosystem. The quality of air and water deteriorates, diseases spread, deforestation increases, the land is degraded, and animal species are extinguished.

Jacques Yves Cousteau (1910–1997) was a French explorer and researcher who dedicated his life to protecting the underwater world and defending the environment from pollution.[†] Cousteau said "The sea, the great unifier, is man's only hope. Now, as never before, the old phrase has a literal meaning: we are all in the same boat."[‡]

---

[*] Peter Singer, "The Drowning Child and the Expanding Circle," *New Internationalist*, April 1997, www.utilitarian.net/singer/by/199704--.htm.

[†] Films and documentary series filmed during his explorations on his ship, the *Calypso*, have been broadcast on television for years, making Cousteau the most celebrated of the underwater world newsmen.

[‡] www.brainyquote.com/quotes/jacques_yves_cousteau.

The physical environment in which we live has been damaged. The overuse of raw materials for production is depleting natural resources, and during the process of transforming these materials into products for sale, harmful things are being introduced into the environment.

When the Dutchman Boyan Slat went diving in Greece a few years ago, he found there were more plastics in the sea than fish. After that experience, Slat devised a plan called "Ocean Cleanup" to eradicate millions of pieces of plastic from the oceans.[*]

World plastic production was around 2 million tons in 1950 and became 407 million tons in 2015.[†]

According to a study by Ipbes,[‡] plastic pollution has multiplied tenfold since 1980. According to the study, 75% of terrestrial ecosystems and 66% of marine ecosystems were altered by human actions.[§]

Every year in the world 500 billion plastic bags are used, and according to data from the Fundación Vida Silvestre Argentina (FVSA, Argentine Wildlife Foundation),[¶] some 8 million tons of plastics are dumped into the oceans per year. For example, in the Sargasso Sea (north of the Atlantic Ocean), in 40 years the density increased from 3,500 to 200,000 plastics per square kilometer.[**]

The tons of plastic that reach oceans every year create a danger to health because pieces of plastic smaller than 5 millimeters that do not biodegrade or break down are found in fishes we consume.[††]

---

[*] To do this, they have built a 600-meter long float that captures the plastic found in the ocean. The plastic is then transported ashore on a ship and recycled into durable products. If this system were to be deployed on a large scale, it could eventually eliminate 50% of the plastic waste from the Pacific Ocean in five or six years.

[†] Victor Ingrassia, "De Que Manera la Basura Plastica Acelera el Cambio Climatico," August 16, 2019, www.infobae.com ("How Plastic Waste Accelerates Climate Change").

[‡] The Intergovernmental Science-Policy Platform on Biodiversity and Ecosystem Services is an independent intergovernmental body established for the sustainable use of biodiversity, long-term human well-being, and sustainable development.

[§] Martin de Ambrosio, "El Mundo al Límite: Hay Un Millón de Especies en Peligro," 6 de Mayo de 2019, www.lanacion.com.ar ("The World to the Limit: There Is a Million Endangered Species," May 6, 2019).

[¶] www.vidasilvestre.org.ar.

[**] "La Peticion para Prohibir el Uso de los Sorbetes de Plastico Consigue una Firma por Minuto," 17 de Mayo de 2019, www.infobae.com/america/medio-ambiente ("The Petition to Prohibit the Use of Plastic Straws Get a Signature Per Minute," May 17, 2019).

[††] "Microplásticos: Científicos Observan que son Millones de veces más Abundantes en el Océano de lo que se Pensaba" ("Microplastics: Scientists Observe that They are Millions of Times More Abundant in the Ocean Than Previously Thought"), Victor Ingrassia, December 22, 2019, infobae.com. "Ahogados por el Plástico: la Contaminación en Mares y Océanos crece de forma Alarmante" ("Drowned by Plastic: Pollution in Seas and Oceans Grows Alarmingly"), Victor Ingrassia, December 3, 2019, infobae.com.

If things continue like this, in 2050 there could be more plastics than fish in the oceans.*

In addition to polluting, plastics contribute significantly to climate change. The production and incineration of plastic emit into the atmosphere the greenhouse gas equivalent of 189 coal-fired power plants with 500 megawatts of power.[†]

Recycling is the process of converting waste materials into new reusable objects. This process reduces energy usage and pollution.

The chemical structure of most plastics renders them resistant to many natural processes of degradation.

Some efforts to reduce the use of plastics and to promote plastic recycling have occurred. Since 2018, the British supermarket retailer Asda Stores has removed 8,000 tons of plastic from its own-brand packaging. The company has pledged to reduce its plastic use and committed to ensuring all its own-brand packaging will be 100% recyclable by 2025.[‡]

Nestle, the world's biggest food company, said it will spend US$1.6 billion to buy two million metric tons of recycled plastic. The company also announced a US$260 million venture fund to invest in start-ups that focus on sustainable packaging.[§]

ISO standards are designed to make products and services better and to make organizations more efficient. There are ISO standards related to recycling and recovery of waste plastics such as ISO 15270:2008.[¶]

The Spanish naturalist Felix Rodriguez de la Fuente (1928–1980) has stated: "The man will be finished when the vital balance of the planet that supports it, ends. Man must love and respect the Earth as he loves and respects his own mother."[**]

Nongovernmental organizations such as the World Wildlife Fund, founded in 1961 in Switzerland, or Greenpeace, founded in 1971 in the

* Victor Ingrassia, "De Que Manera la Basura Plastica Acelera el Cambio Climatico," August 16, 2019, www.infobae.com ("How Plastic Waste Accelerates Climate Change").

† "La Peticion para Prohibir el Uso de los Sorbetes de Plastico Consigue una Firma por Minuto," 17 de Mayo de 2019, www.infobae.com/america/medio-ambiente (The Petition to Prohibit the Use of Plastic Straws Get a Signature Per Minute," May 17, 2019).

‡ Sabrina Barr, "ASDA Launching New Sustainability Store with Refill Stations," www.independent.co.uk, January 16, 2020.

§ Hanna Ziady, "Nestle is Spending Billions to Create a Market for Recycled Plastics," January 16, 2020, www.cnn.com.

¶ www.iso.org/standard/45089.html.

** infovaticana.com/blogs/reflexiones-candil/35-anos-sin-felix-rodriguez-de-la-fuente-reivind ico-su-mensaje-siempre-actual/.

Netherlands, seek to halt environmental degradation, conserve biological diversity, ensure the sustainable use of renewable natural resources, and promote the reduction of pollution and pollutant gases by denouncing those who do not comply with international protocols and agreements.

Palm oil, which comes from the palm's fruit, has become increasingly popular around the world as consumers have demanded fewer chemicals in their cosmetics, food, shampoo, and cooking oil. Palm oil is a substance found in Procter & Gamble's (P&G) line of beauty and household care products.

According to the Worldwatch Institute, an environmental research group based in Washington D.C., palm oil production in Indonesia increased by almost 11 million tons from 2000 to 2009 at a cost of 340,000 hectares of forest. Greenpeace translates those figures to a loss of land equivalent to 140 Olympic-sized swimming pools every hour. The deforestation of the Sumatra jungle has caused endangered species such as the Sumatran orangutan and tiger to face the brink of extinction.

A study published in February 2014 by Greenpeace highlighted serious violations committed by some of the P&G's suppliers; Greenpeace has reported that "the palm oil sector is currently the greatest single driver of deforestation in Indonesia, accounting for about a quarter of all forest loss."[*]

Pressure from Greenpeace, including a protest at the company's headquarters in Cincinnati in 2014 and emails to its CEO demanding action against the destruction of the environment, helped Procter & Gamble commit to stop the deforestation of the jungles of Indonesia to obtain the palm oil used in its products.

Orangutans are in danger of extinction by massive felling of trees and deforestation that destroy their natural habitat. For 15 years the population of orangutans has been decreasing by about 10,000 animals per year.[†]

On YouTube, you can watch a video broadcast by International Animal Rescue, in which an orangutan takes advantage of a fallen tree to confront and hit an excavator destroying the forests of Borneo, Indonesia, in June 2018.

---

[*] Dan Horn and Julie Zimmerman, "Procter & Gamble Targeted in Global Palm Oil Battle," *Cincinnati Enquirer*, March 5, 2014. www.USATODAY.com.

[†] YouTube, "Orangután Tries to Fight Bulldozer Destroying Habitat"; see also, María Aragón, "El Dramático Video de un Orangután Luchando contra la Excavadora que Destroza su Hábitat," June 7, 2018, www.el periódico.com ("The Dramatic Video of an Orangutan Fighting the Excavator that Destroys Its Habitat").

The loss of trees can cause climate change, soil erosion, damage to soil quality, floods, and an increase in greenhouse gases in the atmosphere that increase global warming. Seventy percent of the animals and plants on Earth live in the forests and many do not survive deforestation. Forests cover about 30% of the world's land surface and it is estimated that "the world's rainforests could disappear completely by the year 2115 at the current rate of deforestation."*

Some companies are protecting the environment using renewable energy, that is "renewable" and sustainable, so it will never run out. For example, PepsiCo is using 100% renewable energy for its US operations as part of its goal to cut 20% of its greenhouse emissions by 2030.† Simon Lowden, Chief Sustainability Officer at PepsiCo, said, "Climate change is one of the biggest challenges facing our food system."‡

Corporations are getting more sustainable. AstraZeneca, a British-Swedish pharmaceutical company, announced to have zero carbon emissions from its global operations by 2025.§ Delta Air Lines announced it is investing US$1 billion over the next ten years to become the first carbon-neutral airline.¶ In February 2020, Amazon CEO Jeff Bezos announced that he would be committing US$10 billion to fight climate change through a new fund called the Bezos Earth Fund.** The British newspaper *The Guardian* will no longer accept advertising from oil and gas companies, becoming the first major global news organization to institute an outright ban on taking money from companies that extract fossil fuels.††

Fossil fuels are not renewable and the carbon dioxide released by the combustion of fossil fuels is a leading cause of global warming.

The Kyoto Protocol is an international treaty on greenhouse gas reduction, which came into effect in 2005 and was aimed to reduce 5% of global warming emissions compared to 1990. By 2009, 187 countries had ratified the protocol, although the United States, the largest emitter

---

* Salvador García Liñán, "Deforestación y Contaminación," September 1, 2015, www.elfinanciero. com.mx ("Deforestation and Pollution").

† PepsiCo's operations in nine European countries have already reached 100% renewable electricity.

‡ Dieter Hoger, "PepsiCo Moves to 100% Renewable Electricity in US," January 15, 2020, www. marketwatch.com.

§ George Underwood, "AstraZeneca Commits to Being Carbon Negative by 2030," January 22, 2020, pharmaphorum.com.

¶ news.delta.com/delta-commits-1-billion-become-first-carbon-neutral-airline-globally

** Jay Peters, "Jeff Bezos commits $10 billion to fight climate change," February 17, 2020, www.t heverge.com/2020/2/17/21141132/jeff-bezos-earth-fund-ten-billion-climate-change.

†† "Guardian to Ban Advertising from Fossil Fuel Firms," January 20, 2020, www.theguardian.com.

of these gases, did not ratify it. By 2015 the treaty had reached its ten-year anniversary and achieved a 22.6% reduction in greenhouse gas emissions compared to 1990.

The Kyoto Protocol established commitments only for developed countries but did not include China. In 2015, a global agreement was reached at the Climate Summit, dubbed the Paris Agreement, which was a breakthrough in curbing greenhouse gas emissions. China and the United States, together responsible for 38% of greenhouse gas emissions, ratified the agreement, although it will not enter into force until ratified by at least 55 countries, accounting for 55% of global emissions. The international community agreed on a global average temperature not exceeding 2 °C to avoid (i) extinction of species and ecosystems, (ii) the occurrence of extreme weather events, (iii) problems in water supply and food, (iv) migratory movements and social conflicts, and (v) the disappearance of Greenland ice that would cause a sea rise of about 7 meters.

Chinese President Xi Jinping said his country was fighting the causes of climate change and environmental degradation and pledged to close coal mines and steel mills as part of this effort. "I have said many times that green mountains and clear waters are as good as mountains of gold and silver. To protect the environment is to protect productivity, and to improve the environment is to boost productivity."[*]

The larger the corporation, the greater its commitment to society and part of its corporate agenda should be corporate social responsibility. The Argentine painter Ignacio Alperin has stated that

> ethics is not a philosophy lost in time, but a way of living, supportive and considerate of others and everything around us; and as part of it, we continue to learn that caring for nature is caring for others and our children and grandchildren.[†]

Al Gore, former vice president of the United States, has been one of the most well-known spokespeople on environmental issues, addressing issues such as pollution, global warming, and climate change. In 2006, Gore starred in the documentary *An Inconvenient Truth*, which shows the planetary emergency and the destructive spiral caused by industries that

---

[*] Bingxing Li, "China's President Xi Jinping's Opening Address of G20 Summit: A New Blueprint for Global Economic Growth," September 4, 2016, www.globalresearch.ca/chinas-president-xi-jin pings-opening-address-of-g20-summit-a-new-blueprint-for-global-economic-growth/5543895.
[†] www.ignacioalperin.com.

have generated extreme temperatures, floods, droughts, epidemics, and heatwaves. The film won two Oscars for best documentary and has helped to raise awareness among the international public about the problem of climate change.

In October 2007, the Swedish Academy awarded the Nobel Peace Prize to Al Gore, and in his acceptance speech, Gore said: "The climate crisis is not a political issue; it is a moral and spiritual challenge to all of humanity. It is also our greatest opportunity to lift global consciousness to a higher level."[*]

According to the National Oceanic and Atmospheric Administration, in January 2020, the Earth recorded its hottest January in 141 years of records. Four of the hottest months of January have happened from 2016 to 2020. Scientists say global emissions must be halved to address the climate crisis.[†]

As nobody owns the atmosphere, everybody abuses it.

Carbon Majors is the name of a study carried out by geologist Richard Heede of the Climate Accountability Institute. Carbon Majors's website shows the names of the 90 cement and oil-producing entities that generate almost two-thirds of the global emissions of carbon dioxide and methane. There seems to be a clear relationship between the fuel-extraction industry and climate change.

Degradation of the environment by an external pollutant can cause serious damage and alter survival conditions. This requires companies to have processes to reduce gas emissions and effluents and for the proper deposit and transport of hazardous waste.

There are many pollutants used by companies that have harmful consequences for individuals and communities, including chemicals (such as pesticides, cyanide, herbicides, lead, and asbestos), urban waste, petroleum, leaded gasoline, and ionizing radiation. These pollutants can cause disease and damage to ecosystems. In addition, gaseous pollutants play an important role in different atmospheric phenomena such as the generation of acid rain, the weakening of the ozone layer, and climate change. It is necessary to be aware of this risk and its consequences.[‡]

---

[*] "Environmental Activism of Al Gore," en.wikipedia.org/wiki/Environmental_activism_of_Al_Gore.

[†] "Earth just had Hottest January since Records Began, data shows," www.theguardian.com/environment/2020/feb/13/january-hottest-earth-record-climate-crisis?CMP=Share_iOSApp_Other.

[‡] "The Intergovernmental Panel on Climate Change (IPCC)" is a United Nations entity dedicated to providing an objective view of climate change, its impact, and risks.

In 1986 the German sociologist Ulrich Beck (1944–2015), professor at the University of Munich and the London School of Economics, published a book called *Risk Society: Towards a New Modernity*. In that book, Beck warned about the threats and dangers of industrialization. Beck said, "We are almost unprotected from industrial threats. Dangers become stowaways of normal consumption. They travel with the wind and with the water."[*]

Organizations should prevent pollution by using materials, processes, or practices that eliminate or reduce the generation of these pollutants. Planet Earth has no substitute, belongs to humanity, and must be taken care of. Ken Goodpaster, professor at the University of St. Thomas in St. Paul, Minnesota, wrote, "A business should protect and where possible, improve the environment, promote sustainable development and prevent the wasteful use of natural resources."[†]

Paul Polman, CEO of Unilever, said that in 2016, 60% of the company's inputs came from a sustainable source compared to 10% in 2008. This transformation has allowed Unilever to reduce costs by US$400 million from a policy of zero waste in its factories and green energy.[‡]

Outlined below are some of the catastrophes produced by pollution and the consequences they have generated:

The Seveso Disaster: This was an industrial fire that occurred on July 10, 1976, at 12:37 p.m. in a chemical plant subsidiary of the Swiss pharmaceutical multinational Roche. The municipality of Seveso, which at that time had a population of 17,000 people, is located 25 kilometers north of Milan, Italy.

The fire caused panic in the population when TCDD dioxin was released with a polluting impact on the environment. The subsequent security measures were poorly coordinated; it took a week to announce dioxin had been emitted and another week to begin the evacuation. The European Community reacted with new safety standards for industrial plants using hazardous elements such as the Seveso Directive, which imposed new regulations.

Sandoz: On November 1, 1986, after an accidental fire at the Sandoz chemical consortium located in Basel, Switzerland's industrial zone

---

[*] Ulrich Beck, *La Sociedad del Riesgo* (Paidos, 1998), 13 ("Risk Society").
[†] Ken Goodpaster, "Institutionalizing Ethics in a Global Economy," www.helleniccomserve.com.
[‡] *La Nacion*, May 31, 2016.

Schweizerhalle, about 20 tons of insecticides, fungicides, and herbicides reached the Rhine and contaminated its waters with disastrous results for the flora and wildlife. Heavy metals such as zinc, copper, and cadmium as well as pesticides and nitrogen contaminated the river for more than 500 kilometers. It was an environmental catastrophe.

In 1996 the Chemical Consortium Sandoz merged with Ciba-Geigy to form Novartis and had to pay compensation for damages and losses of 43 million francs to Switzerland, Germany, France, and the Netherlands.*

Prestige: On November 13, 2002, the Greek oil tanker *Prestige* broke apart and sank 3,500 meters deep off the Spanish coast with 70,000 tons of fuel oil and produced a black tide affecting hundreds of kilometers. The discharge of the cargo caused one of the largest environmental catastrophes in the history of navigation, generating an ecological disaster.

The cause of the accident was the poor condition of the ship and the load exceeding the permitted weight. In 2001, an inspection was carried out on the vessel that revealed the corrosion of bulkheads in oil tanks, which required the replacement of 1,000 tons of steel, but only 282 were replaced.

The spill flooded beaches and forced a fishing ban for several months across almost 1,000 kilometers. In the first 9 months after the accident, more than 23,000 oil-filled birds were collected, and the vast majority of them died as a result.

Union Carbide Corporation: Union Carbide is one of the oldest chemical and polymer companies in the United States and became known for a very serious industrial accident, the Bhopal disaster, which took place at its pesticide plant in Bhopal, India. At midnight on December 3, 1984, the plant released 42 tons of methyl isocyanate gas by accident, and the wind carried it to the city.

Upon coming into contact with the atmosphere, the released compound decomposed into toxic gases that formed a cloud that covered the city. It is estimated that between 6,000 and 8,000 people were killed by asphyxiation immediately or during the first week after the toxic escape, and at least 12,000 others subsequently died as a direct consequence of the catastrophe. Another 40,000 people were disabled, maimed, or affected by serious illness. During the crisis, the company's shares declined by about US$900 million.

---

* "The Rhine Has Recovered from the Schweizerhalle Disaster," October 31, 2006, www.swissinfo.ch.

The chemical plant was abandoned after the accident. The tragedy also killed thousands of livestock and domestic animals. The whole environment of the accident site was seriously contaminated by toxic substances and heavy metals that will take many years to disappear. The gas leakage still affects children born with malformations, developmental delays, and deafness due to the consumption of contaminated water or the genetic transmission of affected parents.

Union Carbide India and the Indian government agreed in 1989 to a payment of US$470 million; 93% of the 500,000 people who received compensation obtained about 25,000 rupees (approximately 300 euros). On June 7, 2010, the Indian court sentenced eight company executives to two years in prison and the payment of 500,000 rupees (about US$9,000). The remembrance of the tragedy takes place every December 3 and is known as the World Day of Non-use of Pesticides.

The Chernobyl Disaster: The Chernobyl accident happened on April 26, 1986, at the Vladimir Lenin nuclear power station in Ukraine, 7 kilometers from Chernobyl and 18 kilometers from the city of Prypiat. It remains one of the largest environmental disasters in history.[*]

The accident was the result of a flawed reactor design that was operated with inadequately trained personnel.[†] A human error caused a huge surge in power that caused the overheating of Reactor 4, producing an explosion and generating a giant radioactive cloud.

At first Soviet authorities tried to hide the gravity of the accident in order to avoid alarm, but despite those efforts, the following day a radioactive cloud covered Europe caused by the wind. The security systems of the Forksmar nuclear power station in Sweden (more than 1,000 kilometers from Chernobyl) detected a number of radioactive particles far in excess of safety standards and found they came from Eastern Europe. The level of radioactivity was so high that, at first, the Swedish experts thought that the USSR might have suffered a nuclear attack with an atomic bomb 500 times more powerful than the one dropped on Hiroshima.

After the explosion of the reactor, the workers who were in the nuclear power central were transferred to the hospital of Prypiat, where they died hours later. The workers had strange symptoms: The color of the skin had changed (they looked dark and golden), they urinated blood; they had

---

[*] At that time, Ukraine was part of the USSR.
[†] "Chernobyl Accident 1986," www.world-nuclear.org.

nausea, headaches, and pain in the intestines; their hair was falling out; their eyes were swollen, and their marrow had deteriorated. The skin also had a type of greenish-looking burn. Some operatives died with melted bodies.

Something similar happened with the 31 firefighters who initially moved to the plant to put out the fire without proper protective gear. Their performance was in vain since the fire did not extinguish.

After the explosion, the trees in an area comprising four square kilometers of pine forest near the reactor acquired a brown-orange color, calcined, and fell.

During the first ten days of the incident, several Soviet helicopters dropped a mixture of sand, clay, lead, dolomite, and neutron-absorbing boron on the reactor to prevent a chain reaction and to contain gamma radiation. By the time the emissions stopped on May 13, some 5,000 tons of materials had been dumped into the core.

To curb radiation emissions, a reinforced concrete bunker was built to cover the reactor, known as the *sarcophagus*. The people (military, peasants, and other volunteers) who participated in the construction of the sarcophagus and other disinfection efforts were called *liquidators*. None of them were informed about the danger of exposure to radioactive dust. They were provided with uniforms, boots, and lead masks, which weighed a total average of 30 kilograms, but that did not serve to contain the gamma ionizing radiation.

The liquidators numbered approximately about 600,000, and many of them died prematurely. According to Greenpeace, about 200,000 people died as a result of the catastrophe, and the health of about 100,000 people has been severely damaged. They are considered "Chernobyl invalids."

This contamination multiplied by 74 the cancer index, and the consequences derived from the radiation have become visible with the passage of time. The incidence of thyroid cancer in Belarus, Ukraine, and South Russia has risen notably, especially in children. The incidence of leukemia and other diseases affecting the digestive system and the immune system has also increased. The rate of infant mortality and congenital malformations has also increased.

Europe developed a policy of restrictions on removing food from contaminated areas, but it could not be fully controlled. Still today, especially in Ukraine and Belarus, the population feeds on crops and animals from these soils, and cancers are mainly due to the intake of contaminated food. In 1986, Chernobyl was a city of 43,000 inhabitants and is now abandoned. Some sectors of the scientific community fear radioactivity will not be extinguished in that area up for to 300,000 years.

Fukushima: On March 11, 2011, around 3:00 p.m., a devastating magnitude nine earthquake on the Richter scale and a subsequent tsunami with waves up to ten meters high caused a serious nuclear incident at the Japanese Fukushima nuclear power plant. The total number of evacuees reached 300,000 people. In 2012, the operator of the plant, Tepco, announced that the nuclear accident had released 2.5 times more radiation than initially estimated. In 2013, the company admitted that after the accident, it had poured almost 80,000 gallons of contaminated water into the Pacific Ocean every day. In February 2015, the operator of the Fukushima nuclear power station reported finding a new leak of radioactive water through the drainage of one of the reactors, which caused discharges into the sea.

The Fukushima nuclear accident is the only one that equals Chernobyl on the International Accident Scale (Accident Level 7), constituting one of the largest environmental disasters in recent history.

It is estimated that about 600 tons of nuclear waste must be eliminated, a project that would cost about US$35 billion and take between 35 and 40 years to complete.

A post-tsunami investigation revealed the security procedures of the Fukushima nuclear plant were obsolete and the disaster could have been avoided.[*]

Chevron Corporation: Chevron is an American oil company established in 1911 in California. In June 1997, a gas explosion in Bangladesh destroyed 2.8 kilometers of a forest reserve and, as a result, the government sued its subsidary for environmental damage and claimed compensation of US$650 million.[†]

In Richmond, California, the company owns an oil refinery and processes about 240,000 barrels of crude daily. In August 2012, the Chevron refinery caught fire due to a corroded and worn pipeline. The accident left 15,000 people hospitalized for respiratory problems.[‡]

---

[*] "The Fukushima Nuclear Plant Becomes a Robot Cemetery," March 7, 2017, www.Clarin.com.

[†] This was not the only case involving Chevron outside the United States. Angola also fined the company for a crude oil spill off the coast of the province Cabinda that contaminated its beaches.

[‡] More information on Chevron's environmental problems can be seen in "Chevron's Scandals," October 14, 2013, www.eltelegrafo.com.ec.

US Chemical Safety Board officials noted,

> We have obtained internal Chevron policies that recommend that every segment of pipe in this service should have been included in the pipe inspection program.... There is no indication that this segment of the pipe was inspected for thickness during the most recent November 2011 turnaround.[*]

Anadarko Petroleum: Anadarko Petroleum Corporation is an American petroleum and natural gas exploration and production company headquartered in two skyscrapers in The Woodlands, Texas. The company has been the subject of multiple environmental cases, including one of the largest environmental contamination settlements in American history – the 2014 settlement related to the former Tronox subsidiary of Kerr McGee, a company purchased by Anadarko in 2006. Anadarko settled with the US Department of Justice and the Environmental Protection Agency to pay US$5.15 billion to clean up environmental waste sites around the country.[†]

British Petroleum: British Petroleum (BP) is one of the world's six leading oil and gas companies operating in 80 countries. Its origins go back to 1908 when the Anglo-Persian Oil Company was founded to export oil discovered in Iran. In 1954, the company became British Petroleum. On April 20, 2010, an explosion occurred in the Deepwater Horizon semisubmersible oil rig leased by BP to a subcontractor named Transocean Ltd. operating in the Gulf of Mexico.

The well was located over 5,000 feet beneath the water's surface in the vast frontier of the deep sea – a permanently dark environment, marked by constantly cold temperatures just above freezing and extremely high pressures.[‡]

Within days of the April 20, 2010 explosion and sinking of the Deepwater Horizon oil rig in the Gulf of Mexico, underwater cameras revealed the BP pipe was leaking oil and gas on the ocean floor about 42 miles off the

---

[*] Sarah Phelan, "Chevron Failed to Check Pipes Despite Internal Policies," September 12, 2012, richmondconfidential.org.

[†] en.wikipedia.org/wiki/Anadarko_Petroleum.

[‡] Richard Pallardy, "Deepwater Horizon oil spill Environmental Disaster Gulf of Mexico," www.britannica.com/event/Deepwater-Horizon-oil-spill; The Ocean Portal Team, ocean.si.edu/conservation/pollution/gulf-oil-spill.

coast of Louisiana. By the time the well was capped on July 15, 2010, an estimated 3.19 million barrels of oil had leaked into the Gulf.*

The Deepwater disaster caused the deaths of 11 people and a spill and oil leak at 1,500 meters deep for 87 days, seriously affecting the Gulf ecosystem. During that period, BP also lost more than 50% of its market capitalization.

The CEO of BP at the time said to journalists, "We are sorry for the massive alteration that the spill has caused to their lives. There is no one who wants this affair to end more than I do. I want to get my life back."†

Three weeks later, even as oil poured out of the ocean floor, the CEO was pictured running a race aboard his sailboat in the south of Southampton in the United Kingdom.

The Deepwater Horizon oil spill is regarded as one of the largest environmental disasters in American history. In September 2014, a US District Court judge ruled that BP was primarily responsible for the oil spill because of its gross negligence.‡

On July 2, 2015, BP agreed with the US Justice Department to pay US$18.7 billion in compensation for the oil slick in the Gulf of Mexico, the worst environmental tragedy in US history.§ The agreement was signed by federal authorities as well as the states of Alabama, Florida, Louisiana, Mississippi, Texas, and more than 400 local governments. Payments were to be extended for 18 years. US Attorney General Loretta Lynch said:

> In the case that is approved by the Court, this agreement would be the largest with a single entity in the history of the United States. It would help repair the damage done to the Gulf economy, the fishing industry, marshes, and wildlife.⁵

BP agreed to four years of government monitoring of its safety practices and ethics, and the Environmental Protection Agency announced that BP

---

* Richard Pallardy, "Deepwater Horizon oil spill Environmental Disaster Gulf of Mexico," www.b ritannica.com/event/Deepwater-Horizon-oil-spill; The Ocean Portal Team, ocean.si.edu/conserv ation/pollution/gulf-oil-spill.

† Michael Ritter, *El Valor del Capital Reputacional* (Olivos, Ritter & Partners, 2013), 301 ("The Value of Reputational Capital").

‡ en.wikipedia.org/wiki/Deepwater_Horizon_oil_spill.

§ Of the US$18.7 billion that BP will pay in fines, $5.5 billion responds to civil claims, $7.1 billion will be paid to the federal state and five states affected by the environmental damages, $4.9 billion to compensate for the negative impact on the economy, and $1 billion to pay local authorities.

⁵ July 2, 2015, www.tn.com.ar.

would be temporarily banned from new contracts with the US government. As of 2018, cleanup costs, charges, and penalties had cost the company more than US$65 billion.*

The Lancet Commission on Pollution and Health has reported that pollution is linked to the deaths of more than nine million people in the world each year.

In the face of these disasters and catastrophes, we must reflect on the responsibility of business and government leaders to impose greater controls, in order to protect, not only companies, their customers, and employees, but also to safeguard the planet and its inhabitants from these types of negative externalities that have such detrimental effects that cannot be ignored.

Silent Spring[†] is an environmental book written by the biologist Rachel Carson (1907–1964) and published in 1962. When *Silent Spring* was first published, a chorus of critics called Carson "hysterical" and "extremist." Yet the marine biologist's meticulously documented indictment of DDT led to the birth of the modern environmental movement.[‡]

The book documents the detrimental effects on the environment due to the indiscriminate use of pesticides. Carson argues that DDT not only indiscriminately kills insects, including beneficial species like bees, but also accumulates in the fat of birds and mammals high on the food chain, thinning eggshells and causing reproductive problems. Her chilling vision of a birdless America is still haunting. "Over increasingly large areas of the United States," she writes, "spring now comes unheralded by the return of the birds, and the early mornings are strangely silent where once they were filled with the beauty of birdsong."[§]

The book led to a nationwide ban on DDT for agricultural use and inspired an environmental movement that led to the creation of the Environmental Protection Agency known as the EPA, a US federal government body responsible for protecting human health and the environment: air, water, and soil.

The EPA was created in 1970 and since then has made some achievements including banning chemicals such as the lead additive in gasoline and

---

* en.wikipedia.org/wiki/Deepwater_Horizon_oil_spill.

[†] This book was named one of the 25 greatest science books of all time by *Discovery* magazine. www. discovermagazine.com/2006/dec/25-greatest-science-books. The book was published by Hughton Mifflin.

[‡] discovermagazine.com/2006/dec/25-greatest-science-books.

[§] discovermagazine.com/2006/dec/25-greatest-science-books.

pesticides. Some of the issues investigated by this agency include acid rain, asbestos, carbon monoxide, drinking water, recycling, lead in water and paint, mercury, ozone, pesticides, and radiation.

The *Clean Air Act is* a US federal law designed to control air pollution on a national level. It is one of the United States' first and most influential modern environmental laws, and one of the most comprehensive air quality laws in the world. As with many other major US federal environmental statutes, it is administered by the US Environmental Protection Agency (EPA).*

The previously mentioned Global Compact of the United Nations is also the world's largest initiative for corporate sustainability. Its goal is to mobilize a global movement of sustainable companies and stakeholders to create "the world we want."[†]

Aldo Leopold (1887–1948), a US wildlife biologist and conservationist that was a professor at the University of Wisconsin, said. "We abuse land because we regard it as a commodity belonging to us. When we see land as a community to which we belong, we may begin to use it with love and respect."[‡]

The Intergovernmental Panel on Climate Change (IPCC)[§] issued on August 2019, the "Special Report on Climate Change and Land" prepared by 107 scientists indicating that 25% of the land is degraded.[¶]

When soil is degraded, the amount of plant varieties that can grow in it is reduced, as well as its ability to absorb carbon dioxide. Land overuse is an important cause of climate change and global warming.

The planet Earth is fragile and therefore it is necessary to use it responsibly. Only a drop of oil can turn 25 liters of water into non-potable water. Companies should encourage initiatives that promote greater environmental responsibility and use environment-friendly technologies. For example, by 2020 it is estimated that all taxis in Shenzhen, China, will be electric.

The British businesswoman Anita Roddick, founder and former CEO of the cosmetic company The Body Shop, was known for her campaigning work on environmental issues. Under Roddick's leadership, The Body

---

* https://en.wikipedia.org/wiki/Clean_Air_Act_(United_States).
† www.unglobalcompact.org.
‡ www.aldoleopold.org/teach-learn/green-fire-film/leopold-quotes/.
§ The IPCC is the United Nations body for assessing the science related to climate change.
¶ Nora Bar, "Humanity Has Already Degraded 25% of the Earth's Surface Free of Oceans," August 8, 2019, www.lanacion.com.ar.

Shop avoided the use of animal-derived products and wood from tropical rain forests. Roddick said, "The purpose of business isn't just to generate profits, to create an ever-lasting empire. It's to have the power to affect social change; that helps make the world a better place."[*]

The CDP (formerly the Carbon Disclosure Project) is an international non-profit organization based in the United Kingdom which supports companies and cities to disclose the environmental impact of major corporations. In 2019, over 8,400 companies disclosed through CDP.

CDP's annual "A-Lists" for climate change, forests, and water security name the most pioneering companies on environmental performance. The scoring drives corporate transparency and helps to guide, incentivize, and assess environmental action.[†] For example, HP, L'Oreal, Firmenich, UPM-Kymmene, Tetra Pac, Unilever, and Danone have been highlighted by CDP as world leaders in corporate sustainability, achieving a place on its "A-List" in the three categories: climate change, protection of forests, and water security.

Corporations are getting more sustainable, and investors are benefiting, along with the planet and the rest of its inhabitants. The annual Barron's ranking of America's Most Sustainable Companies makes for a pretty good portfolio: shares of the 100 companies on that list returned 34.3%, on average. The top ten companies in the ranking are the following: Cisco Systems, Agilent Technologies, Texas Instruments, Voya Financial, Tiffany, Best Buy, HP Inc, W.W. Grainger, Avnet, and Autodesk.[‡]

We want a planet where air, water, and food are safe. In some organizations, a director of Environmental Affairs coordinates the company's initiatives related to the environment and monitors the environmental goals set by the corporation. Some of these goals could be the recycling of materials, the reduction of energy and packaging, the use of non-toxic chemicals, the reduction of carbon dioxide emissions, or the criteria for selecting suppliers that are environment-friendly. For example, the global investment corporation BlackRock plans to stop investing in companies it considers an environmental sustainability risk.[§]

---

[*] K. Blanchard, C. Schewe, B. Nelson and A. Hiam, *Exploring the World of Business* (Worth Publishers, 1996), 230. D. Hellriegel and J. Slocum, *Management,* 7th ed (Southwestern, 1996), 229.

[†] www.cdp.net/en/companies/companies-scores.

[‡] Leslie P. Norton, "These Are the 100 Most Sustainable Companies in America — and They're Beating the Market," www.agilent.com/about/newsroom/articles/barrons-100-most-sustainable-companies-2020.pdf, February 7, 2020.

[§] Riva Gold, "BlackRock Aims to Go Green," January 14, 2020, Linkedin.com.

The "green" goals set by the company may be based on the standards published by the International Organization for Standardization (ISO) for a good environmental management system – ISO 14000 and ISO 14001 – and the Leadership in Energy and Environmental Design (LEED) program.

ISO 14000 is a set of environmental standards developed and published by ISO in 1996. This standard helps companies reduce industrial waste and environmental damage. The objective is to help companies manage processes to minimize environmental effects.

ISO 14001 is the most important standard within the ISO 14000 series. ISO 14001 specifies the requirements of an environmental management system (EMS).

The LEED program represents an effort to establish a standard for the construction of "green" buildings. Obtaining the LEED certification requires the fulfillment of certain criteria that affect different aspects, from the selection of the site to the recycling of the construction materials. Buildings with "LEED Certification" are environment-friendly.

Ray C. Anderson (1934–2011) was founder and chairman of Interface Inc., one of the world's largest manufacturers of modular carpet. He was known in environmental circles for his advanced and progressive stance on industrial ecology and sustainability.

Anderson first turned his focus toward the environment in 1994 when he read *The Ecology of Commerce* by Paul Hawken, seeking inspiration for a speech on the company's environmental vision. Hawken argues that the industrial system is destroying the planet and only industry leaders are powerful enough to stop it.

In 2009, Anderson estimated that Interface was more than halfway toward the vision of "Mission Zero," the company's promise to eliminate any negative impact it may have on the environment by the year 2020 through the redesign of processes and products, the pioneering of new technologies, and efforts to reduce or eliminate waste and harmful emissions while increasing the use of renewable materials and sources of energy.

Under Anderson's leadership, Interface was named to CRO magazine's (formerly *Business Ethics* magazine) 100 Best Corporate Citizens List for three years. In 2006, Sustainablebusiness.com named Interface to their SB20 list of Companies Changing the World, and in 2006 GlobeScan listed Interface #1 in the world for corporate sustainability.*

---

* en.wikipedia.org/wiki/Ray_Anderson_(entrepreneur). The Interface story is the focus of the documentary film *So Right, So Smart* (2009) directed by Justin Maine, Guy Noerr, Leanne Robinson-Maine, and Michael Swantek.

The Dalai Lama wrote about the proper care of the environment:

> We are also being drawn together by the grave problems we face: over-population, dwindling natural resources, and an environmental crisis that threatens our air, water, and trees, along with the vast number of beautiful life forms that are the very foundation of existence on this small planet we share.
>
> I believe that to meet the challenge of our times, human beings will have to develop a greater sense of universal responsibility. Each of us must learn to work not for oneself, one's own family or nation, but for the benefit of all humankind. Universal responsibility is the real key to human survival. It is the best foundation for world peace, the equitable use of natural resources, and through concern for future generations, the proper care of the environment.*

Pope Francis, in his speech to the General Assembly of the United Nations on September 25, 2015, also said, "The ecological crisis, and the large-scale destruction of biodiversity, can threaten the very existence of the human species."†

Companies traditionally treated the preservation of the natural environment passively, as a secondary concern. All they had to do was comply with environmental regulations and avoid any major catastrophe that could mean bad press. Nowadays, companies are forced to take an additional approach to help preserve the environment.‡

It is good to remember Robert Hass, ex-CEO of Levy Strauss & Co., who said, companies should be "capable of both reaping profits and making the world a better place to live."§

Sixteen-year-old Swedish activist Greta Thunberg was named a Person of the Year 2019 by *Time* magazine. The adolescent became the most representative voice of the fight against climate change. Her claim at the UN went viral on social networks and millions of young people mobilized as part of the Fridays for Future movement.

---

* www.dalailama.com/messages/world-peace/the-global-community.

† Chris Mooney, "Pope Francis to the UN: Environmental Degradation Threatens the Very Existence of the Human Species," September 25, 2015, www.washingtonpost.com.

‡ K. Blanchard, C. Schewe, B. Nelson and A. Hiam, *Exploring the World of Business* (Worth Publishers, 1996), 9.

§ K. Blanchard, C. Schewe, B. Nelson and A. Hiam, *Exploring the World of Business* (Worth Publishers, 1996), 104.

In January 2019 at the World Economic Forum in Davos, Switzerland, she said: "I want you to panic. I want you to feel the fear I do. Every day. And want you to act. I want you to behave like our house is on fire. Because it is."*

The "World Environment Day," is celebrated on June 5 each year. April 22 is observed the "Earth Day," and the last Saturday of March is celebrated the "Earth Hour." All of them want to raise awareness of the ecological crisis and its consequences.

Ethical organizations are proactive and take action to care for the environment.

---

* "Greta Thunberg Was Chosen as the Person of the Year by *Time* Magazine," December 11, 2019, www.infobae.com/america.

16

Corporate Risks: Unit 4

16.1 MANIPULATION OF ACCOUNTING

Accounting is a technique or system of control and recording of expenses and income and other economic operations carried out by a company.

Accounting records are an ordered source of data to analyze information and make decisions; therefore, those records must be transparent in order to provide a clear picture of the real financial situation of a company.

The Louisiana Purchase was the largest acquisition of land in the history of the United States.* In 1803, Napoleon Bonaparte, French First Consul, sold to the United States more than 2 million square kilometers of French possessions in North America at a price of US$15 million plus interest, which ended up costing to the United States US$23 million. The territory represented 23% of the current area of the United States and was populated by about 35,000 people, a third of them in New Orleans.† The third president of the United States, Thomas Jefferson (1743–1826), decided to buy Louisiana because he did not want France and Spain to have the power to block American merchants from access to the port of New Orleans and because he wanted to control navigation on the Mississippi River. This negotiation opened access to the Pacific Ocean for the United States and substantially increased its territory.

---

* Louisiana was named in honor of Louis XIV, king of France (1643–1715). When René Robert Cavelier de La Salle claimed this territory for France, he called it La Louisiane, which means "Land of Louis."
† The territory sold comprised all or part of the present states of Arkansas, Missouri, Iowa, Oklahoma, Kansas, Nebraska, Minnesota, North Dakota, South Dakota, New Mexico, Texas, Montana, Wyoming, Colorado, and Louisiana.

France wanted to get rid of this colonial territory obtained from Spain two years before since Haiti had declared its independence and the defense of the colony was complicated. Napoleon preferred to sell Louisiana to the Americans and avoid running the risk of losing it to the British. Napoleon said: "This sale is not a big deal for France, but the important thing is that we will give the English a new competitor in their maritime monopoly."[*]

A portion of the payment for Louisiana was made in US bonds, which Napoleon (1769–1821) sold to the British bank Barings[†] at a discount of 87½ for every US$100. Napoleon received US$8,831,250 in cash for Louisiana, and with that sale financed his military campaigns. Years later, the Barings Bank established links with King George V (1865–1936), and a relationship with the British monarchy was born, which would continue until 1995. The Barings Bank was founded in 1762, and the management of its patrimony was entrusted to Queen Isabel.

Between 1992 and 1995 the Barings Bank's activities in Singapore allowed a bank employee, Nick Leeson, to operate without supervision. Leeson generated £10 million or 10% of the bank's total revenue in 1993. Bank authorities rewarded his efficiency with a bond of £130,000. Leeson carried out operations in the futures and options market, reporting to Barings large losses as if they were gains. He hid the losses in the secret account 88888, dubbed an error account.

To turn the results around, Leeson bet aggressively with risky investments, which increased the losses. On January 17, 1995, the Kobe earthquake in Japan knocked down the Asian and Nikkei financial markets, and Leeson's losses amounted to 827 million pounds (more than US$1.2 billion), double the bank's available capital. Baring's internal auditors discovered the computer and accounting manipulation and the huge losses that were reported to the Bank of England.

Barings was declared insolvent on February 26, 1995, and purchased by the Dutch bank and insurance company ING for the nominal sum of £1 and assumed Barings's liabilities.

Leeson tried to flee but was arrested in Germany. He said: "It was scary. My photo was on every front page and on every screen of every airport."[‡]

Barings no longer exists as an independent corporation. Leeson was convicted of fraud and spent two years in a maximum-security prison in Singapore. The trader who broke a bank with more than 200 years of history

---

[*] en.wikipedia.org/wiki/Louisiana_Purchase.
[†] Founded in 1765 by Sir Francis Baring.
[‡] "The Man Who Broke the Barings," December 26, 2005, www.lanacion.com.ar.

is now a frequent speaker. Leeson has said, "If the bank, supervisors and I had done our job better, none of this would have happened. Obviously, I was to blame for everything, but without the contribution of these other factors none of that would have happened."*

Some observers have attributed some of the blame to the poor internal audit practices, accounting controls and risk management of the Baring Bank itself, and its lack of effective control. His losses could have been discovered if his supervisors had asked more questions. This is another example of what may happen if events are permitted to spiral out of control. Companies must take action immediately against the risk of someone distorting numbers to hide problems or improve results, adulterating information, generating non-existent profits, creating apocryphal invoices, overvaluing assets, decreasing liabilities, and falsifying numbers, credits, and/or expenses to cover bribes.

Barings case shows how unethical actions from *a single person* can destroy powerful companies.

The 1999 movie *Rogue Trader*[†] is based on Nick Leeson's 1996 book *Rogue Trader: How I Brought Down Barings Bank and Shook the Financial World.*[‡]

One of the best films about financial markets is *Wall Street*, a 1987 American film[§] that tells the story of a young stockbroker who becomes involved with Gordon Gekko, a wealthy, unscrupulous corporate raider. Gekko became the symbol of greed without limits. A key scene in the film is a speech by Gekko to a shareholders' meeting of Teldar Paper, a company he is planning to take over. In that speech, Gekko says, "Greed, for lack of a better word, is good. Greed is right. Greed works."[¶]

Jordan Belfort is an American former stockbroker who in 1999 was pleaded guilty for manipulating the stock market and had to spend 22 months in prison. In 2013 his story was made into the movie *The Wolf of Wall Street*.[**] One of his most famous phrases is:

---

* www.lavanguardia.com, February 18, 2013.
† The film was directed by James Dearden.
‡ The publisher of the book was Little, Brown & Company.
§ The film was directed by Oliver Stone. Michael Douglas won the Academy Award for Best Actor.
¶ en.wikiquote.org/wiki/Talk: Wall_Street_(1987_film). The defense of greed is a paraphrase of the May 18, 1986, commencement address at the UC Berkeley's School of Business Administration, delivered by arbitrageur Ivan Boesky (who himself was later convicted of insider trading charges), in which he said, "Greed is all right, by the way. I want you to know that. I think greed is healthy. You can be greedy and still feel good about yourself."
** Directed by Martin Scorsese, starring Leonardo DiCaprio, based on the memoirs of Jordan Belfort.

"The real question is this:
Was all this legal?
Absolutely not
But we were making more money than we knew what to
do with."*

At a talk he delivered in Dubai, the United Arab Emirates, on May 19, 2014, Belford stated: "I got greedy... greed is not good."†

Greed is the excessive ambition for money, goods, and wealth. It is a vice that leads people to want more than they really need. This need for accumulation can be translated into actions that may be contrary to ethical behavior, with negative consequences for people, companies, and society. Driven by greed, a person can commit crimes like theft or manipulation of accounts.

Many companies have suffered the manipulation of accounting. Some examples are given below:

Société Générale: The Frenchman Jérôme Kerviel caused the loss of 4.9 billion euros (US$7 billion) for Société Générale due to fraudulent activities.

One of the bank's practices was to buy huge quantities of shares of a company in Tokyo or Hong Kong and sell them immediately afterward in Paris or New York, taking advantage of very small price differences, sometimes euro cents per share. Kerviel pointed out in a long interview exclusive to the newspaper *Le Parisien*,

> From August to December 2007 I win every day.... That creates a sort of addiction.... I lose little by little the real notion of the sums that are at stake.... For me, a day of a million euros was nothing.... I make astronomic profits which sometimes give me orgasmic pleasure.‡

Kerviel lost a lot of money and he used a complex system to hide his losses with false transactions. It was discovered, on January 18, 2008, that Kerviel had made illicit bets that reached 50 billion euros and almost broke the bank.§

---

* www.goalcast.com/2018/10/23/ wolf_wall_Street_Quotes.
† en.wikipedia.org/wiki/Jordan_belfort.
‡ "SocGen Rogue Trader Jerome Kerviel Hit the Jackpot on 7/7 Adam Sage," www.thetimes.co.uk January 23, 2009.
§ Henry Samuel, "Jérôme Kerviel Will Need 177,000 Years to Repay €5 Billion," October 5, 2010, www.telegraph.co.uk.

According to Kerviel, the bank wanted to earn the most money in the shortest possible time. "It was as if I was driving a jet-powered Ferrari. For 365 laps, I overtake everyone else at 3,000 kph. They saw me and they said nothing, is that credible?"*

"My daily existence was about making money for the bank, that was my only objective, at any price, regardless of all moral or ethical considerations," he said before he was imprisoned.[†]

France's banking regulator fined Société Générale 4 million euros over grave deficiencies in its internal controls. The banking commission said it detected "grave deficiencies in the internal control system that made possible the development of the fraud and its serious financial consequences."[‡]

On October 24, 2012, Kerviel was sentenced to three years' imprisonment, found guilty of breach of trust and fraudulent data entry into the computer system.[§]

Jérôme Kerviel, the exchange trader who indebted Société Générale, wrote a book *L 'Engrenage: memories d'un trader.*[¶]

Sumitomo: Yasuo Hamanaka was the main copper trader of Sumitomo Corporation, one of the largest companies in Japan. He was known as "the Lord of Copper" and "Mr. Five Percent," because it was the percentage of the world's copper business his team controlled.

On June 13, 1996, Sumitomo Corporation reported losses of US$1.8 billion in copper trade on the London Metal Exchange.[**] Hamanaka had apparently falsified documents and signatures and had destroyed records to hide losses that lasted for more than a decade. Hamanaka was sentenced to eight years in jail in 1998.

The Bayou Hedge Fund: The investment fund the Bayou Hedge Fund Group also defrauded through accounting by misleading its investors

---

* John Lichfield, "Jérome Kerviel: Secrets of the Rogue Trader," January 23, 2009, www.independent.co.uk.
† Denise Roland and AFP, "Rogue Trader Jerome Kerviel Leaves Prison Less Than Five Months into Three-year Sentence," September 8, 2014, www.telegraph.co.uk.
‡ AFP, "Societe Generale Fined 4 Million Euros for Deficiencies that Led to Rogue Trading," July 6, 2008, www.taipeitimes.com.
§ en.wikipedia.org/wiki/Jérôme_Kerviel; Also, Antonio Jimenez Barca, *The Man of the 5 Billion*, February 1, 2009, www.ElPais.com.
¶ Flammarion, 2010.
** Reed Abelson, "Sumitomo Says It Found Loss of $1.8 Billion," June 14, 1996, www.nytimes.com /1996/06/14/business/sumitomo-says-it-found-loss-of-1.8-billion.html.

about the number of reported profits and losses. Mr. Sam Israel, the founder of the fund, was sentenced to 20 years in prison.

Parmalat: In 1961, Calisto Tanzi, 22, opened a small pasteurization plant in Parma, Italy, and by the beginning of 2000, Parmalat had become a multinational dairy company. The company was the subject of one of the biggest corporate scandals in the history of Europe when it was discovered at the end of 2003 that it had a debt of 14 billion euros,* more than twice what was declared on its balance sheet, and a fictitious account based in the Cayman Islands had non-existent asset of almost four billion euros. The company's founder was arrested after the company declared bankruptcy and was sentenced to 18 years in prison. Most of the company's shares were acquired by the French company Lactalis in 2011.

Subprime mortgage crisis: The US subprime mortgage crisis was a banking emergency occurring between 2007 and 2010 and contributed to the US recession of 2007–2009. The crisis was triggered by a large decline in home prices after the collapse of a housing bubble, leading to mortgage delinquencies and foreclosures and the devaluation of housing-related securities. The United States entered a deep recession, with nearly nine million jobs lost during 2008 and 2009, roughly 6% of the workforce.† In 2007 it was unthinkable subprime mortgages could generate a chain reaction and a domino effect that almost led the entire US financial system to bankruptcy. Some of the banks responsible for the crises received huge fines or disappeared. Here are some examples:

> *Fannie Mae*: The Federal National Mortgage Association (FNMA), known as Washington-based Fannie Mae, was founded in 1938 and is one of the largest financial institutions in the United States. In 2006, an increasing number of borrowers with poor credit were unable to pay their mortgages caused an increase in home foreclosures. In 2006, the Federal Bureau of Housing Supervisors (OFHEO) and the US Securities and Exchange Commission (SEC) imposed on Fannie Mae US$400 million in fines for manipulating their accounts. Regulators labeled the company's corporate culture as "arrogant and

---

* "Parmalat Debt Tops 14bn Euros," *World Business*, January 26, 2004, www.cnn.com/2004/BUS INESS/01/26/parmalat.reut/.
† en.wikipedia.org/wiki/Subprime_mortgage_crisis.

unethical."* By August 2008, shares of both Fannie Mae and Freddie Mac had tumbled more than 90% from their one-year prior levels.†

On December 17, 2011, it was reported that six executives of the mortgage agencies Fannie Mae and Freddie Mac were charged with fraud by the SEC. According to the SEC, although Fannie Mae's high-risk mortgages comprised more than US$43 billion, the mortgage agency reported only about US$4.8 billion.‡

Lehman Brothers: This global financial services company, founded in 1850 in the United States, in 2007 was also affected by the financial crisis of subprime loans, accumulating huge losses in its mortgage-backed securities. Lehman had invested heavily in subprime mortgages and manipulated his balance sheets by generating a US$50 billion accounting fraud. After 158 years of activity, the fourth-largest US investment bank filed for bankruptcy on September 15, 2008, when it had a liability of about US$600 million, the largest bankruptcy order in US history.§

JP Morgan: John Pierpont Morgan (1837–1913) was an important American banker that founded the JP Morgan bank in 1871.⁑ JPMorgan Chase was the result of the merger of JP Morgan and Chase Manhattan Bank in 2000, and is one of the leading banking institutions in the United States, along with Bank of America and Citigroup. On November 19, 2013, JPMorgan Chase received the largest economic sanction in US history up to that time after being embroiled in the scandal of toxic or subprime, high-risk mortgages granted to people with low purchasing power.

In 2008, the increase in loans had increased the delinquency and foreclosures of those mortgages. As banks and mutual funds committed their assets to subprime mortgages, there was a credit crunch, a spiral of mistrust and panic, and a drop in the stock market. Given the possible nonpayment of the debts of the mortgage borrowers, the

---

* Elliot Blair Smith, "Fannie Mae to Pay 400 Million Fine," *USA Today*, May 24, 2006.

† en.wikipedia.org/wiki/Freddie_Mac.

‡ "EEUU acusa a seis ejecutivos de Fannie Mae y Freddie Mac de Fraude," December 17, 2011, http://actualidad.rt.com ("The US accuses six executives of Fannie Mae and Freddie Mac of Fraud").

§ Michael Wolf, "Lehman Brothers Financially and Morally Bankrupt," December 12, 2011, TheGuardian.com.

⁑ In 1900, John Morgan was one of the richest men in the world. Morgan took good care of his money. Once J. P. Morgan asked in a bar for a beer, saying to the waiter, "When Morgan takes, everyone takes." Everyone present then got a beer, and when Morgan finished his beer, he left ten cents on the table, saying, "When Morgan pays, everyone pays."

market was weakened, and insecurity and mistrust spread throughout the financial system.

A *Moral hazard* happens when a person takes more risks because someone else bears the cost of those risks. Moral hazard can occur under a type of asymmetric information where one party to a transaction knows more than the party paying the consequences of the risk. Some large mortgage lenders made loans they knew the borrowers could not afford. These loans were packaged into mortgage-backed securities and sold to investors that took on more risk than they originally thought because they did not have all the information.[*]

Because JPMorgan Chase commercialized toxic mortgages by providing inaccurate information that could lead to deception,[†] on November 19, 2013, after reaching an agreement with the US Department of Justice, the bank was sanctioned with a fine of US$13 billion.

Goldman Sachs: In April 2016 Goldman Sachs settled for US$5 billion for misleading investors about residential mortgage-backed securities. From 2005 to 2007, the company knowingly sold securities that were likely to fall, resulting in the loss of billions of dollars to investors.[‡]

Citi: In 2014 Citigroup settled with federal and state agencies for US$7 billion for its role in the financial crisis. The Department of Justice charged that Citi knew the mortgages it had sold were bad while representing them as good investments.[§]

Bank of America: In 2014 Bank of America paid out US$16.65 billion for financial fraud leading up to the mortgage crisis of 2008. The bank lied to investors about the quality of residential mortgage securities.[¶]

WorldCom: In the mid-1980s, Bernard Ebbers, owner of a Mississippi hotel chain, acquired small communications companies to form a national

---

[*] The term *Moral Hazard* originated in the insurance business. There is a hazard to the insurance company that people's morals won't be strong enough to keep them from giving in to the incentive to act less carefully. Professor Connel Fullenkamp, *The Economics of Uncertainty* (The Great Courses, 2015), 75.

[†] www.StopFraud.gov.

[‡] "Risky Business: Top 10 Corporate Crackdowns," *Censible*, July 20, 2017, www.learn.censible.co/risky-business-top-ten-corporate-crackdowns/.

[§] "Risky Business: Top 10 Corporate Crackdowns," *Censible*, July 20, 2017, www.learn.censible.co/risky-business-top-ten-corporate-crackdowns/.

[¶] "Risky Business: Top 10 Corporate Crackdowns," *Censible*, July 20, 2017, www.learn.censible.co/risky-business-top-ten-corporate-crackdowns/.

network in the United States. This is how LDDS was born, which in the 1990s changed its name to WorldCom and soon merged with MCI. In 1999, the company was listed on the New York Stock Exchange, and in 2002 the telecommunications giant WorldCom was the second-largest long-distance communications company in the United States.

But that year, the value of the company's shares declined sharply after an accounting fraud was disclosed in the company. More than US$3 billion of WorldCom's operating expenses were recorded as investments. As a result of the fraud, their stock prices went from US$60 to 20 cents, and thousands of employees lost their jobs. The lack of an ethical culture and failure in the controls caused the collapse, and the company was finally sold to Verizon.

In an article entitled "A Cultural Asset," professors at North Carolina State University Al Y. S. Chen, Roby Sawyers, and Paul Williams point out that "using quantitative decision-making methods leads managers to worry too much about the technical issues, leaving aside the ethical issues."[*]

Toshiba: Toshiba is a Japanese company dedicated to the manufacture of electrical appliances and was the first company to develop and bring to market the first portable computer in the world.[†] In 2015, it was learned that Toshiba had overstated its earnings in the amount of US$1.2 billion for seven years. The reason was senior management demanded unrealistic profits that led to the adulteration of accounting, so the results match the desire of the bosses.

Hisao Tanaka, CEO, and president of Toshiba was aware of the maneuver and in July 2015 resigned. Toshiba's shares fell in value and the company lost about US$8 billion in market capitalization. The company was then removed from the stock index that includes the best companies in Japan.[‡]

Enron Corporation: Enron was a Houston-based energy company founded in 1985 by the merger of Houston Natural Gas and InterNorth. In 2001 Enron employed 20,000 people. The company was engaged in gas pipeline management within the United States and then expanded its operations as

---

[*] Revista *Gestión*, January–February 1998, 122 (*Gestion* magazine).
[†] Toshiba, Wikipedia.
[‡] en.wikipedia.org/wiki/Toshiba; "Escándalo de Contabilidad que Destronó a Hisao Tanaka, el Todopoderoso Jefe de Toshiba," *BBC Mundo*, July 21, 2015 ("The Accounting Scandal that Destroyed Hisao Tanaka, the Almighty Chief of Toshiba").

an intermediary for natural gas futures and derivative contracts and was involved in the development, construction, and operation of gas pipelines and power plants around the world. Enron then added energy, betting on its deregulation. *Fortune* magazine designated it as the "most innovative company in the United States" between 1996 and 2000.[*]

On October 2, 2000, a *Fortune* magazine article said,

> No company illustrates the transformative power of innovation more dramatically than Enron. Over the past decade, Enron's commitment to the invention – and later domination – of new business categories has taken it from a US$200 million old-economy pipeline operator to a US$40 billion new-economy trading powerhouse.[†]

In the same year, Enron also won the *Financial Times'* "energy company of the year" award.[‡]

In the introductory letter to the Enron Code of Ethics published on July 1, 2000, Kenneth Lay, former president and CEO of Enron, wrote:

> As officers and employees of Enron Corporation … we are responsible for conducting the business affairs of the companies in accordance with all applicable laws and in a moral and honest manner.
>
> We want to be proud of Enron and to know that it enjoys a reputation of fairness and honesty and that it is respected. … Enron's reputation finally depends on its people, on you and me. Let's keep that reputation high.

However, Enron, rather than punish employees making bad decisions, was only interested in the bottom line. As portrayed in the 2005 documentary *Enron: The Smartest Guys in the Room,*[§] two traders in 1987 begin betting on the oil market and diverting company money to offshore accounts. After auditors uncover that scheme, the CEO, Kenneth Lay, encouraged them, "Please, keep making us millions."

---

[*] Bethany McLean and Peter Elkind, "The Guiltiest Guys in the Room," money.cnn.com/2006/0 5/29/news/enron_guiltyest/.

[†] Nicholas Stein, "The World's Most Admired Companies How Do You Make the Most Admired List? Innovate, Innovate, Innovate. The Winners on This Year's List, Compiled by the Hay Group Consultancy, Tell How They Do It," October 2, 2000, http://archive.fortune.com/magazines/for tune/.

[‡] "Rise and Fall of an Energy Giant," November 28, 2001, news.bbc.co.uk.

[§] American documentary film based on the best-selling 2003 book of the same name by *Fortune* reporters Bethany McLean and Peter Elkind. The film examines the 2001 collapse of the Enron Corporation, which resulted in criminal trials for several of the company's top executives. The film was directed by Alex Gibney.

A series of "creative" fraudulent accounting techniques, endorsed by its auditor Arthur Andersen, allowed the biggest business fraud known to date.

Kenneth Lay hires Jeffrey Skilling who used mark-to-market accounting, allowing the company to record potential profits on certain projects immediately after a contract was signed, regardless of the actual profits the deal would generate. Enron recorded sales that supposedly would materialize in the future. This gave the company the ability to give the appearance of being a profitable company even if it wasn't. As the company registered sales that were not being made, the company's sales went from US$13 billion in 1996 to US$100 billion in 2000.

Since many of Enron's "sales" at future energy prices were not being met, they created a network of entities that kept losses off the company's balance sheets. In that network of hundreds of "special purpose entities" (SPEs), they hid assets that lost money so as not to record the losses in the Enron financial statement.

Little by little, Enron's accounting began to attract attention and be questioned. One of the first calls for attention on the validity of its accounting figures comes in March 2001 when *Fortune* magazine published an article by Bethany McLean titled "Is Enron Overpriced?"

A few months later, an Enron internal accountant, Sherron Watkins, alerted CEO Kenneth Ley in an August 2001 letter about possible accounting irregularities in the company. She began her letter saying, "Is Enron a risky place to work?"[*]

When in October of that year the company released the results of the third quarter of 2001, it revealed the black hole and the losses that they had hidden. The SEC began an investigation and found millions of dollars in debt had been hidden in the complex network of SPE entities. Sherron Watkins said: "Enron's tacit message was to make the numbers, make the numbers; if you steal, if you cheat, just do not let them catch you."[†]

Enron's compliance program was on paper, not embedded in the company's culture or operation. When the FBI went to the company's offices, they found a compliance manual in the office of CFO Andrew Fastow, wrapped in plastic.[‡] Enron's code of ethics and its written values of respect and integrity were not enough to create an ethical culture in the company. Ethics codes are of little use without an organizational culture

---

[*] The complete letter can be viewed on the internet. Sherron Watkins letter, Google Images.

[†] Joseph W. Weiss, *Business Ethics* (Thompson, 2006), 31.

[‡] Andrew Fastow was sentenced to six years in prison and is currently a guest lecturer at universities and corporations.

guided by ethical values. If there is no compliance culture, the compliance manuals, policies, and ethics codes will not work.

Enron shares trading at US$90 a share in August 2000, before the fraud was discovered and fell to US$0.40 by the end of 2001. The Enron case shows how anyone can move from a virtuous circle to a vicious one in a very short period of time.

The Enron scandal showed that the leaders of certain organizations seek to maximize profits at any cost. Enron left US$31.8 billion in debt and is yet another example of what can happen when controls do not work, when there is no ethical culture, and when leadership fails. The disappearance of Enron is a symbol of the consequences organizations must face when acting without integrity.*

Jeffrey Skilling, the former CEO of Enron and a graduate of the Harvard Business School, was convicted of fraud related to Enron's financial collapse and sentenced to 14 years in prison. Kenneth Lay (1942–2006), president of Enron Corporation, died of a heart attack within a few months of being convicted of the fraud.

Arthur Andersen: With Enron, Arthur Andersen, one of the world's leading consulting firms that had been Enron's auditor for 16 years, also disappeared.† It was the end of the 88-year-old accounting firm. Trust was lost, and with it, their business.

In 2000, Arthur Andersen charged Enron US$52 million in fees and was probably one of the reasons why the audit firm was too flexible and lacking in independence when conducting audits. Because external audit firms perform lucrative work for their clients, sometimes auditors do not question their clients when they exceed the limits of acceptable accounting.

Professor Kirk O. Hanson of Santa Clara University said:

> Arthur Andersen for years was considered the most ethical and distinguished accounting firm. It does not exist anymore because of Enron. When the company had been caught in a fraud three years earlier, they had promised that if they got caught in another big one, they would allow revocation of their license to do business. ... When they had another serious malfeasance with Enron in 2001 Arthur Andersen had to be dissolved.‡

---

* A good story about the Enron case can be read in Chris Seabury, "Enron: The Fall of the Wall Street Darling," *Investopedia*.

† "The Fallout of Arthur Andersen and Enron on the Legal Landscape of American Accounting," HG.Org.

‡ Kirk Hanson, "The six ethical dilemmas every professional face," speech delivered at the Center for Business Ethics at Bentley University, February 3, 2014.

Arthur Andersen was also accused of destroying thousands of Enron documents that included physical and computer files. After an investigation by the US Justice Department, the firm was indicted on obstruction of justice charges in March 2002. After a six-week trial, Arthur Andersen was found guilty on June 16, 2002.* Thousands of Arthur Andersen employees lost their jobs.

Barbara Ley Toffler, a former Arthur Andersen partner in charge of ethics, explains in her book *Final Accounting*[†] how a culture of arrogance and greed infected the company and caused its values to deteriorate.

US Food Services: This company, a subsidiary of the Netherlands retailer Royal Ahold, recognized and booked promotional allowances and rebates when products were purchased, not when they were sold. The company recognized sales and rebates that did not exist. This accounting treatment allowed the company to show higher income so the employees could get extra bonuses. The company's stock price lost nearly two-thirds of its value when the firm announced a forensic accounting investigation would be launched. The forensic audit revealed fraud at US Food Services totaling over US$850 million.

The philosopher Maria Marta Preziosa has written that "The Greeks pointed out that the excess (Hybris) was the cause of many evils."[‡] Regardless of the size of the organization, if adequate controls are not properly implemented and if there is no ethical culture, the company can sink like the *Titanic*.

The accounting provisions require companies to keep books, records, and accounts in sufficient detail to fairly and accurately reflect the transactions and disposition of the company's assets. These rules seek to ensure a sufficient internal accounting control system that provides reasonable assurance about the transparency and accuracy of the company's financial statements. Internal controls must be effective to ensure transactions are executed in accordance with management's authorization, and their registration complies with generally accepted accounting principles (GAAP).[§]

---

* "The Fallout of Arthur Andersen and Enron on the Legal Landscape of American Accounting," HG.Org.

† Barbara Ley Toffler, *Final Accounting. Ambition, Greed and the Fall of Arthur Andersen*, published by Doubleday, a division of Random House Inc., 2003.

‡ María Marta Preziosa, "Yo Manager, Juro no codiciar," Revista *Empresa*, 195, 2009, 29 ("I Manager, I Swear Not Covet," *Empresa* magazine).

§ "FCPA Spotlight: Books and Records, and Internal Controls," June 10, 2016, create.org/news/.

In recent years, there have been three other cases of false accounting that resulted in million-dollar payments as a result of class action agreements*: Nortel Networks, AOL Time Warner, and Cendant.

Nortel Networks in 2006 agreed to pay US$2.4 billion for creating false accounting showing alleged sales of optical fiber. The value of its stock went from US$124 a share to US$0.47.

AOL Time Warner reported false profits that inflated the value of the company and in 2005 agreed with the authorities to pay US$2.5 billion to close the case.

Cendant, meanwhile, increased its revenues fraudulently by more than US$500 million and in 2000 agreed with the authorities to pay US$3.1 billion to close the case.

A paper by professors Charles Cullinan and Steve Sutton, entitled "Defrauding the public interest: a critical examination of the engineering of audit processes and the probability of detecting fraud," was published in 2002 in *Critical Perspectives on Accounting*. The document shows that of the 276 accounting frauds, the CEOs of the companies participated in 70% of them.[†]

Business leaders should focus not only on financial metrics but also on the limits that legislation imposes on businesses and on the risk of having to pay billions of dollars in fines for non-compliance.

16.2 THEFT

Theft is the taking of another person's property or services without that person's permission or consent with the intent to deprive the lawful owner of it.[‡]

Suzanne Massie is an American writer who met several times with President Ronald Reagan during his tenure and taught him a Russian

---

[*] Class actions are a type of lawsuit wherein one of the parties is a group of people who are represented by a member of the group or consumer organizations. These representatives file lawsuits on behalf of the group when large numbers of people are harmed by the defendant.

[†] Miguel Cano, Rene Castro, Rodrigo Estupinan, "Manipulacion Contable y Fraude Corporativo" ("Accounting Manipulation and Corporate Fraud"), Interamerican-USA.com; Charles P. Cullinan and Steve G. Sutton, "Defrauding the Public Interest: A Critical Examination of Re-engineered Audit Processes and the Likelihood of Detecting Fraud," *Critical Perspectives on Accounting*, 13(3) (June 2002): 297–310. www.sciencedirect.com.

[‡] en.wikipedia.org/wiki/Theft.

proverb that the president used frequently: *Doveryai, no proveryai* (trust, but verify).

The Russian politician Vladimir Lenin (1870–1924) said: "Trust is good, but control is better."*

Juan Domingo Perón (1895–1974), three-time president of Argentina, said, "Man is good, but if he is watched he is better."†

Sam Walton after having experienced robberies in one of his Walmart stores, said: "I learned this very early in the department store business: you have to give people responsibilities, you have to trust them and then you have to control them."‡

Mattel's systems and security engineer has said, "The security cameras make honest people stay that way."§

In 2007, Daniel Kaufmann, director of the World Bank Institute, said,

> If you ask people what they would do if they found an envelope with US$2,000 in a parking lot, 30% say they would take it, 20% say they would give it back and 50% say they would think about it. But if the same question is added that there is a hidden security camera in the place, 67% of the respondents say they would return the money.¶

Employees, customers, and suppliers can steal assets from an organization, and that is why organizations implement control systems, disciplinary sanctions, and legal actions to avoid or prevent theft.

French writer and aviator Antoine Marie Jean-Baptiste Roger de Saint-Exupéry (1900–1944) pointed out, "In the Planet of the Little Prince... there were good and bad herbs. ... If it is a bad plant, the plant should be snatched immediately, as soon as it has been recognized."**

The Parable of the Weed of the Gospel of St. Matthew (13:24–43) in the New Testament in the Bible says that a man had sown good seed in his field, and while he slept, an enemy sowed weed among the wheat. When the wheat budded and produced the grains, the weeds that had been planted also appeared. Jesus said that at the time of harvest, he would say to the reapers, "First collect the weeds and tie them in bundles to be burned; then gather the wheat and bring it into my barn."

---

* "Vladimir Lenin," www.azquotes.com.
† www.sitiosargentina.com.ar/notas/2009/junio/frases-peron.htm.
‡ Sam Walton, *Made in America: Mi Historia* (Imprenta Arredondo, 2001), 152 ("Made in America: My Story).
§ Naomi Klein, *No Logo*, Chap. 11 (Paidos, 2001), 292.
¶ Daniel Kaufmann, 43 Coloquio Anual de IDEA 2007 ("43 Annual IDEA 2007 Colloquium").
** Antoine de Saint Exupéry, *El Principito* (Emece, 1951), 28 ("The Little Prince").

In organizations, as in life, there will always be wheat and weeds and corporate leaders need to tear up the weeds, as soon as they appear, to take care of the good seed.

American lawyer and politician Rudolph Giuliani was the mayor of New York City from 1994 to 2001. His leadership in the city during the attacks of September 11, 2001, led him to be named *Time* magazine "Person of the Year." In an article published by the Argentine newspaper, *La Nación* called "New York, from Chaos to Zero Tolerance,"* Giuliani explains the transformation in New York City in the previous 20 years.

Giuliani was inspired by the "theory of broken windows" of American professors of Harvard University James Q. Wilson (1931–2012) and George L. Kelling that generated a change in the method of combating criminality through the implementation of zero tolerance programs in New York City.[†] According to this theory of criminology, if in an abandoned building there is a broken window and it is not repaired quickly, neighbors will throw stones at the rest of the windows and eventually break into the building, occupy it, and destroy the entire property.

Therefore, it is necessary to promptly repair what is broken or abandoned, in order to prevent problems from multiplying. Because signs of disorder in a business generate misconduct, companies must avoid cluttered and neglected work environments and deal with problems when they are still small.

The "paradox of tolerance" was described by the Austrian-British philosopher Karl Popper (1902–1994) in 1945. The paradox states that if a society is tolerant without limit, its ability to be tolerant will eventually be seized or destroyed by the intolerant. Popper came to the seemingly paradoxical conclusion that in order to maintain a tolerant society, the society must be intolerant of intolerance. In his book *The Open Society and its Enemies*, he said:

> Less well known is the *paradox of tolerance*: Unlimited tolerance must lead to the disappearance of tolerance. If we extend unlimited tolerance even to those who are intolerant, if we are not prepared to defend a tolerant society against the onslaught of the intolerant, then the tolerant will be destroyed, and tolerance with them.[‡]

---

* Manuel J. Torino, "New York, from Chaos to Zero Tolerance," *La Nación*, January 5, 2009.
† This theory is also mentioned in Giuliani's book, *Leadership*, Miramax (2002), 47.
‡ "Paradox of Tolerance," en.wikipedia.org/wiki/Paradox_of_tolerance Popper, Karl, *The Open Society, and Its Enemies, Volume 1, The Age of Plato* (Routledge, United Kingdom, 1945) (1 volume 2013 Princeton ed.).

William Bratton, former New York Police Chief, said: "The police should punish all infractions, no matter how insignificant they may seem, because the sum of these small faults creates a climate of disorder and insecurity that favors the outbreak of crime."*

The New York Police Department deploys a computer system for crime prevention called CompStat, which collects processes and analyzes thousands of real-time crime figures and statistics daily. The results are reflected in a gigantic crime map that allows one to instantly know the most critical areas in the city, to detect trends in new types of crimes, and to evaluate police action block by block. The city of New York had an average of 250,000 car thefts per year, but after implementing this system, annual robberies were reduced to less than 10% of that figure. During his tenure, Giuliani managed to reduce crime by 57% and homicides in the city of New York went from 2,200 to 500 per year.

If bad behaviors are not disciplined, that lack of reaction will only encourage other people to replicate similar actions.

Researchers at University College London, Neil Garrett and Stephanie Lazzaro, in an article published in 2016 in *Nature Neuroscience* investigated how a person's dishonesty works:

> Dishonesty is an integral part of our social world, influencing domains ranging from finance and politics to personal relationships. Anecdotally, digressions from a moral code are often described as a series of small breaches that grow over time. Here we provide empirical evidence for a gradual escalation of self-serving dishonesty and reveal a neural mechanism supporting it. Behaviorally, we show that the extent to which participants engage in self-serving dishonesty increases with repetition.... What begins as small acts of dishonesty can escalate into larger transgressions.[†]

When a person commits a repulsive action for the first time he or she feels fear. But if that incorrect action does not generate a harmful result and, on the contrary, it obtains a personal benefit, the valuation of that act is modified and the next transgression is not considered so dangerous.

As these misbehaviors are repeated, the fear will be less and less and the moral and ethical standards will relax. What produced psychological distress goes attenuating with the repetition of wrongful acts and the moral

---

* Manuel J. Torino, "New York, from Chaos to Zero Tolerance," *La Nación*, January 5, 2009.

† Neil Garret and Stephanie Lazzaro, "The Brain Adapts to Dishonesty," www.nature.com 24 de octubre de 2016.

conscience is being silenced. Unethical acts eventually lose importance and are considered normal acts.*

Fight against theft, be it of employees or third parties, should be part of the prevention work of organization leaders because when the thieves are warned that there are efficient control systems, their interest in stealing declines.

In the book *Business Ethics*, Joseph W. Weiss mentions that "The CNN reported that one out of every three businesses closes due to the theft of employees."[†] Adelphia Communications Corporation, founded in 1952, was one of the largest cable television companies in the United States. In 2002, it filed for bankruptcy because it was learned that hundreds of millions of dollars had been loaned to the controlling family of the company to the detriment of shareholders, and US$2.3 billion of liabilities were hidden.[‡] Adelphia's chief executive was sentenced to more than 20 years in prison.[§]

Next, you will see some historical cases.

Bruce Reynolds and Ronald Gibbs performed a masterstroke on August 8, 1963, when, with more than a dozen hooded bandits, they that night robbed the train that went from Glasgow to London and that carried in a secret convoy the collection of all the banks of the country, £2.6 million.

Eduardo Valfierno (1850–1931) was an Argentine who dedicated himself to selling objects of art and antiques that had belonged to his family.

In one of his regular trips to France, where he called himself "Marques de Valfierno," he met an artist named Yves Chaudron, who was dedicated to forging paintings of the Renaissance. Valfierno and Chaudron reached an agreement, and over 14 months Chaudron made six high-quality copies of *La Gioconda*[ˢ] using sixteenth-century procedures. Meanwhile, Valfierno contacted potential buyers of the artwork with whom they arranged a sale, telling them the painting would be stolen from the Louvre Museum.

---

* Norberto Abdala, "Cómo Funciona la Mente de un Corrupto," August 16, 2018, www.clarin.com.ar ("How the Mind of a Corrupt Person Works").

† Joseph W. Weiss, *Ética en Los Negocios*, 4th ed (Thompson), 11 ("Business Ethics").

‡ "Michael Rigas se declara culpable en escándalo de Adelphia," Associated Press, November 23, 2005 ("Michael Rigas pleads guilty in Adelphia Scandal").

§ The majority of Adelphia's assets were eventually acquired by Time Warner Cable and Comcast in 2006, and the long-distance telephone business was sold to Pioneer Telephone.

ˢ *The Gioconda* is a work of the Italian Renaissance painter Leonardo Da Vinci and property of the French State. Its name, *The Joyful One* in Castilian, derives from the identity of the wife of Francesco Bartolomeo del Giocondo, that was called Lisa Gherardini and from where comes the other name that is given to the painting, Mona (Lady) Lisa.

To carry out the robbery, Valfierno contacted an Italian carpenter, Vincenzo Peruggia (1881–1925), who worked at the Louvre Museum. Valfierno promised him a large sum of money if he would steal the painting, telling him that the work would be "returned to his homeland."*

On August 21, 1911, at 7 o'clock in the morning, the carpenter took down the world's most famous picture, painted by Leonardo Da Vinci between 1503 and 1506, and taking advantage of the absence of the security guard, took it to one of the stairs. With a screwdriver, Peruggia separated the painting from its frame, stripped it of the glass that protected it, hid the painting in its dust coat, and retired from the Museum. At that time the Louvre had over 400 rooms but only 200 guards. Security was poor, as in most museums at that time.†

When the robbery was discovered the next day, the borders were closed and ships and trains were inspected. All the employees were questioned; the poet Guillaume Apollinaire was arrested and jailed on suspicion of stealing La Gioconda and Pablo Picasso was interrogated as a suspect. "Crowds flocked to the Louvre just to see the empty space where the little portrait of that sixteenth-century woman used to be."‡

Peruggia kept the painting for two years, waiting in vain for Valfierno to contact him. As Valfierno had already sold the six copies as originals to five North American buyers and a Brazilian, he no longer needed the original painting.

On December 22, 1913, Peruggia contacted an Italian collector, Alfredo Geri, to whom he offered the painting for half a million lire and the promise that the painting would never return to France.§ When the painting was delivered in Florence, Peruggia was arrested, was imprisoned for a year, and never betrayed his accomplice.

In 1931, Valfierno knew that he had little time to live and wanted to be recognized for having carried out the most important theft in the history of art. He granted an interview to the journalist Karl Decker in which he confessed the origin of his fortune and gave details of the identity of the six purchasers of the paintings whom he had also been swindled out of

---

* Perugia believed that the painting had been stolen by Napoleon when in fact it was bought by Francisco I of France in the sixteenth century.

† Sheena McKenzie, "Mona Lisa: The Theft that Created a Legend," November 19, 2013, www.cnn.com.

‡ Olivia Sorrel-Dejerine, "The Robbery that Made Mona Lisa Famous," December 15, 2013, www.bbc.com.

§ es.wikipedia.org/wiki/Eduardo_Valfierno.

US$300,000 for each painting. The only condition that Valfierno put on the interview was that the story would be released after his death.

William Francis "Willie" Sutton (1901–1980) was a New York–born bank robber who managed to rack up about US$2 million from his robberies. While Sutton was repeatedly captured and imprisoned, he managed to escape from prison on three occasions. When a journalist asked why he stole from banks, he is said to have responded: "Because that's where the money is." This phrase known as Sutton's law is used as a metaphor to focus efforts on a clear objective.[*]

The Frenchman Albert Spaggiari (1932–1989) was a former parachutist who in 1976 carried out what was known as the "Theft of the Century" when he led the assault on the Société Générale Bank of the city of Nice on the French Blue Coast, stealing about 60 million francs from 337 security boxes. After more than a year planning the robbery, he built, with a former-military gang, an 8-meter-long tunnel that ran from the sewer system to the ground below the financial institution. During the Bastille Day holiday weekend, Spaggiari's band pierced the bank floor. They entered on July 17, 1976, and left on Monday, July 20, at 5:00 am, a few hours before the bank opened to the public. Before leaving, Spaggiari wrote on the wall with spray paint: "*Sans arme, sans violence et sans haine*" ("Without arms, without hatred and without violence").[†]

Spaggiari was arrested two months after the spectacular heist. During the trial, he told every detail of the robbery, and after telling it, he ran and launched himself from one of the windows of the courtroom. They believed that he had committed suicide, but he had actually fallen on a mattress-padded roof of a parked van and then climbed onto a motorcycle driven by a friend who was waiting for him.

More than ten years later, on June 10, 1989, Albert Spaggiari was found dead at the door of his mother's house.[‡]

The Jules Rimet Trophy was the original prize for the winners of the Soccer World Cup. Initially called *Victoria*, but usually known simply as the World Cup or "Coupe du Monde," it was officially renamed "Jules Rimet Cup" in 1946 to honor the then FIFA President Jules Rimet (1873–1956) who collaborated to create the competition.[§]

---

[*] In medicine, the phrase is applied to performing first those tests that can confirm or discard the most probable or obvious diagnoses.

[†] es.wikipedia.org/wiki/Albert_Spaggiari.

[‡] The film *The Easy Way* relates to these facts. It was directed by Jean-Paul Rouve (2008).

[§] Designed by Abel Lafleur and made of gold-plated sterling silver with a blue lapis lazuli base, it measured 35 centimeters (14 inches) tall and weighed 3.8 kilograms (8.4 lbs). It consisted of an octagonal cup, supported by a winged figure representing Nike, the Greek goddess of victory.

During World War II, the trophy was retained by the champion of 1938, Italy. Ottorino Barassi, president of the Italian Football Federation, who secretly removed the trophy from a bank in Rome and hid it in a shoebox under his bed to prevent the Nazis from seizing the trophy.

On March 20, 1966, four months before the start of the 1966 World Cup in England, the trophy was stolen during a public exhibition at the Westminster Central Hall. The trophy was found seven days later, wrapped in newspaper at the bottom of a hedge of a suburban garden in Beulah Hill, South Norwood, south London, by a dog named Pickles during a walk with its owner David Corbett.

When the England soccer team won the trophy, as a prize, Pickles was invited to the celebratory banquet and allowed to lick the plates after the inaugural banquet. His owner, David Corbett, collected a prize of £6,000 (based on the increase in average income and inflation would be approximately £169,000 in 2009). An investigation by the *Daily Mirror* in 2018 revealed Sidney Cugullere (1926–2005) stole the cup. Cugullere took advantage that the guards had left to look for coffee and he stole the cup. Upon learning what happened, Sidney's father was frightened and both decided to leave it lying where the dog Pickles found it while walking with his owner.*

On the morning of Friday, September 23, 1994, Mario Cesar Fendrich, deputy treasurer of Banco de la Nación Argentina, Santa Fe branch, greeted his wife and told him after work he would go for fishing with his friends. Actually, he had another plan, to steal from the bank where he worked.

He waited for the arrival of two money transporter trucks; he carried the bags to the treasury but after a while, he left the bank with a box and walked to his car, a red Fiat Duna Weekend.

Before leaving, he left a note to his superior: "I took 3 million pesos and US$187 thousand."

Fendrich became the country's most wanted fugitive for three months.

On January 9, 1995, after 109 days of being a fugitive, he reappeared. Fendrich said he had been kidnapped by a gang and had been forced to withdraw the money.

---

* In 1970 the trophy was handed over to Brazil in property after winning the championship for the third time. In the early morning of December 23, 1983, the cup was stolen again, this time from the headquarters of the Brazilian Football Federation and that same night it was melted to sell the 1.8 kilograms of gold it contained. The trophy that is preserved today is a reproduction made in 1984. "Desvelan la Identidad del Ladrón que Robó la Copa Jules Rimet en Inglaterra en 1966." Mario de la Riva www.as.com, June 12, 2018 ("Reveal Identity of the Thief who Stole the Jules Rimet Cup in England in 1966").

In October 1999, he was given seven years and two months in prison. Fendrich joined the *Guinness Book of Records* for being the author of the largest individual theft in the history.*

The Brazilian Central Bank branch in Fortaleza was assaulted during the weekend of August 6 and 7, 2005. The thieves rented a house across the avenue, facing the bank, and built a 78-meter tunnel. To reach the vault, the thieves drilled through a floor of 1.10 meters of concrete laced with steel mesh. They stole 156 million of reais weighing about 3.5 tons and amounting to about US$68 million.

The first suspects arrested made ostentatious purchases with 50-reais notes. After a judicial investigation, about 50 people were arrested, and authorities managed to recover a third of the money. The bank had not insured the risk because they considered the possibility of theft to be too small to justify the expense of the insurance premium.

The chief of the federal police of the state of Ceara (whose capital city is Fortaleza) said, "This is the biggest assault known in the country. It's kind of a movie"[†] – and the film was made.[‡]

On January 13, 2006, the Banco Rio was robbed in Acassuso, in the Province of Buenos Aires, Argentina. Twenty-three people were taken hostage while 200 policemen had them surrounded. During the time the robbers were in the bank, they asked for pizza and soda and sang the "Happy Birthday" song to one of the hostages. The band of robbers stole around US$20 million and escaped from the bank through a tunnel that ended in an underground channel where two rubber boats were waiting for them to escape.

When the police entered the bank, they came across a message written on one of the walls: "In a neighborhood of rich people, without weapons or grudges, it is just money, there is no love."[§]

Four years after the robbery, a trial began. Fernando Araujo, the mastermind of the assault on the bank of Acassuso, said:

---

* "Murió Mario César Fendrich, el Autor del Robo del Siglo," December 19, 2018, www.lanacion.com.ar José Bordon; "El Robo del Siglo, Murió Mario Fendrich. ¿Quién era?" December 19, 2018, www.elcronsita.com ("Mario Cesar Fendrich, the Author of Theft of the Century, Died"; "The Robbery of the Century, Mario Fendrich Died. Who was?").

† Luis Esnal, "Espectacular Robo en Brasil al Banco Central," August 9, 2005, www.lanacion.com.ar ("Spectacular Robbery in Brazil to the Central Bank").

‡ *Federal Bank Heist* (Portuguese: *Assalto ao Banco Central*) is a 2011 Brazilian thriller film directed by Marcos Paulo Simões.

§ "De Ladrón del Siglo a Joyero," February 9, 2014, www.elmundo.es Juan Ignacio Irigaray ("From Thief of the Century to Jeweler").

Anyone can rob a bank. At least the way I did it. Without violence, taking into account the moral part, thinking every detail, going deep with ideas and studying so there is no margin of error. Stealing a bank is hitting the system. I love the adrenaline: Stealing a bank is a pure adrenaline. … The project to rob the bank I called Donatello Project. Not by the famous Renaissance artist, but by one of the ninja turtles. They were green as cannabis, martial as I'm, they liked the risks and above all things, they were in the sewers.*

The Bible says, "An this know, that if the Goodman of the house had known what hour the thief would come, he would have watched, and not have suffered his house to be broken through."†

To reduce the risk of theft, organizations must be on permanent alert, with processes and controls in place that allow them to be prepared to face it.

As the saying goes, "Always sleep with one eye open."

---

* The Uruguayan Luis Mario Vitette Sellanes was another member of the criminal gang who said "I did not have any money left over from the theft. It was an ugly memory, nothing more. I was imprisoned for 4 years and I spent a fortune in the shade, not free." "Robo Del Siglo," January 14, 2016, www.lanacion.com.ar ("Theft of the Century").
† The Bible: Luke 12:39 and Matthew 24:43.

17

Corporate Risks: Unit 5

17.1 FRAUDS, DECEPTION, AND SCAMS

The word *fraud* comes from the Latin *fraus* and means an action contrary to the truth, a deception that is committed against a person or an organization.

The jurist Servio Rufo (105–43 BC) defined *fraud* as the simulation of doing one thing, when in reality another was done, in order to deceive someone. The Roman jurist Marco Labeon (1 BC) then defined *fraud* as "All cunning, deceit or machination used to surprise, deceive or defraud another."[*]

In the Praetorian Law (Ius honorarium) of the Roman Republic, fraud was considered a vice of the will, because if it had not existed, the other party would not have given its consent to the act.[†]

Donald R. Cressey (1919–1987), American sociologist and criminologist who made innovative contributions to the study of criminal law and organized crime, developed a triangle with the three elements that exist in a fraud. Cressey says, "The perpetrators experience some incentive or pressure that leads them to commit a dishonest act, there must be an opportunity to commit fraud and fraudsters are generally able to rationalize or justify their actions."[‡]

---

[*] "Título 8, De dolo," archivos.juridicas.unam.mx, 217–8; "Actio Doli." Revista Jurídica Electrónica Facultad de Derecho Universidad Nacional de Lomas de Zamora, www.derecho.unlz.edu.ar (Legal Electronic Journal Faculty of Law National University of Lomas de Zamora).

[†] es.wikipedia.org/wiki/Ius_honorarium.

[‡] *Fraude en Tiempos de Crisis* (PricewaterhouseCoopers, 2009), 4 ("Fraud in Times of Crisis").

In organizations, fraud is an act executed in order to seek an illicit benefit to the detriment of the company. The risk of being a victim of fraud is one of the major causes of loss for businesses.

Like the Trojan Horse[*] or the Pied Piper of Hamelin,[†] sometimes organizations are not what they seem. An apple can be very appealing to the eye, but when it is cut in the middle, it can happen that it is rotten or has worms inside.

In 1845, William Thompson, a well-dressed man from New York, used to start conversations with people he did not know, and after gaining their trust, Thompson would ask, "Would you lend some money until tomorrow when I will return it to you without fail?" After receiving it, Thompson disappeared, and the victim did not usually hear from him again. After carrying out many scams, Thompson was brought to trial in 1849.[‡]

The "Cuento del Tio" (Uncle fraud) is the name given to a type of scam that takes advantage of the confidence of people to obtain great benefits. The name comes from the story a swindler tells the victim where he or she has received an inheritance from a distant uncle. Then, the swindler asks for money from the victim to book a trip to secure his inheritance, with the promise the swindler will return the money in an amount several times higher than the amount provided. The scammer leaves and never appears again.

Between 1880 and 1915, some two million Italians settled in Argentina. In 1913, the government of Italy published *The Manual of the Italian Immigrant*, which contained advice and warnings for the citizens who emigrated to Argentina, including a description of a scam:

---

[*] Troy-today, Turkey's territory was a thriving Mediterranean town and famous for its great ramparts. By 1200 BC, the Greek army had tried to conquer it, but they had never been able to cross its walls, and the way to do so was through deception. The "Trojan Horse" was a huge hollow wooden horse that the Greeks left on the beaches of Troy. The Trojans took it as a sign of their victory and took it inside the city, but during the night, warriors hiding inside the horse opened the gates of Troy, allowing the entry of the Greek army, who conquered the city.

[†] The Pied Piper of Hamelin is a German fable, documented by the Brothers Grimm, published in 1816 and tells a story of what happened in the city of Hamelin, Germany, in 1284. The city of Hamelin was infested with rats, and one day a stranger appeared who offered his services to the villagers. In exchange for a reward, he agreed that he would get rid of all the rats. When the unknown flutist began to play his flute, all the rats came out of their holes and began to walk toward where the music sounded. Once all the rats were gathered around the flute player, he began to walk, and all the rats followed the sound of the music. The piper went to the river Weser, and the rats that followed him were fooled and drowned.

[‡] Gregorio Doval, *Fraudes, engaños y timos de la Historia* (Nowtilus, 2011), 190 ("Frauds, Deceptions, and Scams of History").

Be wary.... Do not listen to wonderful stories or pious cases.... Know that there is a remarkable system to deceive the immigrant who has just landed: it is the so-called "tale of the uncle" and in Italy is known as "truffa all' Americana."* It consists of asking the newcomer for money through all kinds of pretexts.... Very often the newspaper's report these cases with rather witty stories.... Do you know the proverb a man warned is half saved? Attention then! Their natural mistrust will be well used in these cases.

At that same time, the train took to Buenos Aires thousands of countrymen that were amazed with the splendor of the city. One of the most famous scams to these naive countrymen was the sale of mailboxes. The scammer stood next to the mailbox (which belonged to the State) and began to talk to the fellow. While they were talking, the accomplices of the scammer left letters in the mailbox and gave money to the scammer. As he received the money, he explained to the countryman that with that job he had already made a fortune and that he wanted to retire and put the mailbox for sale. According to the records of the time, scammers achieved spectacular profits selling mailboxes to countrymen,† being "The Sale of Mailbox," the most famous fraud in Buenos Aires at that time.

In some Latin American countries, but principally in Argentina, it is called "Creole Cleverness" (*viveza criolla*), a way of life that some inhabitants of Buenos Aires used to ignore norms and consideration of their neighbor.

A key highlight from the history of the FIFA World Cups is from June 22, 1986, when Diego Maradona scored both goals for Argentina against England at the Azteca Stadium in Mexico City, in the quarter-finals. After the first goal of Maradona, some English players protested claiming the goal was made using his hand, but the Tunisian referee validated it. The game ended with Argentina winning two goals to one and the Argentine team moved on to the semifinals.‡ Diego Maradona said after the game that the first goal scored "a little with the head and a little with the hand of God." The Argentinian Jorge Valdano who played that game opined

---

* Scam to the American.
† "Vender un Buzón," Significadoyorigen.wordpress.com, June 2, 2010; "De Donde Viene Te Vendemos un Buzón," www.taringa.net/posts/ciencia-educacion ("Sell a Mailbox"; "Where the Phrase 'We Sell You a Mailbox' Comes From").
‡ The second goal that Maradona did in that game is considered "The Goal of the Century" or the best goal in the history of the World Cup. It was decided by a poll on the website of FIFA during the World Cup FIFA 2002.

that "in a game of great symbolic value, Maradona showed the two ways of being Argentine. In the first shot, it shows *the trap, mischievousness* or *creole vivacity*. Maradona's second goal crowns the match with an artwork."*

The Argentine writer Jorge Luis Borges (1899–1986) said that in Argentina the *creole vivacity* was nothing other than dishonesty.

Some phrases that are associated with that philosophy of life are "Made the law, made the loophole," "In the end if I do not steal, someone else will," or "The cunning lives of the sucker, and the sucker lives off the job."†

The famous tango *Cambalache* composed in 1934 by the Argentine musician Enrique Santos Discepolo (1901–1951) said in one of its verses, "There always have been thieves, traitors, and victims of fraud... the immoral have caught up with us... and if you don't steal, you're stupid."‡ Although it was written more than 80 years ago, it still maintains an enormous validity, as a clear reflection of today's society.

The word *deception* comes from the Latin *ignannare*, which means *to entangle someone* or *make fun of him*. Through deception, someone is made to believe something that is not true.

Not everything is as it seems. On November 24, 2009, Michaele and Tareq Salahi attended a White House state dinner for Indian Prime Minister, as uninvited guests. They were able to pass through the security checkpoints and meet President Barack Obama. They pass through the security checkpoints because they "looked the part."§

One of the first lessons of the doctor and academic Jose Letamendi y Manjarres (1828–1897), professor of pathology at the University of Barcelona, was to take the students to see a corpse. Letamendi would say to them:

> A good doctor must have two conditions: 1) not to be disgusted by anything that concerns the sick and 2) to possess, to a great degree, what we call the *clinical eye*, which is a kind of professional intuition that makes us realize, without error, the type of disease that the patient suffers.

Having said that, Letamendi would invite his students to imitate him in everything he did. Letamendi then inserted his index finger into the anus of the body and, without cleaning it, put it in his mouth. Each and every one of the students, conquering their most natural disgust, repeated the action. When everyone finished doing it, Dr. Letamendi told them:

---

* "A 25 años de la genialidad maradoniana ante Inglaterra," June 22, 2011, www.lanacion.com. Mexican photographer Alejandro Carbajal Ojeda immortalized this moment in a photo where it can be seen the blow with the hand ("25 years of Maradona's genius against England").
† "Viveza Criolla," Wikipedia ("Creole vividness").
‡ letrasdetango.wordpress.com/2011/02/15/cambalache/.
§ en.wikipedia.org/wiki/2009_U.S._state_dinner_security_breaches.

Very good and very bad at the same time, although you know how to overcome the natural disgust, as far as the *clinical eye* is concerned, you go very badly. You have used the same finger, without realizing that I have used two fingers, one to insert it in the corpse and the other one to insert it in my mouth.*

But we can go even further back in history. Scottish economist and philosopher Adam Smith (1723–1790) in his book *The Wealth of Nations*, published in 1776, said that before the coins were established, people were always exposed to fraud and deception. Instead of receiving pure metals of silver or copper in exchange for their goods, people received instead metals adulterated with cheaper materials, although apparently pure.

Once the States created the coins that guaranteed the weight and fineness of the metal to facilitate the exchange of goods, over time the States began to decrease the actual amount of metal that these coins originally contained. In this way, princes paid their debts and fulfilled obligations contracted with a smaller amount of metal than they would have needed, defrauding the creditors with a good part of what was owed to them.†

Once, a king of Syracuse asked a goldsmith to make him a gold crown and to do so he gave him a bar of pure gold. When the goldsmith gave the crown to the king, he had doubts about the craftsman's honesty, suspecting that he could have substituted part of the gold with silver to deceive him. Then, to solve the enigma, the king called Archimedes (287–212 BC). This physicist-mathematician was inspired while bathing and, excited about his finding, he ran naked through the streets of Syracuse shouting "Eureka, Eureka." He had discovered that the volume of water that ascended was equal to that of the submerged body. That discovery allowed him to analyze if the crown of Hieron II, king of Syracuse, was made of pure gold. Knowing the volume and the weight, Archimedes could determine the density of the material of the crown. In this way he demonstrated to the king that the goldsmith had deceived him.‡

The deceit, the fraud, the lies, and the lack of ethics have always existed, in every place and in the most diverse fields. It is interesting to review some

---

* Gregorio Doval, *Fraudes, Engaños y Timos de la Historia* (Nowtilus Saber, 2011), 45 ("Frauds, Deceptions and Scams of History").
† Adam Smith, *The Wealth of Nations* (Folio, Biblioteca de Economia, 1996), 68, 72.
‡ This story about the "Principle of Archimedes" appears for the first time in "De Architectura," a book by the Roman architect and writer Marco Vitruvio Polion (80–15 BC) written two centuries after the death of Archimedes. Syracuse was a Greek city in Sicily. It became part of the Roman Republic of Sicily toward 212 BC and in the Siege of Syracuse Archimedes was assassinated.

significant cases of history – some of them are so humorous, incredible, and unreal that they seem to be taken from a cartoon or a science fiction movie. These real stories can serve to remind us that we should not underestimate situations and stay alert and remain vigilant to reduce the possibility of deception, which is always lurking.

Toft, the Mother of Rabbits: Mary Toft (1701–1763), also called Mary Tofts, was an English woman, married and illiterate from Godalming, Surrey.

In 1726, at the age of 25 and three children, she deceived the people of Godalming and several doctors who incredibly believed she had given birth to several rabbits as a result of the sexual assault of a "six-foot rabbit" in the forest.

The subject attracted the attention of Nathaniel St. André, surgeon of the royal house of Jorge I of Great Britain. St. Andre investigated and concluded Toft was telling the truth.

As explained by the Spanish journalist Santiago Camacho Hidalgo,

> When Mary was alone, the patient was replenished from a secret deposit to load her belly. … We do not want to imagine the damage, not to mention the risk of infections of all kinds, which should cause to introduce the small animals in such a delicate part.*

By then already quite famous, Toft was taken to London, where she was studied in depth. Not producing more rabbits, she finally confessed to the hoax and was jailed for a short time.

When Toft died, 40 years later, on her death certificate in the Church she was registered as: "Mary Toft, widow and rabbit impostor."

The Cottingley Fairies: The Cottingley Fairies are a series of five photographs taken by Elsie Wright and French Griffiths, two young cousins living in Cottingley, near Bradford (England) where they appeared performing activities with so-called fairies. In July 1917, when the first two photos were taken, Elsie was 16 years old and Frances, 10.

---

* Santiago Camacho, *Twenty Great Frauds of History* (EDAF, 2008), 81. Camacho mentions that "England of 1726 was to be the scene of the most delirious stories in history. The reign of King George I (1660–1727) was an era in which charlatans and scammers of all fur and condition were born. The king himself was an unusual subject, who never learned English and kept his wife imprisoned for thirty-two years," 71, same book.

Some photographers of the time examined the photos and declared them true. The British writer Sir Arthur Conan Doyle (1859–1930), known for creating the detective Sherlock Holmes, was one of many believers and made the book *The Arrival of the Fairies*, published in 1922.

Just in 1981 in an interview by Joe Copper for *The Unexplained* magazine, the cousins declared the photographs were false. They had pinned fairy clippings.

In 1982 Elsie Wright stated that they had been ashamed to admit the truth after deceiving Sherlock Holmes. Frances said, "I never thought it was a fraud, we were just Elsie and I having a little fun and today I cannot understand how we could deceive them, they wanted us to deceive them."[*]

The Cardiff Giant: On October 16, 1869, the body of a giant of more than 3.1 meters (9.8 feet) in height and 1,360 kilograms in weight was discovered in Cardiff, New York, while a water well was dug on a farm. The giant was buried 2 meters deep. There were those who believed he was a petrified man, and others believed it was a statue created by the Jesuit missionaries. The news was made public, and thousands of people came to see the body.

Twenty-four hours after the discovery, a tent was raised near the excavation, and visitors could see the body by paying 50 cents. The profits were very large, and the figure was eventually sold for US$37,500. A paleontologist from Yale studied the body and declared it a fraud by finding chisel marks on the statue.

The Cardiff Giant was the creation of a gentleman named George Hull, who had ordered the carving of the human figure to be buried in the field of his cousin, William Newell.[†] The idea came to him when he heard the Bible should be interpreted literally, including the Genesis 6:4 passage that says, "There were giants in the earth in those days."[‡]

---

[*] es.wikipedia.org/wiki/Las_hadas_de_Cottingley ("Cottingley Fairies").

[†] The figure is currently at the Farmer's Museum in Cooperstown, New York, and a replica of it can be seen at Marvin's Marvelous Mechanical Museum in Detroit.

[‡] In 1908, while paving in Piltdown, Sussex, England, skeletal remains (a skull, a tooth, and a jaw with teeth) were found and handed over to the amateur archaeologist and lawyer Charles Dawson (1864–1916), who had been investigating that area for years.

Until that time, ancient human fossils had been discovered, but all of them outside of England. The Piltdown finding was immediately accepted by the English scientific community who were reluctant to accept that the first humans were not to be found on their lands (The Dutch anatomist Eugene Dubois (1858–1940), a follower of Darwin's ideas, became famous for his discovery of "Homo Erectus" on the island of Java, Indonesia, in 1891. In 1895 he unveiled his fossil discoveries of a Monkey Man since he considered that the fossils found were half of human and half of apes. Most scientists disagreed with their conclusions that these bones represented those of a monkey man).

Boston Marathon 1980: The athlete Rosie Ruiz, born in Cuba, won the 84th Boston Marathon on April 21, 1980, and became a celebrity for completing the marathon with a world record: 2 hours, 31 minutes, and 56 seconds. Rosie was not among the favorites and her record was the best ever in its

---

Dawson presented the "Piltdown Man" to the British Museum and to the Geological Society of London as the finding of the missing link, the species that related humans to their ape-like ancestors and corroborated Darwin's theory of evolution.

Forty-five years later, and due to the development of new chemical dating methods, it was possible to prove that everything was a fraud. The skull was 500 years old (not 50,000 as suggested by Dawson), the jaw of the skeleton was of an orangutan and the loose tooth of a monkey. The dark color of the bones was due to a chemical treatment to standardize the color differences between the skull and the jaw.

The Israeli biologist Alexander Kohn pointed out that it was "the most elaborate scientific fraud of all that has ever been perpetrated." It is believed that Charles Dawson, deceased in 1916, was the author of the fraud. In spite of the fraud, a monument honoring the discovery has been erected in the place where the bones were found.

www.nationalgeographic.com.es "El Hombre de Piltdown, uno de los mayores fraudes científicos" y www.muyinteresante.es "El Hombre de Piltdown, la gran mentira de la evolución" ("The Piltdown Man, one of the biggest scientific frauds"; "The Piltdown Man, the great lie of evolution").

Santiago Camacho, *20 Grandes Fraudes de la Historia* (EDAF, 2008), 189 ("20 Great Frauds of History").

Another famous fraud was "The Minnesota Ice Man" which depicted a man-like creature, frozen in a block of ice and exhibited at malls, fairs, and carnivals in the United States and Canada in the 1960s and early 1970s. Promoter and exhibitor Frank Hansen stated the Minnesota man was discovered in the Bering Strait, in the Siberia region (he later said he had found him in a Minnesota forest), and his owner was a millionaire from California. In December 1968 the Scottish naturalist and biologist Ivan T. Sanderson (1911–1973) and the French zoologist Bernard Heuvelmans for three days visually examined the creature trapped in the ice block and concluded that it was something extraordinary.

Sanderson, the science editor of *Argosy* magazine, wrote an article on the Iceman in the April 1969 issue that included the headline: "Is this the missing link between man and apes?"

Sanderson also talked about Iceman in TV appearances, and contacted the English primatologist and paleontologist John Russell Napier (1917–1987), asking him to investigate it under the auspices of the Smithsonian Institute.

Napier initiated an investigation and discovered Hansen had commissioned the creation of the Iceman of a West Coast company in 1967.

It was later learned that a paleontologist collaborating with the Smithsonian Institute had rejected in the early 1960s the idea to create a figure "a Man of Cromanon who would later freeze."

Who made the latex figure was the Howard Ball modeler. Ball's widow noted that "we model the body based on an artistic representation of a man from Cromanon."

Napier stated that "The Smithsonian Institution ... is satisfied that the creature is merely a carnival display made of latex rubber and hair."

The creature was purchased in 2013 by the Museum of the Weird, in Austin, Texas.

Massimo Polidoro, *Enigmas y Misterios de la Historia* (Critica, April 2014) 275–6 ("Enigmas and Mysteries of History").

In recent years frauds have been detected on objects that appeared as prehistoric. For example, the antiquity of the "Piedras de Ica," from Peru, which have decorated dinosaur drawings. Scientific studies concluded that the drawings were made in recent years.

The same has been concluded regarding the "Figures of Acámbaro," from Mexico, a collection of thousands of pieces found in 1945 and representing extinct animals.

category. "I woke up with a lot of energy this morning," she said to the media. Rosie was greeted with applause and laurels by the organizers.

Bill Rodgers, the winner in the male category, was surprised to see her get to the press conference almost without sweating and breathing normally while he had not yet had recovered after running 42 kilometers. Rodgers said he did not understand as Rosie was "without sweating and breathing quietly" at the conference.

The organization also suspected and started an investigation. They checked videos and photos taken at different points of the circuit and discovered that she only appeared about the end of the marathon. Two young students recalled an athlete, two kilometers from the finish, moved among people to get to the asphalt. It was learned that Rosie traveled by subway a good part of the circuit to join the squad at 1.6 kilometers from the finish, where she started running for victory. Rosie Ruiz was disqualified for life to run the Boston Marathon and the winner happened to be the Canadian Jacqueline Gareau. The action of cutting the path of a marathon is known ever since as "Making a Rosie Ruiz."*

Armstrong and the Tour de France: According to the International Olympic Committee, doping is a prohibited substance used by athletes to increase physical performance in a dishonest way. Doping goes against sporting loyalty and fair play.

However, athletes decide to dope because of the pressures they are subjected, in order to improve their performance in competitions. The American cyclist Lance Armstrong achieved seven consecutive wins in the Tour de France between 1999 and 2005. But in 2012 the seven wins were withdrawn once it was discovered that he had been doping in those races and he was banned for life. In an interview conducted by journalist Oprah Winfrey in 2013, Armstrong said:

> It was impossible to win the Tour de France without consuming any kind of banned substance. Always I felt a ruthless instinct to win at all costs. Now I see it was not good. Now everything has been discovered. ... I will spend the rest of my life apologizing.†

---

* In 1991 the winner of the Brussels marathon, the Algerian Tehami, was disqualified because his coach started the race but then the Algerian Abbes Tehami finished it. One of the reasons the deception was discovered was that the coach wore mustaches and the Algerian did not.

† "Armstrong: Es Humanamente imposible ganar siete Tour de Francia sin Doparse" (Armstrong: It's Humanly Impossible to Win Seven Tour of France Without Doping), January 18, 2013, www.20minutos.es.

The Greatest Race: In the 1980s the American Carl Lewis, nicknamed "the son of the wind," was the king of athletics after winning four gold medals at the Olympic Games in Los Angeles in 1984. But in 1987 the Canadian born in Jamaica Benjamin "Ben" Johnson set a new record in the 100 meters in the World Championships in Athletics in Rome, and he prepared to beat Carl Lewis in the Olympic Games of Seoul 1988.

On September 24, 1988, in the final of the 100 meters in the Olympics – called "The Greatest Race" – Johnson and Lewis faced each other.

Johnson won the Olympic final in 9.79 seconds, beating by 400ths of a second the world record of 100 meters. At the end, he said, "This record lasted 50 years, maybe 100."*

But 48 hours later, the Olympic Doping Control Center found banned steroids in the urine sample of Johnson. Johnson tested positive in doping for the consumption of Stanozolol, an anabolic that boosts muscle mass. As a result, Ben Johnson was suspended for two years and the gold medal went to Carl Lewis.†

The Man Who Sold the Eiffel Tower: Victor Lustig (1890–1947) was born in the Czech Republic and as a young man used to cheat travelers on a boat to New York, offering them a machine that printed US$100 bills.

In 1925 Lustig was in Paris when he read an article in the newspaper that referred to the city's problems maintaining the Eiffel Tower. Lustig saw a big deal and developed his strategy.

Lustig asked a forger to copy government documents, posed as the deputy director-general of the French Post and Telegraph Ministry, and gathered six major junk dealers at the Crillon Hotel. At that "business meeting," he told them that the tower was very expensive, and he would sell the 7,000 tons of iron as scrap and solicit offers, clarifying the matter was highly confidential, a state secret. Lustig told them that he had been assigned the responsibility of selecting the concessionaire to carry out the task.‡ Lustig confessed that he did not earn much as an official and that

---

* Currently the world record for the 100-meter race is owned by Jamaican athlete specialist Usain Bolt with 9.58 seconds when he ran at the World Athletics Championships held in Berlin in 2009. The Olympic record is owned also by Bolt when he ran the 100 meters in 9.63 seconds in London in 2012.

† At the 2000 Summer Paralympics Games, the basketball team of the Royal Spanish Federation of Disabled Sports Intellectuals won the gold medal. Then it was discovered that except for two of its members, the rest of the Spanish players did not have any type of intellectual disability and Spain had to return the medal.

‡ The Eiffel Tower was designed by the French civil engineer Alexandre Gustave Eiffel (1832–1923) and built for the Paris Exposition of 1889, and should have been moved in 1909 to another location.

"it was necessary to find a way to supplement his income." One of the businessmen named Poisson understood that the deputy director-general was a corrupt official who wanted a bribe. Lustig received from Poisson the funds to win the concession and also a large bribe.

Lustig and his assistant escaped to Vienna, and Poisson did not make any complaint because he felt humiliated. A month later, he returned to Paris and tried again to sell the Eiffel Tower to six other junk dealers, but this time the potential victims went to the police before closing the deal, although Lustig managed to escape before being arrested. In 1935, after numerous scams, he was arrested in New York and sentenced to 20 years in prison on the island of Alcatraz. In 1947, he contracted pneumonia and died.*

Hitler's Diary: In April 1983 the *Stern* newspaper published excerpts of documents called "The Hitler's Diary," which it had acquired for almost US$5 million. They would have been recovered from an aerial accident in 1945.

The Eiffel Tower did not really experience massive and constant success until the 1960s with the development of international tourism. It is visited by more than six million people each year, and it is the symbol of Paris.

* In 1923 the Scottish Arthur Furguson (1883–1938) was in London and observed an American millionaire looking at the statue of Admiral Lord Nelson in Trafalgar Square. He was introduced as the official guide of the square and pointed out: "The government of Great Britain has put it on sale to the highest bidder because of the bad economic situation of the state." The American became interested and asked about the price. Ferguson explained that it was going to be sold for only £6000. The American told Ferguson his interest in the purchase. When the American got in touch with some contractors to be able to pack the monument, they told him that without permission from the authorities they could not do it. When he contacted a Scotland Yard officer, his check had already been cashed.

That same summer, another American complained that he had paid £1000 for Big Ben, and another had made a down payment of £2000 for Buckingham Palace.

During his visit to Paris Ferguson managed to sell the Eiffel Tower as scrap at a price unknown to another American. Since the Americans had been his best clients, he decided to continue his work in that country. In 1925, he leased the White House to a Texas cattle rancher, for 99 years at the price of $100,000 a year, charging him the first year of rent in advance.

In New York, he met an Australian, Ferguson told him that the entrance to the port of New York was going to be expanded and that the United States was willing to sell the Statue of Liberty. Ferguson committed the awkwardness of allowing the buyer to photograph him next to the Statue of Liberty. The Australian took the photograph to the police and Ferguson was arrested and jailed for five years and was released in 1930. "Arthur Ferguson: El hombre que lo vendía todo" ("Arthur Ferguson: The man who sold everything"), www.hdnh.es. Félix Casanova, November 7, 2010.

The American George C. Parker (1870–1936) sold to tourists the Brooklyn Bridge, the Metropolitan Museum of Art, and the Statue of Liberty and as a result of his scams, he was eight years imprisoned.

The documents had been sent to experts in World War II history to corroborate their authenticity. At a press conference in April 1983, they confirmed it. One of them said:

> I can say with satisfaction that these documents are authentic, that the story about their whereabouts since 1945 is true, and that the way in which Hitler's writing habits and personality are now narrated, and perhaps even some of its public actions, must, therefore, be revised.

A couple of weeks later a forensic examination revealed the Journals had been printed using ink and paper used after the year 1945. It was a fraud. Much of the content of the book was excerpts from Hitler's speeches.* The authors were sentenced to 42 months in prison for fraud and 2 editors of *Stern* had to resign.

The Surgeon's Photo: Loch Ness is a large, deep freshwater lake of 56 square kilometers long and 226 meters deep in the highlands of Scotland. This lake is famous because it is said to be inhabited by a creature known as *Nessie*, similar to a plesiosaur animal, a water reptile of the Jurassic period.

The existence of the animal in that lake has rumored for years. For example, in 1868 an article published in the newspaper *Inverness Courier* mentions the existence of a "big fish or other creature" on the lake and in May 1933 the same newspaper published that a couple had seen a huge animal in the lake. London publishers sent reporters to Scotland and a circus offered a reward of 20,000 pounds for the capture of the monster.

In April 1934, the English surgeon Robert Kenneth Wilson drove along the northern coast of the lake and after noticing something strange in the water he stopped his car to take a picture.

On 19 April 1934, the *Daily Mail* published his photo in which appears a high-necked creature hovering over the water.

Hundreds of newspapers spread the "surgeon's photo" on the Loch Ness monster and it was the clearest evidence of the existence of the creature.

In 1994, after 60 years of the photo published, Christian Spurling, 90, confessed that he had participated in a ruse to take the famous photo.

The lie had been devised by Marmaduke Wetherell, a hunter who had been hired by the *Daily Mail* to find the monster and had ended on bad

---

* This fraud was reflected in the mini-series "Selling Hitler" of 1991.

terms with the newspaper. In revenge, he wanted to deceive the newspaper. The silhouette jutting lake monster was actually a sculpture of clay-headed sea serpent placed on a toy submarine submerged in the Loch Ness. The "Surgeon's Photo" was one of the largest photographic hoaxes in history.

The Roswell UFO Incident: The Roswell UFO Incident refers to the alleged crash of an alien ship in New Mexico, USA, in July 1947.

The "official" version said it was one of the observation balloons of the Mogul Project with which they analyzed the nuclear activity of the USSR. However, on May 5, 1995, British producer Ray Santilli presented a 17-minute film at the London Museum, dating back to 1947, where an autopsy was performed on a supposed alien by some doctors. The video showed the dissection of a small biped humanoid with huge eyes.

According to Santilli, the short film was an alien autopsy filmed secretly by military personnel after the New Mexico incident and was broadcast by the Fox network.

Santilli's fraud was executed with a doll made by the sculptor John Humphreys with plaster molds that had ewe brains embedded in raspberry jelly – to look like blood – and chicken entrails.

In one corner of the operating room, a wall phone with a spiral cord had been hung, but in 1947, when the film was allegedly made, the telephone cables were flat.*

Patterson's Bigfoot: Bigfoot or Sasquatch is the name of a simian, ape creature said to inhabit forests in America. The enormous footprint for which the creature is named has become a phenomenon in America.†

No good evidence existed of Bigfoot until October 20, 1967, when Roger Patterson (1933–1972) and Bob Gimlin emerged from Bluff Creek, California's six rivers National Forest with footage of what appeared to be a female Bigfoot.

For more than 30 years the *Patterson-Gimlin Film* was the most important evidence of the existence of the creature, but in 2008 a custom designer named Philip Morris, owner of Morris Costumes of Charlotte

---

* Santiago Camacho, *Veinte Grandes Fraudes de la Historia* (Edaf, 2008), 45 ("Twenty Great Frauds of History").

† According to an article published in *The Washington Post*, 20% of Americans believe in the existence of Bigfoot. Christopher Ingraham, "Study: Americans Are as Likely to Believe in Bigfoot as in the Big Bang Theory," October 24, 2014.

North Carolina, said in 1967 he received a phone call from a guy asking about a gorilla costume.

> The man on the phone, who said his name was Roger Patterson, wanted to buy a gorilla suit. ... He said he wanted something that looked more like Neanderthal. What he wanted was a Bigfoot.

Two weeks after sending out the costume, Morris received another phone call from Patterson:

> He asked me how to hide the zipper in the back and how to make the person in the costume look larger. ... I told him to brush the fur over the zipper and use spray hair to hold it, and then get some football shoulder pads and sticks for the arms to give the illusion of being taller.*

Two months later Patterson was all over the news with a video of Bigfoot while in Northern California. Morris said

> I was watching TV when I saw Patterson and his film on the news. ... I called my wife and said: Look it's our gorilla costume.

In 2004, 36 years after the fact, the man called Bob Heironimus made his confession that he was Bigfoot in the Patterson film in the book *The Making of Bigfoot* by Greg Long.† Heironimus said to the *Washington Post*:

> It's time for people to know it was a fraud. ... It's time to end this. I have been carrying this weight for thirty-six years, watching the movie on television on numerous occasions. There was someone who made a lot of money on this issue. ... [T]he point is that it's time for people to finally know the truth.‡

Patterson (1933–1972) died of cancer in 1972 and maintained that creature in the film was real. Gimlin has always denied being involved in a hoax with Patterson.

Is it a fraud?

---

* "Is There Anyone Left Who Still Believes the 1967 Bigfoot Film Footage Is Real?" www.danger-mind.net.

† "Man Admits: I was Bigfoot," October 3 2004, www.wnd.com; "Lie Detector of Bob "Bigfoot" Heironimus Man in the Suit," February 17, 2012, www.youtube.com.

‡ Santiago Camacho, *20 Grandes Fraudes de la Historia* (EDAF, 2008), 246 ("Twenty Great Frauds of History").

The Philippine's Prehistoric Tribe: In 1971, Philippine government minister Miguel Elizalde announced that on one of the islands in the south of the country, in the forests of Mindanao, appeared a small prehistoric tribe that had never had contact with the world: the Tasaday. The tribe consisted of 26 people who lived in extreme isolation, spoke their own language, dressed in leaves, and lived in caves. The Tasaday did not know the clothes and they were so peaceful that their language did not include words like "war" or "enemy."

A fence of armed soldiers was arranged to prevent the entry of unauthorized persons. The government which was accused of serious violations of human rights received a good press by protecting vulnerable minorities.

The government of Ferdinand Marcos established in the region a reserve of 187 square kilometers to protect them. The story went around the world and appeared on the cover of *National Geographic* in August 1972.

Manuel Elizalde created a foundation that aimed to protect the environment of the Tasaday and received donations from around the world. Elizalde granted some permits to visit the area but in 1976 he announced that no more authorizations would be granted in order to allow the Tasaday to continue their lives without alteration.

The foundation continued receiving donations.

In 1986, a month after the fall of Marcos, the anthropologist Oswald Iten, along with the Philippine journalist Joey Lozano, entered the caves and found them empty. It was discovered that while the Tasaday existed and numbered about 150, they actually lived in houses, used knives, slept in beds, spoke the local dialect, and wore cotton shirts. They were similar to other Southeast Asian tribes. The natives told the journalist that Elizalde had offered them money and arms in exchange for impersonating a primitive tribe. Elizalde, apparently, would have escaped with the money donated to the foundation.*

In an ABC documentary called *The Tribe That Never Was*, the Tasaday explained by means of an interpreter that they had acted on Elizalde's request, and they laughed at the photos taken in the caves by the magazine.†

---

* Guillermo Mónaco, "Los Tasaday: La Tribu de la Edad de Piedra que Duró 4 Años," July 20, 2014, bombillatapada.blogspot.com ("The Tasaday: The Stone Age Tribe that Lasted 4 Years").

† Gregorio Doval, *Fraudes, Engaños y Timos de la Historia* (Nowtilus Saber, 2011), 116 ("Frauds, Deceptions, and Scams of History").

The Atomic Secret of Huemul: In 1948 the Austrian physicist Ronald Richter (1909–1991) presented to the Argentine president Juan Domingo Perón a project to produce energy through the process of controlled nuclear fusion.

On Saturday, March 24, 1951, at ten o'clock in the morning, a group of journalists approached the government house of the Argentine Republic (the Casa Rosada) where President Juan Domingo Perón announced that in the atomic plant of the Island Huemul, eight kilometers from the city of San Carlos de Bariloche, scientists had achieved "thermonuclear reactions under control conditions on a technical scale."[*]

Richter said: "I control the explosion, make it increase or decrease my desire. When an atomic bomb explodes there is astounding destruction. I have managed to control the explosion so that it occurs slowly and gradually."[†]

The announcement provoked a sensation, and Perón presented to society the physicist Ronald Richter, the creator of this feat that placed Argentina in the forefront of the nuclear powers.[‡]

The Los Alamos National Laboratory, where the Hiroshima bomb was manufactured, called for reports to the US Atomic Energy Commission.[§]

Hans Thirring, director of the Institute of Physics in Vienna, made the following statement:

> There is a 50% chance that Peron is the victim of a fanciful person who succumbed to his own illusions; 40% chance that he is the victim of a swindler; 9% chance that Peron is interested in cheating the world; and only 1% chance that this is true.

And he added that if Richter had really succeeded, "then the Nobel Prize would be small."[¶]

---

[*] "Una Insólita Aventura Atómica que Terminó Siendo un Fraude," March 21, 2001, www.clarin.com, ("An Unusual Atomic Adventure that Ended Up Being a Fraud").

[†] "El Gran Fraude de la Isla Huemul," *Angostura Digital*, March 1, 2013 ("The Great Fraud of Huemul Island").

[‡] Richter met Kurt Tank, an aeronautical engineer, in London. Tank later immigrated to Argentina. Recommended to Perón by Kurt Tank, Richter moved to Cordoba, where Tank was developing warplanes for the government. Tank was interested in Richter's proposal to use nuclear power to power them. When Richter was introduced to Perón, Richter proposed a program that would later become known as the Huemul Project.

[§] The *New York Times* mentions it on the cover, and the UN Disarmament Commission received requests to order Perón to reveal the secret.

[¶] Leonardo Torresi, "Una insólita aventura atómica que terminó siendo un fraude," March 25, 2001, www.Clarin.com ("An Unusual Atomic Adventure that Ended Up Being a Fraud").

Richter, an obsessive about security, asked that on Huemul Island there would be a revolving tower with a machine gun in case spies arrived to steal his secret.

On one occasion, Richter forced everyone who worked on the project to watch a fiction film about a nuclear physics investigation where spy agents infiltrated. Later, he imposed that all took target shooting; another day Richter believed that a couple of Germans who lived in the city of Bariloche were spies who watched him by binoculars from a hill. Ritcher had installed powerful light reflectors that worked all night. Colonel Fox, chief of the military garrison of the city of Bariloche, went to inspect the island, but when he appeared there, Richter threw him off the island, pointing a gun at him.[*]

A year later, in 1952, after investing millions of dollars in "Project Huemul," President Perón sent scientists to inspect the island. The investigative commission of scientists, led by the physicist Jose Antonio Balseiro (1919–1962),[†] informed President Perón there was no evidence that any thermonuclear reaction could be demonstrated and that he had been deceived. After a period in prison for the fraud, Richter spent the rest of his life in Buenos Aires.[‡]

Von Filek: Richter was not the only Austrian who deceived the president of a nation. A few years earlier, in 1940, after the Spanish Civil War and in the face of fuel shortages, the Austrian Albert Elder von Filek offered the Spanish general Francisco Franco (1892–1975) an invention that would allow Spain to produce three million liters of non-oil fuel for cars every day. The raw material for the fuel was 75% distilled water, 20% plant ferments, and 5% of "secret ingredients."[§]

Franco paid the Austrian ten million pesetas and ceded land next to the river to build the factory. Franco was told that the trucks that transported

---

[*] www. circuloesceptico.com.ar ("skeptical circle").

[†] Summoned by the government, this young 32-year-old Argentine scientist had to return from Manchester, where he was studying nuclear physics.

[‡] This story is explained in detail in the book *The Atomic Secret of Huemul*, written by my uncle, the Argentine physicist Mario Mariscotti (Sudamericana/Planeta, 1984).

[§] Miguel Angel Villena, "Filek, el Estafador que hizo creer a Franco que podía Convertir el agua en Gasolina en una dictadura chapucera y feroz," April 17, 2018, www.eldiario.es ("Filek, the Scammer that made Franco believe that he could turn water into gasoline into a sleazy and ferocious dictatorship").

the fish to Madrid from the northern ports used that fuel, and even his driver told him his car had used it.

On February 8, 1940, the newspaper *La Vanguardia* announced in a cover note that Spain would have autarky in fuel and would produce three million liters per day.

When the deception was discovered, von Filek and Franco's driver were sent to jail. No more was heard from them.*

The Pyramid Scheme, Ponzi, and Madoff: In the middle of the nineteenth century, the first scam was carried out, known today as a pyramid scheme. The Spanish Baldomera Larra Wetoret (1833–1915) borrowed an ounce of gold from a neighbor, promising one month later she would return it doubled. After the month, Baldomera fulfilled her promise, and then more people began to entrust their money to her. She returned the money with a 30% interest in a month.

By her hands, her "investors" were to spend about 20 million reales until 1876 when Baldomera disappeared and went to live in France under

---

* History shows that there have been many such cases in the last 100 years. For example:

  1 – In 1916, Louis Enricht (1844–1923), an American inventor, claimed to have a substance that, mixed with running water, could be a substitute for gasoline. Enricht was convicted of fraud.

  2 – In 1917, John Andrews offered the US Navy a green powder that, when mixed with water, created fuel for any gasoline engine. His product was not accepted.

  3 – Years later a gasoline pill was introduced by Guido Franch. His invention was a powder that was added to water, which he claimed had been invented by a German scientist named Dr. Alexander Kraft. Franch took money from a number of investors and claimed that the formula for water-based gasoline could not be revealed. He ended up being sued for fraud.

  4 – Heinrich Kurschildgen made some Nazi leaders believe that he could make oil from water. Tried for fraud, he was sentenced to prison.

  5 – In 1983, Wang Hongcheng announced his "Hongcheng Magic Liquid," which could turn regular water into fuel with just a few drops. His ad was widely covered by the Chinese media. He was sentenced to ten years in prison for fraud and deception.

  6 – In 1996, Ramar Pillai of South India (Tamil Nadu) claimed to be able to transmute water to gasoline by an herbal formula that he claimed was the result of a miracle bush. Pillai obtained 20 acres (81,000 square meters) of land to grow his shrub. He was sentenced to prison.

  7 – Between 1992 and 2007, an entrepreneur named Tim Johnston managed to raise more than US$100 million of investors to promote a "magic super pill that would reduce emissions and make fuel last longer." In 2008 the press considered it the largest fraud in Australian corporate history.

  8 – A Soviet agronomist engineer misled Joseph Stalin (1878–1953) with an inexhaustible agriculture project. The name of the engineer was Trofim Lysenko (1898–1976), who led an agricultural campaign known as "Lysenkoism." In 1927, the daily *Pravda* reported that Lysenko, aged 29, had discovered a method for fertilizing the soil without using fertilizers. His theory of how to grow crops in adverse weather consisted of cooling beans before planting them to grow in cold weather. In 1964, nuclear physicist Andrei Sakharov (1921–1989) pointed out in the General Assembly of the Academy of Sciences that Lysenko was "responsible for the shameful backwardness of Soviet biology and genetics."

a false identity. When she was discovered, she was tried, convicted, and sentenced to six years in prison, but she was released in 1881.*

In 1899, a 21-year-old man named William Miller of Brooklyn defrauded 13,000 people for more than US$1 million, a sum equivalent to US$25 million in today's money. Miller operated a business called the "Franklin Syndicate," in which he promised a 10% interest on contributions each week. Miller, who was nicknamed "520 percent" because of the remarkable rate of returns he promised, was sentenced to five years in prison.

Charles De Ville Wells (1841–1922) was an English gambler who visited the Monte Carlo Casino in 1891. With initial stake money of £4,000, he won approximately £60,000 over several visits.† In 1910, under the alias of "Lucien Rivier," he set up a private bank in Paris and promised to pay interest at 365% per annum (1% per day). Some 6,000 investors deposited a total of 2 million francs. Existing customers were paid out of the new investments which "Rivier" received in ever-increasing amounts.

When the French authorities began to investigate his affairs, Charles Wells fled to Britain with his clients' money. The scam was remarkable for its scale, in terms of both the number of investors who lost money and the number of their total losses. A Paris court sentenced him in November 1912 to five years in prison. As a direct result of his crime, the French government introduced more controls on private banks.

Carlo Pietro Giovanni Guglielmo Tebaldo Ponzi (1882–1949) was born in 1882 in Lugo, in the Italian province of Ravenna. In 1907 Ponzi moved to Montreal, Canada, and worked for a bank created by a compatriot named Luigi Zarossi, the Zarossi Bank. "Louis" Zarossi took deposits under the promise of returning them with a 6% interest, twice as much as that offered by the market. The only detail was that these interests were paid with the money provided by the new clients, Italian immigrants. One day Zarossi escaped to Mexico with all the money received.‡

In 1919, in Boston, Ponzi set up an investment operation by which he promised to pay high interest returns to investors who entrusted him with their money. Ponzi used investors' money to buy European postal coupons, known as International Reply Coupon, IRC, at a price equivalent to five

---

* Gregorio Doval, *Fraudes, Engaños y Timos de la Historia* (Nowtilus Saber, 2011), 214 ("Frauds, Deceptions and Scams of History").

† He was famous for the song *The Man Who Broke the Bank at Monte Carlo*.

‡ Rolando Barbano, "El Padre de todos los Estafadores," April 13, 2018, Clarin.com ("The Father of all Scammers").

cents each and then he exchanged them in the United States, obtaining profits of around 10%.

In February 1920, his company, the *Securities Exchange Company*, obtained US$5,000 from investors, and a few months later the income totaled more than US$420,000.*

Ponzi promised a 50% return on 45-day investments or 100% interest on 90-day investments. This was in an environment when banks were paying 5% annual interest. Forty thousand people invested money and the media presented him as an exemplary entrepreneur. In six months, he had become a millionaire in Boston where he bought an air-conditioned mansion, a pool heater, and other extravagant luxuries for the time.†

The *Boston Post* entrusted finance expert Clarence Barron to investigate the Ponzi business. The first thing the specialist discovered was the Italian invested other people's money, but he did not invest his own money. The second piece of data was more complicated, to respond to the investments of its customers Ponzi needed to buy about 160 million postal coupons. But in the world, only 27,000 had been issued.‡ Therefore, Ponzi was not investing the money in the purchase of mail coupons and he was only interested in new investors.

The *Ponzi scheme* or *pyramid scheme* occurs when investors generate benefits to the original participants. The Ponzi or pyramid scheme consists in that the new investors that enter the business generate enough money to pay the original participants. The investments of the new participants are simply passed on to pay the participants who invested before. In order to pay the investment capital and interests to the first participants, the contributions of the last participants are used, all of whom assume their money will be invested. The Ponzi scheme always requires new participants, and that group must be larger than the existing one, hence the name *pyramid*. When the population of potential participants becomes saturated, the benefits of the original participants decrease, and many end up without recovering the money invested. Then, the system collapses when the money of the new participants is not enough to pay the original participants.

The *Boston Post* published its investigation and a crowd of enraged investors gathered in front of the Ponzi office to claim their investments.

---

* Rolando Barbano, "El Padre de todos los Estafadores," April 13, 2018, Clarin.com ("The Father of all Scammers").
† en.wikipedia.org/wiki/Charles_Ponzi.
‡ Rolando Barbano, "El Padre de todos los estafadores," April 13, 2018, Clarin.com ("The Father of all Scammers").

The Italian announced a lawsuit against the authors of the journalistic note and said they criticized him because they did not understand his business. The publicity attracted the attention of the US Attorney General who ordered an audit.

The newspaper also discovered his criminal record and published it. Ponzi had been in prison in Canada for fraud. It is estimated that by then the Italian had obtained more than US$15 million from some 40,000 people, a figure equivalent to about US$225 million today.* The publication stated that despite the high interest rates he paid, Carlo Ponzi did not reinvest the money received and was interested only in new investors.

As a consequence, a multitude of investors appeared in Ponzi's office demanding the return of their money.

Six banks went bankrupt because of his maneuvers, which forced him to face a trial for postal fraud. On November 1, 1920, Ponzi was declared guilty of fraud and sentenced to five years in prison.

He was released from jail after three and a half years and dedicated himself to committing a new scam by selling lands in Florida that were swamps. He was discovered and tried to flee with his head shaved to Italy on a merchant ship, but he was caught in New Orleans and went to prison in Massachusetts.†

Only in 1934 could he leave prison. His wife had left him and he ended up living in Rio de Janeiro, Brazil, where he died alone and poor on January 18, 1949, in a charity hospital.

Carlo Ponzi could have been inspired by Louis Zarossi, or by the schemes of Baldomera Larra Wetoret, the accountant William F. Miller or Charles Deville Wells.‡

Ponzi is studied for defrauding investors with this type of pyramid scheme that would be used years later by Bernard Madoff, a New York investor.

Bernard Lawrence Madoff was the president of an investment firm founded in 1960 and was one of the most important investors on Wall Street. He kept going for more than two decades a fraudulent Ponzi investment scheme worth more than US$35 billion.§ On December 11, 2008, the banker was arrested by the FBI and accused of fraud.

---

* Rolando Barbano, "El Padre de todos los estafadores," April 13, 2018, Clarin.com; es.wikipedia. org/wiki/Esquema_Ponzi.

† es.wikipedia.org/wiki/Carlo_Ponzi.

‡ Charles De Ville Wells (1841–1922) was one of the individuals who broke the Bank at Monte Carlo in 1891. It is also believed that he was also one of the first scammers to use the pyramid system.

§ Of that amount of money, almost 50% could be recovered.

On one occasion an inspector asked him for a report. Madoff created a fake report, "passed it through the refrigerator so it did not look fresh out of the printer, and then tossed it to one another to make it look worn out by the readings."* On June 29, 2009, Madoff was sentenced to 150 years in prison for running one of the biggest financial frauds in US history.†

In the last years, there were many other cases in which the Ponzi scheme was used and which became known by the amount of deceived investors and the high amounts of money involved. Some of them were (i) Allen Stanford or "Sir Allen," who was accused by the SEC of defrauding his investors and sentenced to 110 years in prison; (ii) Tom Petters, chairman of "Petters Group Worldwide" sentenced to 50 years in prison; (iii) Lou Pearlman, sentenced to 25 years in prison; (iv) Gerald Payne, sentenced to 27 years in prison; (v) David Dominelli, sentenced to 20 years in prison; and (vi) Norman Hsu, sentenced to 24 years in prison.

Bre-X Minerals: The Canadian mining company Bre-X Minerals acquired a mine in Indonesia in 1993, and in 1995 announced the discovery of an extraordinary gold reserve known as the Busang Reservoir. According to company founder David Walsh, there were some 6,500 tons of gold in the remote site, equivalent to 8% of world reserves. When the news became known, the value of the company's shares began to rise vertically, in 5 months, from 2 to 275 Canadian dollars, which made the company value about US$6 billion.

In March 1997, the mining company Freeport McMoRan (owner of 15% of Bre-X) decided to inspect the gold mine and contracted an independent consultant named Strathcona Mineral Services. Their report was made public on May 6, 1997, in which they noted: "This site (Busang) purporting to be the biggest find of gold history, is practically a worthless piece of land in the jungles of Borneo." Strathcona's report was very strong and said that "precise amounts of gold dust were added to samples of Bustang in a clandestine laboratory."‡

That same day on the Toronto stock exchange, Bre-X collapsed just over 97% in ten minutes. What hours before was worth US$6 billion was reduced to a few millions. On that day, Toronto broke all the trading

---

* "Se revelan secretos de la pirámide financiera de Madoff," January 12, 2017, www.infoabe.com ("Secrets of Madoff's financial pyramid are revealed").
† Madoff serves his sentence in a prison in the Federal Correctional Complex in North Carolina until November 14, 2139.
‡ "Case Bre-X," www.scribd.com/document/351054276/Expo-Ingles-QAQC-docx.

records seen until then, when almost 50 million shares of the mining company changed hands. It had perpetrated the biggest fraud committed in the history of gold, and that year the company was declared bankrupt.[*]

The Bre-X fraud had an antecedent in the previous century: "the Diamond Hoax of 1872." In 1872, some gold prospectors named Philip Arnold (1829–1878) and John Slack, who were cousins, bought a few diamonds from Arizona Indians and deposited them in a bank vault in California. Several investors were interested in the source of the diamonds. The cousins told several investors that they had obtained the diamonds from a previously unknown deposit and offered it for sale for a figure higher than US$600,000.

The investors interested in the discovery gave them an advance of US$7,000 with which the sellers bought more cheap diamonds in London and Amsterdam for about US$35,000. They showed some diamonds to the investors, who asked to see the deposit. Arnold and Slack placed diamonds in an area in northwestern Colorado, and on June 4, 1872, they took the investors there, who found the gems. After the tour, the investors bought the rights to the field from Arnold and Slack. In October 1872, the American geologist Clarence King (1842–1901) of Yale University inspected the site and concluded that it was a fraud.[†]

Tyco International: Tyco is a company based in Switzerland but with a significant presence in the United States. Its products include electronic components, medical engineering, fire protection, and security systems.

In 2002, a district attorney in Manhattan accused the CEO of having acquired works of art for more than US$13 million and of not having paid the 8.25% tax required by the city of New York.[‡]

In 2002, three senior managers of the firm were accused of stealing millions of dollars from the company.[§]

At Tyco, there was a culture of excesses where loans and million-dollar bonuses were authorized to senior executives.

---

[*] Marion Mueller, "Bre-X Minerals Ltd., the Biggest Scandal in the History of Gold Mining," December 30, 2009, www.OroyFinanzas.com.

[†] Gregorio Doval, *Fraudes, Engaños y Timos de la Historia* ("Frauds, Deceptions, and Scams of History") (Nowtilus Saber, 2011), 191–92. This story was on television as *The Great Adventure* (1963), *The Great Diamond Mines* (1968), and in the first episode of *Maverick* (1958).

[‡] Carlos Manzoni, "The Successful Executive Who with His Extravagances Went to Prison," April 26, 2019, www.lanacion.com.ar.

[§] Report of the BBC Mundo.com of September 13, 2002.

The CEO, who in 1999 had total annual compensation of US$170 million, spent about US$30 million on a department on Fifth Avenue in New York and US$7 million on an apartment on Park Avenue for use by his ex-wife.* He bought a house in Boca Raton, Florida, of 1,393 square meters with a loan from Tyco of US$10 million interest-free.

The executive also used company resources to hold his second wife's birthday party on the island of Sardinia, which cost about US$2 million, with a decoration in the best Roman style and an ice sculpture of Michelangelo's David urinating vodka Stolichnaya, a brand of vodka produced in Moscow.

In June 2005, its CEO and CFO were sentenced to prison for using US$600 million to finance loans, property, donations, and opulent lifestyles.†

Dwight D. Eisenhower (1890–1969), 34th president of the United States, said, "A person that values its privileges above its principles soon loses both."‡

Wells Fargo & Co: Frauds and delusions are sometimes the result of an excessive desire for notoriety or the desire to obtain results, and other times they are the consequence of setting excessively high goals, which generates a very high pressure to comply with the sales plan of financial products previously stipulated.

This is what happened to West Fargo.

Wells Fargo & Co. was founded in 1852 by Henry Wells and William Fargo. It is based in San Francisco, California, and is one of the four largest banks in the United States.§ Wells Fargo has a document called "The Vision and Values," which states that "our values should guide every conversation we have, every decision we make, and every interaction we have. ... We believe in values lived, not phrases memorized."¶

In September 2016, the bank was fined US$185 million by regulatory authorities for creating more than 1.5 million bank accounts not requested by customers to comply with the business plan set by the bank for its employees: open ten bank accounts per day. The *do whatever it takes to meet the goals* emphasis resulted in the firing of 5,300 bank employees

---

* Andrew Ross Sorkin, "Tyco Details Lavish Lives of Executives," *New York Times*, September 18, 2002.
† There was no natural light in the cell. In 2014 he was granted parole.
‡ www.brainyquote.com/quotes/dwight_d_eisenhower_103606.
§ The other three are Citigroup, Bank of America, and JP Morgan Chase.
¶ "The Vision & Values of Wells Fargo," www.damicofcg.com.

and the departure of the company's CEO. John Stumpf, the resigning Wells Fargo CEO said, "Integrity is not a commodity. It is the rarest and precious of personal attributes. It is the core of a person's – and a company's – reputation."[*]

The Office of the Comptroller of the Currency (OCC)[†] announced that former Wells Fargo CEO will be barred from ever working at any bank and will pay US$17.5 million. Joseph Otting, Comptroller of the Currency, said, "The actions announced by the OCC reinforce the agency's expectations that management and employees of national banks…treat customers fairly, and comply with applicable laws and regulations."[‡]

The current Wells Fargo CEO Charlie Scharf said "the company did not have in place the appropriate people, structure, processes, controls, or culture to prevent the inappropriate conduct."[§]

Volkswagen: In 2014, the NGO Clean Transportation began an investigation by which it tried to prove that the environmental controls on automobiles were stricter in the United States than in Europe, and, therefore, the cars in the United States contaminated less than in the old continent. With the help of the University of West Virginia, which had developed a system for measuring pollutant gases that could easily be placed in vehicles, Clean Transportation installed devices in the tailpipes of some vehicles to record their degree of pollution.

To their surprise, they discovered that some Volkswagen cars emitted between 20 and 35 times more nitrogen oxide than allowed in the United States.[¶] In the face of these unexpected results, the NGO sent a report to the US Environmental Protection Agency (EPA), and in May 2014, an investigation was opened against the German automaker to determine if there had been tampering in the certification tests of Volkswagen diesel vehicles.

---

[*] Roger Arnold, "Don't Underestimate Wells Fargo's Woes," October 1, 2016, realmoney.thestreet.com.

[†] It is an independent bureau within the US Department of the Treasury that serves to regulate and supervise all national banks and thrift institutions and the federally licensed branches and agencies of foreign banks in the United States. "Office of the Comptroller of the Currency," en.wikipedia.org.

[‡] Thomas Franck, "Former Wells Fargo CEO John Stumpf Barred from Industry, to Pay US$17.5 Million for Sales Scandal," January 23, 2020, www.cnbc.com.

[§] Thomas Franck, "Former Wells Fargo CEO John Stumpf Barred from Industry, to Pay US$17.5 Million for Sales Scandal," January 23, 2020, www.cnbc.com.

[¶] "Dos ecologistas descubrieron la trampa de Volkswagen por casualidad," September 23, 2015, www.InfobaeAmerica.com ("Two environmentalists discovered the trap of Volkswagen by chance").

The scandal became public in September 2015 when it became known that the world's leading automaker had installed secret software that falsified pollutant emissions data to circumvent environmental controls. This software detected the moment the vehicle was being subjected to the emission control test. It is estimated that 11 million vehicles* could have included such software. Once the scandal broke, Volkswagen shares plummeted 35% in 2 days, and its market capitalization fell by about 35 billion euros.

The company suspended the commercialization of its four-cylinder diesel Volkswagen and Audi vehicles, which represented more than 20% of sales in that market.

The flutter of the butterfly turned into a tornado.

The president of Volkswagen said,

> I am shocked by the events of the past few days. Above all, I am stunned that misconduct on such a scale was possible in the Volkswagen Group. As CEO I accept responsibility for the irregularities that have been found in diesel engines and have therefore requested the Supervisory Board to agree on terminating my function as CEO of the Volkswagen Group. … Volkswagen needs a fresh start. … The process of clarification and transparency must continue. This is the only way to win back trust.[†]

Volkswagen Integrity Chief Hiltrud Werner said, "we are busy analyzing the root of the matter." The company apparently thought it was too big to fail.[‡]

Volkswagen set aside 6.7 billion euros to cover the costs of its rigging of diesel emissions tests.[§] The company agreed to spend up to US$25 billion in the United States to address claims from owners, environmental regulations, states, and dealers and offered to buy back about 500,000 polluting US vehicles.

As a result of this investigation, the government started to review emissions from other diesel vehicles. In January 2017, the US EPA[¶] and

---

* 482,000 vehicles in the United States alone.
† "Statement by Prof. Dr. Winterkorn," September 23, 2015, www.volkswagen-media-services-com; "The Keys to the Volkswagen Scandal," *El Pais*, September 22, 2015.
‡ "Quien es Hiltrud Werner, la Poderosa Mujer Encargada de Acabar con la Corrupción en Volkswagen" ("Who Is Hiltrud Werner, the Powerful Woman in Charge of Ending Corruption in Volkswagen"), *BBC News*, April 5, 2019, www.lanacion.com.ar.
§ Andreas Cremer, "Volkswagen Diesel Scandal Is Starting to Hit Company Where It Hurts," October 28, 2015, www.huffingtonpost.com.
¶ Environmental Protection Agency.

California accused Fiat Chrysler of illegally using undisclosed software to allow excess diesel emissions in 104,000 Jeep Grand Cherokees and Dodge Ram 1,500. Fiat Chrysler's shares fell sharply after Reuters reported the government's plan to file suit. In May 2017, the US government filed a civil lawsuit accusing Fiat Chrysler Automobiles NV of illegally using software to bypass emission controls since 2014.[*]

In 2003, the internal audit department of 3M uncovered evidence that a manager had set up and used a series of fake vendors. The 3M attorney John Stoxen wrote,

> The employee sent himself fake invoices from his fabricated companies, approved them for payment and essentially paid himself more than US$1 million of company funds over several years. When the plot was discovered the employee was fired and he was sentenced.[†]

Knowing stories about fraud helps to become more aware that deception, lies, and lack of ethics have always existed in history, in all activities and, therefore, we must be attentive so both lying and deceit are reduced in organizations. In the footnote, you can see more famous and interesting cases of lies, frauds, and/or possible deceptions.[‡]

The Texas-based Association of Certified Fraud Examiners (ACFE) is the largest anti-fraud organization in the world with more than 75,000 members. The chairman of the board and founder of ACFE is Joseph T. Wells, a former FBI special agent and author of the book *Fraud Fighter*. The mission of the institution is to help prevent and detect fraud and to offer its members a certified fraud examiner to achieve professional excellence in fraud detection and prevention. ACFE considers that an average organization loses 5% of its annual income because of fraud.

---

[*] David Shepardson, "US Government Sues Fiat Chrysler over Excess Emissions," May 23, 2017, www.reuters.com.

[†] John Stoxen, "Fraud Prevention: Using Ethics and Compliance Failures as Teaching Tools."

[‡] Very interesting cases of fraud and possible frauds: (i) George Psalmanazar (1673–1763), the Frenchman who described the island of Formosa; (ii) the Martian attack of Orson Welles in 1938; (iii) the sculptures of the Italian Alceo Dossena (1878–1937); (iv) the Dutch painting forger Han Van Meegeren (1889–1947); (v) the Hungarian painter Elemer Albert Hoffman, known as Elmyr de Hory (1906–1976); (vi) George Dupre (1903–1982) the Canadian tortured by the Nazis; (vii) the Mincemeat operation of the British in World War II; (viii) the contacts with aliens of Travis Walton, George Adamski, or Antonio Villas Boas; (ix) the American Ferdinand Waldo Demara Jr. (1921–1982); the great imposter (x) Frank Abagnale, *Catch Me If You Can*; (xi) Who Wants to be a Millionaire?, the program of September 2001; (xii) Max Higgins, Walt Disney in Argentina; (xiii) the Balloon boy in Colorado of October 15, 2009; (xiv) the private life of Marcial Maciel; or (xv) the German duo Milli Vanilli, the biggest music fraud in history.

KPMG International in its "Global Profiles of the Fraudster" report of 2014 concludes

> more than half (54%) of the frauds were facilitated by weak internal controls. This suggests that if many organizations adjust the controls and supervision of employees, the opportunity to commit fraud would be severely restricted. All too often, organizations are not focused on preventing fraud with proper controls and learn their lesson too late.*

W. Michael Hoffman, founder and executive director of the Center for Business Ethics at Bentley University, says:

> The enemy we are fighting – humanity's capacity to exploit business as a vehicle to extract personal gain at the price of social good – is a wily and creative critter always poised to invent new stratagems for twisting business for its own gain.†

No organization is immune to fraud, and most people who commit this type of crime take advantage of the weakness of existing controls. That is why companies must design and implement fraud prevention control programs to prevent, detect, and respond to this risk. The reasons for fraud can be (i) personal: for example, to overcome financial problems, ambition, or revenge or even to solve "injustices"; or (ii) corporate: for example, from the pressure to achieve goals, to raise the stock price, or to achieve annual bonuses.

Some examples of fraud in companies are: over-invoicing, payment for products and/or services not received; substitution of some products for others (different weight, volume, units); different origin or quality of the product purchased; fictitious suppliers; false commissions, sales and expenses; differences in inventory quantity; incorrect valuations; false receipts; bidding arrangements; handling of discounts and refunds; and frauds with checks.

The Global Economic Fraud Survey conducted by PricewaterhouseCoopers in 2014 said:

> Organizations often do not understand the financial impact of an economic crime until after it happens, sometimes quite a bit later. As in previous years, our survey underscores that the cost of fraud is significant.

---

* KPMG International, *Global Profiles of the Fraudster* (2014).
† Michael Hoffman, "Verizon Visiting Professorship in Business Ethics," February 3, 2014, www.bentley.edu.

These significant losses can be linked to increased incidents of bribery and corruption, frauds that can cost organizations a lot of money, through fines, attorney fees, and billions of dollars.

But the economic loss is not the only concern of companies in the fight against fraud. Our respondents pointed to the damage to employee morale, corporate reputation, and brand.*

In turn, Kroll's "Global Fraud Report" for the years 2013/2014 stated, "There has been increased awareness of fraud, regardless of whether it is linked to cybercrime, theft of information, or expansion into new and higher risk markets. However, fraud protection measures remain limited by budgetary issues and corporate policies."[†]

Some time ago, the Frenchman Gustave Charles invented a treasure-hunting apparatus that consisted of a metal bar at the end of which moved a plate turntable with certain substances that responded to the magnetism sent by gold, silver, and other metals. When he felt their presence, the plate was turned and the speed of the turns indicated the amount of material buried. He sold this invention at a good price and got rich. One day he was asked if anyone had found a treasure with his device.

Charles replied with a smile, "Who knows, I did find one."[‡]

Managers and company employees face temptations; they want to hunt their treasure, and that makes the risk of fraud never go away. It is always latent.

In the 2016 "Global Economic Crime Survey," PricewaterhouseCoopers said, "Today more than ever before, a passive approach to detecting and preventing economic crime is a recipe for disaster."[§]

Fraud is a daily reality that can leave companies weakened and at risk, and therefore it is necessary that organizations implement a proactive strategy to mitigate it.

---

* www.pwc.com.

[†] Kroll, http://fraud.kroll.com/es/.

[‡] Gregorio Doval, *Fraudes, Engaños y Timos de la Historia* (Nowtilus, 2011), 215 ("Frauds, Deceptions, and Scams of History").

At the beginning of the twenty-sixth century, an alchemist wrote a work entitled "Crisopeya or the art of making gold" and presented it to Pope Leo X (1475–1521). The alchemist hoped to be rewarded by giving to the Church a work that taught to make gold. But Pope Leo X gave the alchemist an empty bag for the work. The alchemist asked the pope for an explanation and he replied: "I do not give you the bag full of coins because, without a doubt, it will be easy for you to fill it with your knowledge of alchemy." "Curistoria." Manuel J. Prieto (Evohe Didaska, 2008), 138–139.

[§] "Adjusting the lens on economic crime," Global Economic Crime Survey 2016, www.pwc.com; *Fraud Fighting*, www.fraudfighting.org.

18

Corporate Risks: Unit 6

18.1 BRIBERY AND CORRUPTION

Bribery is a crime that involves the delivery of money or gifts to someone, in an effort to influence their actions for the benefit of those offering the bribe.

Kickbacks and facilitating payments are two forms of bribery.

A kickback involves two parties agreeing to a portion of sales or profits will be improperly given, rebated, or kicked back to the purchaser in exchange for making the deal. For example, a kickback might involve a supplier who offers a company's employee a monthly payment equaling to 3% of the company's purchases as an inducement to the employee to retain the supplier's services.

A facilitating or "grease" payment is a small payment made to a government official to expedite what should be a routine action or service, such as providing police protection or mail service, processing a visa, issuing a permit, or providing utilities like phone service, water, and power.

A facilitating payment does not include official payments, such as those where a government agency has a published fee schedule for a service equally available to anyone and provides a receipt. Most companies prohibit their employees and representatives from making facilitating payments, even if doing so is legal in the country where the payment is taking place.

Someone is said to be corrupt when bribing or being bribed with money or gifts.

The fight against corruption is considered by the World Economic Forum as one of the main challenges for companies.

Rear Admiral Jules Dumont D'Urville (1790–1842) was a French naval officer and explorer. In April 1820, when he stopped in Greece on the island of Melos (Cyclades Islands), he noticed a statue recently unearthed by a peasant named Yorgos Kendrotas who kept it in a goat pen. Dumont recognized the figure of Venus, the Greek goddess of love, who carried in her hand the apple Paris had given her, as the most beautiful among the goddesses. He wanted to buy the statue immediately but could not because of the high amount demanded by the peasant.

A few days later, Dumont convinced the Marquess of Riviere, the French ambassador in Constantinople, to send a diplomat to Melos to buy the statue. When the diplomat arrived on the island with Dumont, the peasant explained he had sold the statue to a Turkish officer and it was already packed. To solve the problem, Dumont said he would give a generous gift to the peasant, who quickly "remembered" he had earlier promised the statue to the French and therefore would not be delivering it to the Turks. The Venus was then transported to the ship of Dumont D'Urville, which was attacked by the Turks, and in that battle, the statue lost its arms.* Later, the statue was delivered to King Louis XVIII.

The word *corruption* comes from the Latin *corruptio* and means *something that breaks, destroys, damages.* Corruption is a plague, a vice, an immoral habit that destroys and breaks ethics in search of a personal benefit. It is, unlike integrity, the fragmentation of what should be united.†

There are authors who have narrowly applied the term *corruption* to abuse of power by only a public official to obtain an illegitimate secret and/or private advantage. For other authors, the term *corruption* is more broadly used to refer to bribes, whether a public official is involved or not. In other words, a bribe between individuals that are not public officials or between private companies would also be qualified as an act of corruption.

Sir Edward Coke (1512–1634) was an English judge and a member of the Parliament, who said, "Though the bribe be small, yet the fault is great."‡

Protestant Pastor Gerald Zandstra has said, "Whoever participates in corruption in some way or another must be aware that it is collaborating with feeding the monster that will finally eat the system."§

---

* "Secretos y Misterios de la Historia, Pelea por Venus," *Reader's Digest*, 1993, 16 ("Secrets and Mysteries of History, Fight for Venus").

† St. Augustine (354–430) in his *Confessions* wrote that "corruption is harm."

‡ "Edward Coke quotes," www.brainyquote.com.

§ Entrevista de Agustina Lanusse, *Diario La Nación. Junio 6, 2005* ("Agustina Lanusse's Interview").

According to PricewaterhouseCoopers's 2009 report,

> The majority of people are essentially honest and do not feel the temptation of unlawful personal gain. However, when someone's livelihood is at stake or the future of the company depends on getting a new commission from a potential client, some people will feel more strongly the pressure to do the wrong thing: paying the bribe that guarantees the financial future or look the other way while others do.*

Corruption has always been a topic considered in movies. The 1942 film *Casablanca* depicts a scene in which Captain Renault and his team shut down a casino inside a cafe. In the middle of the shutdown process, Captain Renault exclaims, "I'm shocked, shocked to find that gambling is going on here," while he is brought an envelope with the profits he has obtained from that gambling.†

The film *The Constant Gardener* (2005) deals with multinational pharmaceutical companies that, through bribes and in complicity with governments, carry out illegal drug tests on children in Africa.‡

The film *Syriana* (2005) is about the oil industry and about how corruption is used to gain business. In one of the scenes, an oilman called Danny Dalton says:

> Corruption is government intrusion into market efficiencies in the form of regulations. ... Corruption is our protection. Corruption keeps us safe and warm. Corruption is why you and I are prancing around in here instead of fighting over scraps of meat out in the streets. Corruption is why we win.§

Illegal payments to government officials are a potential problem for businesses, especially when the government is a customer and the business is subject to many regulations. Ayn Rand (1905–1982), the Russian-American philosopher and writer, said:

> When you see that trading is done, not by consent, but by compulsion – when you see that in order to produce, you need to obtain permission from men who produce nothing – when you see that money is flowing to those who deal, not in goods, but in favors – when you see that men get richer by graft and by pull than by work, and your laws don't protect you against

---

* "Fraude en Tiempos de Crisis," PricewaterhouseCoopers, 2009, 4 ("Fraud in Times of Crisis").
† *Casablanca*, directed by Michael Curtiz.
‡ *The Constant Gardener*, directed by Fernando Meirelles.
§ *Syriana*, directed by Stephen Gaghan.

them, but protect them against you – when you see corruption being rewarded and honesty becoming a self-sacrifice – you may know that your society is doomed.*

René Geronimo Favaloro (La Plata, 1923–2000), an Argentine heart doctor recognized for being the one who developed the coronary bypass using the saphenous vein, in 1999, said, "In every medical act must be present respect for the patient and ethical and moral concepts; then science and consciousness will always be on the same side, on the side of humanity."[†] On July 29, 2000, Favaloro committed suicide at the age of 77. He wrote in a letter the day of his death,

> Corruption has reached levels that I never thought I could witness.... There is no doubt that being honest, in this corrupt society, has its price.... Most of the time I feel alone.... My closest collaborators advise me that in order to save the Foundation we must join the system and accept bribes.... At this age, put to an end the ethical principles that I received from my parents and my teachers is extremely difficult. I cannot change, I prefer to disappear.... This corrupt society has defeated me.... I'm tired of fighting and fighting.[‡]

In the business world, all competitors must follow the rules in force and do everything in their power to do business without falling into corruption.

The problem of bribery and corruption is global. A few years ago, in China, a director of a food and medicine regulatory body was sentenced to death by a court in Beijing for receiving bribes for about US$800,000 in exchange for the approval of several remedies by pharmaceutical companies.

Almost every company, regardless of size, industry, or country of operation, is exposed to some degree of corruption risk.

In the last years there have been regulatory developments in the fight against corruption as follows: (i) the United Kingdom Bribery Act 2010 covers the criminal law relating to bribes to government officials and commercial bribes[§]; (ii) the G-20 established a plan of action to address

---

* "Atlas Shrugged," Chapter 2, Francisco d' Anconia to Bertram Scudder.
† www.Fundacionfavaloro.org.ar Congreso de Bioingeniería, 1999 (Bioengineering Congress).
‡ "The Last Letter of Favaloro Before Dying" (La Última Carta de Favaloro Antes de Morir), October 9, 2013, www.infobae.com.
§ The UK Bribery Act reaches companies that do business in the United Kingdom, regardless of where the act of corruption takes place. Therefore, its jurisdiction extends beyond the United Kingdom.

the problem of corruption*; and (iii) the OECD issued a Good Practice Guidance wherein 44 nations agreed to promote the adoption of ethics and compliance programs.†

Companies also developed anti-corruption programs with the purpose of preventing and detecting inappropriate behaviors and promoting a healthy corporate culture.

Thus, in recent years, organizations devote more resources to the establishment of policies, infrastructure, and processes aimed at combating corruption within their businesses and throughout their supply chains.

Given the risk of a foreign government official being bribed, either by organization personnel or by a third party acting on behalf of the organization, companies began to include in their ethics and compliance programs training on anti-corruption for those who may have to deal with government officials.

Transparency is the opposite of corruption. To combat global corruption, American companies helped create the NGO Transparency International, founded in 1993, based in Berlin, Germany, and aimed at combating corruption. Transparency International defines *corruption* as "the abuse of entrusted power for private gain." The NGO says,

> Our Mission is to stop corruption and promote transparency, accountability, and integrity at all levels and across all sectors of society. ... Our Vision is a world in which government, politics, business, civil society and daily lives of people are free of corruption.‡

On November 8, 2017, the Chair of Transparency International, the Argentine Delia Ferreira Rubio, gave a speech to the UNCAC§ Conference

---

* The Group of 20 (G20) is a cooperative forum of 19 countries, plus the European Union, set up in 1999, wherein regular heads of state (or government), central bank governors, and finance ministers meet regularly to discuss issues related to international financial stability. G20 consists of seven of the most industrialized countries – Germany, Canada, the United States, France, Italy, Japan, and the United Kingdom (G7) – plus Russia (G8) plus 11 newly industrialized countries from all regions of the world and the European Union as an economic bloc. Spain is a permanent guest.

† The Organization for Economic Cooperation and Development (OECD) is an international cooperative organization founded in 1960, made up of 34 states, whose objective is to coordinate economic and social policies to maximize economic growth and to collaborate in its development and that of the countries, not members. Known as the "rich country club," the OECD brings together countries that provide 70% of the world market and 80% of world GNP.

‡ www.transparency.org.

§ The *United Nations Convention against Corruption*.

of the States Parties and she said, "We all want the same thing, a world free of corruption."*

Transparency International annually publishes the Corruption Perceptions Index (CPI), which measures on a scale of zero (perception of very corrupt) to ten (perceived absence of corruption) the levels of perception of corruption in the public sector in a given country. The index is based on various surveys of experts and companies. It is useful for organizations doing international business because it allows taking into account the level of corruption risk and sets off alarms when doing business in countries with high corruption rates, especially when permits and commercial licenses must be made in the governments of those countries or when employees or suppliers are contracted in those countries.

In the 2017 Corruption Perceptions Index, New Zealand, Denmark, Finland, Norway, Switzerland, Singapore, Sweden, Canada, Luxembourg, and the Netherlands are considered the ten least corrupt countries in the world. In Latin America, the best three were Uruguay, Chile, and Costa Rica. The lowest ranking worldwide were North Korea, Libya, Sudan, Yemen, Afghanistan, Syria, South Sudan, and Somalia.[†]

Professor Johann Graf Lambsdorff of the University of Passau says, "Evidence suggests that an improvement in the CPI by one point [on a 10-point scale] increases capital inflows by 0.5 percent of a country's gross domestic product and average incomes by as much as 4 percent."[‡]

Transparency International's greatest success has been to put the issue of corruption on the global agenda and driving awareness. International institutions such as the World Bank and the International Monetary Fund today see corruption as one of the main obstacles to development, whereas before 1990, this issue was not analyzed so thoroughly.

The Open Knowledge Foundation (OKF) is a global nonprofit network based in London that runs the Global Open Data Index (GODI), which measures the state of open government data around the world. Data are hard to find online and GODI creates insights for government's data publishers to understand where they have data gaps. The 2016/17 Report shows that Taiwan, Australia, Great Britain, France, Finland, Canada, and Norway had the best scores in the open data ranking.[§]

---

* www.transparency.org.
[†] www.transparency.org.
[‡] "Persistently High Corruption in Low-Income Countries Amounts to an Ongoing Humanitarian Disaster," www.transparency.org, 2008.
[§] "Open Data Indices," en.wikipedia.org/wiki/Open_Data_Indices; index.okfn.org/about/; https://index.okfn.org/insights/.

Countries have made efforts in recent decades to raise and improve the quality of their anti-corruption legislation.

Previously, some European countries could deduct bribes from their annual taxes, which created a competitive disadvantage for the North American companies. That is why US companies supported the creation of the OECD* Convention on Combating Bribery of Foreign Public Officials in International Business Transactions, adopted on November 21, 1997, where the signatory countries agreed that bribery abroad was a crime under the national laws of the signatory countries and they agreed to abolish the tax deduction for bribes abroad.

The Preamble states, "Considering that bribery is a widespread phenomenon in international business transactions ... which raises serious moral and political concerns, undermines good governance and economic development, and distorts international competitive conditions."[†]

In view of the need to take effective measures to deter, prevent, and combat bribery, Article 1 of the Convention provides that:

> Each Party shall take such measures as may be necessary to establish that it is a criminal offense under its law for any person intentionally to offer, promise or give any undue pecuniary or other advantage, whether directly or through intermediaries, to a foreign public official, for that official or for a third party, in order that the official act or refrain from acting in relation to the performance of official duties, in order to obtain or retain business or other improper advantage in the conduct of international business.[‡]

On 31 October 2003, the United Nations General Assembly adopted the United Nations Convention against Corruption, which entered into force in December 2005. The Foreword to the Convention signed by the secretary-general of the United Nations, Kofi A. Annan (1938–2018) says:

> Corruption is an insidious plague that has a wide range of corrosive effects on societies. It undermines democracy and the rule of law, leads to violations of human rights, distorts markets, erodes the quality of life and allows organized crime, terrorism and other threats to human security to flourish.

---

* Founded in 1961, the Organization for Economic Cooperation and Development brings together 34 countries and has the mission of promoting policies that improve the economic and social well-being of people around the world.

† www.oecd.org/daf/anti-bribery/ConvCombatBribery.

‡ Article 1, "The Offence of Bribery of Foreign Public Officials," www.oecd.org/daf/anti-bribery/ConvCombatBribery.

This evil phenomenon is found in all countries – big and small, rich and poor – but it is in the developing world that its effects are most destructive.

Corruption hurts the poor disproportionately by diverting funds intended for development, undermining a Government's ability to provide basic services, feeding inequality and injustice and discouraging foreign aid and investment.

Corruption is a key element in economic underperformance and a major obstacle to poverty alleviation and development.

I am therefore very happy that we now have a new instrument to address this scourge at the global level.

The adoption of the United Nations Convention against Corruption will send a clear message that the international community is determined to prevent and control corruption.

It will warn the corrupt that betrayal of the public trust will no longer be tolerated. And it will reaffirm the importance of core values such as honesty, respect for the rule of law, accountability and transparency in promoting the development and making the world a better place for all.*

In the Preamble, the States Parties to the Convention agreed to be:

Concerned about the seriousness of problems and threats posed by corruption to the stability and security of societies, undermining the institutions and values of democracy, ethical values, and justice and jeopardizing sustainable development and the rule of law,

Concerned also about the links between corruption and other forms of crime, in particular, organized crime and economic crime, including money laundering,

Concerned further about cases of corruption that involve vast quantities of assets, which may constitute a substantial proportion of the resources of States, and that threaten the political stability and sustainable development of those States,

Convinced that corruption is no longer a local matter but a transnational phenomenon that affects all societies and economies, making international cooperation to prevent and control it essential.†

In order to continue raising awareness of this scourge, the United Nations General Assembly proclaimed in 2003 that an "International Day Against Corruption" be observed. In addition, on December 9, 2009, the OECD published a *Good Practice Guidance of Internal Control, Ethics,*

---

* www.unodc.org/documents/treaties/UNCAC/Publications/Convention.
† www.unodc.org/documents/treaties/UNCAC/Publications/Convention, page 5.

and Compliance to prevent and detect bribes in international business transactions.

In 2008 the International Chamber of Commerce, Transparency International, the United Nations Global Compact, and the World Economic Forum partnered against corruption and published *Clean Business Is Good Business*, wherein they share some thoughts and information. For example:

> Corruption, the abuse of entrusted power for private gain, is the single greatest obstacle to economic and social development around the world. It distorts markets, stifles economic growth, debases democracy and undermines the rule of law.
>
> Estimates show that the cost of corruption equals more than 5% of global GDP (US$2.6 trillion), with over US$1 trillion paid in bribes each year.
>
> Corruption adds up to 10% to the total cost of doing business globally, and up to 25% to the cost of procurement contracts in developing countries.
>
> Moving business from a country with a low level of corruption to a country with medium or high levels of corruption is found to be equivalent to a 20% tax on foreign business.
>
> The international legal framework that companies are facing is changing fast and has been strengthened during recent years. It now includes the following intergovernmental instruments:
>
> - Inter-American Convention against Corruption (1996)
> - OECD Convention on Combating Bribery of Foreign Public Officials in International Business Transactions (1997)
> - European Union Instruments on Corruption
> - Council of Europe Conventions on Corruption (1997–1999)
> - The African Union Convention on Preventing and Combating Corruption (2003)
> - United Nations Convention against Corruption (2003).

Governmental instruments are also increasingly being adopted at the national level, sometimes with global implications to companies, e.g., the Foreign Corrupt Practices Act and the Sarbanes-Oxley Act in the United States.

Why should companies be involved in this issue?

Companies are subject to extortion and some of them pay bribes. Consequently, the private sector is part of the problem, but if the private sector takes necessary precautions, it can also be part of the solution.

What can companies do?

An increasing number of companies are demonstrating leadership by implementing effective anti-corruption programs within their companies.*

The United States–Mexico–Canada Agreement (USMCA) is a free trade agreement between Canada, Mexico, and the United States. It is also referred to as NAFTA 2.0, in order to distinguish it from its intended current predecessor, the North American Free Trade Agreement (NAFTA). The USMCA establishes anti-corruption provisions. In Chapter 27 of the USMCA, the parties recognize the benefits of internal compliance programs in enterprises to combat corruption. The document recognizes the need to build integrity through ethics and compliance programs to prevent and detect bribery and corruption in international trade and investment. The parties recognize the importance of cooperation, coordination, and exchange of information among the respective law enforcement agencies in order to foster effective measures to prevent, detect, and deter bribery and corruption. Each party also encourages companies to establish compliance programs for the purpose of preventing and detecting corruption cases.†

The Defense Industry Initiative on Business Ethics and Conduct (DII) is a nonprofit organization comprised of representatives from nearly 80 member companies, primarily from the aerospace and defense industry that perform US government contracting. DII's mission is the promotion and advancement of a culture of ethical conduct. The DII Principles set out that members of DII must be committed to upholding the highest ethical standards in all business dealings with the government and they shall implement and sustain effective business ethics and compliance programs.‡

China's Anti-Corruption Office reported that in 2009, 106,000 officials were found guilty of corruption. China's federal prosecutors also produced a report that was reproduced by the official Chinese daily newspaper *The Global Times* a few years ago, reporting that 4,000 Chinese officials fled the country with US$50 billion stolen from public funds over the past 3 decades.

Acting against corruption can be dangerous. Sergei Magnitsky (1972–2009) was a Russian lawyer and auditor who investigated a US$230 million tax fraud scheme that involved high-level government officials in Russia. As a consequence, he spent 11 months at the Butyrka prison in Moscow,

---

* www.unglobalcompact.org/library/158.
† Luis Danton Martinez Torres, "USMCA Heralds New Era of Anticorruption and Compliance," October 3, 2018, www.fcpablog.com.
‡ DII Principles are available at www.DII.org.

and during that time, he was tortured and denied appropriate medical attention. He was found dead in his jail cell in 2009.

In 2012, the US Congress passed a law in his name that imposed sanctions on a list of Russian officials believed to be responsible for serious human rights violations, freezing any US assets they held and banning them from entry into the United States.

In an important step for global accountability, in 2016 the US Congress enacted the *Global Magnitsky Act*, which allows the US government to sanction individuals anywhere in the world responsible for committing human rights violations or gross corruption. Those sanctions include (i) denying entry into the United States with visa bans, (ii) asset freezes for funds held in US banks, and (iii) prohibiting doing business with American companies.

In 2012, the Allard Prize for International Integrity was launched, one of the greatest recognitions in the world in the fight against corruption. Every two years, 100,000 Canadian dollars are awarded to a person or organization that demonstrates exceptional courage and leadership in the fight against corruption or the protection of human rights. Some Allard Prize nominees and recipients have been subjected to threats, violence, imprisonment, and other attacks associated with their anti-corruption and human rights activities. The aforementioned Sergei Magnitsky was nominated for this award posthumously.

In November 2017, Ghanaian Patrick Awuah obtained the WISE Prize for Education for having founded Ashesi University College, an institution that fosters academic training with strong ethical leadership. The University was founded by Awuah 15 years ago and has 900 students and more than 1,000 graduates in Africa.

To stop or decrease corruption, it is necessary to strengthen key institutions. An independent and reliable justice system, education in values, and transparent policies should be part of the solution. Countries with low levels of corruption are those with the highest level of development. If corruption increases, productivity, efficiency, equity, and investment decrease.

In the *Mores Maiorum* magazine of the Universidad Catolica Argentina, Professor Carlos A. Manfroni, in charge of the course International Rules against Corruption, stated,

> According to a study carried out by Vito Tanzi while he was managing
> director of the International Monetary Fund, countries with high levels of

corruption make poor strategic decisions. In this way, they acquire assets they do not need or they perform inadequate and oversized works.*

Canada's Huguette Labelle, who was Chair of Transparency International, said in 2008,

> In the poorer countries, corruption levels can mean the difference between life and death when money for hospitals or clean water is in play.... The continuing high levels of corruption and poverty plaguing many of the world's societies amount to an ongoing humanitarian disaster and cannot be tolerated.[†]

Alan Greenspan, former president of the Federal Reserve of the United States, has pointed out that "corruption and fraud are characteristics that exist everywhere...what makes successful economies is to keep it to a minimum. Nobody has totally eliminated these things."[‡]

An Italian judicial investigation carried out in 1992 is known by the name of "Clean Hands" (in Italian *Mani Pulite*). The investigation discovered an extensive network of corruption that involved all the main political, business, and industrial groups. The investigation caused a great commotion in public opinion; known as *the tangentopoli* (*tangent* means bribery in Italian). On April 30, 1993, large demonstrations were organized by the opposition parties. Former Italian Prime Minister Bettino Craxi (1934–2000) left the San Raphaël hotel in Rome, and people reproached him for corruption and threw coins and lyre notes, shouting phrases like "Vuoi pure queste?" (In Italian it means: You also want these?), a gesture as a symbol of stolen money. April 30, 1993, it became a historic moment, a symbolic day of protest against corruption in the history of Italy.[§]

Imelda Remedios Visitacion Romualdez Trinidad, known as Imelda Marcos or the "Steel Butterfly," heard the prison sentence when she was convicted of corruption in 1993. On the verge of breaking into tears, she held a golden rosary in her hands.

---

* Alberto Manfroni, "La lucha contra la corrupción y el aporte de la Universidad," *Revista Mores Maiorum*, UCA, 13 ("The fight against corruption and the contribution of the University").
† Transparency International Secretariat, "Persistently High Corruption in Low-Income Countries Amounts to an Ongoing Humanitarian Disaster," September 22, 2008, www.transparency.org/.
‡ Andres Krom, "Una Empresa Argentina se convirtió en la Primera en Sacar un Certificado Anticorrupción en la Región," July 6, 2018, www.lanacion.com.ar ("An Argentine Company Became the First to Get the Anti-Corruption Certificate in the Region").
§ es.wikipedia.org/wiki/Manos_Limpias_(Italia).

Imelda was a model and singer and in 1954 married a congressman of the Nationalist Party of the Philippines named Ferdinand Marcos (1917–1989), who, 11 years later in 1965, was elected the tenth president of the Philippines. Imelda then became the First Lady of the Philippines during her husband's term of office, 1965–1986.[*]

In 1981, the Marcos couple acquired the Crown building on Fifth Avenue in New York for 39 million euros and then the Herald Mall for 45 million euros. On February 25, 1986, the Marcos family quickly left their country after a popular revolution and went into exile in Hawaii.

In the Palace of Malacañan, the presidential residence of the Philippines, were found 15 mink coats, more than 500 of Imelda's dresses, and her collection of shoes that exceeded 3,000 pairs.

A Swiss bank returned US$475 million deposited by Ferdinand, and about 10,000 people who were victims of human rights violations filed a class action lawsuit against Marcos's estate. Transparency International has estimated that the Marcos family acquired a fortune of close to US$10 billion, of which about US$1.6 billion was recovered.

Imelda's conviction for corruption in 1993 was overturned by the Supreme Court and, therefore, she avoided imprisonment. Years later, in 2010, she was elected a member of the Philippine House of Representatives.

In an interview in 1998, she said, "I was born ostentatious. They will list my name in the dictionary someday. They will use 'Imeldific' to mean ostentatious extravagance."[†]

In 2016, the state seized 15 paintings from her private collection valued in millions of dollars.

Cases of corrupt rulers are numerous, for example:

In Tunisia, Zine Ben Ali had to go into exile and his wife escaped on a plane with a ton of ingots of gold, equivalent to US$60 million.

The former president of Equatorial Guinea, Theodore Obiang, owned a mansion of 107 million euros in Paris and forty cars.

In Malaysia, former premier Najib Razak created a sovereign development fund called 1MBD (1 Malaysia Development Berhad) from which US$4.5 billion disappeared. US$ 681 million were found in his own account. His wife had 550 wallets costing more than US$10,000 each, 453 luxury watches, including one US$850,000 Rolex and 12,000 jewels.[‡]

---

[*] The Beatles toured the Philippines and did not accept an invitation from Imelda. Her anger was such that she caused the Beatles to be driven out of the country.

[†] "Imelda Marcos," en.wikiquote.org.

[‡] Inés Capdevila, "¿Qué Pasa en los Países con Presidentes Abiertamente Corruptos?" August 17, 2018, www.lanacion.com.ar. ("What Happens in Countries with Openly Corrupt Presidents?");

Malaysian businessman Joh Low convinced Najib Razak to create the sovereign fund in 2009. Low, who lived in the United States and is a graduate of Wharton Business School, was the fund's treasurer.

Low had a luxurious lifestyle with ostentatious parties with celebrities and millionaire purchases including real estate, a jet, and a yacht.*

Low bought a white Ferrari of US$325,000 and gave it to a well-known model in 2011. He rented a Boeing 747 to go to celebrate the New Year in Australia and hours later the plane returned to Las Vegas to celebrate New Year again.

This businessman spent 150 million euros for the painting *Les Femmes d'Alger*, by Pablo Picasso, and among his most lavish purchases, was the *Nymphéas* by Claude Monet, a painting acquired for more than US$57 million in an auction.†

Tim Leissner was the Goldman Sachs partner who advised the fund. According to a Goldman Sachs banker, "Tim Leissner brought a lot of money to the bank, and, thanks to that, he enjoyed a lot of freedom in his dealings with clients."‡

Leissner said Goldman Sachs' compliance structure "prioritized deal-making over other weeding out malfeasance."§

Goldman Sachs suspended Leissner in 2016 and the Malaysian government filed claims against the bank totaling US$3 billion. Tim Leissner is accused of corruption and money laundering in Malaysia and the United States. Former premier Najib Razak was arrested in Malaysia and Low is a fugitive.¶

Elias Antonio Saca was president of El Salvador between 2004 and 2009. Shortly after leaving the presidency, Saca built a US$8 million house known as "The Palace of Corruption." They found evidence of money laundering and deviation of about US$275 million and he is in prison since 2016. It is estimated that between Saca and another former president (Funes) diverted

---

Sebastian Seibt, "1 MDB, el Escándalo Financiero Mundial que le costó Miles de Dólares a Malasia," 3 de abril de 2019, www.france24.com ("1 MDB, the Global Financial Scandal that cost Thousands of Dollars to Malaysia," April 3, 2019).

* Maximiliano Fernandez, "Quien es Jho Low, el nuevo lobo de Wall Street," 21 de octubre de 2016, www.infobae.com ("Who is Jho Low, the new wolf of Wall Street," October 21, 2016).

† Maximiliano Fernandez, "Quien es Jho Low, el nuevo lobo de Wall Street," 21 de octubre de 2016, www.infobae.com ("Who is Jho Low, the new wolf of Wall Street," October 21, 2016).

‡ Sebastian Seibt, "1 MDB, el Escandalo Financiero Mundial que le costo Miles de Dolares a Malasia," 3 de abril de 2019, www.france24.com ("1 MDB, the Global Financial Scandal that Cost Thousands of Dollars to Malaysia," April 3, 2019).

§ Richard Bistrong, "How Goldman Sachs Helped a Modern Gatsby Steal $5 Billion," April 30, 2019, FCPA Blog.

¶ The book *Billion Dollar Whale, The Man Who Fooled Wall Street, Hollywood, and the World*, by Tom Wright and Bradley Hope, Hachette Books Group Inc. (2018), recounts the greatest financial scandal in history.

about US$700 million from state coffers, a figure that equals El Salvador's fiscal deficit in 2017.[*]

Other leaders such as Nicolas Ceausescu, from Romania; Saddam Hussein, from Iraq; Isabel Dos Santos, daughter of the president of Angola; Sani Abacha, from Nigeria; Bettino Craxi, from Italy; Mobutu Sese Seko, from Zaire; Zine El-Abidine Ben Ali, from Tunis; Haji Mohammed Suharto, from Indonesia; Hosni Mubarak, from Egypt or Ferdinand Marcos, from the Philippines, they stole hundreds of millions and in some cases billions of dollars.[†]

The United States was the first country to initiate an international action against the bribery of public officials. In 1976, the former president of Lockheed Martin, Archibald Carlisle Kotchian (1914–2008) confessed in the US Senate that he had bribed public officials in Japan and the Netherlands.

In a 1977 profile in *The New York Times*, Kotchian reflected his bitterness at the Lockheed directors who ousted him as a chief operating officer in March 1976 based on his US$38 million of what the board called "questionable payments." Kotchian said:

> Some call it gratuities. Some call them questionable payments. Some call it extortion. Some call it grease. Some call it bribery. I looked at these payments as necessary to sell a product. I never felt I was doing anything wrong. I considered them a commission.[‡]

Kotchian's declaration to the US Senate was one of the main reasons to sanction the Foreign Corrupt Practices Act (FCPA) on December 19, 1977,[§] which established the payment of bribes by the US citizens and companies to foreign state officials constitutes a crime.

The FCPA is a consequence of the actions of hundreds of companies that made questionable or illegal payments to foreign governments to achieve

---

[*] Héctor Silva Avalos, "La Historia del Primer Presidente Latinoamericano que Confesó Como Robo 275 Millones de Dólares," 19 de agosto de 2018, www.infobae.com ("The History of the First Latin American President Who Confessed as a Theft US$275 Million").

[†] Tomas Orihuela, "El Piso de la Corrupción: 12 Infografías de los presidentes que nos Robaron," August 18, 2018, www.infobae.com ("The Floor of Corruption: 12 Infographics of the presidents who stole us").

[‡] en.wikipedia.org/wiki/Carl_Kotchian. Also, see Robert Lindsey, "Kotchian Calls Himself the Scapegoat," *The New York Times*, July 3, 1977, www.nytimes.com/1977/07/03/archives/kotchian-calls-himself-the-scapegoat-kotchian-calls-himself-the.html.

[§] Hugo Alconada Mon, *La Raíz de Todos los Males* (Planeta, 2018), 26–7 ("The Root of all Evils").

commercial advantages. The objective of this regulation was to stop these corrupt practices and restore confidence in the market.

The law meant a competitive disadvantage for American companies compared to others that were not subject to similar legislation. As previously mentioned, when referring to the OECD, some developed countries such as Germany or France argued that the expenses in bribes abroad could be deducted from taxes.[*]

In 1997, the US Senate said that "Corporate bribery is bad business. In our free market system, it is basic that the sale of products should take place on the basis of price, quality, and service."[†]

The FCPA was designed to prevent corrupt practices, protect investors, and provide a fair playing field for those honest companies trying to win business based on quality and price rather than bribes.[‡]

This law seeks to restore integrity in business.

The extraterritorial reach of anti-corruption laws means that organizations doing business in multiple jurisdictions can be prosecuted for acts of bribery committed anywhere in the world.

From 1977 to 2011, more than 400 American companies admitted to making payments to foreign officials.

The FCPA provides that bribes to foreign officials by US companies, their branches or companies listed on the New York Stock Exchange, are prohibited. The law makes it illegal for an employee or agent acting on behalf of the company to offer, pay, promise to pay, authorize payment, or something of value (directly or indirectly, through a third person or company) to a government official to obtain or retain business.

Improper benefits can take many forms, including, but not limited to, cash, gift cards, gifts, travel expenses, entertainment, sponsorships, fake consultancy agreements, employment opportunities, inflated commissions, unauthorized discounts or rebates, and political or charitable donations.

The FCPA sanctions any payment made to third parties with the knowledge that all or part of the payment will be used to bribe a foreign

---

[*] Manuel Solanet, "La Corrupción en las Instituciones Públicas y Privadas" ("Corruption in Public and Private Institutions").

[†] "A Resource Guide to the U.S. Foreign Corrupt Practice Act," by the Criminal Division of the US Department of Justice and the Enforcement Division of the US Securities and Exchange Commission, www.justice.gov/sites/default/files/criminal-fraud/legacy/2015/01/16/guide.pdf, page 9.

[‡] "A Resource Guide to the U.S. Foreign Corrupt Practice Act," by the Criminal Division of the US Department of Justice and the Enforcement Division of the US Securities and Exchange Commission, www.justice.gov/sites/default/files/criminal-fraud/legacy/2015/01/16/guide.pdf, 90.

government official. This situation is considered "willful blindness" or deliberate ignorance of the fact that the intermediary will break the law.

The International Organization for Standardization (ISO), based in Switzerland and founded in 1947, produces international and voluntary standards that companies use as guides to greater efficiency.

On October 13, 2016, it created ISO 37,001, the first standard of good practices for anti-corruption programs to help organizations to prevent and detect bribery. This standard was developed with the help of experts from 45 countries.

The FCPA and ISO 37001 are different efforts toward the same goal: curbing corruption.

Organizations should take special care with donations made to foreign governments or officials to avoid having them perceived as "gifts" in order to obtain or retain business.

Bribes can be used as an illegal means, for example, to reduce tariffs, to hire family members of public officials responsible for conducting inspections, to obtain licensing and permit approvals, or to suspend or make regulatory changes.

The *Huffington Post*, an online newspaper, published a report on corruption in the oil industry in March 2016. According to the report, a company called Unaoil based in the Principality of Monaco and registered in the British Virgin Islands and offering "industrial solutions in the energy sector in the Middle East, Central Asia and Africa," was dedicated to bribing officials from crude oil-producing countries such as Iraq, Syria, Libya, Iran, the United Arab Emirates, Kuwait, Azerbaijan, Kazakhstan, Tunisia, Congo, Algeria, and Angola, in exchange for million-dollar contracts over the last 20 years.

Violation of the FCPA may result in severe consequences for a company, such as fines; return of earned profits; loss of stock value; loss of confidence of customers, investors, partners, and suppliers; negative press reports; and/or the monitoring by a controller of the company's risk control program.

Some companies sign a deferred prosecution agreement (DPA), which is an agreement between the defense lawyer, the defendant, and the prosecutor to dismiss a case upfront, if the accused accepts some conditions. A case of corporate fraud, for instance, might be settled by means of a DPA if the defendant agrees to pay fines, implement corporate reforms, and fully cooperate with the investigation.*

---

* en.wikipedia.org/wiki/Deferred_prosecution.

Some important companies have suffered the consequences of corruption. Some examples are outlined below:

KRB Inc.: Formerly Kellogg Brown & Root, KRB is an American engineering and construction company based in Houston, Texas. On February 6, 2009, the company pleaded guilty to charges related to the violation of the FCPA for its participation in a decade-long scheme to bribe Nigerian government officials with "tens of millions of dollars" in consulting fees to obtain engineering, procurement, and construction contracts.* The CEO was sentenced to 30 months in prison for conspiring to violate the FCPA. KRB pleaded guilty and paid more than US$400 million fine.

Halliburton: In 2009, Houston-based oil company Halliburton agreed with the US Department of Justice and the SEC to pay US$559 million for bribing Nigerian officials to secure a million-dollar contract.

Technip: This company agrees with the US Department of Justice and the SEC in 2010 to pay US$338 million in fines to close an FCPA investigation for alleged bribes to the Nigerian government to obtain engineering contracts.

Siemens AG: The German multinational and the government of Greece were involved in a corruption scandal for bribes in the purchase of security systems for the Athens Olympic Games.

The SEC also found that Siemens made more than 4,280 illicit payments for about US$1.4 billion to carry out bribes to obtain contracts in different countries around the world.† As a result of these illegal actions, Siemens paid about US$2 billion in fines, fees, and investigations around the world.

Under the leadership of Austrian CEO Peter Loscher, the first CEO of Siemens from outside the company, changes were made to the control system and organizational culture, and Siemens became one of the most committed companies with compliance, currently having one of the best ethics and compliance programs in the world.

Baker Hughes: In 2007, Baker Hughes agreed in US federal court to pay US$44 million in fines for FCPA violation as a result of having participated

---

* The US Department of Justice, "Kellogg Brown & Root LLC Pleads Guilty to Foreign Bribery Charges and Agrees to Pay $402 Million Criminal Fine," February 11, 2009, www.justice.gov.
† See Insight's "Recovery from Ethical Lapses – Investigations: Siemens," 2010; "At Siemens Bribery Was Just a Line Item," *New York Times*, 2008.

in possible bribes between 2001 and 2003 through a commercial agent in connection with a project in Kazakhstan. In this case, the fine was based on a lack of due diligence on the supplier.

With respect to the use of intermediaries to perform bribes, the US Department of Justice has stated that it is unlawful to make a payment to a third party while knowing that all or a portion of the payment will go directly or indirectly to a foreign official. The term *knowing* includes conscious disregard and deliberate ignorance.*

BAE Systems: In 2007, the US Department of Justice opened an investigation into the business that the British arms company BAE Systems had undertaken in Saudi Arabia and into possible illicit payments and false accounting. The value of BAE's shares fell 7.5% when the news was disclosed. In 2010, BAE agreed to pay fines of US$400 million and £30 million to close the case. It was the first time that the US and British authorities coordinated a corporate corruption case.

ABB: The Swedish-Swiss group ABB, an engineering and power company, discovered possible bribes to officials in Nigeria between 1998 and 2003 and denounced them.

When bribes made to a Nigerian government official were discovered, the company reported the fact to the Department of Justice and ABB pleaded guilty. The Justice Department ordered it to pay US$10.5 million for the commission of the crime and then had to pay US$5.9 million to the SEC. ABB had to pay 43,000 hours of lawyers' work at an hourly rate of US$400. The SEC requested a controller to investigate the company and obliged it to conduct a global audit of the six years prior to the event.

In 2010, the company pleaded guilty to paying bribes to obtain million-dollar contracts in Iraq and Mexico and agreed with the US Department of Justice to pay fines of US$58 million. ABB lacked internal controls to detect and prevent violations of the FCPA.

IKEA: In 2010, senior officials of the Swedish furniture multinational were fired for bribes by a subcontractor in Russia to ensure the connection of the electricity grid to a shopping center located in St. Petersburg.

---

* "Addressing the Challenges of International Bribery and Fair Competition 2001," the Third Annual Report Under Section 6 of the International Anti-Bribery and Fair Competition Act of 1998, US Department of Commerce, International Trade Administration July 2001, Third Party Payments, page 151.

Avon: Avon Products is a cosmetics and perfume company founded in New York in 1886. In 2010, Avon Products' share price fell 8% in a single day on concerns that the beauty products company had been involved in a bribery scheme with government officials in China. The *Wall Street Journal* reported that Avon had suspended four executives, including three from China's subsidiary, and would strengthen ethics training in an effort to prevent its employees from making illegal payments. "The issue," the article says, "overshadows the reputation of the direct sales industry, which is sometimes seen as a sector where business practices are poorly transparent."*Avon later admitted to handing over gifts worth US$8 million to Chinese government authorities to obtain permission to make direct sales in China. Avon was fined US$135 million.†

Olympus: In 2011, the Japanese magazine *Facta* published a report denouncing the Japanese company Olympus Corporation for the payment of US$687 million in commissions to deal advisers for the purchase of a medical equipment company.‡ Payments were made in the Cayman Islands to companies whose owners had not been identified. Soon the CEO resigned. The value of the company's stock fell 30% and the company lost US$4.6 billion in market capitalization. This case became one of Japan's largest corporate scandals. In 2016, the company agreed with the US Department of Justice to pay a fine of US$643 million for another case of bribery and illegal commissions to doctors in the United States and Brazil.

JGC: The Japanese company JGC Corporation in April 2011 agreed to pay US$218.8 million to settle an FCPA investigation related to the bribery of Nigerian government officials to obtain construction contracts.

Johnson & Johnson: On April 8, 2011, Johnson & Johnson entered into a US$77.9 million global settlement with the SEC, the Department of Justice, and the UK's Sections Fraud Office (SFO). Its subsidiaries in Greece, Poland, and Romania had apparently bribed healthcare providers and probably promoted kickbacks to the former Iraq government.

---

* Ellen Byron and Joann S. Lublin, "Bribe Scandal Overturns Avon's Action," *Wall Street Journal* (April 14, 2010).

† "Multan con US135 millones de Dolares a empresa de cosméticos Avon por sobornos en China," December 18, 2014, www.bbc.com ("US$ 135 million fined by cosmetics company Avon for bribes in China").

‡ Isabel Reynolds and Kirstin Ridley, "Olympus Admits to $687 Million Adviser Fee, Deepening," October 19, 2011, www.reuters.com.

Daimler AG: In 2010, German automotive multinational Daimler AG agreed to pay US$185 million in fines in a bribery investigation into public officials in 22 countries between 1998 and 2008. The US Department of Justice said bribes were made "to secure contracts for the purchase of Daimler vehicles."*

Alcatel Lucent: In 2010, Alcatel Lucent agreed to pay US$137 million to close an FCPA investigation. The French company made illegal payments in Costa Rica, Honduras, Malaysia, and Taiwan. Robert Khuzami, the then director of the SEC's Division of Enforcement, said:

> Alcatel and its subsidiaries failed to detect or investigate numerous red flags suggesting their employees were directing sham consultants to provide gifts and payments to foreign government officials to illegally win business.... Alcatel's bribery scheme was the product of a lax corporate control environment at the company.[†]

The SEC alleged that Alcatel's subsidiaries used consultants who performed illegitimate work to funnel more than US$8 million in bribes to government officials to obtain telecommunication contracts. Alcatel's general counsel said, "We take responsibility for and regret what happened and have implemented policies and procedures to prevent these violations from happening again."[‡]

Tyson Foods: In 2011, the SEC charged Tyson Foods Inc. with violating the FCPA by making illicit payments to two Mexican government veterinarians responsible for certifying its Mexican subsidiary's chicken products. Tyson de Mexico initially concealed the improper payments by putting the veterinarian's wives on its payroll while they performed no services for the company. Those women were later removed from the payroll, and payments were then reflected in invoices submitted to Tyson de Mexico by one of the veterinarians for "services." Two years later, Tyson Foods officials learned about the subsidiary's illicit payments, and its counsel instructed Tyson de Mexico to cease making those payments. Tyson agreed to pay US$5 million to settle the SEC's charges and resolve related criminal proceedings. Tyson

---

* "FCPA Spring Review 2010," April 8, 2010, www.millechevalier.com.
† "SEC Charges Alcatel-Lucent with FCPA Violations: Company to Pay More Than $137 Million to Settle SEC and DOJ Charges," www.sec.gov.
‡ Samuel Rubenfield, Blogs, December 27, 2010, Wsj.com.

Foods failed to implement a system of effective internal controls to prevent the salary payments to phantom employees and the payment of illicit invoices. The undue payments were improperly recorded as legitimate expenses in Tyson de Mexico's books and records.[*]

Alstom: The French engineering company Alstom agreed to pay US\$772 million to settle a corruption case where it paid consultants certain money to make bribes in order to win energy contracts around the world. Using code names such as "Mr. Paris" and "Quiet Man," Alstom tried to hide tens of millions of dollars in bribes to carry out activities that appeared as legitimate. In fact, the consultants were hired to bribe officials in Indonesia, Saudi Arabia, Egypt, Taiwan, and the Bahamas, in a scheme that took place over about 11 years and involved paying more than US\$75 million to secure US\$4 billion in projects.

The US Department of Justice said Alstom falsified its books to mask the bribes and internal emails demonstrated how well company officials knew those payments were illegal.

In 2003, an Alstom finance employee sent an email saying she could not process an invoice for a consultant because there was no proof any services were rendered. A project manager then told her to stop sending such emails unless she wanted to have several people put in jail and instructed to delete all emails about the topic. Patrick Kron, who was the CEO of Alstom until 2016, said,

> There were a number of problems in the past and we deeply regret that. … This resolution with the DOJ allows Alstom to put this issue behind us and to continue our efforts to ensure that business is conducted in a responsible way.[†]

Henri Poupart-Lafarge, Alston's chairman and CEO, in the introductory letter to the Code of Ethics, states, "Our fundamental commitment to ethical conduct. We have an obligation to our employees, customers, shareholders, and other stakeholders to uphold the highest standards of behavior in compliance with all applicable laws and our rules and procedures."[‡]

---

[*] "SEC Charges Tyson Foods with FCPA Violations," February 10, 2011, ww.sec.gov/news/press/2011.

[†] Sarah N Lynch and Doina Chiacu, "Alstom to Pay Record \$772 Million to Settle Bribery Charges with U.S.," www.reuters.com, December 22, 2014.

[‡] www.alstom.com/integrity/our-code-of-ethics/.

Petrobras: Operation Car Wash (Portuguese: *Operação Lava Jato*) is an ongoing criminal investigation being carried out by the Federal Police of Brazil, Curitiba Branch, and judicially commanded by Judge Sergio Moro since 17 March 2014.

Initially, a money-laundering investigation was expanded to cover accusations of corruption in the state oil company Petrobras, where its executives allegedly accepted bribes from construction companies in exchange for awarding contracts.*

The Lava Jato scandal exposed a corruption network at the Brazilian state oil company, Latin America's largest company. The case, with 250 companies involved, is considered the largest investigation of corruption in the history of Brazil. A group of politicians collaborated with the corruption scheme, and it is estimated that between 2004 and 2012, the money diverted exceeded US$8 billion. Brazilian federal judge Sergio Moro asserted that "it was the rule of the game to pay bribes of 1 to 2% of the value of the contract."† More than 200 businessmen and politicians have already been convicted, including former president Luiz Inacio Lula da Silva.

Odebrecht: On December 21, 2016, the US Department of Justice published an investigation into the Brazilian construction company Odebrecht, a Brazilian engineering conglomerate, operating in 27 countries. It is the largest construction company in Latin America and was founded in 1944 by the engineer Norberto Odebrecht Pernambuco. The construction company made bribes totaling US$788 million to a dozen countries in Latin America and Africa to obtain public contracts. Odebrecht created a "Structured Operations Division" or a "Strategic Relations Sector" to disguise bribes.‡

The offshore network of firms that Odebrecht used to carry out the bribes included tax havens such as the Bahamas, the Cayman Islands, and Malta. Some Odebrecht executives revealed to DOJ authorities the Brazilian construction company used offshore firms to launder money and hide the payment of bribes. The former president of the company, Marcelo Odebrecht, has been detained since 2015 and was sentenced to 18 years and 4 months in prison by Judge Sergio Moro. The former

---

* en.wikipedia.org/wiki/Operation_Car_Wash.
† "Las Claves para Entender el Escándalo Petrobras," March 4, 2016, www.elobservador.com.uy ("The Keys to Understanding the Petrobras Scandal").
‡ "Los sobornos de Odebrecht," *Diario La Nación*, February 9, 2017 ("The bribes of Odebrecht").

president of Peru, Alan García, committed suicide when he was about to be detained for alleged money laundering resulting from possible bribes from Odebrecht.

JBS: The world's largest meat processor agreed to pay a US$3.2 billion fine over a 25-year period because its major shareholder, J & F Investments, used US$184 million to bribe hundreds of politicians in Brazil. In May 2017, JBS shares plummeted 25% in value.

Gurtel: The Gurtel case* is the name of an investigation initiated in November 2007 in Spain by the Anti-Corruption Prosecutor and which deals with a network of political corruption linked to the Spanish Popular Party. The case was made public by the newspaper *El Pais* in 2010 and is the largest political corruption plot in Spanish democratic history. Businessman Francisco Correa, sentenced to 51 years in prison, managed to sign public contracts at inflated prices and then some of the money returned to public officials who granted those contracts.†

The Notebooks Scandal: The notebook scandal took place in Argentina in 2018. It was started by the driver Oscar Centeno, who had worked for public officials during the presidencies of Néstor Kirchner (2003–2007) and Cristina Fernández de Kirchner (2007–2015). Centeno revealed an organized corruption scheme. According to notes that he wrote in his personal notebooks, during his work as a driver, he said he often carried bags full of US dollars to several locations, including public buildings and, even, to the house of President Cristina Kirchner. Those bags full of money would be payments for bribes.

Oscar Centeno wrote several notebooks with details of places and hours of several trips he made carrying bags of cash money. Those bags would have been provided to the national government by businessmen benefited with large contracts. The notebooks cover the period of time between the years 2005 and 2015. All the briberies mentioned in the notebooks amount to US$53 million, but the investigators consider that the actual operations may be closer to US$160 million.

---

* Gurtel means a belt in German. The name is Gurtel case because Mr. Correa used to live in Germany and the word Correa in Spanish is associated with a belt. Bruno Vergara, "From Yogi to Gurtel: Why They Are Called Military Operations," May 6, 2014, www.elcorreo.com.

† "What Is the Gurtel Case, the Scandal of Corruption that Cost the Presidency to Mariano Rajoy," June 1, 2018, www.infobae.com; Fernando Perez, "The Illegal Network of Gurtel Condemns the Popular Party," May 25, 2018, politica.elpais.com.

The notebooks came to light, thanks to a secret informant that provided the scoop to journalist Diego Cabot of *La Nación* newspaper. Cabot investigated the case and gave photocopies of the notebooks to the judiciary and returned the notebooks.

Oscar Centeno was detained immediately. He confirmed his authorship of the notebooks, and declared himself guilty. The Argentine "ley del arrepentido" ("Law of the remorseful"), sanctioned in 2016, allows for those involved in corruption cases to receive leniency if their testimony helps to advance in the investigation of the case or get evidence against criminals of a higher hierarchy in the crime.

Several businessmen were detained as a result of the case. The sweep of detentions scared most of the involved businessmen, who quickly pleaded themselves guilty, abiding by the law of the repentant, in exchange for a reduction of penalties. According to the testimonies, the businessmen were forced by government officials to pay bribes.*

Samsung: In February 2017, the heir and president of the multinational Samsung, Lee Jae Yong, was arrested for possible links with a corruption scandal involving former South Korean president Park Geun Hye. Samsung was accused of donating about 43 billion won (US$36.3 million) to nonprofit foundations operated by Choi Soon Sil, who was close to President Park, in exchange for political support for a controversial two-way merger of affiliates of Samsung.

A month later, in March 2017, the South Korean Constitutional Court unanimously approved the removal of the South Korean president, who was implicated in the country's biggest corruption scandal in decades. The former president Park was accused of collaborating with her friend Choi Soon Sil to pressure the large South Korean multinationals to donate large sums of money to the foundations and companies Choi controlled.

FIFA: The International Federation of Associated Football, known as FIFA, is the institution that governs the football (soccer in the United States) federations in the world. It was founded on May 21, 1904, and has its headquarters in Zurich, Switzerland. On May 27, 2015, Swiss authorities stormed the Baur au Lac Hotel in Zurich and arrested seven FIFA executives to face charges of corruption in the US Courts. Charges of the indictment included bribery, fraud, and money laundering. Fourteen

---

* en.wikipedia.org/wiki/Notebook_scandal.

people were charged in connection with an investigation by the Federal Bureau of Investigation (FBI), on suspicion of receiving US$150 million in bribes. The detainees are accused of violating the US RICO law with charges of extortion, bribes, electronic fraud, and money-laundering conspiracies, among other crimes, to enrich themselves through the corruption of international football.

The *Racketeer Influenced and Corrupt Organizations Act*, commonly referred to as the RICO Act or simply RICO, is a federal law of 1970 issued by the United States.

This law opposed the extortion (racketeering) of the American Mafia and the criminal actions within the unions. It is a legal basis to combat and prosecute the criminal activities of criminal organizations.

The RICO Act also allows federal prosecutors to sue people because of their membership in a criminal organization, even if they have only organized or planned the commitment of a crime, and they did not personally execute it. Hence, it was a closed loophole that allowed a person who ordered another to execute an unlawful act to be exempt from a trial, because he or she did not commit the crime personally. The FIFA soccer federation is considered a corrupt organization according to the RICO law.[*]

Chapman University in Orange, California, conducts its annual "American Fears" survey. Surveyed 1,541 participants in the United States in 2015, the result indicates that the main fear of Americans was the corruption of government officials.

The *Financial Times* said, "More and more companies are facing costly investigations for overseas bribery and … what, in their father's generations, might have seemed like harmless acts of foreign palm-greasing, today can cost them millions."[†]

In 2014, the OECD disseminated the "Foreign Bribery Report" that analyzed 427 cases of transnational corruption.

57% of the bribes were paid to obtain a public contract; another 12% to facilitate a customs procedure, and 6% to obtain preferential tax treatment. 41% of the cases analyzed included an intermediary who triangle the bribe between the payer and who received the bribe. In 41% of the cases analyzed, executives at managerial level paid or authorized bribes.[‡]

---

[*] es.wikipedia.org/wiki/Ley_RICO; en.wikipedia.org/wiki/Racketeer_Influenced_and_Corrupt_Organizations_Act.

[†] Patti Waldmeir, "Bribery Is Not Just a Cost of Doing Business," April 4, 2007, www.ft.com.

[‡] Hugo Alconada Mon, *La Raíz de Todos los Males* (Planeta, 2018), 92–3 ("The Root of all Evils"). See also www.oecd.org/daf/oecd-foreign-bribery-report-9789264226616-en.htm.

Pope Francis wrote a twitter on December 9, 2017, in which he stated: "We must fight with force against corruption. It is an evil based on the idolatry of money that hurts human dignity." A few months later, in February of 2018, Pope Francis recorded a video called *Say No to Corruption* where he says, "Corruption is not countered with silence we must speak about it and denounce its evils."

Corruption alters the priorities and the correct way in which corporations and governments should make decisions. It benefits a few and harms the vast majority.

Corruption is a phenomenon that discourages confidence, investment, and the rule of law; favors fraud and tax evasion; avoids free competition between suppliers on an equal footing; and increases the sense of injustice and favoritism.

To fight corruption, it is necessary to permanently improve control systems because when institutions are weak, corruption expands without control.

19

Corporate Risks: Unit 7

PREJUDICE, DISCRIMINATION, EXCLUSION, AND LACK OF DIVERSITY

A prejudice (from the Latin *prae iudicium*, "judged beforehand") is the process of forming a concept or judgment about some person, object, or idea in advance. In psychological terms, it is an unconscious mental activity that distorts perception.*

Prejudices can cause a person to be misjudged.

A lady arrives at the railway station, buys a magazine, a packet of cookies, and a bottle of water, and sits on a bench to wait for the train. While she is browsing a magazine, a young man sits down next to her and begins to read a newspaper. Suddenly, without saying a word, the young man reaches out, takes the package of cookies, opens it, and begins to eat them. The lady does not want to be rude, but with an exaggerated gesture, she takes the package and takes out a cookie, staring at the young man. In response, the young man takes another cookie and brings it to his mouth. Showing annoyance, she takes another cookie. The lady is getting more and more irritated.

Finally, she realizes that there is only one cookie left, and she thinks "he cannot be so cheeky" while looking at the package. Very calmly the young man reaches out, takes the cookie, breaks it in two, and with a kind gesture offers half to his bench mate, who takes the piece of cookie abruptly.

---

* es.wikipedia.org/wiki/Prejuicio (Prejudice).

Then the train arrives. The lady gets up angrily from the bench, gets into her train car, and thinks about how insolent and impolite the young man was. The woman feels her mouth is dry, opens her purse to take out the water bottle, and is shocked when she finds in her purse her package of cookies intact.

A young man over 20 years was traveling on a train with his father. The young man looked out the window of the train and the whole time made comments to his father. He would say, "Dad, look. The trees pass behind the window," or "Papa, the clouds follow us."

In front of them sat a couple, and upon hearing these comments, one of them said to the other, "He should take him to a doctor."

The father heard the comment and said, "We were just at his doctor. My son was blind from birth, and since a few days ago, he can see."

On one occasion a woman commented to her husband that the neighbor always hung out her dirty sheets. The woman made that comment to her husband during breakfast every time she looked out the kitchen window at the neighbor's sheets.

After several days, one morning, the woman was surprised to see that her neighbor's sheets were clean and told her husband, "At last our neighbor has learned to wash her clothes. She must have bought a better soap."

Her husband replied, "No, it's just that I got up early today and washed our window."

These examples can serve to reflect and realize that everyone, in some way, prejudges.

Unconscious bias is created by the environment and our experience. Our mind processes information, and unconscious biases influence our decisions. They affect our perceptions, interactions, and decisions.

Do not quickly prejudge other people because perceptions may be wrong. Prejudging can lead us to make mistakes and to move from prejudice to racism, sexism, and intolerance unless we accept the differences of the other.

Never accept a label in place of a story. We should not judge a book by its cover. When opening the book, we find things we did not imagine.

All human beings are different and from all people, you can learn to grow. The leader must promote diversity, tolerance, and respect among all members of the organization.

Jesus did not make distinctions among men; they were all "neighbors," regardless of religion, nationality, or ideas. Samaritans and Jews were irreconcilable rivals. Luke, the Evangelist, comments on the parable of the Good Samaritan* that Jesus of Nazareth explained the importance of brotherhood with one's neighbor even though there are religious differences:

> A man was going down from Jerusalem to Jericho when he was attacked by robbers. They stripped him of his clothes, beat him and went away, leaving him half dead. A priest happened to be going down the same road, and when he saw the man, he passed by on the other side. So too, a Levite, when he came to the place and saw him, passed by on the other side. But a Samaritan, as he traveled, came where the man was; and when he saw him, he took pity on him. He went to him and bandaged his wounds, pouring on oil and wine. Then he put the man on his own donkey, brought him to an inn and took care of him. The next day he took out two denarii and gave them to the innkeeper. "Look after him," he said, "and when I return, I will reimburse you for any extra expense you may have."
>
> "Which of these three do you think was a neighbor to the man who fell into the hands of robbers?"
>
> The expert in the law replied, "The one who had mercy on him."
>
> Jesus told him, "Go and do likewise."†

Discrimination is an act or omission by which, due to intolerance, rejection, or ignorance, a different treatment is given to a person with negative consequences to that person. Most of the causes of discrimination are given by fear of difference or because people want to show that they are more important or stronger.

John Locke (1632–1704) was an English philosopher, and one of the most influential thinkers of the Enlightenment. Locke said,

> All men by nature are equal in that equal right that every man hath to his natural freedom, without being subjected to the will or authority of any other man; being all equal and independent, no one ought to harm another in his life, health, liberty or possessions.‡

In 1776, the Founding Fathers of the United States used the phrase "all men are created equal" in the Declaration of Independence.§ The phrase

---

* The Bible, New Testament, Luke 10:25–37.

† "The Parable of the Good Samaritan," Luke 10:25–37, www.biblegateway.com.

‡ "John Locke," www.azquotes.com.

§ The quotation "All men are created equal," has been called an "immortal declaration." It appears in the second paragraph of the United States Declaration of Independence: "We hold these truths to be self-evident, that all men are created equal, that they are endowed by their Creator with

summarizes a dream, a vision, and a goal: the desire that all people have the same rights and opportunities to grow and be happy regardless of age, sex, skin color, religion, nationality, political ideas, wealth, or the language they speak.

Human rights are conditions that allow a person to achieve personal fulfillment and include everyone without any distinction. Human rights are irrevocable, non-transferable, and inalienable and are necessary to protect the dignity of people. Every individual must have the same opportunities to grow and overcome challenges with the use of their imagination, creative talent, and freedom of choice.

In 1789, the Declaration of the Rights of Man and of the Citizen of the French Revolution asserted that "men are born and remain free and equal in rights."[*]

In the United States, in 1865, after the Civil War and with the incorporation of the 13th Amendment to the US Constitution, slavery formally ended in the entire North American territory.

In 1948, the Universal Declaration of Human Rights of the United Nations stated that

> all human beings are born free and equal in dignity and rights.[†] ... Everyone is entitled to all the rights and freedoms set forth in this Declaration, without distinction of any kind, such as race, color, sex, language, religion, political or other opinions, national or social origin, property, birth or another status.[‡]

The International Convention on the Elimination of All Forms of Racial Discrimination of 1965 defines racial discrimination as

> any distinction, exclusion, restriction or preference based on race, color, descent or national or ethnic origin which has the purpose or effect of nullifying or impairing the recognition, enjoyment or exercise, on an equal footing, of human rights and fundamental freedoms.[§]

---

certain unalienable Rights, that among these are Life, Liberty and the Pursuit of Happiness. That to secure these rights, Governments are instituted among Men, deriving their just powers from the consent of the governed." en.wikipedia.org/wiki/All_men_are_created_equal.

[*] Article 1 of the Declaration of the Rights of the Man and of the Citizen of 1789, Wikipedia.

[†] Preamble of the Universal Declaration of Human Rights, en.wikiquote.org.

[‡] Article 1, of the Universal Declaration of Human Rights, en.wikiquote.org.

[§] "International Convention on the Elimination of All Forms of Racial Discrimination," Article 1, en.wikipedia.org.

These rules seek to guard and protect the dignity and essential rights of a human person for whom there is no unfair or arbitrary difference. If all people are governed by the same laws, their individual rights and freedoms will be better protected. The rule of law helps a government protect all people in the same way and not violate the rights of a certain group of individuals.

Mankind's journey toward truly recognizing equality for all has taken hundreds of years.

For generations, women had to fight against discrimination based on the supposedly weaker sex.

In prehistory there was a certain division of labor, men hunted and women fished and gathered fruits.

In Greece and Rome, women could not own property and were under the control of the father or the husband.

In ancient Egypt and Mesopotamia, women enjoyed some freedom to gain access to trades and education.

In the Middle Ages, society was divided into the privileged (clergy and nobility) and non-privileged.

During the so-called Holy Inquisition, thousands of women were burned alive, an action defended by a document called *Malleus Maleficarum* ("Hammer of the Witches") of 1486. The document allowed killing those who did witchcraft.*

During the Industrial Revolution, if a woman did not marry, she would enter a convent where she learned to read and write.

In the nineteenth century, women who worked long hours in factories received a salary lower than that of men for the same task.

In the twentieth century, equality between men and women began to be recognized. In the last 200 years, many women stood out as feminist leaders, in their struggle for gender equality. Here are some outstanding examples:

---

* The book was written by Heinrich Kramer (under his Latinized name Henricus Institoris), and first published in the German city of Speyer in 1487. It was a bestseller, second only to the Bible in terms of sales for almost 200 years. The top theologians of the Inquisition at the Faculty of Cologne condemned the book as recommending unethical and illegal procedures. The recommended procedures include torture to effectively obtain confessions and the death penalty as the only sure remedy against the evils of witchcraft. At that time, it was typical to burn heretics alive at the stake and *Malleus* encouraged the same treatment of witches. The book had a strong influence on culture for several centuries. en.wikipedia.org/wiki/Malleus_Maleficarum.

1. In France, Olympe de Gouges (1748–1793) dared to proclaim the equality of the sexes and the rights of women by publishing and disseminating the *Declaration of Women and Citizenship* in 1791. Olympe said, "Man, are you capable of being fair?*... Women are born free and remain equal to men in rights." Olympe said, "A woman has the right to mount the scaffold. She must possess equally the right to mount the speaker's platform."† Her behavior led her to the guillotine.

2. In the eighteenth century, in England, Mary Wollstonecraft (1759–1797) promoted women's rights and wrote a document entitled *A Vindication of the Rights of Woman* (1792), in which she stated that women have the same capacity for reasoning, thinking, and analysis that men have, and they should receive similar education.

3. Sojourner Truth (1797–1883) was an African-American abolitionist who was born into slavery. At nine years of age she was sold as additional to a flock of sheep to a New York landowner. In 1851 she delivered a speech at the Women's Congress in Ohio, called "Ain't I a Woman?" She said, "Look at me! Look at my arms! I had thirteen children and I saw how they were all sold as slaves."‡

4. Margaret Fuller (1810–1850) was an American journalist and women's rights advocate. In July 1845, she published *Woman in the Nineteenth Century*, where she claims the need for equal rights between men and women.

5. Virginia Woolf (1882–1941) was a British writer who wrote an essay in 1923 called "A Room of One's Own"; it was one of the favorite texts by the feminist movement.

6. In 1846 the French writer Flora Tristan (1803–1844) wrote *The Emancipation of Women*.

7. The Polish Rosa Luxemburg (1871–1919) and the German Clara Zetkin (1857–1933) fought for the universal vote and the rights of women. In 1910, the Second International Conference of Socialist Women established on March 8 as the "International Women's Day" to demand women's suffrage and labor nondiscrimination, in commemoration of a demonstration by workers of the Lower East Side seamstress in 1857 in New York. In 1911, after the tragedy of

---

* "Olympe de Gouges," es.wikipedia.org/wiki/Olympe_de_Gouges.
† "Olympe de Gouges," en.wikipedia.org/wiki/Olympe_de_Gouges.
‡ Fernando Soriano, "The Incredible Stories of 30 Icons of Feminism of All Times," *Infobae*, March 8, 2018.

the workers at the Triangle Shirtwaist Co. factory, also in New York, where 146 people died of a fire, a new impulse in the struggle for social justice of working women took place.*

8. The Swiss-Argentine poet Alfonsina Storni (1892–1938), in her work, approached the subject of feminism and the subordination of women to men. She participated in defense of the vote of the Argentine woman. In one of his verses called "Little Little Man" of 1919, she wrote:

Little little man, little little man,
Set free your canary that wants to fly.
I am the canary, little little man,
leave me to fly.
I was in your cage, little little man,
Little little man who gave me my cage.
I say "little little" because you don't understand me,
Nor will you understand.[†]

9. Simone de Beauvoir (1908–1986) was a French philosopher who wrote *The Second Sex* (1949), another of the best-known works of the feminist movement, in which she criticized the education and development of young girls. She said, "One is not born but becomes a woman." She stated that many of the characteristics of women do not come from genetics, but they are a cultural product as a consequence of the education received.

---

* The fire started on March 25, 1911, and took the lives of 146 people (123 women and 23 men). The owners had the doors of the stairs blocked, which was a practice at that time to prevent theft. Many workers who could not escape from the burning building jumped out of the windows. The factory was devoured by the flames. The workers, unable to escape from the burning building, jumped from the eighth, ninth, and tenth floors to the street. The fire led to a change in legislation and improvements in the safety conditions of factories and the birth of the International Ladies "Garment Workers" Union (ILGWU), which fought to improve working conditions. The factory was located at the Asch Building at 23 Washington Place in Greenwich Village in Manhattan. The building today is part of the Brown Building, a piece of New York University.
Three years earlier, in March 1908, the textile factory Cotton Textile Factory, in New York, caught fire and 130 people died. The Cotton workers were on strike, in the same factory building, claiming for the reduction to ten working hours and pay equality with men.

† Alfonsina Storni, "Little Little Man," www.poemhunter.com; www.aboutespanol.com. "Hombre pequeñito, hombre pequeñito Suelta a tu canario que quiere volar. ... Yo soy el canario, hombre pequeñito, déjame saltar. Estuve en tu jaula, hombre pequeñito, Hombre pequeñito que jaula me das Digo pequeñito porque no me entiendes, Ni me entenderás."

10. The Egyptian doctor Nawal El Saadawi wrote *The Woman and Sex*, a book published in 1972 where she criticizes the removal of the clitoris at the age of six. In 1981 she was sent to jail for criticizing the government and in prison, she wrote her memoirs on a roll of toilet paper.

11. Billie Jean King is an American woman who was considered the best female tennis player in the world in the 1970s and who fought for equal compensation for men and women in tennis tournaments. At that time men received prize money of up to eight times the value of women. In 1973, at the age of 29, she participated in a tennis match that was known as "The Battle of the Sexes." Bobby Riggs (1918–1995) had been a world tennis champion in the 1940s and in 1973 he was 55 years old. Riggs began to contemptuously criticize women's tennis, saying that at his age he could comfortably beat any of the best players. King challenged him to play. The match between King and Riggs was one of the most famous tennis events of all time with more than 60 million viewers and a prize for the winner of US$100,000. The game was played at the Houston Astrodome on September 20, 1973, and King won 6-4, 6-3, 6-3.* King became a champion of feminism in the struggle for equality and founded the WTA (Women's Tennis Association) and the Women's Sports Foundation.

According to the United Nations, the average wage gap between men and women in the world is 23%.† On October 24, 2016, the women of Iceland left their jobs at 14:38 to show what would happen if they worked 14% less time than their working hours, exactly the wage gap that exists women and men in that country. The following month French women did the same protest in France. They left their jobs at 16:34 to mark the wage gap with men of 15.1%.‡

Some women excelled in the struggle for equal rights between men and women and confronted the ideology of "Separate Spheres," an old

---

* Mithrandir, "The Battle of the Sexes, September 1973, a Game for Remembrance," September 24, 2014, www.puntodebreak.com; Maria Estevez, "The Battle of the Sexes: A Game for History," November 6, 2017, www.abc.es. A film called *Battle of the Sexes* was released in 2017 directed by Jonathan Dayton and Valerie Faris.

† "ONU Mujeres afirma que la brecha salarial del 23% entre mujeres y hombres es un robo," March 14, 2017, www.un.org ("UN Women affirms that the wage gap of 23% between women and men is a robbery").

‡ Paula Urien, "La Fórmula Nórdica para Saldar una Deuda Histórica con las Mujeres," April 12, 2018, www. lanacion.com ("The Nordic Formula for Settling a Historical Debt with Women").

common law principle that said women were best suited to the domestic sphere. A few stories are pointed out in the footnote.*

In the United States, the struggle of the American woman to obtain the right to vote was difficult and began with Elizabeth Cady Stanton (1815–1902). Stanton was a leading figure of the early women's rights movement and her *Declaration of Sentiments*, presented in 1848, is credited with initiating the first organized women's suffrage movement in the US.†

Another outstanding woman in the fight for the female vote was Susan Anthony (1820–1906). For more than 40 years, she traveled thousands of kilometers throughout the United States and Europe giving hundreds of speeches on the right of women to vote. In 1979, she became the first woman whose image appeared on a circulating US coin.

In 1913, when President Thomas Wilson (1856–1924) assumed the office of the president, Alice Paul (1885–1997) organized the first suffragist parade in Washington, D.C., a march with 8,000 participants that resulted in 200 people being detained.

During World War I (1914–1918), large numbers of women were recruited into jobs vacated by men who had gone to fight in the war. New jobs for women were also created; for example, in munitions factories.‡

---

* A more complete list of leading feminists should also include, for example, the Brazilian Nisia Floresta (1810–1885), who wrote *Women's Rights and Injustice of Men*; the Argentine Virginia Bolten (1876–1960), who founded the newspaper *La Voz de la Mujer*; the Argentine Elvira Rawson (1867–1954), the second Argentine woman to graduate as a doctor in 1892. She said: "We want all the political rights, both as voters and as elected because since we pay taxes, we work for the progress of the country and we are responsible to the laws, we must be able to legislate in everything that concerns the greatness of our country"; the Argentine philosopher Elvira López who made her thesis on feminism in 1901; the Uruguayan Paulina Luisi (1875–1949), who created the magazine *Acción Femenina* and founded two women's unions; the Argentine Eva Duarte de Perón (1919–1952), who promoted the law in Argentina that allowed all women over eighteen years old to vote in 1951. She said: "Women's time has died as an inert and numerical value within society"; the Japanese Yoko Ono, who wrote the manifesto *The Feminization of Society*; the Mexican Comandanta Ramona (1959–2006) who dedicated herself to promoting the social equality of the lower classes in indigenous populations. She was the leader of the Zapatista Army of National Liberation (EZLN). She said: "In the EZLN everything is even, there are no differences, one day men have to prepare food and another day women have to"; the Swedish Gudrun Schyman, who in 2010 burned Swedish currency in a public act, the equivalent of US$13,000, with the argument that the money represented what men earn over what women earn in Sweden; and Pakistani Malala Yousafzai, who was the youngest winner of the Nobel Prize for Peace at 17 years old. She wrote *I am Malala*. Malala has stated that "Feminism is nothing other than equality." See *The Incredible Stories of thirty icons of Feminism of all time*, by Fernando Soriano, Infobae, March 8, 2018.

† "Elizabeth Cady Stanton," Wikipedia.

‡ www.theperspective.com/subjective-timeline/living/womens-right-vote-us-suffrage-movement/.

In the United States, in 1917, during the presidency of Woodrow Wilson (1856–1924), a group of women held a demonstration in front of the White House demanding the president to incorporate an amendment to the US Constitution in order to guarantee the right to the vote of the women in compensation for the support work carried out by them during the war. Because of the claim, some of those women were arrested. From prison they started a hunger strike, which worried Wilson about the negative publicity for his administration.* In 1918, after the war ended, President Wilson said in a speech before Congress, "We have made partners of the women in this war. . . . Shall we admit them only to a partnership of suffering and sacrifice and toil and not to a partnership of privilege and right?"†

In 1919, the US Congress approved a proposed amendment to the Constitution that read, "The right of citizens of the United States to vote shall not be denied or abridged by the United States or by any State on account of sex."‡

When 35 of the 36 necessary states had already ratified the amendment, a vote was taken in Nashville, Tennessee, on August 18, 1920. Tennessee lawmakers voting in favor of female suffrage wore a yellow rose in the buttonhole, and anti-suffragists had a red rose. Lawmaker Harry Burn, 24, wore a red rose but realized that if he voted negatively the vote would be tied 48 to 48 and was reminded his mother had asked him to vote in favor of approving the amendment, so he voted affirmatively. Thus, on August 18, 1920, Tennessee became the 36th state necessary to ratify the amendment and on August 26 of that year, the 19th Amendment of the US Constitution became law, leaving women qualified to vote.§ The 19th Amendment to the US Constitution that gave women the right to vote is also known as the "Susan B. Anthony Amendment."¶

The struggle of women for equal rights did not stop. As mentioned in a previous chapter, on December 1, 1955, Rosa Parks (1913–2005), an African-American dressmaker, 42, refused to give up the seat of a bus to a white man. The laws in Alabama at that time established that black people should sit in the back of buses, and if there were no more seats, they should give the seat to white people. If they refused, the driver could call

---

* www.history.com/this-day-in-history/president-woodrow-wilson-picketed-by-women-suffragists.

† www.theperspective.com/subjective-timeline/living/womens-right-vote-us-suffrage-movement/.

‡ en.wikipedia.org/wiki/Nineteenth_Amendment_to_the_United_States_Constitution.

§ See "The Fight for the Woman's Vote," www.contactomagazine.com/articulo/el woman's vote.

¶ In New Zealand in 1893, the first female suffrage was approved without restrictions, and in 1919, women were allowed to vote and be elected.

the police to get them off the bus or even take them to jail. Parks refused to give up the seat because "she was tired of giving in."* Parks refused to pay a US$14 fine for civil disobedience to be released and was imprisoned for a couple of days.

A boycott led by Martin Luther King Jr. (1929–1968) caused buses to operate nearly empty, and the protest attracted the attention of the whole country. King suffered threats from the Ku Klux Klan;† he was sent to prison and his house bombed. But after 11 months of resistance, on November 13, 1956, the Supreme Court of the United States declared segregation in transportation unconstitutional. In 1999, Parks, the mother of the Civil Rights Movement, received the Congressional Gold Medal.

Muhammad Yunus is an economist born in 1940 in Bangladesh. He developed the concept of microcredit for women who did not have access to the banking system in Bangladesh. Professor Yunus began by lending US$27 to 42 women and in 1976 founded the Grameen Bank. Since then, the bank has grown with more than 2,500 branches, 20,000 employees, and millions of customers. Yunus was convinced that humans have unlimited potential if the system gives them the opportunity and includes them. Yunus says:

> Poverty is not created by poor people. It is imposed on the poor people by the system that we created. Sometimes I give the analogy of a bonsai tree. You take the seed of the tallest tree in the forest and you put it in a flower pot: only a small, one-meter high tree will grow. We call it bonsai. It looks very cute. But it doesn't grow tall. What is the problem? We didn't give it enough soil to grow. Poor people are bonsai people. There is nothing wrong with the seed. Society simply never gave them space so that they can grow as tall as anybody else. A lack of money equates to a lack of space.‡

Recognized personalities have suffered discrimination because of the color of their skin. Next are the stories of Jack Johnson, Jackie Robinson, James Meredith, Carl Maxie Brashear, and Martin Luther King Jr.

---

* "Rosa Parks," en.wikiquote.org/wiki/Rosa_Parks.
† Ku Klux Klan (KKK) is the name adopted by several extreme right-wing organizations in the United States. It was created after the Civil War, and it mainly promotes xenophobia, as well as the supremacy of the white race, homophobia, anti-Semitism, and racism.
‡ Mirjam Gehrke, "Muhammad Yunus: Put Poverty in the Museum," April 29, 2013, www.dw.com.

Jack Johnson: Jack Johnson (1878–1946) was born in Galveston, Texas. His parents had been slaves, and his boxing debut was in 1889. Johnson suffered from racism; he was denied fights because of the color of his skin and received threats from the Ku Klux Klan.

In 1908 in Sydney, Australia, Johnson beat Tommy Burns and became the first black boxing champion to win the heavyweight title which generated an unprecedented controversy.[*]

In 1910, a fight was organized in which Jack Johnson had to defend the title against "The Great White Hope," former champion James Jeffries. Novelist Jack London wrote in those days in a newspaper in New York, "Jim Jeffries must emerge from his alfalfa farm and remove the golden smile from Jack Johnson's face. Jeff, it's up to you! The White Man must be rescued."[†]

"The Fight of the Century" was held in Reno, Nevada, on July 4, 1910. Many of those around the ringside shouted, "Death to the black! Death to the black!" For some, the supremacy of a race was put into play.[‡]

In the 15th round, Johnson knocked Jeffries out of the boxing ring and won a technical knockout (TKO). As a result, there were violent clashes across the country resulting in more than 20 deaths and 300 injured people.

The African-American poet William Waring Cuney (1906–1976) dedicated the poem "My Lord, What a Morning" to him:

> Oh, my Lord
> What a morning,
> O, my Lord,
> What a feeling,
> When Jack Johnson
> Turned Jim Jeffries'
> Snow-white face
> Up to the Ceiling.[§]

---

[*] "He transformed himself from the docks of Galveston, Texas, to early 20th-century glitterati. He had his own jazz band, owned a Chicago nightclub, acted on stage, drove flashy yellow sports cars, reputedly walked his pet leopard while sipping champagne, flaunted gold teeth that went with his gold-handled walking stick and boasted of his conquests of whites – both in and out of the ring. Johnson kept the company of some of his era's most beautiful women, most of them white. Moulin Rouge star Mistinguette. German spy Mata Hari. Sex symbols Lupe Velez and Mae West. Johnson was romantically linked to all." "Johnson boxed, lived on own terms," Ron Flatter, www.espn.com.

[†] Jack London, "Jack Johnson & His Times,", *Project Muse*, muse.jhu.edu/article/5790/summary.

[‡] Mariano Jesus Camacho, "Jack Johnson, the Galveston Giant," September 9, 2014, www.vavel.com.

[§] William Waring Cuney, "My Lord, What a Morning," www.beltwaypoetry.com/cuney/.

On June 10, 1946, when leaving a North Carolina coffee shop where he had been denied entry, Johnson died in a traffic accident at age 68.

Jack Johnson was the only heavyweight champion not received in the White House as was customary at that time; however, over time, his courage and trajectory were recognized and in 1990 the "Galveston Giant" was entered into the International Boxing Hall of Fame.

Jackie Robinson: In 1945, Branch Rickey, the president of the Brooklyn Dodgers, made an offer to the African-American baseball player Jack "Jackie" Roosevelt Robinson (1919–1972). He asked if he would be able to withstand racist insults. Rickey told him, "I'm looking for a ballplayer with guts enough not to fight back.... I know you're a good ballplayer. What I don't know is whether you have the guts."*

On April 15, 1947, Jackie Robinson became the first African-American baseball player to enter Major League Baseball. He broke the racial barrier in baseball, although it was not easy.

Many towns denied Robinson's team permission to train on their fields and even suspended games to prevent them from playing. Some players on his team refused to sit and play with him. The coach, Leo Durocher (1905–1991) told the team, "I don't care if the guy is yellow or black, or if he has stripes like a zebra. I'm his manager of this team, and I say he plays. What's more, I say he can make us all rich."†

The Saint Louis Cardinals threatened a strike because Robinson was going to play, and Robinson had to endure insults from the Philadelphia Phillies. In another encounter in Cincinnati, while the public insulted Jackie, his companion Pee Wee Reese stood next to him and put his arm around him. Reese said, "You can hate a man for many reasons; his color isn't one of them."‡

Robinson continued to receive humiliation wherever he went. They spat on his sneakers, pitchers aimed at his face, and fans threw black cats to the field. In 1949 he was named National League Most Valuable Player. His fame grew until he retired from baseball in 1956.

On October 24, 1972, Jackie Robinson died in Connecticut, suffering from a heart attack caused by diabetes that had left him blind. He was 53 years old, and 2,500 people attended his funeral.

---

* "Jackie Robinson Notecards," quizlet.com.
† "Jackie Robinson," en.wikiquote.org/wiki/Jackie_Robinson.
‡ "Jackie Robinson," en.wikiquote.org/wiki/Jackie_Robinson.

In addition to his outstanding career as a player, Robinson fought for equal rights and against discrimination. He said, "I'm not concerned with your liking or disliking me.... All I ask is that you respect me as a human being."[*]

In 1997 in recognition of Robinson on the 50th anniversary of his debut with professional baseball, all Major League teams withdrew the number 42 from their uniforms in recognition of his talent, dedication, and struggle for human rights.

In 2013 the film *42* was released portraying the life of Jackie Robinson.[†]

James Howard Meredith: On October 1, 1962, James Meredith became the first African-American college student accepted to the University of Mississippi. Meredith had previously been refused admission to Mississippi; therefore, the National Association for the Advancement of Colored People (NAACP) filed a lawsuit. The University of Mississippi only admitted white students under the state's culture of racial segregation.

In September 1962 the Supreme Court of the United States ruled Meredith had the right to be admitted to the state school. The US Supreme Court based its judicial ruling in *Brown v. Board of Education* (1954), which established that segregation in public schools was unconstitutional because public schools were supported by all the taxpayers.[‡]

The University of Mississippi was forced to abide by the decision, but Governor Ross Barnett (1898–1987) blocked Meredith's access to the university. Barnett declared, "No school will be integrated in Mississippi while I am your governor."[§]

Students, encouraged by the governor, made violent demonstrations, and President Kennedy (1917–1963) had to mobilize hundreds of federal police to protect Meredith's right to enter the university. The students attacked the police violently and as a result of the disturbances provoked, President Kennedy sent the army to campus. The clash resulted in burned cars, 2 people killed, and about 200 injured.

On October 1, 1962, after troops took control, Meredith became the first African-American student to enroll at the University of Mississippi. Meredith's admission is regarded as a pivotal moment in the history of civil rights in the United States. He persisted through harassment.

---

[*] "Jackie Robinson," en.wikiquote.org/wiki/Jackie_Robinson.
[†] *42*, Directed by Brian Helgeland.
[‡] "James Meredith," en.wikipedia.org/wiki/James_Meredith.
[§] "James Meredith," en.wikipedia.org/wiki/James_Meredith.

Many students harassed Meredith during his two semesters on campus. Students living in Meredith's dorm bounced basketballs on the floor just above his room through all hours of the night. Other students ostracized him: when Meredith walked into the cafeteria for meals, the students eating would turn their backs. If Meredith sat at a table with other students, all of whom were white; the students would immediately get up and go to another table.*

Meredith graduated with a degree in Political Science on August 18, 1963.†

Carl Maxie Brashear: Carl Maxie Brashear (1931–2006) was a US Navy Sailor. He was the first African-American to attend and graduate from the Diving & Salvage School and the first African-American US Navy Diver, rising to the position in 1970 despite also having an amputated left leg. While attending a diving school in Bayonne, New Jersey, Brashear faced hostility and racism. He found notes on his bunk saying, "We're going to drown you today, nigger!" and "We don't want any nigger divers."

Brashear was motivated by his beliefs that "It's not a sin to get knocked down; it's a sin to stay down" and "I ain't going to let nobody steal my dream."‡

The film *Men of Honor* of 2000 is based on the life of Carl Brashear and reflects his spirit of overcoming all the adversities he had to face due to discrimination.

Martin Luther King Jr.: Dr. King (1929–1968), an American Baptist Church pastor, dedicated much of his life to the struggle for equality and recognition of the civil, political, and economic rights of the African-American population in the United States.

On August 28, 1963, at the Lincoln Memorial in Washington D.C., in front of 200,000 people, he delivered his 17-minutes "I Have a Dream" speech, asking for the end of racism in the United States.§

He said,

> I have a dream that one day this nation will rise up, live out the true meaning of its creed: We hold these truths to be self-evident, that all men are

---

* "James Meredith," en.wikipedia.org/wiki/James_Meredith.
† In 1966, Meredith suffered an attack during the "March Against Fear" and suffered a gunshot wound.
‡ en.wikipedia.org/wiki/Carl_Brashear.
§ As a result of the speech, Dr. King was named Man of the Year by *Time* magazine in 1963.

created equal.... I have a dream that my four little children will one day live in a nation where they will not be judged by the color of their skin but by the content of their character.*

King did crucial work in the United States at the head of the Civil Rights Movement with the goal of ending racial segregation and discrimination through nonviolent means and to gain full and equal rights for Americans of all races. King was awarded the Nobel Peace Prize in 1964 for his work in favor of racial equality and civil rights.

King was assassinated in Memphis in 1968 at the age of 39 while greeting his followers from the balcony of the Hotel Lorraine, which generated riots and at least 50 deaths across the country.

He is remembered as one of the greatest leaders in the history of the United States.

The segregation of races was established by the laws of Jim Crow (laws that advocated racial segregation at all public facilities under the motto "separate but equal"). These racial laws were promulgated at the end of the nineteenth century and they continued to be in force until 1965; they allowed racial segregation in schools, public places, public transportation, restrooms, and restaurants in the United States.

The Pentagon, the headquarters of the Department of Defense of the United States, is located in Arlington, Virginia, and it is a building that has five floors and where 26,000 employees work. It was inaugurated on January 15, 1943, and has 284 bathrooms, double the number of bathrooms needed, because at the time of construction there was a law that required the existence of a bathroom for whites and another for people of color.

Brown v. Board of Education of Topeka, 347 U.S. 483 (1954) was a landmark US Supreme Court case, where it was declared that state laws establishing separate public schools for black and white students were unconstitutional. The Warren Court issued a unanimous (9-0) ruling on May 17, 1954, and established that "separate educational facilities are inherently unequal." As a result of this ruling, racial segregation came to be considered a violation of the Equal Protection Clause of the 14th Amendment to the US Constitution.

The Civil Rights Movement led by Martin Luther King Jr. gets it approved as the *Civil Rights Act* of 1964 (Civil Rights Act) that banned inequality in

---

* "I have a dream," Martin Luther King Jr., March on Washington, www.archives.gov.

voter registration requirements and racial segregation in schools, in the workplace, and in public facilities.*

One year later, the *Voting Rights Act* of 1965 banned literacy tests and other special requirements that had been used to prevent African Americans from voting.

With this legislation, racial segregation became illegal.†

Affirmative Action is the name of the policy of protecting members of minority groups who suffer discrimination. This policy is also known as *Reservation* in India and Nepal, *Positive Action* in the UK, and *Employment Equity* in Canada and South Africa.

The nature of Affirmative Action policies varies from country to country. Some countries use a quota system, whereby a certain percentage of government jobs, political positions, and school vacancies must be reserved for members of a certain group; an example of this is the reservation system in India.

In the United States, affirmative action is a set of laws, policies, guidelines, and administrative practices intended to end and correct the effects of a specific form of discrimination.

The term *affirmative action* was first used in the United States in Executive Order No. 10925, signed by President John F. Kennedy on March 6, 1961, which included a provision that required government contractors to "take *affirmative action* to ensure that applicants are employed, and employees are treated during employment, without regard to their race, creed, color, or national origin."‡

In 1965, US president Lyndon B. Johnson issued Executive Order 11246 which required government employers to take "affirmative action" to "hire without regard to race, religion and national origin."§

Affirmative action or Positive Discrimination in employment and education has been the subject of controversy. In 2003, a pair of US Supreme Court decisions (*Grutter v. Bollinger* and *Gratz v. Bollinger*) established that the use of affirmative action in university admissions is constitutional if the race is treated as a factor among others to achieve a

---

* The Civil Rights Act contains prohibitions against discrimination based on race, color, religion, national origin, and sex.

† Jim Crow's name comes from a caricatured musical show of 1832 called *Jump Jim Crow*, wherein the actor Thomas Rice painted his face black in color. By 1838, *Jim Crow* had already become a pejorative expression for the African-American.

‡ "Executive Order 10925," www.eeoc.gov.

§ "History of Executive Order 11246," Office of Federal Contract Compliance Programs (OFCCP), US Department of Labor, www.dol.gov/ofccp.

"diverse" class, but it does not substitute the individualized revision of each candidate. That is, it is unconstitutional if it automatically increases the applicant's possibilities over others, only because of their race.

In other countries, such as the UK, affirmative action is rendered illegal because it does not treat all races equally. This approach to equal treatment is described as being "color-blind." In the United Kingdom in the *Equality Act* 2010, ss 158–159, the term *Positive Action* is used in the context of employment to allow selection of a candidate from an "under-represented" group, so long as he or she is no less than equally qualified compared to another potential candidate that is not from the under-represented group.

In Sweden, the Supreme Court has ruled that "affirmative action" ethnic quotas in universities are discriminatory and hence unlawful. It said that the requirements for the intake should be the same for all.*

There have always been justifications for different types of discrimination to be exercised, whether by race or ethnicity, religion, socioeconomic conditions, gender, age, or disability.

The United States, in the last 50 years, through laws and Supreme Court rulings, has sought to limit acts of discrimination. The following are some examples:

The Equal Pay Act of 1963 (EPA) prohibits wage disparity based on sex. The law requires employers to pay men and women the same wages for equal work.

In 2009 the *Lilly Ledbetter Fair Pay Act* was sanctioned, a federal statute that establishes a term of up to 180 days to present demands of equal salary with the corresponding readjustments for the discriminatory payment.

In the United States, salary differences are allowed when they are made according to a merit system or by applying a method that measures the gains by quality or quantity of production.

The Age Discrimination in Employment Act of 1967 (ADEA) protects certain applicants and employees 40 years of age and older from discrimination on the basis of age in hiring, promotion, discharge, compensation, or terms, conditions, or privileges of employment.

In 1969, in the court ruling *Bowe v. Colgate Palmolive Co.*, it was decided that women had the right to work in jobs that were historically offered only to men. Hence, companies may not use job classification systems that discriminate on the basis of gender and employees must have the opportunity to demonstrate their suitability for physically demanding

---

* "Affirmative Action," Wikipedia; "Affirmative Action in the United States," Wikipedia.

jobs. Many jobs usually only for men are now also available for women, as long as they meet the physical requirements.

The Equal Credit Opportunity Act (ECOA) is a US law, enacted in 1974, which made it unlawful for any creditor to discriminate against any applicant, with respect to any aspect of a credit transaction, on the basis of race, color, religion, national origin, sex, marital status, or age. Until the ECOA, women could not apply for a loan or credit card without a man co-signing.

The Pregnancy Discrimination Act (PDA) of 1978 is a US federal statute that prohibits sex discrimination on the basis of pregnancy. Until the PDA, women could be fired from their workplace for being pregnant. Pregnancy is considered a temporary disability in the eyes of the law, meaning the treatment of pregnant employees falls under the same jurisdiction as disabled employees. If an employee is temporarily unable to perform her job due to pregnancy, the employer must treat her the same as any other temporarily disabled employee; for example, by providing her light-duty, modified tasks, alternative assignments, disability leave, or leave without pay. PDA made it illegal for employers to pass over qualified female applicants based on the assumption that they might become pregnant.

Head and Master's laws were a set of American property laws that permitted a husband to have the final say regarding all household decisions and jointly owned property without his wife's knowledge or consent. In Louisiana, 1974, Joan Feenstra's husband was incarcerated for molesting their young daughter. To pay his lawyer, he mortgaged their home, which the law did not require his wife's knowledge or permission to do, despite the fact that the wife herself had fully paid for the house. *Kirchberg v. Feenstra* (1981) was a US Supreme Court case in which the Court held that the Louisiana Head and Master law, which gave sole control of the marital property to the husband, was unconstitutional.

After being dismissed from her job at Meritor Savings Bank, Michelle Vinson sued Sidney Taylor, the vice president of the bank. Vinson charged she had constantly been subjected to sexual harassment by Taylor during her four years of work at the bank. *Meritor Savings Bank v. Vinson* (1986) is a US labor law case, where the US Supreme Court recognized sexual harassment as a violation of the Civil Rights Act of 1964. The case was the first of its kind to reach the Supreme Court. The court, for the first time, made sexual harassment an illegal form of discrimination that created a hostile or abusive work environment.

The Americans with Disabilities Act (ADA) became law in 1990. The ADA is a civil rights law that prohibits discrimination against individuals with disabilities in all areas, including jobs, schools, transportation, and all public and private places that are open to the general public. The purpose of the law is to make sure that people with disabilities have the same rights and opportunities as everyone else. The ADA gives civil rights protection to individuals with disabilities similar to those provided to individuals on the basis of race, color, sex, national origin, age, and religion. The ADA also prohibits discrimination on the basis of the disease AIDS.

Apartheid (in Afrikaans means separation) was the system of racial segregation in South Africa until 1992. It consisted of the creation of separate places for different racial groups and the exclusive power of the white race to exercise the vote, as well as the prohibition of marriages between black and white people.

The former South African president Nelson Mandela (1918–2013) was involved in politics as a young man, seeking to end racial segregation and white domination in South Africa. Mandela is an icon of the fight against racism around the world. His activism against racist policies led him to prison in distressing conditions for 27 years, convicted in 1964 for the crime of sabotage to the prevailing racial segregation system in South Africa.

The *apartheid* system in South Africa was expressed in various laws. First, *the separate services law* in South Africa barred people of color from entering the best beaches and parks. Second, the *Population Registration Act* of 1950 established four categories of racial groups: whites, mestizos, Indians, and blacks. There was a clause granting individuals the right to attempt to change their race. A request had to be submitted to a Pretoria agency called *Office for Race Classification*, where several interviews were carried out by white men and women. If the question remained unanswered, the most reliable way of dispelling doubts was the "pencil test." A pencil was inserted into the person's hair, the more hooked into the hair it was, the darker the classification.[*]

In 1960, the Sharpeville massacre took place in Transvaal, when a demonstration of colored people protested against apartheid. They were riddled with bullets by the police. The result was 69 black people died and 180 were wounded. In 1966, the General Assembly of the United Nations proclaimed March 21 the International Day for the Elimination of Racial Discrimination.

---

[*] John Carlin, *Invictus* ("El Factor Humano," Seix Barral, 1999), 129.

Mandela passed 18 out of his 27 years of imprisonment in the Robben Island prison. He was locked in a tiny cell of 2.5 by 2.1 meters with a small barred window of 30 square centimeters that faced a concrete courtyard.

On April 20, 1964, Mandela delivered a three-hour address to the High Court of Pretoria in Rivonia, where he was sentenced to life in prison for sabotage. He ended his famous plea by saying:

> During my lifetime I have dedicated my life to this struggle of the African people. I have fought against white domination, and I have fought against black domination. I have cherished the ideal of a democratic and free society in which all persons will live together in harmony and with equal opportunities. It is an ideal for which I hope to live for and to see realized. But, My Lord, if it needs to be, it is an ideal for which I am prepared to die.*

When he was elected the first democratic president of South Africa in 1994, Mandela sent a message of unity. The enemy was not the white people but the system of apartheid, and he put an end to the racist regime that divided the country. In his autobiographical work, *Long Walk to Freedom*, he wrote,

> No one is born hating another person because of the color of his skin, or his background, or his religion. People must learn to hate, and if they can learn to hate, they can be taught to love, for love comes more naturally to the human heart than its opposite.†

On May 10, 1994, in his inaugural address as president, Mandela spoke of the challenge of reversing apartheid:

> We enter into a covenant that we shall build a society in which all South Africans, both black and white, will be able to walk tall, without any fear in their hearts, assured of their inalienable right to human dignity – a rainbow nation at peace with itself and the world.‡

---

* Nelson Mandela, "I Am Prepared to Die," The Rivonia Trial, en.wikipedia.org/wiki/I_Am_Prepared_to_Die.

† Nelson Mandela, *Long Walk to Freedom* (Little Brown & Co, 1994) en.wikipedia.org/wiki/Long_Walk to_Freedom; Nelson Mandela, "Nelson Mandela on the Nature of Love and Hate," October 1, 1995, berkleycenter.georgetown.edu.

‡ "Nelson Mandela at This Inauguration as President of South Africa, Pretoria," May 10, 1994, www.mandela.gov.za.

His government was dedicated to dismantling the social and political structure inherited from apartheid through the fight against racism and inequality and the promotion of social reconciliation.

Gandhi, Mandela, and Luther King Jr. are universal examples of the defense of human rights and the fight against racial segregation. British philosopher Bertrand Russell (1872–1970) has said that "love is wise and hatred is foolish. We have to learn to tolerate ourselves."[*]

In May 2016, in a speech to the new graduates of Harvard University, film director Steven Spielberg pointed out, referring to racism and religious hatred, that "the world is full of monsters."[†]

The American psychologist Gordon Allport (1897–1967) of Harvard University in his book *The Nature of Prejudice* defines *prejudice* as "an aversive or hostile attitude toward a person who belongs to a group, simply because he belongs to that group."[‡]

In 1957, the American film *12 Angry Men* (1905–1982) was released. The film portrays the exchange of opinions of 12 individuals who are the jury in a trial focused on the possible murder of a young Latino accused of killing his father with a knife. The jury must make a unanimous decision of guilty or innocent; the consent of all 12 jurors is required. If the verdict is guilty, the defendant will be sentenced to death.

The prejudices and influences of society put pressure on the jury when it comes to making a decision. Eleven jurors promptly vote on the defendant's guilt and only one votes in dissent because that juror believes there is reasonable doubt.

The film shows the members of the jury influenced by their prejudices against the accused, which ends up affecting their ability to make fair, correct, and objective decisions.

The jury members with the dissenting vote help the rest examine their own prejudices and objectively evaluate the veracity of the evidence. His reasonable doubt causes individuals to reflect, rethink the problem, and not be conditioned by prejudices, thus saving a perhaps innocent person from the death penalty.

The movie *Philadelphia* (1993)[§] deals with the life of a young lawyer named Andrew Beckett, who is fired from the firm for which he works

---

[*] Bertrand Russell – Face to Face Interview (BBC, 1959), YouTube.

[†] Rachel Gillett, "The World Is Full of Monsters: Steven Spielberg Tells Harvard Grads to Fight Injustice and Create a World That Lasts Forever," May 26, 2016, www.businessinsider.com.

[‡] Gordon W. Allport, *The Nature of Prejudice* (New York, Addison Wesley Publishing Company, 1979), 14–15; David D. Ireland, "The Meaning of Prejudice," www.davidireland.org.

[§] "Philadelphia," directed by Jonathan Demme.

based on his "work performance." But he knows the real reason for the dismissal is he suffers from AIDS. Beckett decides to initiate a lawsuit against the law firm for discrimination, but he has some difficulty hiring a lawyer who wants to represent him due to the prejudices about the disease and its sexual orientation. Finally, he hired a lawyer and he wins the trial and the law firm is required to pay him US$5 million in compensation for discriminatory dismissal.*

The film helps to reflect on the prejudices, the treatment, and the exclusion that society can inflict to some individuals due to their sexual orientation.

The Spanish philosopher Fernando Savater said:

> Humans are gregarious animals and therefore we like to live in flocks. That is, among those who most resemble us. To live in flocks is like living among mirrors: we always see around us faces that reflect ours, that speak like us, that eat the same, who laugh and cry for similar things.
>
> But suddenly there comes someone who does not belong to our clan, who has a different smell or color and that sounds different. Then the gregarious animal inside us is frightened or suspicious, feels threatened, and believes that it is being invaded. In a word, we become aggressive and dangerous.†

The difference generates distance; however, recruitment, training, benefits, and promotion of employees should always be based on their ability and experience, regardless of gender, race, or disability. "Equal opportunities" in hiring practices mean that jobs and promotions are offered without any discrimination based on race, gender, disability, or age.

In the United States, individuals can sue their employers for enormous sums if they are discriminated against.

When workers sue their employers, their chances of winning are slim and about 1% of US Federal Civil Rights lawsuits succeed in Court. Here are some examples of claims won in Court or in which the suit was settled:

Tudor v. Southeastern Oklahoma State University (2010–2017). Rachel Tudor, an English teacher, originally a man, introduced herself as a woman at the university in 2007. In 2010, she sued her employer for promoting

---

* The events in the film are similar to the events in the lives of attorneys Geoffrey Bowers and Clarence B. Cain. Bowers was an attorney who in 1987 sued the law firm Baker McKenzie for wrongful dismissal in one of the first AIDS discrimination cases. Cain was an attorney for Hyatt Legal Services who was fired after his employer found he had AIDS. He sued Hyatt in 1990 and won just before his death.

† Fernando Savater, *Ética para Amador* (Ariel, 2008), 138.

a male at the university. She won the trial and received US$1.1 million. Tudor's was among the first successful lawsuits ruling that transgender people could also be victims of sex discrimination under the Title VII Amendment of the US Civil Rights Act.[*]

Abdallah v. Coca-Cola (1999–2000). A group of African-American employees accused Coca-Cola of routinely paying them less than white colleagues and passing them over for promotions. Coca-Cola did not acknowledge any wrongdoing, but it did pay out more than US$156 million to around 2,000 employees and spent US$36 million on overhauling its policies concerning pay and promotions.[†]

Chopourian v. Catholic Healthcare West (2010–2012). Ani Chopourian was a physician's assistant at Mercy General Hospital in Sacramento, California. She said doctors sexually harassed her. After filing repeated complaints, she lost her job and a jury awarded her US$168 million.[‡]

Juarez v. AutoZone Stores (2007–2014). Rosario Juárez was the store manager of the auto parts retailer "AutoZone Stores" in San Diego, California. When she became pregnant, she sued the company for discrimination, arguing that her supervisor humiliated her, for which she was fired. A jury awarded US$185 million in compensation.[§]

EEOC v. Texas Roadhouse (2011–2017). Restaurant chain Texas Roadhouse was alleged to have refused to employ people over 40 years of age in certain positions as bartenders. The US Equal Employment Opportunity Commission declared this age discrimination. Texas Roadhouse paid US$12 million in settlements to those who applied for front-of-house jobs

---

[*] "The Most Influential US Workplace Discrimination Lawsuits," August 16, 2018, www.bbc.com/capital/story/.

[†] "The Most Influential US Workplace Discrimination Lawsuits," August 16, 2018, www.bbc.com/capital/story/.

[‡] "The Most Influential US Workplace Discrimination Lawsuits," August 16, 2018, www.bbc.com/capital/story/. See also in the same source of information (i) *Ashley v. Aaron's* (2008–2011). Ashley Alford alleged that her manager at Aaron's, a lease-to-own retail chain, harassed, propositioned, and groped her on many occasions. A jury awarded her US$21 million; (ii) *EEOC v. Turkey Service* (2011–2013). Thirty-two male workers at an Iowa turkey plant were underpaid and mistreated for over 30 years. The men, who had intellectual disabilities, received no more than US$65 a month for working at least 35 hours a week. The men were also subjected to physical and verbal abuse. The court ordered the company, based in Goldthwaite, Texas, to pay its former employees lawful wages totaling $1.3 million for jobs they performed; (iii) *Jones v. Clinton* state employee Paula Jones filed a sexual harassment suit against President Clinton when he was governor of Arkansas in 1991; (iv) *Carlson v. Ailes* (2016). Former Fox News host Gretchen Carlson sued her boss Roger Ailes for sexual harassment that was settled for US$20 million.

[§] "The Most Influential US Workplace Discrimination Lawsuits," August 16, 2018, www.bbc.com/capital/story/.

but had been rejected because of their age.* As part of the settlement, Texas Roadhouse had to change its hiring and recruiting practices.

Arnett and EEOC v. Calpers (1995–2003). California police officer Ron Arnett was forced to retire with a back injury but discovered he was not entitled to the same disability benefits as someone who had joined the police at a younger age. Arnett and six other officers argued this was unlawful age discrimination by California's state pension fund. More than 1,700 retired public safety officers in California shared a US$250 million settlement.†

In 1997, the *Texaco oil company* agreed to pay US$176 million as a result of a lawsuit filed by African-American employees. During the previous months, the company had to face the media and activists who called for boycotts. On the occasion of the agreement, the company made many internal changes, including the policy of *zero tolerance for intolerance.*

In 2000, the *Coca-Cola Co.* agreed to pay US$192.5 million to African-American employees who had filed a discrimination lawsuit.

The Equal Employment Opportunity Commission (EEOC) and *Morgan Stanley* announced in 2004 a US$54 million settlement for a discrimination lawsuit initiated in 2001, and as part of the settlement, at least US$2 million would be used for diversity programs designed to improve compensation and promotion opportunities for Morgan Stanley employees.

In 2008, the fashion company *Abercrombie* denied employment as a sales associate to a young woman who used the traditional Muslim veil, because it was not aligned with the company's dress policy. In 2009 the Commission for Equal Employment Opportunities filed a lawsuit, alleging that the company had violated the Civil Rights Act of 1964, which prohibits discrimination based on religious beliefs. The case reached the Supreme Court and in 2015 the US Supreme Court supported the labor rights of Muslim women who did not obtain employment in Abercrombie for interviewing with a black *Hijab.*‡

The following two cases, Pao and Dukes, were dismissed but generated significant publicity.

Pao v. Kleiner Perkins (2012–2015). The claim was for US$17 million. Ellen Pao sued her employer, a Silicon Valley Venture Capital firm, for

---

* "The Most Influential US Workplace Discrimination Lawsuits," August 16, 2018, www.bbc.com/capital/story/.
† "The Most Influential US Workplace Discrimination Lawsuits," August 16, 2018, www.bbc.com/capital/story/.
‡ "Abercrombie, Condenada por Discriminacion," 3 de junio de 2015, elpais.com ("Abercrombie, Sentenced for Discrimination," June 3, 2015).

gender discrimination after she was not granted a senior partner position. Though the jury ruled in favor of Kleiner Perkins on all counts, the case created lots of media attention around the status of women in the tech industry, known as the "Pao effect."*

Dukes v. Walmart (2004–2011). The claim was for US$1 billion. Betty Dukes, a Walmart greeter from Pittsburgh, filed a federal lawsuit against Walmart alleging female employees received lower pay and fewer promotions. Lawyers later expanded the case to represent more than a million people and it was the largest sex discrimination lawsuit in US history. The US Supreme Court threw it out, saying the cases were not similar enough to be grouped this way.†

Thomas Jefferson (1743–1826), third president of the United States, once said, "We should never judge a president by his age, only by his work."‡

Corporate leaders need to promote work environments where everyone feels welcome. The diversity of managers and employees should match the diversity of their community. For example, if you have a factory in San Jose, California, and you don't hire people of Asian origin, or you have a factory in Atlanta and you don't hire African-American employees or you have a factory in Miami and you don't hire Hispanic employees, you take the risk of being sued for discrimination in the United States.

Some employees suffer from *glass ceiling syndrome*§ in some companies; that is, they perceive that there are opportunities in the organization for which they work, but there are always obstacles, apparently invisible, to reach them. They can see the growth opportunities in the organization where they work but cannot reach them, and this limits their job promotion, regardless of their achievements and merits.

Organizational leaders must ensure that promotions, performance evaluations, and staff reduction criteria do not discriminate against any race, gender, age, or religion. Corporate leaders must promote and protect diversity, not only because it is the right thing, but because discrimination can generate high reputational and financial costs. Some companies have a Head of Diversity to monitor, coordinate, and promote diversity initiatives in the organization.

---

* "The Most Influential US Workplace Discrimination Lawsuits," August 16, 2018, www.bbc.com/capital/story/.

† "The Most Influential US Workplace Discrimination Lawsuits," August 16, 2018, www.bbc.com/capital/story/.

‡ Ronald Reagan mentioned this quote from Thomas Jefferson. Ronald Reagan, quotes, www.brainyquote.com.

§ The term *glass ceiling* first appeared in the *Wall Street Journal* in 1986.

Katharine Meyer Graham (1917–2001) was the first woman to become CEO of a Fortune 500 company (*The Washington Post*). In the United States, of the 500 largest companies, only 23 of them have a female CEOs, that's 4.6% of top executives.* And only 38 of the CEOs of America's 675 largest listed firms are women.†

In 1934, Lettie Pate Whitehead Evans (1872–1953) was the first American woman to be named as a board member of a corporation – Coca-Cola – and she held that position for more than 20 years. Fortune 1000 companies are diversifying boards by adding more women and members with international experience.

In 2020, Unilever reached gender balance across its global management ranks. Half of the Anglo-Dutch company's 14,000 managers are now female and about half of Unilever's board is also female.‡ The CEO of Goldman Sachs David Salomon said at the 2020 World Economic Forum, in Davos, Switzerland, that the bank won't take companies public unless they have at least one diverse member on the board, with the focus being mainly on women.§

In the United States women hold one out of every five seats on corporate boards for the 3,000 largest publicly traded companies.¶

Different backgrounds lead to more diversified thinking which enables companies to respond more quickly to changes. Homogeneity, on the other hand, results in many boards failing to see market disruptions and changing customer trends.**

Employees must also be treated within an inclusive environment, and only work factors such as experience and professional performance should be taken into account for promotions.

An American educator divided the students in her class into two groups, the reds and the blues. For some days, the teacher did not take care of the reds, denied them the word, did not recognize them when they did something well, and punished them at the slightest mistake. The blues, on the other hand, were praised, and the teacher forgave them for any behavior outside the norm.

---

* Danielle Wiener-Bronner, "The Ranks of Women CEO's Got Even Smaller This Year," December 18, 2017, http://money.cnn.com.

† "Corporate Headhunters are More Powerful than ever," www.economist.com, February 6, 2020.

‡ "Unilever Reaches Gender Balance Across Management Team of 14,000," by Thomas Buckley, March 2, 2020, www-bloomberg-com.cdn.ampproject.org/c/s/www.bloomberg.com/amp/news/articles/2020-03-03/unilever-reaches-gender-balance-across-management-team-of-14-000

§ Anneken Tape, "Goldman Sachs' New Rule: At Least 1 Woman on the Board or You Can't Go Public," *CNN Business*, January 23, 2020, cnn.com.

¶ Monica Fike, Editor at LinkedIn, "Goldman: No Woman on Board? No IPO," January 23, 2020.

** Homaira Akbari, "Why Boards Need Directors with International Experience," *Financial Times*, August 8, 2018.

Then she reversed roles and favored the reds. In this way, the students experienced both the feeling of power and that of suffering, the frustrations of belonging to a group of the oppressed and excluded, as a way of learning, so that others do not go through the same suffering in the future.*

The world is diverse, and companies that aim to achieve greater diversity among their employees and an environment of job inclusion and trust are more likely to innovate, have creative thinking, and adapt to changes in the market. Organizational leaders must create spaces where heterogeneous talents can maximize their creativity.

Business consultant Stephen Covey (1932–2012) noted,

> The truly effective person has the humility and respect necessary to recognize his own perceptual limitations and to appreciate the rich resources that make available to him the interaction with the hearts and minds of other beings. That person values the differences because those differences increase their knowledge, their understanding of reality.†

This author said that "Strength lies in differences, not in similarities."‡

Leading companies are those that attract talent, respect, develop, and promote them regardless of their cultural background, age, religion, sex, race, nationality, skin color, or physical condition. These companies want different winds to blow in the house.

We speak of "visible diversity" when we refer to age, race, sex, disability, and language; "invisible diversity" refers to religion, work experience, sexual orientation, nationality, and education.

All people are different and each one is special and the coexistence between them is based on the acceptance of the other.

Companies use individual differences and diversity to achieve a greater breadth of ideas, better connection with the needs of customers, and to enrich the organization with creative solutions.

Different backgrounds, mental models, assumptions, and visions about the world generate in companies a competitive advantage that helps to identify new markets and businesses.

Companies that improve the acceptance of diversity and the inclusion of their employees are more likely to achieve greater creativity, innovation, and adaptation to market changes.

---

* Jaime Lopera, *El Pez Grande se Come al Lento*, Intermedio Editores. Colombia. 2003. Páginas 210/211 ("The Big Fish Eats the Slow Fish").
† Stephen Covey, *The 7 Habits of Highly Effective People* (Plural Paidós), 311.
‡ Stephen Covey, www.brainyquote.com.

Smart companies are concerned with micro-messages, those nonverbal signals, often unintentionally many times, but which reveal the feelings of the sender. Stephen Young has published a book* wherein he explains how the tone of voice with which things are said, gestures, glances, body language, or other micro-messages, can affect the place of work, create inequities, and generate exclusion. Whoever receives the message may feel discriminated not only by the words of the issuer but by the way the message is issued. Therefore, effective leaders must not only take care of the words they use but also the ways used to deliver the message.

Companies must remove barriers that may reduce inclusion and diversity, seeking an environment that promotes teamwork, where the right to equity among employees is protected. They must ensure their employees can compete for promotions and areas of responsibility without favoritism or discrimination and within an environment of respect. An inclusive culture allows employees to reach their full potential.

Workgroups are increasingly diverse, and it is natural that there are employees from different backgrounds. Some of them may have prejudices against others.

Discrimination can be a factor that is present not only in daily work relationships but also in the process of recruiting, promoting, and firing employees.

It is the responsibility of an ethical manager or employee to ensure also that no customer is discriminated against. For example, several years ago, lawsuits by angry customers revealed that Denny's restaurant chain discouraged some African-American customers from eating at its restaurants. Some Denny's locked their doors when they saw these customers approaching.†

Organizations should focus on creating a fair work environment where performance is the main factor for promotions and where prejudice and bias do not take place whatsoever.

Companies should fight discrimination not only to avoid unfair treatment, but also because discrimination lawsuits are very expensive for companies in money, resources, and reputation.‡

---

* Stephen Young, *Micromessaging: Why Leadership Is Beyond Words* (McGraw Hill, 2006).

† K. Blanchard, C. Schewe, B. Nelson and A. Hiam, *Exploring the World of Business* (Worth Publishers, 1996), 111; Howard Kohn, "Service with a Sneer," *NYT Magazine*, November 6, 1994, 43–47.

‡ Discrimination by race, religion, origin, sex, disability, and age is prohibited by law in many countries. In the United States in 1978, Congress enacted *The Pregnancy Discrimination Act*, which prohibits discrimination based on pregnancy in the workplace.

On November 7, 1982, Pope John Paul II in Montjuic, Spain, addressed entrepreneurs and industrialists, saying:

> The company is called to carry out, under your impulse, a social function – which is deeply ethical – to contribute to the perfection of man, of every man, without any discrimination; creating the conditions that make possible work that, while developing personal capacities, achieve an efficient and reasonable production of goods and services.*

In 2001, consultant McKinsey & Company published a work titled *The War for Talent*[†] wherein talent was presented as a strategic challenge and the most important asset of organizations to achieve success.

Dr. R. Roosevelt Thomas Jr. in his article "From Affirmative Action to Affirming Diversity," published in *Harvard Business Review* in 1990, noted that a diverse group benefits organizations and American companies should try to incorporate talent to compete successfully in markets where they operate.[‡]

The globalization of business has created a super-competitive environment and, to grow, it is necessary for companies to launch new products and services addressing the particularities of consumers in each market. For example, Kraft Foods' Oreo cookies are different in the United States and China. The Coca Cola Company offers different flavors of its drinks in different countries; at the Coca-Cola Museum in Atlanta, you can taste the drinks offered by the company in different regions of the world. McDonald's produces a different hamburger in India. There, a cow is a sacred animal, and the company has tried with chicken and vegetarian products. Coach, a leading portfolio designer, conducts thousands of inquiries each year to understand trends and the preferences of its customers, in style, color, and price.

If the client changes, the company's business model must also change. Diversity, then, becomes a competitive advantage, because new preferences, tastes, and tendencies in the different sectors of society are more likely to be perceived more quickly by a diverse group than by a homogeneous one.

---

* Ambrosio Romero Carranza, *Enrique Shaw y sus Circunstancias* (ACDE, 1984), 243 ("Enrique Shaw and his Circumstances").

† Ed Michaels, Helen Handfield-Jones and Beth Axelrod, *The War for Talent* (Harvard Business School Press, 2001).

‡ R. Rooevelet Thomas, Jr., "From Affirmative Action to Affirming Diversity," *Harvard Business Review*, March–April 1990, hbr.org/1990/03/from-affirmative-action-to-affirming-diversity.

Different voices get new and diverse ideas. Mattel takes advantage of those ideas its employees can suggest, thanks to a culture of inclusion. For example, a few years ago Mattel launched a doll line aimed at African-American customers. Prior to its manufacture and in order for the dolls to be accepted by their clients, the company sought advice from a group of African-American employees to give feedback on the product. This group made suggestions on skin tone, hair color, name, or aspects of the face, helping to make the product culturally accepted.

The French writer Jules Verne (1828–1905) said that "everything that one man can imagine, other men can make real."*

Companies committed to diversity understand the unique value of each of their employees and appreciate the individuality of every member of their team. Each person brings a unique talent. The Austrian management consultant Peter Drucker (1909–2005) stated that "Nobody ever commented, for example, that the violinist Jascha Heifetz probably couldn't play the trumpet very well."†

In innovative companies, all employees participate in the decision-making process with ideas and proposals, contributing from their different experiences, perspectives, and points of view.

World War II US Army General George Patton (1885–1945) stated, "If everyone is thinking alike, then somebody isn't thinking."‡

James Cameron, the film director of *Terminator*, *Titanic*, and *Avatar*, is known for creating an inclusive work environment where everyone participates with ideas.

The goal should be to achieve greater diversity and perspective among employees and an environment of inclusion where all are welcomed, listened to, and respected.

In a global and changing market, a diverse workforce constitutes a competitive advantage because customers are diverse. Heterogeneous groups are more effective and creative at solving problems than homogeneous groups.

According to the Italian writer Umberto Eco (1932–2016), who received an honorary degree from the Hebrew University of Jerusalem in 1994, "It is necessary to teach young people living in contact with persons of

---

* "Jules Verne," www.goodreads.com.
† "Peter Drucker," www.azquotes.com.
‡ "George S. Patton quotes," www.brainyquote.com/quotes/george_s_patton_130444.

different origin, that their reciprocal diversity is not an obstacle to life in common, but rather a source of mutual enrichment."*

The collision of perspectives, experiences, and points of view leads to innovation, something that companies need because the future requires change and constant reinvention. Sony launched the Walkman in the 1980s, the Discman in the 1990s, but the next step came from Apple, who understood that digital music would be consumed, and the iPod was created.

Professors Don Hellriegel of Texas A&M University and John Slocum Jr. of Southern Methodist University explain how Ernest Drew, who was CEO of Hoechst Celanese, became a champion of diversity at work:

> I was participating in the 1990 conference for 125 Hoechst executives and divided executives into groups to solve problems. Some groups were mixed and some were all white men.
>
> When the teams presented the findings to the problems, Drew remembers, it was obvious that the diverse teams had broader solutions, ideas that I had never thought of. For the first time, we realized that diversity was strength in relation to problem-solving. We used to think of diversity as the number of minority groups and women that there should be in the company, through affirmative action policies. We now know that we need diversity at every level of the company where decisions are made.†

Neville Isdell, former president of Coca-Cola, believed diversity was not only a moral goal but it was also good for business and would make Coca-Cola a stronger company. He said, "Our Company and our leadership must be inclusive just like our brands.... As talent proliferates; ideas and innovation flourish as well."‡

On January 9, 1979, UNICEF organized an inclusive concert in the United Nations General Assembly Hall in New York to mark the beginning of the International Year of the Child;§ and a similar thing happened in 1985 when a group of outstanding musicians sang "We are the World,"¶

---

* Jaime Lopera, *El Pez Grande se come al Lento* (Colombia, Intermedio Editores, 2003), 210 ("The Big Fish Eats the Slow").
† D. Hellriegel and J. Slocum, *Management* (Southwestern, 1996), 182.
‡ Neville Isdell, *Inside Coca-Cola* (New York, St. Martin's Press, 2011), 189.
§ UNICEF included the Bee Gees; ABBA; Olivia Newton-John; Andy Gibb; Earth, Wind & Fire; Rod Stewart and Donna Summer among other artists.
¶ The song was released on March 7, 1985, and the songwriters were Michael Jackson and Lionel Richie.

this time to collect funds to fight hunger in Ethiopia.* These are some examples of the success of teamwork when diverse talents are included.

Steve Jobs (1955–2011) pointed out the origin of wealth was the mind and imagination. He told the story that when he was a boy, an octogenarian neighbor showed him how a stone-polishing machine worked. The neighbor took some stones from the garden and placed them in the machine; the engine began to work and produced a loud noise due to the collision of the stones, which were well polished. Steve Jobs used this metaphor to tell what happens to a work team that is passionate about a goal; it argues, makes noise, and creates tension with their different perspectives, but by working together and rubbing their ideas against each other, what they finally get are precious polished rocks.†

Jobs said that

the source of wealth … is the human mind … the human imagination … when we inspire our people, we take advantage of their creativity … we nourish ourselves from a fertile soil where the seeds of innovation can flourish for sustainable growth.‡

Diversity of thought generates an innovative mentality that allows for achieving the objectives through different points of view. Diverse teams are enriching and make the organization more competitive and successful on a global scale. Different experiences, perspectives, and background are crucial to fostering innovation.

Diversity with inclusion consists of accepting variety and differences. Every human being has a different perspective that, if there is an inclusive corporate culture, can foster creative solutions. Teamwork, cooperation between the parties, complementarity, inclusion, and acceptance of differences is what allows achieving better results.

Henry Ford (1863–1947) said, "Coming together is a beginning; keeping together is progress; working together is a success."§

---

* Performing for the Concert USA for Africa were, among others, Ray Charles, Kenny Rogers, Lionel Richie, Diana Ross, Paul Simon, Michael Jackson, Tina Turner, Billy Joel, Stevie Wonder, Cyndi Lauper, Bob Dylan, and Bruce Springsteen.

† Philip Elmer-DeWitt, "Steve Jobs: The Parable of the Stones," November 11, 2011, www.fortune.com.

‡ Donald Fan, *Do Diverse Teams Solve More Problems Than Homogeneous Teams?* (Diversity Inc., 2012), 130.

§ Erika Andresen, "21 Quotes from Henry Ford on Business, Leadership and Life," May 31, 2013, www.forbes.com.

Ted Mathas, Chairman of New York Life, has said, "In my experience, an environment that encourages diversity of background, perspective, experience, and viewpoint is one that attracts the best people and leads to consistently better decision-making."*

John Pepper, a former CEO of Procter & Gamble, said,

> Our success as a global company is a direct result of our diverse and talented workforce. Our ability to develop new consumer insights and ideas and to execute in a superior way across the world is the best possible testimony to the power of diversity any organization could ever have.†

Bill Gates has said, "The collaborative energy that is created when talented people from different backgrounds come together to focus on innovation has helped fuel Microsoft's success for more than 30 years."‡

It does not matter the origin of the human resource, but the value that adds. Diversity is variety, it is a difference, and it is an opportunity to be more competitive. Diversity is more.

Numbers are Arabic; democracy is Greek, the car is Japanese, the shirt is from Thailand, the watch is Swiss, pizza is Italian, the creator of WhatsApp was born in Ukraine, and Albert Einstein was from Germany. About half of Silicon Valley residents are foreigners, and 40% of the 500 largest companies in the United States were founded by immigrants or their children.

The importance of the diversity of talent can be seen in this story told by advocates of capitalism and free-market:

> John was loading gas to my Mercedes when a man approached him and said, "Do you know how many people could be fed with the money your car cost?" John replied, "I do not know how many, but I am sure, food for many families in Stuttgart, Germany, where they manufactured it, and it has also fed people. In Japan to those who worked to make the tires; and in Guanajuato, Mexico, to many workers who made the internal components; in Chile, to the people of the copper mine with whom they made the electric cables; and has fed the people who made the trucks that transported the copper and has fed the drivers of those trucks; surely it has fed the

---

* "Diversity Leadership: Ted Mathas, New York Life," April 25, 2013, www.diversityinc.com/ted-mathas.
† Juan Lopez, "My Diversity Journey," *The Diversity Calling*, The Diversity Community Exchange Group (DiCE Group); Joe-Joe McManus (2011), 39.
‡ Bill Gates, www.beyourfuture.net Microsoft, From Inspiration to Reality Build on.

cattlemen who sold the leather of the seats, to the workers of the automobile agency of this city, to the seller who sold me the car and to the person in charge of the cleaning of the salesroom; and with the taxes I pay for having it and using it, the government pays salaries for police, teachers and other public servants." The man who asked the question turned around and left.

The American philosopher Leonard Read (1898–1983) published in 1958 an essay called "I, Pencil: My Family Tree as Told to Leonard E. Read," which details the complexity of making a pencil, enumerating all its components, the division of labor, and the thousands of persons involved in producing it. Leonard Read says:

> These people live in many lands, speak different languages, practice different religions, may even hate one another – yet none of these differences prevented them from cooperating to produce a pencil.*

The American economist Milton Friedman (1912–2006), Nobel Prize for Economics in 1976, said of this work: "I do not know of any piece of literature that is so succinct, persuasive and that actually illustrates … the importance of dispersed knowledge."† Friedman says:

> Look at this pencil. There is not a single person in the world that can manufacture it … the wood of which it is made comes from a tree that was cut in Washington, to cut that tree a saw was needed, to make the saw steel was necessary, to have steel, iron was necessary. The pencil mine, compressed graphite, comes from some mines in South America. The eraser is rubber that comes from Malaysia, where the rubber tree is not even original; it was imported from South America by some businessmen with the help of the British government. I don't know where the bronze comes from, or the yellow paint, or the paint that delineated the black lines, nor the glue that holds all the pencil together. Thousands of people cooperated to make this pencil. People who do not speak the same language, who practice different religions …"

The importance of understanding talent's diversity can also be seen in this letter sent by a school principal in Singapore to the parents before the exams:

---

* Leonard E. Read, "I, Pencil: My Family Tree," http://oll.libertyfund.org/titles/read-i-pencil-my -family-tree-as-told-to-leonard-e-read-dec-1958; also see, en.wikipedia.org/wiki/I, Pencil.
† "I, Pencil," Afterword by Milton Friedman, Nobel laureate, 1976, FEE, Foundation for Economic Education, fee.org/resources/i-pencil/.

Dear Parents:

The exams of your children are to start soon. I know you are all really anxious for your child to do well. But, please do remember, amongst the students who will be sitting for the exams there is an artist, who doesn't need to understand Math.... There is an entrepreneur, who doesn't care about History or English literature.... There is a musician, whose Chemistry marks won't matter ... there is an athlete whose physical fitness is more important than Physics*

The National Society of High School Scholars of the United States conducted a survey of 13,000 millennials (high school students, college students, and young professionals) and asked them several questions, including what the main benefit of a diverse and inclusive company would be. Of the respondents, 41% answered that a diverse and inclusive company helped the organization to generate new ideas and creative solutions, and 34% said that the main benefit was showing respect for each individual.[†]

Leading companies ensure that their employees are united in diversity and manage to establish a corporate culture where everyone is respectful of the opinions of others, there is equal treatment, differences are tolerated, and all have the same possibilities for growth and development.

In an inclusive and diverse culture, everyone enjoys equal treatment or opportunities regarding jobs, training, promotions, continued employment, or any other aspect of working life.

Adecco, the leading Swiss company in human resources worldwide, has stated, "Increasing the diversity of human capital is a business imperative to compete in this global economy."[‡]

Lee Scott, CEO of Walmart Stores between 2000 and 2009, said: "Diversity is very important in our commitment to our customers and associates. Treat them with justice and respect, be their lawyers, be sensitive to their concerns, value their differences and help them the best we can."

Effective leaders recruit a diverse workgroup and promote an inclusive work environment. They create a culture where all employees can give their best and have a sense of belonging to the organization, which makes it possible to maximize their potential and innovative mentality. Why not let all employees contribute their best to the growth of the organization?

---

* Abby Jackson, "The Internet Is Freaking Out over This Note a Principal Sent to Parents during the Exam Week," November 21, 2017, www.businessinsider.com.
† People born between the years 1980 and 2000 are also known as Generation M or Generation Y.
‡ ADECCO, "The Emerging Hispanic Workforce," 2007, www.adeccousacom.

Verna Myers wrote an article in *NALP* (the Association for Law Placement) magazine in 2011 that said, "Diversity is being invited to the party. Inclusion is being invited to dance."*

Peruvian consultant Andres Tapia said, "Diversity is the mix; inclusion is making the mix work."†

Leaders must work to ensure that the corporate culture ensures, throughout the organization, that all employees are heard and valued. Therefore, training managers at least annually on the importance of diversity and inclusion is critical.

If the *inclusion* of *diversity* is one of the roots of innovation, companies must include diversity as a strategic priority and eliminate discrimination, prejudice, and unconscious bias that prevent companies from developing their full potential.

Business leaders that foster a work environment that promotes the integration of diversity get a better working environment where there is a culture of tolerance and respect for people and the ideas of others.

An inclusive work environment for cultural diversity generates greater confidence and openness to new points of view, which will result in a greater variety and quantity of ideas; and therefore, greater innovation and competitiveness.

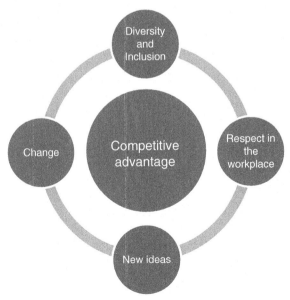

---

* *NALP Bulletin*, 23, no. 7 (July 20, 2011).
† "Why Diversity Is Upside Down," Tedx Talk, Tedx Indianapolis, YouTube.

20

Corporate Risks: Unit 8

20.1 ABUSE AND HARASSMENT

Writer and lecturer Dale Carnegie* (1888–1955) was the author of *How to Win Friends and Influence People*, first published in 1936.[†] Carnegie emphasizes the importance of kindness and dealings with dignity.

Carnegie commented on the following fable in his book:

> They discussed the Sun and the Wind about which was stronger, and the wind told the Sun, I will prove to you that I am the strongest. Do you see that old man wrapped in a cloak? I'll bet you I'll have the coat removed faster than you. The sun was hidden behind a cloud and began to blow the wind, more and more until it was almost a cyclone, but the more it blew the more the man was covered in the cape. At last the wind subsided and declared itself defeated.
>
> Then the sun came out and smiled upon the old man. It did not take long until the old man, heated by the warmth of the sun, took off his cloak. The Sun then showed the wind that softness and friendship are more powerful than fury and severity.[‡]

---

* Dale Carnegie changed the spelling of his last name from Carnagey to Carnegie at a time when businessman Andrew Carnegie (1835–1919) was widely recognized. See "Dale Carnegie," en.wikipedia.org/wiki/Dale_Carnegie.

† It has sold more than 15 million copies. All his books have sold more than 50 million copies in different languages, and more than 7 million people have attended the Dale Carnegie courses.

‡ Dale Carnegie, *How to Win Friends and Influence People* (Out of Pocket, 2006), 180; also see "The Wind and the Sun," The Harvard Classics, www.bartleby.com.

Lao Tzu, also called Lao Tse, was one of the most relevant philosophers of Chinese civilization and lived between the fourth and sixth centuries BC. Lao Tzu said, "Water is the softest thing, yet it can penetrate mountains and earth. This shows clearly the principle of softness overcoming hardness."*

Organizational leaders must treat their employees with respect and dignity to make them feel appreciated, respected, valued, and heard. One way to do this is by asking employees to contribute with suggestions that help the company improve.

J. Willard Marriott (1900–1985), the founder of the Marriott Corporation, has said, "Take good care of your employees and they'll take good care for customers, and the customers will come back."†

Herb Kelleher, founder and former CEO of Southwest Airlines, has said:

> If employees are first, then they will be happy.... A motivated employee treats clients well. The customers will be happy and they will come back.... It is not a mystery; it is how things are.... If employees are treated well, they will treat customers well. If the clients are treated well, they will return and the shareholders will be happy. The employees go first. The customers go second. The shareholders go third.‡

The Spanish writer Fernando Savater said,

> The happier and happier you feel, the less you will have to be bad. Is it not prudent to try to encourage as much as possible the happiness of others instead of making them unhappy and therefore prone to evil? He who collaborates with the misery of others or does nothing to remedy it... is looking for it.§

Savater mentions in his book the English novelist Mary W. Shelley (1797–1851), who in 1818 wrote the novel *Frankenstein*, which tells the story of Victor Frankenstein, a young Swiss medical student who creates a body from the union of different parts of dissected corpses. He intends to create a human being of superior intelligence and long life. The experiment concludes when Frankenstein, through an electric spark, gives life to a humanoid that is 2.44 meters tall. The situation becomes out of control. As the creature is rejected, despised, and disgusted because of his appearance,

---

* "Laozi Quotes about Water," www.azquotes.com.
† "J. Willard Marriott Quotes," www.azquotes.com.
‡ Robert Simons, "Stress Test Your Strategy," *Harvard Business Review* (November 2010): 96.
§ Fernando Savater, *Ética para Amador* (Ariel, 1998), 92–93 ("Ethics for Amador").

he wants to destroy everything in his path and confesses to his repentant inventor: "I am malicious because I am miserable."*

George Elton Mayo (1880–1949) was a sociologist and industrial psychologist specializing in the theory of organizations and human relations. Elton Mayo showed there is a relationship between organizational climate and productivity. When people feel valued and happy, they produce more.

It is known as *the Hawthorne effect*, a series of experiments coordinated by Elton Mayo, realized between the years 1924 and 1932 at the Hawthorne Works factory in the United States.† Mayo showed if workers are not heard or considered by their superiors, it is very difficult to reach the established objectives. An increase or decrease in productivity is due to factors such as employee morale, the existence of positive interrelations among the members of a workgroup, the sense of belonging, and an administration capable of motivating and communicating.

When workers receive special attention, their productivity is likely to improve. Therefore, the workforce produces more in the same period of time or produces the same in less time.

Mayo's main idea was to modify the mechanical model of organizational behavior and replace it with another that takes into account the feelings, attitudes, and motivations of human beings.

When people are challenged, motivated, and recognized, when people feel important, productivity grows. Milliken & Company, founded in 1865 by Roger Milliken (1915–1980), is an industrial manufacturer located in South Carolina, USA, that created a successful business process to increase productivity, quality, and efficiency in a way that engages and listens to employees' proposals, resulting in a long-term sustainable improvement.‡

There is a growing need to improve the way people work together. As David Rock, co-founder of the Neuroleadership Institute says, "When you meet someone who makes you feel better about yourself, provides clear expectations, lets you make decisions, trusts you and is fair, you will probably work harder for them as you feel intrinsically rewarded by the relationship itself."§

---

* Mary Wollstonecraft Shelley, Quotes, www.goodreads.com.
† The factory on the outskirts of Chicago where Mayo performed the experiment.
‡ www.performancesolutionsbymilliken.com.
§ David Rock, "SCARF: A Brain-Based Model for Collaborating with and Influencing Others," www.neuroleadership.org, qrisnetwork.org.

Erich Fromm (1900–1980), a prominent German psychoanalyst, said, "The danger of the past was that men became slaves. The danger of the future is that men may become robots."*

The military strategist and philosopher of ancient China Sun Tzu (544–496 BC) is considered the author of the book *The Art of War,* a treatise on military strategy. Sun Tzu said that "when orders are reasonable, fair, simple, clear and consistent, there is a reciprocal satisfaction between the leader and the group."†

Akio Morita (1921–1999), Japanese physicist and entrepreneur, founder of Sony Corporation, understood that Sony's success was nothing magical; the secret was in the treatment this company gave its employees. In his biography, *Made in Japan,*‡ Morita says: "The most important mission of the Japanese manager is to establish a healthy relationship with their employees, create a family atmosphere in the company, the feeling that employees and managers share the same fate."§

The philosophical idea of human dignity has been especially highlighted by the German philosopher Immanuel Kant (1724–1804). For Kant, human beings deserve a special and dignified treatment that enables their development as people. Kant affirms man is an end in himself, not a means for uses of other individuals, which would turn him into "a thing." People are worthy of all moral respect.¶ For Kant, when people are used to fulfilling purposes, they must be respected as human beings.

Companies that seek to be more competitive and global must guarantee a work environment of respect and equity where attention is paid to employees because the lack of such attention and recognition is one of the main reasons employees quit their jobs.

Global studies reveal that 79% of people who quit their jobs cite a lack of appreciation as their reason for leaving.**

Recognition is the number one thing employees say their manager could give them to inspire them to produce great work.††

Happy employees are more productive, and the best leaders are those who turn their talent into performance.

---

* "Erich Fromm Quotes," www.brainyquotes.com.
† "The 101 Best Phrases of Sun Tzu," Life Persona, www.lifepersona.com.
‡ The book was first published by Dutton Books in 1986.
§ J. Stoner, R. Freeman and D. Gilbert Jr, *Administration,* 6th ed (Pearson, 1996), 411.
¶ "La Conciencia Moral," La dignidad humana según Kant, recursostic.educacion.es ("Moral Conscience," Human dignity according to Kant).
** David Sturt and Todd Nordstrom, "10 Shocking Workplace Stats You Need to Know," March 8, 2018, www.forbes.com.
†† David Sturt and Todd Nordstrom, "10 Shocking Workplace Stats You Need to Know," March 8, 2018, www.forbes.com..

Gandhi (1869–1948) said, "Life has shown me that people are courteous if I am courteous... people smile if I smile... that people get mad if I am mad; that people are grateful if I show gratitude... Life is like a mirror; if I smile, the mirror returns the smile. The same attitude I have towards life is what life will have towards me."*

Canada's Isadore Sharp is the founder and president of the Four Seasons hotel chain with 99 hotels in more than 30 countries and, according to *Fortune* magazine, is one of the 100 best companies to work for. According to Sharp, the secret is in the quality of customer service, which is achieved only if the employees are happy. Sharp says, "It all boils down to a principle that transcends time and geography, religion and culture. It's the golden rule: treat others as you would like them to treat you."†

The Golden Rule mentioned by Sharp is a general and powerful moral principle that can be expressed,

> treat others as you would want them to treat you (in their positive way) or do not do to others what you do not want them to do to you (in its negative form, in this form also known as silver rule).

It is found under different formulations in all cultures, religions, and philosophies, as a fundamental rule.‡

Hinduism says, "One should be always treating others as they themselves wish to be treated."§

Buddhism says, "Hurt not others with that which pains yourself."¶

The Chinese teacher and philosopher Confucius (551–479 BC) said, "What you do not wish for yourself, do not do to others." Zi Gong [a disciple] asked him: "Is there any one word that could guide a person throughout life?" The Master replied: "How about 'reciprocity'! Never impose on others what you would not choose for yourself."**

The Confucian virtue called *Ren* denotes the good feeling a virtuous human experiences when being altruistic. Yan Hui, Confucius's favorite disciple, once asked his master to describe the rules of *Ren*. Confucius replied, "One should see nothing improper, hear nothing improper, say nothing improper, do nothing improper."††

---

* "The mirror of Gandhi," Joose Scharenberg, January 29, 2014, sloyu.com/blog/english/2014/01/29/mirror-gandhi/.

† "El éxito de Isadore Sharp, fundador de Four Seasons," *BBC Mundo*, October 19, 2016 ("The success of Isadore Sharp, founder of Four Seasons").

‡ es.wikipedia.org/wiki/Regla_de_oro_(ética).

§ www.thegoldenrule.net/quotes.htm.

¶ www.thegoldenrule.net/quotes.htm.

** en.wikipedia.org/wiki/Confucius.

†† en.wikipedia.org/wiki/Ren_(Confucianism).

Ren relies heavily on the relationships between two people, but at the same time represents an inner development toward an altruistic goal, by noting one is not alone and there are interhuman relationships one can support, such as family, society, and the world in general.

Ren has been translated as "benevolence," "perfect virtue," "goodness," or even "human-heartedness." When asked, Confucius defined it by the ordinary Chinese word for love, *ai*, saying that it meant to "love others."*

Confucius argued that all humanity should be treated with love and if we all practice "Xiao" (loving attention, care), the society will operate with greater care and mutual respect.†

The Bible says "Love your neighbor as yourself"‡ and also says, "So in everything, do to others what you would have them do to you."§

As Professor Clancy Martin of the University of Missouri-Kansas City wrote:

> Let's use the Golden Rule as a touchstone against some moral dilemmas. You wonder if is ever permissible to lie. Simply ask yourself if you like being lied to. None of us likes being lied to, especially if a lie is being used to manipulate us or lead us to believe false situations.¶

What did Sam Walton (1918–1992) think about the treatment of employees? Walton said:

> At Walmart, we must treat our people with respect and courtesy. Our employees are not numbers. They are real people and deserve to be treated like that.
>
> We have to know them – their families, their problems, their hopes, their ambitions – if we are going to help them grow and develop. We must thank them daily.
>
> Leaders must put their people first before themselves. ... If you want a successful business; your people should feel that you work for them, not that they work for you. And it must be that way.
>
> As a leader, your most important job is to help your people be the best they can be to reach their full potential. No one can lose with a group of motivated and happy people working hard to reach their individual goals.**

---

* en.wikipedia.org/wiki/Ren_(Confucianism).
† Clancy Martin, *Moral Decision Making*, The Great Courses, Guidebook, University of Missouri-Kansas City, Lesson 14.
‡ The Bible, Mathew 22:37–40.
§ The Bible, Mathew 7:12.
¶ Clancy Martin, *Moral Decision Making*, The Great Courses, University of Missouri-Kansas City, Lecture 9, 52.
** Michael Bergdahl, *The 10 Rules of Sam Walton* (John Wiley & Sons, Inc., 2006), 243.

One of the first people to have a salary of more than US$1 million annually in the United States was the entrepreneur Charles Michael Schwab (1862–1939), who was elected, at 35 years of age in 1897, by the businessman Andrew Carnegie (1835–1919) to be the president of the Carnegie Steel Company. The writer Dale Carnegie (1888–1955) comments as follows:

> Why did Andrew Carnegie pay more than US$1 million a year to Charles Schwab?
> Was he a genius? No.
> Did he know more about making steel than other people? No. Charles Schwab told me that he had many men working who knew more than Schwab about the manufacture of steel.
> Schwab said he received that salary because of his ability to deal with people. He said that the most important asset that he possessed is to appreciate and motivate people.*

Neville Isdell, a former CEO of Coca-Cola, inspected the bathrooms on their tours to the bottling plants. If they were not clean, it was a sign that the company did not take care of or pay attention to their employees.†

Leadership writer and consultant James Hunter in his book *The Servant*, states:

> If we focus only on the task and not the human relationship, we find permanent changes in personnel, rebellion, lack of quality, low level of commitment; low confidence level and other equally undesirable symptoms.... Businesses that work all have to do with working relationships. Great truth leaders have the art of building relationships that work.‡

Walt Disney (1901–1966), Chicago-born producer, director, screenwriter, innovator, and icon of the entertainment industry, said, "You can design and create, and build the most wonderful place in the world. But it takes people to make the dream a reality."§

Deterioration of the work environment and mistreatment reduce productivity and the commitment of the employees, and they generate more absenteeism and rotation of personnel. But the problem should not

---

* Dale Carnegie, *How to Win Friends and Influence People* (Cedar, 1995), 46–47.
† Neville Isdell, *Inside Coca-Cola* (New York, St. Martin's Press, 2011), 77.
‡ James C. Hunter, *La Paradoja* (*The Servant*) (Ediciones Urano, 2013), 66–67.
§ www.brainyquote.com/quotes/walt_disney_131631.

be reduced to absenteeism. *Presence* is also a problem if the employee is unmotivated because if he or she does not have a good experience at work, he or she will not achieve his or her maximum potential.

In the previously mentioned survey conducted by the National Society of High School Scholars of the United States with 13,000 millennials,[*] they were also asked about the main factor in selecting a company as their employer, and 73.1% responded it was "to treat their employees fairly."[†]

Everyone wants to be treated as an individual, even in *moments of truth*, those moments of crisis when one is in the eye of the storm. It is easy to criticize, mistreat, and lose self-control. It takes character not to do so.

> Smart companies make certain that their managers know how to balance being professional with being human. Bosses who fail to really care will always have high turnover rates.... It is impossible to work for someone for eight-plus hours a day when they aren't personally involved and don't care about anything other than your output.[‡]

If, when an employee makes mistakes or does not comply with plans, and his or her boss explodes furiously and transforms into the Incredible Hulk, the worker will receive negative energy and perceive a work environment where mistrust, fear, lack of motivation, and lack of commitment will prevail.

Sometimes people are frustrated, they are filled with anger, and they need to find someone to turn their bad mood into good mood and throw away all the trash they have accumulated and carry inside. They externalize this behavior through bad treatment and insults. In a situation like this, it is necessary to exercise patience, control reactions, and avoid confrontation until peace returns and the emotional imbalance disappears. As William Ury, the American negotiating expert, says, "One of the greatest powers we have in negotiation is the power not to react."[§]

---

[*] People born between 1980 and 2000, also known as Generation M or Generation Y.

[†] NSHSS Scholar 2016 Millennial Career Survey Results, The Emerging Workforce: Generational Trends, www.nshss.org/media/29076/2016-nshss-millennial-career-survey.pdf.

[‡] Travis Bradberry, "8 Bad Mistakes that Make Good Employees Leave," September 7, 2016, www.forbes.com.

[§] Bernardo Barcena, *Trato Hecho* (Ediciones B Argentina, 2015); William Ury – Conflict Resolution, www.whatsbestnext.com/2012/08/william-ury-conflict-resolution/.

Ury says:

> When the other person says no or launches an attack, you may be stunned into giving in or counterattacking. So, suspend your reaction by naming the game. Then buy yourself time to think. ... Throughout the negotiation, keep your eyes on the prize. Instead of getting mad or getting even, focus on getting what you want. Don't react: Go to the balcony.*

Do not underestimate the power of actions and words, each day you can leave a mark or mark on someone.

Insult, humiliation, and abuse leave scars that last forever and even forgiveness does not cure them. The verbal offense is as harmful as physical.

Anna Eleanor Roosevelt (1884–1962), who served as the First Lady of the United States during President Franklin D. Roosevelt's terms in office, said, "To handle yourself, use your head; to handle others, use your heart."†

The poetess and American author Maya Angelou (1928–2014) said, "I have learned that people will forget what you said, people will forget what you did, but people will never forget how you made them feel."‡

For the Stoics, the way to achieve tranquility was to control the emotional reactions. Zenon de Citio, a founder of Stoicism, said that people should achieve peace of mind.§

The Spanish Saint Teresa of Avila (1515–1582), a religious founder of the Discalced Carmelites, prayed, "Let nothing disturb you. ... All things are passing away. ... Patience obtains all things."¶

Business consultant Donald T. Phillips explains how Abraham Lincoln (1809–1865) controlled his frustration and anger:

> Although from time to time he experienced a burst of anger and lost his temper, he did it in private. To avoid such manifestations, the president would sit in his office and write long letters of reply to what had irritated him, which he then kept instead of sending them to the addressee. The letters only served as a means of getting rid of the emotional feelings repressed inside.**

---

* "Getting Past No – The Five Steps of Breakthrough Negotiation," www.williamury.com/the-five-st eps-of-breakthrough-negotiation/.
† www.goodreads.com.
‡ "Maya Angelou Quotes," www.goodreads.com/quote.
§ Among the most famous Stoics are Epictetus, Seneca, and the Roman emperor Marcus Aurelius.
¶ "Prayer of Saint Teresa of Avila," www.ewtn.com/devotionals/prayers/StTeresaofAvila.htm.
** Donald T. Phillips, *Lincoln on Leadership* (Deusto, 1993), 101.

As the recruiting expert, Barb Bruno said, "You can't control what happens to you, but you have 100% control over how you react to it."*

One day, at a high school, a new student named Peter walked home with his books. A group of companions ran toward him, and when they reached him, they threw all his books out of his arms and pushed him to the ground, and his glasses flew through the air.

Peter looked up at the sky with sadness in his eyes. Another companion named Tom, who saw what had happened, ran to help him. Tom helped Peter with the books, brought him his glasses, and accompanied Peter to his house. Over the next four years, Peter and Tom became great friends.

Graduation day came, Peter had been selected to give the commencement speech and he said:

> Graduation is a good time to thank all those who have helped us through these years: your parents, your teachers, your brothers, some coaches ... but mainly your friends. I am here to tell you that being friends with someone is the best gift that we can give and receive, and for this purpose, I am going to tell you a story.

Peter began to tell his story of the first days at school and the weekend he planned to commit suicide. He talked about how he had taken all those books with him after school so that his mother would not have to go later to pick them up at school. Peter stared at Tom and said, "Fortunately I was saved. My friend saved me from doing something irremediable."

Actions and words are not carried away by the wind, actions and words have the power to heal, but also to harm.

A young man had a bad character and would lose his patience very easily. Everything angered him. One day his father gave him a bag of nails and told him, "every time you lose your patience, you must hammer a nail behind the door."

The first day, the boy nailed ten nails behind the door.

With the passing of days, as he managed to control his character, the young man was nailing fewer nails in the door and after a few weeks, one day he informed his father that he had not nailed any in two days, because he had begun to control his character better.

---

* Barb Bruno, Top Producer Tutor (Good as Gold Training Inc.), www.topproducertutor.com/login.

His father then suggested that he remove a nail for each day he could control his character. The days passed and one day the young man told his father that there were no more nails to remove at the door.

His father then went to the door and said, "You worked hard, my son, but look at all those holes in the door. It will never be the same. Every time you lose your patience, you leave scars like those ones here at the door."

Effective leaders know how to control their feelings and impulses. They have self-discipline and manage to govern their emotions. Be careful with actions and reactions because people are not anybody's doormat.*

We are not in the years of King Henry VIII (1491–1547).†

Organizational leaders should avoid falling into arrogance, vanity, abuse, and the narcissistic individualism of some individuals who reach power.‡

Effective leaders are not only interested in achieving results and being task-oriented, but they are also interested in their employees.

The 1994 movie *Swimming with Sharks*§ shows how a boss can be cruel and ruthless and humiliate and abuse an employee.

If a person mistreats a US$100 bill, the bill still has the same value: 100 dollars. Sometimes the circumstances of life leave people in difficult times and feel devalued; however, despite the mistreatment and abuse of authority that may be suffered by an employee; the value of being a "person" is never lost. Your value doesn't decrease based on someone's inability to see your worth.

As the American motivational speaker Leslie Brown says, "Other people's opinion of you does not have to become your reality."¶

The Nicaraguan poet Félix Rubén García Sarmiento (1867–1916), known as Ruben Dario, wrote a poem called "La Calumnia" in which he expresses that however much a person is slandered and defamed, he or she will not lose his or her value. It reads as follows:

---

* In an extreme example in Japan in 2015, a boss dipped the face of one of his employees in a pot of boiling water. The video was recorded at a New Year's Eve party and was posted on the *Shukan Shincho* magazine's website. The victim filed a criminal complaint against the president of the company. "Workplace Abuse: A Chief Submerged the Face of an Employee in a Boiling Water Pot," November 23, 2018, www.infobae.com.

† King Henry VIII (1491–1547) had servants like Sir Henry Norris (1482?–1536), who was the "Groom of the Stool" and his task was to wash the king after going to the bathroom.

‡ In Greek mythology, Narcissus was an egomaniac teenager who fell in love with his image reflected in the water. Narciso got so close to the water to admire himself that he fell into the water and drowned. "Narcissism," Wikipedia.

§ Directed by George Huang, the movie is also known as *The Boss* or *Buddy Factor*.

¶ Les Brown, Quotes, www.brainyquote.com/quotes/les_brown_104662.

A drop of mud
Can fall on a diamond;
And thus, it can also
Obscure its radiance
But although the diamond
Is full of mire,
The value that makes it good
Will not be lost for even a moment,
And it must always be diamond
Even if is stained by mud.*

The Liberator of Argentina, Chile, and Peru, the military Jose de San Martin (1778–1850), said that "Arrogance ... often affects poor unhappy mortals who find themselves with a miserable share of power."† Power seduces, and to preserve it, humans have sometimes endured the abuse of the authority.

Power exposes ordinary people to extraordinary temptations. Lord Acton (1834–1902), historian and English politician, said that "power tends to corrupt and absolute power corrupts absolutely."‡

The influence on people is not always exercised from formal power. One person cannot always resist the pressure of a group of people, which can lead that person to behave erroneously.

In 1951 the Polish-American psychologist Solomon Asch (1907–1996) conducted a series of experiments to try to show how social pressure can lead certain people to make bad decisions, modifying their thinking, behavior, and convictions.

Asch's experiment consisted of gathering a group of seven to nine participants in a room to perform a vision test where they would compare the length of certain lines that appeared in some cartons.

The subjects of the experiment were shown a card with a line of a certain length and then they were asked to choose among three other lines, which had the same length as the one shown above. The process was carried out 18 times with different comparisons on the size of lines.

---

* Edwin de Paula, *From Zero to Infinity* (WestBow Press, 2015), 19.
† "Diez Frases Célebres de José de San Martin," www.lanacion.com.ar/2163026-diez-frases-celeb res-de-jose-de-san-martin-en-su-aniversario ("Ten Famous Phrases of Jose de San Martin").
‡ "Lord Acton Quotes," www.brainyquote.com.

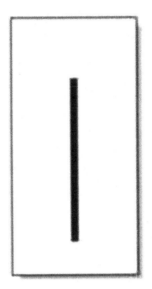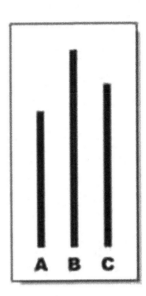

What one of the participants in the experiment did not know was the rest of the group were not subjects of the experiment like him, but their answers had been planned in advance to determine if the response of the non-accomplice subject could be conditioned by the wrong opinion of the majority. Asch's accomplices were instructed to answer 12 incorrect answers.

Each member spoke aloud and was heard by all the participants. Thus, in the first two comparisons, all participants responded correctly. But from the third test, the accomplices began to respond incorrectly.

After several incorrect answers from the accomplices, the subject under examination also began to respond erroneously as the others.

The experiment allowed testing the effects of social pressure on the behavior of human beings and how 30% of those who participated in these tests were influenced by the views and the clearly incorrect opinion of others.*

To avoid the consequences the Asch experiment demonstrated, organizational leaders must keep in mind that ethics training can help people resist the pressures of certain groups to act in an unethical manner.

---

* "Asch's Experiment: Bases, Procedures, and Results." www.lifeder.com; Solomon Asch Experiment: Group Pressure to Force Compliance with the Established. https://liberacionahora. wordpress.com; The Asch Conformity Experiment, YouTube.

In the 1960s, Stanley Milgram (1933–1984), American psychologist, conducted a study to know if people were able to inflict damage when required by an authority figure.* Milgram's idea arose from the trial in which Otto Nazi SS Lieutenant Colonel Adolf Eichmann (1906–1962) was sentenced to death in Jerusalem for crimes against humanity during the Nazi regime. Eichmann was directly responsible for the transfer of the deportees to the German concentration camps during World War II.†

During the trial, Eichmann expressed surprise at the hatred shown by the Jews. He stated he had only received orders, and obeying those orders was what he had to do. In his diary in prison, he wrote, "Obeying an order was the most important thing to me."‡

Eichmann appears to have no bitterness against the Jews, and six psychiatrists testified that he was healthy.§

Why did he participate in the Holocaust? Just for obedience? Milgram wanted to find out. The aim of the experiment was to measure the willingness of a participant to obey the orders of an authority, even if they might conflict with their personal conscience and moral principles.

Three people participated in the experiment: The *experimenter* (a university researcher), the *teacher* (a voluntary participant), and the *student* (an accomplice of the experimenter, an actor). The activity was that the experimenter would try to persuade the teacher to deliver what the student thought were electric shocks to the learner sitting in a chair. The learner was an actor who pretended to receive electric discharges with cries of pain every time he or she answered a question incorrectly. For every wrong answer of the student, the teacher increased the shock by 15 volts.

If the teacher, after several "electric shocks," was afraid to continue providing those shocks because of the heart-rending cries of the student (the actor), the experimenter replied, "Please continue, the experiment requires that you continue."

---

* The experiment was described in 1963 in an article published in the *Journal of Abnormal and Social Psychology* under the title "Behavioral Study of Obedience" and summarized in 1974 in his book *Obedience to Authority: An Experimental View*.
† Eichmann took refuge in 1945 with false documents in Argentina under the name of Ricardo Klement. In 1957, the Israeli secret service, the Mossad, located and kidnapped him in an operation called "Operation Garibaldi." Eichmann was hanged on May 31, 1962.
‡ Roger Cohen, "Why? New Eichmann Notes Try to Explain," August 13, 1999, www.nytimes.com.
§ After the Crimes Against Humanity trial, he was sentenced to death by hanging, and in 1962, he was executed in Ramla Prison, Israel.

Milgram summarized the experiment in his 1974, "The Perils of Obedience," writing, "I set up a simple experiment at Yale University to test how much pain an ordinary citizen would inflict on another person simply because he was ordered to by an experimental scientist."* The question was to what extent the participant (the *teacher*) would follow the instructions before refusing to perform them because it conflicted with his conscience.

The result of the experiment was that 65% of participants obeyed the order and administered electric shocks to the maximum level of 450 volts despite understanding the harm they caused and the supplications of the receiver. The conclusion was that obedience to authority prevailed over the moral principles of the participants of not to hurt others.[†] Milgram wrote,

> Ordinary people, simply doing their jobs, and without any particular hostility on their part, can become agents in a terrible destructive process. Moreover, even when the destructive effects of their work become patently clear, and they are asked to carry out actions incompatible with fundamental standards of morality, relatively few people have the resources needed to resist authority.[‡]

These conclusions lead us to reflect on the predisposition of an employee to commit illegal or immoral acts, at the request of his or her boss.

In 1999, Thomas Blass, a professor at the University of Maryland, published an analysis of all similar experiments conducted up to that point and concluded that the percentage of participants who applied very high voltages was above 60% regardless of the year or the locality of the experiment.

Humans are predisposed to comply with any order from an authority, and most of the time, what leaders ask will be executed, even if not right, fair, ethical, or legal. It will be executed because the authority asks for it.

As people tend to obey blindly those who have the authority, this can lead to serious consequences since people fail to exercise their own independent ethical judgment.

---

* "Milgram Experiment," e.wikipedia.org/wiki/Milgram_experiment.
† Milgram filmed a documentary showing the experiment and its results entitled *Obedience*. Also see *The Milgram Experiment*, a 2009 film by the Brothers Gibbs, that chronicles the story of Stanley Milgram's experiments.
‡ "Milgram experiment," en.wikiquote.org/wiki/Milgram_experiment, "The Perils of Obedience," *Harper's Magazine* (1974).

In order to better understand the causes of conflict in US prisons, a researcher and psychologist at Stanford University, Philip Zimbardo, conducted an experiment in 1971, ten years after the Milgram experiment, on the behavior of men in a fictional prison installed in the basement of the Department of Psychology at Stanford University.

Zimbardo selected 24 university participants and offered to pay them US$15 per day for a study on life in prison.* Twelve participants were assigned the role of prisoners, while the other 12 were assigned the role of guards. Zimbardo took on the role of the superintendent.

Participants who were guards received caps, military-inspired khaki uniforms, and mirrored glasses.

Participants who were prisoners, meanwhile, wore only robes and sandals with rubber heels and were identified by numbers sewn to their uniforms rather than by their names. Prisoners also had to wear nylons stockings on their heads to simulate skinheads and a chain around their ankles to remember his imprisonment.

The day before the experiment, the guards attended a brief orientation meeting with vague, fuzzy instructions. They were told it was their responsibility to direct the prison without physical violence.

The prisoners were "arrested" at their homes and "charged" with armed robbery. The local Palo Alto police department assisted Zimbardo with the arrests and conducted full booking procedures on the prisoners, which included fingerprinting and taking mug shots. The prisoners were transported to the mock prison from the police station, where they were strip-searched and given their new identities.

The small mock prison cells were set up to hold three prisoners each. The prisoners were to stay in their cells and the yard all day and night until the end of the experiment. The guards worked in teams of three for eight-hour shifts. The guards were not required to stay on-site after their shift.

Some guards felt the need to show their dominance even when it was not necessary. Their behavior put them in situations many times dangerous and psychologically damaging situations. One-third of the guards were judged to have exhibited genuine sadistic tendencies, while many prisoners were emotionally traumatized.

A few days into the experiment, some prisoners were exhausted, and after being subjected to repeated humiliations, some of them suffered serious emotional disorders, including severe depression. Two of the prisoners suffered severe trauma and had to be replaced.

---

* About US$90 in 2019.

One of the replacement prisoners, prisoner number 416, was horrified by the treatment of the guards. He began a hunger strike and he was locked in solitary confinement in a small compartment for hours.

The guards enjoyed their role, and most prisoners accepted the submission. One student, Christina Maslach*who visited the installations to conduct interviews, objected to the conditions in which the experiment was taken place.

After Maslach confronted Zimbardo and persuaded him that he had been passively allowing unethical acts to be performed under his supervision, Zimbardo concluded that both prisoners and guards had become grossly absorbed in their roles and realized that he had likewise become grossly absorbed in his own, and he terminated the experiment after just six days, eight ahead of schedule.†

According to Lombardo, under certain conditions, "good people can be induced, seduced, and initiated into behaving in evil ways. They can also be led to act in irrational, stupid, self-destructive, antisocial, and mindless ways."‡

The experiment had questionable ethics, the most serious concern being that it continued even after participants expressed their desire to withdraw.

Zimbardo was faced with the ethical dilemma that the experiment could possibly return outstanding results if continued, but it might also adversely affect the participants' well-being if not halted.§

The Stanford experiment came to the same conclusions as to the Milgram experiment regarding the willingness of people to abuse the exercise of power if the circumstances or the environment allows it to occur.

The results of these two experiments should help business leaders to understand the need to control the work environment and the use of the authority by managers and directors, ensuring a corporate culture that

---

* Lombardo's future wife.

† The film *The Experiment* (2010), directed by Paul Schuring, is based on the Stanford experiment. In 2015 was released *The Stanford Prison Experiment*, directed by Kyle Patrick Alvarez, also based on the same experiment.

‡ "Philip Zimbardo," Psychology Unlocked, June 10, 2018, www.psychologyunlocked.com. The question of people's social behaviors directed much of Zimbardo's research and led to key books, such as *The Lucifer Effect*, considering how good people perform evil behaviors.

§ The Stanford Prison Experiment led to the implementation of rules to preclude any harmful treatment of participants. Before they are implemented, human studies must now be reviewed and found by an institutional review board to be in accordance with the ethical guidelines set by the American Psychological Association. These guidelines involve consideration of whether the potential benefit for science outweighs the possible risk for physical and psychological harm. "Stanford Prison Experiment," ethical issues, n.wikipedia.org/wiki/Stanford_prison_experiment.

reinforces respect for the individual has a control system to prevent abuses and takes into account the human factor.

In June 2003, Amnesty International, a London-based nongovernmental organization focused on human rights, published reports of human rights abuses by the US military and its coalition partners at detention centers and prisons in Iraq. These included reports of brutal treatment at Abu Ghraib prison, which had once been used by the government of Saddam Hussein and had been taken over by the United States after the invasion.

On November 1, 2003, the Associated Press presented a special report on the massive human rights abuses at Abu Ghraib and in April 2004, a *60 Minutes* news report was aired by CBS News, describing the abuse, including pictures showing military personnel taunting naked prisoners.

The administration of George W. Bush asserted that these were isolated incidents, not indicative of general US policy. The Red Cross, Amnesty International, and Human Rights Watch stated the abuses at Abu Ghraib were not isolated incidents but were part of a wider pattern of torture and brutal treatment at American overseas detention centers. The US Department of Defense removed 17 soldiers and officers from duty.[*]

When acts of prisoner torture and abuse at the Abu Ghraib prison in Iraq were publicized, in March 2004, Zimbardo himself, who paid close attention to the details of the story, was struck by the similarity with his own experiment. He was dismayed by official military and government representatives shifting the blame for the torture and abuses in the Abu Ghraib American military prison onto "a few bad apples" rather than acknowledging the possibly systemic problems of a formally established military incarceration system.[†]

In organizations with a mature ethical culture, employees know the values and principles that guide the company and know that in case of receiving incompatible orders in contradiction to or in conflict with those values and principles – even from their own bosses – processes will be available to challenge those requests or orders.

American professor and total quality expert William Edwards Deming (1900–1993) said, "A bad system will beat a good person every time."[‡]

A strong ethical culture will enable organizations to better confront any attempt at the authoritarian use of power.

[*] "Abu Ghraib torture and prisoner abuse," en.wikipedia.ort/wiki/ Abu_Ghraib_torture_and_ prisoner_abuse.

[†] "Stanford prison experiment," en.wikipedia.org/wiki/Stanford_prison_experiment.

[‡] "Quote by W. Edwards Deming," quotes.deming.org/authors/W. Edwards_Deming/quote/10091.

Whoever occupies a position of leadership must be able to control his or her emotions under pressure and avoid abusive behaviors that psychologically destroy people. As the French novelist Albert Camus (1913–1960) said, "a man without ethics is a wild beast loosed upon this world."*

The French psychiatrist, psychoanalyst, and psychotherapist Marie France Hirigoyen points out that "through a process of moral harassment or psychological abuse an individual may be able to shatter another person."† She also said, "For a company, the economic consequences of harassment are not negligible. The deterioration of the work atmosphere leads to a significant decrease in the efficiency or performance of the group"‡ and she also wrote that "A pervert acts more easily in a disorganized and poorly structured company."§

Brazilian novelist Paulo Coelho has sold more than 140 million books translated into 80 languages and sold in more than 150 countries. Coelho says, "from among all the weapons that man has been able to invent; the most terrible, the most powerful, is the word."¶

Heinz Leymann (1932–1999) was a doctor in pedagogical psychology born in Germany and a pioneer in the disclosure of bullying or *mobbing* in the workplace. Mobbing consists of humiliating and discrediting a person in order to destabilize the person psychically. Psychological or moral harassment submerges the person in a depressive and toxic spiral that destroys the dignity and respect for the individual. Mobbing can occur in any context, in the family, at school, in the workplace, in the neighborhood, in the community, or online.

When emotional abuse occurs in the workplace, through rumors, intimidation, humiliation, discredit, and isolation, with the aim that the harassed person leaves his job; it is also known as general, non-sexual, and non-racial harassment.**

---

* "Albert Camus Quotes," www.brainyquote.com/quotes/albert_camus_118026.

† Marie France Hirigoyen, *El Acoso Moral*, 22nd ed (Paidos, 1998), 11 ("Moral Harassment").

‡ Marie France Hirigoyen, *El Acoso Moral*, 22nd ed (Paidos, 1998), 75 ("Moral Harassment").

§ Marie France Hirigoyen, *El Acoso Moral*, 22nd ed (Paidos, 1998), 64 ("Moral Harassment").

¶ Paulo Coelho, *La Quinta Montana* (Planeta, 2006), 73 ("The Fifth Mountain").

** The Austrian zoologist Konrad Lorenz (1903–1989), in his book entitled *On Aggression* (1966), first described mobbing among birds and animals, attributing it to instincts rooted in the Darwinian struggle to survive. In his view, humans are subject to similar innate impulses but capable of bringing them under rational control. In the 1970s, the Swedish physician Peter-Paul Heinemann (1931–2003) applied Lorenz's conceptualization to the collective aggression of children against a targeted child. In the 1980s, a German professor and practicing psychologist Heinz Leymann (1932–1999) applied the term to ganging up in the workplace. "Mobbing," en.wikiped ia.org/wiki/Mobbing#Mobbing_as_human_bullying_behaviour.

When one person harasses or annoys another, he or she is committing some form of harassment. The verb *harass* refers to an action or behavior that generates discomfort in the other. For example, deliberately preparing a person to make a mistake, or to be humiliated, intimidated, or physically or socially isolated (the so-called "silent treatment").

Psychological or moral harassment immerses the person in a depressive and toxic spiral that destroys his or her dignity and self-respect. Thus, organizations must prevent through training and control any bullying situation.

Sexual harassment is referred to as sexual intimidation or the promise of rewards in exchange for sexual favors. The Latin phrase *quid pro quo* means to substitute one thing for another ("something for something"). It is currently used to mean an exchange of favors. *Sexual harassment quid pro quo* refers to the requirement of sexual favors in exchange for obtaining a job or promotion in an organization.

Directive 2002/73/EC of the European Parliament defines *sexual harassment* as follows:

> Sexual harassment: where any form of unwanted verbal, non-verbal or physical conduct of a sexual nature occurs, with the purpose or effect of violating the dignity of a person, in particular when creating an intimidating, hostile, degrading, humiliating or offensive environment.*

Sexual harassment can take many forms, such as sexual advances, inappropriate physical contact, requests for sexual favors, sexually oriented jokes, pictures or messages, degrading comments about appearance, or display of sexually suggestive pictures or pornography.

Sexual harassment is a problem in workplaces. In a recent survey carried out by the Trades Union Congress,[†] 52% of the women said that they had experienced some form of sexual harassment at work. Almost a quarter had unwanted contacts and a fifth of the respondents had experienced unwelcome verbal sexual advances during the workday. The same survey found that only about one in five affected women report sexual harassment

---

* "Directive 2002/73/EC of the European Parliament and of the Council of 23 September 2002." Article1.3: Harassment and sexual harassment within the meaning of this Directive shall be deemed to be discrimination on the grounds of sex and therefore prohibited.

† Trades Union Congress (TUC) is a national trade union center, a federation of trade unions in England and Wales, representing the majority of trade unions. en.wikipedia.org/wiki/Trades_U nion_Congress.

and those who reported said that the results were poor: 80% said that nothing changed.*

In 1998, Mitsubishi agreed to pay US$34 million to resolve a claim of sexual harassment initiated by female employees of the Illinois factory.

In 2011, an employee of Aaron got US$40 million after claiming in court that the store manager sexually harassed her.

At the time Susan Flower was an Uber engineer, she received inappropriate messages from her manager and reported the situation to Human Resources. Flowers was told that even though the messages received were sexual harassment, the manager was a "high performer" and they wouldn't feel comfortable punishing him for what was "probably just an innocent mistake on his part." She was informed she had to make a choice: (i) find another team or (ii) stay on the team although she would probably receive a poor performance review.†

In December 2019 Uber agreed to pay a total of US$4.4 million to settle claims of gender discrimination brought by the US Equal Employment Opportunity Commission. An investigation into the company found that it "permitted a culture of sexual harassment and retaliation against individuals."‡

A research in 2018 revealed that while one in three Australians have experienced workplace sexual harassment in the past five years, only 17% made a formal report or complaint.§

Employers must ensure that their organizations foster a culture in which harassment is clearly unacceptable. *Time* magazine conferred the "Person of the Year 2017" annual title to a group of individuals who broke their silence and shared their stories about sexual harassment.¶

The Me Too movement or *#MeToo* spread virally in October 2017 as a hashtag used on social media to help demonstrate the widespread prevalence of sexual assault and harassment, especially in the workplace. On October 15, 2017, the American actress Alyssa Milano used this phrase

---

* Hannah Freeman, "Sexual Harassment in the Workplace: A Widespread Problem," November 15, 2017, www.oldsquare.co.uk/news-and-media/articles/sexual-harassment.

† In February 2017 Flowers wrote an article about her story at Uber called "Reflecting on One Very, Very Strange Year at Uber," www.susanjfowler.com/blog/2017/2/19/reflecting-on-one-very-strange-year-at-uber.

‡ Patrick McGee, "Uber to Pay $4.4 M to Settle Gender Discrimination Claims," December 18, 2019, www.ft.com.

§ Natalie MacDonald, "20 Big Ideas that Will Change Your World in 2020," December 10, 2019, LinkedIn.

¶ Stephanie Zacharek, Eliana Dockterman and Haley Swetland Edwards, "The Silence Breakers," 2017, Time.com.

in the context of an awareness campaign tweeting: "If all the women who have been harassed or sexually assaulted made a tweet with the words *Me Too*, we could show people the magnitude of the problem." The phrase was tweeted more than 700,000 times on October 15 and 16. On Facebook, the hashtag was used by more than 4.7 million people during the first 24 hours.[*]

Organizations are responsible for omission if they receive a report of sexual harassment and do not initiate a diligent investigation. Failure to act on sexual harassment can cause it to escalate into sexual abuse, i.e., any kind of sexual activity between two people without one person's consent.

Business leaders should be aware the organization also assumes the risk of being punished for acts of harassment by its employees.

Dr. Walter Doyle Staples, an American consultant, with a Ph.D. in behavioral psychology, mentions Professor Peter Koestenbaum, a philosopher who works for the Ford Motor Company and who advises treating people with respect to creating an atmosphere in which employees feel proud and motivated to develop and contribute.[†]

"Mafalda" is the name of a 6-year-old girl from a comic strip translated into 26 languages, created by the Argentine comedian known as Quino.[‡] The character's reflections as an adult were so successful that Mafalda's books sold millions of copies. Mafalda says: "Understanding and respect are the important things to live with others and above all, you know what? Do not believe that one is better than anyone."[§]

Maria Montessori (1870–1952) was a famous Italian educator and founder of the *Montessori Method*, which taught that if work were done without joy, there would be less creativity and productivity.

The Spanish religious leader Saint Ignatius of Loyola (1491–1556) advised the Jesuit directors to govern with all possible love, respect, modesty, and charity in a way that would bring more love than fear:[¶] "Organizations, armies, sports teams, and companies do their best when team members respect each other. ... Individuals also do their best when

---

[*] es.wikipedia.org/wiki/Me_Too.

[†] Walter Doyle Staples, *Piense Como un Ganador* (Atlántida, 1991), 303 ("Think Like a Winner").

[‡] His name is Joaquín Salvador Lavado Tejón. They called him *Quino* to differentiate him from his uncle Joaquin.

[§] thinkaboutworld.wordpress.com/2014/06/23/comprension-y-respeto-eso-es-lo-importante-para-convivir-con-los-demas-y-sobre-todo-sabes-que-no-creer-que-uno-es-mejor-que-nadie-quino/ 23 de junio de 2014.

[¶] Bernardo Bárcena, *El Liderazgo de Francisco* (Ediciones B.), 159 ("Francis' Leadership").

respected, esteemed and trusted by someone who genuinely cares about their well-being."[*]

The Italian Saint Francis of Assisi (1181–1226) said:

> "Lord, make me an instrument of your peace;
> Where there is hatred, let me sow love;
> Where there is injury, pardon;
> Where there is discord, union;
> Where there is doubt, faith;
> Where there is despair, hope;
> Where there is darkness, light;
> Where there is sadness, joy."[†]

Catholic social teaching is a set of principles and norms based on the Gospel and the teaching of the Catholic Church. According to this Doctrine:

> Social justice can only be obtained by respecting the transcendent dignity of man. ... What is at stake is the dignity of the human person, whose defense and promotion has been entrusted to us by the Creator and by those who are rigorously and responsibly indebted men and women at every juncture in history.[‡] Contribute to give back to the human person the dignity that God granted him from the beginning.[§]

For Saint Teresa of Calcutta (1910–1997), the world's worst poverty is that of the heart, where there is a need for affection, understanding, and love:

> It is not height, weight, beauty, title or much less money that makes people great. It is their honesty, their humility, their decency, their kindness and respect for the feelings and interests of others. The major disease today is not leprosy or tuberculosis, but to feel unloved, disregarded and abandoned.[¶]

---

[*] Chris Lowney, *Liderazgo al Estilo de Los Jesuitas* (Buenos Aires, Editorial Norma, 2013), 32. Mentioned by Bernardo Bárcena in *The Leadership of Francis* (Editions B., 2014), 159 ("Leadership in the Style of the Jesuits").

[†] "Peace prayer of Saint Francis," www.loyolapress.com.

[‡] *Sollicitudo Rei Socialis*, no. 47.

[§] Pio XII Radiomensaje, "Con Sempre," no. 35.

[¶] Diario La Hora, "Santa Madre Teresa de Calcuta," October 22, 2016, lahora.gt/santa-madre-teresa-calcuta/; http://devocionpoetica.blogspot.com/2014/03/frases-de-la-madre-teresa-de-calcuta.html, March 9, 2014; www.filosofiahoy.com/cartas_al_editor/ampliar/129, May 2, 2015 ("Holy Mother Teresa of Calcutta").

The French-Argentine entrepreneur Enrique Shaw (1921–1962) was the manager of Cristalerias Rigolleau factory in Argentina, and he supervised more than 2,000 employees. Shaw said,

> Entrepreneurs are agents that overcome social differences. We must unite men.... It is essential to improve social coexistence within the company. It matters a lot if the company leader is accessible. The factory has to be humanized. To judge a worker one must love him.[*]

At the end of his life, when workers at his factory knew that Shaw would be operated on, they lined up at a clinic in Buenos Aires to donate blood. Shaw said, "Now I am happy because through my veins is coursing workers blood."[†]

The dean of the faculty of Juridical, Business, and Social Sciences of the Francisco de Vitoria University in Madrid, Spain, Jose Maria Ortiz Ibarz, said, "Being the best does not consist in annihilating others; only becomes leaders who are not afraid that those around them will be leaders too."[‡]

The English corporate guru Simon Sinek said in a TED talk:

> If you have hard times in your family, would you ever consider laying off one of your children? We would never do it. Why we would consider laying off people inside our organization?
>
> Great leaders would never sacrifice their people to make the numbers; they will sacrifice the numbers to save people.
>
> When people feel safe and protected by the leadership in the organization, the natural reaction is to trust and cooperate.
>
> We call them leaders because they go first... and because they want to sacrifice for their people. [§]

For Sinek hiring people is like adopting a child and therefore we have to take care of them and give them a good environment to develop.[¶]

---

[*] www.enriqueshaw.com.

[†] "Enrique Shaw: The Argentine Businessman Whom Francis May Soon Beatify," www.catholicnewsagency.com/news/enrique-shaw-the-argentine-businessman-whom-francis-may-soon-beatify -52592; "Enrique Shaw, el Empresario con Sangre Obrera que Humanizo los Negocios," www.amexcorporate.com.ar/.

[‡] Braulio Fernandez B, "La Ética como Competencia Laboral," http://es.catholic.net ("Ethics as Labor Competence").

[§] Chip Cutter, "Simon Sinek: Great Managers Don't Lay Off Employees," March 21, 2014, www.linkedin.com.

[¶] Simon Sinek, "Treat Hiring as Adopting a Child," The Entourage.

To increase trust and commitment over the long term, managers may have to sacrifice profits in the short term. They may have to find an alternative to employee layoffs as a cure for a short-term drop in sales or profits.*

Good shepherds always take care of their sheep. When the bad times come, instead of abandoning them through massive layoffs, great leaders look for other solutions to protect them.

Konosuke Matsushita (1894–1989) was a Japanese businessman, founder of Matsushita Electric Industrial Company Ltd., and one of the most prominent figures in the history of the industry in that country. In 1929, the mass dismissal of workers was a common practice in companies around the world. However, Matsushita maintained the employment and salary of its workers. The strategy was a resounding success and the employees created a special bond with the company.†

A caring work environment will help employees develop their skills and their commitment for the benefit of the company.

A friend told me that years ago he offered a lady a job as a babysitter to help with the care and attention of his young children. The lady had at that time another job where she earned more money than my friend offered, but nevertheless, she accepted the job offer because in the other house "she was treated like a dog."

Bob Hoover (1922–2016) was an American pilot recognized as one of the best in history for his acrobatics and has been called the "pilot's pilot." In World War II, he was imprisoned by the Germans and managed to escape by stealing an FW-190, with which he flew to Holland. In 1948, he left the army to work in civil aviation as a test pilot. On one occasion, he was going from San Diego to his house in Los Angeles, piloting a propeller airplane that was a relic of World War II. This is what happened:

> A hundred meters high the two engines suddenly went out. Thanks to his ability, Hoover landed, but the plane was seriously damaged. None of the occupants were injured.
>
> The first thing Hoover did after the emergency landing was to inspect the fuel tank. As he suspected, the old propeller had been loaded with jet fuel, instead of ordinary gasoline. When he returned to the airport, he asked to see the mechanic who had taken care of the plane.

---

* K. Blanchard, C. Schewe, B. Nelson and A. Hiam, *Exploring the World of Business* (Worth Publishers, 1996), 17.
† Konosuke Matsushita, Wikipedia.

The young man was terrified of his error. Tears ran down his cheeks as he approached Hoover. His mistake had caused the loss of a very expensive plane and could have caused the loss of three lives.

It's easy to imagine Hoover's anger. It is possible to suppose the verbal storm that could cause such carelessness in this superb pilot.

But Hoover did not reproach him... not even criticism. Instead, he put his arm around the boy's shoulders and said: "To prove that I'm sure you'll never do it again, I want you to take care of my F-51 tomorrow."*

A person demonstrates his greatness in how he is controlled in situations of high crisis and tension. Great leaders know how to manage their emotions well and their success is not only due to *what* they do but *how* they do it. How good it would be that in crises, all leaders could control themselves, set an example, and motivate as Hoover did.

The American banker and philanthropist John Templeton (1912–2008) said, "It's nice to be important, but it's more important to be nice."†

British author J. K. Rowling is the creator of the Harry Potter series of books that have sold more than 450 million copies.‡ Rowling has said that "if you want to see the true measure of a man, watch how he treats his inferiors, not his equals."§

Ella Wheeler Wilcox (1850–1919) was an American poet who wrote:

It is easy enough to be pleasant,
When life flows by like a song,
But the man worthwhile is one who will smile,
When everything goes dead wrong."¶

Punch was the name of a British illustrated magazine founded in 1841 that in 1850 published a definition of *sportsman* that became famous:

Sportsman is one who has not only invigorated his muscles and developed his resistance by the exercise of some great sport, but in the practice of this exercise he has learned to repress his anger, to be tolerant of his companions, not to take advantage of a vile advantage, to feel deeply as a dishonor

---

* Dale Carnegie, *How to Make Friends and Influence People* (Debolsillo, 2006), 42.
† "John Templeton Quotes," www.brainyquote.com/quotes/john_templeton_392069.
‡ Rowling is one of the richest women in Britain with a fortune over 500 million pounds and was *Time*'s "Person of the Year" in 2007.
§ J. K. Rowling Quotes, www.brainyquote.com/quotes/j_k_rowling_178389.
¶ Ella Wheeler Wilcox, "Poems of Sentiment," www.ellawheelerwilcox.org/poems/pworthwh.htm.

the mere suspicion of a trap and to carry with height a cheerful countenance, under the disenchantment of a setback.*

The French writer and pilot Antoine de Saint Exupery (1900–1944) wrote, "I have no right to say or do anything that diminishes a man. ... Hurting a man in his dignity is a crime."†

US consultants Kenneth Blanchard and Spencer Johnson point out that people who feel appreciated produce more and better results. The authors say, "Helping people to feel good is the key to achieving more. I am very hard with low performance, but only with the performance. I'm never hard on the person."‡

Mexican entrepreneur Carlos Kasuga, president of Yakult Mexico, has said, "It is necessary to make the human being feel useful, necessary and wanted in the company. ... It is not machinery or technology, but human beings that improve an organization."§

Daniel Goleman is an American writer and psychologist who gained fame after the publication of his book *Emotional Intelligence* in 1995.¶ For Goleman, the emotional coefficient allows us to understand the feelings of others, to be sensitive and empathetic with the other. Thus, success does not necessarily depend on the intellectual coefficient or the academic career, what matters most is the level of emotional intelligence, that is, the level of management of one's own emotions and of an understanding of one's point of view and feelings.

The word *empathy* comes from the Greek word *empatheia*, which means *thrilled*. Empathy is the ability to understand the feelings and emotions of another individual. When one person is placed in the situation of the other, feels like the other, and tries to see the world from their perspective, that person can more easily understand the behavior and the way of thinking of the other person.

An effective leader knows how to handle stress, he or she knows the power of emotional intelligence, and is aware of how to control his or her emotions. An empathetic person knows how to listen to others and understands their problems and emotions.

---

* In 1925, that definition was reproduced by Sir William Burton, VP of the Yacht Racing Association.
† "Antoine de Saint-Exupery Quotes,", www.goodreads.com/quotes/102664-i-have-no-right-to -say-or-do-anything-that.
‡ Kenneth Blanchard and Spencer Johnson, *The One Minute Manager* (New York, Berkley Books, 1982), 96.
§ Marisol Garcia Fuentes, "10 Minutos con Carlos Kasuga," January 4, 2012, www.entrepreneur. com ("10 Minutes with Carlos Kasuga").
¶ His book was on *The New York Times* Best Seller list for a year-and-a-half.

Jesus of Nazareth when walking on the shore of the Sea of Galilee saw the fishermen Simon (called Peter) and Andrew and he told them, "Follow me and I will make you fishers of men."* The two left what they were doing and followed him. Pope John Paul II achieved an enormous connection with the faithful with his smile and his charisma, Freddie Mercury achieved great empathy during the *Live Aid* concert to raise funds for the benefit of Ethiopia and Somalia in 1985. The president of South Africa, Nelson Mandela, put on a cap and jersey of the rugby team of South Africa on June 24, 1995, at the Ellis Park stadium in Johannesburg, before the final match of the Rugby World Cup between South Africa and New Zealand. While walking through the center of the field, 65,000 white fans cheered his name: "Nelson, Nelson, Nelson." In a television interview, the then captain of the South African team, François Pienaar, said: "When he entered into the locker room to wish us good luck, he turned around and my number was on his back. It was an incredible feeling."† The film *Invictus* is about the events in South Africa before and during the 1995 Rugby World Cup, a tournament organized after the dismantling of the segregationist apartheid system.‡

The most effective leaders are those who are distinguished by their emotional intelligence and empathy. These leaders are attentive people and more sensitive than the average person, they are influenced by the emotions of other people, and they feel what others feel.

There are, on the contrary, people who over the years learn to solve problems, but they never learn to feel.

Henry Ford (1863–1947) pointed out, "If there is any secret of success, it lies in the ability to get the other person's point of view and see things from that person's angle as well as from your own."§

John D. Rockefeller (1839–1927), one of the most successful entrepreneurs in the history of business in the United States and founder of Standard Oil, said, "I will pay more to those who have the ability to deal with people than for any other ability under the sun."¶

---

* The Bible, Matthew 4:19.
† "El Día Que Cambió la Historia con una Camiseta de Rugby," December 6, 2013 (The Day that the History Changed with a Rugby Shirt), www.eldia.com.
‡ *Invictus*, a film released in 2009, directed by Clint Eastwood and starring Morgan Freeman and Matt Damon. The story is based on the book *Playing the Enemy* by John Carlin.
§ "Henry Ford Quotes," www.brainyquote.com.
¶ K. Blanchard, C. Schewe, B. Nelson and A. Hiam, *Exploring the World of Business* (Worth Publishers, 1996), 250; and en.wikiquote.org/wiki/John_D._Rockefeller.

Kazuo Inamori is a billionaire Japanese entrepreneur* and Buddhist priest who believes if the staff is happy, they will work better and, as a result, the profits of the company will grow. Inamori says, "If you want eggs, take care of the hen."[†]

The founder of Walmart, Sam Walton (1918–1992), said, "If you love your work, you'll be out there every day trying to do it the best you possibly can, and pretty soon everybody around will catch the passion from you – like a fever."[‡]

James Goodnight is an American businessman who in 1976 co-founded the SAS software company and has since been its CEO. His leadership style and the work environment he has created for SAS has been studied by academics and companies. Says a Deloitte report on SAS:

> The SAS software giant was recently ranked as the best place to work for the Great Place to Work Institute. SAS is very successful with 37 consecutive years of records earnings.
>
> SAS has identified trust as a critical cultural attribute and regularly surveys its employees on elements of trust: communication, respect, transparency and being treated as a human being.[§]
>
> When our employees are happy, they keep our customers happy. There is a direct correlation between our culture and the success of our business. SAS recently celebrated 39 uninterrupted years of growth in sales and profits. It is a virtuous circle. Treat your employees well … create happy customers, happy customers generate sales, and sales allow you to reinvest in employees. It makes sense.
>
> The work environment affects productivity and retention. 95% of my assets come out the door every afternoon. It's my job to maintain a work environment that makes these people come back every morning. If you treat your employees as making the difference, they will make a difference.[¶]

An article called "Secret Boss: The Discoveries Made by a CEO Infiltrated in His Own Company" says, "A leader has to create an environment

---

* At the age of 27, Inamori founded Kyocera Corporation, which is now a multinational hi-tech conglomerate employing thousands of people and supplying cell phones and cameras. In 1984, Inamori founded KDDI, Japan's second telecommunication network.
[†] November 7, 2015, julzcards.wordpress.com.
[‡] Colin Dodds, "Sam Walton: Most Influential Quotes," www.investopedia.com.
[§] *Global Human Capital Trends 2016* (Deloitte University Press), Shape Culture, 40, www2.deloitte.com.
[¶] www.futureofbusinesstech.com.

of trust. It's harder to turn a good executive into a good person, than a good person into a good executive."*

A Gallup poll of 7,000 workers showed that the main reason why workers change jobs is to get away from their boss.†

Comparably is the name of a platform that provides anonymous data about companies' culture. The 2018 Comparably's list shows companies with best managers and was based on information sent by three million employees working in 45,000 American companies. According to the survey results, some of the best managers come from Costco, Facebook, Netflix, Google, and T-Mobile. The report says, "The managers of these companies express empathy and concern for their employees as individuals. There is a feeling that they are fair when they deal with people."‡

Stanley Gault (1926–2016), CEO of Goodyear, said,

> We discontinued use of the word "employee," and we instituted the word "associate," because that was a leveling action. Regardless of your station in the organization, you are an associate. It is particularly important to women and minorities because they feel that the word "employee" means you work for someone. Well, we don't work *for* each other, we work *with* each other.§

Sam Walton (1920–1992), the founder of Walmart, was a very effective humble leader who achieved great empathy with his employees.

In November 1980 Sam Walton wrote,

> Every human being has the same basic needs. Among them is the desire to be appreciated and respected. As managers of people, we need to put ourselves in others' shoes. We should try to understand their needs, desires, and strivings from *their* point of view.¶

---

* Sofía Terrile, *La Nación*, May 31, 2017.
† Zameena Meija, "The 25 Companies with the Best Managers in America According to 3 Million Employees,", June 7, 2018, www.cnbc.com.
‡ Zameena Mejia, "The 25 Companies with the Best managers in America According to 3 Million Employees," June 7, 2018, www.cnbc.com.
§ K. Blanchard, C. Schewe, B. Nelson and A. Hiam, *Exploring the World of Business* (Worth Publishers, 1996), 30.
¶ He made these comments after reading an article written by Theodore V. Houser, former chairman of the board of Sears.

A successful leader is one who cares and helps his employees to grow and develop professionally within an environment of good treatment and respect. Commit to your employees and promote a culture free of harassment. Professional relationships are built on trust and commitment. Employees who know their company cares for them perform better.

The Spanish Joan Antoni Melé, a recognized educator in the banking sector, has stated, "I firmly believe that another world is possible: putting the center of the economy in the human being, not profit. The way of conducting business has not respected the human being or human dignity or the planet."*

David Packard (1912–1996), an electric engineer and co-founder of Hewlett-Packard, said,

> When we discuss supervision and management we are not talking about a military-type organization where the man at the top issues an order and it is passed on down the line until the man at the bottom does as he is told without question (or reason). That is precisely the type of organization we do not want. We feel our objectives can best be achieved by people who understand what they are trying to do and can utilize their own capabilities to do them. I have noticed when we promote people from a routine job to a supervisory position; there is a tremendous likelihood that these people will get carried away by the authority. They figure that all they have to do now is tell everyone else what to do and quite often this attitude causes trouble. We must realize that supervision is not a job of giving orders; it is a job of providing the opportunity for people to use their capabilities efficiently and effectively. ... We must provide a means of letting our employees know they have done a good job. You as supervisors must convey this to your groups. Don't just give orders. Provide the opportunity for your people to do something important. Encourage them.†

William James (1842–1910) was an American philosopher with a long career at Harvard, where he was a professor of psychology. James said, "The deepest principle of human nature is the craving to be appreciated."‡

---

* "Marks Can Make Ethics a Global Trend" (Las Marcas Pueden Hacer de la Etica una Tendencia Mundial) *La Nacion*, September 8, 2017.
† Christina Bonnington, "The HP Way: How Bill Hewlett and I Built Our Company," Speech by Dave Packard to HP Managers, May 8, 1960, gizmodo.com.
‡ www.brainyquote.com/quotes/william_james_125466.

Claude Michel Steiner (1935–2017), a French-born American psychotherapist and writer, has said that to develop, humans need stroking.
The Saratoga Institute, a leading global human capital consulting firm
at PricewaterhouseCoopers, says that "losing an employee... often costs
the equivalent of six months to one year of paid salary."[*] This calculation
does not seem unreasonable if we think that with the departure of the
employee, the company loses productivity and institutional knowledge,
the morale of other employees falls, and the costs of recruitment and
training, overtime, and temporary employment increase.

The former First Lady of the United States, Michelle Obama, has said that
"success isn't about how much money you make; it's about the difference
you make in people's lives."[†]

Businessman Guillermo Murchison said in 2007 at the IDEA Colloquium
that "the problem of this age is that we love things and use people, and we
have to love people and use things."[‡]

So, if mistreatment brings inconvenience, distrust, rotation, rumors,
grudges, and risks. Why then not treat employees well so that they are
loyal and dedicated to their work?

Westminster Abbey is an Anglican Gothic church the size of a cathedral
located in the city of London next to the Palace of Westminster. It is the
traditional place for the coronations and burials of the British monarch.
It contains the graves of members of the royal family and illustrious
personalities such as Newton, Darwin, or Dickens. The Argentine writer
and politician Rafael Bielsa mentions in one of his books, a classic story
about the Abbey of Westminster:

> "Why is the grass of the Abbey so green?" they asked the
> gardener.
> "Because we water it every Wednesday," the gardener
> answered.
> "Only that?" the curious ask.
> "Yes, in addition to what we have been doing for the last five
> hundred years," the gardener answered.[§]

---

[*] Roger E. Herman, *Keeping Good People* (Oakhill Press, 1999), 330; Retention Management, Saratoga Institute, and the American Management Association, January 1998.

[†] September 5, 2012, www.elephantjournal.com/2012/09/michelle-obama-inspires-tears-success-isnt-how-much-money-you-make-but-how-much-of-a-difference-you-make-in-peoples-lives/.

[‡] Guillermo Murchison, inaugural speech as president of the IDEA Colloquium of 2007.

[§] Rafael Bielsa, *Argentina una luz de almacén: Reflexiones sobre un país en penumbras* (Editorial Sudamericana, 2001), 125 ("Argentina a warehouse light: Reflections on a country in twilight").

Like a garden, the workplace needs the constant care and attention of the leader. As Gil Stricklin, CEO of Marketplace Ministries Inc., says, "If you want to have a good bottom line, you must take care of your top line, that is, your employees."*

When work relations are developed on the basis of honesty, respect, and integrity, there is effective communication, a bond of trust, and some emotional connection between the employee and the company. This kind of labor relations generates enthusiasm. As the American poet Ralph Waldo Emerson (1803–1882) said, "Nothing great was ever achieved without enthusiasm."†

Clarence Francis (1888–1985), who was the chairman of General Foods, said:

> You can buy a man's time, you can buy a man's physical presence at a given place, you can even buy a measured number of skilled muscular motions per hour or day. But you cannot buy enthusiasm, you cannot buy initiative, you cannot buy loyalty, you cannot buy the devotion of hearts, minds, and souls. You have to earn these things.‡

To take care of the work environment, leaders must protect the culture of respect and create processes that alert them of any type of abuse or mistreatment.

Hence, we should avoid reacting like did the president of the Spanish electricity company Iberdrola, Ignacio Sánchez Galán, who, losing patience, interrupted his presentation before investors to claim those who were in charge of adjusting the light of the stage and said: "Please can you lower the light? ... Do not think please, do not think, execute, ... others think, don't worry."§

Employees should feel from their bosses they are not only a resource for an end but mainly human beings. Each person is valuable, and leaders must promote and guarantee good treatment to employees.

Corporate leaders should thank, respect, understand the needs of employees, and accept different opinions. They must be able to manage

---

* Gil Stricklin, speech made on February 22, 2018, at Cross Church Pinnacle Hills in Rogers, Arkansas at The Summit.
† Ralph Waldo Emerson quotes, www.brainyquote.com.
‡ www.goodreads.com.
§ "La Regaña del General Galán a los Soldados que Incordiaban con la Luz," *El Confidencial*, March 21, 2019, blogs.elconfidencial.com ("The anger of General Galán to those who handled the Light").

and contain their emotions and exercise patience and respect even in times of crisis and stress.

As the American philosopher and poet Ralph Waldo Emerson (1803–1882) said, "Good manners are made up of petty sacrifices."*

Fred Mc Feely Rogers (1928–2003) was an American television personality and host of the preschool television series *Mister Rogers' Neighborhood*, which ran from 1968 to 2001. Rogers taught young children about civility, tolerance, the value of loving one another, and being a good person in society. Mr. Rogers said:

> As human beings, our job in life is to help people realize how rare and valuable each one of us really is, that each of us has something that no one else has – or ever will have – something inside that is unique to all time. It's our job to encourage each other to discover that uniqueness and to provide ways of developing its expression.†
>
> There are three ways to ultimate success: The first way is to be kind. The second way is to be kind. The third way is to be kind.‡

Organizations need leaders like Mr. Rogers and his lessons of kindness.

The British American author Simon Sinek shared a story about a former Under Secretary of Defense who at a large conference, took his place on the stage, took a sip of coffee, smiled, and said:

> You know, I spoke here last year. I presented at this same conference on this same stage. But last year, I was still an Under Secretary.
>
> I flew here in business class and when I landed, there was someone waiting for me at the airport to take me to my hotel. Upon arriving at my hotel, there was someone else waiting for me. They had already checked me into the hotel, so they handed me my key and escorted me up to my room. The next morning, when I came down, again there was someone waiting for me in the lobby to drive me to this same venue that we are in today. I was taken through a back entrance, shown to the greenroom and handed a cup of coffee in a beautiful ceramic cup.

---

* www.azquotes.com/Quote/524195.

† Geoffrey James, "45 Quotes from Mr. Rogers that We All Need Today," August 5, 2019, www.inc.com/geoffrey-james/45-quotes-from-mr-rogers-that-we-all-need-today.

‡ Robin Zlotnick, "Amazing Quotes from Mr. Rogers that Will Improve Your Whole Day,", https://twentytwowords.com/incredibly-inspiring-mr-rogers-quotes-that-will-brighten-your-day/.

But this year, as I stand here to speak to you, I am no longer the Under Secretary, I flew here coach class and when I arrived at the airport yesterday there was no one there to meet me. I took a taxi to the hotel, and when I got there, I checked myself in and went by myself to my room. This morning, I came down to the lobby and caught another taxi to come here. I came in the front door and found my way backstage. Once there, I asked one of the techs if there was any coffee. He pointed to a coffee machine on a table against the wall. So, I walked over and poured myself a cup of coffee into this here Styrofoam cup.

It occurs to me, the ceramic cup they gave me last year … it was never meant for me at all. It was meant for the position I held.*

In best companies, all employees are treated similarly, regardless of functions.

On one occasion, at the nursing school, the professor gave a surprise exam.

One of the students quickly read all the questions until he reached the last one that said: What is the name of the woman who cleans the school?

The student had seen this woman several times, but how was he to know her name?

The student took the exam without answering the last question, which was probably a joke.

Then another student asked the teacher if that question counted for the grade.

"Of course," the professor replied. "In your career, you will meet many people. All are important. They all deserve attention and care."†

It is important to keep people motivated and to support them. If motivation and support are missing, the productivity of the company shall decrease significantly.

Human relationships are complex, but a hostile work environment has a very high cost for any organization. Leaders must ensure that people who work at all levels of the organization feel appreciated, respected, valued, and heard.

---

* "How Humility Can Be Your Secret Weapon as a Boss," Simon Sinek, Inc.com.
† Jaime Lopera Gutierrez and Maria Ines Bernal Trujillo. *La Culpa es de la Vaca* (Colombia, Intermedio Editores), 53 ("It is Cow's Fault").

Results should not be obtained at the expense of the people, but with people. A person is not a number.* For Saint Therese of Lisieux (1873–1897), the world was like a Garden of God and each person a flower.

Just as flowers require an adequate environment to grow and develop, organizational leaders must build and maintain good work environments so that employees can grow, develop, and reach their full potential. By helping to create a good work environment, a leader is also helping the employees also act ethically.

Putting oneself in the situation of the other, controlling emotions, and achieving empathy and connection with people will result in increased enthusiasm, commitment, productivity, and, therefore, results.

On one occasion a customer walked into Walmart with an item to return. The customer was upset and Mr. Sam happened to be up at the front of the store to greet the customers.

Mr. Sam asked the customer how he may help him. The gentleman opened up the plastic bag and proceeded to tell Sam how upset he was with the fact that he had purchased a rotisserie chicken and it was not fully cooked.

After seeing the rotisserie chicken which was obviously uncooked, Mr. Sam took the bag and told the customer he would refund him the money and replace the chicken. He said, "I don't ever want you to go back to our competitor."

The rotisserie chicken still had the competitor's label on the case. Even though the customer did not purchase the item at Walmart, Mr. Sam wanted to ensure customers felt 100% satisfied with any merchandise they purchased and build a brand around satisfaction guaranteed.

As seen, experts in human resources agree on the advantages of fostering a good working environment and a culture that shows care and respect among employees. An ethical company with a good reputation and a good working climate brings multiple benefits. It increases dialogue, trust, and commitments of people. It reduces stress, reduces absenteeism, reduces employee turnover, and improves innovation. All this leads to the company being more productive and profitable.

---

* As the religious María Josefina Llach says, "the most important in the world: a person," *Un Sol para mi Pueblo: Vida de Santa Rafaela María* (Buenos Aires, Paulinas, 1995) ("A Sun for my People: Life of Saint Rafaela María").

In ethical organizations, employees are less likely to be deceived, mistreated, discriminated, or pressured to carry out illegal actions.

Section 4

Control

21

Designing an Effective Ethics and Compliance Program: Unit 1

A leader must know how to plan, execute, and control.

How can you plan and execute effectively and at the same time reduce unpleasant risks and surprises?

The answer is to build an ethics and compliance strategy.

Compliance programs consist of a set of actions, initiatives, and internal processes carried out by organizations to promote, supervise, and control ethical conduct and compliance with laws and policies and to detect and correct irregularities and unlawful acts.

A compliance program helps to deal with a constantly changing environment and to overcome obstacles that block the way to achieving business goals.

Companies design these programs to prevent risks.

In 1572, Prince William of Orange was sleeping and did not notice the danger of enemy Spanish troops entering his camp. However, the barks of his white dog saved his life.[*]

Like the Prince of Orange or the mice of Odo de Cheriton (1185–1247),[†] businesses need an effective system of alarms and internal controls to help them detect, control, and respond to threats.

---

[*] William of Orange has been portrayed at different times with his dog at his side. Manuel Prieto, *Curistoria 2*, 2017, 165.

[†] In the thirteenth century, the Catholic theologian and poet Odo de Cheriton (1185–1247) wrote *The Book of the Cats*, in which a group of mice tries to find a solution to the deaths caused by the attack of a gray cat. The mice come to the conclusion that the solution is to put a rattle on the cat so that when it moves, they can hear it and the cat cannot attack them by surprise. All the mice agree that this would be the solution to the problem, but when it comes time to choose the mouse to carry out putting the bell on the cat, each mouse makes excuses to avoid performing this risky action. Who is going to put the bell to the cat?

How can a business plan reduce unpleasant surprises? The first step is to create a compliance strategy.

Then, the correct implementation of integrity or compliance programs is an ideal means to prevent the commission of crimes and to promote and strengthen an ethical culture in the organization.

The relationship is inversely proportional: The more effective the compliance program in the organization, the lower the risk of suffering damages related to ethics and compliance risks.

Mary Gentile in her book *Giving Voice to Values* says, "If we approach our business careers with the expectation that we will face values conflicts and if we anticipate some of the most common types of conflicts... we can minimize the disabling effect that surprise can have."[*]

The best way to prevent and detect fraud is by knowing the enemy. As global business risk becomes more complex, all organizations must enhance their risk management in order to achieve their business strategy.

For Ernst and Young, "The fight against crime develops day by day and the time and effort it demands must be in line with the rest of the efforts and times that the company dedicates to carry out its business plan."[†]

A risk control program should integrate compliance activities into the business process, so each business area is responsible for the specific aspects of compliance related to its area.

The US Department of Justice, Criminal Division, and Fraud Section has created guides of specific factors prosecutors should consider in conducting an investigation to evaluate a corporate compliance program. These factors, known as "Principles of Federal Prosecution of Business Organizations" or "the Filip Factors," include the existence and effectiveness of the corporation's preexisting compliance program and the efforts to implement an effective corporate compliance program or to improve the existing one. Some of the questions that the Fraud Section has frequently found relevant in evaluating a corporate compliance program are:

What is the company root cause analysis of the misconduct at issue? What systemic issues were identified?

Were there prior opportunities to detect the misconduct in question, such as audit reports identifying relevant control failures or allegations, complaints, or investigations involving similar issues?

---

[*] Mary Gentile, *Giving Voice to Values*, Chapter 4 "It's Only Normal" (The McGraw-Hill Companies, 2010).

[†] Ernst & Young, *Fraud Report, Second National Survey 2007*.

What is the company's analysis or why such opportunities were missed? What specific changes has the company made to reduce the risk so the same or similar issues will not occur in the future? What specific corrections emerged from the problems identified in the root cause, and was the opportunity analysis lost?

In 1992, COSO* published the first report to help companies in their internal control systems and in 2004 this Committee published a second report called "Enterprise Risk Management" that extended the concept of internal control to risk management.[†] In this document it was defined that *internal control* consists of five interrelated components: (i) control environment (integrity and values), (ii) internal and external risk assessment, (iii) control activities (e.g., policies and procedures), (iv) information and communication, and (v) supervision and monitoring (checking the control system).[‡]

The main guide to designing an effective US compliance program is the US Sentencing Commission's Federal Sentencing Guidelines,[§] which set out certain recommendations that the US government uses to evaluate the quality of ethics and compliance and to determine the amounts of fines for non-compliance.

Corporate fines for non-compliance can be mitigated if the company has implemented an effective ethics and compliance program that helps prevent and detect violations of laws and demonstrates the organization has made efforts to manage an ethical culture. Other factors mitigating the amount of the fines are cooperation with the authorities or the company self-reporting to the authorities a possible case of corruption or criminal conduct within the company.

Fines, on the other hand, can be aggravated if (i) the organization has a prior history of similar conduct and does not make internal changes

---

* Since its founding in 1985 in the United States, COSO (Committee of Sponsoring Organizations of the Treadway Commission) seeks to improve internal controls within organizations. COSO studies the factors that can lead to fraudulent financial information and makes recommendations. They integrate COSO: The American Accounting Association, The American Institute of Certified Public Accountants, Financial Executives International, the Institute of Internal Auditors, and the Institute of Accountants and Finance Professionals.
† The "Enterprise Risk Management" (ERM) evaluates the total universe of business risks, including risks for inflation, insecurity, earthquakes, operational risks, threats from competitors, lack of certain products for sale, etc.
‡ In 2013, COSO published the third version of this report.
§ The United States Sentencing Commission is an independent agency of the Judicial Branch of the US government and is responsible for articulating the Sentencing Guidelines for use by the Justice Department of the United States. It was created in 1984. See www.ussc.gov.

to prevent it from occurring again; (ii) the organization obstructs an investigation; and (iii) the organization and its leaders were tolerant of or participated in the act of corruption.

The Federal Sentencing Guidelines encourage companies to promote an organizational structure that encourages ethical behavior and compliance with the law. According to the guidelines, an effective corporate compliance program is one that includes the following elements: board and management oversight and governance; adequate organizational structure with accountability; an ethical culture, periodic risk assessments and prioritization of risks; policies, procedures, standards, internal controls and training; monitoring and auditing of the program; mechanisms for reporting, responding to, investigating complaints, and corrective actions.

The Department of Justice of the United States and the Securities and Exchange Commission have also published documents that serve as a guide to attacking corruption; for example, "A Resource Guide to the US Foreign Corrupt Practices Act"* or a document called "Evaluation of Corporate Compliance Programs."†

Other resources to design compliance programs are ISO 19600 "Compliance Management System-Guidelines" (2014) and ISO 31000 "Risk Management" (2009), which are compliance standards introduced by the International Organization for Standardization (ISO)‡ and help organizations establish, develop, evaluate, and maintain a compliance management system.§

Failing to have the right controls and culture in place could mean "forking out millions in fines."¶

Both the Federal Sentencing Guidelines and the ISO standards seek to provide certain principles, guidelines, contributions, best practices, and recommendations to companies to maintain a culture of integrity.

Leaders must ask themselves if the company has a sufficiently robust plan to face the risks.

Is their house in order?

The distinction between ethics and compliance may seem like an academic exercise since these are terms sometimes used interchangeably, but the respective areas deal with different, complementary issues.

---

* www.documentcloud.org/documents/515229-a-resource-guide-to-the-u-s-foreign-corrupt.html.
† www.justice.gov/criminal-fraud/page/file/937501/download.
‡ The ISO was founded in 1947 and promotes worldwide industrial and commercial standards. ISO has its headquartered in Geneva.
§ www.iso.org.
¶ www.iso.org.

Ethical culture aims to make decisions and choices made by company employees aligned with the principles and values of the organization.

Compliance, on the other hand, not only seeks to create an awareness of the multiple risks that exist when operating an organization but also is responsible for designing tools for protection from, prevention of, and reaction against those risks to avoid or reduce their damage. Compliance refers to the development of policies, systems, training, and supervision to avoid regulatory risks.

Ethics issues, on the other hand, are more related to the specific training in the code of ethics and to the promotion and communication of the values and principles of the organization. Within this area is also the whole system of reporting allegations and investigations for violation of the code of ethics and queries related to that code.

Ethics issues are more related to events that have *internal* consequences such as situations of conflict of interest, fraternization issues, and harassment situations *versus* compliance issues that usually result in *external* consequences, such as possible fines from regulatory bodies (e.g., environmental issues, bribes, food safety, or antitrust) or requests for reports, the presence of auditors, the closure of establishments, and news in the media.

This differentiation is not always as sharp because, for example, the area of ethics is also responsible for the analysis of internal frauds which, when serious, can have external consequences such as the intervention of regulatory agencies.

Ethics and compliance programs do not release the company from all the ills and sins, but they help to achieve greater transparency in the organization and detect problems to manage them immediately. These programs inform about existing behaviors that can harm the company.

The savings achieved by avoiding and reducing theft and fraud justify the total cost of these integrity programs that let one see with more clarity what's going on in the organization. In order to sell products and services, a marketing plan is created; similarly, to reduce the company's illegality and misconduct, a compliance plan is created.

The elements and techniques recommended by the Federal Sentencing Guidelines have proven successful in combating risks. Companies must create building blocks for compliance and ethical infrastructure that prevents and protects them.

Integrity programs should be tailored to each company taking into consideration their needs, characteristics, and the context in which they operate. The content of the program is adapted according to the industry where each organization operates. All businesses are different and, therefore, there is no one-size-fits-all compliance program, but there are some recommended practices considered important and necessary to the complex and interconnected risks faced by organizations.

Section 3 of this book presents different risks that organizations face. In Section 4, you will see some good practices and essential elements of an effective ethics and compliance program that, if implemented in a coordinated way, make up an effective strategy that helps companies mitigate risks.

21.1 LEADERSHIP: THE TONE COMES FROM THE CEO

On April 19, 1998, my grandfather, the architect Ventura Mariscotti (1908–1999), delivered a speech to his grandchildren and great-grandchildren on the eve of his 90th birthday. He finished his message by saying, "I tell you, just be useful and good people."* He left his legacy to his grandchildren and great-grandchildren: the culture of effort, the value of truth, solidarity, justice, and integrity.

In companies, as in families, the tone comes from above, shows the way forward, and creates the footprint.

Children look to elders and employees to their bosses.

Ethical behavior must flow from top to bottom. Lower level employees will find it very difficult to act ethically if they are under pressure from their bosses to achieve results without emphasizing ethical behavior.

Management must articulate an ethical vision as part of the company's objectives to avoid pressures to obtain short-term benefits. For example, a salesperson under pressure to achieve a stretching sales goal may inflate profits or sales or use deceptive sales tactics to produce the requested results.

The CEO is primarily responsible for leading a culture of ethics and compliance and observing high standards of ethical conduct. But without

---

* This was the last sentence of his message: "To my grandchildren and grandchildren, children of my children, doubly children, thank you for the happiness you give me; And my great-grandchildren, the children of my children's children, who came to me as evening declined, the beautiful reality of a long dream. And today they have come to prolong my life, my name, and my memory; I tell you, be useful and good people."

credibility, the CEO will not be able to lead. Therefore, to build trust, he or she must lead by example, conduct himself or herself ethically, and be a preacher, promoter, and an ambassador of corporate morality. The best leaders not only act ethically but also encourage employees to behave ethically.

In addition to building trust by listening and taking care of employees, the CEO is responsible for building and maintaining a culture that insulates the company against ethics breaches and lack of integrity. The CEO must be the first to commit to zero tolerance of corruption and to support the integrity program.

As the authors, Kouzes and Posner say, "The center of gravity for business loyalty is the personal integrity of the senior leadership team."[*]

It is not enough for the CEO to say the right thing; he or she must be authentic in words and actions. CEO's words and actions must be consistent with values. There should not be an inconsistent morality in word and deed. Gandhi said that happiness occurs "when what you think, what you say and what you do are in harmony."[†]

Albert Einstein (1879–1955) said, "Setting an example is not the main means of influencing others, it is the only way."[‡]

Ethical behavior must be exemplified and modeled by the leader. Kent Druyvesteyn, executive of General Dynamics Corporation once said:

> People in leadership need to … set the tone by the example of their own conduct. We could have had all the workshops in the world. We could have even had Jesus and Moses and Mohammed and Buddha come and speak at our workshops. But if after all of that, someone in a leadership position then behaved in a way which was contrary to the standards that instance of misconduct by a person in a leadership position would teach more than all the experts in the world.[§]

CEOs live like in a "glass house"; all the employees look at how they behave and look for guidance and leadership. Therefore, CEOs must be very careful with their conduct and their reactions in good and bad times, not only during the time in the office but also in their private life.

---

[*] J. Kouzes and B. Posner, *Leadership the Challenge*, 3rd ed (Jossey-Bass, 2002), 34.
[†] "Mahatma Gandhi Quotes," www.brainyquote.com.
[‡] Einstein, www.goodreads.com.
[§] Linda Trevino and Katherine Nelson, *Managing Business Ethics*, 5th ed (John Wiley & Sons, Inc., 2011), 180.

If the CEO is not committed to compliance and ethical issues, the compliance officer will be a voice that preaches in the desert. The number one is the organization's face and must have the determination to make ethics and compliance a cornerstone of the business operation. It is part of his or her task to plant the seed, live the values, promote honest communication, and show respect for employees.

Senior managers have a leadership role in the implementation of the integrity program and the prevention of ethical failures. They must act prudently and diligently, allocating sufficient resources for compliance and ethics departments.* A CEO must be the first interested in the existence of an ethical culture in the organization and should never be satisfied with the actions that the company can take to help employees to do the right thing every day.

This individual must be a strategist to pilot complexity and do what is right even if it is not the most popular decision. He or she must be a leader who inspires, motivates, and be committed to integrity policies.

Embedding compliance in the behavior of the people working for an organization depends above all on leadership at all levels, clear values, and in the implementation of control measures.

The top management must openly and continually communicate the message of honesty and integrity and express its support and commitment to zero tolerance for corruption. Tim Cook, CEO of Apple Inc., has said that "it is up to the company's leaders to set the tone. Not only the CEO but all the leaders of the company."[†]

If the CEO, his or her direct reports, supervisors, and managers consider ethics and compliance issues to be a priority, the rest of the employees are more likely to do so as well. They have the power to influence the conduct, training, and knowledge of the members of the organization.

If the head of the organization does not transmit an ethical culture, the body will not either. Corporate values must be demonstrated by the behavior of corporate leaders. To create an ethical culture, senior leaders should be an example of behavior and should periodically conduct discussions with their teams on business ethics.

Managers must put moral concerns on the table because such actions reduce employee reluctance to raise ethical issues.

Sometimes managers suffer from *moral muteness*, a reluctance to discuss ethical questions with others. In a workplace environment where

---

* "The 4 Key Business Ethics Themes You Need to be Aware of in 2018," Simon Webley IBE Research Director, Institute of Business Ethics, March 2, 2018.
† Apple CEO Interview, *La Nacion*, April 14, 2015.

ethics is seldom discussed, people who do bring up ethical objections may be seen as preachy, self-righteous, and even disloyal. As a result, ethical considerations may be completely suppressed in a discussion.*

If ethical considerations are not explicitly valued and promoted within a firm, they are likely to be downgraded and avoided. An employee at National Semiconductor described how the company started breaking rules on the testing of semiconductors, for which it was fined in 1984.

As demand for semiconductors grew between 1979 and 1981, managers faced intense pressure to take shortcuts in meeting contract schedules. The company slowly began to omit required tests on the products and then falsified records to cover the omissions. Over time, more than 100 employees participated in this falsification. They knew it was unethical but there was not an ethical culture in the organization to stop the falsifications.†

The ethical message should also be directed to the suppliers and partners with whom the organization conducts business in order for them to understand the culture of the company.

CEOs lead the ship and must face the challenges and risks that come from all directions. It is the responsibility of the CEO to take the measures and decisions to reduce the vulnerability of the organization.

Business leaders are evaluated by the decisions they make. A single mistake and a single person are enough to put at risk the company. Therefore, ethics is an important issue on the CEO's agenda.

An excess of optimism and innocence can lead to underestimating the risks and having an attitude that "everything will be fine," which can cause preparation to fail in the face of unforeseen events.‡

Top management must ensure companies provide employees with all the tools to make the right decisions and to find help when they need it. The CEO, as a sponsor of the program, must ensure that the ethics and compliance area has enough budget in terms of structure, systems, training, travel expenses, and communication tools.

---

* K. Blanchard, C. Schewe, B. Nelson and A. Hiam, *Exploring the World of Business* (Worth Publishers, (1996), 124. "The Moral Muteness of Managers," *California Management Review* (Fall 1988): 228–44.

† K. Blanchard, C. Schewe, B. Nelson and A. Hiam, *Exploring the World of Business* (Worth Publishers, 1996), 124.

‡ Eugenio Andres Marchiori and Andres Hatum, "Lo que no hay que Hacer: Nueve Personajes que Pueden Costarle la Carrera a un Ejecutivo" ("What not to do: Nine Characters that Can Cost an Executive to Run,"), October 10, 2019, www.lanacion.com.ar.

CEOs have so much influence on the company culture they lead. Their opinions are often interpreted as orders, and their habits are replicated by the employees.

The chief legacy of CEOs will be their behavior and moral impact and, second, the results of their management. If they fail with their behavior, their know-how will be of no importance. In July 2018, the CEO of Texas Instruments resigned after seven weeks. The company said in a statement, "The violations [of the company's code of conduct] are related to personal behavior that is not consistent with our ethics and core values."[*]

As Kenneth Goodpaster, professor at the University of St. Thomas, St. Paul, Minnesota, said in a speech at the Center for Business Ethics at Bentley University, "The future of the corporation is tethered to the future of responsible management."[†]

You cannot ask employees to do something the person asking for it is not willing to do. The best motivation and teaching is of a leader who sets the example and is consistent between what he or she says and does. The audio must match the video.

Aesop (600–564 BC) was a famous fabulist from ancient Greece who told this story:

> One day a crab saw his son moving sideways, and he tried to correct him so he would walk forward. The young crab said to the father, "I do what you do. I think you should correct your walking first so that I follow suit. If you want me to walk forward, do it so I can imitate you."[‡]

The SEC Commissioner Cynthia Glassman has said that "adopting a Code of Ethics means little if the CEO or its directors make clear through their conduct that it does not apply to them."[§]

Employees expect from the CEO honesty, fair decisions, and transparency. Employees will not trust and follow the CEO if this person does not have a good reputation. Without trust and respect, the CEO will not be able to lead or fulfill company objectives.

Dwight Eisenhower (1890–1969), the 34th president of the United States, said, "To have followers, the leader must be reliable. Therefore, the supreme

---

[*] Julia Horowitz, "Texas Instruments CEO resigns over 'personal behavior,'" July 17, 2018, money. cnn.com.

[†] Kenneth E. Goodpaster, "Tenacity: The American Pursuit of Corporate Responsibility," Center for Business Ethics at Bentley University, February 4, 2013, www.bentley.edu.

[‡] The Spanish writer Felix Samaniego (1745–1801) has also written a similar fable about crabs.

[§] April 7, 2003, www.sec.gov.

quality of a leader is his unquestioned integrity. Without it, there is no real success possible."*

Jeffrey E. Garten, a professor at the Yale School of Management, says, "Trust is the glue that holds everything together. Without an Executive Director who has confidence and who inspires it, the company is in danger."†

Writer Donald T. Phillips says,

> Trust, honesty, and integrity are exceptionally important qualities because they strongly affect followers. Most individuals need to trust other people, particularly their bosses. The subordinates must see in their leader an honored person at all times if the leader wants them to commit.‡

Part of the task of a CEO, as the organization's chief ethical leader, is to educate, promote, and protect the culture of the company. The person in that role must develop a reputation for ethical leadership inside and outside of the company.

Ben Heineman Jr., a former senior GE executive and the leader of the design of the ethics and compliance program at that company, says, "To achieve an organization with high performance and integrity, the CEO has the fundamental role of leading a culture of values that can influence how employees think and behave."§

John William Gardner (1912–2002) explains that "The leaders whom we admire most help to revitalize our shared beliefs and values. They have always spent a portion of their time teaching the value framework."¶

Berkeley professor of sociology Philip Selznick (1919–2010) in his book *Leadership and Administration* wrote that "The leader is primarily an expert in promoting and protecting values."**

Hundred percent of compliance should be the goal. As Ben van Beurden, CEO of Shell, says, "Anything less than 100% compliance undermines our performance and risks high costs that would hurt our bottom line as well as our hard-earned."††

---

* John Maxwell, *Developing the Leader within You* (Nelson, 1993), 38.
† Jeffrey E. Garten, *The Mind of the CEO* (Editorial Norma, 2001), 158.
‡ Donald Phillips, *Lincoln y el Liderazgo* (Deusto, 1993), 73.
§ Ben Heineman Jr., *High Performance with High Integrity* (Harvard Business Review Press, 2008), 25.
¶ Walter Gmelch and Jeffrey Buller, *Building Academic Leadership Capacity* (Jossey-Bass, 2015), 179. John William Gardner was Secretary of Health, Education, and Welfare under President Lyndon Johnson. Also see, John Gardner, *El Liderazgo* (Grupo Editor Latinoamericano, 1989), 30.
** Thomas Peters and Robert Waterman Jr., *En Búsqueda de la Excelencia* (Ed. Atlantida, 1994), 86.
†† "Our Code of Conduct," Making the Right Decisions. Shell.

However, there is always a gap between the results sought (100% integrity and compliance) and what you get. Being in 100% compliance in a large company every day, in all business units, and by all employees, and all suppliers does not seem possible. There will be failures. But what is feasible is to reduce the lack of compliance.

Enron's slogan was "Respect, Integrity, Community, and Excellence," but its leaders did the opposite. The CEO must procure that values live within the organization. Including matters such as integrity and risk issues in business plans and strategy meetings, the CEO shows that these issues are not a slogan; he or she sets the tone and makes clear the importance of business ethics. CEOs and managers must comply with policies and participate in ethics training like any other employee.

Larry Bossidy, who was the CEO of Honeywell International, a multinational engineering services conglomerate, said, "When I select a new business manager, the first thing I say is that you should behave with the highest integrity. This is a subject where there is no second chance. ... If you break the rules you are fired."[*]

Santa Clara University, a Jesuit University located in Silicon Valley, asked hundreds of organizational managers which were the most important characteristics of admired leaders. Managers first considered "a leadership style of honesty and integrity" and only secondly "a forward-looking vision for the company."[†]

In another study of 195 leaders over 30 global organizations published by *Harvard Business Review*, participants were asked to choose the most important leadership competences from a list of 74. The most important competence chosen was "high ethical and moral standards."[‡]

Competition can create opportunities for unethical behavior. Pressures to achieve results test leaders' commitment to the culture of integrity. The pressure is great to get more sales, get ahead of the competition, and accelerate growth. Leaders must watch carefully to ensure they are not rewarding unethical behaviors.

As the British-American motivational speaker Simon Sinek says,

---

[*] Larry Bossidy and Ram Charan, *Execution: The Discipline of Getting Things Done* (New York, Crown Business, 2002).

[†] "Follower-Oriented Leadership," Characteristics of Admired Leaders, James M. Kouzes, Barry Z. Posner, Santa Clara University (2004), 495.

[‡] Sunnie Giles, "The Most Important Leadership Competencies According to Leaders Around the World," *Harvard Business Review* (March 15, 2016), hbr.org/2016/03/the-most-important-leadership-competencies-according-to-leaders-around-the-world.

Effective leaders must have courage. It is difficult, it is difficult to resist the pressure and have the courage to do the right thing even if by doing so you can lose your job. The best leaders have that courage, only the best.*

There is no point in achieving a short-term success in sales and growth if that goal is not achieved within the norms, policies, and codes of ethics that regulate and set limits to the actions of the organization.

During the decision-making process, the only focus of managers should never be just the profitability and the bottom line. Great leaders make decisions based on financial and ethical analysis.

The best leaders handle the tension between business objectives and company values and subordinate *what* needs to be done to *how* to do it. Results and profits can be obtained only through ethical-legal behavior, overcoming any pressure and/or temptation. The CEO cannot be dominated by the pressure of making the numbers without considering the ethical and human side of every decision.

Decisions should not be limited to financial calculations. The organizational culture must be based on values and not on a monetary purpose. As Professor Jorge Etkin says, it is necessary to integrate the economic dimension with the human one, because "when the economy is above the social, the organization is sick."†

Professors Linda Trevino and Katherine Nelson write,

> Employees need to know that executive leaders in their organization care about ethics at least as much as financial performance. An ethical leader makes it clear that strong bottom-line results are expected, but only if they can be delivered in a highly ethical manner.‡

In large corporations, accountability and controls might be improved when the roles of CEO and Chairman are under different people. This governance method allows a system of checks and balances that makes it more difficult for CEOs to get away with controversial acts. What happened with the former Chairman and CEO of Renault-Nissan-Mitsubishi could

---

* Simon Sinek, "Love and Relationships," September 18, 2017, beinspiredchannel.com/alarms, YouTube.

† Jorge Etkin, Conference at the Faculty of Economic Sciences of the University of Buenos Aires, Amartya Sen Seminar, April 2015, www.youtube.com.

‡ Linda Trevino and Katherine Nelson, *Managing Business Ethics*, 5th ed (John Wiley & Sons, Inc., 2011), 166.

be an example of where a split Chairman and CEO role could have deterred some of his decisions.*

Carlos Ghosn is a Brazilian-born businessman who was the chairman and CEO of the Nissan-Renault-Mitsubishi Alliance for several years, until November 1, 2018. Ghosn was arrested at Tokyo International Airport (Haneda) on November 19, 2018, on allegations of under-reporting his earnings and misuse of company assets.† The allegation included, among others, misuse of private plans, and expenses in apartments and houses in Amsterdam, Beirut, and Tokyo.‡

Nissan Motors has filed suit against Carlos Ghosn, seeking ten billion yen (US$91 million) in payback for claimed damages inflicted through alleged financial misconduct. Nissan said in a news release: "The financial damages by Nissan are linked to Ghosn's breach of fiduciary duty as a company director and his misappropriation of Nissan's resources and assets."§

The board of directors must be involved in the evaluation and supervision of the integrity program and as the final controller of the program, it should receive at least a quarterly update on the progress of the ethics and compliance program in training, policy changes, improvements in controls, resources, identified new risks, ethical survey results, benchmark, and trends. In other words, the program must be on the directory's discussion agenda. It is also advisable to keep the board informed of the most serious ethical issues, comparisons made with industry standards, and emerging risks.

Once the decision to implement an ethics and compliance program has been taken, the CEO should delegate to a specialist its design and implementation: the Compliance Officer.

21.2 ETHICS AND COMPLIANCE OFFICER, ORGANIZATIONAL STRUCTURE, AND REPORTING LINES

The leader in charge of the compliance department must have a specialized work team with the following functions: (i) the operation and supervision

---

* Betsy Atkins, "Business Ethics And Integrity: It Starts With The Tone At The Top," February 7, 2019, www-forbes-com.cdn.ampproject.org.
† en.wikipedia.org/wiki/Carlos_Ghosn.
‡ Business Insider, Meira Gebe, Taylor Nicole Rogers, January 6, 2020.
§ "Nissan Seeks 10 Billion Yen in Damages from Former Chairman Carlos Ghosn over Misconduct and Fraudulent Activity," global.nissannews.com.

of the integrity program; (ii) supervision of contacts with the ethics office, complaints and consultations on ethics and compliance issues; (iii) the evaluation of trends on the basis of the information received; (iv) leadership and general coordination and resolution in a reasonable time of complaints and investigations; (v) training in ethics and compliance; (vi) marketing and communication tools on reporting lines; (vii) the preparation, execution, and follow-up of the risk assessment process; (viii) the implementation of related policies, due diligence, systems, and procedures related to the different risks of the organization; (ix) coordination of the Integrity Committee and participation in the executive committee.

In order to define the program design, certain factors should be considered, such as the size of the organization, the countries in which it operates, the laws applicable to the particular industry, and the history of the company in terms of risks, fines, and litigation.

In recent years, the compliance area has had a growing influence on companies in approving and authorizing businesses.

In an article entitled "Why do all companies look for a legal compliance officer?" published in the Spanish newspaper *La Vanguardia* on May 29, 2015, attorney Alain Casanovas Ysla, partner of KPMG, said,

> Today to be the administrator of a company is a risky profession and no manager wants to risk breaking a rule by the action of an employee or by the simple ignorance of the existence of a specific rule in a country. Therefore, they hire an expert who cares about regulatory compliance.*

Effective leaders focus on processes and designs, and the compliance officer is in charge of designing, implementing, coordinating, and supervising the ethics and compliance program. In its role as a guardian angel of the organization, the compliance officer must implement controls and processes to prevent and reduce risks and threats to the security of the company. Part of the tasks of the compliance officer is to think strategically about tomorrow's risks and manage adequate controls to detect, prevent, and respond to compliance failures.

The compliance officer must keep senior management informed of the risks to which the company is exposed and how to prevent or avoid them. In his role as an arbitrator, he must clearly indicate to the company's leaders what the limits of action are within the law and internal policies.

---

* "¿Por qué Todas las Empresas Buscan un Legal Compliance Officer?" *La Vanguardia*, July 15, 2014, www.tribunadelcompliance.com ("Why do all Companies look for a Legal Compliance Officer?").

A major challenge for the compliance officer will be to obtain the approval and support of the CEO and the board of directors in their task of creating and maintaining an adequate ethics and compliance infrastructure. It is necessary that the compliance officer has the appropriate tools and resources to respond to risk prevention.

Whoever occupies the position must have interpersonal relations, be proactive, and manage the issues with confidentiality.

The compliance officer must also have knowledge and experience in the analysis of cases. It is also convenient that he or she should be certified as an ethics and compliance expert.

The compliance officer is the second line of defense for the company against risks. The first line of defense is formed by the leader of the area or department where the risk arises and the third line of defense is the area of internal audit.

The Aspen Institute is an international non-profit organization founded in 1949 and based in Washington D.C. It is dedicated to promoting exemplary leadership and appreciation of eternal ideas and values, as well as open dialogue in contemporary problems.

Judith Samuelson, founder and executive director of the Aspen Business and Society Program, said in 2003,

> Managers with the courage and skill set to rise the right questions and sound the right bell, not just when there is an ethical or legal problem in the firm but when the problems and the implications to risk management and reputation lie far outside the gate, these managers are going to be in great demand.*

The compliance officer must have the independence of judgment and even oppose the decisions of the CEO when deemed necessary. He or she should give voice to values and defend them in all circumstances. Because what is wrong, it is wrong even if the CEO and the managers in the company do it, and what is right, it is right even if nobody does it.

The compliance officer should question what are the ethical dilemmas related to business initiatives and how to solve them.

The general administrator of railways of the Argentine State, Engineer Pablo Nogues (1878–1943), refused a request from Argentine President

---

* Judith Samuelson, "Leadership and Values: Moving Beyond the Ethics Debate," September 22, 2003. Judith Samuelson is the founder and executive director of the Aspen Institute's Business and Society Program.

Agustin Pedro Justo (1876–1943) to hire a specific person. Nogues replied, "The only vacant post is mine."* That kind of independence of criteria and invulnerability to pressures is what a compliance officer should have.

The referee Horacio Elizondo's decision to expel the French soccer player Zinedine Zidane from the game for using his head to hit the chest of the Italian Materazzi in the final of the World Cup of 2006 was not influenced by the fact that Zidane was the captain and idol of France, nor that he was playing his last game with 34 years of age, nor that it was the World Cup final.

The independence of criteria that Elizondo showed to evaluate the facts and apply the regulation is the one that should prevail in any compliance officer.[†]

To ensure the independence of judgment and action in the different geographic areas where the organization operates, the local compliance officers working in other countries should report to the global or regional compliance officer and only indirectly (dotted line) to the general manager that leads the business of the company in that country. This structure seeks to ensure the officer's position, salary, or benefits are not dependent exclusively on the decision of the country's general manager of the company where the compliance officer works so that compliance officer's independence of judgment and supervision are not affected.

In addition, the compliance officer must have an alternative reporting line for critical cases; for example, where the responsibility of one of his or her bosses is involved. Only sufficient guarantees of independence will be given when, if the situation requires, he or she can communicate directly with the company's Board of Directors or the CEO.

A practice some organizations use to ensure transparency and objectivity in communicating risks is for the board to meet periodically with the global compliance officer without the presence of the global CEO.

Compliance officers must participate in the strategic planning of the company, so they can express their opinion and question *how* the projects are carried out. Also, the ethics and compliance officer must be a member of the executive committee of the company where he or she acts and must sit at the executive table with the rest of the country general manager's direct reports.

---

* Raúl Mariscotti, *El Modelo Federal* (Ediciones Nueva Técnica, 1993), 251 ("The Federal Model").
† Zidane's actions made headlines all over the world, the front page of *L'Equipe* asked, "What should we tell our children, for whom you have become an example for ever? … How could that happen to a man like you?" en.wikipedia.org/wiki/Zinedine_Zidane.

If the compliance officer is seen as part of senior management, he or she is more likely to enjoy greater credibility by peers and receive the internal support required to effectively discharge his or her role.

In some organizations, the area of compliance is included within the responsibilities of the legal department. In others, there is a compliance officer with the same hierarchical position as the head of the legal area or the head of the internal audit area.

Does the ethics and compliance officer need to be a lawyer? The American Bar Association recommends that the director or vice president of the legal area of a company listed on the stock exchange in the United States be primarily responsible for the issues of ethics and compliance.*

The complexity of legislation and regulations can justify the desirability of an attorney in these duties because he or she is familiar with reading legal reports on corruption issues, regulations, and evaluation of evidence.

Some organizations seek compliance to position an internal executive with knowledge on the history and culture of the company and the operation. Other companies prefer instead – and usually after a crisis – to recruit an expert outside the organization who brings new perspectives and ensures the professional independence in order to avoid having the executive be tied to old loyalties.

The ethics and compliance officer, in charge of the direction and coordination of the compliance program, is responsible for transforming facts in patterns, identifying and assessing risks, coordinating mitigation plans, implementing internal reporting processes, coordinating investigations, recommending disciplinary sanctions, and presenting reports periodically to senior management.

The head of compliance must understand the business he or she controls in order to build trust among the members of the company; know the rules and policies; and cultivate a productive relationship with employees and peers. Effective leadership is based on relationships and to foster trust leaders need to be approachable.

The compliance officer must always consider the ethical implications of business initiatives.

The ethics and compliance officer is the leader and coordinator of a group of experts in risk areas and operators who must monitor compliance with laws and procedures in the different areas of the business.

---

* See James Cheek III, *Report of the American Bar Association, Task Force on Corporate Responsibility* (2003), www. Abanet.org/buslaw.

Compliance and ethics directors and/or vice presidents should be also distributed in certain markets and international regions where the company operates, professionals who have experience and ability to decide on a multiplicity of issues related to the day-to-day business. All of them should work as a team, collaborating and interacting together with the business areas to understand the risks and problems they face in order to achieve the objectives in the most efficient way possible.

Those who lead the areas of legal, security, audit, human resources, and finance should work as partners of the ethics and compliance officer as guardians of the organization.

Finally, when restructuring companies, it is important to measure the consequences of cutting areas of effective control that do not generate sales. Changes in the structure made by companies without considering the impact on the safety of employees or the environment can generate serious inconveniences and collateral effects.

21.3 ETHICS AND COMPLIANCE COMMITTEE OR INTEGRITY COMMITTEE

The Ethics and Compliance Committee is a vehicle that allows managers to take notice and discuss business risks. This committee oversees the integrity program and makes recommendations to identify, monitor, and mitigate risks. It also facilitates the development and implementation of the measures considered appropriate.

In short, the Integrity Committee acts as an advisory body that analyzes and debates compliance issues.

These committees should be composed of the CEO and his or her direct reports, globally, regionally, and in each market where the company operates. Ideally, the committee should meet every one or two months and analyze the follow-up on risk mitigation plans, training status, new regulations, statistics, and, eventually, ethics surveys.

The issues discussed should include metrics on trends in ethics cases, number of contacts received, cases closed and tested, percentage of anonymous cases, average time to conduct investigations and close cases, and systems and processes that need to be improved and modified as a result of investigated and substantiated allegations, the number of disciplinary sanctions and dismissals for ethics problems, and classification of allegations by category of conduct (e.g., fraud, theft, illegal use of inside information, money laundering, harassment, violence at work, conflict of interest, corruption, commercial bribery, etc.).

Any relevant information on new legislation, permits and licensing status, harassment, fraud, and/or theft should also be shared in these committee meetings.

These meetings should avoid mentioning specific allegations against any of the organization's leaders, or, even, situations of sexual harassment, which are dealt with in meetings with the human resources leader and/or the CEO.

The committee must have a work agenda and keep a record of the meetings that it carries out.

21.4 CODE OF ETHICS

A code of conduct or ethics is a core part of an integrity program and applies to all employees, including the CEO and the board of directors.

This document sets out the expectations the company has about how its employees should behave and guides them in making ethical decisions. The code reflects the values, principles, and beliefs of the organization and against them, any decision or action made by employees may be collated. This document emphasizes the commitment of the organization to compliance and business ethics.

In the 1980s, less than 10% of large corporations in the United States had a code of ethics. The Sarbanes-Oxley Act of 2002 forced US-listed companies to have an ethics code and today almost 100% of the 1,000 largest companies in the United States have an internal document on business ethics.

In May 2012, a Harvard University professor noticed abnormalities in some of the answers on the exam. An investigation was initiated that resulted in the expulsion of 70 students for cheating on the exam. The dean of the undergraduate college described the case as "unprecedented in scope and magnitude."* In 2014, the Harvard Academic Integrity Committee drafted a Code of Honor.

---

* Richard Perez-Pena, "Harvard Students in Cheating Scandal Say Collaboration Was Accepted," August 31, 2012, www.nytimes.com.

The code of ethics or conduct defines the company and establishes the treatment that must exist with its customers, suppliers, and employees. The document communicates values and the organizational culture, establishes expectations of conduct, and promotes the ethical culture and the commitment to compliance with the law. In addition, the code should include questions, queries, and ethical dilemmas and their responses. It is similar to a guide, beacon, or control tower that prevents the plane from crashing.

It is like a GPS employee uses to make correct decisions aligned with the organization's culture. This document is like a compass that helps employees navigating the decisions they make at work.

Codes of ethics are an important but not sufficient tool. Just as in the countries there are criminal codes but still lawbreakers, a code of ethics is not enough if it is not accompanied by a clear commitment of the top management to the values that are proclaimed.

A code of conduct establishes standards of conduct, is written in the official language of the organization, and must be translated into all the languages of countries where the company operates and has employees. Kirk O. Hanson, professor of ethics at Santa Clara University, said in 2014,

> About five or six years ago … I started to ask big American companies with operations in China if they had translated their code of conduct into the Chinese language. For most of them, the answer was no. I would say, how the hell can you communicate the company's commitment to compliance or ethics if you don't even have it in the local language?*

A generic code or a copy of codes must be avoided because the code must include the identity of each organization. Its content varies depending on the type of industry, its history, its corporate culture, and the regulatory environment.

The draft code should be reviewed by the legal department and by the legal departments of the different countries where the company operates.

It is recommended that the introduction to the code be preceded by a letter from the CEO, where the tone of the organization is clearly established. The letter should emphasize the importance of good behavior for the achievement of business objectives.

---

* Kirk Hanson, "The six ethical dilemmas every professional face," speech delivered at Center for Business Ethics at Bentley University, February 3, 2014.

Code of ethics should be communicated to as many employees as possible, and their writing style should be simple, direct, and include examples. Ideally, a printed version should be distributed to each employee. Large companies, with thousands of employees, can create a webpage or an app, for the purposes of digital communication of the code of ethics.

It should be kept in mind, however, that in some regions of the world many employees do not have access to the technology that allows them to access the digital version.

The best code designs are those that use colors, large letters, photos, and graphics that maximize understanding. PepsiCo, Walmart, Lockheed Martin, Kimberly-Clark, Johnson & Johnson, Dow Corning, and Wells Fargo & Co. are good examples of such codes.

The document should make clear how to raise complaints and how to ask advice or opinions of the office of ethics. It should include the e-mail addresses and telephone contact numbers where an employee can make complaints. It should be clarified that complaints may or may not be anonymous and if an employee violates the provisions of the code of ethics, he or she will be sanctioned.

The code must clearly communicate the organization does not accept reprisals against employees who make good-faith complaints. The fact that a complaint is not verified after being investigated does not imply that the employee who made the complaint acted in bad faith.

It is good practice for employees to sign an acknowledgment of receipt of the code and the commitment to read and fulfill it.

The code should be reviewed and updated periodically – every three or five years – because it is a document that must remain in force in the face of constant changes in business and employee behavior. The document responds to the issues and risks that are emerging over time and incorporates new processes and changes in regulations.

21.5 INTERNAL POLICIES

Internal policies are minimum global standards for company operations that establish the expectations of the organization consistently in the face of situations that may arise. They are written statements of governing principles designed to address specific risks.

The company can count on policies and codes of ethics, but if they are not observed or respected, it is as if they were "pictures hanging on the wall."* Any organization should consider at least the following internal policies:

(I) Anti-corruption: Bribes and improper payments are prohibited, with zero tolerance for the payment or acceptance of bribes, even if this implies loss of money or project delays. The interaction with public officials must be explained in detail in the internal policy to reduce the risk of corruption. Organizations must create internal policies and processes to regulate donations to political campaigns and sale of products to governments – national, provincial, or municipal – including prior approval controls related to the delivery of gifts to public officials. Consultants or agents chosen to mediate with foreign governments should be selected carefully. It is advisable to know the opinion of the embassy and/or the consulate and ensure that the consultant is a recognized company in the market. It would be a warning if the company requests that the payment for its services be made in a bank account in a tax haven or if it demanded that the payment be made in cash. Companies should conduct due diligence of their current and potential suppliers and partners. Companies must also implement financial control procedures to ensure that expenditures are detailed and actually reflect the transactions performed, which are legal and in compliance with the organization's anti-corruption policies.

(II) Financial Controls and Accounting: Books and records should be accurate and detailed. The accounting process must capture all transactions, and the financial control must register all donations that take place.† The amounts, descriptions, and prices recorded must be correct, as well as the period in which the transaction is performed. Registered information must be accurate and reliable.

(III) Non-discrimination: Any type of discrimination in the selection, promotion, and dismissal of employees must be prohibited. Adopting global standards of non-discrimination in the employment of

---

* Jackie Wills, "Cómo se Logra un Buen Comportamiento," *Revista Gestión*, July–August 1996, 140. ("How a Good Behavior is Achieved").

† For large corporations, the issue of donations is relevant. For example, Walmart and Walmart Foundation donate more than US$1 billion a year.

personnel is necessary for a diverse and transnational enterprise. The principle of non-discrimination is not only important to give all employees the same opportunities in a company, but also to recruit minority groups and talented people.

(IV) Safety at Work: Business units (factories, stores) must provide safety to workers. Accidents or factory fires must be prevented or avoided, introducing new requirements and processes that improve the health and safety of workers (company or suppliers) and reduce the risk of accidents. These policies are necessary to establish a minimum standard of occupational safety. Policies on banning alcohol, tobacco, and certain drugs are recommended to reduce the risk of accidents, improve the working environment, and reduce absenteeism. Businesses have an obligation to keep the workplace safe, and alcohol and gambling can affect the judgment of employees. Organizations must provide employees with the necessary protection equipment for certain tasks.

(V) Environment: Product development and pollution reduction in the manufacturing process is an important issue for the community, for customers, and for the image of the company. Protecting and preserving the environment is central to achieving sustainable development and there are OECD Guidelines on these topics. These recommendations provide principles and standards for responsible business conduct of multinational corporations.* A company is committed to the environment when it takes into account the environmental impact of its activities. The Canadian market research firm Corporate Knights lists the 100 most sustainable companies in the world, giving as an example the multinationals that care and commit themselves to the environment, for which they implemented programs of energy-saving and control of toxic waste and pollution. Reviewing this list allows delving into the best practices these companies apply and incorporate them into the internal politics of the company. To help communicate business action to the community and the shareholders, the Global

---

* The OECD Guidelines for Multinational Enterprises recommend that managers of enterprises give appropriate attention to environmental issues in their business strategies and day-to-day operations. Organization for Economic Cooperation and Development (OECD), "Guidelines for Multinational Enterprises," www.oecd.org (Better Policies for Better Lives); The Business for a Better World, www.bsr.org/. See also "OECD Guidelines for Multinational Enterprises," en.wikipedia.org/wiki/OECD_Guidelines_for_Multinational_Enterprises.

Reporting Initiative (GRI)* created the first global standard for the development of sustainability reports for companies wishing to assess their economic, environmental, and social performance.† Many companies publish a sustainability report, also known as a corporate social responsibility (CSR) or environmental, social, and governance (ESG) report. GRI's framework for sustainability reporting helps companies identify, gather, and report this information in a clear and comparable manner. First launched in 2000, GRI's sustainability reporting framework is now widely used.‡

(VI) Conflicts of Interest: Employees of the organization must report annually if they have equity participation in competing companies and/or suppliers, if they have family members working in the company (and their position), and if they have relatives working in competing companies or suppliers.

(VII) Background Check: Companies should review the background of potential employees and employees they want to promote. The purpose of this background analysis is to identify candidates whose past behavior is inconsistent with company values. The organization should not promote and/or hire those who have a past with unlawful or unethical conduct.

(VIII) Computer Security or Cybersecurity: Computer security refers to the protection, storage, transport, and good use of information and data. The organization must establish processes to safeguard, control, and store information.§ The information stored in the company's computers and cell phones is owned by the organization. Precautions should be taken in relation to cyber-attacks. For example, the policy will establish the use of passwords, the firewall system to block unauthorized access, the use of antivirus and antispyware software, the updates of antivirus and software, file

---

* The Global Reporting Initiative was founded in 1997 in Boston, USA. It is an international independent standards organization that helps businesses, governments, and other organizations understand and communicate their impacts on issues such as climate change, human rights, and corruption. en.wikipedia.org/wiki/Global_Reporting_Initiative.

† Issues reported in sustainability reports include surveys, audited suppliers, money invested in education and training, compliance and ethics structures, compliance matters, etc.

‡ "Global reporting initiative," en.wikipedia.org/wiki/Global_Reporting_Initiative.

§ The ISO 27001 standard establishes standards for the security of information. The ISO 27018 standard allows certified cloud service providers to communicate to their clients that the protection and privacy of the data are guaranteed.

encryption, cloud storage, backup copies on external disks, avoid apps that do not come from Apple Store or Google Play, approval of the level of computer security of providers, cybersecurity insurance, avoid public Wi-Fi networks to reduce the risk of a man-in-the-middle (MITM) attack that could insert malware or steal data, etc. Computer security serves to guarantee the privacy of the information and the continuity of systems. Some companies use the COBIT model to control the flow of information.* The organization must also create response protocols in case of computer attacks.

(IX)   Money Laundering: There should be a policy to prevent and detect money laundering that establishes limits on the use of financial products and the monitoring of suspicious transactions. No employee shall knowingly engage in or assist any person or entity in any activity that involves money laundering or transactions in order to avoid disclosure to governmental authorities.

(X)   Anti-monopoly: Antitrust policies protect competition and prohibit agreements that restrict trade. They establish procedures to set prices and contact competitors. These policies are based on laws that seek to avoid the creation of monopolies.

(XI)   Food Safety: Ensure food products come from suppliers with GFSI certifications,† establish processes for product recall and to maintain adequate temperature, verify pest controls, avoid cross-contamination processes, and ensure the maintenance of the cold chain. Establish processes of reception, storage, separation, and rotation of food products.

(XII)   Employment: Implement systems that control the entry and exit of employees, and correct payment for working hours.

(XIII)   Licenses and Permits: Document the required licenses, monitor the licenses of suppliers and partners, and establish procedures and management systems to secure them and prevent them from expiring.

---

* COBIT stands for Control Objectives for Information and Related Technology. It is a framework created by ISACA (Information Systems Audit and Control Association) for IT governance and management. It was designed to be a supportive guideline for managers that can be applied to any organization in any industry. COBIT ensures the quality, control, and reliability of information systems in organizations. See "COBIT," en.wikipedia.org/wiki/COBIT.

† The Global Food Safety Initiative (GFSI) is a private organization, established and managed by the international trade association, the Consumer Goods Forum in May 2000. The GFSI maintains a scheme to benchmark food safety standards for manufacturers as well as farm assurance standards. en.wikipedia.org/wiki/Global_Food_Safety_Initiative.

(XIV) Tenders: Develop a procedure to regulate the transparent purchase of goods and the contracting of services above certain amounts.

(XV) Internal investigations: Internal investigation actions must respond to a protocol that ensures and guarantees the dignity of the person interviewed. It is not appropriate to inquire about private aspects of the interview (sexual, political, religious, union, or cultural preferences). The information stored in the cell phones and computers of the company can be used in internal investigations.

Employees are not expected to memorize internal policies, but rather to have a basic idea of the issues covered by those policies. To do so, training is used.

22

Designing an Effective Ethics and Compliance Program: Unit 2

22.1 TRAINING

Ethics should not remain in statements of principles; it is necessary to promote educational actions and create internal spaces for discussion. Training is a fundamental tool to transfer knowledge and information and to impact the thinking and behavior of individuals. It helps to think, mobilize people, and plays an important role in the process of raising awareness about corporate ethics and risks and for the creation of a culture of integrity in any organization.

The Italian philosopher and jurist Cesare Beccaria (1738–1794), at the age of 25, wrote a short work titled *On Crimes and Punishments*, an essay that was important in the development of criminal law.

In the book, the author expresses the best method to prevent crime is education. Beccaria argues that if people were educated and knew what the illegal behavior is, many would not commit it and for that he recommends clear laws, written in the language of the people subject to them.

Former Argentine president Domingo Faustino Sarmiento (1811–1888) said that "all problems are problems of education."*

In teaching processes, there are different ways and methods to improve learning.

---

* Domingo Faustino Sarmiento, akifrases.com/frase/144355.

For example, the Greek philosopher Socrates (470 BC–399 BC) used the *maieutic method*, a teaching technique based on questions that forced his disciples to think and find a solution to moral problems.

The Italian priest John Bosco Occhiena (1815–1888), known as Don Bosco, developed a preventive educational system for the training of young people at risk. The Salesian Preventive method teaches the virtues and guides youth toward a future with fewer risks, insisting on the importance of young people knowing and understanding regulations, so they know how to distinguish good from evil. Don Bosco said, "Educate young people to become ... honest citizens."*

Osvaldo R. Agatiello, professor of International Economics and Governance, Geneva School of Diplomacy and International Relations, says, "The teaching of moral principles fosters reasoning and dignified behavior and helps identify potential conflicts between individual ethics and everyday business practices."†

The American writer Ralph Waldo Emerson (1803–1882) said, "Thought is the seed of action.‡ ... The mind, once stretched by a new idea, never returns to its original dimensions."§

Carlos Kasuga, a Mexican businessman, and son of Japanese immigrants, president of Yakult Mexico, said, "We must educate companies since the only way to generate wealth is through education. ... The foundation of Yakult's success lies in educating its colleagues to be quality men."¶

Training is one of the main protections against risks. Sometimes employees end up making wrong decisions for the simple reason company leaders do not encourage ethical decision-making and occasionally the pressure to do something wrong might be strong.

The training does not pretend that the members of the organization become morally superior beings, but it does intend that the employees obtain more information and ask questions to help them act ethically before making decisions.

---

* "Few words and a lot of action, an introduction to the working style of Don Bosco": 25. www. donboscoyouth.net.
† Osvaldo Agatiello, "De Taylor a Matsushita: El Empresario Socialmente Responsable," 1992, 53 ("From Taylor to Matsushita: The Socially Responsible Businessman").
‡ Ralph Waldo Emerson, www.goodreads.com/quotes/307921-thought-is-the-seed-of-action.
§ Ralph Waldo Emerson, www.goodreads.com/quotes/37815-the-mind-once-stretched-by-a-new-i dea-never-returns.
¶ Luis Valls, "Carlos Kasuga, el líder detrás de Yakult," July 6, 2013, www.forbes.com.mx/carlos-kasuga-el-lider-detras-de-yakult/. See also Marisol Garcia Fuentes, "10 minutos con Carlos Kasuga," www.entrepreneur.com/article/264879 ("Carlos Kasuga, the leader behind Yakult"; "10 minutes with Carlos Kasuga?").

Organizations have the need to train their members to develop ethical reasoning and to be better prepared to successfully face the ethical dilemmas and risks that may arise in their jobs.

Employees should analyze ethical cases, identify the key facts and conflicting values and then, communicate the values and principles that influence their position.

For example, at the Ethics Institute at Kent Place School, in New Jersey, USA, secondary school students discussed the case of an individual who enters a coffee shop wearing a T-Shirt with a Swastika, which clearly offends other customers. What should the manager do? How does one balance the right to freedom of expression with the rights of the community?*

Ethics education improves performance and reasoning abilities and helps employees to test and reflect on their own values. Ethics training helps individuals understand what the company expects of them; to behave appropriately in every situation that comes their way.

Employees will find themselves in situations where the course of action is not clear and where they will have to face dilemmas and decide between doing the right thing or opting for the wrong.

There are situations in which acting out of ethics can appear to be a good business in the short term. To avoid bad decisions, companies must permanently train their employees and must be clear in the commitment to always act within ethics.

Organizations that do not provide ethical training to its employees are failing to do that which should be done. The lack of ethics training can be considered deliberate misconduct or omission or indifference of corporate leaders.

Ethical guidance is important to control employee's behaviors. Professors Linda Trevino and Katherine Nelson have written that "organizations that neglect to teach their members ethical behavior maybe are tacitly encouraging unethical behavior through it."[†]

Tom Butz of Koch Industries said that "bad decisions come from either gap in knowledge and skills or gap in values and beliefs. For knowledge and skills gaps, employees may get more training or better tools. For values and beliefs gaps, employees may be dismissed."[‡]

---

[*] Linda Flanagan, "What students Gian from learning ethics in school," May 24, 2019, KQED.ORG.
[†] Linda Trevino and Katherine Nelson, *Managing Business Ethics*, 5th ed (John Wiley & Sons Inc., 2011), 18.
[‡] Linda Trevino and Katherine Nelson, *Managing Business Ethics*, 5th ed (John Wiley & Sons Inc., 2011), 250.

It is management's responsibility to provide guidance in an ethical direction. Companies must train their employees to prevent falling into the temptations that exist in business life.

Therefore, it is necessary to educate about ethical principles and standards of conduct regarding what the organization expects from its employees. One way to do this is by identifying those potential risks and challenges employees may face in their work. Once these challenges have been identified, the members of the organization should be trained on the existence of those risks so that they know (i) how to act if the situation presents itself and (ii) the consequences of not acting ethically.

Training helps to overcome temptations, to improve employees to analyze problems from an ethical perspective, to reflect on the morality of acts and to reinforce the need to act within the rules of business. Ethical training helps to make the right decisions and to protect the organization from fraud, theft, and misconduct.

Education in values and in the culture of compliance is an advisable process for individuals to incorporate ethics into their way of thinking and improve behavior in the company.

It is important for organizations to help develop the analytical capacity of their members so they can understand more clearly the consequences of their decisions, from an ethical perspective.

This will allow that before making a decision, the person considers the course of action to take, not only from the commercial or financial aspect but also from the ethical angle.

Ethical training helps people decide what actions are right and activates the reasoning process to understand the ethical dimension of behaviors and that values are not confused. Immoral behaviors and the loss of ethical values can be reversed with training.

Moral reasoning is improved with training. Those who are trained in the ethical conscience are more likely to understand the possible consequences and risks associated with a particular decision and, therefore, are more likely to be able to recognize moral issues and, consequently, make good ethical choices.

It is advisable to train on the basis of dialogue and discussion of ethical issues and dilemmas to encourage reflection by employees. During the training, real or hypothetical cases must be analyzed to practice the process of ethical decision-making in difficult situations.

Without training in ethics individuals may not be aware of when faced with a moral dilemma.

Because those who are part of a company are permanently faced with ethical dilemmas, it is necessary they are prepared before they appear, in order to be better protected against risks.

Bernardo Kliksberg, pioneer of ethics for development and business social responsibility, has said that "if a society systematically cultivates its ethical values, it harvests results."* In an article published in 2004, Kliksberg pointed out that the German sociologist Amitai Etzioni had raised acute questions about the reasons why executives failed with ethics.

> In a shocking article published by *The Washington Post*, Etzioni recounts the resistance he found as a professor of MBA's ... to teach ethics that looked superfluous and unnecessary. By emphasizing the teaching of profit ... perverse incentives were produced.[†]

Ernst Friedrich Schumacher (1911–1977) was a German intellectual and one of the most influential economic thinkers of the last century. In his book *Small is Beautiful*, Schumacher said, "In ethics, we are totally ignorant, we are not educated. It is an issue that, of all that one can think of, is the most important."[‡]

Companies should be concerned with maintaining an ethical culture in the organization, and each employee entering the organization should receive an induction course on the culture of the company before starting to perform the functions for which he or she was hired. Or said another way, "No train, no game."

Ethics training will also help you to protect yourself from mistakes good employees might make, because "doing the right thing" is not always easy and sometimes requires training and an ethical culture to help ethical employees avoid mistakes in their decisions.

It is perceived that an ethical culture exists in an organization when its employees can make the decision to steal products from the company in which they work without being discovered, but they choose not to do so because it is not the right thing to do.

Training must be constant because it is necessary to raise awareness about the risks and the possibility of fraud.

Training is essential to improve ethical performance. With more training, the better the performance. Talking about ethics helps people understand their personal boundaries.

---

* Alejandro Melamed, *Empresas más Humanas* (Editorial Planeta Booket, 2010), 272 ("Business more Human").

† Bernardo Kliksberg, *La Nacion*, March 28, 2004.

‡ E. F. Schumacher, *Small Is Beautiful* (Vintage Books, 1993), 79.

The Spanish philosopher Jose Ortega y Gasset (1883–1955) has said that "if you want to take the advantages of civilization, but you do not defend and sustain it, you will quickly run out of civilization."*

Carlos Rozen, a partner of BDO, has indicated that "15% of people commit fraud, another 15% will never do it and the remaining 70% may cross the wrong line depending on the circumstances."†

The compliance area must inform the other areas of the company about applicable regulations and the consequences of noncompliance.

Employees need to know the laws and policies to reduce the risk of noncompliance by ignorance. You have to learn the rules of the game and then you have to play. It is the responsibility of the company to inform employees about the rules of the game and about changes in policies and legislation related to the activity they perform.

It is advisable to have annual training of two types: (i) a general training program for all employees, on the code of ethics and the principles and values that govern the organization, and (ii) a specific training program focused on the areas that they require a specific training on risks and regulations related to the task they develop. It is necessary to have deeper training for those who, due to their functions, have greater possibilities of facing corruption cases.

For example, San Francisco City law requires that the Public Works director, deputy directors and all staff involved in contracting and purchasing take an online ethics training course. The ethics training follows the arrest of a former director on federal corruption charges.‡

General training aims to: (i) convey the content of certain laws, code of ethics, and internal policies; (ii) report on complaints, how to make allegations, how the investigation is conducted and the prohibition of reprisals for filing an allegation, (iii) report the main risks to which the organization is exposed, (iv) report on the analysis of ethical problems, and (v) inform about the risks of discrimination, (vi) sexual harassment, and (vi) the contamination of the environment.

Training must be dynamic and participatory. Hypothetical ethics cases should be discussed and reflected in groups of employees. You can ask

---

* José Ortega y Gasset, *La Rebelión de las Masas* (Andrés Bello, 1996), 123 ("The Rebellion of the Mass").
† "Responsabilidad Penal de las Personas Jurídicas para Delitos de Corrupción. Cambios Significativos en las Reglas de Juego." Carlos F. Rozen, April 31, 2018, www.iaef.com.ar/publicaciones ("Criminal Liability of Legal Entities for Crimes of Corruption. Significant Changes in the Rules of the Game").
‡ "Corruption investigation means ethics training for all SF Public Works staff," Phil Matier, March 4, 2020, www.sfchronicle.com/bayarea/philmatier/article/Corruption-investigation-means-ethics-training-15102957.php

questions, for example, (i) When was the last time you had to make a tough ethical choice? (ii) Describe a situation in which the pressure to compromise your integrity was the strongest you have felt. (iii) Have you ever witnessed unethical behavior by a colleague or supervisor? How have you reacted?*

Professor Denis Collins of Edgewood College also recommends employees discuss and propose what things would change to reduce the risk of potential fraud or theft in the organizations they work.†

Specific training should focus on policies and procedures; for example, (i) the anti-corruption law for areas related to public officials; (ii) the management of toxic waste and pollution for those working with such materials; (iii) antitrust training for the procurement department in the organization; (iv) security in food handling for those related to the sale of food products; (v) job security for employees in distribution centers or factories; (vi) money laundering for financial services; and (vii) insider trading for managers and directors who receive shares of the company as part of their benefits package.

All employees to whom a particular set of policies and procedures is applicable must agree that they understand the company's policy and that they are committed to complying with the procedures.

On the internet, there are websites that provide training in ethics and those present moral dilemmas. Some examples are "The Moral Sense Test" and "Moral Machine."‡

Training helps to know right from wrong and to make the right decisions in crises.

On January 15, 2008, pilot Chesley Burnett Sullenberger III successfully landed an Airbus 320 (US Airways Flight 1549) in the frozen waters of the Hudson River in New York after birds hit the fuselage and engines of the airplane. Thanks to the experience and training of the pilot, he was able to perform this emergency maneuver three minutes after taking off the 155 passengers and the crew survived and were removed safely from the plane.§

One way to prevent negative situations is to allow debate about values and encourage critical thinking about ethics, challenging employees with examples of moral dilemmas. During these sessions, employees may disclose potential problem situations presented to them.

---

* Destree Rickard, "Avoiding the bad apples," Ethisphere.com, 25.
† Denis Collins, "Business ethics: How to create an ethical organization," Udemy.com.
‡ moral.wjh.harvard.edu and moralmachine.mit.edu.
§ In 2016, Clint Eastwood directed a filmed version of the story of the flight called *Sully*.

Johnson & Johnson's code of business conduct says, "Know the 3 D's: Disclose, Discuss and Decide."* By asking questions employees help organizations stop or prevent misconduct.

General Electric has a Center of Excellence to analyze training needs and uses new technology for its compliance program. The company uses all available information and data to understand the causes of noncompliance and anticipate risks.

Training programs should be recorded, reviewed, and updated frequently, incorporating lessons learned, to be more effective. Multinational companies must also train in different languages.

Online sessions are useful since it facilitates the distance training of thousands of employees distributed in different countries and regions.

This type of training has the advantage of the consistency of the message and the flexibility to take the training; however, it has the disadvantage that sometimes it does not reach the whole universe of employees due to technical issues of the computer network. In these cases, you can resort to the use of videos. For example, the University of Texas at Austin created a series of ethics videos called Ethics Unwrapped.†

Teaching with a facilitator has the advantage of interaction with employees and the possibility of asking and answering questions. Within its limitations, there is a lack of flexibility in time and space for training and potential inconsistencies in the messages of different instructors.

Training by an internal instructor (an employee of the company) allows a greater alignment with the values and culture of the company. An *external* instructor, on the other hand, may not have a deep knowledge of the organization and this can generate some distrust with the employees of the company.

It becomes essential to promote ethics in organizations to strengthen a moral mentality in employees. The ethics training should be a tool at the service of the organizations so the ethical culture progresses. As the Argentine philosopher Jose Ingenieros (1877–1925) said, "Ethical progress is slow, but it's sure."‡

From each session, something always remains. Someone wrote:

---

* Code of Business Conduct, 34, www.jnj.com/sites/default/files/pdf/code-of-business-conduct -english-us.pdf.
† ethicsunwrapped.utexas.edu.
‡ José Ingenieros, *El Hombre Mediocre* (Linkgua, Red Ediciones, 2012), 101 ("The Mediocre Man").

Teach them to fly, but they will not fly your flight.
Teach them to dream, but they will not dream your dream.
Teach them to live, but they will not live your life.
Nevertheless, in every flight, in every life, in every dream,
The print of the way you taught will always remain

St. Matthew, the Evangelist, one of the twelve apostles chosen by Jesus of Nazareth, wrote The Parable of the Mustard Seed: "It is the smallest of all seeds, yet it grows into the largest of garden plants and becomes a tree."[*] It is convenient to plant the seed of ethics so that the culture of integrity expands and grows among employees in ways that impact their thoughts, words, decisions, actions, and omissions.

Thomas Koulopoulos, CEO and founder of the Delphi Group, mentions that few organizations have the sort of obsession with teaching and learning Amazon does, "The plain truth is that if you invest in training and teaching, it becomes the single most important determinant of your culture."[†]

Ethics conduct should not be taken for granted, "Transgressions occur because people are people and can make poor choices."[‡]

Sometimes a rational person acts irrationally, and bad decisions are made by people with good intentions.[§]

Ethical training helps strengthen the moral foundations of companies. In organizations, as well as in trees, the stronger their roots are, the more they will grow and bear fruit.

Ethics and compliance training helps develop an ethical antenna, an ability to recognize the risks and the potential consequences that a company may face if one does not react in time.

---

[*] The Bible, Matthew 13:32.
[†] Thomas Koulopoulos, "In just 2 words, Jeff Bezos sums up what separates winners from dreamers," April 19, 2018, www.inc.com.
[‡] John Baldoni, "How to deliver moral leadership to employees," April 12, 2018, www.forbes.com.
[§] Good intentions and bad results are something that can also be seen in politics. For example, in 1990 the US Congress passed a "luxury tax," an extra sales tax on expensive luxury items like personal airplanes and boats. Members of Congress went along with the tax since it did not affect the majority of working people. After all, most people can't afford to buy a new airplane or boat. A luxury tax seemed likely to bring in lots of extra money for the government. It was estimated an extra US$6 million in 1991. But by the end of 1991, the total money raised stood at only US$53,000. What happened? The case of Beech Aircraft Corp provides a clue. Its sales were 80 planes short of what management expected in 1991. It lost US$130 million in expected sales and had to cut 480 jobs that year. A customer survey revealed that most people avoided buying new planes because of the luxury tax. And similar results drove many US boat builders out of business in the early 1990s. *Exploring the World of Business*, Blanchard, Schewe, Nelson, Hiam, Worth Publishers (1996), 62.

Ethics and compliance training helps elude sirens singing, avoid temptations, and prevent bad decisions and that a small problem becomes large and difficult to control.

22.2 CORPORATE COMMUNICATION

It is said that the German mathematician Carl Gauss (1777–1855) was much focused on his work when he was told that his wife was dying, Gauss replied, "Ask her to wait a moment, I'm almost done."[*]

Communication is the process of transmitting information from a sender to a receiver, but *effective* communication occurs not when the message is sent but also when it is understood.

The functioning of organizations requires a clear exchange of information because bad communication complicates the interaction of people, causes frustration, demotivates and generates mistrust. Management pioneers Chester Barnard (1886–1961) and Mary Parker Follett (1868–1933), argued that an effective authority relies on cooperation and effective communication.

Efficient organizations have a culture of open communication that seeks to integrate all employees under the corporate project of the company. The best leaders share business and financial information with their teams and achieve a work environment where concerns can be discussed.

Consultant Tim Irwin has written that "isolation is what contributes to the derailment."[†]

Malcolm Gladwell is a journalist and sociologist who was born in England and studied in Canada. In his book *Outliers*, he explains that plane crashes are often generated by a lack of communication among the pilot, copilot, and control tower.

Flight 52 of Avianca Airlines was scheduled to fly from Bogota, Colombia, to New York City. The Boeing 707 crashed on January 25, 1990, at 9:34 p.m. after running out of fuel before landing at John F. Kennedy International Airport. It crashed into a hill on the north shore of Long Island. Of the crew members 8 of the 9 and 65 of the 149 passengers on board died.

According to the National Transportation Safety Board (NTSB) report, the crew did not adequately state the fuel emergency, so air traffic controllers underestimated the gravity of the situation.

---

[*] E.T. Bell, "Men of mathematics," 1937, en.wikiquote.org/wiki/Carl_Friedrich_Gauss.
[†] Tim Irwin, *Derailed* (NelsonFree, 2009), 187.

The crew never used the word "emergency" because of low fuel levels as determined by the International Air Transport Association (IATA) guidelines. This made air control unable to understand the seriousness of the problem.

The Avianca plane crash is used as an example in pilot training to improve communication with your copilot and control tower in crisis situations. Extreme respect for hierarchies and authority creates a culture of silence that can lead to chaos.

Knowing the consequences that bad communication can generate, the airlines have a training called Crew Resource Management (CRM), whose objective is to improve the communication skills of the crew. According to Gladwell, "Many airlines teach a standardized procedure for copilots to challenge the pilot if he or she thinks something has gone terribly awry."[*]

Gladwell says,

> The kinds of errors that cause plane crashes are invariably errors of teamwork and communication. One pilot knows something important and somehow doesn't tell the other pilot.[†] ... Planes are safer when a least experienced pilot is flying because it means the second pilot isn't going to be afraid to speak up.[‡]

The American surgeon Atul Gawande pointed out that teaching communication skills helped to achieve a substantial reduction in the high level of mortality of moms and babies at birth centers in Uttar Pradesh, India. Hundreds of nurses were trained in the practice of speaking up when the baby mask was broken, the gloves were not clean or out of stock, or when someone was not washing their hands.[§]

In efficient companies, employees are not afraid of the consequences of expressing disagreement with their bosses, raise their points of view and highlight what they think is wrong. If top management demands overly ambitious profit targets, it generates such managerial pressure that it can induce them to misreport and falsify accounting to achieve the objectives.

That is what happened at Toshiba in 2015. The company had declared US$1.2 billion in false profit.[¶] Within Toshiba there was "a corporate culture in which one could not contradict the wishes of superiors."[**]

---

[*] Malcolm Gladwell, *Outliers*, chap. "The ethnic theory of plane crashes" (Back Bay Books, 2010), 197.
[†] Malcolm Gladwell, *Outliers*, chap. "The ethnic theory of plane crashes" (Back Bay Books, 2010), 184.
[‡] Malcolm Gladwell, *Outliers*, chap. "The ethnic theory of plane crashes" (Back Bay Books, 2010), 197.
[§] "Want to get Great at Something? Get a Coach," Atul Gawande, TED Conferences, www.youtube.com, January 30, 2018.
[¶] "Learning from the Toshiba scandal," *The Japan Times*, July 23, 2015, www.japantimes.co.jp.
[**] "El Escándalo de Contabilidad que Destronó a Hisao Tanaka, el Todopoderoso jefe de Toshiba," *BBC Mundo*, July 21, 2015 ("The Scandal of Accounting that Dethroned Hisao Tanaka, the Almighty Chief of Toshiba")

The fallout from the scandal hit employees directly; the company cut 7,800 jobs as part of a major restructuring plan.*

Organizations should promote open, frank, and sincere communication in order to get to know the problems in a timely manner and avoid serious crises. Lack of communication creates a void that is filled with a lack of confidence, disinterestedness, and demotivation.

Active listening is one of the most important aspects of communication because it contributes to invigorate the self-esteem of the listener or receiver.

The *Journal of the American Medical Association* (JAMA) conducted an investigation into medical malpractice. It was observed that one group of physicians was regularly sued for child deaths in childbirths and another group of physicians was not, despite having participated in similar tragedies. In this investigation, it was concluded that those who were frequently sued were perceived as bad communicators, carefree and distant, while non-sued physicians were considered to be accessible for people with a listening capacity.

Companies use different methods and training so their employees can communicate better and more effectively.†

The importance of effective communication generally ranks among the key qualities for leaders' success. It is not necessary to become a speaker like the Greek politician Demosthenes (384–322 BC),‡ or the Romans Marcus Tullius Cicero (106–43 BC),§ or Marcus Antonius (83–30 BC)ˢ but a corporate leader must master the art of communication and the

---

* Tom Warren, "Toshiba cuts 7,800 jobs following an accounting scandal," December 21, 2015, www.theverge.com.

† For example, companies use specialized services in the development of communication skills such as Toastmasters International, Dale Carnegie or The Ammerman Experience, just to name a few top consulting firms. Companies also use techniques like the Hartman color code, the five-coin test, the STROOP effect, the Helium Bar test, the SBI model, the GROW model, the LAST model, the three-meter rule, the BLOCK model, the Marshmallow Challenge, to name a few.

‡ Demosthenes grew up with a stuttering problem, and to reinforce his voice, he practiced on the beach with a stone in his mouth.

§ Cicero is considered one of the greatest prose stylists in the Roman Republic. He opposed the dictatorship of Caesar. He was an enemy of Marcus Antonius and beheaded, and according to the Roman historian Cassius Dio, the wife of Marcus Antonius, Fulvia, furious with Cicero, grabbed his head with his hands, spat, and ripped out his tongue.

ˢ Marcus Antonius was an important collaborator of Julius Caesar when Caesar was assassinated by a group of senators led by Gaius Casio and Marcus Bruto. Five days later was the funeral at which spoke Brutus and then Marco Antonius. During his speech, Marcus Antonius listed Caesar's deeds and concessions in his will in favor of the Roman people, showing great talent for rhetoric and dramatic interpretation. Antonio showed the 23 wounds in the body of Caesar and raised the Roman town against the murderers.

way of transmitting ideas, because they are fundamental tools in an organization.

Winston Churchill (1874–1965) wrote in an essay called "The Scaffolding of Rhetoric," "Of all the talents bestowed upon men, none is so precious as the gift of oratory. He who enjoys it wields a power more durable than that of a great king."*

Aristotle (384–322 BC) described three components for speakers to succeed in persuading the audience: ethos, logos, and pathos. *Ethos* refers to the importance that the speaker has the credibility to be more effective in front of the audience. *Logos* is related to the way in which the argument is presented so that it is more convincing. And finally, *Pathos* had to do with the importance of inspiring emotions in the audience to achieve a good connection.

Bobby Kennedy's announcement of the assassination of Martin Luther King on April 4, 1968, is an example of effective communication and it is considered to be among the most moving speeches in US history.[†]

Bobby Kennedy (1925–1968) was campaigning to earn the Democratic Party's presidential nomination and made his remarks while in Indianapolis, Indiana. Despite fears of riots and concerns for his safety, Kennedy went ahead with plans to attend a rally in the heart of Indianapolis's African-American area.[‡]

Kennedy began his speech by announcing that Dr. King had been killed. He then mentioned the assassination of his brother, President John F. Kennedy (1917–1963), by a white man. Kennedy then delivered one of his most well-remembered remarks:

> What we need in the United States is not division; what we need in the United States is not hatred; what we need in the United States is not violence or lawlessness, but love and wisdom, and compassion toward one another, and a feeling of justice towards those who still suffer within our country, whether they be white or whether they be black.[§]

Rather than exploding in anger at the tragic news of King's death, the crowd exploded in applause and enthusiasm.

---

* winstonchurchill.hillsdale.edu/the-scaffolding-of-rhetoric/.
† Professor Kenneth G. Brown, *Influence: Mastering Life's Most Powerful Skill* (The University of Iowa, The Great Courses, The Teaching Company, 2013), 70.
‡ en.wikipedia.org/wiki/Robert_F._Kennedy%27s_speech_on_the_assassination_of_Martin_Luther_King_Jr.
§ en.wikipedia.org/wiki/Robert_F._Kennedy%27s_speech_on_the_assassination_of_Martin_Luther_King_Jr.

The following stories show the importance of effective communication.

The Blind Man: A man was sitting on the sidewalk with a cap on his feet and a sign in chalk saying "Please help me: I am blind."

A marketing man stepped in front of him, stopped, and noticed that in the cap there were almost no coins. Without asking the blind man for permission, the marketing expert wrote another message on the other side of the poster; he put that message visible in front of the blind man and left.

In the afternoon, he passed again in front of the blind man, and his cap was full of bills and coins. The blind man recognized his footsteps and asked if he had been the one who had written something on the poster and, if so, what he had written. The marketing man replied that he wrote the same thing as was written before but in different words, and went on his way.

The blind man never knew, but his new sign said: "We are in spring and I cannot see it."

The Sultan: Once a sultan dreamed that he had lost all his teeth, and when he awoke, he sent for a fortune-teller to interpret his dream.

"What misfortune, my lord!" exclaimed the soothsayer. "Every fallen tooth represents the loss of a relative of your majesty."

"What insolence!" cried the enraged sultan. "How dare you say such a thing to me? Get away from here. Guards, give him a hundred lashes!"

Later the sultan ordered another diviner to be brought to him and again told him the dream.

The latter, after listening to the sultan closely, said, "Excellency, sir! Great happiness has been reserved for you. The dream means that you will survive all your relatives."

The Sultan's face lit up with a big smile, and he shouted, "Give him a hundred gold coins!"

When the soothsayer left the palace, one of the courtiers said to him,

> It is not possible! The interpretation you have made of the dream is the same as the first soothsayer. I do not understand why the sultan paid the first with a hundred lashes and you with a hundred gold coins.

"Remember," replied the second fortune-teller, "it all depends on the manner in which the communication takes place."

The Pope: Former Siemens executive and consultant Michael Ritter attributes to the American psychologist Gordon Allport (1897–1967), the following story:

Two priests debated whether it was appropriate or not to smoke and pray at the same time, and because they could not agree, each one individually wrote to the Pope for his advice. After receiving the answers of the Supreme Pontiff, they were perplexed since apparently the responses were contradictory. They then compared the manner in which each had asked the Holy Father his question.

One of them had asked him if it was appropriate to smoke while he was praying, to which the Pope replied, "Certainly not," explaining that praying was a very serious matter during which there should be no distractions.

The other priest had used a slightly different formulation. He asked if it was appropriate to pray while smoking. "Certainly," replied the Pope. "Prayer is always convenient."[*]

To communicate a message, care must be taken in how it is formulated so that the receiver interprets it correctly.

The Oracle: The Greek historian Herodotus (484–425 BC) and Marco Tulio Cicero (106–43 BC) wrote a story about Cresus, the last king of Lydia (now Turkey).

It was said that Croesus was the richest man of that time. Croesus sent a messenger to the oracle of Delphi, a place of consultation with the gods in Greece, in the present villa of Delphi, at the base of Mount Parnassus.[†]

The oracle replied to the king's messenger, "Croesus, if you cross the river Halis you will destroy a great empire." The oracle's answer was interpreted favorably; that is, the great empire that would be destroyed would be the Persian. But the empire destroyed was Croesus's, in the battle of the river Halis (547 BC), and Lydia was conquered by the Persians.

Napoleon: When Napoleon died on the island of St. Helena on May 5, 1821, a messenger rushed to tell King George IV of England (1762–1830), "Your Majesty, your worst enemy is dead." The English king asked him, "What happened to my wife?"[‡]

---

[*] Michael Ritter, *El valor del Capital Reputacional* (Olivos, Ritter & Partners, 2013), 35 ("The value of Reputational Capital").

[†] To consult the oracle, one had to go to that sacred place and offer Apollo a honey cake and sacrifice a goat that was burned in a bonfire. If the animal's body trembled during the offering, it meant that Apollo was going to speak. The oracle was in charge of a priestess (an old woman, the Pitia) and a prophet. After the question of the petitioner, the priestess communicated with the god while chewing laurel leaves, sprinkling flour and drinking swallows of water from a sacred source. If his words were unintelligible, the prophet interpreted them.

[‡] Manuel J. Prieto, *Curistoria: Curiosidades y Anécdotas de la Historia* (Evohe, 2008), 46 ("Curiosities and Anecdotes of History").

Los Rodeos: On March 27, 1977, the Spanish airport of Los Rodeos was the scene of the greatest tragedy of civil aviation in history when two Boeing 747S, one from KLM and one from Pan Am Airways, collided at the airport in Tenerife while performing takeoff maneuvers. Five hundred and eighty-three people died.

The KLM commander communicated with the control tower and told them, "We are now at the takeoff position." The controller thought that KLM was "ready" to take off and replied, "OK."

But the KLM commander believed that he had been "authorized to take off" and began the takeoff.

Due to the intense fog, the KLM aircraft pilot who accelerated to take off was able to see the Pan Am aircraft, which was on the airstrip in front of them, only about eight seconds before the collision. The accident could not be seen from the control tower due to the fog.

As a consequence of the tragedy, changes were introduced to improve control and communication in airplane takeoffs, for example, certain words and preset terms that must be used between the cockpit and the control tower. The word *takeoff*, which generated confusion between the control tower and the pilot, can now be used in air navigation to *start the takeoff*.

To communicate a message, one must take care of the way in which it is formulated, so that the receiver interprets it correctly. Communication is a double process. On the one hand, someone sends a message – the sender – and on the other side, there is a receiver, that is, someone who receives that message and who must understand or decipher it.

Corporate communication must always include messages that should be repeated as if reading the Gospel in church or a speed limit sign on a route. This is necessary for organizations with a high level of employee turnover and also after the acquisition of companies. However, it must be taken into account that it is not convenient to repeat exactly the same thing all the time because we must capture the receiver's attention. Therefore, stories can be used that help to connect people with values and to keep ideas fresh and interesting.

The organization must keep its employees and business partners informed of its principles, policies, and procedures. The dissemination of the ethical culture must be continuous and the values must be consistently communicated so that they can be embedded in the daily work.

The principles and policies written on the company's website or in the code of ethics alone are not sufficient but must be constantly communicated not only from the compliance office but also from senior management, in order to integrate ethics and the business and to achieve greater impact. Many repetitions of the same statement are necessary for the message to be internalized. Repetition is the mother of learning.

Dale Carnegie (1888–1955) explained the importance of repeating a message as follows:

> Let's not expect a quick reference to one or perhaps two examples to produce the desired effect. … Experience must be accumulated over experience until the same weight sinks the idea deep into brain tissues. Then it becomes part of it and neither time nor events can erase it. And the principle by which this occurs is called Accumulation.*

Attorney Leslie Caldwell said in 2014:

> I once represented a company that had an A+ compliance program. But then acquired a Chinese subsidiary, and for several years failed to communicate to their new – and not so new – Chinese employees the need for FCPA compliance. The predictable result: The Chinese employees continued doing business in a way that was familiar to them. And the US parent found itself in deep violation of the FCPA.†

Communication should be also simple and limited to a few points. What is not simple is not understood and is not done well. Lecturer Jürgen Klaric has pointed out that "the more basic and simple the communication, the more effective it can be. … The brain loves simple and basic. In English KISS: Keep it Simple Stupid."‡

Integrity Awards or Ethical Courage is another initiative that helps to reinforce and motivate employees to do the right thing and helps the organization to convey a strong message about the importance of acting ethically and to reflect the organization's values in concrete behaviors. With these awards, companies like Walmart or Lockheed Martin promote and recognize actions that inspire others to always do the right thing. By sharing stories, the program fosters the integrity-based culture.

---

* Dale Carnegie, *Como hablar bien en Público* (Sudamericana, 2004), 316 ("The Art of Public Speaking").
† Assistant Attorney General for the Criminal Division Leslie Caldwell, speech at the 22nd Annual Ethics and Compliance Conference, Atlanta, Georgia, October 1, 2014.
‡ Jurgen Klaric, "Sell to the mind, not the people," *Places* (2016): 140, 175.

Employees are voted on by other employees as role models by demonstrating exceptional commitment to company values. The proposed stories are selected by a committee, and the winners participate in a recognition ceremony led by the CEO of the company and/or by the chairman of the board. Examples of ethical courage include situations when the individual does the right thing even when it is risky or difficult or when the person reports unethical or illegal conduct, despite the pressure to remain silent.

The winners of the ethical courage award, when returning to their business units around the world, will be able to share and communicate their experience at the event and become part of a network of ethical ambassadors to help promote the culture at a regional and global level.

Compliance expert Joe Murphy shared in the business ethics publication *Ethikos* another best practice from Lockheed Martin:

> Lockheed Martin staged a contest inviting employees to develop their own videos to promote ethics in the workplace. Employees submitted two-minute videos. There were twenty videos submitted from all areas of the business, with three finalists selected and invited to the annual meeting for the company's ethics officers in Orlando. This event called the Ethics Film Festival, awarded statues to the top three, and portions of those videos were included in the company's ethics training video.*

Another way to communicate and disseminate ethical culture is to create a "guide" that the ethics office sends monthly to business units with examples to share with employees. The document, translated into several languages, is distributed to the business units so that the managers discuss hypothetical work situations with the employees in their weekly or monthly meetings.

Gary Di Bianco, a partner at law firm Skadden Arps, Meagher & Flom, said:

> Firms often have fairly rigorous training for their domestic employees in the United States, but that does not always communicate or translate outside the United States. It's important when they do anti-corruption training at non-US subsidiaries so companies can make sure that training is

---

* "Lights, Camera, Action! Lockheed Martin's Ethics Film Festival," *Ethikos*, 8 (January–February 2004).

understandable to people, using the local language and the legal concepts they are familiar with.*

Global companies cannot have a centralized program in a single language because the communication must be clear and precise so that the recipient understands it.† In India alone, there are more than 20 languages, and the most prominent of them, Hindi, is spoken by only 28 percent of the population.

Organizational leaders should follow the advice of Nelson Mandela (1918–2013), who said, "If you talk to a man in a language he understands, that goes to his head. If you talk to him in his language, that goes to his heart."‡

Language differences can be a great barrier to effective communication.

Legend has it that when the English conquerors led by the British navigator and explorer James Cook (1728–1779) arrived in Australia, as they traveled the vast territory, they were amazed to see strange animals that jumped very high. Cook asked an aboriginal with signs of what that animal was. The native replied, "Kan Ghu Ru", Kan Ghu Ru"; therefore, the conquerors called the animal *kangaroo*. Linguists determined many years later that what the Natives were saying with "Kan Ghu Ru" was "I do not understand what you are telling me."

A few years earlier, in 1517, Spanish explorers asked some indigenous Mayans the name of the region where they were. The Maya replied, "Yu ka t'ann," which in Mayan means "Listen how they talk." The Spaniards interpreted that the zone was called *Yucatán*, and the zone was

---

* Melissa Klein Aguilar, "Latest FCPA action spotlights foreign units," February 2008, www.complianceweek.com.
† Tradition tells us that many years before Christ, only one language was spoken on Earth. The whole population of the land was in the region of Sema-ar (Iraq). Defying the authority of God, the inhabitants of Sema-ar planned to build a tower that would reach Heaven. That tower, which became about sixty meters high, was known later as the Tower of Babel. According to the Bible, to punish the people for their arrogance, God said, "Confuse their language so that they do not understand each other" (The Bible, Genesis 11:1–9). Then, as people did not understand each other, they began to disperse on Earth. *Babel* derives from the Hebrew verb *balbal*, which means to confuse, and for that reason, the Tower was called so because it was where God confused the tongues of all men. The Tower of Babel is identified as the cradle of communication and represents the spread of the more than 6,000 languages in the world. There are 6,912 languages spoken by people in the world, and most of them come from Papua New Guinea in Oceania, one of the most culturally diverse countries in the world, where 836 different languages have been counted in a population of almost eight million inhabitants.
‡ Nelson Mandela quotes, www.brainyquote.com/quotes/nelson_mandela_121685.

denominated *Peninsula of Yucatán*, which divides the Gulf of Mexico and the Caribbean Sea.

It would be easier for global companies to use a common language, a universal code that everyone can understand. That was the goal of the yellow and red cards in soccer. Previously, the referee communicated to the players that they were expelled.

The yellow and red cards were an idea of the wife of a former referee called Ken Aston who was a referee at the 1962 World Cup in Chile. In that championship, Aston had been the referee of the match between Chile and Italy and had suffered the players' incomprehension because they did not speak English. That is why he thought of the need to create a universal code that all players could understand, similar to the traffic lights that first prevent with yellow and prohibit moving forward with red. After commenting his concern to his wife Hilda, she showed him two pieces of cardboard, one yellow and one red, and suggested that the referees carry them in their pockets. In the 1970 World Cup in Mexico, the cardboards were used for the first time.*

If the company wishes to communicate something with relative success at a global level, the message must be adapted to the culture of the recipient's country, using the language of the place where the company operates.

Professor Bernardo Bárcena says that "the context defines the text."† Bárcena mentions the American business consultant Chris Lowney, who explains how The Jesuits adapted to the different cultures they intended to evangelize:

> In Europe Vatican officials condemned the Bible and prayer books in ver-
> nacular languages, but "The Jesuits prepared original translations of Tamil,
> Japanese, Vietnamese and many other languages to be able to present their
> Gospel in native languages to local populations."‡

To communicate ideas, some leaders use examples, stories, metaphors, analogies, and tales. Jesus Christ conveyed his ideas with more than 60 parables and sermons.

---

* "Una Mujer, Clave en la Creación de las Tarjetas Amarillas y Rojas en el Futbol," July 7, 2018, www.lanacion.com.ar ("A Woman, Key in the Creation of Yellow and Red Cards in Soccer").
† Bernardo Bárcena, *El liderazgo de Francisco* (Ediciones B., 2014), 124 ("Francis' Leadership").
‡ Bernardo Bárcena, *El Liderazgo de Francisco* (Ediciones B., 2014), 70. Bárcena mentions the American writer Chris Lowney who explains the way the Jesuits adapted to different cultures. *Liderazgo al estilo de los Jesuitas* (Buenos Aires: Editorial Norma, 2013), 30. Lowney was formerly a managing director of JP Morgan ("Francis' Leadership"; "Leadership in the style of the Jesuits").

An old English expression says, "A picture is worth a thousand words."* The sixteenth president of the United States, Abraham Lincoln (1809–1865), stated,

> They say I have too many stories. I think they are right; but I have learned from long experience that people … are allowed to be influenced more easily by a simple and humorous illustration than by the use of any other procedure.†

The French thinker and historian Alexis de Tocqueville (1805–1859) in his book *Democracy in America* said, "There is nothing more unproductive for the human mind than an abstract idea. So I hasten to run toward facts. An example will cast light on my thoughts."‡

Creating a video with the CEO and his or her direct reports or members of the board talking about the history of the company and its values is another great tool to communicate ethics inside and outside the organization.

Other options are the Leadership and Integrity Talks where the company leaders share with the employee's experiences and situations they have lived and answer questions from the attendees. Shared experiences allow people to learn from each other and improve team performance.

Part of a good leader's job is to inspire the people around him to be better; lead by example; practice what you preach, and share your stories. That way the corporate leader will be reliable in the eyes of employees.

As Ginni Rometty, president and CEO of IBM, says, "In a company, your value is not what you know, but what you share."§

The leaders of each business unit should also participate annually in an integrity and compliance presentation where the ethics and compliance area reports on the main risks, mitigation plans, types of complaints received, the status of training programs, ethics survey results, communication strategies, trends, and statistics. Some large companies do that, for example, General Electric conducts *integrity reviews*, and Siemens conducts *integrity dialogues*.

In the face of a crisis, good, transparent, and honest communication to the media, the community and employees are of vital importance.

---

* en.wikipedia.org/wiki/A_picture_is_worth_a_thousand_words.
† Donald Phillips, *Lincoln y el Liderazgo* (Deusto, 1993), 190 ("Lincoln on Leadership").
‡ Alexis de Tocqueville, *Democracy in America* (Folio, 2001), 207.
§ "IBM employee highlights," March 16, 2013, www.ibmemployee.com/Highlights130316.

Silence is consent. If nothing is communicated or communicated poorly, late or bad, the crisis may be aggravated.

Earlier I said that Johnson & Johnson handled communication well in the Tylenol crisis. The same thing happened with Pepsi. On June 10, 1993, three people in Washington State claimed that they had discovered hypodermic syringes inside a Diet Pepsi can. In two days, the company received 10,000 calls and when the issue went to the media, the event affected the company's sales.

Pepsi quickly created videos to inform how Pepsi cans were filled and the safety of their production. These videos were watched by more than 150 million viewers in the following days. Then it was proved that the incident had been sabotage. After the videos were broadcast and the case was clarified, Pepsi sales grew 7%.

If the situation escalates into a serious crisis, social networks, journalists, unions, lawyers, prosecutors, the government, and Wall Street can create a tsunami that could seriously affect the company's reputation.

To avoid appearing weak, the CEO needs to stand up within the first 48 hours of the beginning of the crisis.

Has the person who should speak to the media been trained?

Are you going to apologize?

What should you do if a customer of your restaurant finds a dead rat in a salad?

What is the communication plan and what are the protocols in case of serious crises?

As I mentioned earlier in this book, during the Bridgestone Firestone tire crisis in the Ford Explorer, 6.5 million tires had to be replaced after 148 deaths that were apparently caused by a defect in the tires.

The way in which CEO Yoichiro Kaizaki handled the crisis was widely criticized and as a result, the value of Bridgestone's shares fell by 50% and Kaizaki resigned.

After the oil spill in the Gulf of Mexico, BP's former CEO told the BBC, "If I had done a degree at RADA (Royal Academy of Dramatic Art) rather than a degree in geology, I may have done better."[*]

Rupert Younger is the founder and director of the Center for Corporate Reputation at the University of Oxford. Younger is an expert

---

[*] Dan Berman, "Former BP CEO has no regrets," *Politico*, November 10, 2010, www.politico.com.

in strategic communication. He says, "My advice is to act decisively in a crisis to restore the feeling that you understand the seriousness of the issue."*

April 9, 2017, was the date of the ticketing incident of United Airlines flight 3411 – mentioned earlier in this book – in which Air Safety Officers forcibly expelled and seriously injured a 69-year-old passenger. He had bought his ticket to the airline and was reluctant to get off the plane. A day after that event, the CEO of United Airlines sent a statement to the employees in which he pointed out, among other things, the following:

> This is an upsetting event to all of us here at United. I apologize for having to re-accommodate these customers.
>
> Like you, I was upset to see and hear about what happened last night aboard United Express Flight 3411 headed from Chicago to Louisville.
>
> While I deeply regret this situation arose, I also emphatically stand behind all of you, and I want to commend you for continuing to go above and beyond to ensure we fly right.
>
> I do, however, believe there are lessons we can learn from this experience, and we are taking a close look at the circumstances surrounding this incident. Treating our customers and each other with respect and dignity is at the core of who we are, and we must always remember this no matter how challenging the situation.
>
> He was approached a few more times after that in order to gain his compliance to come off the aircraft, and each time he refused and became more and more disruptive and belligerent.
>
> Our agents were left with no choice but to call Chicago Aviation Security Officers to assist in removing the customer from the flight. He repeatedly declined to leave.
>
> Chicago Aviation Security Officers were unable to gain his cooperation and physically removed him from the flight as he continued to resist – running back onto the aircraft in defiance of both our crew and security officials.†

---

* Constanza Capdevilla de la Cerda, "La Reputación Corporativa es Clave para Cualquier Organización y su Manejo es mucho más que la Relación con los Medios," April 21, 2018, www.economiaynegocios.cl/noticias/noticias.asp?id=462095 ("Corporate Reputation is Key to Any Organization and its Management is much more than the Relationship with the Media").

† Erin McCann, "United's apologies: A timeline," *The New York Times*, April 14, 2017, www.nytimes.com.

In that first statement, the CEO did not perform any self-criticism of the violence used, did not show compassion, did not take responsibility for what happened and only apologized for having to "re-accommodate" the passengers. That is, he called "re-accommodating" dragging and hurting an unconscious passenger.

The CEO considered that they complied with the pre-established procedures and clearly showed some lack of emotional intelligence and disconnection with what had happened. The incident plus the CEO's statement put United Airlines in a serious crisis that damaged its brand and reputation.

After the criticism his statement received, the following day, in a second statement, the CEO said that the airline took full responsibility for the episode:

> The truly horrific event that occurred on this flight has elicited many responses from all of us: outrage, anger, disappointment. I share all of those sentiments and one above all: my deepest apologies for what happened. Like you, I continue to be disturbed by what happened on this flight and I deeply apologize to the customer forcibly removed and to all the customers aboard. No one should ever be mistreated this way.
>
> I want you to know that we take full responsibility and we will work to make it right.
>
> It's never too late to do the right thing. I have committed to our customers and our employees that we are going to fix what's broken so this never happens again. This will include a thorough review of crew movement, our policies for incentivizing volunteers in these situations, how we handle oversold situations and an examination of how we partner with airport authorities and local law enforcement. We'll communicate the results of our review by April 30th.
>
> I promise you we will do better.*

The CEO on ABC's "Good Morning America" program said he felt embarrassed when he saw the video of the client being dragged from the flight, and said, "This can never – will never – happen again on a United Airlines flight. That's my premise and that's my promise."[†]

---

* Erin McCann, "United's apologies: A timeline," *The New York Times*, April 14, 2017, www.nytimes.com.

[†] Erin McCann, "United's apologies: A timeline," *The New York Times*, April 14, 2017, www.nytimes.com.

Communication affects the profitability of organizations; therefore, it is necessary to analyze not only its content but also the most appropriate way to deliver the message.

Business consultant Peter Drucker (1909–2005) said that "60% of problems in business are the result of poor communication."*

Good communication, internal and external, improves the competitiveness of the organization, as well as motivation, commitment, and the work climate.

Organizational values must be present in the communicative process because the ethics of the company is the guide to which employees must appeal when faced with complex situations.

---

* Alberto Dominguez, "Change your work environment today and avoid communications problems in the workplace," September 19, 2017, Ehorus.com.

23

Designing an Effective Ethics and Compliance Program: Unit 3

23.1 RISK ASSESSMENT, SWOT, SCORECARD, AND SCENARIO PLANNING

The success of a compliance program lies in a profound analysis of the internal root causes of risks. To do that it is necessary to carry out an exhaustive investigation.

The risk assessment is an effective process used to identify, analyze, evaluate, and prioritize the risks faced by an organization, which allows having a holistic view of them, and to attack their causes.

The evaluation of risks is a process that allows knowing the vulnerable points of the operation of a business. The activities of evaluation, design, and implementation must be carried out starting from a deep self-diagnosis.

The risk assessment process incorporates the contributions of the leaders in charge of different areas, functional leaders who have a better knowledge of the risks to which the organization is exposed.

This process prioritizes risks according to the probability of occurrence (that an event happens within a foreseeable timeframe), the impact it can have on the organization (the calculation of all the negative consequences that can occur if the risk occurs) and the factors that contribute to it.

Based on this evaluation, companies allocate the necessary and sufficient resources to prioritize and address the most significant compliance risks. Through this process, existing controls are evaluated, hidden threats are detected and action plans are defined to mitigate the risks.

The next step is to prioritize.

The Italian sociologist, philosopher, and economist, Vilfredo Pareto (1848–1923) explained in 1906 that 20% of the Italian population owned 80% of the property, an observation that would be known as the Pareto Principle or Rule 80-20. The principle can be applied to different activities. For example, if we know that 20% of our customers generate 80% of our sales, we will focus on that group.*Following Pareto, the expert in quality management, Romanian Joseph Moses Juran (1904–2008) analyzed which 20% of the causes generated 80% of the problems.

Applying this principle, once all risks are identified and listed, 20% of the risks that can generate the greatest damage to the company in terms of probability of occurrence and potential impact are prioritized and entered into the risk assessment matrix in order to visualize the organization's priority risks, the existing controls, the improvement plan and the area in charge.

The risk assessment includes review of (i) company policies; (ii) applicable legislation; (iii) fines received; (iv) major litigation; (v) internal and external audit reports on controls and risks; (vi) information on ethics complaints; (vii) the main consumer complaints; (viii) the subpoenas of national, provincial, and municipal governments; (ix) existing risk controls; and so on.

To mitigate risks, for example, training activities are carried out, policies and procedures are created, audits are carried out, new technologies are adopted to improve controls, certain lines of products are discontinued, activity is suspended in some regions and/or countries and/or certain suppliers or partners.

A risk matrix shows a quadrant in which the risks must be located taking into account their likelihood of occurrence and potential impact. The most critical risks should be included in the upper right quadrant.

In addition to the risk assessment, another tool known as the SWOT matrix can be used, which refers to the strengths, opportunities, weaknesses, and threats an organization faces. The goal is to visualize the risks of compliance and the mitigation procedures defined in the risk assessment from another angle.

The SWOT internal origin allows for knowing the quality of existing processes and controls. *Strengths* are the elements the program has and

---

* British consultant Richard John Koch, author of several books on the Pareto Principle, points out "What really fascinates me about the Principle is its asymmetry, its imbalance. In most important areas of life, a small number of events has a disproportionately large effect." Richard Koch, *The 80/20 Leader* (Aguilar, 2013), 41.

must be maintained, while the *weaknesses* are all those controls that the organization does not have and that should be part of an ethics and compliance program.

The SWOT external origin identifies the main opportunities and threats of the external environment. The *opportunities* are those tools of ethics and compliance the market offers and that should be incorporated into the program. *Threats* are external risks that can undermine the survival of the organization and on which adequate mitigation strategies must be designed.

Just as the risk assessment matrix allows the company's risks to be prioritized based on the degree of likelihood and potential impact, the compliance SWOT matrix allows a clear view of the existing and missing elements of an ethics and compliance program, as well as the main risks – classified as threats – already identified in the risk assessment.

Likewise, the strength of a compliance program can be analyzed by creating a *compliance scorecard* where (i) the potential risks that the organization can face are listed and (ii) the existence and quality of internal policies and training programs related to each type of identified risk.

For each one of the risks identified, a red, yellow, or green circle is placed on the scorecard, depending on the strength of each of the two items (internal policies and training), to face each risk analyzed.

The scorecard allows a clear vision, as in a chessboard, of the risks where the efforts should be prioritized.

Scenario planning also called scenario thinking or scenario analysis is a strategic planning method some organizations use to develop long-term plans. It is in large part an adaptation and generalization of methods used by military intelligence.*

This method helps a firm to anticipate the impact of different scenarios in identifying weaknesses. When identified years in advance, these weaknesses can be avoided or their impacts mitigated more effectively than if similar real-life problems were considered under duress of an emergency.†

The idea of scenario planning arose from the early work of nuclear strategy theorists, the American Herman Kahn (1922–1983) who became famous for developing scenarios about nuclear war in the 1950s.‡

---

* Scenario Planning, Wikipedia, en.wikipedia.org/wiki/Scenario_planning.
† Scenario Planning, Wikipedia, en.wikipedia.org/wiki/Scenario_planning.
‡ Professor Stanley Ridgley, *Strategic Thinking Skills*, Course Guidebook (Drexel University, The Great Courses, The Teaching Company, 2012), 172.

In the 1970s, scenario planning was introduced at Royal Dutch Shell by the French oil executive Pierre Wack (1922–1997). As a result, the Anglo-Dutch oil giant was able to anticipate not just one Arab-induced oil shock during that decade, but two.*

Scenario Planning improves the quality of thinking about the future. Scenarios can be as simple as asking yourself a series of *What if?* questions based on the various ways certain situations might play out.†

Gary Klein is an American research psychologist famous in the field of decision-making. In 2007, he wrote an article in *Harvard Business Review* called "Performing a Project Pre-Mortem."

A *pre-mortem* is a process by which a management team imagines an event has already occurred and the project has failed. Management analyzes all possible reasons for this failure, identifying everything that could potentially lead to the failure of the project. Each person on the management team is asked to write down all the reasons they believe that failure occurred.

The technique facilitates a positive discussion about the threats and this is another layer of protection for the organization since it enables the main threats to be identified in advance to prevent the "death" of the project and/or the organization.

Klein wrote:

> Projects fail at a spectacular rate. One reason is that too many people are reluctant to speak up about their reservations during the all-important planning phase.
>
> Research conducted in 1989 by Deborah J. Mitchell, of the Wharton School; Jay Russo, of Cornell; and Nancy Pennington, of the University of Colorado, found that prospective hindsight – imagining that an event has already occurred – increases the ability to correctly identify reasons for future outcomes by 30%.
>
> We have used prospective hindsight to devise a method called a pre-mortem, which helps project teams identify risks at the outset.
>
> A pre-mortem is the hypothetical opposite of a postmortem. A post-mortem in a medical setting allows health professionals and the family to learn what caused a patient's death. Everyone benefits except, of course,

* Pierre Wack 1985 articles "Scenarios: Uncharted Waters Ahead" and "Scenarios: Shooting the Rapids" are considered among the first to bring the thoughts and theories of futurist Herman Kahn into business strategy. Pierre Wack, Wikipedia, en.wikipedia.org/wiki/Pierre_Wack.
† Professor Stanley Ridgley, *Strategic Thinking Skills*, Course Guidebook (Drexel University, The Great Courses, The Teaching Company, 2012), 172.

the patient. A pre-mortem in a business setting comes at the beginning of a project rather than the end, so the project can be improved rather than autopsied.

Unlike a typical critiquing session, in which project team members are asked what might go wrong, the pre-mortem operates on the assumption that the "patient" has died, and so asks what did go wrong. The team members' task is to generate plausible reasons for the project's failure.

A typical pre-mortem begins after the team has been briefed on the plan. The leader starts the exercise by informing everyone that the project has failed spectacularly. Over the next few minutes, those in the room independently write down every reason they can think of for the failure, especially the kinds of things they ordinarily wouldn't mention as potential problems, for fear of being impolitic.

Next, the leader asks each team member, starting with the project manager, to read one reason from his or her list; everyone states a different reason until all have been recorded. After the session is over, the project manager reviews the list, looking for ways to strengthen the plan.*

Finally, the *cause-effect* methods mentioned in Chapter 11, like the *Ishikawa Fishbone Diagram* or the *Five-Way method*, developed by Sakichi Toyoda, help team members display, categorize, and evaluate all the possible causes of an effect.

The team begins by agreeing on the effect. Then, the team identifies all the factors or categories that contribute to the problem and finally, they reach an agreement on the top root causes in each category.

The use of the cause and effect diagram encourages individuals and teams to spend time searching for root causes and this effort reduces people's tendency to identify symptoms as causes.†

The compliance risk assessment, the compliance SWOT, the compliance scorecard, the pre-mortem project analysis, and the cause-effect methods should be included as part of the compliance program of any organization.

What are the causes for which a business can be interrupted?

What are the possible scenarios that may happen?

What should the organization do to prevent these scenarios from happening?

---

* Gary Klein, "Performing a project premortem," *Harvard Business Review* (September 2007), hbr.org/2007/09/performing-a-project-premortem.
† K. Blanchard, C. Schewe, R. Nelson and A. Hiam, *Exploring the World of Business* (Worth Publishers, 1996), 287.

These analysis tools allow showing more clearly the degree of vulnerability of the organization against risks.

23.2 OPEN DOORS AND ETHICS LINES

The term *Open society* was introduced by the French philosopher Henri Bergson (1859–1941), and the idea was further developed by Austrian-born philosopher Karl Popper (1902–1994). In open societies, the government is expected to be responsive and tolerant, and its political mechanisms, transparent. In an open society each citizen has freedom of thought and expression and the cultural and legal institutions facilitate this.*

The central characteristic of an open society is the transparent way in which knowledge is obtained and transmitted to improvements or reforms because knowledge is never complete but is in constant development. In a free and open society, you can freely and creatively express what leads to innovation and progress. Each citizen engages in the practice of criticism with a wide freedom of thought and expression, supported by a legal and cultural apparatus that facilitates this exercise.

Leaders must ensure that there are necessary conditions for an "open society" in organizations so that employees can express themselves without fear of reprisals and have the freedom to tell what they observe. Sharing not only the good but also the bad, that is, telling the full truth.

Organizations with a strong ethical culture are those in which employees feel free to speak openly about ethical issues with their bosses. As Professor Clancy Martin says, "If people do not speak out in the face of moral wrong, they not only compromise themselves but also encourage immoral behavior."†

When Alan Mulally arrived at Ford as the CEO, he discovered that executives were afraid of admitting failure. Their presentations at Thursday morning meetings highlighted only successes (color-coded green), never problems (color-coded yellow or red). Mr. Mulally asked how everything could be so rosy when the company was losing billions. The next week, everybody's chart was like a rainbow.‡

---

* "Open Society," en.wikipedia.org/wiki/Open_society.
† "Moral Decision Making" Professor Clancy Martin, *The Great Courses*, Guidebook, Lecture 3, University of Missouri-Kansas City.
‡ Robert Simons, "Stress test your strategy," *Harvard Business Review* (November 2010): 100.

The Latin adage *Ubi Dubium ibi Libertas* means *Where there is doubt there is freedom*. The adage shows that limited knowledge takes more advantage of a free system through debate.*

The company makes the most of the freedom of expression and thought of its employees when the communication channels are opened in the company, and the employees can express opinions and get rid of doubts.

It is necessary for the organization to establish and facilitate an internal channel so that employees and third parties can report possible violations of the code of ethics or illegal acts in a confidential manner and without fear of reprisals. The more complex the company, with a greater number of employees distributed in different offices and regions, the greater the need to have an ethical channel. The complaint channels used by the organization must be secure to protect the confidentiality of the information and personal data.

Companies should use all means at their disposal to facilitate the communication of any facts of which employees are aware of and contrary to the culture of the organization.

Many things happen in organizations that leaders don't know. If employees observe or know about potential unethical behaviors that are taking place, they should report them. The earlier the problem is detected, the less expensive the solution will be.

The ethics line is a great tool to discover problems and eliminate hidden practices.

In some organizations that have a history of tolerating ethical abuses, employees do not report unethical behaviors they observe because they find it risky for fear of reprisals.

In an organization with a mature ethical culture, if the employee learns of a possible problem, he or she reports it without hesitation and has an active role in working to solve it.

Employees must report acts done outside the law or ethics knowing that this action will not be reproached and their voice will be heard.

Companies must give *voice to values*, as Professor Mary Gentile says.†
For this reason, the organization must provide a variety of channels for employees, suppliers, and even clients to make complaints, send questions, and report violations of company policies or laws.

---

* Alberto Benegas Lynch (h), "En Torno a la Teoría del Caos," March 5, 2016, www.opinion.Infobae. com ("Around the Chaos Theory").

† Sr. Advisor at Aspen Institute and Professor at the University of Virginia – Darden.

All employees should be informed about how they can communicate ethical concerns and potential wrongdoings.

The most important reporting process is the "open door" policy whereby the employee talks to his or her supervisor and openly discusses potential or current problems. If the employee approaches the supervisor to speak and the person who initiates the process is not satisfied with the response, or in case his or her supervisor is part of the problem, he or she may go and talk to the next managerial level. This process does not imply the opinion of who initiates the open door will prevail or that it will obtain the expected response, but the employee is guaranteed to be heard by his or her hierarchical superiors.

Ethical organizations have a policy that clarifies no complaint in good faith can be retaliatory to the complainant, even if it is not well founded or the complaint is not verifiable; otherwise, no employee would raise complaints. If the existence of reprisal is proven to the person who made the complaint, disciplinary actions must be taken toward the person who made the retaliation.

The ability of employees across the organization to be able to ask questions and raise inquiries or complaints about ethical matters without fear of reprisal forms the basis of an effective system of ethics and compliance. It means employees perceive their complaints, and inquiries are welcome and they will be analyzed and investigated professionally. When people believe they will be heard, their level of trust in the organization increases.

If managers do not want to discuss ethical issues, they will create a culture of silence and as a result, employees will hesitate to communicate ethical problems because they will not want to be considered troublemakers.

As a leader, you must ensure that employees feel comfortable discussing ethical issues. A culture of fear, absolute obedience, or indifference deteriorates relationships and affects the productivity of organizations.

Each employee must work in an inclusive environment where everyone has the right to ask and be heard. It should be made clear that the organization does not support the culture of silence, the main cause of many of the conflicts of interest and scandals.*

Leaders must create an organization with a culture where no one is afraid to share their opinion and recommendations. Organizational

---

* "Boeing's top lawyer spotlights company's ethical lapses," Law blog, January 31, 2006, *Wall Street Journal* Online, http://blogs.wsj.com/law/2006/01/31/boeings-top-lawyer-rips-into-his-company.

leaders must be humble and always be open to receiving advice, so employees are not reluctant to share their opinions. The honesty and respect of organizational leaders are necessary to achieve organizational trust. Leaders should encourage a transparent culture where their work teams always provide feedback because that will allow the organization to improve continuously.

As the entrepreneur Betsy Atkins suggests, at team meetings, observe how people interact – do they look engaged, do they ask questions? These indicators provide important insights into your organization's culture. Invite them to challenge your thoughts, and to bring a diversity of ideas and opinions to the table. When employees feel that they are being heard and when they know that their concerns are being noted, they will be more engaged, productive, and innovative.*

Complaints can be uncomfortable, but efficient companies see them as a contribution to improve and evolve.† As the consultant, Jaime Lopera Gutiérrez says, "A complaint is a gift when it is used to solve problems."‡

A simple complaint or feedback that is not given due attention can lead to a serious conflict.

The Boeing Company is an American multinational corporation that designs, manufactures, and sells airplanes. Boeing employs more than 130,000 people and has thousands of suppliers. The 737 MAX jet is one of Boeing's most important airplanes. However, after two Boeing 737 MAX aircraft crashed in October 2018 and March 2019, causing 346 deaths, the aviation authorizations grounded the 737 MAX. Boeing temporarily suspended its production and, therefore, lost millions of dollars. Due to the crisis, Boeing's CEO had to resign.

When analyzing why things happen, it is about determining the cause-effect relationship.

Internal employee communications were provided to congressional investigators and covered a five-year period before the crashes. The investigation revealed that while Boeing was going through the certification process, some problems arose in the MCAS (Maneuvering Characteristics

---

* Betsy Atkins, "Business Ethics And Integrity: It Starts With The Tone At The Top," February 7, 2019, www-forbes-com.cdn.ampproject.org.
† In the same way, for example, a 360-degree survey where the boss, peers, and subordinates evaluate the employee, or an audit report marking the opportunities for improvement in the different business units, can be uncomfortable but can also help continuous improvement.
‡ Jaime Lopera, *El Pez grande se come al lento* (The Big Fish Eats the Slow) (Colombia, Intermedio Editores, 2003), 189–90.

Augmentation System) automated control software system, but the warnings were disregarded.*

In 2014, an employee working on the MAX training materials told Boeing's chief technical pilot that the training material should include more information about how to handle certain emergencies. The chief technical pilot didn't relish that idea because it might lead the FAA (Federal Aviation Administration) to require more extensive training for MAX pilots.[†]

As David Gelles says in an article in *The New York Times*, "the culture of Boeing appears to be broken, with some senior employees having little regard for regulations, customers, and even co-workers."[‡]

From the review of employee internal communications, it was learned that one person wrote, "I honestly don't trust many people at Boeing."[§]

Sara Nelson, the president of the Association of Flight Attendants Union, said the messages revealed a "sick culture" at Boeing, noting that the "trust level was already in the toilet."[¶]

The 737 MAX crisis reminds us again of the importance of maintaining a culture of trust and compliance where employees can scale their problems and concerns without fear or pressure: a corporate culture where security is more important than profitability.

Companies must ensure employees share their concerns, enabling communication channels so employees have the opportunity to express their concerns.

For example, it is estimated that 70% of situations of violence occurring in workplaces could be prevented if the previous behaviors of the aggressors were duly taken care of. If the organization had known the previous behaviors, violence would probably have been avoided.

As the company cannot solve problems it does not know about, it is the responsibility of each employee to report immediately any type of irregular situation or violation of ethics they become aware of. This open

---

* BBCNEWS MUNDO, "Boeing 737 MAX 8: las demas acusaciones contra la empresa en el Congreso de EEUU por los accidentes del controvertido modelo de avion," ("737 MAX 8: the other accusations against the company in the US Congress for the accidents of the controversial aircraft model"), October 30, 2019, www.bbc.com.

† Matt Kelly, "How Pressure Invades Corporate Culture," January 12, 2020, radicalcompliance.com.

‡ David Gelles, "I Honestly Don't Trust Many People at Boeing: A Broken Culture Exposed," January 13, 2020, nytimes.com.

§ David Gelles, "I Honestly Don't Trust Many People at Boeing: A Broken Culture Exposed," January 13, 2020, nytimes.com.

¶ David Gelles, "I Honestly Don't Trust Many People at Boeing: A Broken Culture Exposed," January 13, 2020, nytimes.com.

communication allows the organization to bring to light the most secret actions and learn about emerging problems.

It is important that the problems, difficulties, and bad news not be hidden and to do so, leaders must ensure a culture where voices are protected.

Punishing an employee who does not report an irregular situation he or she may have knowledge of may seem unfair, but some companies believe it is better to do so because the integrity of the organization is achieved with the input of all members. Some organizations prefer to differentiate between the *obligation* to report an unethical activity and the *obligation* to collaborate in an investigation for potential unethical behavior. Organizations are usually stricter in the latter cases.

The Lebanese-American author Nassim Taleb said, "If you see fraud and do not say fraud, you are a fraud."*

Some people may be uncomfortable in the position of the accuser; however, ethic lines or helplines are a great tool for receiving anonymous complaints and raising questions about ethical or unethical conduct. All information received must be treated with the utmost confidentiality.

New technology has the potential to bring to light inequities and unethical acts and should be used to the maximum extent possible by the ethics and compliance programs so the reality is visible and problems are confronted before they grow.

US legislation regulates that companies listed on the stock exchange must have an ethical line available for employees to report complaints related to internal controls or accounting.†

A whistleblower is a person who exposes any kind of information or activity deemed illegal, unethical, or not correct within an organization that is either private or public.‡

The Whistleblower Protection Act of 1989, as amended, is a US federal law that protects federal whistleblowers who work for the government and report the possible existence of an activity constituting a violation of law, rules, or regulations, mismanagement, a gross waste of funds, abuse of authority, or a substantial and specific danger to public health and safety. A federal agency violates the Whistleblower Protection Act if agency authorities take (or threaten to take) retaliatory personnel action against any employee or applicant because of disclosure of information by that employee or applicant.§

---

* Nassim Nicholas Taleb, Quotecatalog.com.
† Section 301, Sarbanes-Oxley Act, 2002.
‡ en.wikipedia.org/wiki/Whistleblower.
§ en.wikipedia.org/wiki/Whistleblower Protection Act.

The Dodd-Frank Wall Street Reform and Consumer Protection Act of July 2010 created a rewards program for people who report to the SEC violations of security laws that lead to legal enforcement of SEC regulations.*

Section 922 of the Dodd-Frank Act provides the Commission shall pay awards to eligible whistleblowers who voluntarily provide the SEC with original information that leads to a successful enforcement action yielding monetary sanctions of over US$1 million.†

According to this law, a *whistleblower* is an individual who, being employed by a publicly traded company, provides the SEC with information related to a possible violation of securities laws, for example, allegations of false or misleading statements about prices or quantity of shares, misappropriation of funds or securities, manipulation of price or volume of securities, fraudulent offer or sale of securities, bribery of foreign officials, and any other fraudulent activity. This law helps to improve fraud detection and internal control systems.

The National Whistleblower Center is a nonprofit organization that provides education on whistleblower laws and a number of programs in support of whistleblowers.‡

Posters must be placed in all the business units and in the internal web-page briefly explaining open door policies and the option of the helpline. Posters must include telephone numbers and local and international email addresses (for multinational companies) where to file complaints.

Small pocket cards can also be distributed to employees with contact information from the ethics office.

It is convenient to use an ethical line where complaints can be reported 24 hours a day, and every day of the year. For example, a 1-800 telephone number handled by an external operator, who can answer calls in different languages and who can categorize the complaints and submit a report to the company within 24 hours of receiving the complaint

However, a disadvantage of the external line managed by a provider is the employees of the receiving provider do not understand the organization's internal areas and/or lexicon in depth, and the complaints may not be well transcribed in the reports.

---

* Under this Act whistleblowers can receive as much as 30% of any monies that the SEC recovers from a rule-breaking company.
† US Securities and Exchange Commission, "Whistleblower program," www.sec.gov/spotlight/dodd-frank/whistleblower.shtml.
‡ www.whistleblower.org.

An internal helpline or a voice-mail administered by the company may be a cheaper option, but anonymous whistleblowers generally prefer their voices not be recorded.

Although one of the advantages of an internal telephone line is the person who answers the calls has better knowledge of the business and is likely to understand the informant better; this process may not be seen as independent or impartial and those who report may feel confidentiality is compromised or their voices might be recognized.

Some people are also using anonymous social sharping apps like Whisper to break news. This app is a form of anonymous social media, allowing users to post and share photos and video messages anonymously. Whisper was the source when the CEO of American Apparel stepped down, accused of unethical conduct.*

To react as quickly as possible to mitigate and manage crises more effectively, some companies are using the AI platform Dataminr, a global real-time information Discovery company that is used as a source of breaking news alerts. Datarminr detects signals from public data sets, giving its clients an early line of sight into relevant breaking news and emerging risks, in real-time.†

The ethics office that receives and responds to inquiries and complaints must maintain the independence of judgment and confidentiality, and it must be fair and consistent in its decisions. This is extremely necessary in order to gain employee trust when making inquiries and complaints.

Complaints, inquiries, and responses given by the ethics office must be registered with an identification number in an electronic system so they can be tracked and identified quickly. Electronic complaint management systems are an invaluable source of information and enable the organization to analyze trends and data. This is a great source to maintain consistency in decision-making.

The ethics office's advisory service is intended for employees to seek help, advice, and guidance before taking any action.

Anonymous complaints should never be discredited. Organizations must treat all reports and complaints seriously and confidentially, regardless of their origin.

---

* Betsy Atkins, "Business Ethics And Integrity: It Starts With The Tone At The Top," February 7, 2019, www-forbes-com.cdn.ampproject.org.
† info.dataminr.com.

The ratio of complaints and queries received *versus* the number of company employees varies according to the culture of each country and company and the maturity of ethics and compliance program.

The Ethics & Compliance Initiative (ECI) is a leading provider of independent research about workplace integrity, ethical standards, and compliance processes. According to a research called "State of Ethics in Large Companies," created by the Ethics Research Center (ERC), the research arm of ECI, when the largest companies invest resources in ethics and compliance, gets impressive results:

> Large companies can dramatically improve their integrity by implementing effective ethics and compliance programs to reduce employee misconduct and improve every key measure of workplace behavior. On average, large companies with effective programs face half of the rules violations as those without effective programs. Their employees experience less retaliation for blowing the whistle on rule-breaking and feel less pressure to compromise standards.
>
> The study also credits effective programs and strong ethics cultures for making it more likely that employees will report wrongdoing when they see it. Nearly nine out of ten employees (87 percent) who observe violations at large companies with effective programs report those violations for action by higher-ups, compared to just 32 percent who report wrongdoing when programs are lacking. That's significant because reporting is essential for identifying and eliminating potential ethics risks.
>
> In companies with effective ethics and compliance programs, only ... 4% have suffered retaliation for reporting. This compares with ... 59% of those who experience reprisals when programs are ineffective and weak.*

ECI CEO Patricia Harned says, "Companies that invest in ethics reap an enormous return. ... Better workplace ethics cuts business risks by reducing the chance that serious ethics problems will throw companies off course and distract them from their core business."†

Due to the cases of sexual abuse of minors in the Catholic Church, in March 2019, the Vatican announced that it will implement a confidential and anonymous system to report misbehavior, similar to the ethical line used by the Church in Boston to denounce violations of the code of

---

* "When the largest companies invest resources in ethics and compliance, they get impressive results," www.ethics.org/ecihome/research/nbes/nbes-reports/large-companies.
† "Large companies can boost ethical performance, cut business risks," March 26, 2015, www.ethics .org/ecihome/research/nbes/nbes-reports/large-companies.

conduct. In a letter addressed to the faithful of the Archdiocese of Boston, Cardinal O'Malley said, "The crisis of sexual abuse by clergy is the greatest failure of the Church in my lifetime. It has eroded our moral authority."*

We all share in the responsibility to defend and live the organizational values every day. That includes keeping an open dialogue by asking questions when we don't know what to do and reporting concerns related to business activities.

It is an obligation to inform if someone is breaking the law or the code of ethics, regardless of the person's position in the company or whether the person is a vendor, customer, or temporary worker.

Raising concerns shows commitment to act ethically and fosters a culture of compliance.

23.3 PROTOCOL ON COMPLAINTS, INVESTIGATIONS, SANCTIONS, AND CASE MANAGEMENT

The fact that a complaint or inquiry is reported to the ethics office does not mean that the issue is treated as an ethical case. The ethics office analyzes the information received and, if applicable, it will start an investigation.

If there are long delays in the resolution of the case (for whatever reason), the lack of action or results may be perceived by the complainant as lack of interest, and confidence in the reporting and investigation system may be adversely damaged, which could, in turn, affect the effectiveness of the system. Investigating complaints in a timely manner is an important aspect of building trust.

The purpose of the investigation is to know what has happened and to correct processes to avoid similar situations in the future. Each organization must have a protocol established whereby the most significant and riskiest complaints are immediately communicated to the ethics office of the headquarters.

The company must define in a protocol, situations that qualify for the escalation system. Thus, for example: (i) allegations of fraud or internal

---

* Patricia Ynestroza, "Iglesia en Boston Crea Línea Telefónica Directa para Denunciar Abusos" ("Church in Boston Creates Direct Telephone Line to Report Abuses"), *Vatican News*, March 12, 2019, www.vaticannews.va; "O'Malley Introduces Whistleblower System for Complaints Against Boston Bishops," *CNA-Catholic News Agency*, catholicnewsagency.com; "Cardinal Sean P. O. Malley's Lenten Letter," www.bostoncatholic.org.

theft that imply a significant financial impact on the organization (for example, any allegations of fraud or internal theft above US$100,000 must be reported to the home office within 24 hours of being informed of the fact); (ii) allegations that may cause serious damage to the reputation or image of the company, published in the media; (iii) allegations involving senior executives in the organization; (iv) allegations that may generate strong negative publicity for the organization; (v) reports of active or passive bribes involving public officials; (vi) allegations about commercial bribery; (vii) allegations about manipulation of the financial statements; and (viii) allegations of theft of confidential data.

Certain allegations can be very serious and generate a high risk; therefore, it is advisable that the CEO be informed before the investigation begins.

The company needs to have a trained and specialized area for investigations, to carry out the inquiry efficiently and fairly. Internal investigations should not affect the dignity, intimacy, or privacy of the interviewed. One should not inquire, for example, about political, religious, or sexual preferences. There must always be a balance between the right to investigate and the protection of the interviewed to privacy and dignity.

The policy must include access to: (i) the corporate mail the company assigns to the worker; (ii) the call log of the cell phones or telephone lines provided by the company; (iii) the satellite tracking record of the company's vehicles; (iv) the internet search history from company's computers; (v) the company's lockers and drawers; (vi) video surveillance in office spaces, parking lots, and/or factories; (vii) inspections of clothes, bags, and cars in the entrance and exit of workplaces; and (viii) interview employees to carry out internal investigations. Employees must be informed in advance that the information stored in those sources is the company's property.*

The life cycle of a case investigated should not exceed 90 days or 120 days for those matters of greater complexity where external investigation services are used and/or when document translation is required. The ethics office supervises the investigation and receives the support of experts to carry out the fact-finding whose responsibility falls in lawyers, investigators, and/or personnel from the security and/or the human resources area, depending on the case.

---

* "Lineamientos para la Implementación de Programas de Integridad," www.argentina.gob.ar/ sites/default/files/lineamientos_de_integridad_para_el_mejor_cumplimiento_de_lo_estableci do_en_los_arts_22_y_23_ley_27.401_0.pdf ("Guidelines for the Implementation of Integrity Programs").

An internal policy must state that the accused must be informed of the allegation, the topics the investigation report must include, and the format the report must-have.

Whoever is the object of an investigation must have the opportunity to be heard and has the right to the "presumption of innocence" until proven guilty.

The Latin locution *In dubio pro reo* (in case of doubt in favor of the accused) expresses the legal principle that in case of lack of sufficient evidence, the accused will be favored.

During the investigation, all the interviewees must be made aware of the duty to maintain confidentiality during and after the investigation is completed, as well as the obligation to cooperate and to tell the truth.*

An investigation typically analyzes physical and electronic documentation, reviews policies, sets interviews, and documents the ascertainment obtained. These days, more than 90% of the information is generated electronically.†

The ethics office has the role of general supervisor of the investigation and receiver of the investigation report, which must include the presentation of facts, witnesses interviewed, and policies, laws, regulations, and/or code of ethics that could have been violated.

The ethics office determines if there is sufficient information in the report received from the investigators to consider the case closed. Subsequently, the ethics office informs the business management about the results of the investigation and recommends the course of action, including, if necessary, disciplinary sanctions.

The business area decides how it wants to close the case, although most of the time it coincides with the recommendation of the ethics office due to the experience of this office in the administration of cases and the need to ensure consistency in the decisions taken.

The credibility of the entire process depends on the objectivity of the decisions based on proven facts and taking into account preexisting cases and similar decisions, in order to achieve consistency and justice.

Once the investigation is concluded and the actions are defined, the complainant must be notified of the conclusion of the investigation of the case, in order to establish trust and credibility in the company's complaint system.

---

* Good information on good practice in investigations can be obtained from the Council of the Inspectors General on Integrity and Efficiency, www.ignet.gov.
† One gigabyte of data is equivalent to 100,000 pages of documents.

The entire complaint reporting system may not achieve its objective if the complainants perceive their complaints are not investigated or are not taken seriously.

The accused person must receive information about the result of the complaint, but not about the data of the complainant. If the complaint was closed due to a lack of substantiation, the complainant and the defendant must also be notified.

It is usual that due to the allegation, processes, policies, or controls that should be improved are identified and, therefore, the investigation process helps to prevent similar situations.

The source of the problem must be corrected to prevent it from being repeated in the future and should be communicated to internal audit and to the business area and, as the case may be, it should be included in future training sessions.

The ethics office must keep a record of the different allegations, investigations, and measures taken. Said registry must be periodically audited to correct errors and ensure the quality and veracity of the data.

Companies must sanction employees who fail to comply with laws or internal company policies, or who do not cooperate with an investigation. Disciplinary sanctions may include, for example, the need for training, a verbal or written warning, demotion, or dismissal. The severity of the offense, the intent, the impact of the offense and whether there are mitigating circumstances are taken into account, for example, if it is the first time the individual has committed the offense or if he or she is a repeat offender.

The organization must maintain a commitment to justice (organizational justice), whereby similar infractions receive similar sanctions, regardless of who commits them. Disciplinary sanctions send a strong message about the organization's commitment to ethics and compliance and the consequences of noncompliance with the code of conduct and the laws are consistent, without regard to hierarchies or favoritism.

In 1959, in an interview, the British philosopher Bertrand Russell (1872–1970) was asked what advice he could give to future generations and, he said:

> When you are studying any topic, ask yourself, what are the facts and what is the truth that those facts reveal? Never let yourself be diverted either by what you want to believe or by what you think would bring you to benefit if it were believed, only observe what the facts are.*

---

* Bertrand Russell – Face to Face interview (BBC, 1959), YouTube.

That advice must be used by all those who must resolve situations every day. Employees will agree with the decisions made if there is organizational justice. When a fair process is exercised, people trust.*

Employees must know the code of conduct exists to be complied with, and its violation will involve disciplinary sanctions, including dismissal. Employees involved in unethical behaviors should be disciplined; otherwise, the other employees may assume that if they also act unethically, they would not be disciplined.

Finally, since what is measured can be compared and improved, it is convenient to keep statistics of the allegations received; the disciplinary sanctions applied; the cases received versus closed; the number of allegations and contacts received by a certain number of employees; the duration of the cases, measuring how many cases are open less than three months and how many are delayed in closing between 90 and 120 days; and, in addition, a record of the questions and answers provided by the ethics office.

It is also convenient to make this measurement and comparison by countries or regions where the company operates.

With this information, you can measure the efficiency of the whole system and make the necessary changes to improve it continuously.

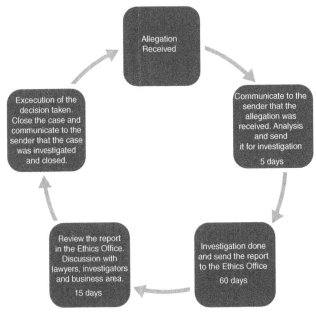

---

* W. Chan Kim and Renee Mauborgne, *Blue Ocean Strategy* (Harvard Business School Press, 2005), 175.

23.4 ELECTRONIC FILES

It is desirable organizations record, in addition to complaints, contacts, ethical opinions, and research, all communication and education activities developed to promote an ethical culture in the company. A good electronic file system helps to identify the content of information, facilitates access to it, and preserves it. It allows quick responses to unexpected requirements from the CEO, the board of directors, the Justice, or the Government, facilitates the presentation of evidence, and reduces the risk of fines for not providing the information required by the authorities in the required time.

A file maintenance program should include an internal policy on the handling of document files, and its classification by type of complaints received, ethical opinions provided, and dates.

23.5 ETHICAL SURVEYS, FOCUS GROUPS, AND EXIT INTERVIEWS

Annual Ethical Climate Questionnaires and focus groups allow knowing the opinion of employees regarding the ethical conduct of the organization and the degree of confidence in the system

Also, they are very useful to know:

1. How the leaders of the company are perceived in matters of integrity
2. If they consider that the company treats employees with respect
3. If they consider that there is justice in the decisions made (organizational justice)
4. If employees trust that the allegations will be investigated
5. If employees are afraid of retaliation in case of sending complaints

Surveys identify the strengths and weaknesses of the ethics program and determine if the program is effective in promoting and sustaining the ethical culture in the organization. By identifying areas for improvement, surveys generate information to carry out action plans. For example, the company should implement ethical plans in facilities or departments with lower integrity scores.

From these surveys, it is possible to know if employees are afraid of reprisals, what they are subject to, and if they work in an environment where they can express themselves in an open and transparent way.

Employees, customers, and suppliers can see the company differently than one sees it, and surveys are a useful tool to know how the company is perceived, and what aspects should be improved to develop action plans.

Surveying the organization's ethical culture sends also a message to the employees that ethics is important.

Human resources departments should conduct "exit interviews" with employees leaving the company. Employees who leave the organization are more willing to report any unethical behavior or compliance problem they know.

The areas of opportunity are analyzed and specific action and correction plans are created.

23.6 ANNUAL WORK GOALS, PERFORMANCE APPRAISALS, BONUSES, AND BUSINESS PLANS

Work goals can be red flags and put people and companies at risk. The objectives, although they must be challenging, must be also attainable.

Amazon recorded 9.6 serious injuries per 100 workers at its distribution centers in 2018, compared to the industry average of 4 serious injuries per 100 workers. Some Amazon workers said they broke the rules to keep up with "ruthless quotas."*

As mentioned in Chapter 13, Domino's Pizza had guaranteed that customers would receive their pizzas within 30 minutes of placing an order. In 1993 a woman was injured when a Domino's delivery driver ran a red light and collided with her vehicle.

If the company establishes an "extraordinary bonus" reward to employees who achieve certain "extraordinary results" (e.g., sales and/or contracts, profit margins, business openings.), it is necessary to reinforce the message that if these "extraordinary" results are obtained in violation of laws or ethical conduct; instead of an award, they will receive a sanction. Incentives must be always aligned to performance with integrity.

If work goals set are almost impossible to achieve, some people may want to act dishonestly to accomplish the goals and obtain the bonus.

---

* "Happy holidays? Workers injuries spike at amazon warehouses seasonally, data shows," December 3, 2019, www.marketplace.org.

In the annual goals of managers and directors, it must be stated that their actions must be in accordance with the policies, principles, and values of the organization, following the guidelines of the code of ethics.

Goals should not be only numerical or quantitative; they should include the qualitative component. In performance evaluations we can ask the following questions:

Have we treated people with dignity?

What kind of actions and initiatives did we carry out to promote diversity?

Did we comply with the rules and procedures to achieve the objectives?

Sometimes executives realize how they are perceived after receiving feedback from their bosses and other employees either from 360-degree evaluations or from annual performance evaluations.

Business plans must be realistic, otherwise, the pressure to get results can be significant and counterproductive.

For this reason, the ethics and compliance cultural component should be included in business plans (for example, if business units are to be opened in a short period of time, a clear explanation of how the permits, licenses, and approvals shall be obtained within the framework of the law and within the period mentioned in the business plan).

Leaders have an irreplaceable role in strengthening their teams to fulfill objectives within ethical conduct and in compliance with regulations and internal policies.

Specific objectives of ethics and compliance should be part of the annual performance evaluation processes of the company's leaders.* These could be expressed as follows:

I'm committed to complying with the law, regulations, internal policies and the highest standards of ethics and integrity. This is not optional. If there is a conflict between doing the right thing and fulfilling the business plan, we will do the right thing. I will create an open environment where associates are treated with consideration and respect and are empowered to come forward and report concerns without retaliation. All of this is necessary to build and sustain a culture that protects our employees and the company.

---

* Some companies do it, "Boards Tie Executive Pay to Sustainability Goals at Duke, Baxter" ("The Week's News from Other Boardrooms," May 7, 2007); "Boards Tie Top Executive Pay to Enterprise Risk Management Objectives," www.AgendaWeek.com/.

Siemens implemented incentives to comply with good governance, and 17.5% of executives' awards are linked to compliance.* Other multinational companies also have tied their performance appraisal system directly to competencies like respect, integrity, trust, and honesty. These actions help ensure that the culture of results with integrity is branched across the organization and its importance for the company is clear.

As Keith Darcy, senior adviser to Deloitte, says, "Failure to align ethics and values to business strategies and operating plans bears potentially heavy costs."[†]

Novartis, the Swiss drug manufacturer, decided its employees will only receive a bonus if they meet or exceed expectations of ethical behavior. The company believes ethical culture is a priority after costly bribery scandals or legal settlements in South Korea, China, and the United States. The CEO of Novartis, Vas Narasimhan, said, "Novartis wants to have the right balance between pay for performance and having the right behavior."[‡]

23.7 DUE DILIGENCE OF SUPPLIERS, THIRD PARTY INTERMEDIARIES, AND PARTNERS

Considering the risks related to the supply chain, factories, compliance with labor laws, occupational safety and health, money laundering, bribery, and so on, it is advisable to conduct thorough due diligence of companies that may become or are suppliers, third-party intermediaries or partners of the organization to reduce reputational risk.

Corporate criminal responsibility can be triggered when a bribe is paid by a third party. Therefore, companies must analyze transactions made by certain third parties, to avoid the risk of third parties bribing on their behalf.

Due diligence is a valuable tool to analyze and better know the trajectory, reputation, and background of potential suppliers, partners, or future companies to be acquired. The due diligence process allows us to

---

* Michael Ritter, *El Valor del Capital Reputacional* (Olivos Ritter & Partners, 2013), 323 ("The Value of Reputational Capital").

† "Building world-class ethics and compliance programs: Making a good program great," www.deloitte.com.

‡ John Miller, "Novartis links bonus to ethics in bid to rebuild reputation," September 17, 2018, www.reuters.com.

analyze the structure of the third party, its experience in the industry, and verify possible conflicts of interest, wrongful acts or irregularities, its financial solvency, its professional suitability, and the existence or not of a compliance program and anti-corruption policies.

Thanks to this due diligence process, it is also possible to know if the company was previously investigated for violations of anti-corruption laws. In the case of acquired or merged companies, this process allows us to know if inappropriate payments were made to public officials or if hidden liabilities were detected in violation of the anti-corruption policies of the acquiring company, and in such cases, immediately report them to the competent authorities.

There are international legal and consultancy firms specialized in the due diligence process; for example, KPMG, Dun & Bradstreet, Kroll, Deloitte, or Ernst & Young.

The World-Check database of Politically Exposed Persons (PEPs) and heightened risk individuals and organizations is used around the world to help identify and manage financial, regulatory, and reputational risk. In financial regulation, "politically exposed person" (PEP) is a term describing someone who has been entrusted with a prominent public function. A PEP generally presents a higher risk for potential involvement in bribery and corruption by virtue of their position and potential influence.*

Organizations can also consult the OFAC list to make a previous checklist of potential suppliers and partners. The Office of Foreign Assets Control (OFAC) is a financial intelligence and enforcement agency of the US Treasury Department. It administers and enforces economic and trade sanctions in support of US national security and foreign policy objectives. OFAC was founded in 1950 and is a financial intelligence agency of the US Department of the Treasury. It applies economic and commercial sanctions in support of national security and foreign policy objectives of the United States. This agency has the power to impose significant penalties against entities that defy its directives, including imposing fines, freezing assets, and barring parties from operating in the United States.

---

* Initially, World-Check's intelligence was used by banks and financial institutions as a comprehensive solution for assessing, managing, and remediating risk. However, as legislation has become increasingly complex and its reach has become increasingly global, the demand for such intelligence has grown beyond the financial sector to include organizations from all sectors. World-Check's research team monitors emerging risks in more than 60 languages, covering over 240 countries and territories worldwide. en.wikipedia.org/wiki/Politically_exposed_person; see also en.wikipedia.org/wiki/World-Check.

The OFAC publishes a list of Specially Designated Nationals (SDNs), which lists people, organizations, and vessels with whom US citizens and permanent residents are prohibited from doing business. As of October 7, 2015, the SDN list had more than 15,200 entries from 155 countries. Of those, 178 entries were for aircraft and 575 entries were for ships ("vessels"). The remaining 14,467 entries were for designated individuals and organizations.*

In 2008, Apple entered into a development agreement with SIS, a Slovenian company, without noticing that SIS and its majority shareholders were on the SDN list. Apple's detection software did not identify SIS or its main shareholder. Apple made several payments to SIS and when the company discovered the violations, in February 2017, Apple reported them to the OFAC. Apple had to improve the detection software of the SDN list, instituted mandatory training for employees, and paid a fine of US$467,000 to the OFAC.†

The OFAC list differs from the list maintained pursuant to Section 314(a) of the Patriot Act. The US Patriot Act is an Act of Congress signed into law by US president George W. Bush on October 26, 2001.‡ In accordance with this law, all financial institutions that conduct business in the United States must identify any person seeking to open a bank account.

In addition, the regulation imposes the obligation to maintain the records of this verification process for five years after the account is closed and the customer's name must be compared with those on the list. Individuals and entities listed in the Patriot Act have sanctions imposed by the US government.

In 2011, the World Economic Forum's Partnering Against Corruption Initiative (PACI) developed Good Practice Guidelines on Conducting Third-Party Due Diligence. The guidelines are aimed at helping organizations mitigate the risk of becoming involved in corruption through third parties (e.g., agents, consultants, suppliers, distributors, joint-venture partners, or any individual or entity that has some form of business relationship with the organization).

---

* en.wikipedia.org/wiki/Office_of_Foreign_Assets_Control.

† Michael Volkov, "Apple agreed to pay OFAC $467K for Violations of the Foreign Narcotics Kingpin Sanctions Regulations," December 2, 2019, https://blog.volkovlaw.com/2019/12/apple-pays-467k-to-ofac-for-sanctions-violations/.

‡ With its ten-letter abbreviation (USA PATRIOT) expanded the Act's full title is "Uniting and Strengthening America by Providing Appropriate Tools Required to Intercept and Obstruct Terrorism Act of 2001." en.wikipedia.org/wiki/Patriot_Act.

Conducting risk-based due diligence on third parties has become a legal expectation in many countries that have ratified the OECD Anti-Bribery Convention and/or the United Nations Convention against Corruption, and it helps organizations decrease the risk of criminal culpability for corrupt third-party conduct.

Companies are responsible for the actions of any third party acting on behalf, in representation or in the interest of the companies, whether or not they have entered into a written contract to represent them.

As companies cannot outsource corruption, it is necessary to know their partners in business. However, as the PACI Guidelines say, not all of an organization's third parties must be subject to anti-corruption due diligence:

> Large and even medium-sized organizations can have thousands of third-party business relationships, and many of these are subject to little or no corruption risk. Submitting all of these third parties to corruption due diligence would not only be burdensome and costly in terms of time and resources, but much of the effort would add little value to the organization's anti-corruption efforts.
>
> The key to effective third-party due diligence is knowing which third parties pose the most corruption risk to the organization and targeting them for the thoughtful review.*
>
> As organizations consider which third parties need to go through due diligence, they may also need to determine how far down the supply chain their due diligence efforts should go. Indeed, an organization's third party may itself use another third party to perform its contract, thereby pushing corruption risks further down the supply chain.†

When dealing with potential suppliers there are some red flags to consider:

- Does the third party operate in an industry or geographic location perceived to have higher corruption risks?
- Did you find the reputation for integrity issues related to the third party in internet searches?
- Will the third party have interaction with government officials in the course of doing work for the organization?

---

* "Good Practice Guidelines on Conducting Third-Party Due Diligence," Partnering Against Corruption Initiative (PACI), 13, World Economic Forum.
† "Good Practice Guidelines on Conducting Third-Party Due Diligence," Partnering Against Corruption Initiative (PACI), 14, World Economic Forum.

- Is the retention of the third party encouraged or required by a government official?
- Is the third party wholly or partly (directly or indirectly) owned by a government official/entity or does it have direct or indirect links with government officials/entities?
- Does the third party have family or business ties with government officials?
- Does the third party require payment by unusual means (e.g., split into small amounts or in a country or currency not related to the transaction)?
- Does the third party require that its compensation takes the form of a political or charitable contribution?
- Does the third-party request discretionary authority to handle local matters alone?
- Is the third-party candidate the most suitable candidate in terms of quality, price, and expertise?
- Does the third party plan to use any other entities or individuals, including subsidiaries, affiliates, partnerships, or joint ventures, to perform services under the proposed agreement?
- Does the third party, or its key employees, possess the necessary professional degrees, experience, regulatory licenses, and certificates to perform services under the proposed agreement?
- Has the third party made comments to the effect that any particular payment, contribution, or other activity is needed to "get the business"?
- Has the third party, or any key employee or senior management member of the third party, ever been convicted of a felony, misdemeanor, or any other crime? Has the third party made any settlements out of court for matters related to corruption, facilitation payments, or fraud?
- Is there negative press coverage or findings in publicly accessible registers or filings indicating any regulatory or legal proceedings of this nature pending against the third-party organization or any of its key employees or senior management?
- Does the third party, or any of its key employees or senior management, appear on a denied-party or denied-person list (e.g., OFAC list)?
- What is the general reputation of the third party according to its business/bank references and the opinion of other parties interviewed?

- Is the third party incorporated offshore with no evidently legitimate reason?
- Do the third party use bank accounts in third countries (i.e., neither in the country of service nor in the country of the third party's incorporation) and lacks any evidently legitimate reason to do so?
- Does the third party ask for cash payment, or advance payments (where advance payments are not customary), or for the splitting of the payment in several small installments (each of which seems to fall below the usual de *minimis* thresholds for anti-money laundering checks conducted by banks).
- Is the third party reluctant to answer due diligence questions, in particular, questions of ownership or affiliations, or answers relevant questions evasively?
- Does the third party suggest, in the course of negotiations, to suddenly contract not with itself but instead with another third party affiliated with it, or suggests the use of an unnecessarily complex transaction structure whose legitimate purpose is not spontaneously clear?
- Does the third party want to work without a contract?
- Is the third party hesitant to make anti-corruption compliance certifications?
- Does the total amount to be paid for goods and services appear to be unreasonably high or above the customary or arms-length amount?

All documentation relating to the due diligence processes, risk indicators, and red flags should be retained by the organization. Once the data has been collected and properly verified and validated, organizations should request to include the following provisions in their contractual agreements with third parties:

- A written agreement by the third party to comply with the organization's anti-corruption policies and programs and/or with applicable laws and regulations
- A written confirmation that the third party has read the organization's Code of Conduct and agrees to satisfy its requirements
- A provision obligating the third party to maintain accurate books and records, and an effective system of internal controls
- A "right to audit" provision, providing access to the third party's relevant records

- A contractual right of termination in case of breach of anti-corruption laws or any clause of the contract
- Provisions limiting the third party's ability to act on behalf of the company and/or have interactions with government officials
- A right to implement ethics and anti-corruption training to the third party
- A provision providing for the cooperation of the third party in case internal investigations are carried out
- A request for the third party to submit an annual certification of compliance with applicable anti-corruption laws

Many reputational risks due to lack of ethics and compliance come from partners, suppliers, and third-party intermediaries; therefore, these mitigation tools such as due diligence, anti-corruption certifications, ethical and anti-corruption training, affidavits and audits are recommended.*

The due diligence actions and all those activities carried out to execute an integrity program, must be duly documented, as evidence of the efforts made by the company to comply with regulations.

The compliance department should monitor the third-party's due diligence process and periodically review its suitability and effectiveness.

The organization's top leadership should make clear that the appointment of or partnerships with third parties should be subject to risk-based due diligence to mitigate potential corruption risks.

Following these practices, organizations will minimize the risk of being involved in corruption through their third parties.

23.8 MONITORING AND INTERNAL AUDIT

An ethics and compliance program requires permanent monitoring of the effectiveness of the program's prevention and detection of unethical and illegal activities. It is necessary to measure the impact and progress of the program in relation to the objectives set. Through monitoring, the compliance team reviews and identifies strengths and gaps in the processes and acts quickly to remedy them.

---

* "Ethic Intelligence," for example, since 2006 collaborates with companies with certifications to prevent corruption.

Integrity programs should be reviewed periodically to verify if the main risks of the industry where the company does business are analyzed and if the controls applied to mitigate them are effective.

The Japanese word *kaizen* means "change for better." Kaizen is a Japanese quality system that focuses on processes of continuous improvement. Compliance programs must follow that philosophy and always evolve, because of risks, business and technology changes.

The internal audit evaluates existing controls to prevent, detect, and mitigate risks; conducts a retrospective and periodical review of transactions for compliance with applicable laws and policies; and analyzes (i) whether the company has implemented the elements of the program suggested by the Federal Sentencing Guidance and (ii) the effectiveness of controls to reduce the risks detected in the risk assessment.

The following should be monitored and audited:

1. The degree of execution of the action plans arising from the risk assessment
2. The affidavits of conflict of interest
3. The accuracy of the information on existing complaints
4. The contacts and opinions recorded in the case management system
5. The integrity of investigations
6. The consistency in sanctions
7. The training carried out
8. The operation and effectiveness of procedures to report or conduct ethical consultations
9. That posters with ethical information are placed in all units and in visible locations
10. Accurate and active email addresses and telephone numbers
11. Timely response to messages and, where appropriate, their investigation in accordance with internal policies

Robert Klitgaard, Ph.D. at Harvard and anti-corruption consultant has pointed out that audits should focus on those areas or people that have great decision-making power.*

Program audits should be documented and annually submitted to the compliance and ethics committee members and to the CEO.

The internal audit may include recommendations; collaborating with the improvement of the ethics and compliance program.

---

* "Dónde está la Corrupción," Robert Klitgaard, 2013, YouTube ("Where is Corruption?").

There are organizations that audit integrity programs and certify them according to certain generally accepted quality standards. The specialized external analysis of the integrity program and its validation and certification are good practices to strengthen the process of continuous improvement.

In 2018, Edesur* became the first company in Latin America to receive the certification of ISO 37001: 2016 ("Anti-Bribery Management System") granted by Intertek Group.[†]

23.9 BUILD AND IMPLEMENT YOUR "PROTECTIVE SHIELD"

Roberto Sanchez (1945–2010) is a popular Argentine singer who has sold more than eight million albums. Sandro tried to keep his private life away from journalists. He said, "I have nothing to hide but I have a lot to protect."[‡]

Sustainable companies, like Sandro, have nothing to hide but a lot to protect.

In organizations it is not enough to only create integrity programs, it is also necessary to implement them. As the president of Transparency International, lawyer Delia Ferreira Rubio says, "what we need is AIRE (Action, Implementation, Report, and Evaluation)."

"Implement a program that manages risks, prevents crimes and fines, promotes business ethics, and protects the reputation of the company" must be a priority for companies.

Hiding from problems under the rug doesn't make them go away. Like Carlos Rozen, partner of BDO Global firm says, "In some companies, a fraud is happening at this time, although perhaps we never know it."[§]

Just as financial investors reduce stock market risk diversifying and combining their investments, in the same way, corporate risks are diminished when the tools to combat them are diversified.

---

* Distributor of electric power in Argentina.
[†] Andres Krom, "Una Empresa Argentina se convirtió en la Primera en Sacar un Certificado Anticorrupción en la Región," July 6, 2018, www.lanacion.com.ar ("An Argentine Company became the first to obtain an Anti-Corruption Certificate in the Region"). To achieve certification, Edesur underwent a thorough audit. Intertek Group is an English company, founded in 1888, that audits the quality of products, processes, and systems. www.intertek.com.
[‡] He was the first Latin American artist to sell out a show at the Madison Square Garden in New York. "The Argentine Elvis Dies," wrote the *New York Times* and the *Washington Post*. "A un Año de su Muerte, Fanáticos Homenajearon a Sandro," January 4, 2011, www.ambito.com ("One year after his death, fans paid tribute to Sandro").
[§] Carlos Rozen, partner of BDO Argentina, "Hay Más Casos de Fraude en las Empresas y los Montos cada vez son Mayores," September 10, 2015, www.clarin.com.ar ("There are More Cases of Fraud in Companies and the Amounts are Increasing").

An old African proverb says that "several webs united can catch a lion."* Companies must create an infrastructure for the prevention of and reaction to risks that makes illegal and unethical behavior difficult.

Savater says, "In countries where there is less corruption it is simply because it is more difficult. It is not a moral issue; it is a problem of institutions."†

The elements or tools of an ethics and compliance program can be classified into:

1. *Preventive* measures, such as a culture of integrity, training, and policies and procedures
2. *Detection*, for example, risk assessments, ethics, audits, and SWOT
3. *Response*, for example, investigations and sanctions.

Each industry and business has its particularities and will apply the elements that it considers most effective to achieve an effective program.

Austrian psychiatrist Viktor Frankl (1905–1997) said that a person can choose "one's attitude in any given set of circumstances, to choose one's own way."‡

American Christian Pastor Charles Swindoll says, "Life is 10% what happens to you and 90% how you react to it."§

How should one react to the risks faced by the organization?

You must go ahead with the changes your company needs.

As Ramiro Cabrero, Baker Hughes' compliance officer says, "there are cultural changes that are born of conviction and there are changes that are born of necessity."¶ In any case, any company must be prepared to face corporate risks to which it is inexorably exposed.

In a highly regulated world with so many and varied risks, an effective program of ethics and compliance – although imperfect – is an indispensable tool of corporate governance.

Ernst & Young (EY), one of the largest professional services firms in the world, said in its 2007 fraud report that

---

* Robin Sharma, *The Monk Who Sold His Ferrari* (South American, 2010), 158.
† Guadalajara International Book Fair in Mexico, November 29, 2011, cultura.elpais.com.
‡ www.goodreads.com/author/quotes/2782.Viktor_E_Frankl.
§ www.brainyquote.com/quotes/charles_r_swindoll_388332.
¶ Ramiro Cabrero, "Hay Cambios Culturales que nacen de la Convicción y otros de la Necesidad," September 30, 2018, www.lanacion.com.ar ("There are Cultural Changes that are born from Conviction and others from Need").

Preventing fraud increases the chances of successfully crowning the efforts of the vast majority of executives who daily give the organization its personal effort and talent. ... Preventing fraud, companies are simultaneously protecting the interests of their employees, customers, shareholders and society in general.*

Ernst & Young (EY) published also a 2018 report called "Integrity in the Spotlight, The Future of Compliance." In its introduction, Andrew Gordon, EY Global Leader, wrote:

Between October 2017 and February 2018, we interviewed 2,550 executives from 55 countries and territories. The interviews show that fraud and corruption in business are not going away.

We found that many businesses have reached a certain level of maturity in their compliance programs, with the vast majority of executives interviewed aware of anti-corruption policies, procedures, and intent from management. However, we see a mismatch between this awareness and employee behavior – and we continue to see ethical failures, business losses, and consequent reputational damage.

The survey results suggest that the benefits of demonstrating organizational integrity go beyond the avoidance of penalties and can actually improve business performance. This makes sense: doing the wrong thing is a lost opportunity to do the right thing.†

Professor Lynn Sharp Paine has written about Martin Marietta, a company that merged with Lockheed Corporation in 1995 to form Lockheed Martin:

Martin Marietta Corporation, the US aerospace and defense contractor implemented an ethics program in 1985. ... Today top-level managers say the ethics program has helped the company avoid serious problems and become more responsive to its more than 90,000 employees. The ethics network, which tracks the number and types of cases and complaints, has served as an early warning system for poor management, quality and safety defects, racial and gender discrimination, environmental concerns, inaccurate and false records and personal grievances regarding salaries, promotions, and layoffs. Martin Marietta is able to take corrective action more quickly and with a lot less pain. In many cases, potentially embarrassing

---

* Ernst and Young, 2007 Fraud Report.
† Ernst and Young, Global Fraud Survey 2018, fraudsurveys.ey.com/ey-global-fraud-survey-2018/in troduction/.

problems have been identified and dealt with before becoming a management crisis, a lawsuit or a criminal investigator.*

The organization obtains success in compliance when the risks are permanently monitored.

The company must always be prepared to act in the face of the worst possible scenario. Therefore, with the aforementioned elements, the organization must build a compliance shield in order to protect itself.

23.9.1 A Protective Shield against the Risk of Lack of Ethics and Compliance

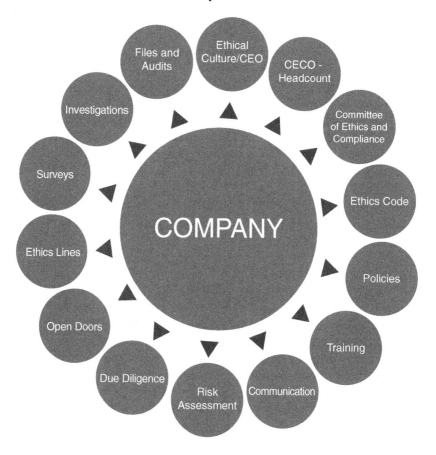

---

* Lynn Sharp Paine, "Managing for organizational integrity," *Harvard Business Review* (March–April 1994): 114.

If an integrity plan is designed and implemented with the elements recommended in this book and where priority is given to compliance with laws and good treatment of employees over numbers, the company will have a competitive advantage, it will be more protected, will make better decisions and will have greater possibilities of controlling the damage and survive in an increasingly volatile, fast, uncertain, and dangerous business environment.

Therefore, to achieve a more sustainable company it is advisable to meet these four stages:

1- Build an ethical culture in the organization
2- Design an integrity program
3- Identify the main risks
4- Implement the program

24

The Importance of Ethics and Compliance in Corporations

Ethics and Compliance are the platforms for the sustainable growth of successful companies.

Below are some examples that help us to become aware and understand better how ethics and compliance are an essential part of the long-term growth strategy of large corporations.

This selection of statements of leading companies, from the most varied industries, can be a mirror to look for those business leaders who strive to spread the ethics, values, and compliance in their organizations.

Johnson & Johnson has been a leader in integrating values into the corporate culture. Robert Wood Johnson took the management of the company in 1932 and 11 years later wrote a one-page document known as "Our Credo." The values that guide decision-making in J & J are in this document.

The Johnson & Johnson creed states that the company's primary responsibility is with people who use its products and services, the second is with employees, the third is with the community and the environment and, finally, the fourth is with shareholders. If the first three responsibilities are fulfilled, the shareholders will benefit.

The document helps the company create a culture of alignment of employee behavior with company values. The Credo says:

> We believe our first responsibility is to the doctors, nurses, and patients, to mothers and fathers and all others who use our products and services. In meeting their needs everything we do must be of high quality. We must constantly strive to reduce our costs in order to maintain reasonable prices. Customers' orders must be serviced promptly and accurately. Our suppliers and distributors must have an opportunity to make a fair profit.

We are responsible to our employees, the men, and women who work with us throughout the world. Everyone must be considered as an individual. We must respect their dignity and recognize their merit. They must have a sense of security in their jobs. Compensation must be fair and adequate, and working conditions clean, orderly and safe. We must be mindful of ways to help our employees fulfill their family responsibilities. Employees must feel free to make suggestions and complaints. There must be equal opportunity for employment, development, and advancement for those qualified. We must provide competent management, and their actions must be just and ethical.

We are responsible to the communities in which we live and work and to the world community as well. We must be good citizens – support good works and charities and bear our fair share of taxes. We must encourage civic improvements and better health and education. We must maintain in good order the property we are privileged to use, protecting the environment and natural resources.

Our final responsibility is to our stockholders. Business must make a sound profit. We must experiment with new ideas. Research must be carried on, innovative programs developed and mistakes paid for. New equipment must be purchased, new facilities provided and new products launched. Reserves must be created to provide for adverse times. When we operate according to these principles, the stockholders should realize a fair return.*

Alex Gorsky, chairman, and CEO of Johnson & Johnson said in an introductory letter to the Code of Business Conduct:

Every day, our products and services touch the lives of one billion people around the world – what I view as not only a great privilege but a great responsibility. Our Company's global reach is a testament to the high quality that our customers have come to expect from Johnson & Johnson, but also speaks to the tremendous amount of trust customers have in each of our businesses. As the world's largest health care company, we've been building that trust for more than a century.

I am proud to lead a company that has a long history of high ethical business practices. ... In a world that is increasingly complex, we all must remain vigilant that our words and actions reflect the right behavior.†

The company says,

---

* "Our credo," www.jnj.com/credo/.
† "Code of business conduct," 3, www.jnj.com/sites/default/files/pdf/code-of-business-conduct
 -english-us.pdf.

The values that guide our decision-making are spelled out in Our Credo. Put simply, Our Credo challenges us to put the needs and well-being of the people we serve first. ... Our Credo is more than just a moral compass. We believe it's a recipe for business success. The fact that Johnson & Johnson is one of only a handful of companies that have flourished through more than a century of change is proof of that.*

Abbott Laboratories is an American health care company founded in Chicago in 1888. Abbott also a global company and it conducts business in over 150 countries around the world and its employees are citizens of nations with diverse cultures and beliefs. Abbott is subject to different laws and regulations that vary across the countries in which it operates. Miles D. White, chairman of the board and CEO, has written in the introductory letter to the Code of Business Conduct:

The fundamental message of the Code is straightforward: it is up to each of us, as Abbott employees, to build our company and our brand by holding ourselves to the highest ethical standards and by living our values and continually operating with honesty, fairness, and integrity.

We earn our reputation every day by the decisions we make and the actions we take.

We all share in the responsibility to live our values every day. That includes keeping a watchful eye on our business activities and reporting concerns in good faith without fear of retaliation.

Our products affect people's health and lives in the most crucial ways. That obliges us to not just follow the letter of the laws that govern our work, but also the spirit and the ethical expectations that come with being a leader in a business as important as ours.†

Siemens was founded in Germany in 1847 by Werner von Siemens (1816–1892) and is the largest engineering company in Europe. In the introductory letter to the Code of Ethics (Siemens Business Conduct Guidelines), Joe Kaeser, CEO of Siemens, says:

I'm sure you're aware of the fact that sometimes a small tone can trigger a major landslide. The same goes for unclear business practices. The misconduct of one individual can jeopardize the reputation and existence of an entire company, putting hundreds of thousands of jobs on the line.

---

* "Our credo," www.jnj.com/credo/.
† "Abbott code of business conduct," webstorage.abbott.com/cobc/ebook_us.html#pNum7.

Siemens learned this the hard way. In 2006, the corruption scandal had pushed the company to the brink of the abyss. The financial damage was enormous, but the loss of our good name was a far heavier burden.

Since then, we've gotten most things right: Today, our compliance culture and our commitment to integrity in business are recognized around the world.

Today and in the future, only clean business is Siemens business.

I urge you to read our Business Conduct Guidelines. They offer guidance for our daily business. They make it easier for us to decide how to behave in tricky situations. They tell us who we can turn to for advice.

Ultimately, it's about playing fair. Fairness is good for society. And fairness is what Siemens should stand for – everywhere and at all times.*

Siemens has set globally binding principles and guidelines that require all employees and managers to behave in an ethical, law-abiding manner. Siemens says:

Being a responsible company is our foundation. We want to establish compliance in the minds and actions of all Siemens employees.

We have zero-tolerance for corruption and violations of the principles of fair competition.

Siemens conducts business responsibly and in compliance with the legal requirements and governmental regulations of the countries in which we operate. Under no circumstances, therefore, will illegal or non-compliant behavior be tolerated in the company.†

General Electric is a conglomerate founded in 1892 by American inventor Thomas Alva Edison (1847–1931). In its Code of Ethics, "The Spirit and the Letter," the former CEO, Jeffrey Immelt, said:

For more than 125 years, GE has demonstrated an unwavering commitment to performance with integrity. At the same time, we have expanded into new businesses and new regions and built a great record of sustained growth, we have built a worldwide reputation for lawful and ethical conduct.

This reputation has never been stronger. In several surveys of CEOs, GE has been named the world's most respected and admired company. We have been ranked first for integrity and governance

---

* "Siemens business conduct guidelines," www.siemens.com/content/dam/internet/siemens-com/g lobal/company/sustainability/compliance/pdf/business-conduct-guidelines-e.pdf.
† "Code of conduct for Siemens suppliers," www.aan.siemens.com/compliance/Documents/Code.

GE must seek to earn this high level of trust every day, employee by employee.

All GE employees must comply not only with the letter of these policies but also their spirit.

Do not allow anything – not "making the numbers," competitive instincts or even a direct order from a superior – to compromise your commitment to integrity.

GE leaders are also responsible not only for their own actions but for fostering a culture in which compliance with GE policy and applicable law is at the core of business-specific activities. Leaders must address employees' concerns about appropriate conduct promptly and with care and respect.

There is no conflict between excellent financial performance and high standards of governance and compliance – in fact, the two are mutually reinforcing. As we focus on becoming the pre-eminent growth company of the 21st century, we must recognize that only one kind of performance will maintain our reputation, increase our customers' confidence in us and our products and services, and enable us to continue to grow, and that is performance with integrity.[*]

General Electric says:

Every day, everyone at GE has the power to influence our company's reputation – everywhere we do business. The Spirit and The Letter helps to ensure that, after more than 125 years, we still conduct our affairs with unyielding integrity. For well over a century, GE employees have worked hard to uphold the highest standards of ethical business conduct. We seek to go beyond simply obeying the law – we embrace the spirit of integrity.[†]

Microsoft Corporation is an American multinational technology company with headquarters in Redmond, Washington, USA. The CEO of Microsoft, Satya Nadella, wrote the following introductory letter to the Standards of Business Conduct:

I have always said that each one of us shapes our culture.

At Microsoft, we strive to build a diverse and inclusive culture that embraces learning and fosters trust – a culture where every employee can do their best work.

---

[*] "The spirit & The letter," www.shrm.org/ResourcesAndTools/hr-topics/behavioral-competencies/Documents/TheSpirit_26TheLetter.pdf.

[†] "The spirit & The letter: Guiding the way we do business." www.shrm.org/ResourcesAndTools/hr-topics/behavioral-competencies/Documents/TheSpirit_26TheLetter.pdf.

Making good decisions and ethical choices in our work build trust in each other and with our customers and partners. You should never compromise your personal integrity or the company's reputation and trust in exchange for any short-term gain.

We are more likely to make ethical choices when integrity, honesty, and compliance guide our decision making. We should always be transparent about our motives, learn from our mistakes, and ask for help when faced with a difficult situation. I expect leaders and managers to foster a culture where employees feel free to ask questions and raise concerns when something doesn't seem right.

Our Standards of Business Conduct emphasizes the role that each of us plays in building trust and the approach you should take in making decisions. When we apply these principles, we can move forward with confidence in our ability to make good decisions that build trust and empower our customers and partners.*

In the section "Our Values and Culture," the company states that when faced with a difficult decision or situation the employees should follow these steps:

1. Pause

 Does a situation make you uneasy? Are your instincts telling you something is not quite right? Pause and consider how to approach the situation.
2. Think

 Is your approach consistent with Microsoft's culture and the values in these Standards? Does it build or maintain trust? Never sacrifice long-term reputation and trust for a short-term benefit.
3. Ask

 Ask questions and get help.†

Cisco Systems is a North American company based in San Jose, California, founded in 1984 and dedicated to the manufacture and sale of telecommunications equipment. At the beginning of the Code of Business Conduct, Chuck Robbins, in his welcome message as chairman and CEO, said:

---

* www.microsoft.com/en-us/legal/compliance/sbc/default.aspx.
† www.microsoft.com/en-us/legal/compliance/sbc/values-culture.

One thing that will always remain constant is our longstanding commitment to maintaining the highest standards of business and professional conduct and compliance. Our customers, partners, and stakeholders around the world trust us, and the products and services that we deliver, because we consistently uphold strong values and always strive to make the right choices in how we conduct business.

Our culture of integrity comprises all of our business dealings and interactions, including how we treat one another in the workplace. I am proud that Cisco's culture is based on zero tolerance for harassment of any kind, and it is important that you feel confident and safe in sharing any concerns without fear of retaliation.*

The Code of Business Conduct states:

Innovative ideas, emerging technologies, strategic acquisitions – we work in an industry where the pace is fast and change is constant. But some things will never change, like our commitment to doing business honestly, ethically and with respect for one another. At Cisco, we put our values into practice every day. Doing the right thing is just part of our DNA.

Make good choices. When you are faced with an ethical dilemma, you have a responsibility to take action. It may seem easier to say nothing or look the other way, but taking no action is, in itself, an action that can have serious consequences.

Our continued success depends on your ability to make decisions that are consistent with our core values.... Your individual commitment to doing the right thing will strengthen our reputation as a trusted global brand.†

As an employee, you have an obligation to speak up promptly about anything you believe, in good faith, may constitute a violation. We also encourage you to come forward with situations that "just don't feel right."‡

Our inclusive workplace is welcoming, positive, creative and rewarding – an environment that promotes individual and team expression, innovation and achievement.... I recognize my duty to act responsibly, be a team player and treat others with respect and dignity. Valuing everyone strengthens our collaboration and productivity.§

---

* "2018 code of business conduct," www.cisco.com/c/dam/en_us/about/cobc/2018/code-of-busin ess-conduct-fy18.pdf.
† "Code of business conduct, I am ethical," www.cisco.com.
‡ "Code of business conduct, I share my concerns," www.cisco.com.
§ "Code of business conduct, I respect others," www.cisco.com.

Colgate-Palmolive is a North American company founded by William Colgate in 1806, is present in more than 220 countries, and is dedicated to the manufacture, distribution, and sale of oral hygiene products, personal, and household cleaning products.

The Colgate Code of Conduct, translated into more than forty languages, promotes the highest ethical standards in all business of the company.

These are some paragraphs of the letter from Ian Cook, former CEO of the company, in the Code of Conduct:

> Ethical leadership has never been more important...Our reputation matters deeply to Colgate people, to our consumers and customers, to our investors and to our business partners.
>
> Since it was launched nearly 30 years ago, our Code of Conduct has guided us with a set of principles that reflect Colgate's values and established standards that guide our ethical behavior.
>
> As a truly global company operating in numerous countries around the world, all of us must ensure that our behavior and decisions live up to our ideals and values as stated in our Code.
>
> Each of us makes decisions every day that may have personal, financial, community or ethical implications. As a member of the Colgate family, it is important that you read, understand and fully comply with our Code to ensure that we make our decisions guided by our personal responsibility to act with integrity and the highest ethical standards.
>
> Colgate people are expected to consistently demonstrate ethical behavior through their actions and words. This includes "Speaking Up" to challenge behavior that conflicts with our Code, as well as other Colgate policies or applicable laws.
>
> Colgate people take great pride in our business results. Results do matter, but so does the way in which we achieve those results.*

The Kellogg Company, founded in 1906, is a multinational American agribusiness company that is dedicated to the manufacture of cereals and biscuits and is based in Michigan. The founder of the company, Will Keith Kellogg (1860–1951), left a legacy of integrity and doing business correctly that lasts until today. John Bryant, Kellogg's CEO, wrote a letter to employees in the company's global code of ethics, where he says:

> Our values guide us in the way we pursue our goals, tackle challenges and find answers to the tough questions that can arise for a company doing business around a dynamic, complex and hyper-connected world.

---

* "Living our values, a message from our chairman, president and CEO," www.colgatepalmolive.com.

Our continued success and reputation depend upon each of us living our values and acting ethically, responsibly and in compliance with the law. Our Global Code of Ethics, titled "Living Our Values," represents the culture we've built and the commitment we've made to continue earning the trust of those who love our brands.

This important document is a guidebook for the journey we're on. I would ask you to consult it regularly, ask questions and raise any concerns you might have – with me personally, if you wish. That's how seriously I take the standards for conduct we have set.

Thank you for Living Our Values and doing your part to maintain Kellogg's legacy of trust.*

The company says in its Code:

Today, as Kellogg Company pursues its Vision and Purpose in more than 180 countries, the world has never been more interconnected or more interdependent. This means the actions of a single individual have the potential to affect more people in more ways than ever before. This creates huge opportunities for Kellogg – but also risks. It's why we have to be more focused than ever on how we do what's right.

Our values are part of our DNA. They guide the way we work with our business partners, within our communities and with each other. Living Our Values is Kellogg Company's Global Code of Ethics.

Our reputation and success depend upon the decisions and actions of our people, all over the world. We are committed to ensuring that every action we take honors our K Values and is in full compliance with the law and this Code.

As employees, we are all responsible – individually and collectively – for how Kellogg does business and the impact Kellogg has in the world. We pursue our Vision and Purpose and honor our founder's legacy of integrity through the right behaviors, which always involve:

- Acting with integrity – honoring our commitments, upholding this Code, obeying the law and acting responsibly and in good faith.
- Showing respect – valuing the diversity of thought and opinions, encouraging open and frank dialogue, and considering the impact of our decisions on stakeholders.
- Building trust – seeking fair resolutions, making decisions based on the merits, dealing fairly and honestly with all stakeholders and maintaining the appropriate level of transparency in our decision making.†

---

* "Living our values, Kellogg company's global code of ethics," Message from John Bryant, www.kelloggcompany.com.

† "Living our values, Kellogg company's global code of ethics," www.kelloggcompany.com.

L'Oréal is a French personal care company founded in 1909. It is the world's largest cosmetics company and in its Code of Ethics "The Way We Work," it says:

As a business our strategy for leadership is based on continuous investment in our research and development. This enables our brands to deliver to our consumers' products that are innovative, highly effective, practical and pleasant to use, and which are manufactured to the most demanding standards of quality and safety. We place great value on honesty and clarity: our consumer advertising is based on proven performance and by scientific data. We are committed to building strong and lasting relationships with our customers and our suppliers, founded on trust and mutual benefit. We respect the stakeholders of our business environment, including our competitors. We do business with integrity: we respect the laws of the countries in which we operate and adhere to good corporate governance practices. We maintain high standards in accounting and reporting and support the fight against corruption. We deliver long-term, sustained shareholder value by protecting and making the most effective use of Company assets. We aim for excellence and constantly challenge ourselves and our methods.

As an employer we aim to make L'Oréal a great place in which to work. We know that our employees are our greatest assets. They are entitled to a safe and healthy working environment: one in which personal talent and merit are recognized, diversity is valued, privacy is respected, and the balance between professional and personal life is taken into account. We believe in offering our employees a stimulating environment, exciting personal opportunities and a chance to make a difference. We encourage an atmosphere of openness, courage, generosity and respect so that all our employees feel free to come forward with their questions, ideas and concerns.

As a responsible corporate citizen we play our part in creating a world of beauty and fairness. We are mindful of our impact on the natural environment, including biodiversity, and constantly seek to reduce it: we are determined to avoid compromising tomorrow for the sake of today. We make a positive contribution to the countries and communities in which we are present and respect local cultures and sensitivities. We are committed to the respect of Human Rights. We want to help end the exploitation of children in the workplace and the use of forced labour. We want an end to animal testing in our industry, and we contribute to the development and acceptance of alternative methods. We actively seek out and favour business partners who share our values and our ethical commitments.*

---

* loreal-dam-front-corp-fr-cdn.damdy.com/ressources/afile/130772-e2c64-resource-code-of-ethics-english.pdf.

PepsiCo Inc. is a North American beverage and snack company that was created in 1890 in North Carolina. PepsiCo renewed its Global Code of Conduct in 2012. Indra K. Nooyi, former chairman and CEO, pointed out in the introductory letter to the Code:

> Our Code continues to be a declaration of the highest standards of ethics and integrity in all that we do, uniting all of us at PepsiCo with one set of values that guide our daily decisions and actions.
>
> Our Code defines how we do business the right way – guided by Performance with Purpose, our commitment to sustainable growth. It describes the "purpose" behind our performance and is designed to help us meet our obligations, show respect to one another in the workplace and act with integrity in the marketplace.
>
> PepsiCo's outstanding reputation rests on how each of us conducts ourselves and how we conduct ourselves collectively as a company. Nothing is more important to PepsiCo, to me personally, and I hope to each of you than preserving PepsiCo's good name by embracing the principles of our Code of Conduct.[*]

Ramon Laguarta, the current chairman and CEO of PepsiCo, says:

> Integrity is one of PepsiCo's most valuable assets. It is key to maintaining the trust of our stakeholders, sharpening our competitive advantage, and driving long-term growth. Just as we hold ourselves to the highest levels of excellence, we must also hold ourselves to the highest standards of integrity.
>
> And while a culture of integrity and ethics takes years to build, it takes just a moment to lose. So, that culture cannot be taken for granted. We must invest in it consistently, day after day, year after year.
>
> Thank you for your commitment to this critical effort – a commitment that will help ensure PepsiCo remains one of the most respected, ethical, and successful companies in the world.[†]

The company also says:

> Our Code is our roadmap and our compass for doing business in the right way.

---

[*] "Pepsico, global code of conduct," Performance with Purpose, www.pepsico.com.
[†] /www.pepsico.com/docs/album/global-code-of-conduct/pepsico-global-code-of-conduct/english_letter_global_code_of_conduct_booklet.pdf?sfvrsn=68014c63_18.

Our reputation for acting ethically and responsibly is built one decision at a time, every day, by each of us

Each of us, especially leaders and managers, must act with integrity and inspire trust.

While all employees are expected to act ethically, each manager and leader at PepsiCo has the increased responsibility of leading by example. We expect our leaders and managers to serve as positive role models and inspire others

It is your responsibility to ask questions and raise concerns when compliance issues arise. If you are aware of something that may be a violation of our Values, our Code, our policies or the law, you should speak up and report it so it can be addressed.

Our success can be achieved only when we treat everyone, both within and outside our company, with respect. Respect in the workplace, along with individual excellence and collaborative teamwork, is how we will accomplish our goals.

We strive to attract, develop and retain a workforce that is as diverse as the markets we serve, and to ensure an inclusive work environment that embraces the strength of our differences.

You play an important role in creating a work environment in which employees and business partners feel valued and respected for their contributions. You promote diversity and inclusion when you:

- Respect the diversity of each other's talents, abilities, and experiences
- Value the input of others
- Foster an atmosphere of trust, openness, and candor

We will better understand the needs of our consumers and foster innovation if each of us embraces diversity and inclusion in all aspects of our business.*

Xerox Corporation is a North American company based in Connecticut, founded in 1906, and is the world's largest supplier of photocopiers. Ursula Burns is its chairman and CEO, and she says in the introductory letter to employees for the Code of Business Conduct:

We are committed to being a role model for corporate ethical behavior. This commitment is enabled by the personal actions and accountability of each and every one of us. Our greatest successes over the years have been driven by our allegiance to our long-standing core values. Our reputation rests on what we do and how we act every day.

---

* "Pepsico, global code of conduct," Performance with Purpose, www.pepsico.com.

Nothing we do is more important than maintaining our personal integrity and our collective financial and business integrity in the name of Xerox. This Code of Business Conduct is a guide. It is not intended to be a compendium of all policies. Use it as a tool to enable dialogues with co-workers and managers and to find the appropriate policies, tools, and other resources to help you do the right thing every day.[*]

The code says:

> The Code of Business Conduct is designed to assist us in aligning our actions and decisions with our core values and compliance requirements as we pursue our Xerox mission. It is intended to help us recognize ethics and compliance issues before they arise and to deal appropriately with those issues that do occur.
>
> As a global enterprise, we operate in over 160 countries worldwide. We conduct our business activities in compliance with our Code of Business Conduct, policies, standards, guidelines and procedures as well as with the laws and regulations of the countries where we do business. Our Code is designed to meet or exceed existing legal and compliance requirements.
>
> We are committed to earning and maintaining our customers' trust through fair, honest and lawful dealings and by delivering great value.
>
> We do not tolerate misrepresentation, fraud or deliberate omission of information in our sales or marketing activities.[†]

Marriott International is an American chain of luxury hotels and was founded in 1927. In the letter to employees found in the Code of Ethics, chairman and CEO, J. Willard Marriott Jr., says:

> Marriott's reputation and continued success as a global hospitality leader are grounded in our commitment to service and business integrity and in our application of consistently high standards to everything we do.
>
> Since the very beginning, a fundamental commitment to hard work, fair business practices, and respect for others has shaped our everyday decision making and has guided our relationships with all of our stakeholders – associates, owners, business partners, franchisees, customers, and the communities in which we work.
>
> Our commitment to being a responsible corporate citizen has not changed since 1927. Decisions that do not reflect our fundamental values

---

[*] "Code of business conduct," Connecting with Our Core Values, www.xerox.com/downloads/usa/en/i/ir_Code_of_Conduct_EmployeeHandbook.pdf.

[†] "Code of business conduct," Connecting with Our Core Values, www.xerox.com/downloads/usa/en/i/ir_Code_of_Conduct_EmployeeHandbook.pdf.

of integrity, honesty, and fairness can compromise our competitiveness, lead to significant financial losses, and harm our associates.

Because our business relies upon integrity and good judgment, this Business Conduct Guide and related Company policies were developed to provide all members of the Marriott community with guidance on not only what is legal but also what is right.

This Guide supports our pledge to uncompromising business standards and a fair and ethical workplace.

All of us who act on behalf of Marriott are responsible for upholding ... Our Tradition of Integrity.*

The code says:

Every day, we are confronted with situations that test our values, our beliefs, and our judgment. The reputation of Marriott is built upon the actions of all of us who act on behalf of Marriott. It is vitally important for each of us to understand our legal and ethical responsibilities so that we can make the right decisions every day.†

Thomson Reuters is an information company. Its operating headquarters is in Manhattan, New York, and operates in more than 90 countries. Its CEO, Jim Smith, wrote a letter to the employee that appears in the company's Code of Ethics. Some of the paragraphs of the letter say:

Our business depends on transparency and our determination to do the right thing. Our customers count on the accuracy of our information, the reliability of our systems and the integrity with which we operate. Trust is our currency.

This Code of Business Conduct and Ethics expresses our commitment to compliance and integrity with a renewed emphasis on the values and principles that define who we are. It lays out the expectations we all should have of ourselves and of each other, and it provides enhanced resources to guide our decisions. We operate from an incredibly principled position. Our success depends on it.‡

The company says in the Code of Ethics:

---

* "Marriott business conduct guide," Our Tradition of Integrity, www.marriott.com/Multimedia/ PDF/CorporateResponsibility/Marriott_Business_Conduct_Guide_English.pdf.

† "Marriott business conduct guide," Our Tradition of Integrity, www.marriott.com/Multimedia/ PDF/CorporateResponsibility/Marriott_Business_Conduct_Guide_English.pdf.

‡ "Trust matters, code of business conduct and ethics," ir.thomsonreuters.com.

Thomson Reuters is built on a legacy of integrity and performance. For more than 150 years, we have delivered vital information and expertise that empowers customers all over the world. We use our much strength to fulfill this purpose. However, if there is one single quality that binds, empowers and defines us more than any other, it is Trust.

With thousands of employees around the world, Thomson Reuters operates under a wide variety of laws and regulations. At times, we tailor our decisions and actions to specific facts and situations. But wherever we operate, our values and principles will not change.

Bribes, corruption, and illegal payments all have a deeply damaging impact on our society. They can harm economies, destabilize governments and undermine public trust. These types of actions can result in Thomson Reuters being prohibited from bidding on contracts. In addition, they can result in both personal and company fines and even imprisonment. As a team of thousands of professionals working around the world, we have both the power and the obligation to fight bribery and corruption wherever we encounter it. By embracing this responsibility with the business partners with whom we engage on a daily basis, we continue to bolster the reputation of Thomson Reuters.*

Marks and Spencer plc, founded in 1884 by Michael Marks and Thomas Spencer, is an English company specializing in the sale of clothing, household goods, and food. The introduction of the Code of Ethics and Behaviors, says:

At Marks & Spencer, we are committed to our core values of Inspiration, Innovation, Integrity, and In Touch. They are key to the way we work and interact with our customers, suppliers, and colleagues across the business and underpin our customer promise of "Enhancing Lives, Every Day." Our Code of Ethics and Behaviours (the "Code") outlines the standards and behaviours that help to shape and strengthen our culture. All colleagues are expected to uphold these high standards wherever in the world we conduct business, ensuring that honesty and integrity are maintained.

This Code, although not addressing every situation you may face as an employee, does provide a guide to the values, behaviours, and ways of working which are core to M&S and which each of us is responsible for upholding as an employee. You should read the Code carefully and refer to it if facing an ethical dilemma at work. It is essential to create a supportive environment in which you feel able to raise concerns internally without

---

* "Trust matters, code of business conduct and ethics," ir.thomsonreuters.com.

fear of disciplinary action. If you have any concerns or something you come across doesn't feel right, speak up.*

Marks and Spencer's Code of Ethics also states:

Our values of Inspiration, Innovation, Integrity, and In Touch have been shaped by building on the core values that have characterized M&S since it was founded in 1884. They are at the heart of everything we do as a business and provide the direction and sense of common purpose that ensures we are doing the right things in the right way, to deliver for our customers.

- Inspiration – we aim to excite and inspire our customers;
- Innovation – we are restless in our aim to improve things for the better;
- Integrity – we always strive to do the right thing;
- In Touch – we listen actively and act thoughtfully.

We all have a responsibility to protect the Company's reputation in everything we do and say. This also includes:

- Complying with the applicable laws and regulations in all countries in which we operate;
- Conducting ourselves in a professional manner with the highest standards of honesty and integrity;
- Following Company policies and procedures;
- Working with our suppliers, third parties and agencies to ensure our high ethical standards are maintained;
- If in doubt, seeking guidance and always doing the right thing.

We're also on a journey to make our business more sustainable. We believe a successful business must also be environmentally and socially sustainable.†

Levi Strauss and Co. is an American company founded in 1853 in San Francisco by Levi Strauss, a German immigrant. The Company is a producer of clothing and jeans. Charles Victor Bergh, president and CEO of Levi Strauss & Co., says in his introductory letter to the Code of Business Conduct:

We established the first code of conduct for apparel manufacturers, ensuring the people who make our product work in a safe environment and are treated with dignity and respect. And we work to build sustainability into

---

* "Code of ethics and behaviours," corporate.marksandspencer.com.
† "Code of ethics and behaviours," corporate.marksandspencer.com.

everything we do. Ask an employee what makes this company different, and they'll tell you. It's our values: empathy, originality, integrity, and courage. These guide every decision we make and every action we take. And they fuel our commitment to drive profits through principles.*

Starbucks Corporation, the American company founded in 1971 in Seattle, Washington, is the largest coffee company in the world, with more than 17,000 locations. Howard Schultz, the former CEO of Starbucks, says in his introductory letter to the Standards of Business Conduct:

> We are all entrusted to make decisions that impact our reputation and relationships with each other, our customers, our business partners, and our communities. Conducting business ethically, with integrity and transparency, is essential to preserving our culture and protecting our brand.
>
> The *Standards of Business Conduct* provide guidance to help all of us make ethical decisions at work. It is up to each of us to live our values through our actions. That means asking for help if you have a question or concern and if you are unsure of what to do in a situation, please speak up.†

Mattel Inc., founded in 1945, is one of the largest toy companies in the world and is headquartered in California in the United States. The Mattel Code of Conduct says:

> At Mattel, our values are:
>
> Play Fair: Act with unwavering integrity on all occasions. Treat each other with respect and dignity. Be accountable for the impact of every action and decision. Trust each other to make the right decisions.
>
> Play Together: Work as a team to realize our full potential. Form lasting partnerships and productive relationships. Enrich the communities where we work and play.
>
> Play with Passion: Use unparalleled innovation and creativity to make a positive impact on the lives of children and families around the globe. Have the ingenuity, commitment and confidence to drive change.
>
> Play to Grow: Pursue inventive thinking and take smart risks. Reward innovation in every part of our business. Be leaders, deliver superior quality and surpass goals. The Values Statement includes a commitment to act with unwavering integrity.

---

* "Worldwide code of business conduct," http://levistrauss.com/wp-content/uploads/2017/03/CodeofConduct_English.pdf.

† livingourvalues.starbucks.com/letter-from-howard.

Leaders should foster an environment of ethical behavior by • acting as role models, demonstrating ethical behavior in the performance of their own duties, • making sure that employees understand that business results are never more important than compliance with the standards for ethical behavior, • ensuring that employees are familiar with the standards for ethical behavior in the Code of Conduct and Company Policies that are relevant to the performance of their duties, • encouraging open communication regarding business practices and ethical issues, • acting to address incidents of unethical behavior, including training, counseling and disciplinary action where appropriate, and • recognizing and rewarding ethical behavior.

Failures to act ethically and violations of the Code of Conduct and Company Policies can impact Mattel's business and reputation and can have serious consequences for all Mattel stakeholders, including employees, shareholders, consumers, business partners, and our communities.

Whenever Mattel becomes aware of a violation of the Code of Conduct, Company Policy or the law, we will act to correct the problem and prevent future occurrences. Depending on the circumstances, the corrective and preventive steps might include training, counseling and disciplinary actions up to and including termination of employment and civil or criminal prosecution.

You have a responsibility to speak up when you are in a situation which you believe may violate or lead to a violation of the Code of Conduct, Company Policy or the law.*

Glaxo Smith Kline is a UK-based pharmaceutical, dental and healthcare company and is the sixth-largest pharmaceutical company in the world. The code of conduct says:

At GSK, we believe it's not just what we achieve that counts, it's also how we achieve it. We believe in making good choices and taking responsibility and accountability for them so that we can become one of the world's most innovative, best performing and trusted healthcare organizations, and positively impact the lives of our patients and consumers. It goes beyond simply following laws and rules.

We gain our patients' and consumers' trust by focusing on their needs. That means always thinking from their perspective. We put their safety first, provide them with clear, up-to-date information and promote our products appropriately and ethically.

---

* Code of Conduct Mattel, Introduction, www.corporate.mattel.com/about-us/pdf/CoC/Code%20of%20Conduct%20-%20English%20(2015).PDF.

We are honest and transparent about what we do and how we do it. This improves how we collaborate with each other and enhances the way we are seen by the communities we work with. It demonstrates that we are open to challenge and discussion and want to improve the way we operate. We are also mindful of our responsibilities. We care about our communities and the wider world and are committed to human rights and a sustainable approach in all that we do.*

United Parcel Service, Inc. (UPS) is one of the world's largest package carriers, delivering more than 14 million packages to more than 200 countries each day. UPS's headquarter is in Atlanta, Georgia. The company was founded in 1907. The UPS Code of Business Conduct states:

UPS has a long tradition of transforming and adapting to the needs of our customers, but our commitment to integrity remains steadfast. We remain committed to a set of beliefs that guided our founders and their successors, and currently guide employees and representatives of UPS.

It is this commitment that will continue to move us forward.

More than 100 years ago, UPS Founder Jim Casey began building our company by asking retailers for their trust. They entrusted us with their business, and every day, UPS people honored that trust and maintained relationships with customers by acting with integrity. We have preserved this philosophy over the years, and it has become our guiding principle.

Today, UPS employees and representatives continue to uphold our strong brand and the legacy of integrity that Jim started.

This requires us to conduct business fairly, honestly, and ethically.

For our company to survive and remain successful, we must have a sound set of beliefs that serves as the foundation for our decisions and actions. We must remember that our success, reputation, and brand were developed over many years and can be damaged if we do not act responsibly with an uncompromising set of common beliefs.

A commitment to integrity is about creating a climate for continued success. It is about creating an environment where people can make good decisions. It is about doing the right thing in every business situation. By using good judgment and respecting others, UPS's commitment to integrity will endure.

UPS's reputation for ethical behavior has enabled us to attract and retain the best people and loyal customers; it has opened doors in new and emerging global markets and allowed us to transform our business to meet changing customer needs.

---

* "Living our values and expectations," www.gsk.com/media/4800/english-code-of-conduct.pdf.

Compliance with our legal and ethical obligations is the responsibility of every UPS employee and representative, as is the responsibility to report potential violations of those obligations. Reporting may be accomplished directly through a discussion with a member of the management team or by using the UPS Help Line.[*]

The Clorox Company, based in California, is an American global manufacturer and marketer of consumer and professional products. Benno Dorer, chair and chief executive officer, in the introductory letter to the Code, says:

> Do the right thing. Those four words are a core value here at The Clorox Company. They've shaped how we do business from our founding in 1913 through today. Honest and ethical business practices are the foundation of our long-term success.
>
> We all have a shared responsibility to speak up and report any violation of our Code of Conduct or Clorox policies. We investigate any report of misconduct. We also prohibit any retaliation against individuals who in good faith report suspected misconduct.[†]

The code says,

> Each of us is personally responsible for supporting our core values, which require compliance with the law as well as ethical conduct. Clorox is strongly committed to doing business ethically and in compliance with all applicable laws. We have policies, processes, and training in place to support ethical and legal decision-making. Personal integrity, practiced on a daily basis, is the foundation of corporate integrity.[‡]

Royal Dutch Shell is an Anglo-Dutch hydrocarbons company with business in the oil and gas sector. It was founded in 1907 and is one of the largest multinationals in the world. There is an introductory message from the CEO of Shell, Ben van Beurden.

> Welcome to our Code of Conduct (the Code). It has been designed to help every one of us make the right decisions and remain true to our core values and Business Principles.

---

[*] www.ups.com/media/en/code_bus_conduct.pdf.

[†] www.thecloroxcompany.com/wp-content/uploads/2019/03/2019-Code-of-Conduct-Policy_External_English.pdf.

[‡] www.thecloroxcompany.com/wp-content/uploads/2019/03/2019-Code-of-Conduct-Policy_External_English.pdf, 5.

These core values and principles are at the very heart of our company. They are not optional. Anyone who chooses not to follow them is making a choice not to work at Shell.

All of us believe we are ethical, but our world and business environment are constantly changing. It is never safe to assume we know everything or that we are not at risk.

The Code helps by highlighting your responsibilities so you can identify the risks relevant to your role.

Whether you are a manager, an employee or contract staff, I encourage you to read and use our Code to make sure you are doing your part to sustain an ethical culture and protect the future of Shell.

A personal commitment to ethics and compliance is something over which we each have absolute control. Anything less than 100% compliance undermines our performance and risks high costs that would hurt our bottom line as well as our hard-earned reputation. By following this Code, you are helping to make Shell credible, competitive and affordable.

See the Code as your guide, helping you to refresh your knowledge and giving you sound advice. You might find something surprising – a new risk might have emerged or perhaps you will discover that changes in your job have exposed you to risks you were not previously aware of. Don't let complacency put you at risk of breaking the rules and creating an unacceptable risk for you, your colleagues or Shell. If you have any reason to doubt your understanding, always seek advice as set out in the following pages or contact the Shell Ethics & Compliance Office.

Thank you for your commitment to ethics and compliance.[*]

Lockheed Martin is an American multinational aerospace and military company founded in 1995. Marilyn A. Hewson is the president and CEO of Lockheed Martin and in his letter to the company's employees in the code of conduct, says:

Our core values, to "Do What's Right," "Respect Others," and "Perform with Excellence," are fundamental to who we are and how we operate as a corporation.

They not only define us, but they are also the key to our future – building bridges of trust with customers and colleagues.

Our Code not only sets clear ethical standards in critical areas, but it also explains how we should conduct ourselves when acting on behalf of the company. For instance, our Code makes it clear that Lockheed Martin has zero-tolerance for corruption, and we encourage employees to step forward

---

[*] "Our code of conduct," Making the Right Decisions. Shell.

and speak up whenever they suspect actions or behavior inconsistent with our values and expectations.

Thank you for your efforts to understand and uphold the high standards that make Lockheed Martin a special place to work. Together, we can ensure that ethics and integrity are never compromised at our corporation.*

Citigroup is one of the largest financial services companies in the world, founded in 1812 and headquartered in New York City. Mike Corbat is its chief executive officer, and in the letter to employees in the code of conduct, he says:

> Our Mission and Value Proposition captures our vision of an interconnected world – a network across the world making up our global bank and through which we serve as a trusted partner to our clients, shareholders, and colleagues. That vision relies on our commitment to live our values and to lead others in doing the same.
>
> To preserve the trust of our stakeholders and to fulfill our Mission and Value Proposition, we all must hold ourselves to the highest standards of ethics and professional behavior. This latest update to our Code reflects our continued commitment to the standards and values that have made Citi a successful enterprise and a trusted partner for over 200 years. Please carefully read the Code. … It provides guidance on the behaviors we are all expected to follow, regardless of region, business, job function, or seniority.
>
> I urge you to use the Code to inform your daily work and the choices you make. However, no one document can anticipate every situation we may encounter. Our license to do business depends on all of us exercising good judgment by ensuring our decisions pass three tests – that they are in our clients' interests, create economic value, and are always systemically responsible. We must also be certain that our decisions are guided by a strong sense of personal accountability.
>
> Exercising good judgment also includes speaking up when we have a concern that behavior violates the values and principles outlined in this Code. If you encounter a situation that you feel is not right, or if you have any questions about the best course of action in a particular situation, it is critical that you raise the issue to your manager or seek help from any of the other resources listed in the Code.†

---

* www.lockheedmartin.com/content/dam/lockheed-martin/eo/documents/ethics/code-of-conduct.pdf.
† "A message from Mike Corbat," www.citigroup.com/citi/investor/data/codeconduct_en.pdf.

Founded in 1892, the **Coca-Cola Company** based in Atlanta, Georgia, USA, is the manufacturer of the most-consumed soft drink in the world. The Code of Business Conduct says:

> What makes Coca-Cola one of the most admired brands in the world? It is not just our products. It is also how we do our work and the integrity of our actions. Ingrained in our culture, integrity inspires our work and strengthens our reputation as a Company that does extraordinary things and always does what is right. Integrity is the essential ingredient to our success.
>
> Sometimes, you might face a situation where the right thing to do is not obvious. That is where our Code of Business Conduct can help. It is always here as your guide to preserving our reputation and living our values. While the Code cannot answer every question, it can show you where to go for guidance when the answer is not clear.
>
> It does not matter where you work or what you do for the Company – you have a responsibility to use good judgment and follow our Code. That includes every full-time or part-time employee at every level of the Company, all the way up to the executive suite. The Code also applies to controlled subsidiaries and entities in which the Company either owns a majority interest or manages operations (all of the above are referred to throughout this Code as "the Company"). All employees and any others subject to the Code must acknowledge that they have read and agree to uphold the Code.
>
> Anyone who works on the Company's behalf (including suppliers, consultants, and other business partners) must share our commitment to integrity by following the principles of our Code when providing goods and services to the Company or acting on our behalf. Suppliers, as a condition of working with us, must comply with our Supplier Code of Business Conduct and our Supplier Guiding Principles.[*]

McDonald's, the California-based fast-food chain, was founded in 1940 and serves 60 million customers per day in more than 33,000 establishments worldwide.

Brothers Dick and Mac McDonald created the company in 1940 in San Bernardino, California, but its qualitative leap was in the year 1955 when a salesman by the name of Ray Kroc (1902–1984) joined the company as a franchise agent and opened his first Mc Donald's restaurant.

In 1958 Ray Kroc said,

---

[*] www.coca-colacompany.com/investors/code-of-business-conduct.

The basis of our entire business is that we are ethical, truthful and dependable. It takes time to build a reputation. We are not promoters. We are business people with a solid, permanent, constructive ethical program that will be in style … years from now even more than it is today.[*]

McDonald's president and CEO Steve Easterbrook wrote a letter to employees in the Standards of Business Conduct. He says:

It is our privilege and responsibility to be stewards of one of the world's greatest brands.

As we grow our business, we must always honor the trust of our customers and many other stakeholders have placed in McDonald's. This means doing the right thing. That's what we have done for over 60 years, and we will continue to hold ourselves accountable to the highest standards.

We recognize that today we are competing and adapting during a time of rapid change. We must continue to comply with complex laws and regulations. Sometimes we'll face situations where the choice between right and wrong may not be immediately clear. When this happens, take a moment to consider what is in the best interest of McDonald's. If you are unsure, you have many resources to guide you.[†]

The Walt Disney Company was founded on October 16, 1923, by Walt Disney. Robert Iger is the CEO of the company, and in the introductory letter to the Standards of Business Conduct of the company, he says:

Throughout the years, we have earned the trust of guests, audiences, consumers, and shareholders because of our commitment to high standards in everything we do, everywhere we operate. Integrity, honesty, trust, respect, playing by the rules, and teamwork – these define not only the operating principles of our company but also the spirit of our diverse global workforce and how we function.

Our Standards of Business Conduct provide the information, the resources, and the tools necessary to conduct ourselves ethically and in compliance with the law. As a Cast Member or employee, you are expected to read and be familiar with the Standards and to use them to guide the way you act.

Always remember that in every interaction, you are the face of our Company. Act responsibly in all of your professional relationships, in a

---

[*] "Standards of business conduct," https://corporate.mcdonalds.com/content/dam/gwscorp/corporate-governance-content/codes-of-conduct/US_English_Sept_2018.pdf.

[†] "Standards of business conduct," https://corporate.mcdonalds.com/content/dam/gwscorp/corporate-governance-content/codes-of-conduct/US_English_Sept_2018.pdf.

manner consistent with the high standards we set for our business conduct, and speak up whenever you have a question or concern. As we continue to create Disney Magic, make sure your actions reflect your pride in yourself, those you work with and the Company.*

The Disney Standards of Business Conduct also states:

We recognize that our continued success depends upon a commitment to conduct business with honesty, integrity and compliance with the law everywhere we operate.

Keep in mind, no document can address every situation you may possibly face in your everyday work. We rely on you to use these Standards as well as your good judgment to guide your behavior and to ask questions if you are ever unsure of the proper course of action.

Remember, one of the best resources for solving an ethical dilemma is your conscience. If an action you're contemplating feels dishonest, unethical or illegal, it probably is.

Our Company is committed to open, free and effective channels of communication, so promote an "open door" policy, be a good listener and work to earn the trust of your co-workers.

One of our greatest assets is our reputation. We're known for operating with high ethical standards everywhere we do business. Our continued success depends, in part, on your commitment to doing the right thing and speaking up if you see or suspect someone is violating our Standards. You have the right and the responsibility to protect our Company from conduct that can threaten our day-to-day operations, our reputation and our future growth.

Our Company does not tolerate any form of retaliation (including separation, demotion, suspension or loss of benefits) against anyone who makes a good faith report of potential misconduct or helps with an investigation. We want you to be free to ask questions and raise issues without fear of retaliation, secure in the knowledge that you did the right thing in coming forward. Sometimes, it may seem easier to keep quiet or look the other way when someone violates our Standards, but doing nothing can, in itself, result in serious consequences. When you speak up about unethical and illegal behavior, you're saying that an honest and ethical workplace matters to you.†

---

* "Standards of business conduct," The Walt Disney Company, ditm-twdc-us.storage.googleapi s.com/DIS-SBC-CM.pdf.
† "Standards of business conduct," The Walt Disney Company, ditm-twdc-us.storage.googleapi s.com/DIS-SBC-CM.pdf.

American Airlines was founded in 1930 and is headquartered in Texas. Doug Parker, chairman and CEO, wrote an introductory letter to his colleagues in the Standards of Business Conduct:

> Building the greatest airline in the world requires a strong commitment to our customers, shareholders, business partners and, of course, each other. That commitment is founded on a value system we all share, one based on integrity, honesty and the absolute dedication that every decision we make is a responsible and ethical one. We know that you embrace these values, and continue to make smart, sound decisions every day.
>
> Consider these Standards part of our moral compass that sets clear expectations for each of us, and tells the world how we conduct business. Please read the new Standards carefully and ask questions if there is something you don't understand.
>
> Our Standards of Business Conduct do require us to comply with the law. But the Standards ask for more: that we all work together to ensure that American Airlines is a company that we and all of our stakeholders can count on to do the right thing.*

The Ford Motor Company was founded in 1903 in Detroit, Michigan, USA, with US$28,000 contributed by 11 investors, including Henry Ford. In the Ford Code of Conduct Handbook, Bill Ford, executive chairman, says:

> Henry Ford once said, "There is a most intimate connection between decency and good business." He believed that the main purpose of a corporation should be to serve customers, employees, and communities. By staying true to those values, he was able to build the greatest business enterprise of the 20th century.
>
> Today, the values of a company are even more critical to its success. As we move into the 21st century, expectations are higher and processes are more transparent. Now, more than ever, companies must not just proclaim the highest standards, they must live them every day.
>
> The Code of Conduct Handbook will help Ford Motor Company personnel around the world understand and follow our policies and procedures. It builds on our heritage of corporate citizenship, and it updates our business practices so that we can compete ethically and fairly in all circumstances.

---

* "American Airlines. Standards of business conduct," www.aa.com/content/images/customer-service/about-us/corporate-governance/standards-of-business-conduct-for-employees.pdf.

I urge all personnel to learn and follow these standards. By doing so, you will help us earn the trust and respect that are essential for building a great Ford Motor Company for the next 100 years and beyond.*

The company reports the following in its Code of Conduct:

Ford Motor Company is committed to conducting business fairly and honestly. This commitment to integrity requires each of us to act ethically. Each of us is expected to act, at all times and in all circumstances, with the highest sense of integrity on behalf of the Company. We are expected to act in a manner that protects and enhances the Company's corporate reputation.

All personnel must know and comply with the spirit and the letter of all Company Policies and legal requirements related to their work. If you supervise any personnel, you are expected to take reasonable steps to ensure that they, too, know and follow Company policies and any applicable legal requirements.

Remember, anyone who violates the law or a Company Policy may be subject to disciplinary action, up to and including termination or release. Violations of the law can expose the Company, and even the individual violator, to fines, penalties, civil damages, and, in some cases, imprisonment. Additionally, violations could damage the Company's reputation and result in lost sales and profits.†

Walmart was founded on July 2, 1962, in Arkansas. Doug McMillon, its president and CEO, at the beginning of the Global Statement of Ethics, says:

Our unique culture drives our purpose of saving people money so they can live better, and the foundation of our culture is a commitment to operating with integrity. Even as we change to meet the needs of our customers, Walmart will stay true to the values, beliefs, and behaviors that have guided us over the last 50 years.

Regardless of where each of us works in our global company, this Statement of Ethics is the guide to exemplifying integrity as a Walmart associate. It's a daily resource for making honest, fair and objective decisions while operating in compliance with all laws and our policies. This Statement of Ethics applies to me, the board of directors and all associates at every level of our organization.

---

* "Ford code of conduct handbook," www.fcs.ford.com/coc/pdfs/coc_english.pdf.
† "Ford code of conduct handbook," www.fcs.ford.com/coc/pdfs/coc_english.pdf.

Through your ethical behavior and willingness to speak up for the highest standards, we earn and keep the trust of our customers, each other and our local communities. We believe in everyday low cost and everyday low prices, but only if accomplished through our everyday integrity.

Thank you for your commitment to our Statement of Ethics. It means more than making ethical decisions; it demonstrates you care about Walmart, our reputation and our customers.*

The Global Statement of Ethics says:

Since Sam Walton founded our company it always has been a values-based, ethically led organization. Our beliefs are the values that guide our decisions and our leadership.

Respect for the Individual: We value every associate; own the work we do and communicate by listening and sharing ideas.

Service to our Customers: We're here to serve customers, support each other, and give to our local communities.

Striving for Excellence: We work as a team and model positive examples while we innovate and improve every day.

Act with Integrity: We act with the highest level of integrity by being honest, fair and objective, while operating in compliance with all laws and our policies.†

These benchmarks with some of the world's largest and most successful corporations can help us to become more aware of the emphasis placed by large corporations on caring for and protecting their ethical behavior. The ethical and compliance culture is the pillar on which organizations must build their activities and businesses in order to protect their reputation, their finances, and their future.

If organizations do not have adequate risk control systems in place and solid ethical culture, the photo may change within a few hours.

No company is perfect, and a successful past does not imply a successful future in the battle against risks. As already said, a good reputation takes years to get, but it can be destroyed in an instant. It all depends on how the risks are controlled.

Everything depends on the success obtained in the control of risks.

---

* Doug McMillon, "A message from our chief executive officer," Walmart Global Statement of Ethics. www.walmartethics.com/content/dam/walmartethics/documents/statement_of_ethics/Walmart_Statement_of_Ethics_English.pdf.

† "Global statement of ethics," www.walmartethics.com/uploadedFiles/Content/U.S.%20-%20English.pdf.

25

Ethics Opinions and Ethics and Compliance Organizations

25.1 ETHICS OPINIONS: QUESTIONS AND ANSWERS

Although some ethical problems are easy to solve, others are more difficult. The debate that occurs during ethics training helps clarify these issues. Below you can find selected examples of frequently asked questions and their answers, published in the Code of Ethics of some of the corporations mentioned in the previous chapter. You will see how ethics and compliance officers answer ethical concerns.

25.1.1 Confidential Information, Privacy, and Data Protection

1.1 What should I do if I receive a call or an inquiry online from someone asking me about the latest news from Abbott? The person who called me seemed very professional, and indicated that he is doing a formal survey across the health care industry about current industry developments. Am I allowed to participate?

Providing information that is non-public about Abbott's business could be a problem. Some people contacting Abbott for information of this nature are trying to piece together information from different sources to gain an insider view of what is happening at our company. Until Abbott is ready to publish its results or other information about our business, you should keep information about your work confidential.*

1.2 I am taking a vacation where I want to completely disconnect. Is it okay if I leave my laptop with my administrative assistant to handle

---

* Abbott Code of Business Conduct, http://webstorage.abbott.com/cobc/ebook_us.html#pNum59, 58.

any approvals in the various company systems on my behalf? I trust this person completely so I don't mind sharing my password.

No. Employees should never give their personal password to anyone. Some systems allow you to delegate certain actions to others; other systems escalate issues to your manager in case of absence. If you bypass these controls you are undermining the security of our systems, avoiding your own responsibilities, and putting your assistant in the position of also violating company policy.*

1.3 I am trying to find a new supplier for office materials. The first one I contacted offers a good service, but at a high price. The second isn't quite as good, but he's cheaper (mainly because he's made a significant discount in an effort to win L'Oréal business). Can I tell the first supplier what price the second guy quoted, in order to try to get his price down?

You can tell the first supplier in very broad terms that you have a better price elsewhere, but without revealing the identity and price of the second supplier. Otherwise, you would be giving the first supplier confidential information about his competitor, which is unethical, and, in many countries, against the law.†

1.4 I am in the process of supplying our products to a new client. A consultant who works for this client contacted me and told me he could help me by providing me with confidential information about this client.

You must refuse this offer and inform your manager. It will also probably be necessary to tell your client that a third party is trying to sell you confidential information belonging to them.‡

1.5 The other day, I was taking a potential customer to a meeting. On the way to the meeting room, we walked past a colleague's office. His door was open, and he was talking to another customer about our pricing conditions on his speakerphone. Just as we passed, we could

---

* "Code of business conduct," Johnson & Johnson, www.jnj.com/code-of-business-conduct, 25.

† "Code of ethics, the way we work," L'Oreal, https://loreal-dam-front-corp-fr-cdn.damdy.com/res sources/afile/130772-e2c64-resource-code-of-ethics-english.pdf, 13.

‡ "Code of ethics, the way we work," L'Oreal, https://loreal-dam-front-corp-fr-cdn.damdy.com/res sources/afile/130772-e2c64-resource-code-of-ethics-english.pdf, 19.

hear him offering some special deals – all within my customer's hearing! Shouldn't he be more careful?

We all need to take the necessary measures to protect the confidentiality of information, even within the workplace: for example, by following a "clean desk" policy, locking files away, changing passwords regularly, and exercising caution when using speakerphones. You can never know who may be passing, and even among L'Oréal employees, commercially sensitive information should only be shared on a "need-to-know" basis.*

1.6 During a professional trip, my suitcase containing a USB key with customers' personal data was stolen. Unfortunately, it was not encrypted, but I don't see what the "thief" could do with it.

The loss of personal data may result in legal action, which can damage L'Oréal's reputation and may adversely affect people whose data have been lost. Identity theft based on personal data loss in this way is becoming more and more common. Therefore, it is crucial to respect the internal rules and procedures for data encryption. Wherever it is possible, make the personal data anonymous or use code names.†

1.7 I must transfer personal information on consumers to an agency in another country. Whom should I ask for advice?

The best thing would be to contact your Legal Director. Laws vary greatly from country to country. Moreover, we should not transfer personal information to a third party without ensuring they have signed a commitment to respect our Standards for protecting personal data.‡

1.8 May I use the information I learned from my former employer in my new role with Kellogg?

Maybe not. If that information is not generally known outside of your former employer and would give Kellogg a competitive advantage, that information is very likely a trade secret, and you may face civil

---

* "Code of ethics, the way we work," L'Oreal, https://loreal-dam-front-corp-fr-cdn.damdy.com/res sources/afile/130772-e2c64-resource-code-of-ethics-english.pdf, 20.

† "Code of ethics, the way we work," L'Oreal, https://loreal-dam-front-corp-fr-cdn.damdy.com/res sources/afile/130772-e2c64-resource-code-of-ethics-english.pdf, 22.

‡ "Code of ethics, the way we work," L'Oreal, https://loreal-dam-front-corp-fr-cdn.damdy.com/res sources/afile/130772-e2c64-resource-code-of-ethics-english.pdf, 22.

and criminal prosecution if you disclose it. Check with the Legal and Compliance Department for guidance on what types of information can and cannot be used in your new role.*

1.9 Marriott recently hired a former employee of a competitor who had been exposed to the competitor's confidential and proprietary information.

The new associate and the business unit where he works should ensure that all legal and ethical obligations are observed during the associate's transition and employment by Marriott. He should not divulge to Marriott non-public information he received while working for the competitor or use the competitor's confidential information in his work.†

1.10 A customer offers a Marriott associate a copy of a written proposal from a competitor and asks if Marriott can improve on the competitor's terms.

The associate may not review the competitor's proposal without first determining whether its disclosure to Marriott is in violation of a confidentiality agreement or other duty that the customer owed to the competitor. If in doubt, the associate may not share or use the information without consulting with the Marriott Law Department.‡

1.11 I recently joined Thomson Reuters from a competitor, and I have knowledge about some of this competitor's processes. Some of this information is confidential, and some, I believe, is not. What can I use in my work or share with my Thomson Reuters colleagues?

You must not keep or share documents – in any format – related to the competitor's business that you possessed as an employee of that competitor. Even in the case of information you simply remember, if the information is confidential, you have a personal legal obligation to your former employer to protect it from disclosure, just as you

---

* "Kellogg company's global code of ethics," www.kelloggcompany.com/content/dam/kellogg-company/files/KGlobalCodeofEthics.pdf, 38.

† "Marriott business conduct guide," www.marriott.com/Multimedia/PDF/CorporateResponsibility/Marriott_Business_Conduct_Guide_English.pdf, 13.

‡ "Marriott business conduct guide," www.marriott.com/Multimedia/PDF/CorporateResponsibility/Marriott_Business_Conduct_Guide_English.pdf, 13.

would with Thomson Reuters confidential information if you left the company for a competitor. Sharing such information with Thomson Reuters could also put you and us at risk legally. For the information you recall that you believe is not confidential, it is best to contact a company lawyer before revealing it to anyone.*

1.12 A local events company asked me for the names and addresses of my team members in order to invite them to a party. Is it OK to give that information out?

No. Sharing personal information about LS&Co. employees violate company policy.†

1.13 A salesperson for a competitor and I are friends. Occasionally we talk about marketing plans. Should I be concerned?

Yes. You are revealing confidential information that Starbucks has invested time and money to develop. You also may be violating competition laws that ban discussions of marketing and pricing.‡

1.14 I am able to get an early start on my day by returning calls during my train ride to work. Is this a problem?

You must be careful not to discuss non-public company information in public places where others may overhear you, such as taxis, elevators, or at conferences and trade shows. When it is necessary to conduct a telephone call in a public place, be mindful of your surroundings.§

1.15 What do we do with a consumer's personal information that we collect?

Privacy laws vary by country. If you have access to consumers' personal information, you should be aware of the laws that apply to your use of that data in the country where the data originates and any other country where it may be used. You may use consumers'

---

* "Code of business conduct and ethics," ir.thomsonreuters.com/static-files/f4169de5-ee8c-4c28-9 971-75b0baf97365, 41.

† "Worldwide code of business conduct," http://levistrauss.com/wp-content/uploads/2017/03/ CodeofConduct_English.pdf, 10.

‡ "Standards of business conduct," Starbucks, http://en.starbucks.com.cy/media/SoBC-2017-En glish_tcm55-10746.pdf, 15.

§ "Standards of business conduct," Starbucks, http://en.starbucks.com.cy/media/SoBC-2017-En glish_tcm55-10746.pdf, 19.

personal information solely for legitimate business purposes and consistently with any representations Mattel has made, such as the representations made to users in Mattel's online privacy statements.*

1.16 A potential supplier is eager to do some work for Mattel. In the latest bid process, he asks you to share with him the lowest price offered by the other bidders. Can you tell him what the other bidders offered?

If bidders have been asked to submit confidential bids, you may not disclose information to this bidder about another bidder's submission. Sharing this information would provide an unfair advantage to this bidder to the detriment of the other bidders, and would undermine the entire bid process.†

1.17 My supervisor travels a lot and is very busy. During one of her business trips, she asked me to log into a company system that has highly restricted information using her user ID and password to retrieve some reports that I would not otherwise have access to. Is that okay?

No. It is against company policy to share passwords. Also, access to highly restricted information should be limited only to those who are authorized to have access. You should refuse the request and remind the supervisor that you do not have access to this system and this information due to its sensitivity. Immediately report this to your manager, your Local Ethics Officer, the Ethics & Compliance Office or Ethics Line, any of which can help you address this situation properly. In instances where you would otherwise be authorized to access the information, steps should be taken to provide you with appropriate access without using the password of another user.‡

1.18 Someone accidentally emailed me a HR report that includes names, government IDs, and passport numbers. Should I just close it and forget I saw it?

---

* "Code of conduct," Mattel, Introduction, www.corporate.mattel.com/about-us/pdf/CoC/Cod e%20of%20Conduct%20-%20English%20(2015).PDF, 24.

† "Code of conduct," Mattel, Introduction, www.corporate.mattel.com/about-us/pdf/CoC/Cod e%20of%20Conduct%20-%20English%20(2015).PDF, 32.

‡ "Code of business conduct," Coca Cola, www.coca-colacompany.com/content/dam/journey/us/ en/private/fileassets/pdf/2018/Coca-Cola-COC-External.pdf, 12.

No. If it was accessed by you, it could be accessed by others without the proper authorization or need to know. Contact the privacy department, legal, or the Compliance Office to help ensure the appropriate protections are put in place.*

1.19 I just returned from a regional meeting where I learned about McDonald's exciting new product plans and excellent financial results that will be announced soon. I am very proud of McDonald's success and am eager to share the news. Can I tell my family or answer questions if a reporter contacts me?

No. This information has not been released to the public and is confidential. Unauthorized disclosure could have serious consequences. For example, McDonald's could be placed at a competitive disadvantage or exposed to legal liability. Never disclose confidential company information to reporters or anyone outside McDonald's.†

1.20 I found a vendor's confidential five-year plan in one of our conference rooms. What should I do?

Do not read the information or share it with others. Deliver the plan promptly to the Legal Department for follow-up.‡

1.21 At the end of every quarter, a friend who works at a hedge fund asks me what I think our quarterly earnings are going to be. Can I tell my friend before the press release?

No. You can't tell him, or other colleagues who don't need to know this information to do their jobs. This is confidential information, and the SEC takes leaks of financial information very seriously. Even if no one trades on leaked confidential information, disclosure still violates our policy and may violate the law.§

1.22 I used to work for one of our competitors. Can I share details about the competitor's sales strategy with members of my group?

* "Code of business conduct," Coca Cola, www.coca-colacompany.com/content/dam/journey/us/en/private/fileassets/pdf/2018/Coca-Cola-COC-External.pdf, 31.
† "Standards of business conduct," https://corporate.mcdonalds.com/content/dam/gwscorp/corporate-governance-content/codes-of-conduct/US_English_Sept_2018.pdf, McDonald's, 17.
‡ "Standards of business conduct," The Walt Disney Company, http://ditm-twdc-us.storage.googleapis.com/DIS-SBC-CM.pdf, 20.
§ "Standards of business conduct," American Airlines, www.aa.com/content/images/customer-service/about-us/corporate-governance/standards-of-business-conduct-for-employees.pdf, 7.

No. You have a responsibility to protect the confidential information of your prior employer just as you would have a responsibility to protect our confidential information if you left American. If you're unsure, don't disclose the information until you have discussed it with the Ethics Office.[*]

1.23 A co-worker of mine has recently given her resignation. Since then, she's been emailing supplier contact information to her home computer so she can start her own business. Is this a violation?

Yes. The supplier information she obtained through her position at Walmart is considered confidential company information. She should not be using it for her personal business.[†]

1.24 I have an anonymous blog that I write on a regular basis. Can I post the information I've learned based on my job?

While posting information online can be a great way to communicate with others, it's important to consider some of the risks and rewards that are involved. Maintain the confidentiality of business information related to Walmart and its partners, and the personal information of associates and customers. Don't reveal anything that is not public. Ultimately, you're responsible for what you post.[‡]

25.1.2 Fair Competition

2.1 I've found out that one of our main competitors will be launching a new product shortly that could have serious implications for our sales and marketing strategies. We desperately need to find out more about it, whatever it takes. Given how crucial this is, can we hire someone to sort through their trash in search of clues as to their launch strategy?

No. This is wholly unethical behavior, which could be severely damaging to our reputation for integrity. L'Oréal can never be a party to such activities. We can only collect competitive information through

---

[*] "Standards of business conduct," American Airlines, www.aa.com/content/images/customer-service/about-us/corporate-governance/standards-of-business-conduct-for-employees.pdf, 19.

[†] "Global statement of ethics," Walmart, www.walmartethics.com/content/dam/walmartethics/documents/statement_of_ethics/Walmart_Statement_of_Ethics_English.pdf, 30.

[‡] "Global statement of ethics," Walmart, www.walmartethics.com/content/dam/walmartethics/documents/statement_of_ethics/Walmart_Statement_of_Ethics_English.pdf,31.

legitimate means. Such means include examining our competitors' products and using publicly available sources, such as promotional leaflets, annual reports, competitors' displays at trade shows, and aggregated industry data that does not disclose company-specific information.*

2.2 While visiting a client, he gave me information on my competitors' recommended prices as well as their launch plans. Can I also ask him for information on the in-store set-up for these launches?

You should not collect non-public sensitive information (prices, product launches, market shares, advertising budget, etc.) on our competitors whether directly from our competitors or indirectly, namely through our clients. Doing so poses a risk for both L'Oréal and the client.†

2.3 Six months ago, I hired someone who used to work for a competitor. While there, she gained some hugely valuable research expertise in a really key area for us. Indeed, that experience was one of the main reasons I hired her. Obviously, I've taken great care to ensure she doesn't pass on any confidential information to us, but surely there's a time limit, after which she can share her knowledge freely? Otherwise, it would just be taking all this confidentiality stuff to extremes, wouldn't it?

No. There is no time limit on protecting confidential information. Your recruit should have been hired on the basis of her skills, and not because of her past work for our competitor. It may even be appropriate to transfer her to a different department, where she won't feel under any pressure or tempted to pass on confidential knowledge.‡

2.4 A sales director from a competing company reached out to me to discuss the price of our respective products.

You should never enter into a discussion with competitors about the price of our products or other proprietary information. If you receive

---

* "Code of ethics, the way we work," L'Oreal, https://loreal-dam-front-corp-fr-cdn.damdy.com/res sources/afile/130772-e2c64-resource-code-of-ethics-english.pdf, 14.

† "Code of ethics, the way we work," L'Oreal, https://loreal-dam-front-corp-fr-cdn.damdy.com/res sources/afile/130772-e2c64-resource-code-of-ethics-english.pdf, 14.

‡ "Code of ethics, the way we work," L'Oreal, https://loreal-dam-front-corp-fr-cdn.damdy.com/res sources/afile/130772-e2c64-resource-code-of-ethics-english.pdf, 15.

a call from a competitor, or if someone unknown to you approaches you to discuss pricing, make it clear that you will not discuss the price of our products with competitors. Politely end the conversation and report the incident to the Law Department.[*]

2.5 I was recently at a trade association meeting and overheard one of our competitors talking about their pricing strategy. I immediately left the room. Was that the right thing to do?

Yes. Removing yourself from the meeting reduces the risk that someone might think you were trying to fix prices or engage in other inappropriate activities. Contact the Legal and Compliance Department immediately to report the incident and to receive instructions – and don't share the information with anyone else unless told otherwise. While we never underestimate our competition, we always demonstrate a commitment to integrity and ethics in the marketplace.[†]

2.6 I ran into one of our competitor's representatives at a trade show recently. Over a drink in the bar, he mentioned that his company would soon implement a price increase on several key products. This is really useful intelligence! Who should I tell about it so we can take full advantage?

We do not share or exchange prices or bid information with competitors. This includes pricing policies, discounts, promotions, royalties, warranties, and terms and conditions of sale. If a competitor volunteers such information, you should bring the conversation to a close sensitively but immediately, and alert your management and the Legal Department. You should of course also not share this information with anyone. While the exchange may be intended innocently, it also could create the appearance of price-fixing or bid-rigging which is unethical and, in most countries, illegal.[‡]

2.7 Marriott and a competitor are planning to build hotels in an emerging market. At an industry meeting, the competitor's employee casually

---

[*] "Code of business conduct," Johnson & Johnson, www.jnj.com/sites/default/files/pdf/code-of-business-conduct-english-us.pdf, 12.

[†] "Kellogg company's global code of ethics," www.kelloggcompany.com/content/dam/kellogg-company/files/KGlobalCodeofEthics.pdf, 33.

[‡] "Code of ethics, the way we work," L'Oreal, https://loreal-dam-front-corp-fr-cdn.damdy.com/resources/afile/130772-e2c64-resource-code-of-ethics-english.pdf, 14.

suggests to a Marriott associate that the two hotel chains should coordinate the sites of their new hotels to avoid "crowding."

Associates should be on heightened alert when interacting with competitors. The conversation above could violate competition laws. The Marriott associate would be prudent to change the subject, remove himself from the conversation, and contact the Marriott Law Department for guidance.*

2.8 I mentioned to several competitors that we would soon be increasing ticket prices. I just learned that these competitors have now increased their prices. Did I do something wrong?

Yes. Discussions with competitors about commercial or competitive matters carry significant antitrust risk. Regulators may use these discussions to allege that industry members reached a tacit agreement to violate the law. And violations can be serious criminal matters resulting in severe fines for our company and fines and imprisonment for individuals.†

2.9 A friend at a competitor has offered to share their confidential price list with me. This could help us be more competitive. Should I accept it?

No. We want to win in the marketplace, but it would be unethical to accept the price list. It might also be illegal and subject you and our company to civil or criminal penalties. You should refuse the offer and contact our antitrust attorneys.‡

25.1.3 Conflicts of Interests and Gifts

3.1 I work in Finance and, because of my academic performance, I have always been in contact with the academic world, so a University has contacted me to teach classes on Analysis and Evaluation of Financial Statements. I've discussed with my manager and we agree that it is a job where the functions are completely independent of those in

---

* Marriott Business Conduct Guide, www.marriott.com/Multimedia/PDF/CorporateResponsib ility/Marriott_Business_Conduct_Guide_English.pdf, 12.
† "Standards of business conduct," American Airlines, www.aa.com/content/images/customer-service/about-us/corporate-governance/standards-of-business-conduct-for-employees.pdf, 15.
‡ "Standards of business conduct," American Airlines, www.aa.com/content/images/customer-service/about-us/corporate-governance/standards-of-business-conduct-for-employees.pdf, 16.

Abbott; the work schedule does not interfere with my Abbott work and it does not require the disclosure of confidential information from Abbott. Is this a conflict of interest?

Because outside employment could pose a conflict of interest, you were correct to disclose the potential conflict of interest and discuss it with your manager. After you've consulted with your manager, evaluated the situation together, and determined that the new job does not affect the performance of duties for Abbott, this situation would not be considered a conflict of interest.*

3.2 What if I have a side business that has been determined by Cisco to not be a conflict of interest? Is it okay for me to use my Cisco email, phone, or other resources?

Business use of company assets is only for Cisco business. Employees are not permitted to use company assets to support a second job, self-employment venture, or consulting effort.†

3.3 A new vendor is grateful for the work I did to expedite the execution of their Kellogg contract and sent me a bottle of champagne valued at US$40. Since it's not very expensive and was unexpected, is it okay to accept it?

No, you should politely return the gift to the vendor. Procurement employees or employees who can influence or determine vendor selection have to be especially careful to avoid the appearance of impropriety. Accepting gifts beyond a nominal value, like inexpensive notepads, calendars, and pens, could create the impression that such gifts influenced your decision. Oftentimes with conflicts of interest, perception is the reality. Make the tough call, and avoid the situation altogether.‡

3.4 My son owns a really good local hotel, and lots of companies in the area use it for lunches and functions. It would be an obvious choice

---

* Abbott "Code of business conduct," http://webstorage.abbott.com/cobc/ebook_us.html#pN um59, 57.

† Cisco, "Code of business conduct," www.cisco.com/c/dam/en_us/about/cobc/2018/code-of-busin ess-conduct-fy18.pdf, 15.

‡ "Kellogg company's global code of ethics," www.kelloggcompany.com/content/dam/kellogg-co mpany/files/KGlobalCodeofEthics.pdf, 22.

for our event. Given that it compares well on price and quality with other options, is there any obstacle to me making a booking?

Given the competitive price and popularity of the venue, it may well be acceptable for the company to arrange functions there. However, it would not be right for you to have a say in the matter, as there is an obvious conflict of interest here. As with all such cases where a close family member works for a current or potential supplier or other business partners, you should disclose this fact to your manager. Then he or she can take the necessary steps to avoid placing you in an awkward situation.*

3.5 A member of my team has been dating his subordinate for a couple of months. They were pretty discreet about it at work but people eventually found out. I'm not supposed to know about it officially. It has started off all sorts of rumors. Of course, I am keeping an eye on things to make sure there can be no evidence of favoritism – but what if they split up and it all gets nasty? Should I do something about it, and if so, what?

This is a very sensitive situation. At L'Oréal, we respect employees' private lives, and therefore we do not need or want to know about their romantic relationships. However, we do have a legitimate interest in their professional relationship, namely when one reports to the other or is in a position of authority or control over the other person. The situation you describe is not appropriate because there is a conflict of interest. A manager cannot be expected to judge his/her subordinates objectively if he/she is romantically involved. You should consult your manager or your Human Resources Manager in order to discuss how to handle this. Ideally, one of the employees should change jobs, and we would endeavor to make sure that this could be achieved tactfully. Depending on the facts and circumstances, there may also be a sexual harassment issue.†

3.6 As part of my job, I organize numerous business meetings, trips, and conventions. Now a hotel where I often book rooms for L'Oréal

---

* "Code of ethics, the way we work," L'Oreal, https://loreal-dam-front-corp-fr-cdn.damdy.com/res sources/afile/130772-e2c64-resource-code-of-ethics-english.pdf, 16.
† "Code of ethics, the way we work," L'Oreal, https://loreal-dam-front-corp-fr-cdn.damdy.com/res sources/afile/130772-e2c64-resource-code-of-ethics-english.pdf, 17.

employees has offered me a free weekend for my parents' wedding anniversary. It's a sweet gesture. Can I accept it?

No. Even if you are not personally going to benefit from the gift, accepting the offer makes it difficult to remain impartial when you arrange future hotel accommodation for L'Oréal. Even the appearance of such a conflict of interest is inappropriate and should be avoided by politely declining the offer, and making clear why you're doing so.*

3.7 A Marriott associate with responsibility for making purchasing decisions receives a watch, valued at US$750, as a gift from a vendor who has done recurring business with the associate's department for many years. May the manager approve acceptance of the watch?

The manager should consider the value of the gift, the ongoing nature, and recurring award of the business, the associate's role in the procurement process, and appearances. Weighing these factors, the manager must direct the associate to return the gift.†

3.8 A member of the Finance department is married to an outside auditor assigned to LS&Co.

It may make it difficult for the employee to perform his or her work objectively and effectively.‡

3.9 An employee gives sample clothing to a relative, who sells the samples on eBay.

The employee and the family member are receiving improper benefits as a result of the employee's position with LS&Co.§

3.10 A supervisor starts a relationship with a subordinate.

This creates opportunities for favoritism and unfair advantages being given to the subordinate.¶

---

* "Code of ethics, the way we work," L'Oreal, https://loreal-dam-front-corp-fr-cdn.damdy.com/res sources/afile/130772-e2c64-resource-code-of-ethics-english.pdf, 18.

† "Marriott business conduct guide," www.marriott.com/Multimedia/PDF/CorporateResponsib ility/Marriott_Business_Conduct_Guide_English.pdf, 15.

‡ "Worldwide code of business conduct," http://levistrauss.com/wp-content/uploads/2017/03/ CodeofConduct_English.pdf, 5.

§ "Worldwide code of business conduct," http://levistrauss.com/wp-content/uploads/2017/03/ CodeofConduct_English.pdf, 5.

¶ "Worldwide code of business conduct," Levi Strauss, http://levistrauss.com/wp-content/upload s/2017/03/CodeofConduct_English.pdf, 5.

3.11 I want to start my own accessories business, working on the weekends. Is that OK?

Any outside employment, even your own business, needs the approval of your manager. In addition, this proposed business could be considered a competitor, posing another conflict of interest. You should talk with your manager or a member of the HR or Legal team before starting your own business.[*]

3.12 We're accepting bids for a new vendor. One candidate offered to donate $1,000 to one of the company's favorite charities as a thank you for all of the meetings during the RFP process. Is this OK?

No. Even if the vendor is donating in good faith, the timing could be seen as an effort to influence our decision. You should thank the candidate for the gesture but decline the donation.[†]

3.13 I have a relative I'd like to hire to do some work at Starbucks. Since it's a legitimate project that needs to be done, and my relative is trained to do this type of work, is it okay if I hire her?

Although the work is legitimate, this situation creates the appearance of a conflict. The circumstances of this situation should be raised with Ethics & Compliance so that an independent review can be done prior to committing to a contract. This will help protect you, your relative, and Starbucks if the relationship ever comes into question.[‡]

3.14 I am interviewing companies that are bidding on a potential project. One of the bidders has offered to take me to the SuperBowl, all expenses paid. May I attend the game?

No. A trip to the SuperBowl is of significant value and may influence your decision to award business to that company. To determine what types of gifts may be acceptable, you should contact your manager and Legal Services.[§]

---

[*] "Worldwide code of business conduct," Levi Strauss, http://levistrauss.com/wp-content/uploads/2017/03/CodeofConduct_English.pdf, 6.

[†] "Worldwide code of business conduct," Levi Strauss, http://levistrauss.com/wp-content/uploads/2017/03/CodeofConduct_English.pdf, 6.

[‡] "Standards of business conduct," Starbucks, http://en.starbucks.com.cy/media/SoBC-2017-English_tcm55-10746.pdf, 11.

[§] "Code of conduct," The Clorox Company, https://www.thecloroxcompany.com/wp-content/uploads/2019/03/2019-Code-of-Conduct-Policy_External_English.pdf, 12.

3.15 I am responsible for planning a big meeting at our facility and need a caterer. Coincidentally, my sister just started a catering business. This event would be a big help to her. I know she would do a great job and offer great pricing. Can I hire her?

No, not without approval from your Local Ethics Officer. Even though there may be legitimate reasons for hiring her, it could look to others that she was awarded the job just because she is your sister.*

3.16 When my department hosts special events, my team puts me in charge of catering because my daughter-in-law owns a local restaurant that provides great food at a discount. Is that okay?

No, even if the restaurant offers a great meal at a great price, selecting your daughter-in-law's business without prior approval from the Management Audit department may give the appearance that we chose her business because of your family connection.†

3.17 Someone told me I cannot own stock in a supplier. Is this correct?

Maybe. The restriction is that you may not have any direct financial interest in a supplier whose business you have direct or indirect influence over in your position at Walmart. There are no restrictions against financial interests in suppliers whose business you do not influence.‡

3.18 I recently joined Walmart and I own more than US$20,000 of stock in a key competitor. Must I sell this stock?

You should disclose the information to your manager and Global Ethics. Global Ethics will advise you regarding any potential conflicts of interest.§

3.19 There's a contracting company I do business with as part of my position with Walmart. They've asked me if I know of an engineer

* "Code of business conduct," Coca Cola, www.coca-colacompany.com/content/dam/journey/us/en/private/fileassets/pdf/2018/Coca-Cola-COC-External.pdf, 21.
† "Standards of business conduct," The Walt Disney Company, http://ditm-twdc-us.storage.googleapis.com/DIS-SBC-CM.pdf, 11.
‡ "Global statement of ethics," Walmart, www.walmartethics.com/content/dam/walmartethics/documents/statement_of_ethics/Walmart_Statement_of_Ethics_English.pdf, 17.
§ "Global statement of ethics," Walmart, www.walmartethics.com/content/dam/walmartethics/documents/statement_of_ethics/Walmart_Statement_of_Ethics_English.pdf, 18.

they could hire. My son is qualified and would like to work for this company. May I refer my son for the position?

No. Even though the contracting company sought your recommendation, it could be interpreted that you are using your position with Walmart to get your son a job. That would be a conflict of interest that could compromise your reputation as a representative of Walmart.*

3.20 Our market electronics team is attending a training session, hosted by a supplier, to understand a new item the supplier is launching. The supplier said we will each get free t-shirts for attending the training. Can we accept t-shirts?

Since the t-shirts are coming from the supplier and are not related to the product, and understanding of the product, they cannot be accepted. Politely decline the t-shirt and explain our gifts and entertainment policy to the supplier.†

25.1.4 Bribery and Facilitating Payments

4.1 How do I tell the difference between a bribe and a legitimate payment to get service performed more quickly, like when I want to apply for a visa or seek customs clearance on a "fast-track" basis?

Some differences include the amount of documentation and whether the same option is always available to every applicant. Fees for legitimate "fast-track" options are normally published, with a set fee, and accompanied by clear, standard documentation such as an application form and receipt from the fee issuing entity. Abbott policies and procedures do not allow "facilitation payments," which are different from such legitimate "fast-truck" options. If you are unsure whether a payment to get services performed more quickly is permitted, you should contact your manager, OEC (Office of Ethics and Compliance) or Legal.‡

---

* "Global statement of ethics," Walmart, www.walmartethics.com/content/dam/walmartethics/documents/statement_of_ethics/Walmart_Statement_of_Ethics_English.pdf, 18.

† "Global statement of ethics," Walmart, www.walmartethics.com/content/dam/walmartethics/documents/statement_of_ethics/Walmart_Statement_of_Ethics_English.pdf, 18.

‡ Abbott, "Code of business conduct," http://webstorage.abbott.com/cobc/ebook_us.html#pNum59, 59.

4.2 A consultant we use to facilitate government relations in a particular locale added a significant "facilitation" fee to her charges to Cisco. I am concerned she may intend to pass along this extra money to local officials. What should I do?

Cisco does not condone bribing of government officials, either directly or through a third party, and in fact, Cisco can be legally liable if there are "red flags" that bribery may be occurring. If you suspect this consultant may pass along this payment inappropriately, contact ethics@cisco.com or Legal.*

4.3 During a company social event, a local government representative whose office approved our operating permits came over to me, expressed her delight at having Kellogg operating in her region, and then handed me an envelope containing the curriculum vitae of her nephew. She then said, "Many of our young people are having a hard time finding jobs in our economy, and I thought you might be able to help. Of course, you are under no obligation." I reviewed it, and her nephew is qualified for a number of open positions. What should I do?

Contact our Legal and Compliance Department immediately. Situations like this need to be handled with care to avoid harmful legal repercussions.†

4.4 I am negotiating an increase in our shelf space with a customer. My contact is refusing to examine our proposal, arguing that our competitors are "nicer" to him. I have the impression he wants me to give him a gift but he has not asked me for anything specific.

Let your management know about your doubts. It might be necessary to talk with your customer's management because it is unlikely that they encourage this type of behavior from their employees. In any event, do not give way to temptation. Healthy negotiation with our customers is based on the quality of our products and on our price policy, and not on our capacity to give gifts to their employees.‡

---

* Cisco, "Code of business conduct," www.cisco.com/c/dam/en_us/about/cobc/2018/code-of-busin ess-conduct-fy18.pdf, 27.

† "Kellogg company's global code of ethics," www.kelloggcompany.com/content/dam/kellogg-co mpany/files/KGlobalCodeofEthics.pdf, 36.

‡ "Code of ethics, the way we work," L'Oreal, https://loreal-dam-front-corp-fr-cdn.damdy.com/res sources/afile/130772-e2c64-resource-code-of-ethics-english.pdf, 18.

4.5 I've been told I should hire a local "consultant" to help get all the necessary permits that we need from a foreign government. This consultant requested a large retainer and said that he would use the money to "help move the process along." Since we don't really know where the money is going, do we have to worry about it?

Yes. If you suspect that any agent is acting improperly, you must not pay any such retainer or any other sum until you have determined that no improper payments have been or are being made.*

4.6 I am setting up a new office and the local authorities requested a small gratuity before they will install our phone lines. May I make this payment?

No. If the payment is not a legitimate installation fee, you must not pay it.†

4.7 A Marriott associate is responsible for obtaining a necessary land use permit for a Marriott hotel. All of the legal conditions for the permit have been satisfied. The government official responsible for reviewing Marriott's application says he will approve in exchange for US$50.

Associates may not give or receive bribes no matter how small the sum. The associate should seek guidance from the Marriott Law Department.‡

4.8 A Marriott hotel's General Manager in a Latin American country has been told by the government official in charge of health inspections that a cleaning service company run by his cousin provides excellent services. The inspector informs the GM that other hotels using his cousin's service have never been charged with a local health violation.

The health inspector's suggestion contains many "red flags" that require analysis by the Marriott Law Department. Even if competitive

---

* "Code of ethics, the way we work," L'Oreal, https://loreal-dam-front-corp-fr-cdn.damdy.com/res sources/afile/130772-e2c64-resource-code-of-ethics-english.pdf, 19.

† "Code of ethics, the way we work," L'Oreal, https://loreal-dam-front-corp-fr-cdn.damdy.com/res sources/afile/130772-e2c64-resource-code-of-ethics-english.pdf, 19.

‡ Marriott Business Conduct Guide, www.marriott.com/Multimedia/PDF/CorporateResponsib ility/Marriott_Business_Conduct_Guide_English.pdf, 20.

bid procedures were followed, the propriety of the relationship is questionable.*

4.9 We engaged a local agent with good connections to help us secure a government contract. He wants to give a bottle of expensive liquor to the government official who signed off on the contract and insists that it's customary to do so. Could we get in trouble for that?

Yes. Thomson Reuters can be held responsible for the actions of the agents we hire. You must tell the agent from the start not to give gifts to a public official. More importantly, before engaging such a person, it's important to conduct due diligence on the agent and get a contractual assurance that no improper payments will be made on behalf of Thomson Reuters.†

4.10 A consultant handling the permits for a new store outside the United States asked for a US$40,000 retainer. He says the money is needed to "make sure the permitting goes smoothly." Should I be concerned?

Absolutely. You need to know where, how, and why the $40,000 is being spent. LS&Co. needs to be sure the money won't be used as a bribe. Raise this issue with your manager or the Legal Department.‡

4.11 We use an agent to facilitate relations with local government officials. Recently he asked us to increase his commission, and I suspect he wishes to pass this money on to the local officials. What should I do?

If you suspect that the agent is making illegal payments on Starbuck's behalf, the company is under an obligation to investigate whether this is the case and to halt any such payments. You should report your suspicions to your manager or Ethics & Compliance.§

4.12 A local official is the key decision-maker in an international business deal. He has invited you to join him and his family for dinner. You have been told that it is customary to bring a gift on such an occasion. What should you do?

---

* Marriott Business Conduct Guide, www.marriott.com/Multimedia/PDF/CorporateResponsib ility/Marriott_Business_Conduct_Guide_English.pdf, 20.
† "Code of business conduct and ethics," ir.thomsonreuters.com/static-files/f4169de5-ee8c-4c28-9 971-75b0baf97365, 34.
‡ "Worldwide code of business conduct," http://levistrauss.com/wp-content/uploads/2017/03/ CodeofConduct_English.pdf, page 6.
§ "Standards of business conduct," Starbucks, http://en.starbucks.com.cy/media/SoBC-2017-En glish_tcm55-10746.pdf, page 14.

We have to be especially careful in dealings with foreign government officials, to avoid violations of the US Foreign Corrupt Practices Act and similar anti-bribery laws of other countries. Although it may be the customary practice to offer a small gift of nominal value, even such a small gift could be construed as a violation of these laws. You must seek prior approval from Mattel's Law Department.*

4.13 After receiving prior written approval from the Law Department, you took several foreign officials to dinner. Now you are preparing your expense report and you plan to record the expense as a meal for yourself and several business associates. Is this sufficient?

No. To comply with the recordkeeping requirements of the Foreign Corrupt Practices Act, you must record the expense accurately and completely as a meal provided to foreign officials, including the names and titles of each individual present and the purpose of the meeting.†

4.14 I need to obtain a non-discretionary approval for a project. The government employee I contacted has offered to speed up the process if I pay him a "small fee." May I make a small payment to a government employee to speed up the approval process?

No. This type of payment is known as a "facilitation payment" and is prohibited by Clorox. You may not offer or pay any amount to government officials to facilitate government approvals even if it will speed up a project. You should notify your manager and Legal Services of this request for a facilitation payment. In certain cases, official payments paid directly to government agencies (not to government officials) for expedited services may be permissible but check with Legal Services first.‡

4.15 A congressman and his family are flying to London for vacation. They want to leave a week later and ask you to waive the change fees. Should you do it?

---

* "Code of conduct," Mattel, Introduction, www.corporate.mattel.com/about-us/pdf/CoC/Code%20of%20Conduct%20-%20English%20(2015).PDF, page 13.
† "Code of conduct," Mattel, Introduction, www.corporate.mattel.com/about-us/pdf/CoC/Code%20of%20Conduct%20-%20English%20(2015).PDF,31.
‡ "Code of conduct," The Clorox Company, https://www.thecloroxcompany.com/wp-content/uploads/2019/03/2019-Code-of-Conduct-Policy_External_English.pdf, 11.

No. Waiving the fees is a gift to a government official and is prohibited unless approved by the Compliance Office.*

4.16 I just learned that the spouse of a high-ranking government minister is on my flight. Can I offer him an upgrade to the First-Class cabin?

No. Family members of government officials are usually subject to the same rules as government officials. Contact the Compliance Office if you have any questions.†

4.17 A government official that controls landing slots has asked that we make a sizable contribution to a local charity. Since we're giving the money to a charity, and not to the government official, is this okay?

No. Donating money to a charity to influence a government official to take or refrain from taking an official act is illegal.‡

4.18 An official at the Ministry of Transportation has asked that we hire his daughter as a consultant. Can we do this?

No. Paying or promising to pay something of value to a family member of a government official to influence a government official to take or refrain from taking an official act is illegal. Contact the Compliance Office immediately.§

4.19 Small payments to government employees are common in my country, and the bribery laws are never enforced. Do I still need to follow the law?

Yes. We obey the US anti-bribery laws and our company policy regardless of whether local laws are enforced. And even if local laws are not enforced, US and UK law enforcement agencies may be able to prosecute you and our company.¶

---

* "Standards of business conduct," American Airlines, www.aa.com/content/images/customer-service/about-us/corporate-governance/standards-of-business-conduct-for-employees.pdf, 11.
† "Standards of business conduct," American Airlines, www.aa.com/content/images/customer-service/about-us/corporate-governance/standards-of-business-conduct-for-employees.pdf, 11.
‡ "Standards of business conduct," American Airlines, www.aa.com/content/images/customer-service/about-us/corporate-governance/standards-of-business-conduct-for-employees.pdf, 17.
§ "Standards of business conduct," American Airlines, www.aa.com/content/images/customer-servi ce/about-us/corporate-governance/standards-of-business-conduct-for-employees.pdf, page 18.
¶ "Standards of business conduct," American Airlines, www.aa.com/content/images/customer-service/about-us/corporate-governance/standards-of-business-conduct-for-employees.pdf, page 18.

25.1.5 Supplier Selection

5.1 Your low-cost supplier offers good quality and reliable delivery at prices that can't be beaten. But you are uncomfortable with the working and living conditions it provides its workers. Shrug it off, or make an issue of it?

Don't shrug it off. It's a big issue – GE's reputation depends on doing business only with suppliers that deal responsibly with their workers and with their local environments.*

5.2 Someone told me confidentially that one of our overseas suppliers is under investigation following allegations of forced labor. The supplier hasn't told me any of this, and on previous site visits, there's been no reason for concern. Should I ignore these rumors?

No. You should investigate, starting by asking the supplier for information. If you are in any doubt, consider including them in L'Oréal's Social Audit programme, which involves sending an external auditor to verify the facts around employment practices, working conditions, and other issues. If the audit reveals scope for improvement, we will inform the supplier and try to get him to agree to a corrective action plan. Of course, in case of severe noncompliance with our Standards which we do not think we can fix immediately or if the supplier does not improve, we must end the relationship.†

5.3 I am part of the sourcing team at one of the company's non–US-based concentrate supply facilities and have been asked to purchase sour cherries from a supplier in Iran. The supplier is designated as a "Blocked Person" and appears on the US government Specially Designated Nationals list. Since the facility where I work is outside the United States and I am not a US national, is it ok for me to purchase this product from the supplier? If not, can I have an independent third-party source this item on the company's behalf?

No. Our Trade Sanctions Policy and the law make clear that all "US Persons" must comply with applicable trade sanction laws and regulations. The definition of a US Person generally includes our company

---

* "GE code of conduct," https://www.shrm.org/ResourcesAndTools/hr-topics/behavioral-compe tencies/Documents/TheSpirit_26TheLetter.pdf, page 17 and 20.

† "Code of ethics, the way we work," L'Oreal, https://loreal-dam-front-corp-fr-cdn.damdy.com/res sources/afile/130772-e2c64-resource-code-of-ethics-english.pdf, 13.

and its employees, regardless of where they are located. Additionally, it would be a violation of our Policy and the law to authorize a third party to make this purchase on our behalf.*

5.4 Local police officers have recently stopped trucks leaving our distribution center and threatened to delay deliveries unless the driver pays US$50 in cash to the officer. My manager said we should carry $50 gift cards with us. Is it permissible?

Walmart's policy prohibits even small unofficial payments to government officials to influence government action. This prohibition applies to cash, gifts, or other things of value. Immediately report this matter to the Legal Department or the Global Ethics Office.†

25.1.6 Money Laundering

6.1 A longtime GE customer recently opened a new import/export company in Nevada. Her company wants to purchase medical equipment for a private clinic in the Middle East. She offers to pay via a wire transfer from an account held in the name of a British Virgin Islands company at a bank located in a Pacific island nation. Should I be suspicious?

Yes, you should be suspicious if a transaction involves transferring funds to or from countries or entities unrelated to the transaction or not logical for the customer. Moreover, requests to transfer money to third parties also raise red flags that need to be investigated to ensure the legitimacy of the transaction. Consult with company counsel or a GE anti-money laundering specialist before proceeding.‡

6.2 One of our customers has asked if they can pay through a mix of different accounts, using a combination of cash and checks. Is that OK? What should I do?

You should be especially careful with these sorts of transactions. It could be money laundering, a process in which funds obtained

---

* "Code of business conduct," Coca Cola, www.coca-colacompany.com/content/dam/journey/us/en/private/fileassets/pdf/2018/Coca-Cola-COC-External.pdf, 28.
† "Global statement of ethics," Walmart, https://www.walmartethics.com/content/dam/walmartethics/documents/statement_of_ethics/Walmart_Statement_of_Ethics_English.pdf, page 28.
‡ "GE code of conduct," www.shrm.org/ResourcesAndTools/hr-topics/behavioral-competencies/Documents/TheSpirit_26TheLetter.pdf, 23.

through illegal means (e.g., drugs, bribery, prostitution, etc.) are concealed or made to look legitimate. You must take all possible steps to ensure that this is a bona fide transaction. These payments can only be accepted under exceptional circumstances and after having received approval from your manager. Among the red flags to look out for are: payments made from currencies other than that specified in the invoice; attempts to make payments in cash; payments made by someone who is not a party to the contract; payments to and from an account other than the one used in the normal business relationship; and requests to make an overpayment. If the account is not in the name of the contracting company, the payment must be refused.*

25.1.7 Insider Trading

7.1 I was chatting with my brother and mentioned that I had an upcoming business trip to close the deal for GE to acquire company X. Could this create a problem?

Yes, if company X is a public company and the possible acquisition of company X has not been publicly announced. If your brother trades company X stock based on your tip, both of you could be charged with insider trading.†

7.2 What if I become aware of Cisco's quarterly earnings results before they have been publicly announced? May I purchase company stock, knowing that information?

No. This information is considered "material non-public information," and the purchase of Cisco stock would be a violation of the Cisco policy and a potential violation of federal securities laws.‡

7.3 A vendor presented a new product it plans to introduce soon. My team agreed the product would not be useful for Cisco, but I think it

---

* "Code of ethics, the way we work," L'Oreal, https://loreal-dam-front-corp-fr-cdn.damdy.com/res sources/afile/130772-e2c64-resource-code-of-ethics-english.pdf, 25.

† "GE code of conduct," www.shrm.org/ResourcesAndTools/hr-topics/behavioral-competencies/ Documents/TheSpirit_26TheLetter.pdf, 54.

‡ Cisco, "Code of business conduct," www.cisco.com/c/dam/en_us/about/cobc/2018/code-of-busin ess-conduct-fy18.pdf, 27.

will be a real breakthrough for other industries. Can I buy stock in the vendor's company before the product launch?

No, you may not buy this stock until information about the new product is known to the public. Otherwise, it would be considered insider trading, which is illegal.[*]

7.4 I realize that I can't buy L'Oréal stock based on inside information myself. But what if I just "happened to mention" to my girlfriend that now might possibly be a good time to buy. Would that be OK?

No. It would be as unacceptable as if you were buying it yourself. As well, even if your girlfriend did not follow your advice, the simple fact of passing on a rumor is a violation of our ethics and the law.[†]

7.5 My family and friends often ask me about Starbucks and whether they should buy stock. Usually, I tell them what I know about our business and suggest they buy stock. Is this a problem?

The same rules about inside information apply whether you buy or sell the stock yourself or if you give the information to someone else – known as "tipping." If a relative or friend buys or sells stock based on non-public information that you give him or her, both of you could be liable for the violation of securities laws. Furthermore, you could be in violation simply for sharing material non-public information, regardless of whether or not he or she uses it or benefits from it.[‡]

7.6 You are asked to join a meeting with a potential business partner to explain a product under development. Afterward, your supervisor tells you that the deal is a sure thing and will be announced soon. Based on the information, you would like to buy Mattel stock. Would this be a violation of insider trading laws?

Yes, because the information is material information that is not yet public. You should not trade in Mattel's stock or the stock of the

[*] Cisco, "Code of business conduct," www.cisco.com/c/dam/en_us/about/cobc/2018/code-of-business-conduct-fy18.pdf, 27.

[†] "Code of ethics, the way we work," L'Oreal, https://loreal-dam-front-corp-fr-cdn.damdy.com/resources/afile/130772-e2c64-resource-code-of-ethics-english.pdf, 26.

[‡] "Standards of business conduct," Starbucks, http://en.starbucks.com.cy/media/SoBC-2017-English_tcm55-10746.pdf, 17.

other company until an announcement has been made and the public has had time to absorb the information.*

7.7 Sometimes my friends and family ask me about buying Clorox stock. May I tell them what I know about our business and suggest they buy stock?

No. If a friend or relative buys or sells stock based on non-public information that you give him or her, both of you could be liable for the violation of securities laws. Furthermore, you could be in violation simply for sharing material non-public information, regardless of whether or not he or she uses it or benefit from it.†

7.8 I have inside information about a product that will be released by another public company. Can I buy that public company's stock?

No. Any stock sale or purchase based on material non-public information is considered insider trading.‡

7.9 Could I encourage a friend to buy that public company's stock?

Encouraging others to purchase the stock would still be considered insider trading and is commonly referred to or known as "tipping." The friend would be liable for insider trading if he or she purchased shares based on your tip, and you would be liable for insider trading for giving the tip even though you did not buy any shares of the public company's stock.§

7.10 I've just heard that L'Oréal is about to acquire another company. This sounds like an excellent time to buy stock in one or the other – or both since the values are bound to rise when the deal is announced. Is it OK for me to go ahead and do so?

No, you cannot. As a L'Oréal employee, you are most likely to be considered an "insider" and therefore cannot buy or sell stock in either

* "Code of conduct," Mattel, Introduction, www.corporate.mattel.com/about-us/pdf/CoC/Cod e%20of%20Conduct%20-%20English%20(2015).PDF, 30.

† "Code of conduct," The Clorox Company, https://www.thecloroxcompany.com/wp-content/u ploads/2019/03/2019-Code-of-Conduct-Policy_External_English.pdf, 14.

‡ "Global statement of ethics," Walmart, www.walmartethics.com/content/dam/walmartethics/do cuments/statement_of_ethics/Walmart_Statement_of_Ethics_English.pdf, 23.

§ "Global statement of ethics," Walmart, www.walmartethics.com/content/dam/walmartethics/do cuments/statement_of_ethics/Walmart_Statement_of_Ethics_English.pdf, 23.

L'Oréal or the other company until the deal has been announced to the public.*

25.1.8 Safety, Quality, and Contamination

8.1 I have a safety concern. But if I bring it up now, it will slow down production and we may miss our deadline. I don't want my supervisor to be upset with me. What should I do?

Deadlines are important, but health and safety always come first. So, we make tough calls when necessary. The company always wants you to bring up health and safety concerns immediately, even if that may mean slowing production, missing a deadline, or losing a business opportunity.[†]

8.2 I work on the production line. I've noticed some defective finished goods. A machine may be generating some quality problems. I know we're supposed to stop production when that happens, but my supervisor has not taken any action. I know that the production schedule is very tight. Should I trust that she knows what she's doing in ignoring it?

L'Oréal has put in place quality controls at each stage of the manufacturing process to ensure that our customers obtain the highest quality products. Quality comes first, regardless of production schedules. You should put that line on hold without any hesitation, openly share the problem with your manager, and work with her and the rest of the team to fix the issue, before carrying on with production.[‡]

8.3 My production supervisor has instructed me to exceptionally disable a safety device that slows down the production line. What should I do?

You should never bypass, disconnect, or disable any safety device or monitoring equipment without the proper prior approval of a safety representative. If your production supervisor insists, you must refuse

---

* "Code of ethics, the way we work," L'Oreal, https://loreal-dam-front-corp-fr-cdn.damdy.com/res sources/afile/130772-e2c64-resource-code-of-ethics-english.pdf, 26.

† "Kellogg company's global code of ethics," www.kelloggcompany.com/content/dam/kellogg-co mpany/files/KGlobalCodeofEthics.pdf, 14.

‡ "Code of ethics, the way we work," L'Oreal, https://loreal-dam-front-corp-fr-cdn.damdy.com/res sources/afile/130772-e2c64-resource-code-of-ethics-english.pdf, 10.

and inform the site management and your HR. Safety is an absolute commitment that should not be compromised by production schedules or for any other reason.*

8.4 A colleague often works more than four feet off the ground without wearing required fall protection equipment. What should I do?

Everyone is responsible for safety. You should encourage him to use the proper safety equipment. If he does not, tell a manager or supervisor.†

8.5 An associate is asked to dispose of several containers of damaged household cleaning chemicals. He knows there is a standard operating procedure that governs the proper disposal of those kinds of items, but instead of following it, simply moves the chemicals outside the building and leaves them there. How should this be handled?

Chemicals never should be stored outside and subjected to the elements, especially if they are damaged. They may leak or deteriorate, allowing the chemicals to be released into the environment. Associates should ensure all chemicals are stored safely in approved areas with proper containment to prevent releases to the environment. Associates always should follow corporate standard operating procedures regarding environmental issues. If an associate discovers a leaking or improperly stored chemicals, he should immediately notify management and contact the Compliance Hotline or report the information to Global Ethics.‡

8.6 While working in the back room, I noticed associates were placing boxes or pallets in front of the emergency exit, blocking the door. I reported this to my manager who stated he saw no problem with the practice since it was just temporary and the items would be moved when the merchandise went out on the sales floor. Is this a problem?

* "Code of ethics, the way we work," L'Oreal, https://loreal-dam-front-corp-fr-cdn.damdy.com/res sources/afile/130772-e2c64-resource-code-of-ethics-english.pdf, 29.
† "Standards of business conduct," American Airlines, www.aa.com/content/images/customer-service/about-us/corporate-governance/standards-of-business-conduct-for-employees.pdf, 6.
‡ "Global statement of ethics," Walmart, www.walmartethics.com/content/dam/walmartethics/do cuments/statement_of_ethics/Walmart_Statement_of_Ethics_English.pdf, 30.

Yes. Blocking emergency exits endangers associates and customers should an emergency occur at the store. In addition, we may face potential fines and liabilities for safety hazards such as the blocking or locking of emergency exits. It is crucial that emergency exits be accessible for immediate use in the event of a fire or other emergency. You should immediately report the information to the Compliance Hotline or Global Ethics.*

8.7 The pollution control device on a critical piece of manufacturing equipment is faulty. I've just learned it will take three days to obtain parts and make a repair. Can we really afford to halt production when we have a huge backlog of orders to fulfill?

We have no choice. Our commitment to environmental good practice takes precedence over short-term profits or production schedules. The machine must not be run without the required pollution controls. You must notify your management to help you work out a solution.†

25.1.9 Harassment, Discrimination, Working Conditions

9.1 Lately my store has been very busy and it has been hard to find time to do routine cleaning. At this morning's store meeting, our manager told everyone that if they don't complete their tasks before they punch out, they will have to stay "off the clock" to do so. Is it okay for our manager to ask this of us?

No. Working "off the clock" is strictly prohibited by Starbucks. Starbucks is committed to ensuring that all partners are accurately compensated for all work performed. Any requests to work "off the clock" must be reported to Partner Resources or Ethics & Compliance.‡

9.2 I keep receiving "joke of the day" emails from a friend in another department, some of which are very funny. I'd like to send them on

---

* "Global statement of ethics," Walmart, www.walmartethics.com/content/dam/walmartethics/do cuments/statement_of_ethics/Walmart_Statement_of_Ethics_English.pdf, 29.
† "Code of ethics, the way we work," L'Oreal, https://loreal-dam-front-corp-fr-cdn.damdy.com/res sources/afile/130772-e2c64-resource-code-of-ethics-english.pdf, 36.
‡ "Standards of business conduct," Starbucks, http://en.starbucks.com.cy/media/SoBC-2017-En glish_tcm55-10746.pdf, 8.

to my colleagues and give them a smile on a Monday morning, but I'm not sure if my manager will approve. What should I do? Leave her off the list?

You shouldn't forward these "jokes." Remember that not everyone has the same sense of humor. In particular, you should bear in mind that the company's email and internet access systems must never be used to access, store, send, or publish any material which is inconsistent with the L'Oréal Spirit – especially when it comes to respect for individuals. This includes, of course, pornographic or sexually explicit images, political or religious content, racist comments, or anything that promotes violence, hatred, or intolerance.[*]

9.3　My manager can be highly intimidating. I know she's pushing us hard to deliver quality work, but at times she can really humiliate people, and it's affecting the morale of the whole team. Is there anything I can do about it?

Your manager is expected to challenge and drive her team to deliver the quality of work we expect at L'Oréal. This may mean that she will criticize or comment on team members' performance. However, a manager is also expected to treat team members with respect and act with due sensitivity. If you feel that you are not being treated in a professional manner, you should try and speak to your manager. You can also consult your Human Resources Manager. A good working environment can only occur with the support and involvement of us all – managers and staff alike.[†]

9.4　I have a meeting with a client and he's always touching me and making comments about my figure and how he'd buy more from us if I went to dinner with him. It's a client, not another L'Oréal employee so I'm not sure L'Oréal will do anything about it.

You should speak to your manager or your Human Resources Manager. L'Oréal's policy is to ensure that its employees are not subject to sexual harassment including from business partners.[‡]

---

[*] "Code of ethics, the way we work," L'Oreal, https://loreal-dam-front-corp-fr-cdn.damdy.com/resources/afile/130772-e2c64-resource-code-of-ethics-english.pdf, 24.

[†] "Code of ethics, the way we work," L'Oreal, https://loreal-dam-front-corp-fr-cdn.damdy.com/resources/afile/130772-e2c64-resource-code-of-ethics-english.pdf, 32.

[‡] "Code of ethics, the way we work," L'Oreal, https://loreal-dam-front-corp-fr-cdn.damdy.com/resources/afile/130772-e2c64-resource-code-of-ethics-english.pdf, 33.

9.5 My colleague has a habit of sending me off-color jokes via email that I find highly offensive. I don't want to get her angry at me, but I really don't care about the material. What's more, I fear I may get in trouble for even having such material on my computer.

You certainly have a right to be concerned. Inappropriate use of Xerox information systems is a serious matter and can have serious consequences. Sending jokes using our email system can potentially create a hostile, unproductive work environment. You should ask your colleague to stop sending you the jokes or if you feel uncomfortable directly confronting her, you should report the behavior to your manager, Human Resources, or the Ethics Helpline.[*]

9.6 I've noticed that one of our customers keeps making mildly sexual comments that seem to make one of my colleagues uncomfortable. If that colleague never makes a complaint to the company, is there anything I can do? Do we have to accept the behavior to maintain the customer relationship?

Even if an apparent target of the behavior does not make a complaint, he or she still may be uncomfortable. You should talk to Human Resources. While Thomson Reuters is always mindful of customer relationships, we never want our employees to be in an uncomfortable work environment. The company will take appropriate steps to address the behavior.[†]

9.7 A co-worker has made repeated references about a colleague's sexual orientation, including derogatory names. When the co-worker was confronted, he said it was only a joke. The behavior has not stopped. What should be done?

"It was only a joke" is not an excuse for inappropriate behavior. This incident, or any concern about workplace behavior that may violate Mattel's Policies and other guidelines prohibiting harassment or discrimination, should be reported to your HR Representative. Retaliation toward any employee who in good faith reports an integrity or ethical concern or issue will not be tolerated.[‡]

---

[*] "Code of business conduct: Connecting with our core values," Xerox, https://www.xerox.com/downloads/usa/en/i/ir_Code_of_Conduct_EmployeeHandbook.pdf, 15.

[†] "Code of business conduct and ethics," ir.thomsonreuters.com/static-files/f4169de5-ee8c-4c28-9971-75b0baf97365, 18.

[‡] "Code of conduct," Mattel, Introduction, www.corporate.mattel.com/about-us/pdf/CoC/Code%20of%20Conduct%20-%20English%20(2015).PDF, 21.

9.8 My supervisor makes several of us uncomfortable with rude jokes and comments. What should I do?

Talk to your supervisor about how you feel. If you are uncomfortable talking directly to your supervisor, you can talk to another manager, the Shell Ethics and Compliance Office, Human Resources, or call the Global Helpline. Harassment or a hostile work environment in which employees feel threatened or intimidated will not be tolerated.*

9.9 I overheard a co-worker use insulting language when referring to someone on our team. What should I do?

A language that is disrespectful of a person's race, religion, color, sex, or any other protected class doesn't fit in a workplace that values diversity. If you feel comfortable doing so, say something to your co-worker to express your concern. If you don't, speak to your supervisor, your Human Resources representative, or call the Guideline.†

9.10 My manager asks me to gather carts each evening on my way out to my car. Is this acceptable?

No. You should tell your manager you have already clocked out and it is a violation of company policy for you to work "off the clock." You also should report the issue to management through the Open-Door process or contact Global Ethics.‡

9.11 Should I report suspected non-authorized workers if they're technically employed by a contractor and not Walmart?

Yes. We require our contractors to use only work-authorized employees at our facilities. If you suspect there are unauthorized workers at our worksites, please contact the Global Ethics Office.§

9.12 One of my colleagues did not select a supplier who, in my opinion, seemed to meet all our expectations. Given comments made by this

* "Our code of conduct," Shell, https://s03.static-shell.com/content/dam/royaldutchshell/document s/corporate/code-of-conduct-english-2016-bw.pdf, 13.

† "Standards of business conduct," The Walt Disney Company, http://ditm-twdc-us.storage.googlea pis.com/DIS-SBC-CM.pdf, 9.

‡ "Global statement of ethics," Walmart, www.walmartethics.com/content/dam/walmartethics/do cuments/statement_of_ethics/Walmart_Statement_of_Ethics_English.pdf, 17.

§ "Global statement of ethics," Walmart, www.walmartethics.com/content/dam/walmartethics/do cuments/statement_of_ethics/Walmart_Statement_of_Ethics_English.pdf, 29.

colleague, I suspect that it is due to the supplier's nationality and ethnic origins. What should I do?

Any discrimination based on skin color, nationality, or ethnic origin is unacceptable to L'Oréal. It denies the respect that each of us deserves. Try to talk about it with your Diversity Correspondent, and otherwise, you should raise the matter with your manager or Purchasing Manager.*

9.13 I like to wrap up the working week with a Friday evening team meeting so that we can discuss any issues that came up during the week. I know that this creates difficulties for two members of my team who, for religious reasons, prefer to leave early on Fridays. Is this indirect discrimination?

It could be indirect discrimination if you do not have a legitimate need to hold the meeting on Friday evenings, or if there are more appropriate ways to meet your needs. You appear to have a legitimate need for the meeting (monitoring your team's progress and being available for their questions) – but do you really have to hold it on a Friday evening? Could you not obtain the same result by holding the meeting earlier in the day – or first thing Monday morning?†

9.14 I keep hearing that diversity is important for the Group. Does that mean I should only hire or promote women or people from ethnic minorities?

No, this is not what is expected. At L'Oréal, we hire on the basis of merit, and therefore you should select the best candidate for the job. But remember that diversity is not just limited to women and ethnic minorities. It includes other groups who are often discriminated against, such as disabled people, older people, and so on.‡

9.15 I am about to go on maternity leave and am concerned about what will happen when I come back and my future career opportunities. Who should I ask for advice?

---

* "Code of ethics, the way we work," L'Oreal, https://loreal-dam-front-corp-fr-cdn.damdy.com/res sources/afile/130772-e2c64-resource-code-of-ethics-english.pdf, 30.

† "Code of ethics, the way we work," L'Oreal, https://loreal-dam-front-corp-fr-cdn.damdy.com/res sources/afile/130772-e2c64-resource-code-of-ethics-english.pdf, 31.

‡ "Code of ethics, the way we work," L'Oreal, https://loreal-dam-front-corp-fr-cdn.damdy.com/res sources/afile/130772-e2c64-resource-code-of-ethics-english.pdf, 31.

L'Oréal's policy is to support employees during their maternity leave. In addition to paid maternity leave, L'Oréal guarantees the reintegration of employees at the end of their maternity leave, in their former position or at an equivalent position in terms of status and salary. You should discuss the matter with your Human Resources Manager before you go on maternity leave.*

9.16 I reported an allegation six months ago. Ever since my manager stopped including me in several meetings. Is this retaliation?

Significant changes in how you're treated can be viewed as retaliation. If your manager treats you differently since you reported an allegation, you should raise your concern to management through the Open-Door process or to the Global Ethics Office.†

9.17 One of my associates called the Helpline and made a false claim against me this past year. I think they did it to hurt my career. Can I score them lower on the "Integrity" section of their evaluation since they're obviously trying to spread lies about me?

We should believe that associates who report concerns do so in good faith. Therefore, taking action against an associate for reporting a concern would be viewed as retaliation, and could result in disciplinary action for you as a manager. Retaliation will not be tolerated at Walmart. It prevents an open reporting environment and encourages a culture of fear.‡

25.1.10 Financial Statements

10.1 My manager has asked me to purchase some equipment we need in our testing lab. The equipment will cost more than he is authorized to approve. He told me just to split the order so that he can approve the purchase without obtaining his manager's approval since his manager is traveling for the next two weeks and we really need the equipment ASAP.

---

* "Code of ethics, the way we work," L'Oreal, https://loreal-dam-front-corp-fr-cdn.damdy.com/res sources/afile/130772-e2c64-resource-code-of-ethics-english.pdf, 31.

† "Global statement of ethics," Walmart, www.walmartethics.com/content/dam/walmartethics/do cuments/statement_of_ethics/Walmart_Statement_of_Ethics_English.pdf, 10.

‡ "Global statement of ethics," Walmart, www.walmartethics.com/content/dam/walmartethics/do cuments/statement_of_ethics/Walmart_Statement_of_Ethics_English.pdf, 10.

Taking shortcuts in the purchasing process to save time may get you and your manager in a lot of trouble. One example is splitting requisitions. Let's say your manager can only sign up to US$25,000, but you need US$32,000 worth of goods. Splitting the purchase requisition into two separate requisitions that are each below the US$25,000 approval level is against corporate policy and could lead to both you and your manager facing disciplinary action, up to and including termination. If you are doing business with a supplier, be sure both to submit a requisition for the entire dollar amount that represents the full nature of the transaction and to get the right level manager to approve it in total.*

10.2 A manager is working on two projects – Project A which is under budget, and Project B which is over budget by a small amount. So that he can report that Project B was within budget, he recorded a very small amount of the expenses incurred on Project B to the under budget Project A. Is this acceptable?

No. The manager may not distort the purpose of expenses, no matter how insignificant the amount.†

10.3 An associate submits an expense report to his manager for approval. A meal expense on the report does not include an explanation of its business purpose, and the receipt amount and date do not match those stated on the expense report. The manager does not carefully review the report and approves it for reimbursement. Who is responsible?

The associate and his manager are both responsible for the report's inaccuracy. When approving transactions, managers have a duty to ensure expenses are valid, are properly supported, and have a bona fide business purpose.‡

10.4 A contractor has asked us to make a payment to a company for his services instead of to him personally. We previously engaged the contractor in his own name. Is this permissible?

---

* "Code of business conduct: Connecting with our core values," Xerox, https://www.xerox.com/dow nloads/usa/en/i/ir_Code_of_Conduct_EmployeeHandbook.pdf, 12.

† Marriott Business Conduct Guide, www.marriott.com/Multimedia/PDF/CorporateResponsib ility/Marriott_Business_Conduct_Guide_English.pdf, 9.

‡ Marriott Business Conduct Guide, www.marriott.com/Multimedia/PDF/CorporateResponsib ility/Marriott_Business_Conduct_Guide_English.pdf, 9.

No. Payments to vendors and contractors must be supported by appropriate documentation. They also must be accurate and complete, which includes making payments to the same person or company that we engaged in.*

10.5 I received a vendor invoice for an amount that exceeds my authority limit. Can I split the amount into two separate payments that I am able to authorize?

No. Splitting an invoice into separate payments in order to meet an authorization level is considered a circumvention of our internal controls. If the vendor payment amount exceeds your authorization level, the next-level approver in your management chain will need to approve the expense.†

10.6 A colleague told me that his supervisor asked him to submit an inflated expense account. I wasn't involved. Do I have an obligation to report this?

Yes. It's your responsibility to report an incident that may be a violation of the Code of Conduct. You don't have to have been an eyewitness or be absolutely certain of the situation. When you report something like this, it allows us to investigate. You're doing your part to make sure LS&Co. and our employees act with integrity.‡

10.7 Can I get fired if I report that I think our financial statements are incorrect?

No. This would be considered retaliation for doing what this Code asks you to do. We never discharge, demote, threaten, or discriminate against anyone who has made a good faith report about accounting or auditing matters. What's more, federal and state laws protect employees who raise concerns about this kind of misconduct.§

* "Code of business conduct and ethics," ir.thomsonreuters.com/static-files/f4169de5-ee8c-4c28-9 971-75b0baf97365, 50.
† "Code of business conduct and ethics," ir.thomsonreuters.com/static-files/f4169de5-ee8c-4c28-9 971-75b0baf97365, 51.
‡ "Worldwide code of business conduct," http://levistrauss.com/wp-content/uploads/2017/03/ CodeofConduct_English.pdf, 10.
§ "Worldwide code of business conduct," http://levistrauss.com/wp-content/uploads/2017/03/ CodeofConduct_English.pdf, 11.

10.8 An associate near me says she makes adjustments to our financial information so that our "good months" will help out our "bad months." Could this be an issue?

The manipulation of accounts and allowances is not only intentionally dishonest but also is a financial integrity concern that can have serious consequences both personally and as a company. You should report this immediately to Global Ethics.*

10.9 Our team did not utilize all of our approved project budgets this year. In order to maintain this level of funding in the future, is it okay to ask a supplier to pre-bill us this year for one of next year's projects, referencing a current-year purchase order?

No. Doing this would falsify expenses recorded in our books and records, misrepresenting the timing of actual spend. The law requires us to maintain accurate records and management relies on accurate financial records to steward the business and make decisions. This action would constitute a violation of our Code.†

10.10 I work in Sales and am currently trending below my volume target. I was thinking about asking a customer to order a product that they do not need now, telling them that they can always return it after the period closes. Is that okay?

No. Manipulating the recording of revenue would violate our Code. The request would likely also put the customer in a terrible position that could damage the relationship.‡

25.1.11 Taxes, Theft, and Improvements

11.1 To avoid paying customs duties in its country, an international customer has asked that I sign an origin declaration or certificate of origin identifying that the company's products originate in Mexico. I know the product was bottled in Mexico, but I am not aware of the manufacturing process. Can I sign the declaration/certificate of origin?

---

* "Global statement of ethics," Walmart, www.walmartethics.com/content/dam/walmartethics/documents/statement_of_ethics/Walmart_Statement_of_Ethics_English.pdf, 23.

† "Code of business conduct," Coca Cola, www.coca-colacompany.com/content/dam/journey/us/en/private/fileassets/pdf/2018/Coca-Cola-COC-External.pdf, 15.

‡ "Code of business conduct," Coca Cola, www.coca-colacompany.com/content/dam/journey/us/en/private/fileassets/pdf/2018/Coca-Cola-COC-External.pdf, 15.

You can sign only with prior approval from the Corporate International Trade Group. Origin declarations and certificates of origin are governed by local and international laws and require a detailed analysis of the manufacturing process under an established set of rules. An incorrect statement may result in false declarations to the customs authorities and subject the company to significant fines and penalties, even when we are not the importer or exporter.*

11.2 I believe one of our imported items was incorrectly classified on the paperwork. What should I do?

Contact your manager and the Legal Department immediately. There are fines and additional tariffs in many countries for misclassifying import information on products.†

11.3 An associate who has access to a Marriott cash bank needs a short-term loan. Without anyone else's knowledge, he takes US$50 from the cash bank and pays the money back the next day.

Although the associate returned the money, the unauthorized "loan" is theft of Marriott's property.‡

11.4 I think my supervisor lists expenses on his expense report that he didn't incur. Should I say something to someone?

Yes. Lying on an expense report is not only a violation of our Standards, but is plainly wrong. Report your concern to your Human Resources representative, the Management Audit department, or contact the Guideline.§

11.5 "Yesterday, my supervisor asked me to do something that violates our Standards. I'm not sure what to do."

You have a responsibility to comply with our Standards, even if your supervisor asks you to do otherwise. No one – not even your

* "Code of business conduct," Coca Cola, www.coca-colacompany.com/content/dam/journey/us/en/private/fileassets/pdf/2018/Coca-Cola-COC-External.pdf, 28.
† "Global statement of ethics," Walmart, www.walmartethics.com/content/dam/walmartethics/documents/statement_of_ethics/Walmart_Statement_of_Ethics_English.pdf, 32.
‡ Marriott Business Conduct Guide, www.marriott.com/Multimedia/PDF/CorporateResponsibility/Marriott_Business_Conduct_Guide_English.pdf, 26.
§ "Standards of business conduct," The Walt Disney Company, http://ditm-twdc-us.storage.googleapis.com/DIS-SBC-CM.pdf, 23.

supervisor – has the authority to tell you to do something illegal or unethical. Talk to someone else in management or contact your Human Resources representative, the Guideline, or the Legal Department for help.*

25.2 ETHICS AND COMPLIANCE ORGANIZATIONS

Several organizations specialize in helping companies maintain a culture of ethics and compliance. Some examples follow:

The Society of Corporate Compliance and Ethics (SCCE) is an association that provides resources for ethics and compliance professionals through publications, training, and conferences, and provides ethics and compliance certifications.†

The Ethics and Compliance Officer Association (ECOA) aims to improve the quality of ethical conduct through training that promotes ethical leadership. ECOA also offers certifications in ethics and compliance.‡

W. Michael Hoffman Center for Business Ethics at Bentley University in Massachusetts is a nonprofit educational and consulting organization whose mission is to provide leadership in the creation of organizational cultures that align effective business performance with ethical business conduct. The center helps to educate a new generation of business leaders who understand from the start of their careers the importance of ethics in developing strong business and organizational cultures. It is one of the world's leading research and educational institutes in the field of business ethics.§

The Ethisphere Institute aims to measure the ethical standards of businesses and the promotion of good practices. Each year, the institute announces the winners of the "The World's Most Ethical Companies," which gives companies the opportunity to be recognized for their Global Ethics and compliance programs.⁵

---

* "Standards of business conduct," The Walt Disney Company, http://ditm-twdc-us.storage.googlea pis.com/DIS-SBC-CM.pdf, 2.
† www.corporatecompliance.org/AboutSCCE/AboutSCCE.aspx.
‡ www.ecoafoundation.org.
§ www.bentley.edu/centers/center-for-business-ethics.
⁵ www. ethisphere.com.

Markkula Center for Applied Ethics at Santa Clara University assists leaders in creating trustworthy organizations and applying a framework of ethical reasoning to everyday decisions and emerging issues driven by social and technological change.*

The Institute for Global Ethics (IGE), founded in 1990, is a nonprofit organization that provides tools to build ethical fitness and cultures of integrity in the workplace and in society. IGE is headquartered in Madison, Wisconsin, USA.†

Navex Global provides solutions to prevent detect and remedy the lack of integrity, and help businesses to maintain an ethical culture. It provides an annual report called "Corporate Governance and Compliance Hotline Benchmarking Report" that helps to identify good practices and assess the health of Organizations.‡

Ethics and Compliance Initiative (ECI) is a nonprofit organization that empowers companies to build and sustain high-quality ethics and compliance programs. ECI provides leading ethics and compliance research and best practices, networking opportunities and certification to its membership, and conducts an annual survey called ECI's National Business Ethics Survey (NBES) that provides business leaders information about trends and best practices related to work ethics. Since 2010 ECI annually grants the Carol R. Marshall Award for Innovation in Corporate Ethics. ECI is comprised of three nonprofit organizations: The Ethics Research Center, the Ethics and Compliance Association, and the Ethics and Compliance Certification Institute.§

The Ethics Resource Center (ERC) is one of the oldest nonprofit organizations in the United States devoted exclusively to the advancement of high ethical standards and practices in public and private institutions. Through independent, nonpartisan research, ERC publishes resource materials on business and governmental ethics for policymakers, ethics and compliance officers, students, scholars, nonprofit professionals, and other readers from around the world.¶

TRACE International Inc. is a global provider of anti-bribery compliance support, risk-based due diligence, and anti-bribery training.

---

* www.scu.edu/ethics/.
† www.globalethics.org.
‡ www.navexglobal.com/en-us.
§ www.ethics.org/about/about-eci/ and www.ethics.org.
¶ berkleycenter.georgetown.edu/organizations/ethics-resource-center.

Trace-certified entities are seeking to do business with transparent business practices. TRACE members include hundreds of multinational companies.*

LRN, founded in 1994, is an American company that provides advising and educating on ethics, regulatory compliance, and corporate culture to other organizations.†

Institutional Shareholders Services (ISS) is an organization with more than 30 years of experience advising shareholders on governance issues. ISS developed a "Quality Score" to help the financial community and institutional investors assess corporate governance risks. Therefore, a score of 1 indicates the highest level of governance quality and the lowest level of governance risk and a score of 10 means high risk in governance.‡

ETHIC Intelligence, founded in 2001 by Philippe Montigny, certifies company anti-corruption programs since 2006 and it helps companies to strengthen and promote their efforts to prevent corruption.§

International Business Ethics Institute, founded in 1994 and headquartered in Washington, D.C., works on developing Global Ethics programs and it has delivered training in over 60 countries. It has formed a strategic partnership with the *Institute for Business Ethics* in London.¶

The Center for Ethics and Corporate Responsibility, formerly known as the Southern Institute for Business and Professional Ethics, is one of the United States' leading centers promoting professional integrity and global corporate responsibility. Founded in 1993 by leaders in business, education, and the professions, the center is a unit of the J. Mack Robinson College of Business at Georgia State University.**

The European Business Ethics Network (EBEN) has a mission to promote ethics and excellence in business to increase awareness about ethical challenges in the global marketplace and to enable dialogue on the role of business in society. EBEN has a portfolio of activities that include, among others, an annual conference and a European Business Ethics Forum.††

---

* www.traceinternational.org.
† lrn.com/about/.
‡ www.issgovernance.com.
§ www.ethic-intelligence.com/en/.
¶ business-ethics.org.
** ethics.robinson.gsu.edu.
†† eben-net.org.

The Josephson Institute of Ethics, located in Los Angeles, California, wants to improve the ethical quality of society by changing personal and organizational decision-making and behavior. The institute promotes leadership effectiveness to create an ethical business culture that enhances growth while reducing the risk of reputation-damaging lawsuits and scandals.*

Business for Social Responsibility (BSR) is a global nonprofit organization that works with its network of more than 250 member companies to build a just and sustainable world.†

The Institute of Business Ethics (IBE). Since 1986 IBE has published more than 50 books on applied business ethics topics; conducted surveys, developed training programs, and promoted the study of business ethics.‡

Center for the Study of Ethics in the Professions. Founded in 1976, it is one of the leading centers on practical and professional ethics. The mission of the center is to educate students as responsible professionals, to reflect on the wider implications of scientific progress, and to contribute to the shaping of technology in accordance with fundamental human values.§

CEB Compliance and Ethics Leadership Council,¶ *Gartner,*** the *Association of Corporate Counsel,*†† *Ethical Corporation* magazine,‡‡ *Compliance Week,*§§ and the *Open Compliance and Ethics Group* (OCEG)¶¶ are other organizations that provide excellent information and valuable services.

---

* josephsoninstitute.org/.

† www.bsr.org.

‡ www.ibe.org.uk.

§ www.iit.edu.

¶ news.cebglobal.com/home.

** www.gartner.com/en/about.

†† www.acc.com.

‡‡ www.ethicalcorp.com.

§§ www.complianceweek.com.

¶¶ www.oceg.org/about/what-is-oceg/.

Conclusions

Winston Churchill (1874–1965) said that writing was comparable to building a house, "the foundations have to be laid, the data assembled, and the premises must bear the weight of their conclusions."*

Throughout this work, the historical and global importance of culture and ethics has been analyzed and presented as an overview of the multiple hazards to which the organizations are exposed due to internal and external behavioral problems.

The first step in change is to discover your own weaknesses and recognizing there is always something to improve.

Corporate risks are difficult to control and there is a high probability of occurrence, so it is necessary to prevent or limit the damage and the impact they can make.

Strange situations happen all the time. While I finish writing this book, an American investment bank is in talks with the US government to pay a billion-dollar fine related to the 1MBD (Malaysian State Fund) corruption scandal, Russia was banned for four years from international sporting events by the World Anti-Doping Agency (WADA), France has imposed Google with more than US$100 million fine for abusing the dominant position in the online ad market, and Mexico ordered its Ambassador in Argentina to return home after a video showing he may have tried to steal a book from *El Ateneo*, a Buenos Aires bookstore.

Compliance is not optional. Lack of ethics and compliance is a real risk that has hurt many organizations. Leading companies consider this issue a priority because their businesses are exposed as never before.

The pursuit of greater profits, more customers, new business and markets, and the need to grow rapidly can cause leaders to lose touch with values.

The technological revolution has put mistakes organizations make on a global stage for all to see. The exposure is very high; everything is recorded and uploaded to the internet.

---

* Winston Churchill, "A roving commission: My early life," /quoteinvestigator.com/2017/11/18/p lanning/.

The regulatory and sanctions revolution has also exponentially increased the cost of fines for noncompliance.

Organizations must train their employees on the ethical and legal boundaries that exist in business management to help them make the right decisions in their work and reduce the risk of noncompliance.

The corporate message must be business and profits make sense *only* if they are ethically performed and comply with all standards.

Ethics has a profound influence on our behavior. Ethics and compliance must be part of the organizational culture and companies have to build an infrastructure of integrity, control, and prevention of risks in the different business units and countries where they operate.

A behavior aligned with moral values and ethics is the basis for building a successful and sustainable company over time.

A strong ethical culture acts as a filter or funnel in decision-making, favoring the company, in all its levels, and helping its members to make fewer mistakes.

Ethics must prevail over financial results when leaders make decisions.

There are other impacts and derivations such as the environment, safety, or the effects of a bad decision on people, which should also be considered. The analysis of all the potential consequences of any decision is a critical part of the thought process.

Organizations transmit the values of their leaders. When problems, conflicts, and strategies are discussed, values such as honesty, justice, and dignity must always be present.

Organizations currently not subject to corruption, theft or fraud, may be so in the future. Therefore, it is necessary to be prepared for what may come, for the unlikely events that by their impact can move the board and create company instability.

A program of ethics and compliance helps to raise moral issues, identify problems, anticipate and prevent risks; to "feel" their presence and react quickly. If a negative event happens, the program immediately triggers the necessary mechanisms of self-defense.

The best companies train employees in respectful treatment because it is important *how* they are led, *how* results are generated, and *how* employees are treated. Therefore, leaders should focalize not only on results but also on the right processes to get those results.

A mature ethical culture protects the company against abuses of the authority of chiefs, supervisors, managers, or directors. The humanity of the company makes a difference. A leader must plant the tree to generate the shade under which employees can work with peace of mind. Organizations must assure work environments where employees have the freedom to communicate their concerns, opinions, and doubts, where there is diversity, inclusion, and respect.

The culture of silence and fear leads to collapse and can be fatal to the company. Employees should feel free and safe to report unethical or illegal activities of which they are aware, without fear of reprisals from their bosses. Reporting those acts is a corporate duty.

To be able to identify problems when they are still a threat of crisis; organizations must have control systems and processes to proactively detect these risks.

In a nonlinear and continuously changing world, better controls are required, because the small can become dangerous and if actions are not taken quickly, a simple threat or symptom can grow and generate great chaos. Controls help leaders to be informed quickly of the dangers, crises, and irregularities that happen in the organization, facilitating the discovery of problems.

The more a leader climbs the corporate ladder of an organization, the less contact he or she has with the reality of what is happening or being achieved in the business units. An ethics and compliance program adds transparency to the information received and allows leaders to have a realistic vision of what happens in the different corners of the company. Integrity programs act as an alarm that gives greater predictability to management.

Leaders want to execute their plans, and the challenge is to avoid unexpected events that might breach business objectives and strategies. It is their responsibility to review and renew the quality of the controls and the status quo on a permanent basis because threats change, and it is necessary to update prevention systems with new technology, processes, and training.

CEOs who do not invest in compliance structures are probably not sufficiently informed of the magnitude, potential impact, and variety of risks, damages, and hazards to which companies are exposed. As if they were in a cave, they do not understand clearly what happens behind their backs.

The integrity program does not free from all evils, nor is it perfect, but it is the best way to detect, mitigate, and reduce illegal acts and reduce exposure to multiple organizational risks.

Leaders must anticipate, and act proactively. The possibility of negative events should never be underestimated. Sooner or later the company can be threatened on any of its fronts and it is necessary to be prepared for the worst scenario.

In this world of uncertainty, it is imperative and necessary to have some peace and security.

Why accept having the sword of Damocles over your head?

Why should we be overcome by risks?

There are two elements to the sustainable success of any company. Paradoxically, they are the two sides of the same coin, which lead to the growth of the organization in the long term:

Profit and values.
If the organization is profitable but does not act correctly, success will be ephemeral, short term and will not be sustainable.
If the company has a culture of ethics and compliance but is not profitable, it will not be sustainable either.

Therefore, both conditions, profitability and values (what and how), are necessary to achieve a sustainable company. Profit alone is not enough.

Because a company has not experienced problems in the past, it does not imply in any way that it will not have them in the future. The risks should not be underestimated. Hundreds of companies misperceived reality and learned the lesson at a very high cost.

An organization in which there is a strong ethics culture will achieve greater retention and commitment of its employees, attract investors, maintain a good reputation, and be more productive and reliable. The company will enjoy the loyalty of its employees, suppliers, and customers and will have built the foundations for a sustainable business.

A leader is not just an observer. A leader must manage the present and build a long-term vision. A leader must propose solutions, change and move the organization to bridge the gap between what is and what should be. A leader must look to the future.

Every company must be prepared to be able to anticipate and solve crises that arise. Leaders cannot relax or ignore the risks. Like the owl in the painting *The Garden of Earthly Delights* of Hieronymus Bosch (1450–1516), Satan is always on the prowl.

It is not always possible to discover and anticipate all the problems and risks that threaten organizations; however, companies can implement systems, processes, policies, and a culture that prevents or mitigates risks when they emerge and become visible. Intel leader Andy Grove said, "Only the paranoid survive."*

Making the right decisions and being able to make the changes on time makes the difference between success and failure. The book *Who Moved My Cheese?* says, "If you do not change, you can become extinct."†

An ethical crisis can put the whole organization at risk, even when the sales, profits, or growth plans have been fulfilled.

It is necessary to face the problem and corporate leaders should commit themselves and include ethics and compliance in the strategic agenda so that they are integrated into the daily management of the organization.

This work stems from the need to promote the idea that organizational leaders must pursue an ethical and compliance culture. One of the most important goals of every corporate leader must be to build an ethical organization. If you implement the best practices mentioned here, you will reduce unethical behaviors and their costs.

Corporate risks are controlled not only by designing internal policies, processes, training, and systems, but also with leadership so ethics and compliance programs are duly executed and obeyed.

I hope the information presented in this book can be a turning point that helps you to think – and eventually change – processes, policies, trainings, behaviors, and the culture of your organization.

As the Bible says, "Remember therefore how thou hast received and heard."‡

Put into action what you have read and implement an integrity program in your organization.

The company's journey in search of its business goals is full of dangerous obstacles and an anti-risk shield makes the road safer and the organization more sustainable.

---

* Andrew Grove, *Only the Paranoid Survive: How to Exploit the Crisis Points that Challenge Every Company* (Doubleday, 1996).
† www.goodreads.com/work/quotes/3332594-who-moved-my-cheese.
‡ The Bible, Apocalypse 3:3.

Thank you for reading this book. I hope you liked it.

If you want, send me your comments, observations, and suggestions to:

risksandleadership@gmail.com

Index

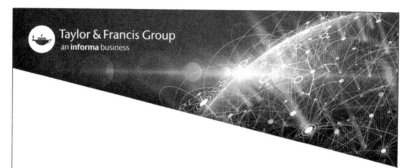

Printed in the United States
by Baker & Taylor Publisher Services